OXFORD HISTORY OF
THE CHRISTIAN CHURCH

Edited by
HENRY AND OWEN CHADWICK

RELIGION
IN ENGLAND
1688–1791

GORDON RUPP

CLARENDON PRESS · OXFORD
1986

Oxford University Press, Walton Street, Oxford OX2 6DP
Oxford New York Toronto
Delhi Bombay Calcutta Madras Karachi
Petaling Jaya Singapore Hong Kong Tokyo
Nairobi Dar es Salaam Cape Town
Melbourne Auckland
and associated companies in
Beirut Berlin Ibadan Nicosia

Published in the United States
by Oxford University Press, New York

Oxford is a trade mark of
Oxford University Press

British Library Cataloguing in Publication Data
Rupp, Gordon
Religion in England 1688–1791.—(Oxford history
of the Christian Church)
1. England—Church history—Modern period, 1485–
I. Title
274.2 BR755
ISBN 0–19–826918–8

Library of Congress Cataloging in Publication Data
Rupp, E. Gordon (Ernest Gordon), 1910–
Religion in England, 1688–1791.
(Oxford history of the Christian Church)
Bibliography: p.
Includes index.
1. England—Church history—18th century.
2. England—Church history—17th century.
I. Title II. Series.
BR758.R87 1986 274.2'07 85–13886
ISBN 0–19–826918–8

Set by Hope Services, Abingdon

Printed in Great Britain
at the University Printing House, Oxford
by David Stanford
Printer to the University

TO

JACKIE and MARTIN

ANDREW

CHRISTOPHER and PETER

PREFACE

To describe the Christian religion in England in the period between 1688 and 1791, that is, between the non-juring crisis and the death of John Wesley, brings its problems and surprises to one who, like myself, has turned from the sixteenth to the eighteenth century. But there is perhaps something to be gained from coming to the Age of Reason, the Evangelical Revival, and the Latitudinarian Establishment from behind, so to speak, and to see these events as emerging from their background, rather than in the light of the hindsights—which are not always the insights—of the nineteenth and twentieth centuries. And then, I too was among the company of students whom Norman Sykes encouraged to pursue their studies in Church History, and he might have been amused to know that at the end of the day I would return from a far country to the period in which so many of his pupils in London, Oxford, and Cambridge have made distinguished contributions. My debt to some of them, to the Very Revd Edward Carpenter, the Revd Dr G. V. Bennett, and Dr John Walsh in particular, is very evident in these pages. In considering the Free Churches I might hope that Ernest Payne would not have disapproved what I have said about the Baptists, and I have profited much from re-reading the meticulous and scholarly writings of Dr Geoffrey Nuttall. I have come once again to appreciate the worth of some of the older Methodist historians, beginning with Luke Tyerman, as well as from the more recent studies of Dr Frank Baker, R. E. Davies, and A. R. George. Dr Eamon Duffy has graciously initiated me into the writings of the brilliant company of English Catholic historians of which he is an eminent member.

Among particular acknowledgements first mention must be made of my friend and former student, the Revd Martin Evans-Jones, who went to great pains to translate and read to me portions of Derec Llywd Morgan's fine study of the Welsh Revival. Dr Ronald Gray, Fellow of Emmanuel College, Cambridge, read the section on William Law. I am grateful to the librarian of Westminster–Cheshunt College for permission to quote from the letters of the Countess of Huntingdon which are so beautifully housed in the college, and for permission from Dr Williams's Library to quote from the Walton–William Law MSS.

I owe many thanks to the librarians of Wesley House, Fisher House, and the Divinity School, Cambridge, and to Emmanuel College with its splendid collection of eighteenth-century writings, to the University Library of Cambridge, and not least the swift courtesies of the Rare Book Room. But I remember the sub-librarian in one college who raised a kindly eyebrow at the numbers of books I ferried to and fro, but excused me on the ground that 'after all, they don't seem to be books much in demand by the students at this college'. And perhaps that is one justification for attempting this book at a time when the young men like to leap from the Reformation to the nineteenth century which they suppose to be more 'relevant' to their ministry in the modern world.

I have always thought it must be a great moral support for the Lord Mayor of London, in Guildhall, to have behind him the giant figures of Gog and Magog, and it has been a great encouragement to me to have the giant figures of the general editors of this series encouraging me, and from time to time bestowing kindly apocalyptic warnings about time running out.

Expressions of gratitude to spouse or secretary are a common enough art form, but I have no ordinary thanks to offer my wife who acted in both capacities. Like the Psalmist, I have coveted hands to war and fingers to fight in many a losing battle with a battered typewriter. But she, encompassed with infirmities and with cheerful patience, transcribed the whole into a smooth and impeccably typed version.

Cambridge
All Saints' Day 1983

CONTENTS

ABBREVIATIONS

ARG	*Archiv für Reformationsgeschichte.*
BQ	*Baptist Quarterly.*
BJRL	*Bulletin of the John Rylands Library, Manchester.*
CH	*Church History*, published by the American Society for Church History.
CRS	The Catholic Record Society.
DNB	*Dictionary of National Biography from the earliest times to 1900.*
DTC	*Dictionnaire de théologie catholique*, Paris 1903 ff.
ERE	*The Encyclopaedia of Religion and Ethics*, ed. J. Hastings, Edinburgh.
LQHR	*London Quarterly and Holborn Review.*
PWHS	*Proceedings of the Wesley Historical Society.*
RGG	*Die Religion in Geschichte und Gegenwart*, 3rd edn. Tübingen 1962.
TRHS	*Transactions of the Royal Historical Society.*
VCH	*Victoria County History.*
Wesley's Works (OE)	The Oxford Edition of the Works of John Wesley, 1975–.

PART I

'NAMES AND SECTS AND PARTIES'

Those odious and unhappy Names of Difference which some years ago sprang up among us, the Devil knows how, did seem whilst a common danger threaten'd us, to be quite dead and buried: But no sooner was the danger over, but by a kind of *miraculous* infatuation, behold a sudden *Resurrection* of them with greater heats and animosities than before . . . Did we well and wisely before our late happy Revolution when we united for our common defence against a common danger and did let those *unlucky* names of distinction fall, so that they seem'd to be quite extinguish't? And can it now be wise to take them up again?

J. TILLOTSON, *The Way to prevent the Ruin of a Sinful People.* Jer. VI.8.
A Fast Sermon preached before the Lord Mayor, etc. Wednesday 18 June 1690.

THE Restoration seemed to have ensured the triumphant re-establish-
ment of the Church of England, the resumption of the ancient alliance
between Church and State in which a national Church nourished
godliness and learning and administered discipline over the whole
Christian nation.

Puritanism had been repudiated and discredited. No doubt there were
still underground continuities, for like Alph the sacred river, lost causes
have a way of running underground through caverns measureless to
man, surfacing in this case in the persistence of Calvinist notions, a
Covenantal view of the terms of salvation, the English Sunday, and a
national addiction to sermons. The threat from Rome seemed reduced
to manageable proportions. Beyond the sea it was another matter,
where Protestantism was still fighting desperately for its existence.

It has been said that 'the Church of England what it is, none but her
lovers know.' And in that age she had many lovers. Men of differing
parties would have agreed with Archbishop Sharp that

the Church of England is undoubtedly both as to the doctrine and worship the
purest church that is at this day in the world: the most orthodox in faith, the
freest on the one hand from idolatry and superstition and on the other hand
from freakishness and enthusiasm.[1]

There was evident a patriotism of the Church at least as deep as that
towards the English nation. More low-keyed, but from a Non-Juror
even more impressive, is the confession of Charles Leslie that

tho' the Events of my Life have given me occasion to take a nearer view of the
Doctrines and Worship of other Christian Churches, yet from thence I have
been confirm'd in my belief that the Church of *England*, Abuses notwithstand-
ing, is the most agreeable to the institutions of *Christ* and his Apostles.[2]

Yet though the Church of England might seem to be indeed

> urbs coelestis, urbs beata
> super petram collocata
> urbs in portu satis tuto,

she had by no means come into still waters, or arrived safely in the

[1] T. Sharp, *The Life of Archbishop John Sharp*, ed. T. Newcome (2 vols., 1825), i. 354.
[2] *The Theological Works of the Reverend Mr. Charles Leslie* (2 vols., 1721), Introductory
Epistle.

haven where she fain would be. As the long, swelling waves succeed a hurricane, so the tempest of the Puritan Revolution was followed by continuing disturbances. Within a generation the Church of England was once more to be torn by conflict, immersed in a new church struggle.

Yet the Church had sorely needed a breathing space, a few years of peace. Its machinery, not least its discipline, though continuing to work more effectively than older historians believed, was creaking and groaning, in need of overhaul and repair.

Lay patronage and the political appointment of bishops, pluralities, and non-residence, the inequalities between the higher and lower clergy, too many clerics chasing too few jobs, the rubs of economic and political involvement, these were medieval problems surviving in a Church which had known no Council of Trent. If these things did not shock the mind of the eighteenth century, since they were part of an order of society shot through and through with inequalities and anomalies, they none the less distorted the instruments of pastoral care, and made much more difficult the primary business of a Christian Church, the cure of souls, and the evangelical mission. The parochial structure was out of date and out of gear, and ill adapted to the movement of population in the growing towns, in the swelling metropolis of London, or in the missionary situation in North America. There was need for revision of canons and liturgy, as well as for the consideration of measures of comprehension and toleration which might perhaps win back all but a rump of the Nonconformists. Such a Church was in no situation to cope with the 'clear air turbulence' which shook the nation in a series of crises in the reign of James II.

I

THE NON-JURORS

THE term 'Non-Juror' has blurred edges, like the even more tantalizing word 'Jacobite'. To understand it, we shall best proceed chronologically, showing how stubborn obedience to conscience led to deprivation and suffering, and how these in turn led to separation, and the formation of a sect, increasingly introverted and fissiparous, a prey to personal quarrels in a communion where all the principal characters knew one another. Yet they influenced the religion of England in a way out of all proportion to the smallness of their numbers, and their ranks included notable Christian men, clerical and lay, whose influence on godliness, learning, and Christian worship was impressive and lasting.

The occasion of the non-juring schism was simple.[3] It was the refusal of the Archbishop of Canterbury and a group of his episcopal colleagues to swear allegiance to the intruding William and Mary, on the ground that they had already sworn inviolable oaths of allegiance to James II. In consequence they were first suspended and then deprived of their offices, as were some 300–400[4] inferior clergy and an unknown number of laity who followed them.

But this was no 'once for all' affair. There were recurring problems of conscience, in 1701 when James II died, and on the deaths of William III, Anne, and George I, and the '15 and '45 rebellions. Oaths were involved at university level, for fellowships and university posts, and those like Hearne at Oxford and Baker at Cambridge, like the Fellows of St John's College at Cambridge, and the many Jacobites at Oxford, counted the cost and paid the price.

The question of oaths was primary, but other problems were soon involved. The Church of England was in schism, from the non-juring point of view, but even so, were its orders and its sacraments necessarily invalid? Was it lawful to attend the parish church, and if so what of the prayers for the King? 'Query', wrote Robert Nelson, 'whether a man may hold communion with such a church and join in all points of worship with such a church, as use of unlawful prayers, without guilt or dissimulation?'

---

[3] T. Lathbury, *A History of the Non-Jurors*, 1845; J. H. Overton, *The Non-Jurors: Their Lives, Principles and Writings*, 1902; H. Broxap, *The Later Non-Jurors*, 1924.

[4] These are Leslie's figures and more probable than the 400–500 generally given.

A point of conscience indeed, though it might be resolved in the not edifying sight of Non-Jurors taking snuff or having a coughing fit, or even turning their backs at the reprobated portions of the liturgy. But these were matters where the Non-Jurors were themselves divided, between the hardliners like Hickes and Brett and the more eirenical like Frampton and Thomas Ken who continued to attend the public prayers.

To high-church historians of the nineteenth century, the Non-Jurors were the heralds of the Oxford Movement, nobly upholding the spiritual autonomy of the Church as a divine society, opposing in the eighteenth century the Erastians as they in turn withstood liberalism. It is a view which modern historians have challenged. 'The real interest of the non-juring schism', wrote Laski, 'was political rather than religious, and its roots go out to vital events in the past.' 'The non-juring protest', commented Norman Sykes, 'was political in principle, looking backwards to the obsolescent doctrine of divine indefeasible hereditary right.'

It does not invalidate this judgement that none of the Non-Jurors, from the first 'deprived fathers' to the last lone clerics a century later, would have accepted such a view. For them the root of the matter was a crisis of Christian conscience, grounded in a Christian view of Church and Society. A long list of passages might be quoted from Hickes, Kettlewell, Leslie, Brett, and Deacon which stress this spiritual independence of the Church.

Yet it is true that the fact of Establishment, and the 'state point' of the oaths of allegiance was at the centre of the protest, and a concept of obedience to a Christian prince—something for which there was no precedent in the pre-Constantinian primitive Church.

To begin with the abstract principles is legitimate, if we remember, too, that for these first Non-Jurors, those principles were bound up with personal relationships in a historical situation. The first principle was that of Christian obedience to divinely instituted temporal authority. This was of course no seventeenth-century discovery. It was the ancient gloss on the Epistle to the Romans (chapter 13) and the First Epistle of St Peter, underlined by the Fathers, and notably St Augustine. To it Martin Luther had appealed in repudiation of the violent rebellion of Thomas Müntzer and Luther's famous 'Leiden! Leiden! Kreuz! Kreuz!' —'Suffering, suffering: the Cross! the Cross!' anticipated that 'doctrine of the Cross' which Thomas Ken confessed on his death-bed.

But the repudiation of rebellion and the duty of passive resistance, as these doctrines emerged from the Civil War, might not have led to collision, had they not been combined with belief in the divine right of a hereditary monarchy, a monarchy whose rule was generally conceived in absolutist terms. This was the baroque notion which Macaulay dismissed as a 'superstition as stupid and degrading as the Egyptian worship of cats and onions'. But in the seventeenth century, and in the neighbourhood of the French monarchy, it was not bizarre. There is perhaps a third dimension. The Non-Jurors shared with the great majority of their fellow countrymen a Protestant, anti-Roman consensus. However vehement Sancroft might be against doctrinaire Calvinism, he was firmly Protestant. 'I can by no means as our brethren seem to do,' he wrote to Dr Cowel at The Hague in 1684, 'give up the whole Protestant cause as lost and desperate and ready to breathe its last. No! God hath by the Reformation kindled and set up a light in Christendom which I am fully persuaded shall never be extinguished.' He and Ken were active in support of the Huguenot refugees, and considered as a menace the France of Louis XIV.

Sancroft in 1688 instructed the clergy to 'take all opportunities of assuring and convincing "the Protestant dissenters" that the bishops of the Church of England are really and sincerely irreconcilable enemies of the errors, superstitions, idolatries and tyrannies of the church of Rome.' Thus in their loyalty to the Reformation, in their refusal to accept such doctrines as Transubstantiation and the Real Presence, the Non-Jurors looked backward to Laud rather than forward to Hurrell Froude. How simple, yet how impossible it would prove, even for the extreme Jacobites among them, to cut the knot of their problems, and surrender to the Roman Church, even in its Gallican form, and thus to reunite their loyalties to altar and to throne. Instead, in ones and twos they took their place among the exiles in Saint-Germain, Florence, or Rome, bearing ridicule from the Catholics among whom they lived, dwelling in Mesech and having their habitation among the tents of Kedar, clinging obstinately to a definition of 'catholic' which to all but themselves seemed an absurd sectarianism.

Nor did the Non-Jurors, at a time when the 'appeal to history' was a mark of learning, fail to recognize the temporal authority of the State and the powers of a Christian prince. John Kettlewell gave large powers to an established Church:

In Christian kingdoms, the Church is incorporated into the State, and by the benefit of this incorporation, Bishops and Pastors have their spiritual ministrations backed with secular effects and censures. All these secular fortifications, jurisdictions and encouragements in their ministrations, conferred on Bishops and Pastors of an incorporate Church are the gifts of a State and are secular additions to what spiritual powers they received from Jesus Christ. And what the State gives, the State when it sees fit may deprive them of.[5]

[5] L. M. Hawkins, *Allegiance in Church and State* (1928), p. 126.

The right to make canons without the approval of the Crown was one which the Church had surrendered and Kettlewell further admitted that, while clergy might not be deprived of their orders, they might have their jurisdictions and temporalities taken away.

Perhaps the most persuasive statement of the Non-Jurors about the independence of the Church as a divine society came from Charles Leslie in his treatise: *The Case of the Regale and of the Pontificate stated in a conference concerning the Independency of the church upon any power on earth, in the exercise of her purely spiritual power and authority.*[6]

Charles Leslie (1650–1722) was one of the ablest apologists and sturdy spirits among the first generation of the Non-Jurors. An Irishman of Scottish extraction he was ordained in 1680, but withdrew to London after the crisis of 1689. He was a devoted Jacobite, and had to spend much time in hiding, at one time disguised in regimentals. After 1715 he went to the Stuart court and followed his prince loyally from Saint-Germain to Italy. He was allowed to return to England in 1721, but was by then worn out and he died the following year. Though one of the most widely respected of the body, he was not chosen as a bishop.

Among his many writings were doughty defences of the Catholic faith against Quakers, Jews, Dissenters, Deists, and Socinians. He may or may not deserve Dr Johnson's famous comment that he was the only 'reasoner' among the Non-Jurors, but certainly his treatise of the *Regale* leans over backwards in an attempt to persuade (he even speaks of Burnet as 'judicious'—the last adjective even his best friends would have applied to him). In this work he blends the contemporary appeal to history with learned instances, but there is also a continuing appeal to the New Testament and to the living, active presence of Christ in his Church. In a new preface which he wrote at the end of his life, and in the light of the great argument which had arisen during the Convocation controversy, he could claim that even White Kennett and Wake were with him in the main contention—'both parties do now happily agree in the original and inherent rights of the Church deriv'd from Christ, as a society distinct from and independent upon the state, even when the state is Christian.'[7]

In his attempt to keep quite distinct the rights and properties of the temporal and the spiritual powers, Leslie was aware of the long centuries of conflict between them. But he was able to illustrate his point from the Fathers, from the Middle Ages, from the Old Testament, and, somewhat surprisingly, with detailed illustrations from the history of the Church in Sweden.

[6] Leslie, *Works*, i. 586.   [7] Ibid.

At times Leslie comes nearer than he knows to Luther's distinction between the Two Kingdoms, and his antagonism towards those who would mix one with the other.

Our blessed Saviour . . . gave to *Caesar* all that was *Caesar's*: But the things of God and the administration of the spiritual Kingdom of Heaven upon Earth, that he left in the hands of his church and accountable to none but himself: That as it is rebellion and usurpation in the church to extend her commission to civil power, so it is the highest sacrilege and rebellion against Christ for the civil power to extend their commission into the spiritual Kingdom . . . it is confounding of Heaven and Earth: These agree best at the distance God has plac'd them. To bring them together would be a new *Chaos* and contradiction irreconcileable. Such is the attempt of blending the sacred and civil powers together. While each move in their own Sphere, there is concord and harmony.[8]

But perhaps, as with Luther, the distinction was inevitably blurred in theory by the notion of the Christian Prince, and of the role of the State as protector of the Church, as well as by the prescriptive usages of many centuries. It was plausible enough for Leslie to protest against the appointment of bishops by Court or Ministers, but there was lay interference at every level of the Church's life, in lay patronage, for example, and in the impropriation of tithes. Where Leslie was strong, and where the Non-Jurors had more to say than modern defenders of the eighteenth-century Church admit, is in the secularizing effect of Erastianism.

We find by experience that the State particularly in *England*, have been out in their politicks, in reducing the church to so low an ebb of credit and authority with the People: for we have seen that Laws and Constitutions have prov'd too weak to restrain the unruly passions and ambition of designing Men. The State has no security as great as the Principles of the People when they are taught to obey for conscience sake and to believe that Rebellion is a damning Sin: which the church cannot inculcate into them farther than her credit reaches with them. And when they see Bishops made by the Court, they are apt to imagine that they speak to them the Court-language and lay no farther stress upon it than the charge of a Judge at the Assizes who has received his instructions beforehand from the Court.[9]

Thus religion itself has come into disrepute and the Erastian principle 'had turned the Gentry, Deists: and the common people, Dissenters.'

The principle of the *Regale* . . . does beget a secular Spirit in the Clergy. Those of them who are possess'd with it look not farther than unto the place whence their preferments come: and to which they are accountable, even for the administration of their spiritual office: And that whereon they so absolutely

[8] Ibid. i. 609.   [9] Ibid. i. 610.

depend they come in time to think the original and fountain of their power and that they are oblig'd to defend it as such. This makes them turn Courtiers, those at least that have a mind to rise: and to acquaint themselves with all the pretty arts there, of insinuation, flattery and address. This soon eats out the evangelical Spirit of Christian Simplicity.[10].

The first generation of the 'deprived Fathers', the eight bishops (soon reduced by death to five) with Archbishop Sancroft at their head, were bred in the teachings of the Caroline divines and in the Laudian mode. They had lived through the Commonwealth and had already suffered for their refusal of the Puritan oaths. Of this first generation, William Sancroft, ageing and ill, was a formidable relict. Bred in the moderate Puritan tradition of Emmanuel College, Cambridge, and its Biblical learning, where his uncle had been Master, his attitude came to harden against his Puritan contemporaries whom he denominated, 'the children of disobedience'. For him there was no attraction in the way of the Cambridge Platonists or those moderate men like John Worthington who were unwilling to take sides. In 1648 he confessed 'I cannot look upon this bleeding kingdom, this dying church with the same indifference as I would read the history of Japan or hear the affairs of China related',[11] and he warned,

If once I see the fatal blow struck I shall think of nothing but trussing all up and packing away and nothing but your command [he wrote to his father] shall stay me in a nation which I am persuaded will sink to the centre if it suffers so horrid a wickedness without chastisement.[12]

For him the death of Charles I was

the martyrdom of the best Protestant in these kingdoms and incomparably the best king upon earth, Charles the pious and glorious with whom fell the church and the kingdom, religion and learning, and the rewards of both, and all the piety and honesty the nation could hope for in the world.[13]

At the restoration he was able to direct Emmanuel College into new paths. To the end of his life he dabbled in building (he was a friend of Christopher Wren) and the new college chapel at Emmanuel was in a special sense a reorientation, for the building reflected the image of the future college much as the new St Paul's, of which he became Dean, suited the coming age.

But he felt that, for all its new look, learning had suffered, and in Emmanuel the age of Bedell and Holdsworth and Tuckney was over:

---

[10] Ibid. i. 644.
[11] G. D. D'Oyly, *The Life of Archbishop Sancroft* (2 vols., 1821). i. 35.
[12] Ibid. i. 42.   [13] Ibid. i. 44.

the Hebrew and Greek learning being out of fashion everywhere . . . and the rational learning they pretend to being neither the old philosophy nor steadily any one of the new . . . divers of them are very good scholars and orthodox (I believe) . . . yet methinks I find not that old genius and spirit of learning in the college which made it once so deservedly famous.[14]

And, perhaps more than he knew, this was a tribute to those Puritan children of disobedience who, in a way not his, obeyed the truth.

He himself stood consciously and gratefully in a learned tradition, could pen voluminous memoranda and amass a fine library; like Cranmer, Parker, and Grindal among his predecessors, he knew how to 'switch off' to his books amid the pressure of events, and perhaps, like them, could be inhibited by a donnish confusion of sympathy and stubbornness.

Nevertheless the conflict between the Bishops and James II, when the future of the Church of England was at stake, found him speaking with forthrightness and acting with courage, and for a fleeting moment, in an increasingly anti-clerical age he and his companions became national heroes, a kind of magnificent seven samurai.

With the flight of James II, Sancroft found he was isolated amid a small minority who took seriously the idea, long mooted, that there should be a Regency, so that when William and Mary arrived he took care not to meet them, and made it plain that while he would swear no new oaths, he had no intention of resigning his authentic Primacy. He himself had always adhered to these doctrines of obedience, and of the divine appointment of a hereditary monarchy. He had not only sworn allegiance to James, but had put the royal crown upon his head. He retired to his house in Lambeth which he stubbornly refused to surrender, in a rather futile gesture of defiance. But when he had to go, and had retired to Fressingfield in Suffolk, his old serenity returned, as his correspondence bears witness, and he occupied himself in his rebuilding plans. But he was determined to perpetuate lawful authority in the Church of England and on 9 February 1691 drew up an instrument consigning his archiepiscopal powers to Lloyd, the deprived Bishop of Norwich.

In his view, not he and his friends, but the great majority of the Church of England were the troublers of Israel. He was prepared to follow the logic of this, and to approve the steps taken by Hickes and others to perpetuate a non-juring episcopate, and consequently schism. Thus it was with his approval that the old act of Henry VIII was followed, in the creation of two Suffragan Bishops of Thetford and

[14] Ibid. i. 128.

Ipswich, named in the act, but the more appropriate because it was the Bishop of Norwich to whom Sancroft had delegated his authority, though Sancroft himself died before the consecration took place.

More eirenical, and less rigorist towards old friends and colleagues, were two others who had also grown up under the Commonwealth, Thomas Ken (1637–1711) and Robert Frampton (1622–1708). When Charles I was executed, Ken was a schoolboy creeping willingly about his beloved Winchester. But for him too, loyalty to the Stuarts was no mere abstract principle. Ken, small, fiery in the pulpit,[15] had been a Nathan to Charles II and a procession of willing Bathshebas and complaisant Uriahs. But he had also rebuked the household of the Prince of Orange, and won the amused admiration of both princes. He had seen a good deal of James II and admired his genuine affection for his children, his daughters Mary and Anne. At the Dutch Court, as chaplain to Mary, he followed the examples of Compton and George Hooper, by conducting a tug of war for her soul, against Calvinists and Papists—keeping the young woman (as devout a Christian as her sister, if less of an Anglican) well supplied with such prophylactic reading as the works of Eusebius and Richard Hooker. How deep was his impression on the Princess Anne appears from her note to Francis Turner, Bishop of Ely:

I hear the Bishop of Bath and Wells expounds this afternoon at your chapel, and I have a great mind to hear him: therefore I desire you would do me a favour, to let some place be kept for me where I may hear well, and be the least taken notice of: for I will bring but one body with me and desire I may not be known. I should not have given you the trouble but that I was afraid if I had sent anybody, they might have made some mistake.[16]

But he preached with splendid eloquence, and during the crisis 1687–8 drew excited audiences, at sermons which James II no longer attended, and where the Princess Anne received the three bows at the end of the Whitehall sermon. Evelyn described how on Passion Sunday, 1688, after Stillingfleet had preached the first sermon,

The H. Communion followed, but was so interrupted by the rude breaking in of multitudes, zealous to hear the second sermon to be preached by Dr. Ken . . . that the latter part of the holy Office could hardly be heard or the Sacred Elements distributed without great trouble. . . The Princesse being come, the Bishop preached on 7 Micah: 8.9.10 . . . This he preached with his accustomed

---

[15] Ken could be venomous at times, about Dutch Calvinists or about the preferment of men of latitude like John Wilkins.

[16] W. Benham (ed.), *The Prose Works of the Rt. Rev. T. Ken, D.D.*, p. 111.

action, zeale and Energy so as people flock'd from all quarters to heare him.[17]

It was a fine oration, one of a sadly small number of his sermons which have survived. His preaching style belongs to an older generation, and the beautiful passages, in which he loves to repeat a key word, have a haunting and melodic quality unlike that of the new preaching age. Hardly less notable is his tribute to his spiritual protégée, the saintly Lady Mainard, while his sermon on the Prophet Daniel (1685) is fit for any anthology of great sermons.[18]

One feels that the political crisis brought him to the centre of the stage at the height of his powers and that he was affected in more ways than one by the anticlimax of 1689. The apparent levity of Mary on taking over at Whitehall (exaggerated by gossip, an unhappy, but well-intended gesture to please her husband) was something he never understood or forgave. But committed to the Stuarts as he was, and so a firm Non-Juror, he could see more sides to the question than either Sancroft or Hickes. Sancroft had said—it became a famous phrase—that he was not one to worship the rising sun. The sad truth was that he and his friends were paying tribute to the sunset. But Ken would not write off the Church of England as wholly schismatic or repudiate old friends who did not scruple at the oaths, with the result that he became more and more estranged from those who, like George Hickes, would cut off the Church of England as apostate. Though he was repelled (perhaps on personal grounds) by the intruded Kidder (for whom there is a lot more to be said than is generally written), he was quite ready to accept George Hooper as his successor, and to recognize that in fighting for the Nicene faith Hooper was engaged in a more important cause than that of perpetuating a protest which must end in schism.

The last years of Ken's life were spent racked with arthritic infirmity, 'under the cross' in more ways than one, and not least by reason of the savage reproach of the extremer Non-Jurors. He found refuge in retreat and in the companionable minds of godly women, as he had often done—the Lady Mainard and the ladies of Naish. Thomas Ken, like William Law, was not a typical Non-Juror, and indeed not a 'type' at all, unless it be in that tradition of holiness to which George Herbert belonged, and he takes his place with those whose heart lay not in polemic, but in 'practical divinity' (his library contained many French and Spanish devotional writings). His devotional works, which began with his prayers for Winchester school and his Catechism, were mainly written before he became a Non-Juror. No other

---

[17] J. Evelyn, *Diary*, ed. E. S. de Beer (6 vols., Oxford 1955), iv. 577.
[18] Benham, *The Prose Works of Thomas Ken*, pp. 57–111.

contemporary catechism has such a 'devotion of rapture' which recalls the medieval 'Bone Jesu' tradition, but is an authentically seventeenth-century devotion—Puritan as well as Caroline. We take leave of him, remembering the little figure at his prayers, singing aloud, and accompanying himself on his organ, or better still, his lute. He has left to the Catholic Church those lovely morning and evening hymns which have been for many Christians since something so precious that, once known and got by heart, neither dawn nor dusk can ever be quite the same again.

Robert Frampton[19] (1622–1708), Bishop of Gloucester, belonged to the Sancroft generation. He was nearly seventy when the deprivations took place. But he retained his poor living of Standish and continued to preach and catechize the children. He seems to have been the only bishop seriously to consider easing the situation by resignation, and in the last years of his life ceased correspondence which would involve him in controversy with the more extreme Non-Jurors. He had no sympathy with the more militant Jacobites.

If one were to divide the non-juring leaders by temperament, then Frampton might head the eirenical, and George Hickes (1642–1715) the spleeny, Non-Jurors. But it is only when we see the career of this dour Yorkshireman as a whole that his strength of character appears. The crisis of 1689 found him a 'coming man': a well-known pamphleteer, a chaplain to Lauderdale in Scotland, then incumbent of a city living in London, and thereafter Dean of Worcester already surrounded by the rumour of impending episcopacy. On his deprivation, he nailed a vigorous protest to his cathedral door, but unlike Luther, there he could not stand, but went into hiding. He found refuge with—of all people—White Kennett (the Judas of the Welton altar-piece) with whom he sustained one of those clerical friendships which are very cordial as long as both parties keep off religion and politics. Kennett did his not ineffectual best to keep Hickes's attention fixed on antiquarian and linguistic studies.

Hickes did not mince words or dodge the logic of his principles. He said of the conforming clergy in words which pre-echo the Ultra-montanism of a Manning a century later:

They can perform no valid acts of priesthood: their very prayers are sin: their sacraments are no sacraments: their absolutions are null and void: God ratifies nothing in heaven which they do in his name upon earth: they and all that adhere to them are out of the church.

It should be said that his bark was worse than his bite and that, like some

[19] Lathbury, T. 194; Overton, pp. 69ff.; *DNB* s.v.

other extreme Non-Jurors, he kept up friendships across the divide of parties. But he could certainly bark, not only at Burnet and Tillotson, whom he blamed for the schism, but at those who, like Ken and Dodwell, were prepared to bring it to an end. He was the only formidable leader among them, and it was natural that it should be he who should carry out the negotiations with the exiled James II for the perpetuation of the episcopal succession which led, 24 February 1693, to the consecration of himself as Suffragan Bishop of Thetford, and Thomas Wagstaffe as Bishop of Ipswich. Though the fact of these consecrations was secret, the leadership of 'Father Hickes' was widely acknowledged, and he dominated the movement after the return to the Church of the 'Shottesbrooke group' of laymen.

But his ecclesiastical career and the episcopal office, which he sought strenuously to discharge, are but half the man. It is as a scholar that he complements his work as a leader of men and as a polemic divine. He took a manful part in the astonishing burst of learning, of antiquarianism in the best sense, which was a glory of the age. It was in Saxon studies that he made his mark, with his seminal grammar (1689) and the great folio volumes of his monumental *Linguarum Veterum Septentrionalium Thesaurus*. He presided benevolently at the centre of a spider's web of scholars, guiding, inspiring, encouraging, working with them in a true catholicity of learning which crossed all boundaries. This was the more impressive since he was no recluse, no Gilbert White nor William Law studying to be quiet, but one often on the run, often in hiding, ever immersed in the conscientiously fulfilled burdens of his pastoral office.[20]

Eminent among the first generation of Non-Jurors was a group of distinguished laymen. Henry Dodwell (1641–1711) was an Irishman, educated at Trinity College Dublin, but settling first in London, then in Oxford, where he was appointed Camden Praelector of Ancient History, a post he resigned at the Revolution for his non-juring principles. He retired to the pleasant Thames-side village of Cookham, one day to be inhabited by the artist Stanley Spencer, one also given to eccentric eschatology. For Dodwell, besides writing his share of non-juring pamphlets, wrote a number of works dealing with the nature of the soul and of immortality, which almost deserve the ridicule which Macaulay poured upon them. Certainly his notion of immortality was very conditional indeed, and in his zeal to combat the pagan notion of the natural immortality of the soul, and to deny to Dissenters the possibility of true sacramental grace, he seems to have supposed that Dissenters would be granted immortality in order to be damned. It has to be remembered that in this time, the aftermath of Descartes,

[20] Overton, pp. 91–112, D. C. Douglas, *English Scholars 1660–1730* (1951), ch. 4.

Malebranche, and Henry More, there was a good deal of often confused and confusing speculation about the relation of the material and spiritual, and about the nature of the soul. But Dodwell was soon drawn to the not distant village of Shottesbrooke, where the squire was the admirable Francis Cherry (1665–1713), [21] a sanctified Roger de Coverley, whose seventy-bedroomed house was Liberty Hall to Non-Jurors on the run. To them were joined the chaplain Francis Brokesby, [22] who was to be Dodwell's biographer, and the scholar Thomas Hearne. Hearne (1678–1735)[23] was a vehement spirit whose conscience closed the doors of the Bodleian Library against him, and deprived him of his office as under-librarian. But he produced a fine series of carefully edited medieval texts, while his *Collections* of vast information and malicious gossip have continued to profit and titillate scholars ever since. Robert Nelson[24] (1656–1715) was a man of truly catholic spirit and practical compassion who deserves our close attention on a later page. These men, with the exception of Hearne, were deeply concerned to end the schism at the earliest moment and Dodwell in his *Case in View* (1705) raised the question what should happen when the deprived bishops died? When this became the *Case in Fact* (1709), the Shottesbrooke group decided that enough was enough, and to the joyful ringing of the church bells the first period of the non-juring movement may be said to have ended.

The return of the Shottesbrooke laymen and the death in 1715 of George Hickes mark the end of the first, primarily confessing, side of the movement. What followed was the growth of a resistance group, under pressure, with the classic results of division and bitter conflict, within a leadership about evenly composed of saints and awkward squads, the two categories, alas, not quite exclusive.

Before Hickes died he had engineered important consecrations and ordinations. The Scottish non-juring movement will not concern us, but Hickes had to turn to Scotland for the canonical minimum of three bishops to consecrate, and these he found in Archibald Campbell and James Gadderer, the first an inveterate trouble-maker. On Ascension Day 1713 'in Dr. Hickes's oratory' there were consecrated Jeremy Collier, Samuel Hawes, and Nathaniel Spinckes. Notable converts were the layman, Roger Laurence, who won fame by a learned assault on lay baptism, and Thomas Brett, LL.D., the movement's greatest liturgical scholar.

---

[21] Overton, pp. 238–40.   [22] Ibid., pp. 206–7.
[23] Ibid., pp 177–8; Douglas, pp. 177–94.
[24] Overton, pp. 381–4; C. F. Secretan, *Memoirs of the Life and Times of the pious Robert Nelson*, 1860.

Jeremy Collier (1650–1726) was the natural leader to succeed Hickes, and he accepted a little too readily the title of 'Primus'. His famous onslaught on the immorality of the contemporary theatre made him widely known. But his *Ecclesiastical History of Great Britain* was a major event in historical learning, 'the most comprehensive account of the medieval church since the days of Fuller' and his view of the medieval church struggles of Becket and Anselm was a salutary antidote to the Erastian interpretation which had prevailed since the days of Henry VIII. His second marriage, to a dragon named Cecilia, nicknamed 'Pope Joan' by Non-Jurors of the baser sort, made him stepfather to Thomas Deacon, one of the last notable figures in the movement, and whose early ordination by his stepfather won him the name 'the boy priest'.[25]

The less the Non-Jurors were involved in politics, the more they were immersed in internal problems which led to further divisions in their ranks. There were those, of whom Thomas Bell was the most articulate, who were Protestant, and not simply in an anti-Roman sense. They defended the Reformation, the Thirty-nine Articles, and the Book of Common Prayer. Not so the high churchmen. Convinced as they were that the Church, as a spiritual society, was able to make its own rules, they became more and more critical of the English liturgy as their attention and admiration, stimulated by the learning of Dodwell, Collier, and Brett, focused on the primitive Church, defined as the Church of the first four centuries.

This preoccupation they shared with a wide spectrum of Anglican divinity, with William Wake and Ernest Grabe, William Cave and William Whiston. But they had their own special interest as Non-Jurors in the Church as a sacramental society. While they rejected Roman doctrines, Transubstantiation, and the Corporal Presence[26]—in the technical sense of the presence of the humanity as well as the divinity of Christ—they believed in a eucharistic sacrifice. This was the more remarkable since it did not derive from Roman theories of the Mass, but from the study of the Fathers, and of the ancient liturgies, those of the Eastern Church being especially favoured, and above all the document known as the *Apostolic Constitutions*, which most of them regarded as primitive and apostolic. Just as the Cambridge Platonists had been misled by misdating the Hermetic writings and those of Pseudo-Dionysius, so the Non-Jurors, and the wider circle who shared their general theological approach, mistakenly gave to the *Apostolic Constitutions* a normative value. The effect of this is not diminished by the fact that William Whiston outwent them in his reverence for it, and that he

[25] Overton, pp. 121–9; Douglas, pp. 200–2.
[26] G. Williams, *The Orthodox Church of the East in the Eighteenth Century*, 1868.

drew from it what to them were outrageous and heretical conclusions, or by the fact that some non-juring scholars had their reservations about its apostolicity.

They attacked the liturgical competence of the English Reformers, considering that Cranmer and Ridley had been perverted by the influence of such 'foreign divines' as Martin Bucer and Peter Martyr (as though Augustine had been a Yorkshireman, and Chrysostom a Man of Kent!). Yet those four Reformers were closer to them than they could know, sharing their own addiction to the Eastern Fathers, and an overall patristic knowledge as deep and perhaps wider than their own. (Deacon wrote to John Wesley that his knowledge of the Fathers was liturgical and did not extend to their moral theology.) The high-church doctrine of the eucharistic sacrifice was put forward most learnedly by John Johnson of Cranbrook, and particularly in his *Unbloody Sacrifice* (1714). Their studies in the ancient liturgies convinced them that the Prayer Book was defective, if not corrupt, though some of them found a half-way house in the First Prayer Book of Edward VI, which seemed to countenance, if not to imply, what came to be called the Four Usages. These were:

1. The oblation of the elements in the Eucharist;
2. The invocation of the Holy Spirit upon the elements;
3. The removal of the word 'militant' so that the prayer for the whole estate of the Church might include the living and the dead;
4. A mixed chalice, i.e. water mingled with the eucharistic wine.

There were those who regarded these four usages as necessary or essential, and they became known as the 'essentialist' Non-Jurors. Those who opposed them altogether were known as the 'Non-Usagers'. The argument split their communion down the middle, bishops, clergy, and laity and provoked a violent pamphlet war—facilitated by the contemporary furore for dashing into print at the slightest provocation (a century before, divines had been much readier to exchange memoranda). Nor was this a simple division, for there were those who would be content with some revision of the Prayer Book, and others who favoured an entirely new rite more consistent with the liturgies of the primitive Church.

The party of the 'Usagers' had found a redoubtable and expert leader in Thomas Brett (1677–1744). His conversion to the Non-Jurors was a curious by-blow of the Sacheverell case. He brought his learned pen to bear on what he considered the 'trimming' Church of England, and against such diverse exponents of its doctrines as Hoadly and Waterland. His liturgical polemic was crowned by his massive and immensely expert *Dissertation on Liturgies* (1720) and its defects were not so much his, as the state of historical criticism of his age.[27] The liturgical studies and creations of Thomas Brett and of Thomas Deacon have much more than sectarian interest and have rightly been judged of importance in the progress of liturgical learning.

Despite their claim to be the true Catholic remnant in England, the Non-Jurors could not but feel their isolation. Utterly opposed to Rome, detesting the Lutheran and Reformed Churches, counting the English Dissenters as little better than heathen men and publicans, the Non-Jurors found it difficult to give practical expression to their zeal for the unity of all Christians, so often declared, and like some modern successors, made up for their lack of service towards their separated brethren at home, by compassing sea and land to love the brethren they had not seen. Naturally they turned towards the Orthodox Churches whose historic liturgies they found so congenial. The visit to England in 1714 of the Archbishop Arsenius of Thebais, gave them the opportunity to open negotiations, via the Tsar of Russia, with the four eastern patriarchs.

Arsenius, whose purpose was to solicit gifts to pay off the colossal debts of the Patriarch of Alexandria (Queen Anne had promised £200 George I £100) was eager to make friends with any mammon of unrighteousness and no doubt encouraged a too optimistic view of the prospects of Orthodox–Non-Juror unity.

The most startling proposal of the Non-Jurors was that union should take place under the primacy of the Church of Jerusalem, to which the other patriarchs must agree to accord primacy of jurisdiction. They believed (and here their belief in hereditary monarchy is reflected) that the primitive Church had begun with a monarchical episcopate from Jerusalem under a succession of kinsmen of the Lord. They also probably accepted Grabe's view that the liturgy in Book VIII of the *Apostolic Constitutions* was the liturgy of the Church of Jerusalem. They knew sadly little of the history of the Byzantine centuries and the long-drawn-out struggles about primacy and jurisdiction or they would have known that such a proposal was the ecumenics of cloud-cuckoo-land. To it in fact the Orthodox patriarchs replied with their habitual immovable courtesy. 'It has the face of an innovation: whereas our Oriental Church, the immaculate Bride of Christ, has never at any time admitted any novelty.'

The non-juring reply to this point is revealing, for it goes to the heart of their appeal to the primitive Church. 'We desire that their patriarchal Lordships would please to remember that Christianity is no gradual

[27] Overton, pp. 138–47; Broxap, p. 18 and refs. ad loc.; W. J. Grisbrooke, *Anglican Liturgies of the Seventeenth and Eighteenth Centuries* (Alcuin Club, No. 40, 1958), pp. 88ff.

religion, but was entire and perfect when the Evangelists and Apostles were deceased, and therefore the earliest traditions are undoubtedly preferable.'

In matters of doctrine and devotion there was a similar impasse. In an astonishing gesture, the Non-Jurors had begun the dialogue by making conciliatory noises about the controverted 'filioque' clause in the western version of the Creed, and in one of the memoranda it is clearly stated that 'Filioque . . . shall be laid aside . . . it will need no great matter of debate.'[28] Even more remarkable and a puzzle for nineteenth-century high churchmen[29] was their rejection, not only of Transubstantiation, but of the Corporal Presence. Their first statement in which they pressed the view that the mode of presence should not be defined had been greeted with the comment 'Blasphemy!' from the Orthodox side, but their fuller statement quotes the patristic passages alleged in the sixteenth century by Oecolampadius, and may be correctly described by George Williams as 'virtualism', whereas in their reply the Orthodox fathers retort that by 'Body' they mean the body born in Bethlehem and by 'blood', the blood shed on the Cross. They attacked also the invocation of saints, angels, and the Virgin Mary and about these, too, the Orthodox Fathers were adamant, irritatingly excusing their new friends 'for being born and educated in the principles of the Lutheran Calvinists'. The Non-Jurors' vision of a building in London to be called 'Concordia' where in a united Church Non-Jurors and Orthodox might worship together was not to be fulfilled and their mental fight to build the Patriarchate of Jerusalem in England's green and pleasant land came to nothing. When Archbishop Wake, through his man in Constantinople, got wind of all these goings on, he wrote a forthright letter to the Patriarch of Jerusalem, warning him that the Non-Jurors, so far from being the Catholic Church in England, were a schismatic rump.[30] Though himself much given to ecumenical ploys, he was realist enough to know where in the eighteenth century eirenical lines could profitably be drawn.

Divisions, wrangles, nasty gossip, intrigues, and manifestos continued to bedevil relations between the leading Non-Jurors until a patched-up peace was achieved in 1732 by the two Thomas Bretts, and the Non-Usagers Rawlinson and Gandy. We must surely agree with

[28] G. Williams, *Orthodox Church*, pp. 7, 132.

[29] 'The Real Presence was manifestly an article of faith with all the Non-Jurors' (Overton). But the position taken in the conversations is rightly diagnosed by G. Williams, *Orthodox Church*, p. xxxiii.

[30] Overton, pp. 464ff.; Lathbury, p. 307; N. Sykes, *William Wake* (2 vols., Cambridge 1957), ii. 179–80.

Broxap and Grisbrooke that it was a victory for the Non-Usagers, but for this reason it was followed, not by peace, but by another division led by Archibald Campbell. It is an intricate story, a rigmarole of personal relations, and time would fail us to tell of the lesser figures, of Gandy and Gadderer, Campbell and Blackburne, Rawlinson, Laurence, and Mrs Wagstaffe—are they not all written in the book of Broxap?[31]

Consecrations and ordinations intermittently followed, many of them in private oratories, or rooms, and invariably with a secrecy so that there is a Nag's Head aura about them which is probably unjust, since they went to great trouble to see that the ancient canons were observed. Both parties 'begat' successors. On 25 January 1720 the Non-Usagers Spinckes, Hawes, and Gandy consecrated Hilkiah Bedford and Ralph Taylor. On 25 November 1722 the Usagers, Collier, Brett, and the Scot, Campbell, raised John Griffin to the episcopate. Anomalous was the consecration of Henry Doughty in Edinburgh by four Scottish bishops. On Ascension Day 1725 John Blackburne was consecrated by the Non-Usagers and, soon after, Henry Hall. In 1727 Thomas Brett the younger was consecrated by the Usagers and in the following year Richard Rawlinson by the Non-Usagers. In 1728 George Smith was consecrated by the Non-Usagers. The last two bishops in their line were Timothy Mawman and the Scot, Robert Gordon. About the last bishops of the remaining line, Brown, Cartwright, Garnett, and Booth, our information is as shadowy as the number and the doctrines of their flocks. But it seems that they were less and less politically involved. After the '45, and still more after the accession of George III, the Jacobite cause, which had been a ground bass of the movement, disappeared and the movement itself languished, dying the death at a time which it is almost impossible to ascertain.

The Non-Jurors did not exhaust their energies in internal controversy. Some of them, Hickes, Leslie, Dodwell, Brett, and above all William Law, contributed to wider learning, and to the defences of the Christian faith against heresy and scepticism. In the realm of 'practical theology' their contribution was outstanding. Catechesis, pastoral care, and eucharistic devotion were their concern and about these they wrote from personal experience. Thus they contributed to the educational revival, tools much needed for the charity schools, the missionary work of the SPCK, and Dr Bray's libraries. Thomas Ken's devotional writings, especially his exposition of the church catechism was widely used in the eighteenth century. Some of John Kettlewell's tracts were concerned to nourish eucharistic devotion, while his *Practical Believer: or*

---

[31] Broxap, *The Later Non-Jurors*.

the Articles of the Apostles' Creed drawn out to form a true Christian heart and practice ran into many editions. In 1749 a selection of his works was published as The True Church of England Man's Companion.

Robert Nelson's first work was The practice of True Devotion . . . with an office for Holy Communion and he followed this with a manual for family worship. But his outstanding writing was the Companion for the Festivals and Fasts of the Church of England which had run to thirty-six editions by 1826. Nathaniel Spinckes wrote devotional tracts which mirror his deep if sombre piety, the Sick Man Visited—dialogues and prayers, and a tract about dying well, in the long 'Ars moriendi' tradition, while his True Church of England Man's Companion to the Closet, known popularly as Spinckes's Devotions was reprinted several times. William Law we shall consider on a later page, but of seminal importance were his two masterpieces, his Practical Treatise upon Christian Perfection and the great Serious Call to a Devout and Holy Life.

But the lasting importance of the Non-Jurors was in their liturgical studies. At a time when the Church of England was preoccupied with other matters, and when liturgical revisers such as Simon Patrick and Samuel Clarke made appalling concessions to what might have been called 'contemporary English', they pursued their search for a primitive liturgy in truly learned investigations, and notably those of Bishop Brett and Thomas Deacon. Unlike the liturgies of William Whiston and John Henley, the 1718 liturgy of the Non-Jurors did not lean too heavily on the Apostolic Constitutions and what they produced was a seminal rite which, according to Grisbrooke, 'has a claim to be regarded as a primary source of all the Anglican rites descended from the Scottish liturgy of 1764.'[32]

It was in the writings of Thomas Deacon (1697–1753) that the doctrines of the Usagers found their logical conclusion. As the young 'boy priest', his precocity won him dangerous renown as the author of the last words on the scaffold of two Jacobites of '1715', Hall and Paul. He migrated from London to Manchester about 1720 where he practised medicine, and is attractively known to us from his correspondence with his friend, John Byrom. In 1734 he published in two volumes A Compleat Collection of Devotions, both Publick and Private, taken from the Apostolical Constitutions, the Ancient liturgies and the Common Prayer book of the Church of England. In his preface he claimed that the way to Christian unity lay in the adoption of two principles. The first is that the best method for all Churches to follow is to 'submit to all the doctrines, practices, worship and discipline not of any particular, but of

---

[32] Grisbrooke, pp. 109–12.

the Ancient and Universal Church of Christ, from the beginning to the end of the fourth century'. The second (supported at the end of his work by a catena of passages from Whiston, Bingham, and Grabe):

That the liturgy in the Apostolical Constitutions is the most ancient Christian liturgy extant: that it is perfectly pure and free from interpolation: and that the book itself called the Apostolical Constitutions contains at large the doctrines, laws and settlements which the three first and purest ages of the gospel did with one consent believe, obey and submit to and that as derived from Apostolical men.

To the Non-Usagers its new offices, for Penitents, Energumens, its reintroduction of chrism, milk, and honey for the candidates for Baptism must have seemed like the sheet in Peter's vision, full of all manner of creeping things. But others, like John Wesley who contributed to the work a new grouping of the Psalms for the monthly rota, and a piece on stationary fasts, in which he was helped by William Whiston, found them impressive.

It would be foolish to concentrate on how much the Non-Jurors got wrong, and how much they were led astray, in mistaking a Syrian liturgy of the fourth century for an Apostolic rite, and not to pay tribute to their insights, to their recognition of the wealth of devotion in the early liturgies. One has only to look at modern liturgies to see how much that they fought for is now widely accepted. In their conceptions of invocation and oblation they rested on a doctrine of eucharistic sacrifice, appealing to Scripture and tradition, and yet distinct from the rationale of the Roman Mass, and their doctrine of the eucharistic sacrifice has not perhaps yet been fully explored, or its ecumenical implications finally assessed.

The Non-Jurors were a proscribed community, on whom the authorities might swoop as they did in dangerous times, as 1715 and 1745 when oaths would be proffered them, on pain of arrest and fine, if not imprisonment. While some continued to worship in the parish church, others preferred to meet in their own assemblies. There were dozens such in London, in Holborn, in Aldersgate, in Spitalfields, in Whitechapel in the east, and Great Ormond Street in the west. Others were scattered throughout the country and there was a notable concentration in Manchester and its collegiate church, with which Clayton, John Byrom, and Thomas Deacon were associated. We hear occasionally of gatherings of several hundreds, and of other congregations forced to worship in twos and threes.

There were those who were sufficiently well off to bear the problems of their way of life. But there were clerics who had to turn a hand to medicine or teaching. And among the inferior clergy there were those reduced to desperate straits. Thus we hear of non-juring bishops meeting at the Essex Coffee house to discuss their problems. But Kettlewell, who organized a fund to help them, knew what might go on among a dispossessed clergy driven into the clerical proletariat of London.

> The clergy here who have no business, but stay in town as the best place of gifts, may be sent into the counties where they will be much better maintained at half the charge and where they may do service. And others will have no excuse to spend most of their time in coffee houses and hunting after gifts: but when they are not employed in their holy functions may follow their studies to improve themselves.[33]

Touting for gifts and patronage alongside the hacks of Grub Street and a grisly underworld of the talented impecunious must have had a contaminating effect even if there were but few who were drawn to the 'very wicked shifts' hinted at by Dr Johnson. There were a few peers and gentlefolk among the laity, such as Heneage Finch, the Earl of Winchelsea, a kind of godparent to the movement, or Sir Thomas Yarborough of Snaith Hall, Yorks.

We could bear to know more about the non-juring women. They were doubtless not all the Mrs Proudie type of the second Mrs Collier or Mrs Wagstaffe. There is the splendid Mrs Mary Harbin, a true prototype of Miss Beale and Miss Buss, who was the first mistress of the girls' school in St Martin's parish who had

> taken the sacrament once a month, since that once a week: has read besides the Bible, Bishop Taylor's, Dr. Scott's, Dr. Horneck's and Dr. Sherlock's Books: has for these 20 years past brought up several children and has made it her chief business to instruct them in religion, so that all but one being brought to the minister received communion at 15 years of age: writes a very good hand and understands knitting and plain work.

She was dismissed, however, in 1717 because she would not teach her girls to pray for King George.[34]

There was the Lady Yarborough of Snaith Hall, sister to the famous Margaret Blagge, on whom John Evelyn doted, that rare thing, a religious woman at the Court of the last Stuarts. It is in connection with her that we get an unexpected glimpse of the pastoral machinery of the Non-Jurors at work and of the episcopal oversight of George Hickes.

---

[33] Overton, p. 15.
[34] M. G. Jones, *The Charity School Movement* (Cambridge 1964), p. 107.

We shall quote at some length because it illustrates several facets of English religion at the beginning of the eighteenth century. What had been thought by many to have been garbled apocrypha about the Wesley family was confirmed when some of Hickes's papers turned up at a sale in the 1950s.[35]

To the Lady Yarborough,
Saturday night, March 7th, 1701–2

I'm infinitely obliged to your ladyship for your charming civility to a person so utterly unworthy of your favours, but oh Madam, I must tell your ladyship you have somewhat mistaken my case. You advise me to continue with my husband and God knows how gladly I would do it, but there, there is my extreme affliction, he will not live with me. 'Tis but a little while since he one evening observed in our family prayers I did not say 'Amen' to his prayer for K.W. [King William] as I usually do to all others: upon which he retired to his study and calling me to him asked me the reason of my not saying 'Amen' to the Prayer. I was a little surprised at the question and don't well know what I answered but too well I remember what followed. He immediately kneeled down and imprecated the divine Vengeance upon himself and all his posterity if ever he touched me more or came into a bed with me before I had begged God's pardon and his for not saying 'Amen' to the prayer for the King.

This Madam is my unhappy case. I've unsuccessfully represented to him the unlawfulness and unreasonableness of his Oath: that the Man in that case has no more power over his body than the Woman over hers: that since I'm willing to let him quietly enjoy his opinions he ought not to deprive me of my little liberty of conscience . . . I should be eternally obliged to your Ladyship would you be pleased to consult one of our Divines about it that might be trusted with such an important secret . . . I am inexpressibly miserable, for I can see no possibility of reconciling these differences, though I would submit to anything in the world to oblige him to live in the house with me. I appeal to your Ladyship if my circumstances are not strangely unhappy. I believe myself an Original of misery. I don't think there's any precedent of my case in the whole world: . . . I . . . most humbly beg your Ladyship's direction.

I am etc. S. Wesley . . .

My Master is for London at Easter when I hope to be able to wait on your Ladyship if I can live so long, and in the meantime earnestly desire your prayers and direction.

Lady Yarborough now turned to her bishop, George Hickes, to whom in April Susanna Wesley addressed herself.

My master will not be persuaded he has no power over the conscience of his wife and though I believe he is somewhat troubled at his oath, yet cannot be

---

[35] See R. Walmsley, 'John Wesley's Parents: quarrel and reconciliation', (*PWHS* xxix. 3 (Sept. 1953)), 49ff. for the following correspondence.

persuaded 'tis not obligatory. He is now referring the whole to the Archbishop of York and Bishop of Lincoln.

She added a revealing postscript: 'My master is at London and the extreme difficulty of receiving a letter when he's at home without his knowledge, is the reason I most humbly beg the favour of a speedy answer.'

Hickes replied in a letter 29 April roundly condemning Samuel, for making such an oath

wholly contrary to the prior obligation of his marriage promise, and the relative duties of a husband resulting from thence. It was perjury of him to make it and will be a continuance of perjury for him to persist in the performance of it.

He too recommended a consultation with the Archbishop of York, Dr Sharp (a good friend to the Wesleys), and he concluded: 'Wherefore, Madam, stick to God and your conscience, whatever you may suffer for adhering to them.'

It is to be noted that Samuel Wesley, in a characteristic explosion, had made a solemn vow, which in that age was far from being an idle word, to be repented and withdrawn at leisure. He took it and its consequences seriously. Though a high churchman (his son John believed his father had composed the defence speech of Dr Sacheverell) he was devoted to William and Mary, and claimed to have been the first to go into print in their defence in 1688. It is also to be noted that Susanna Wesley was a practising Non-Juror and not simply a sympathizer, for she asks Lady Yarborough to consult 'one of our Divines'. On 15 March she wrote again, Lady Yarborough having in the meantime submitted this case of conscience to an unnamed divine who counselled Susanna to 'persevere in following the dictates of my own conscience'. Samuel was now threatening to leave home altogether and become a naval chaplain (with the blind spot about leaving his six children which seems characteristic of the Wesley men in regard to their women, and was perhaps a mark of the age). 'I've offered since I last writ to put this business to a reference, provided I might choose one referee and my Master another, but I fancy he'll never agree to it . . . when he is gone I hope to be able to wait upon your Ladyship.'

However, on 30 April Susanna was able to give dramatic and joyful news. Samuel had indeed set off, but perhaps not unwillingly had allowed himself to be talked into returning home by a clergyman he had met, and to whom he had unbosomed his troubles. Hardly had he got home than the rectory was severely damaged by a serious fire (perhaps caused by arson). This seems to have shattered Samuel, for whom it must have seemed that his oath had had dire consequences, and he caved in. The church historian holds his breath at this point, for had Samuel not returned home, there would have been no John or Charles Wesley! So, be it noted, Susanna had won, as she perhaps often did, when her husband's squalls had blown themselves out. We do not know how long Susanna continued as a Non-Juror, but in 1709 it is plain that she still upheld their principles. 'I cannot tell how to think that a King of England can ever be accountable to his subjects for any maladministrations or abuse of power but as he derives his power from God so to him only must be the answer for using it.'

It would be interesting to know if her notions had any influence on her children, since we know that they took her theological ideas seriously. Samuel junior was a protégé of Atterbury, Charles had much to do with John Byrom before and after his return from Georgia and was much taken with his shorthand system which he commended to John. John seems to have gone through a phase at Oxford, where he was very close to John Clayton in the Holy Club and when he took an interest in the practices (e.g. the mixed chalice and a doctrine of eucharistic sacrifice) of the 'essentialist' Non-Jurors. He shared their misdating of the *Apostolic Constitutions*, and collaborated with Thomas Deacon by suggesting the Psalms to be included in his new prayer book (*Compleat Devotion*). But he seems to have had no sympathy with their Jacobite notions.[36] Finally it may be said that the well-authenticated poltergeist at the Epworth Rectory, Old Jeffry, was wont to give hefty and doubtless disapproving raps on the wall during prayers for the King and must be regarded as the only known non-juring ghost.

The non-juring movement has therefore a considerable interest and deserves the attention we have given it, however much Burnet or Wake might have objected to such serious attention to a small and irritating schism. There are interesting parallels to their story in modern church struggles, in the effects of pressure on dissident minorities, parallels to the tense, heroic in-fighting of the German Confessing Church. For however eccentric some of their leaders, and for all their doctrinaire rigidities, there were throughout those who suffered for their convictions: old Sancroft brought in tears to his grave, Thomas Ken deprived of influence, Leslie condemned to perpetual traipsing about Europe in attendance on his Prince. They were not all Jacobites, but the movement suffered in consequence of events in 1715 and 1745.

[36] L. Tyerman, *The Oxford Methodists* (1873), pp. 24ff. John Wesley, *Letters* (OE), i. 331, 352, 355 (abridged, see Tyerman, p. 35), 433. Charles Wesley has an enigmatic reference to a 'Jacobite' sermon by John Wesley on the 'one thing needful', but there is nothing treasonable or politically provocative in the copy of the sermon which has survived.

We may wonder at Thomas Brett, out of his impoverishment sparing money to send his grandson to Rome to be touched for the 'King's Evil' by James III, but who could not but be moved by the poignant fate of Thomas Deacon? His three sons were members of that Manchester regiment, in the '45, so hated by Government, one of whom died while being taken to London for trial, one was transported to the West Indies where he died within ten days of the yellow fever, and the other was executed and his head exposed on Manchester Exchange, before which his father bowed in prayer. There were enough eccentrics among them to recall a saying of Dean Inge in another connection, 'non angeli sed anguli', but there were saints and scholars of high degree among them, and in the field of Christian devotion, education, and philanthropy they played a worthy part, while in liturgical studies their work was impressive and of lasting influence.

2

LATITUDINARIANS

i. 'Latitude Men'

THE labels of the parties which bitterly polarized at the end of the seventeenth century had their origins in earlier decades. The term 'Latitudinarian' had its beginning in Cambridge soon after 1660 when a number of theologians conformed, who had remained at their academic posts, sometimes precariously, during the Commonwealth. Moderate men, they were attacked by their Puritan teachers, but were also resented by the returning Royalists of the Laudian school, like Wren and Gunning. The most illuminating account of them, and the earliest, is the published letter of Simon Patrick—*A Brief account of the new sect of 'Latitude Men' together with some reflections on the New Philosophy* (1662).[1] It is a reply to an enquiry from an Oxford friend, one 'G.B.' who had written (15 May 1662): 'I can come into no company of late but I find the chief discourse to be about a certain new sect of "Latitude Men" ' and adds 'I can meet with nothing distinct concerning them, but that they had their rise at Cambridge.' They are said to be 'as a party very dangerous both to the King and Church'.

This explicitly Cambridge origin seems to exclude from its pedigree the Oxford thinkers, Lord Falkland, Chillingworth, and the Tew circle. Patrick's letter abounds in good phrases and shrewd perceptions. Many Cambridge scholars have often wanted to say what Patrick says of his friend's invitation to him to come to Oxford, 'Truly it is as far from Cambridge to Oxford as it is from Oxford to Cambridge, and therefore you must hold me excused.' There is the famous reference (an echo of Donne and Herbert) to the 'vertuous mediocrity which our church observes between the meretricious gaudiness of the Church of Rome, and the squalid sluttery of Fanatick conventicles', and the fine phrase

---

[1] The letter, by 'S.P.' is generally accepted as the work of Simon Patrick though he never refers to it in his *Autobiography*, and never achieved anything as sparklingly impressive in any of his later writing. A useful reprint is that of the Augustan Reprint Society No. 100, University of California 1963, ed. A. T. Birrell. The editor's suggestion that the letter was a by-product of the struggle over Patrick's abortive election to the Presidency of Queens' College, quashed by a royal *mandamus* in favour of Dr Sparrow, is perhaps unlikely, but it is true that Sparrow represents the Royalist reaction against these new men.

about the Church's 'old loving nurse, the Platonick philosophy'. Patrick insists on the vagueness of the term: 'A Latitude man therefore, (according to the best definition that I can collect) is an image of clouts that men set up to encounter with, for want of a real enemy—it is a convenient name to reproach a man that you owe a spight to.' But the real clue is his reference to 'such whose fortune it was to be born so late as to have their education in the University since the beginning of the unhappy troubles in this Kingdom, where they ascended to their preferments by the regular steps of election.'

The Latitude Men and the Cambridge Platonists—the groups overlap, but are to be distinguished, for while most Cambridge Platonists were latitudinarian in temper, many even of the first Latitudinarians (Tillotson and Patrick for example) were not Platonists. Centred in Emmanuel and Christ's colleges, the Platonists seem to have been students in the 1630s—the Mastership of Richard Holdsworth at Emmanuel may be significant—Fellows in the 1640s, and Heads of Houses in the 1650s, a group of massively learned men who somehow survived successive academic purges (Worthington and Whichcote absented themselves from Cambridge when the Covenant was taken). They had made it their chief business to pursue sound learning in a dissolving political society.

Though reacting sharply against their Puritan teachers, they represent the last flowering of Puritan humanism. Milton might bitterly criticize that for its narrowness, but his own learning attests its depth, the formidable combination of classical learning with technical study of the sacred languages, and ancillary middle-eastern tongues. To this must be added the solid grounding in logic, rhetoric, and philosophy, never merely backward looking, which gave them an impressive power of argument, a rationalism which was not their least contribution to the Christian apologetic of the coming age.

Patrick shares their emphasis on 'reason' and cites the favourite text of the Platonists when he says that reason is 'that faculty whereby a man must judge of everything, nor can a man believe anything except he have some reason for it . . . and those principles which are the candle of the Lord set up in the soul of every man that hath not wilfully extinguished it.'

At the Restoration these men had conformed to the Church of England and this had roused the resentment of the returning high churchmen of the Old Guard.[2] But Patrick defends them:

---

[2] See Ken's onslaught on 1,342 'factious ministers lately ordained' in his *Ichabod* (1663). Ken, *Prose Works*, ed. Benham, ch. iv, pp. 23 and 25.

It seems very strange that any son of the Church should be displeased to see the number of her children to increase beyond expectation.

I fear if the Fathers of the Church were not wiser than some of their angry sons, who must needs be thrusting some of their younger brethren out of doors, if (I say) all that have been reproached with the name of Latitude should be disowned by the Church, that the remains would be the least party of any one denomination in England.

But the Latitude Men are genuinely Church of England men. They not only love its liturgy and accept its government, but they 'think that our Church may easilyer be marred than mended . . . but they presume no man would have them to think that the whole weight of religion lies in externals, or that they are of greater account than the eternal and indispensable laws of good and evil.' Here is a return, as against Puritan scholasticism, to the view of Christianity as primarily a way of life and a vision of God.

Lastly for the Doctrine of the Church, they do cordially adhere to it, as doth sufficiently appear by their willingness to subscribe to the thirty-nine articles, and all other points of Doctrine contained either in the Liturgy or book of Homilies, and particularly (whatever may be privately whispered to the contrary) they do both devoutly adore the Blessed Trinity in the Letany and make solemn profession of the orthodox faith, both concerning it and other points in the three creeds, not excepting that which is commonly ascribed to *Athanasius*, nor is there any article of Doctrine held by the Church which they can be justly said to depart from, unless absolute reprobation be one, which they do not think themselves bound to believe.[3]

These men looked back across Puritan and medieval scholasticism to the Church of the first centuries 'nor is there any point in divinity where that which is most ancient doth not prove the most rational, and the most rational, the ancientest.'

The relation of the Cambridge Platonists to 'that old loving nurse, the Platonick philosophy' was both philosophical and religious. It was a tradition which may have persisted in Cambridge throughout the sixteenth century and it turned gratefully back to the Florentine Platonists, to Ficino and Pico della Mirandola, with their roots in the Neo- and Middle Platonists, and their addiction to the Hermetic writings and the Cabbala. It was their strength and their weakness that they lived in the half-light of a dawning age, where much that was bogus, pseudo-science, and the occult, alchemy, even white magic, existed alongside new discoveries and the widening horizons of mathematics and science. They were aware that new questions

---

[3] Patrick, *Brief Account*, p. 9.

demanded new answers, and accordingly 'Aristotle and the schoolmen are out of request with them.'

Patrick lists the fields in which new truth has been discovered—astronomy, magnetism, anatomy. In the middle of his letter he has an intricate humorous parable about a farmer's broken clock, and the various attempts to put it right—it is the Latitudinarian who succeeds. He quotes with approval the attempts of Descartes and others to provide a rationale for the new world view. With fine perception he defends this new openness of mind, a forward-looking mentality which these men contributed to the Cambridge tradition. 'There is an infinite desire of knowledge broken forth into the world, and men may as well hope to stop the tide or bind the ocean with chains as to hinder free philosophy from overflowing.'[4]

His words were indeed prophetic, for in the coming century the Church would more than once be caught off balance, driven back on the defensive, using old arguments to meet new challenges.

Nor will it be possible otherwise to free religion from scorn and contempt, if her priests be not as well skilled in nature as the people, and her Champions furnished with as good Artillery as her enemies. How shall the Clergy be able to maintain their credit with the ingenuous Gentry who begin generally to be acquainted with the *Atomical Hypothesis*, and know how to distinguish between a true Gemme and a *Bristol* diamond, or how shall they encounter with the witts (as they are called) of the age that assault Religion with new kinds of weapons? Will they acquiesce in the authority of *Aristotle* or *St. Thomas?*—or be put off with '*contra negantem principia*'? Let not the Church send out her soldiers armed with Dock leaves and Bullrushes, to encounter Swords and Guns, but let them wear as good brass and steel as their enemies, and fight with them at their own weapons: and then, having Truth and Right on their side, let them never despair of victory.[5]

ii. Stillingfleet, Patrick, Tillotson, Kidder

Burnet's description of the first Latitudinarians continues where Patrick's 'Latitude Men' had left off. He speaks of the affluence of the Church regained at the Restoration, an elderly leadership 'loaded with many livings and dignities' so that 'an overset of wealth and pomp . . . came on men in the decline of their parts and age' and he adds 'if a new set of men had not appeared of another stamp, the church had quite lost her esteem over the nation.'[6]

These new men were the Latitudinarians, a label which by the end of

---

[4] Ibid., p. 23.　　　　[5] Ibid., p. 24.
[6] G. Burnet, *History of My Own Time* (1753), i. 260.

the century had become a dirty word in the vocabulary of the high churchmen, but which, slightly polished, was to remain a handy description for historians, of the temper of the eighteenth-century Establishment. They themselves would have preferred the word 'moderate'—for a tradition which eschewed extremes and went back in Cambridge through John Worthington, Samuel Ward, and William Bedell to Joseph Mede who was perhaps the spiritual father of them all.

If 'the Spirit of Man is the candle of the Lord' (Prov. 20:27) was the Platonist text, then Phil. 2:5, 'Let your moderation be known to all men', was the Latitudinarian watchword.[7]

They loved the constitution of the Church and the liturgy [says Burnet]. They wished that things might have been carried on with more moderation, and they continued to keep a good correspondence with those who differed from them, and allowed a great freedom both in philosophy and divinity: from whence they were called men of Latitude, and, upon this men of narrower thoughts and fiercer tempers fastened upon them the name of Latitudinarians.[8]

He names the most eminent of the Latitudinarians as Tillotson, Stillingfleet, and Patrick. They had been young men during the latter part of the Commonwealth and 'coming men' in the reign of Charles II. They arrived at eminence and reputation in time to take a manful share in the church struggle under James II. They shared with their high-church contemporaries a rejection of Calvinist doctrines, though the word 'Arminian' has little relevance applied to them. But they also had little room for the high-church doctrines of passive obedience to a hereditary monarch, and were able conscientiously to accept and support the Revolution under William III and loyally to serve both Mary and William, to the fury of their opponents. At the same time they were accused of being too friendly towards the Dissenters, and insufficiently guarded in their defence of the historic faith of the Church.

Of the three named by Burnet, Edward Stillingfleet (1635–99)[9] deserves first mention, for he was the first to get into print, as a young man of twenty-four, winning for himself an early and almost awesome prestige, remaining almost unchallenged amid many not inconsiderable

---

[7] John Worthington claimed to be devoted to a 'moderation' which he believed might have averted the Civil War. A sermon by Wilkins on Phil. 2:5 was reprinted during the Hoadly controversy. The text appears on the title page of Stillingfleet's *Irenicum*. It was a favourite text for Benjamin Hoadly.

[8] Burnet, *My Own Time*, p. 263.

[9] Burnet, p. 264; J. Tulloch, *Rational Theology and Christian Philosophy in Europe in the Seventeenth Century* (3 vols., 1872), 411ff.; A. T. Hart, 'The Age of Reason', in *A History of St. Paul's Cathedral*, ed. W. R. Matthews and M. Atkins (1957), p. 215.

contemporaries as 'Ecclesiae Anglicanae Defensor semper invictus'. A Dorset man, he was educated at St John's College, Cambridge, where he became a Fellow in 1653. We sometimes underrate the extent to which in a Europe and a Britain rent by violent religious wars the development of European culture went on—the enormously wide-ranging correspondence between Samuel Hartlib and John Worthington is an eloquent testimony to its continuance. Stillingfleet was bred into this Cambridge learning, in its depth, in respect both of technical equipment in the sacred languages and ancient history, and of a training in logic and dialectic which made him a formidable apologist. He was aware not only of the Platonist inheritance, but of the new challenges of the age of Descartes and Robert Boyle. Like many young contemporaries, he began as a private tutor, in the household of Sir Roger Burgoyne, who in 1657 presented him for the living of Sutton. In 1665 he became Rector of St Andrew's, Holborn, and thereafter Archdeacon of London, Dean of St Paul's, and in 1689 Bishop of Worcester. It is likely that only infirmity prevented him from succeeding John Tillotson as Archbishop of Canterbury.

Every now and then a young scholar pulls off an intellectual feat which sets the academic dovecote murmuring. This Edward Stillingfleet achieved with his *Irenicum* in 1659. It was an appeal to all parties to seek unity, in an episcopal polity in which Presbyterian and Independent principles were embodied; it implied the rejection of 'de jure divino episcopacy'. When it appeared it looked like an impressive olive branch. But within a few months, it all looked very different, and twenty-five years later Stillingfleet had repented of this effort of his salad days. 'The writing of his Irenicum', said Burnet, 'was a great snare to him: for to avoid the imputations that brought upon him, he not only retracted the book but went into the humours of a high sort of people beyond what became him, perhaps beyond his own sense of things.'[10] Certainly his famous sermon on the 'Mischief of Separation' represents the common front of the London clergy in 1680 and possibly, too, what Burnet calls his 'haughty temper' has something to do with the coldness towards Dissent that marks that sermon. As a polemic divine he was of the artillery rather than the cavalry, bombarding opponents with massive learning, defending the Church of England against atheists, Dissenters, and Roman Catholics. His *Origines Sacrae*—written when he was twenty-seven—is perhaps even more impressive than his first work. It shows that he had a sound historical sense, which took him into the available sources of ancient learning, and makes his defence of the Bible

[10] Burnet, *My Own Time*, p. 265.

and its accuracy a genuinely comparative study of ancient history and religion. In between the linguistic and historical points there is taut and persuasive reasoning, and, like Tillotson, he distinguishes between the kind of certainty which mathematical demonstration brings, and the certainty of faith. He is up to date enough to note that the authenticity of the Hermetic writings have been discredited by critical investigation, yet has no notion how damaging this methodology might be when applied to Holy Writ. Here he can do no other than affirm the historical accuracy of Genesis, arguing from the height of mountains on the earth ('no mountains much above three miles perpendicular') and the dimensions of the Ark, and the fewness of animal species, to the veracity of the account of the Flood. His later writing, the *Origines Britannicae*, is perhaps his best work, and places him high in the goodly company of historians and antiquaries of the day. His polemic against the Roman Catholics is more commonplace, and his attacks on John Locke whose empiricism raised his Platonist hackles, and whose Christology he suspected, has been generally regarded as less successful. As Tillotson would summarily write off the medieval schoolmen, so Stillingfleet in *A Discourse Concerning the Idolatry Practised in the Church of Rome* (1672)[11] poured scorn on the Catholic mystical tradition for irrational fanaticism. He jeered at Cressy's edition of the *Revelations of Divine Love* of Mother Julian of Norwich, as a collection of 'fopperies' and 'blasphemous tittle-tattle', and thought that the whole vocabulary of 'abstractedness of life, mental prayer, passive union, a deiform fund of the soul' must end in either enthusiasm or madness. No doubt he was attacking emotional jargon, but it is plain that his 'Latitudinarianism' has moved from that of John Worthington, Henry More, and John Smith among the Cambridge Platonists. He set the fashion for Anglicans like William Nichols who in 1701 published a translation of St Francis of Sales's *Introduction to the Devout Life* with a preface denouncing the 'mystical stuff of Teresa . . . Sancta Sophia' and the Mechthilds and Gertrudes of Helfta, with St Bridget of Sweden as 'Bedlam Divinity'.[12] Bishop Lavington and 'John Smith' would use similar language when writing to John Wesley.[13] As a writer his style was mannered and old-fashioned, nearer to Jeremy Taylor than to Tillotson.

Simon Patrick (1625–1707) is one whose fame lies in the field of what the age called 'practical theology'. His early writings were published

[11] pp. 224, 284.
[12] T. A. Birrell, 'English Catholic Mystics in non-Catholic circles', *Downside Review*, Jan. 1976.
[13] See below, pp. 383–6.

anonymously. They included a university sermon, *The Hypocritical Nation* (1657), preached on a Fast day. It must have been unbearably tedious to listen to, but is massive in its Biblical learning, well splashed with Hebrew, and it is kindest to think of it as a young academic showing off. A Lincolnshire man, he was deeply influenced at Queens' by the paragon of the Cambridge Platonists, John Smith. Like Stillingfleet and Tenison, he had sought episcopal ordination during the Commonwealth and in 1658 became Vicar of Battersea. In 1662 he became Rector of the newly formed parish of St Paul's, Covent Garden, and exercised there a devoted ministry, refusing to exchange it for the more celebrated and more demanding St Martin-in-the-Fields, though as a prebend of Westminster and Treasurer of the Abbey he did accept wider responsibilities.

Despite that university sermon, he became a notable preacher, though perhaps he tended to go on and on, and his attempted revisions of the Collects for the Liturgical commission of 1689 are generally regarded as something from which the Church of England may be grateful for having been saved. But his edifying writings were attractive and popular, and ran into many editions, among them his *Parable of the Pilgrim* (1664)—which has nothing save the image in common with John Bunyan—a sensitive *Letter to a Friend*, and his *Christian Sacrifice*. This last is not concerned with the new interpretations of the eucharistic sacrifice of Brevint, Bull, and Johnson and the Non-Jurors, but is part of the eucharistic renewal to which the London divines were devoted. Each section of the work ends with extended prayers, similar to those which adorn the devotional writings of his neighbour, Anthony Horneck of the Savoy. He took a prominent part in the great confabulations of clergy and bishops during the critical months of confrontation with James II, and in 1688 was made Bishop of Chichester, being translated to Ely in 1691.

John Tillotson (1630–94)[14] was five years younger than Patrick, and as a student and Fellow of Clare in the 1650s was involved in the theological dichotomy which had split the college down the middle. His father had been an Independent, and he himself seems at first to have favoured Thomas Goodwin's Calvinism rather than the new attitudes of Ralph Cudworth. But a study of Chillingworth moved him, and he became for many, and notably for his enemies, the epitome of what they called 'Latitudinarianism'. It was as a preacher that he came to fame, at St Lawrence Jewry in the City and at the Inns of Court, and then more and

[14] J. Tillotson, *Works* (with Life by A. T. Birch), 3 vols., 1752. Hart, 'The Age of Reason', p. 219.

more in Court preaching before Mary and William. 'I never knew any clergyman so universally esteemed and beloved as he was for above twenty years',[15] said Burnet.

Of the quality of his mind we shall speak in a later chapter, but it may be said here that his worth as a theologian has been underrated. If, like St John Chrysostom whom he much admired, his was the faith of a moralist, it was because there was a cause. In an age of dissolving moral standards there was abundant need for plain and solid teaching. If in the next generation there was some improvement in manners and morals, it was because of Tillotson and his friends.

William and Mary admired and liked him, and though he would willingly have rested on his laurels as Dean of St Paul's, he yielded to William III's insistence that he succeed Sancroft, the deprived Archbishop, in 1691. Though in poor health (he had had a stroke some years before), he struggled to fulfil his duties, though they brought upon him the unrestrained fury of the high churchmen and especially the Non-Jurors. They taunted him with his Nonconformist background, doubted whether he had ever been baptized, and magnified every utterance which could be twisted into Socinianism and even the 'atheist' doctrines of the detested Thomas Hobbes. He got into trouble when, with characteristic fairness, he stated the views of those who believed in annihilation rather than eternal punishment, yet he plainly rejected their views, and though he opposed the statutory use of the Athanasian Creed, and albeit he was the friend of the Socinian conformist and philanthropist, Thomas Firmin, he was no Deist nor Arian. It did not help his reputation after his death that he was quoted by Samuel Clarke and Anthony Collins. There is no doubt that this sensitive man was deeply wounded by the venom of the attacks upon him. But his own catholic spirit extended to men of all parties and of none, and he died in the arms of his non-juring friend and unflagging admirer, Robert Nelson.

The career of Richard Kidder (1633–1703)[16] is an illumination of what could happen to a Latitudinarian transplanted into a high-church environment. He was born in East Grinstead, and enough money was found to send him to Emmanuel College, Cambridge, where William Sancroft was his friend. Like his contemporaries John Worthington and Benjamin Whichcote, he refused to swear the Puritan oaths, and, like Simon Patrick and Edward Stillingfleet, received Anglican orders, from

[15] Burnet, *My Own Time*, p. 264.
[16] *The Life of Bishop Kidder, D.D.*, ed. A. Robinson, Somerset Record Society, vol. xxxvii, 1924.

Bishop Brownrigg. He became a Fellow of his College, but resigned on succeeding to a living which he was forced to surrender in 1662 when he refused to swear to the Prayer Book, on the stubborn ground that he would not swear to what he had not in fact seen. There followed a sojourn in Essex where three of his little boys died (he lost another three a few years later). A key to his ills is the phrase in his autobiography 'surpriz'd by the gout'. Henceforth it was always present, at times crippling him entirely. As a bishop he had to be carried into his first ordination, and because of it in his early career he turned down the notable livings of St Helen's, Bishopsgate, and St Paul's, Covent Garden. But he was a worthy member of the goodly company of London divines in this period and shared in their frequent gatherings to plan Biblical commentaries and anti-Roman apologetic. In his small parish of St Martin Outwich he had affluent friends who showed their esteem by sending him pupils, who included William Dawes, the future Archbishop, and George Harbin, a leading high churchman. He was a noted Hebraist and Old Testament scholar, a Boyle Lecturer, on the Liturgical Commission of 1689. Like others of the group, he wrote in favour of frequent communion, and their celebrations raised large sums of money. Kidder shared with these friends a concern for the poor. 'I was wont when I had my feet, to go to the ends of the town, Southwark and Whitechapel, and to go from one poor house to another and leave them such relief as I judged necessary.'

He became Preacher at the Rolls Chapel, a royal chaplain, and Dean of Peterborough, where he lived happily with his fellow clergy. Then, under pressure from the Government, and very unwillingly, he consented to be made Bishop of Bath and Wells, in place of the deprived Ken. It would have been difficult to follow any one of the seven bishops, but quite hopeless to expect to succeed in place of the beloved Ken who was near at hand, and who protested vehemently at his displacement. Kidder found himself among Jacobites and high churchmen, and his Archdeacon, Sandys, refused to recognize him (his wife was noted for standing when prayers were made for William III). He might have settled down quietly with his books, but he was a stubbornly conscientious man and soon stirred up trouble with his dean and chapter. No doubt in this almost medieval wrangle about the provisions of its Elizabethan charter, there was as much to be said for the dean and chapter as for the bishop. But nobody can doubt that there were plenty of abuses about the place, and the infiltration of the Creighton family into the dignitaries, and their preferments, is but one example of the ills of the time.

He became immersed in a series of unsavoury wrangles which he meticulously recorded in his note book, and an almost *opéra bouffe* rumpus with a colourful character, Claver Morrice, the ambitious local doctor. Morrice became involved with Kidder's daughter—she whose broken-handed effigy today points to her father's memorial in Wells Cathedral. He seems to have tried to extort a large settlement from her parents, and, so her father thought, played fast and loose with her affections. Morrice was involved in a long squabble with George Hooper in later years, and all, and perhaps rather more than all, that can be said on his behalf is inscribed on his massive memorial in the cloisters of the cathedral, over which his bust stares truculently.

On the night of 26–7 November 1703 there occurred the worst recorded storm in English history. The fleet was shattered, the Eddystone Lighthouse destroyed. In London a terrified German chaplain told how he clung to his bed while the whole room soared up and down with the gale. In Wells the wind funnelled down from the Mendips to the Bishop's Palace and the great chimney-stack fell, crushing Kidder and his wife to death, dragging them in its fall to the lower floor from which they were dug out next day. Ken was soon telling his non-juring friends how miraculously he had been spared, amid creaking rafters, but perhaps those on whom the Tower of Siloam fell were not sinners above all others in Jerusalem and Kidder, sad, scholarly man, beset with bodily pain and frequent sorrows, has deserved to be more generously remembered than he was by the high churchmen of his cathedral and his diocese.

3

SOME DIVINES OF THE CITY OF LONDON

THE City churches of London, and their clergy, played an important role in the seventeenth century. Here the great Puritan preachers had their influential pulpits, as incumbents or as lecturers. The first half of the century had left the nation sermon prone, and London was the magnet for the preachers. Benjamin Whichcote, ousted from Cambridge, happily settled for St Lawrence Jewry in London. There is the comic story of Isaac Barrow, renowned in Cambridge, turning up to preach a supply sermon at St Dunstan's-in-the-West, where his insignificant presence and scruffy appearance emptied the church in a rowdy scramble within seconds of his appearing in the pulpit, leaving a tiny group of hearers, who, however, included Richard Baxter. Then, in 1666 came the Great Fire, and within hours, of the ninety-seven parish churches within the walls, only a dozen damaged buildings remained, the parishioners turned overnight into wandering, homeless refugees, as did John Worthington's congregation at St Bene't Fink.

And if, as in the aftermath of the Blitz in 1940, recovery was marvellously swift, many famous bells had been silenced, and many churches had to find temporary accommodation, like St Lawrence Jewry, whose congregation met in the chapel of Guildhall. St Paul's, which had been in disrepair even before the fire, was to make do amid the rubble and rebuilding for the rest of the century before Sir Christopher Wren's dome could stand out above a renewed city and a vista of fine new steeples. London had been growing eastward and westward (less quickly to the north and south) for a whole century, despite repeated efforts of Crown and Government to prevent the growth of suburbs. Soon the line from the City along the Strand was continuous to Westminster. And while something of the unplanned variety of an enormous village persisted, so that gentry, merchants, tradesmen, and the poor lived often side by side, there were new fashionable squares in the Holborn area, but also grievous slums appearing in Westminster and in the area surrounding the two key parish churches of St Martin and St Giles-in-the-Fields.[1]

At this time these churches, with their affluent and overflowing

[1] N. G. Brett-James, *The Growth of Stuart London*, 1935; M. D. George, *London Life in the Eighteenth Century*, 1976; G. Rudé, *Hanoverian London*, 1971.

congregations, were served by a group of exceptional men, splendid preachers, devoted in pastoral care, pioneers in some of the most impressive educational and philanthropic projects of the time. Historically and geographically they were in the forefront of the confrontation with Popery, and also with the defence of the faith against the cultivated scepticism and ridicule of the 'witts' of the Court. And right manfully they acquitted themselves. If there was indeed a renewal in the Church, however temporary and limited, and a revival of manners, then these London clergy are gratefully to be remembered. Most of them, when they had become bishops and archbishops, maintained a high level of episcopal devotion which would not be equalled for another century.

The most distinguished of these City preachers were royal chaplains, and the sermons before the King and Court at Whitehall and elsewhere were at the heart of this concentration of divinity. At a time when the Royal Court was becoming a byword for dissoluteness, never perhaps had a court been subjected to such an incessant barrage of edification. It may be doubted whether the Elizabethans, the Puritans, or the Caroline divines at their considerable best could surpass the performances of these preachers whose sermons and great audiences were chronicled in the journals of a Pepys, an Evelyn, a Thoresby. Stillingfleet, Sherlock, South, Tillotson, Sharp, Lloyd, and Ken preached sermons no longer wrapped up in florid and baroque symbolism, but which spoke directly and very plainly about the evils of the day. When that Christian Prince Charles II entered the sanctuary to take Communion, preceded by the three young peers who were his illegitimate sons by three different mothers, the sermons before and after may have kept clear of texts about the Prophet Nathan or St John Baptist, but they were plain enough.

The population of the parishes was out of all proportion to the provision for worship. It is said that St Martin-in-the-Fields had pews for 400, though Evelyn speaks of a communicating congregation of 1,000 on at least one occasion, but what was this among so many as 40,000? Soon it had to be subdivided, and new parishes were formed in St Paul's, Covent Garden (1662), St James's, Westminster (1685; later known as St. James's, Piccadilly), and St Anne's, Soho (1686). St Martin-in-the-Fields[2] claimed to be the most important parish church in England, its incumbent's income between £900 and £1,000 a year. It faced towards the Court and St James's, and its flourishing congregation included such characters as Nell Gwynn, Sir Edmund Berry Godfrey,

[2] J. McMasters, *St. Martin-in-the-Fields*, 1916; K. Esdaile, *St. Martin-in-the-Fields*, 1944.

and the Duke of Monmouth. To the north was the ancient parish of St Giles, bordered by the new fashionable squares of Bloomsbury, but already a seedy and unsavoury area, with its slums, and their notoriously swarming cellars, and a high proportion of unprosperous Irish immigrants.

The older City churches continued to provide important pulpits for learned incumbents like Beveridge, Cave, Fowler, Clagett, and for still-prized lectureships like the Friday lectureship at St Lawrence Jewry, while the Inns of Court retained their reputation as intellectual audiences. St Paul's dominated the scene with its distinguished preaching deans, Stillingfleet, Tillotson, and Sherlock.

But in the period 1670–88 our attention centres on a remarkable group of parish clergy in the churches without the walls. They were exceptionally gifted men, all bound for high preferment. They came from all parts of the Kingdom, Lloyd from Wales, Tenison from East Anglia, Sharp from Yorkshire, Patrick from Lincolnshire. And they were men in their prime, before their capacities had been straitened by the manifold chores of high ecclesiastical office, and before they had been crippled by age or illness. Lloyd and Tenison came to St Martin's in their forties, and John Sharp at St Giles was just turned thirty. We tend to remember Lloyd at his latter end, as a doddering Merlin, clutching the Book of Revelation, pin-pointing apocalyptic prophecies which convinced only himself: or Tenison, his true greatness obscured by the years of painful sickness, thwarted again and again by lesser men.

William Lloyd (1627–1717) was instituted in St Martin-in-the-Fields in December 1676, though he soon left for a spell in Holland as chaplain to Mary. But he was back in time to be at the centre of the furore about the Popish Plot and it was he who, flanked by two ecclesiastical muscle-men in the pulpit, preached the sensational sermon on the murder of his parishioner, Sir Edmund Berry Godfrey, on the text 'Died Abner as a fool dieth?' Despite the affluence of his congregation, the building was in sad disrepair and it was not until the end of the century that measures were taken to pull it down and build the lovely Gibbs church.

Lloyd was one of those parsons who, as the saying goes, mind their pews and keys, and even after he left, he still kept a concern for a hierarchical arrangement of seating as nicely differentiated as the circles in Dante's *Paradiso*. He wrote to Lord Hollis in March 1681—'I remember your Lordship did . . . speak of putting a lock upon the seat, which I would by no means permit . . . at last I did consent upon condition that your Lordship would keep the key, and not lend it to any person, nor lock that seat yourself, but just when you sat there.' He added that it was his rule to 'keep all the chancel seats free for the use of them that came to serve God, and not to take any rent nor to suffer anything to be paid but what people were pleased to give freely to the chancel-keeper for his attendance, which is all that he has for keeping the place clean and decent.'[3] And though this rule was indeed honoured in its observance rather than its breach, he could not prevent the development of pew-renting, and even tipping of a kind which turned the seating in the still more fashionable St James's, Westminster, into that of an exclusive club.[4]

Thomas Tenison (1636–1715) was born at Cottenham, near Cambridge, and went to Corpus Christi College. He was ordained privately by Bishop Duppa in 1659, and after holding two or three livings outside London was in 1680 appointed Vicar of St Martin-in-the-Fields. Here he was placed at a focal point in the church struggle in dangerous and exciting years, when the leaders of the Church faced a crisis of conscience, of a rather modern kind—whether to obey when pulpits were ordered to be silent, whether to read, at the State's behest, statements from the pulpit. If Bishop Compton was the Niemöller and St Paul's the Dahlem, then St Martin's was a Marienkirche and Tenison its Probst Grüber. Tenison was a serious man, as were many seventeenth-century clerics, but we may take with reservation Swift's dismissal of him as a dull dog. Both he and his wife had a great deal of ill health to cope with. But his ministry at St Martin's was even more signal than William Lloyd's. John Evelyn wrote of one of his sermons (21 March 1683):

Dr. Tenison on 1 Cor. 6. 12 . . . concluding in a most heavenly exhortation, almost rapturous: I esteem the doctor to be absolutely the most profitable preacher in the Church of England, being likewise of a most holy conversation, very learned and ingenious: but the insuperable pains he takes and care of his parish will I fear wear him out, which were an unexpressible loss.[5]

As a pastor he was attacked by the rigorists, among whom Thomas Ken belonged. It was Tenison who preached at the funeral of Nell Gwynn and, when complaint was made, threatened to put her in the grave intended for himself. This Ken could barely put up with, who on a famous occasion had refused her lodging, but he was still more enraged with Tenison for administering comfortable words to the dying Queen Mary, and for not insisting on an act of penitence for her ungrateful disobedience to her father, James II. Admirable and saintly as the leading

[3] A. T. Hart, *William Lloyd* (1952), p. 37.

[4] J. P. Ferguson, *An Eighteenth Century Heretic: Dr. Samuel Clarke* (Kineton 1976), p. 200.

[5] J. Evelyn, *Diary*, ed. de Beer, iv. 307.

Non-Jurors were, they were not the kind of people to have with you on the scaffold, or at a death-bed, unless you were a Jacobite.

Tenison was at the geographical centre of the London Roman Catholic crisis, and fitted by learning and by his power of preaching to take a lead in the sharp controversy which now reopened. It was played out against an audience of clubs and Court and coffee houses, so that a few conversions to either side roused great excitement. There were barely decorous debates and confrontations in some of which Simon Patrick and Dr Jane were involved. But the liveliest concerned the Jesuits of the Savoy, who in 1684 had opened a college, and the leading Jesuit in England, Andrew Pulton, and Thomas Tenison became engaged in a tug of war for the soul of an apprentice boy. There was a series of arguments before excited audiences, and a flurry of pamphlets best summarized by the newsletter which reported:

On Thursday last was held a conference between Dr. Tenison of St. Martin's and Mr. Pulton, a Jesuit of the Savoy, upon the subject of a Brazier's son in Long Acre who had embraced the Roman Faith, it being to render satisfaction to the parents of the lad, but it being managed with great heat, it came to little effect.[6]

Tenison carried through two admirable educational projects. Libraries were a subject in the air at this time as the contemporary foundations by the Lancashire merchant, Humphrey Chetham, show, but Tenison felt there was a special need in London where 'there are a great number of Ministers and other studious persons and especially in the parish of St. Martin's where beside the Vicar and his assistants, there are several Noblemen's chaplains perpetually residing.'[7] Tenison planned the library with John Evelyn and Sir Christopher Wren, himself bore the whole cost of the building and the furniture, giving part of his own ever-growing collection of books and manuscripts. Patrick suggests that the charity schools were sparked off by the Jesuits:

The romish priests were then so busy that they set up a school to teach youths for nothing: which we thought might draw many into their snare and therefore we agreed to do the same, which we did in St. Martin's churchyard adjoining to the library which proved a flourishing school under the care of an excellent master, Mr. Postlethwait, now master of St. Paul's school, London.[8]

But the Jesuit school does not appear to have opened before 1687, and Tenison was busied about a school in 1683. Moreover a merchant named Skelton had left money for a school in the parish of St Giles in the

---

[6] E. F. Carpenter, *Thomas Tenison* (1948), p. 55.   [7] Ibid., p. 24.
[8] S. Patrick, *Autobiography* (Oxford, 1839), p. 128.

1670s,[9] so that it is difficult to pin-point the beginning of the charity-school movement. But if any pioneer can be named, it must surely be Tenison, who not only founded the St Martin's school, but another in the new parish of St James, and a school for girls at Lambeth and a school at Croydon. His concern for learning was lifelong and when the Boyle Lectures languished he came to the aid of this important platform for the new learning, and later directed its progress with sympathy and wisdom.

We have already drawn attention to the similarly devoted pastoral ministry of Simon Patrick at St Paul's, Covent Garden, where, too, there had been a eucharistic renewal, and as a result greatly increased offerings for the poor. 'Having very often great communions and sometimes large offerings (more than once near twenty pounds and on Easter Day five and twenty) I was very solicitious to dispose of such money.'[10]

When the immediate needs of the sick and poor had been met, the question arose what to do with the remainder. Patrick forbade his ingenuous churchwardens to employ it for the relief of the poor rate, and formed a trust out of whose funds a curate might be employed to read prayers.

Some pious persons indeed had desired prayers at the hours of ten in the morning and three in the afternoon, which they maintained by a voluntary contribution—these therefore were ordered to be at six o'clock in the morning and seven at night in the summer time (before trading was begun and when it was done) that servants might resort unto them. Which they did very much, and I hope will continue to do so. The other prayers also still continue at ten and three to which the gentry and better sort of people who maintain them are wont to come.[11]

John Sharp (1645–1714)[12] was just turned thirty-one years of age when he was installed as Rector of St Giles-in-the-Fields (having already served as a locum tenens for some months). Not only had he the advantage over his neighbours of youth, but he had the precious charisma of personal charm without which archbishops, as Tenison could ruefully have told him, are accounted as dead before princes. A Yorkshireman, he went up to Christ's in the heyday of the two most learned of the Cambridge Platonists, Ralph Cudworth and Henry More. Despite the wide range of his interests, he was not perhaps cut out for Academe, and

[9] R. Dobie, *The History of the United Parishes of St. Giles-in-the-Fields and St. George's Bloomsbury*, 1829.

[10] Patrick, *Autobiography*, p. 88.   [11] Ibid., p. 90.

[12] T. Sharp, *Life of Archbishop John Sharp*; A. T. Hart, *The Life and Times of John Sharp, Archbishop of York*, 1949.

when he failed to obtain a fellowship it was not all loss. Future episcopal colleagues were perhaps cumbered with too much learning and at any rate, in becoming tutor to the sons of Sir Heneage Finch, he had found a patron of growing influence, for the Finch family were bound, as they say, right for the top. Although he was to become the leader of the high churchmen, he was not partisan in his friendships. Tillotson was his friend and the one who obtained for him the notable Friday lectureship at St Lawrence Jewry. Richard Baxter consented to his marriage (Sharp's mother-in-law-to-be doted on Baxter, and insisted on it), and it says much that Richard Baxter, a very choosy sermon-taster, frequented his services. And his preaching won him fame. It was lucid, moralistic, and if he lacked the *gravitas* of Tillotson, it was all gain that he spoke simply in the pulpit as a man speaketh to his friends. Taught by his mother to love the liturgy, his prayers were as striking as his sermons:

distinct, nervous, devout and indeed seraphic was his elocution on these occasions, that he not only disposed the congregation present to seriousness and reverence, but inspired them with some degree of that devotion, life and comfort which he expressed himself. [13]

He had a flair for moral theology in the tradition of Jeremy Taylor, and his two tracts, giving an analysis of conscience, were much read. From his pastoral skill in this ministry of sixteen years in London, he acquired a great fund of pastoral experience, and his letters of spiritual counsel, for which he was solicited by people of all ranks, are of the highest order.

There were grim corners of his parish, not least the Irish immigrants and the notorious 'cellarers'. But though he had a team of well-paid curates (he gave them between £100 and £120 a year) he never sent them where he had not been himself and he knew the dark alleys at first hand. He was concerned for his young people and himself regularly catechized them on Sunday afternoons, and these were the only occasions when he spoke extempore. When, in 1682, he was made Dean of Norwich, he had perforce to leave more and more to his assistants. When he came to leave St Giles, he preached a moving farewell sermon on Phil. 4: 8, exhorting his parishioners to take heed to family prayers and family worship—stressing the great importance of keeping sanely and Christianly the Lord's Day which he believed was a great bulwark against the moral confusion of the age, and stressing the importance of frequent Communion. On 24 June 1688 he underwent a deep spiritual experience, which he was wont to commemorate annually, and from that time there seems to have been a new depth to his spiritual life.

[13] Hart, *Life of Sharp*, p. 77.

It is relevant, if slightly anachronistic, to mention two other notable London ministries at this point. White Kennett (1660–1728)[14] entered upon the impropriated living of St Botolph's, Aldgate, in 1700 and had to struggle for many months to gain authority and win acceptance by patron and by parish. Here, at the East End of London, 24,000 people lived in 1,300 dwellings. With the assistance of a reader he laboured hard. In 1707, his last year in the parish, there were 162 marriages, 569 baptisms, and 698 burials. He preached twice a Sunday to a great congregation, read prayers once a week, and was a persistent visitor. His leading layman, Samuel Brewster, praised him and the congregation for 'constant attendance on the sermons and other divine ordinances, how great the number of communicants who do duly frequent the holy sacrament: how decently your children of both sexes have been clothed and how well instructed.'[15]

At the other end of the town William Wake (1657–1737)[16] was appointed to St James's, Westminster, a church which was to remain the temple of an affluent society and almost to deserve what was said of a fashionable church in Manchester, that it was 'a carriage-way to heaven'. But he exercised a conscientious ministry there for ten years. He had already made his reputation as a preacher before the lawyers of Gray's Inn and as a chaplain preaching before King and Queen, and the Princess Anne. His sermons are garnished with learning, and the ills of the Roman Church figure prominently in his published sermons. But his farewell sermon on Michaelmas Day 1706, shows how much his congregation meant to him, while the printed sermon has an illuminating appendix of the finances and extensive charities of his congregation. He, too, took seriously his weekly catechism class, and, as at St Paul's, Covent Garden, there were two sets of public prayers, one at hours convenient for servants and the others for their employers. Tenison, as incumbent of the newly formed parish, had promptly founded a charity school. But Wake added two more, one for fifty boys and another for sixty girls.

Behind the London clergy stood that doughty Protestant champion, their bishop. Henry Compton (1632–1713)[17] was a colourful character whose great qualities outweigh some obvious flaws. Nobly born, of a staunchly royalist family he seemed, in modern jargon, to have everything going for him. Entered as a nobleman at Queen's College, Oxford, he did not tarry long during the Commonwealth period, and as

---

[14] G. V. Bennett, *White Kennett, 1660–1728,* 1957.   [15] Ibid., p. 181.
[16] Sykes, *William Wake,* i. 58–61; W. Wake, *Sermons and Discourses on Several Occasions,* 1690.
[17] E. F. Carpenter, *The Protestant Bishop,* 1956.   [18] Ibid., pp. 61ff.

a theologian was *autodidactos*. But he took a commission in the Blues, and the persona of a Guards' Officer was always more obvious from his speech and bearing than that of the theologian. Into it he happily and boisterously relaxed in the famous incident when, to protect the escaping Princess Anne, he rode in his blue cloak at the head of his troop. He had travelled widely in France and Italy, had mastered the tongues and made contacts, and acquired interests which stood Protestant refugees in good stead when the times of persecution came. He had close connections with the Court, supervising the education of the royal princesses, and when Mary went as a bride to Holland, kept a watchful eye on her through a succession of chaplains who reported to him. He was perhaps a little green-eyed, and resented the intrusion when Gilbert Burnet turned up in Holland, a rival for the royal attention and whose person and churchmanship were uncongenial. But he fully earned the title 'the Protestant Bishop' and came into direct confrontation with James II, in bitter and personal hostility. Compton encouraged his learned brethren to the defence of the Protestant cause, and crisis came when James reissued the *Injunctions for Preachers* which his brother had sent out in 1662 in an attempt to muzzle preaching. The parish of St Giles-in-the-Fields, with its large and often obstructive Irish and Catholic population, presented special problems, and John Sharp determined to deal with the menace to Protestantism in a series of sermons, the second of which (9 May 1686) was judged by his enemies to have reflected on the King. The King ordered Compton to suspend him forthwith, but though Sharp, a little scared, was reduced to silence, Compton refused to suspend him, and calling on the highest legal aid and, backed by powerful members of the nobility, he withstood, though in vain, the members of James's Ecclesiastical Commission.

The result was Compton's own suspension. It was no wonder that this forthright man should be the only bishop to sign the invitation to William III. But he had shown that he could be awkward and somehow was not trusted by William or even by Mary, and he was twice passed over for the Primacy which had once seemed his destiny. Though he rallied under disappointments, something of bitterness may underlie his increasing support of the more extreme high churchmen, Atterbury and Sacheverell.

Though not himself a man of learning, he gathered round him a team of theologians who shared his own deep concern for the renewal of the Church. The modern Church, which sometimes seems to believe in Salvation by Conferences, might be inclined to overvalue the importance of Compton's pastoral conferences, but they are, on any showing, impressive, and he presided over these gatherings of clergy in London and Westminster, giving the opening address and summing up at the end (his archdeacons arranged similar gatherings in the countryside and villages).[18]

There were twelve major consultations of this kind between 1678 and 1702, and they dealt with practical and pastoral theology, with the administration of the sacraments, with confirmation and catechizing, and the visitation of the sick, while later conferences went through the disciplinary canons.

We do not know how closely Compton himself was involved in the preparation and publication of a number of volumes of collected essays. But they were the work of this inner group of London clergy, men who knew one another well, who regularly dined together and who had a common mind about the apologetic needs of the Church.

Towards the end of this year [wrote Simon Patrick in 1669] several divines met and dined together intending to consult how they might most efficaciously promote true religion by their ministry . . . and it was agreed that each of them, who were in number as I remember, sixteen, should write a little plain book of a shilling or eighteen pence on such subjects as were misunderstood as about the knowledge of Christ, Faith, Justification, Repentance, Mysteries, Temptation, Desertions etc. and every one chose his subject, but said they would excuse me if I would prepare a prayer book to fit most occasions, and they gave me heads, to which I consented.[19]

Ten years later he described the planning of another symposium. 'In the summer of 1681 several ministers met together and combined to make a short commentary on the Bible and everyone had his part assigned.'[20]

Here were men with a common mind forming a common front. They were aware the Church was under attack from many directions, of which the most serious was the dissolution of faith under the satirical and intellectual attacks of sceptics, and of the threat to orthodoxy from growing Socinianism. They had also to face the problems posed by the continuance of Dissent, both before, and especially after, the Act of Toleration in 1689. And above all there was the polemical demand of the controversy with Roman Catholicism. They had obviously given priority to positive measures, and while giving polemic divinity its due place, were even more insistent that what were needed were better instruments of pastoral care and catechesis, and above all, clear and plain material for the study of the Bible.

The persistence of Dissent, and the problem of Occasional Conformity, led them to make a reasoned statement of the case of the Church of England at this time. It is obvious that Stillingfleet's famous

[18] Ibid., pp. 61ff.   [19] Patrick, *Autobiography*, p. 65.   [20] Ibid., p. 98.

sermon to which we have already referred, was not idiosyncratic, but expressed a common front. This was expressed in a volume *A Collection of Cases and Other Discourses lately written to Recover Dissenters to the Communion of the Church of England* by 'Some divines of the City of London', which was published in 1698 and dedicated to Henry Compton.[21] The tracts had in fact been written over the previous twenty years. They included the two discourses on Conscience which John Sharp had written in 1683–4. The most learned essay was a powerful defence of Infant Baptism by George Hickes, and there were essays on the menace of Rome from Tenison, a defence of preaching by Simon Patrick, and a sermon by John Tillotson on frequent communion. The older items of controversy, the sign of the Cross, extempore prayer, kneeling at Communion, were dealt with in separate essays.

One would look in vain through this volume, or indeed in the much wider field of Anglican apologetic, for any expression of regret or pity, still less of penitence, from any eminent Church of England leader, about the pains inflicted on the Nonconformists, or any unease about the cultural apartheid within which they were now compressed. But at least a volume like this represents an appeal to dialogue.[22] The fact is that they believed the whole onus of separation rested squarely on the shoulders of the Dissenters themselves, who had incurred the guilt of schism. For they did not separate from the Church of England because it denied the essentials of the faith. The Occasional Conformists, who attended Communion and who would worship at their parish churches, showed that they were obstinately witholding from worship in a true Church. What the authors show no awareness of, is that for a century and a half there had been in existence communities of English Christians with their own patterns of worship and community life, which had by now the depth of a rooted tradition.

We can hardly blame these seventeenth-century divines for not considering the uses and practicalities of a pluralist Christian society, since two and a half centuries later the English Churches have so little studied the problems and opportunities involved and are still obsessed by a feeling that unity must mean, not diversity, but uniformity. None the less the *Collection of Cases* shows an awareness that moral theology was involved at a high level and that a learned and rational apologetic

---

[21] Often referred to as 'The London Cases against Dissent'.

[22] There was at least one reply: *Several of the London Cases Considered*. It may have been written by J. Colinges (cf. J. O'Higgins, *Anthony Collins, the Man and his Work* (The Hague 1970)), p. 66.

could not be evaded. There is some evidence that it was not without effect.

Much more extensive was the continuing apologetic against Rome. In 1738 Bishop Edmund Gibson thought it timely to reprint the tracts which had been written by the London clergy in the 1680s and these he printed in three enormous folio volumes each of a thousand pages of close print entitled a *Preservative Against Popery*. They perhaps invite the retort that they were not so much preserved as mummified discourses and it is true that much of their content rehearses ancient arguments repeated again and again in the previous century and a half.

But that is perhaps to do insufficient justice to the rationality of this polemic, to its grounding in Scriptures and the Fathers, and its appeal to history. There is formidable scholarship in the volumes, from Stillingfleet's analysis of the Council of Trent, to Wake's masterly essay—the most impressive apologist, surpassing even Tenison in this field. And if the arguments against Transubstantiation, against the Papacy, about Mariology, were hoary, there were some up-to-date reflections on Roman missionary methods, while the volume included Tenison's famous translation of the French treatise of J. de la Placette, *Of the Incurable Scepticism of the Church of Rome*.

The Roman Church might be small in numbers, but under Charles II, and finally under James II, it came near to capturing the springs of political power. We may easily forget the genuine fear that for the second time in a century the Church of England stood on the edge of irretrievable disaster. These churchmen, who deeply loved the Church of England, who believed that it was the best of all Churches, who could point to a splendid tradition over a century and a half in spirituality and divinity, stood shoulder to shoulder in its defence. But more important than their words in preaching and in writing was their holy conversation in living, the attention they gave to a renewal of the Church in piety and edification, which they made the centre of their own arduous and devoted pastoral care. Between the troubled years that followed the Restoration and the too secularized Church which was to follow, these London divines were a luminous interlude and contributed in no small degree to what we might call 'the Small Awakening'.

For some of them, Tenison and Wake especially, it is possible these were their happiest years spent in the prime of life, and in full vigour of mind and body as members of a company of parish priests, all of uncommon gifts and outstanding devotion, older and younger ones linked in friendship. Later, as eminences, worried by high politics, drawn into a maelstrom of political events and into conflict which ran quite contrary to their temperaments and inclination, wearied and weakened by painful illness—for the gout may have influenced church history as much as Convocation—they appear as tired men, always under strain. In the history of Christ's Church Militant, as in other campaigns, it is the captains, rather than the generals, who enjoy their wars.

4

THE HIGH CHURCH PARTY
(1688–1715)

THE High Church Party represented a formidable combination of ideas, a backward-looking appeal to tradition, and a forward-looking and sometimes radical programme. On the one hand, the watchword was a fervent 'Stare super antiquas vias', the return to the concept of a national Church in a Christian realm, the clergy exercising spiritual discipline over the whole nation, supported by the laity acting through Parliament. But in fact the events of the last half-century had made this dream impossible to realize. There was not only the survival of Dissent, despite the Clarendon Code, and unabated by the Toleration Act, a body of convictions much further removed than the Church of England, a little obsessed by the Occasional Conformists, could realize. There was, outside and within the Churches, a European-wide ferment of ideas, which could no longer be contained, or suppressed, about which the renewal of censorship would have been as futile as ineffective.

Yet it seemed to a large number of the clergy and their friends among the laity that the old partnership might yet be made to work. 'The heart of the high church movement' says Dr G. V. Bennett, 'was a simple belief that the conditions of the old establishment could be restored by firm political action.'

If the phrase 'high church' came into use in the last decades of the century, and then as an antithesis to 'low church' or Latitudinarian, there was behind it a coherent and continuous tradition going back through the Laudian and Caroline divines to the Henrician clergy at the beginning of the Reformation. In the reign of Elizabeth it included those who opposed the Biblical Calvinism of men like Chaderton and Whittaker and who, like the *émigrés* Peter Baro and Adrian Saravia, championed the doctrine of *de jure divino* episcopacy. In the field of spirituality and poetry John Donne and Lancelot Andrewes, George Herbert, Henry Vaughan, and Nicholas Ferrar represent the flower of a Church of England spirituality distinct from that of Counter-Reformation Catholicism or of Continental Protestantism.

A succession of learned theologians had produced an impressive rationale of the Church of England as a *via media* between Puritanism and Rome, with its roots in the primitive tradition of the first Christian centuries. They differed from the men of the Oxford Movement, who regarded them with fond nostalgia, in being firmly Protestant. Thomas Tenison, no high churchman, could say of the earlier assaults of the Church of Rome that 'we owe a part of the stability of men in those times to God's blessing on the writings of Archbishop Laud, Mr. Chillingworth, Dr. Bramhall, Dr. Cosin, Dr. Hammond and others'.[1]

The Laudians had been Royalist to a man, and went into prison, exile, or hiding during the Commonwealth. At the Restoration they made short shrift of the middle sort of men, such as the Cambridge Platonists. They held the old doctrines, with a new emphasis, on passive obedience, passive resistance, and devotion to hereditary monarchy, and abhorred all populist or republican notions. We have already seen how the events of 1688 threw them off balance. For those unable or unwilling to follow the Non-Jurors, there was still a crisis of conscience, and frustration shown in anger against those who found no difficulty in accepting the new regime, and especially those like Burnet, Sherlock, and Gibson, who seemed to have ratted on their earlier convictions. And though there were great and good among them, at all levels, there were too many whose spiritual fervour was not of a high order, and who, gathered together, seemed almost to be a caricature of the caricaturists, of Bumbury, or Rowlandson, or Hogarth, plump, choleric, and pompous. The rustling gowns of this cohort of angry middle-aged men, echoing back and forth across the floor of Westminster Abbey, flourishing their papers and memoranda in the face of a wearied and exasperated Archbishop, was not an edifying spectacle, and this high-church faction, so staunch in its loyalty to 'primitive Christianity', and in its defence of the divine right of episcopacy, came at length rather to resemble the mutinous presbyters of the *Epistle of Clement*, or the rigorists Novatus and Novatian than spiritual heirs of St Athanasius and St John Chrysostom.

It is not easy to assess the extent to which their ranks were permeated by Jacobitism. But most of them disliked William III and tried to maintain their loyalty to the House of Stuart, first for the person of Queen Mary and then of Queen Anne.

They were alarmed at the large numbers of the Dissenters, growing in strength despite the Clarendon Code. The failure of the Comprehension Bill in 1689, while it pleased them, had resulted in an unlooked-for situation, for the Toleration Act had not envisaged a situation where large bodies of Nonconformists remained outside the Establishment.

---

[1] *A Collection of Cases*, p. 488.

Yet between the years 1691 and 1710, 2,356 places of Nonconformist worship were licensed. More offensive still to their pious minds was the fact that the Toleration, or 'Indulgence' as they preferred to call it, had been taken as an excuse by non-Dissenters for absence from parish churches, and this was shown in a sharp drop in attendance at divine service and the eucharist. As the Archdeacon of Norwich complained,

a liberty being granted, more lay hold of it to separate from all manner of worship, to perfect irreligion than go to their meeting houses . . . no church warden or constable will present any for not going to church, though they go nowhere else but to the ale house, for this liberty they will have.

They were thus sharply opposed to the Whigs, who favoured toleration and were friendly towards Dissent, to whom the preservation of the Protestant Succession was a paramount concern. This was to be the guiding element in the policy of Tenison, and after him of Edmund Gibson. But to the high churchmen what was more evident was the fact, admitted frankly by Gilbert Burnet, that among the Whig ranks there were too many anti-clericals, many who looked to see the power and influence of the clergy and the Church diminish, as well as those who were giving the word 'Latitudinarian' its new sense, sympathy for the novel and horribly fashionable scepticism and heresy. The High Church Party found its strength in the support of the country gentry and the inferior clergy. But those clergy themselves included great numbers of those sadly handicapped in the scramble for benefices and preferments, who lacked patrons, or who were inferior in education and manners, and they included a servile minority who, in their employment as chaplains, were treated as inferior servants, for the Heneage Finches and the John Sharps were but a tiny minority.

On the death of Anne there were many who regretted the accession of the House of Hanover, who would have welcomed the exiled Stuarts had one of them shown any readiness to return to the Church of England, and who in 1715 and in 1745 would have greeted the victory of the invader with relief. The latter end of Atterbury himself suggests that he was not just an isolated leader, while even more startling is the frankness with which John Byrom describes the attitude of Manchester Tories, not all of them Non-Jurors, during the brief space of time when the Pretender held court in the north. On the other hand there were always those among the high churchmen, like Samuel Wesley and John Sharp, who loyally supported the Revolution.

But there is no doubt that the defection of the non-juring bishops and the elevation in their room of Latitudinarian clergy, gifted and worthy as they were of high office, polarized the divisions between the higher

Whig clergy and the lower House of Convocation, and that this cleavage exacerbated the 'Convocation controversy' which now took place. This has been admirably summarized and discussed in a series of modern studies. It would take an unseemly relish for *Schadenfreude* to embark on another blow-by-blow description of a conflict which shows the clerical character at its lamentable worst, amid scenes which would have been out of place among the boys of Westminster School, but which were played out by senior clergymen within the walls of Wesminster Abbey.

i. The Convocation Controversy

In an apparently casual decision which changed history, Archbishop Sheldon in 1664 agreed with Lord Clarendon to waive the ancient right of the clergy to be taxed separately. The unforeseen result was to make Convocation 'unnecessary to the Crown', and it did not meet between 1664 and 1689. When it was summoned in 1689, the Lower House expressed furious opposition to the proposed measures of Comprehension and Toleration with a firm 'Nolumus leges Angliae mutari' which produced another prorogation. Thenceforward, while Parliament grew daily in stature and prestige, it seemed that Convocation must wither away, leaving the lower clergy with no medium to express their convictions and get rid of their frustrations.

One man thought he saw the opportunity and need of the hour, and was ready to lead a campaign to preserve the rights of Convocation. It took the form of that most insidious of all radicalisms, innovation based on an appeal to tradition, to a past that never was.

Francis Atterbury (1622–1732)[2] was a brilliant and dangerous man, prevented only by flaws of temperament from becoming the Newman of the high-church movement. He had splendid gifts, but they were marred by a headiness of judgement, and an inability to brook opposition, or control his wrath when his behaviour was questioned or his authority thwarted. Eloquent as were his utterances in speech and in writing, dazzling his polemic, yet the appearance of great learning was illusory, lacking depth of earth, and in the end he withered.

Educated at Westminster School under the redoubtable Dr Busby, he was one of a generation which produced Philip Henry, Christopher Wren, and John Dryden and would soon nurture Samuel and Charles Wesley. Busby, who encouraged gifted loners, kept a kindly eye on

---

[2] G. V. Bennett, *The Tory Crisis in Church and State, 1688–1730*, Oxford 1975. Among the many virtues of this admirable study, the affairs of the Church are at each point related to the changing political situation, and to party politics.

Atterbury. The school had prized entrance facilities for Trinity College, Cambridge, and Christ Church, Oxford, and Atterbury went to Christ Church, among such high-church contemporaries as George Smalridge and Henry Aldrich.

His first adventure into print was an eloquent defence of Martin Luther against a surprisingly knowledgeable attack by the Catholic, Abraham Woodhead (1687).[3]

What brought Atterbury into prominence was his defence of a protégé of the college, the Hon. Francis Boyle. The young man, who seems to have resembled a character from P. G. Wodehouse, had produced a half-baked edition of the *Epistles of Phalaris* which drew down on him the wrath of Dr Bentley, the giant, or perhaps the ogre, of Trinity, Cambridge. It was felt that Christ Church had lost face, and Atterbury launched a counter-attack, behind a smokescreen of satire and invective, with a colour of learning sufficient to deceive even the elect. In vain did Bentley go on to produce his prodigious *Dissertation on Phalaris* (1699), for in the popular view, Atterbury had won hands down. It was a heady success, and it provided an ominous methodology which was to bedevil the Convocation controversy.

In 1696 Atterbury wrote up the ideas of a high-church and Tory group in an anonymous *Letter to a Convocation Man*. From this and the literary war which followed, it became plain that Atterbury's aim was to establish the Lower House of Convocation as the spiritual counterpart of the House of Commons, to free it from dependence on the Upper House and the control of the Archbishop, and to give the lower clergy complete freedom to debate, re-establishing their due place among the instruments of government of a Christian nation. He asserted that the Convocation, historically, was a national synod and saw this confirmed in the 'Praemunientes' clause of the royal writ which bade bishops bring their representative clergy with them to Parliament. So far from having been muzzled by the Act of Submission (25 Henry VIII), they had in fact full leave to debate, and needed only the final sanction of the Crown for their decisions. The pamphlet was a sensational success, and a greatly perturbed Archbishop Tenison turned to William Wake, the Rector of St James's, Westminster, who produced a learned, but rather heavy, treatise on *The Authority of Christian Princes over their Synods*. It was not well received, and the ironic ripostes which had perhaps been intended to enliven the discourse were much criticized, as was the overall Erastian flavour.

Yet Wake had exposed the weak points of the Atterbury case. He

[3] F. Atterbury, *An Answer to Some Considerations on the Spirit of Martin Luther, and the Origins of the Reformation, published at Oxford, A.D. 1687*, repr. 1728.

showed that there had been two types of Convocation. There had once been an assembly which was summoned by the King, in order to grant taxes, but this was distinct from the ancient provincial synod. Atterbury had indeed confused a provincial synod with a national assembly (it was a great weakness of his entire case that the Convocation of York also existed and was kept quietly out of the trouble by John Sharp, its Archbishop). But Atterbury was roused, and spent the next two years rummaging in archives and registers, producing another *tour de force* in the volume, also published anonymously, *The Rights, Powers and Privileges of an English Convocation*. From its 600 odd pages, further implications were drawn from the original arguments, and it was now argued that not the clergy, but the Archbishop of Canterbury, had been reduced in status by Henry VIII, since he became simply a royal messenger to Convocation, which under its own elected Prolocutor could manage its own affairs, and meet and adjourn as it willed. Wake, who had been the immediate object of Atterbury's attack, took seriously the task of a further rebuttal, and it was three years before he could produce a massive work *The State of the Church and Clergy of England in their Councils, Synods, Convocations and Other Public Assemblies*.[4] But it was Bentley all over again, and once more Atterbury's rhetoric had triumphed. Tenison realized that some shorter and more succint reply was urgently needed, and turned to two younger medievalists for help. One was Dr White Kennett, who in 1701 produced his *Ecclesiastical Synods and Parliamentary Convocations in the Church of England Historically Stated*, in time to be read before the meeting of a new Convocation. More effectual was the work of Edmund Gibson, Tenison's librarian and chaplain, who, shutting his ears to the surrounding hubbub, dug deep in the historical records and produced a series of writings which culminated in the definitive study *Synodus Anglicana, or the Constitution and Proceedings of an English Convocation* (1702).[5]

Soon Atterbury's interpretation of history became received doctrine among high-churchmen, and there is a revealing sentence in the Diary of Bishop Nicolson: "Tis a common practice in ye young Oxford divines to pray (before sermon) for ye House of Commons and ye convocation."[6]

If there were any notion that this was a mere theoretic or antiquarian dispute, the events of the Convocation which met in February 1701

---

[4] Sykes, *William Wake*, i, ch. 2; G. Every, *The High Church Party*, 1688–1718, 1956; Bennett, *The Tory Crisis*, pp. 48ff.

[5] N. Sykes, *Edmund Gibson* (Oxford 1926), ch. 2.

[6] *Bishop Nicolson's Diaries* (*Transactions of the Cumberland and Westmorland Antiquarian and Archaeological Societies*, 1903), p. 220.

disprove it. Atterbury himself had had but modest preferment. He was chaplain to the hospitals of Bridewell and Bethlehem, but the combination of a royal chaplaincy and a lectureship at St Bride's, Fleet Street, enabled him to display his great preaching talent. The Tory bishop. Trelawny was his friend, and he was enabled to enter the Convocation of 1701 as Archdeacon of Totnes. During subsequent Convocations he would be promoted Dean of Carlisle, Dean of Christ Church, and finally Bishop of Rochester. But he did not straightway become the head of the high churchmen in Convocation and it was to be some hindrance to his campaign that George Hooper, able, learned, but flappable, was elected Prolocutor.

Atterbury soon attracted the attention of the politicians, first of Lord Rochester, then of the more important Robert Harley who sought him out, and found him a useful ally but no passive tool, so that during the Whig ministries Atterbury had no support from Government, and even Tory statesmen were not as fully committed as he thought they should have been. Though Anne was generally sympathetic to the High Church Party, there were only a few months in 1710–11 when she acted strictly in accordance with Atterbury's designs, and her dislike of extremities, and concern for her own prerogatives, prevented her giving him her whole trust. That she would give only to Archbishop Sharp.

When the Convocation met, Tenison was indecisive, while Atterbury was quite clear about his objective 'not just to harass the Archbishop but to make of Convocation an instrument by which urgently needed measures could be taken to restore the authority and status of the Church.'[7]

The Lower House soon showed its teeth. It ignored a notice of prorogation, continued to debate, and adjourned itself. It set up committees to examine Toland's *Christianity not Mysterious* and began to make threatening noises about Burnet's *Exposition of the Thirty-Nine Articles*. On 28 February 1701 they began their session in Henry VII's Chapel, without first assisting the Bishops in Jerusalem Chamber at prayer. Tenison pounced on the irregularity as calculated to 'break the union of a provincial synod'. On 31 March they voted by 66 to 24 that the Lower House had power to adjourn itself. Atterbury was feeling thwarted by the half-hearted actions of the Prolocutor and unwisely led a deputation across the Abbey without him. But the Archbishop stood firm, demanded the presence of the official spokesman, and when he appeared, read them a lecture on the due and canonical subordination of the presbyterate. He then, but in an eirenical spirit, adjourned the Convocation until May.

[7] Bennett, *The Tory Crisis*, p. 57.

The Lower House, however, continued to hold its intermediate sessions, despite the protest of a group of high churchmen of quality, who included Beveridge, Bull, and Sherlock. The supporters of the Archbishop were led by White Kennett whose pungent speech generally raised, rather than lowered tempers.[8] Nor was this merely a controversy within four walls, and in private. Atterbury on the one hand and Kennett on the other kept up printed running commentaries designed to reach the clergy throughout the land.

With a new session in May, the Bishops proposed a joint committee to examine the records of Convocation, but the Lower House would not collaborate. They continued to press for the examination of Burnet's teachings, but the Archbishop refused to discuss such things until the main issue of their irregularities had been dealt with.

To mass demonstrations there were added nasty personal confrontations. For the Bishop of Bangor, Tenison's accredited emissary, the road from Jerusalem Chamber to Jericho was not one in which wayfaring men, yea, bishops could safely err. When he was met by an excited Hooper, clutching documents, he got an equivocal answer to his question whether the documents concerned the irregularities, and when they proved to be about the Burnet business, Bangor felt Hooper had deceived him. The result was that the word 'liar' was to be recorded in the Minutes of the Upper House while Burnet's cry of 'Insolence!' a little later led the Lower House to record the fact that they too had been affronted.

The Archbishop behaved with firmness and patience, prepared to compromise at many points for the sake of peace, but was baffled by unyielding and hostile truculence from his sons in the gospel. One wonders what might have happened had he had a larger sense of humour, the rarest, alas, of clerical virtues in that age, or had there been in existence a group of really moderate men anxious only to get both sides to 'cool it' and so defuse the atmosphere of battle.

It used to be said of the older kind of Wesleyan Superintendent minister, that he might not be much of a leader, but that it was almost impossible to get round him, if he stood firm and in the way. The same seems to have been true of Archbishops of Canterbury; it was surely true of Tenison. If the Queen turned to Archbishop Sharp for counsel, and if Tenison found himself bypassed in the matter of preferments and episcopal appointments, if, an ageing invalid, he withdrew more and more from Court and Parliament, 'Old Totius' stood his ground. His

---

[8] He was specially hated of high churchmen, as the notorious Weldon altar-piece at Whitechapel showed, in which he was portrayed as Judas Iscariot.

protégé and disciple, Edmund Gibson, was quite sure that Tenison had a clear policy and that he kept to it.

There is no way [he wrote to Nicolson] to preserve the Church but by preserving the present establishment in the state, and there is a far greater probability that the Tories will be able to destroy our present establishment than that the Dissenters will be able to destroy our establishment in the Church. This I understood to be the reasoning of my old master: upon which he acted in the whole course of his administration, and from which he could never be driven by the continued claims of the Tories about the danger of the Church. If he and the bench had regarded the noise, where had we been at this day?[9]

He had, of course, some tactical weapons. The Archbishop used his power of prorogation with effect. He was able to take the death of a prolocutor as a valid excuse for prorogation, and on another occasion was able to declare an absentee prolocutor contumacious. Despite the fierce and damaging personal attacks and the attempt to reduce his status to that of a mere official, he was nevertheless Archbishop, and the Upper House was constituted of bishops all conscious of the dignity of their order. In the end the Lower House was often reduced to the status of His Majesty's Opposition in later times—they had only words where it was power that mattered. And there was evident among the 'high-flying' churchmen a distaste for the royal authority which led them more than once to overstep the mark, and which led the Queen herself to protest in 1706 that she 'was resolved to maintain her Supremacy and the due subordination of Presbyters as fundamental parts thereof' and in the following year to complain that a protest by the Lower House was a 'plain invasion of her Royal Supremacy'.

It is interesting to consider what might have happened had Tenison given way and given in, if the High Church Party had been thoroughly united, or if it had been fully supported by the successive ministries, or even by Robert Harley. After all, it had been possible for the House of Commons to grow and change, and to develop into a new instrument of government, a new pillar of the constitution. Might not the Lower House of Convocation have similarly 'evolved', to become the clerical counterpart of the lay House of Commons, partners together in government? That the past history of Convocation was not as described by Atterbury had been demonstrated by the learning of Wake, Kennett, and Gibson. But it would not have been the first or the last time that an unhistorical mythology became the basis of a bid for the future. What would have been the result had the Lower House achieved its independence; been allowed to meet and adjourn itself, and to discuss

[9] Sykes, *William Wake*, ii. 119.

freely an agenda worked out in collaboration with ministry, and with the consent of the Queen?

There were obvious reasons why this could not come about, for such a development of one house of only the Canterbury Convocation would have overthrown the very nature of an ecclesiastical synod and broken the canonical subordination of presbyterate to episcopate (itself a high-church doctrine). Such a clerical assembly at this time could never have overcome a more than latent anti-clericalism, while the power base of the country gentry, lower clergy, and the London mobs could never have offset the spirits which the Whigs could conjure from the vasty deep. And there is perception in Tenison's overruling conviction that the safety of the Protestant Succession could not have been left to the high-church Tories.

But there was a point in the years 1710–11 when such possibilities seemed not too fanciful. The upheaval of the Sacheverell trial and the subsequent political triumph of the Tories, put the High Church Party in an ascendancy which a weary Tenison could no longer withstand. The Queen sent a letter to Convocation which represented Atterbury's wishes. They were to deliberate the state of religion, and to consider the amendment of church law and discipline.

The long-demanded committees were formed, and began rather cumbrous deliberations, spending much time on the heretical doctrines of William Whiston. The young Tories of the October Club were to present to the Queen a 'Representation of the State of the Nation' and it was thought it might be timely to present a similar 'Representation of the State of Religion'. Atterbury as Prolocutor of the Lower House of Convocation was at this time working closely with Bromley, Speaker of the House of Commons. Of this collaboration there had already been an impressive first-fruit, the Act for the building of fifty new churches in the cities of London and Westminster, the money for which, following the precedent of the rebuilding after the Great Fire, was to come from a tax on coal.

This document was entrusted to a committee of both houses, the representative of the Upper House being the Bishop of Peterborough, and four Welsh bishops.[10] It is generally thought that its chief author was Atterbury. But though it passed the Lower House, it was rejected by the Upper, and though printed and circulated, it was not formally presented to the Queen. Dr G. V. Bennett calls it a 'classic represen-

---

[10] *A Representation of the Present State of Religion, with regard to the late excessive Growth of Infidelity, Heresy and Profaneness. Unanimously agreed upon by a Joint Committee of Both Houses of Convocation of the Province of Canterbury,* 1711.

tation of Tory ecclesiastical doctrine'.[11] And it is true that behind it is the conception of one Christian realm, exercising moral and spiritual authority over the Church through the clergy, reinforced by the legislative sanctions of a Christian parliament. But it is a far from doctrinaire document, and is indeed something of a manifesto. Atterbury begins with a lament for 'the late excessive growth of infidelity heresy and prophaneness' the responsibility of which he places on the 'long unnatural rebellion'. This was the normal high-church opening gambit, which never mentioned the ill effects of the Restoration and the evil examples of monarch and Court. Credit is given for recent attempts at amendment; the religious societies, the charity schools, royal proclamations, and the royal example. But these have proved ineffectual. The author then examines the growth of heresy and unbelief: attacks on the doctrines of the Trinity and of the person and work of Christ, the assault on the authenticity of Scripture. There are specially sharp comments reserved for Unitarians and for the 'damnable errors' of the Quakers.

There had been what was even worse, a growth of complete unbelief, ridicule of sacred things, contempt for the clergy. Defective belief must lead to defective practice. 'From the wicked principles thus disseminated . . . wicked practices have followed.' There follows the familiar catalogue of public vices attacked by all the moralists, High, Low, Dissenter, which include the abuse of the Lord's Day and the corruptions of the stage. But a dominating item of the indictment is the circulation of heretical and blasphemous books and it is important to note that the one explicit demand for legislation is 'That by your Royal Interposition an Act may be obtain'd for restraining the present excessive and scandalous Liberty of Printing wicked books at home or importing the like from abroad'—with which the document closed.

When one looks at this document as a programme, it is gloomy and ominous and puritanical. Heresy is to be tackled by Convocation which would indict any doctrine that would endanger the faith: but it is clear from their addition of Burnet to Toland, and Hoadly to Whiston that these matters would not be immune from party prejudice. Nor was it at all clear what in fact the legal machinery was for the investigation of heretical pravity, in the light of the Royal Supremacy and of the power of Parliament, and the disrepair of the ecclesiastical courts, or what the penalties might be, beyond excommunication, and how and if the secular arm could reinforce them.

[11] *The Tory Crisis*, p. 137.

As we have seen, the climax of the adumbrated programme was the demand for the return to a strict and effective censorship, to be exercised as of yore, under clerical supervision.

Such a demand was simply impracticable in the new age of Swift, Defoe, and Addison, still less of Hobbes, of Locke, Mandeville, and Newton. The result could only have been a further pent-up explosion of unbelief and anti-clericalism. The fabric of church discipline was in disrepair, despite the efforts of bishops, and the determined effort of an Edmund Gibson to restore and refurbish it.

It was as well perhaps, that the document of 1711 was rejected, and that this kind of programme could not be enforced, even though support for many of its demands was wider than the High Church Party, and included such bishops as Wake and Gibson. But it seemed that the experience of the Sacheverell affair and its political aftermath had been in some degree cathartic, for Convocation began to simmer down, and to do useful work, tackling real and urgent problems, until the writings of Benjamin Hoadly once again roused Atterbury (who had been exercising his flair for agitation in the diocese of Carlisle). With the resuscitation of old and new doctrinal tensions, the matter of lay baptism, the revived doctrines of passive obedience, things went on the boil again, and in the end precipitated the wrath of Government which, to save Hoadly, suspended Convocation, a prorogation which was to last for 130 years. In the last months of the reign of Anne, however, the high churchmen had a small real victory when the long-attempted Occasional Conformity and Schism Acts were passed.

ii. 'The Bloody Flag Officer': The Case of Henry Sacheverell

Before the end of the Convocation controversy there intervened a fateful interlude—the case of Dr Sacheverell. The meridian line of the High Church Party seems to run through the flamboyant personality of this man. His convictions, unoriginal and superficially thought out, were so caught up into the events in which he became involved as to whip into ecstasy the passions of his party.

An unpopular Fellow of Magdalen College, Oxford, Sacheverell was quarrelsome, tactless, a bully of the inferior classes, and a heavy drinker. He was also esteemed enough by fellow high churchmen for Samuel Wesley to send the young John Wesley to seek his testimonial. In 1701 he wrote a venomous onslaught against the Latitudinarians, *The True Character of a Low Churchman*. A 'Low Churchman' he defined as 'a trimming villain' who was loyal only 'so long as the reigning prince shall please him and his party'.[12] But the main point of the caricature is to attack Latitudinarian belief, or rather lack of it.

A Low Churchman is one who though he professes himself to be of the communion of the Church of England and sometimes joins in its religious offices, yet he has that tender regard to weak brethren, that upon occasion he can see the inside of a conventicle, be of any synagogue but that of Satan and can show more signs of devotion at the heat and rapture of an extempore cant than at the flat forms of the ungifted liturgy.[13]

A Low Churchman is so far from being given to superstition that he believes nothing at all in religion . . . he believes very little or no revelation and had rather lay his faith up upon the substantial evidence of his own reason than the precious authority of divine testimony.[14]

He is an utter enemy to precise technical explanations of the person of Christ and

the scholastic jargon of the Trinity will ill suit with one of so polite a genius and he had rather be a Deist, Socinian or a Nestorian than to affront his own understanding with believing what is incomprehensible and be so rude as to obtrude on others what he cannot himself explain.[15]

'He thinks the articles of the church too stiff.' He is in fact 'full of malice and hypocrisy'.

Sacheverell had a handsome presence, always winning the sympathy of the female element in the congregation. He was tall, well dressed in correct, but modish, style, and he had the piercing eyes of the true spellbinder. In the pulpit he spoke with authority. In 1702 he preached a fierce sermon against Dissenters, Occasional Conformists, and Whigs who were indeed, if the inept phrase be pardoned, the King Charles's head of all his sermons, but his final call on this occasion to 'hang out the bloody flag and banner of defiance' earned him from Defoe the name of 'the Bloody Flag Officer'. More notable was a sermon preached on 23 December 1705 on *In Perils from False Brethren* for it was a pre-run of a more sensational preachment. In 1709 he obtained the chaplaincy of St Saviour's, Southwark, the prize of a city pulpit, and an overflowing congregation. An assize sermon at Derby, preached in August 1709 attracted attention when it was published in October under the title *The Communication of Sin* in which he attributed the Great Rebellion to Puritans deceived by a 'masquerade' of Jesuits, thus killing two birds with one stone.

In the modern St Andrew's, Holborn, rebuilt after the Blitz, a tablet commemorates the fact that Henry Sacheverell, when Rector, had

---

[12] p. 1.   [13] p. 3.   [14] p. 5.   [15] Ibid.

beautified the house of the sanctuary. But the text could hardly be applied to the sermon he delivered in a still-scaffolded St Paul's on Saturday 5 November 1709 at the behest of the new Lord Mayor, Sir Samuel Garrard. It was a good congregation, even apart from the officials, and included a high proportion of clerics, some of whom had come to scoff, and a number of devotees who looked upon him as 'the cherub with the flaming sword'.

If ever a sermon could have set the Thames on fire this would have done it. A four-year-old sermon is generally extinct, but this renovated diatribe breathed fire and slaughter from the beginning to the end.

It is not necessary to analyse the sermon on *The Perils of False Brethren in Church and State*, for it was to be put under a legal and theological microscope, line by line and word by word, by the acutest minds in the kingdom. No secondary study can be a substitute for the enthralling record of the trial which followed it and which was published by order of the House of Lords, but Geoffrey Holmes's scholarly analysis is of great use. Here we need only select one or two points. In his preamble the preacher coupled Gunpowder Plot not so much with 5 November 1688 as with 30 January 1649 and thus laid all blame for national ills on the makers of the Rebellion and their heirs, the Dissenters. He next turned his attention to St Paul's situation at Corinth and the catalogue of his sufferings, the culmination of which was to be in peril 'from False Brethren'. What followed was a rhetorical rag-bag into which all the watchwords, clichés, and invectives of the High Church Party were thrown, little scraps of history followed at each stage by contemporary side-swipes.

The first set of false brethren are those who deny the faith—'the upstart Novelist, or Self Conceited Enthusiast' and without naming names, he attacked heterodoxies charged upon Whiston, Tillotson, Burnet, and Stillingfleet—interspersing rhetorical questions: 'Who best deserve the Name of Churchmen, those that . . . maintain the Catholic doctrine . . . or those who would Barter them for a Mungril-Union of all sects?'

He turns on those Latitudinarians who are not above attending Dissenting services—who 'slide privately into a Conventicle and look as Demure as the slyest saint amongst them'.

Had he preached only the first part of this sermon, no more might have been heard of it. But when he turned to 'False Brethren with relation to the State, Government or Society' he was on more delicate ground, and, intentionally or not, there were sentences of confused ambivalence. Thus, half-way through he raised aloft the banner of high-church doctrine, declaring that the very pillar of government was 'obligation to an absolute and Unconditional obedience to the Supreme Power and the utter Illegality of Resistance upon any Pretence whatsoever'. Having said this, he could hardly avoid a reference to the Glorious Revolution:

they urge the Revolution of this day for their defence. But certainly they are the greatest Enemies of that and his late Majesty, and the most ungrateful for the Deliverance who endeavour to cast such black and Odious Colours upon both. . . . How often must they be told that the King himself solemnly disclaimed the Least Imputation of Resistance.

In recurring attacks, increasing in vehemence, 'Occasional Conformists and Dissenters' are assaulted and there is one bit of sheer humbug when he, the author of the malicious *Character of a Low Churchman* accuses the Dissenters of inventing the term: 'have they not lately villainously divided us with Knavish distinctions of High and Low Churchmen?'

But it was the attack on the politicians which suddenly leaped out of a fog of vague insinuations, in a plain reference to 'the crafty insidiousness of such wilely Volpones'. For this was the well-known nickname of the First Minister, Godolphin. Moreover Godolphin's brother was the Dean of St Paul's who, doubtless warned by a dream, had absented himself. So Sacheverell moved to his peroration, and the invectives piled up: 'Let us despise the Sneaking, Shuffling Compliances of such as consult their safety' and he ended with a flourish of resonant Biblical rhetoric, and the affirmation that in the end the Church cannot be brought to disaster from false brethren for 'there is a God that can and will raise her up'.

The outraged Whigs among the City Fathers reacted sharply, forbidding the usual vote of thanks and the formal request that the sermon be printed. But in an interview with Sir Samuel Garrard, 'unter vier Augen' which both interpreted differently, Sacheverell decided he had been commanded to print. This was what he needed. Not for him to waste his fierce sweetness on a preprandial somnolence of divines. He had been playing to a greater whispering gallery. The prints, reprints, and pirated editions seem to have reached 100,000 copies, and may have been read by as many as a quarter of a million people. He was a national talking point, and it was impossible to ignore him. Professor Holmes[16] has vindicated the Government from the charge of slipping foolishly into disaster, and has shown how limited were the legal options of an action they could not now avoid. The result was the impeachment of Sacheverell, for crimes and misdemeanours, by trial before the Bar of

---

[16] G. Holmes, *The Trial of Dr. Sacheverell*, 1973.

the House of Lords, at which the House of Commons would be present as a whole committee, to take place in Westminster Hall on Monday 27 February 1710.

What followed was a great spectacle, as they say, pure theatre. Within the ancient walls of Westminster Hall there was a setting devised by Sir Christopher Wren. To it all society thronged from the Queen and the Duchess of Marlborough downwards. It became a cross between No. 1 Court at the Old Bailey, and the Centre Court at Wimbledon, and the quality fought, connived, and bribed for tickets. And how splendid was that audience. Perhaps not often in our national history would fine ladies and fine gentlemen have shown to such advantage in their coloured silks, brocades, and velvets and the men with all the additional *gravitas* of their great wigs. And at the heart of it there was the House of Lords in all its finery, and the more sombre but impressive ranks of the House of Commons. For it the finest lawyers in the country had been engaged, some of them future Chancellors who would make their reputations in the next days. At least two of them, Sir Thomas Parker for the Prosecution and Sir Simon Harcourt for the Defence, were accomplished orators.

From the moment when the Serjeant-at-Arms called out for silence and in the hush cried 'Oyez, Henry Sacheverell, Doctor of Divinity, come forth, save thee and thy bail or thou forfeitest thy recognizance' drama unfolded, and though it would be untrue to suggest there was never a dull moment, for in fact there were many bones of legal argument and most of them were very dry, there were some remarkable and memorable ones. The indictment had been framed in four articles, which did not quote Sacheverell's own words, and referred to other sermons and writings beside the 'False Brethren' sermon. Apart from the speeches by the lawyers, there was an impressive utterance from Robert Walpole and, towards the end, some notable speeches from bishops, from Burnet and Wake and Trimnell, and a short but characteristic speech from Sharp who said what he could for the defendant, affirming that the times called for 'bold shepherds' and that 'a skilful surgeon always searches to the bottom of a wound before he applies a healing plaster . . . so a true pastor of the church must tell his hearers their faults and the danger thereof', though he took away some of the strength of his defence when he added 'however, I humbly submit to what this wise assembly shall think fit to determine in this matter'.

Through it all the ebullient Sacheverell, outwardly unruffled, showed no sign of being awed. His own speech in defence, when it came was a *tour de force*. It was restrained in word and argument, dignified in refusal to retract, and in fact so different in temper from the offensive sermon as to make many believe that at least Atterbury and Smalridge had a hand in it. Nor can the repeated statement of John Wesley, that it was written by his father, Samuel Wesley, be brushed aside.[17] But the climax was pure Sacheverell, and as the emotional temperature soared, handkerchiefs were dabbed at running eyes among sentimental ladies and the more susceptible peers in a geometric progression which those can best understand who have met the same phenomenon in a Baptist service in Moscow, or a girls' school prize day which got out of hand.

Outside Westminster Hall there was uproar enough. On the night of 1 March the violence of the London mobs broke out in a frenzy of arson and looting. During it the fine new Dissenting chapel of Daniel Burgess in Lincoln's Inn was pulled down piece by piece almost over his head—a house of the sanctuary not beautified by Sacheverell. At last the peril to the Bank of England touched hearts unmoved by the roughing up of Dissenters, and the cavalry rode in.

Condemnation had always seemed probable, and it came in the vote of the House of Lords on 20 March by a vote of 69 to 52. But, thanks to Tory manoeuvres, the majority was whittled away in the next days and the result was that there was no condign punishment, but a trivial sentence, the inevitable burning of the sermon, and a mere three years' moratorium on Sacheverell's ecclesiastical advancement. There followed an extraordinary and nation-wide celebration, on the part of gentry, clergy, and common people, with bells, bonfires, junketings, and Sacheverell himself on an almost regal progress; and as in each place he was dined and caroused by all the 'top people', he could serenely contemplate his future through claret-coloured spectacles. In 1713 the Queen gave him the rich living of St Andrews, Holborn, where high churchmen and Non-Jurors were thick on the ground. So once again Sir Christopher Wren supplied the scenery. The death of a wealthy kinsman and his marriage to the widow meant that when the pother had died down, he could still be very much at ease in Zion. He died in 1724.

The political consequence of the trial was catastrophic for the Whigs, and resulted in an electoral landslide in favour of the Tories. Anne, devoted to the Church of England, had a healthy distrust of extremists, but now gave her ear to Atterbury, as well as to John Sharp, and in 1713 Atterbury was made Bishop of Rochester and Dean of Westminster. But for Atterbury there would be no comfortable sunset. His happy days were his middle years, in the quiet, lovely house at Chelsea and the fine study, into which men like Swift and even his old adversary

---

[17] John Wesley, *A Concise History of England* (1776), iii. 72ff. 'It was wrote by the Rector of Epworth in Lincolnshire.' Wesley also stated this in the presence of Alexander Knox: J. Telford, *John Wesley* (1886), p. 30.

Nicolson could come for good talk and good cheer. He had now become entangled in dangerous broils, at Christ Church where, as Dean, he behaved outrageously to old friends, and in Carlisle. But after the death of Anne his frustrations took a desperate and overtly Jacobite turn, and he fell into high treason, and after a trial more deftly managed than that of Sacheverell was exiled. Here he lived among the Catholic Jacobites, an entirely committed Church of England man, dying at last poignantly isolated from his followers and friends, buried almost furtively in Westminster Abbey, the fine voice which from boyhood had echoed through its precincts silent at last.

It would be quite wrong to judge the High Church Party by the ill manners of the Convocation controversy, or by the Sacheverell agitation, or even by those leaders who most caught the public eye. Atterbury, for all his brilliance, was an ecclesiastical comet, and there was something bogus about Sacheverell. Their rhetoric and invective give no real impression of where the strength of their party lay. It was not altogether foolish to believe that the Church was in danger in the middle years of the reign of Anne, and it was certainly not wrong to be appalled at the surrounding and terribly swift dissolution of Christian verities, or to be alarmed at the flood which poured through the broken dam of censorship and governmental press control. The high church-men shared with their Whig and Latitudinarian contemporaries a patriotism of the Church such as no other communion possessed, but in their case it was a vision rooted in the long succession of Christian centuries and in the Apostolic Church.

If some of the Tory leaders were stuffy, and old-fashioned, like the Sprats, Trelawnys, and Comptons of the day, there were some of them, like George Hooper, who were men of considerable learning and great experience, and above all there was the Archbishop John Sharp.

Sharp indeed is the one with whom to leave a last impression of the quality of the English high-church tradition, with its deepest root in 'practical theology', in devotion and in spirituality. These qualities he shared with men like Bull and Brevint, and laymen like Robert Nelson. He feared the menace, as it seemed to him, of the incorrigible Dissenters with their ominously successful seminaries. But when it came to personal relations, as in the case of the oft hounded Nonconformist Principal Richard Frankland, the matter ended in a friendly haze of tobacco smoke and cordial. Not a great scholar, but civilized in his learning, wide in the range of his intellectual interests, a great collector of coins and antiquities, the care with which he drew up his great inventory of his archdiocese reflected his own pastoral care for all his people, and notably of his clergy.

He has a special place among those learned and devoted bishops who served the Church at the turn of the seventeenth century. It was no wonder that Queen Anne turned to him as her confessor and spiritual director, from that first interview when he promised her: 'I would always act according to the best sense I had . . . if she would give me leave to say it, I loved her—for which she thanked me.' Poor, solemn, stiff Tenison, plagued with the absence of health from his dwelling, with the illnesses of his wife, and with his own lingering afflictions, could not compete with this. And though Sharp's advice was not always taken, and Tenison was not always bypassed, Sharp was rightly regarded as the most distinguished leader of the High Church Party. But his heart was not in attendance at the courts of princes, or even in his home amid the comforts of tobacco, good wine, and conversation with many friends. It came more and more to be in the invisible world, where he loved best to pray in temples not made with hands, in the green countryside, or in his home-made oratory at Bishopthorpe, the little grass plot walled on all sides by yews and hornbeam, or praying alone on the long coach rides. When he died, aged sixty-nine, in February 1714, he had on his lips the words of George Herbert which reflect the slightly sombre blend of penitence and praise which was at the root of the Caroline devotion:

> All my sour sweet days
> I will lament and love.

5

CHURCH OF ENGLAND MEN

i. *The Underlying Consensus*

THE great struggle which had agitated Church and nation, 1640–60, had lasting consequences, in a hardening of attitudes and the erection of mythologies on both sides. The fathers had eaten sour grapes and the teeth of their children and of their children's children were set on edge. There was the usual legacy of bitterness which civil wars bequeath, mass emotions and loyalties, irrational and beyond the capacity of reason to change. The result was that both sides viewed the past through distorting mirrors. Mistrust, suspicion, readiness to believe the worst were the order of the day, and nowhere among those in high places a deep desire, in Winston Churchill's words in 1945, 'to wipe a sponge over the past' and make a fresh start. There had been in fact a mutual excommunication between two coherent patterns of Christian faith and order.

The many-sided debate of which the Westminster Assembly had been the focus, had been but a half-dialogue from which the leadership of the Church of England was virtually excluded. Now, at the Restoration, things were reversed, and it was the Dissenting cause which would cease to count. The Church of England had survived dire peril, and was again to be in danger in the 1680s from an opposite direction. In modern jargon, it now emerged from an identity crisis, more concerned to stress the inheritance from the Caroline divines than those it shared with the first English Reformers or the considerable body of Church of England Puritans.

It was ironical that at a time when its scholars had traced with new exactitude the origins of the episcopate in the primitive Church, if not to the Apostles' time, at least to the sub-apostolic age, the historic episcopate in England was undergoing yet another of its diverse incarnations, and was to be embedded in party politics. The evidence for episcopacy in the *First Epistle of Clement* and in the Ignatian epistles had been brought into prominence by learned editors. Dr Fell's edition of the works of Cyprian was seen to reinforce the case for monarchical episcopacy in a way which shook the presbyterians. Except in Stillingfleet's *Irenicum*, evidence on the other side did not come into prominence.

The changes in the English Constitution after 1688 saw an immense reinforcement of the power of Parliament, new tensions between the Crown and the various ministries, and two political parties, divided by principles indeed, but even more as groups of competing political and economic interests.[1]

Inevitably, and, arguably quite properly, the leaders of the Church were sucked into all these pressures, since for almost a thousand years bishops had acted as counsellors of state. But now they were commanded to attend parliamentary sessions less and less widely spaced in time, and to devote many months each year to residence in London, which some of them would have preferred to spend in their dioceses. They were expected to give the services of vote and voice in favour of the political programme of the party to which they owed their elevation, though in fact most of them were by no means passively inclined to vote 'just as their leaders tell 'em to' and Tenison, Wake, Sharp, and Gibson could on occasion act contrary even to royal behest. But those who make friends of the mammon of unrighteousness give hostages to fortune. Times of sharp political conflict such as recurred during the reigns of William III and Anne must needs have influenced ecclesiastical affairs and even theological controversy. They put pressures on the leaders of the Church (draining a sick man like Tenison of energy), and robbing them of time, and Burnet's critical attitude to Archbishop Sharp in his later years may have truth in it, for he may not have been unscathed by the cruel necessities of politics. Statesmen like Danby, Rochester, Nottingham, and Harley might care for the welfare of the Church, but there were enough 'wilely Volpones' about who were less interested in feeding the flock than in the distribution of the loaves and fishes.

Two essays by G. V. Bennett and Norman Sykes have illuminated the background of the choice of bishops under William III and Mary.[2] The flurry of high-level correspondence at each set of appointments was much more than the inevitable and endemic gossip of the 'old boy network' where all the eminent at least knew about the others. When Anne broke away from her political advisers and made her own appointments, the furore caused was because the political balance was upset. The Whig party expected to share the ecclesiastical rewards of office as well as the political, at a time when every vote in the House of Lords might count, and when in

[1] J. H. Plumb, *The Growth of Political Stability in England, 1675–1725*, 1967; J. Cannon (ed.), *The Whig Ascendancy*, 1981.

[2] G. V. Bennett and J. Walsh (edd.) 'King William III and the Episcopate', in *Essays in Modern English Church History in Memory of Norman Sykes*, 1960; N. Sykes, 'Queen Anne and the Episcopate', *EHR* 1935.

fact there were some very close divisions. In their dioceses the Bishops were not less politically relevant than in the House of Lords, though the heavy interventions in local elections of Lloyd at Worcester, Burnet at Salisbury, and Nicolson at Carlisle were unexpectedly counter-productive. The political involvement therefore of the Church in the new party conflicts was operative at all levels, even though there were some clerics who enjoyed politics more than others.

But it would be wrong to suppose that the men who led the English Church in this period were primarily moved by party or political concerns, or to forget the coherent body of convictions which for Church of England men cut across the labels 'Whig', 'Tory', or even 'high church' and 'low church'. Dr Bennett has shown how in the reign of William III the influential London clergy, Tenison, Sharp, Wake, Patrick, were far from being 'Latitudinarian Whigs' as some historians conceived them to be.[3] And if he perhaps exaggerated the influence upon their actions of the fact that they were a 'Nottingham connexion' they obviously owed something to the wide patronage of the Lord Chancellor. But they were men of note, marked out by uncommon gifts, so that Burnet could put their names on the list he gave to William III without any consideration of their involvement with the Earl of Nottingham.

Tenison, Sharp, Wake, and Gibson do not altogether fit the party labels. Tenison supported the Whigs, because his over-riding concern was for the Protestant succession. 'Bishop Gibson', said Norman Sykes, 'was designed by Providence to be a high church Tory "sans peur et sans reproche": the accident of the Revolution and the taint of Jacobitism which clung to the Tories drove him into political alliance with the Whigs.'[4] Sharp, Tenison, and Wake shared views on the alliance between Church and State in a Christian nation, which separated them from a Benjamin Hoadly. Wake had opposed, and almost sunk single-handed, the anti-clerical Vestry Bill which would have wrested philanthropy from church control and handed it to the Justices of the Peace, and he opposed, as Sharp would have done, the repeal of the Occasional Conformity and Schism Acts and the measures to give more liberty to the Quakers.

All three men were reluctant to give new liberties to the Dissenters, and Gibson echoed the view of Sacheverell that the Nonconformists should be grateful for the Toleration Act, and that they should not try to move outside its orbit. Sharp and Gibson were at one about the need to reinforce Sabbath observance, while Wake agreed with Collier and Atterbury that something needed to be done about the corruption of the stage. It was Wake who was furious when his tenant, Mrs Juxon, sub-let the Palace of

---

[3] Bennett, op. cit., p. 132.   [4] Sykes, *Gibson*, p. 182.

Canterbury to a troupe of strolling players who intended to perform within the precincts during Lent.

Christian men as they were, they had to accept the limitations imposed upon their ministries by the structures of political power. Tenison and Wake and Gibson may have found, as Matthew Parker and Thomas Cranmer before them, that attendance at Court was uncongenial, and indeed damaging, so that each of them withdrew more and more in later years.

Thus although it was a high-church dream to return to a true *Corpus Christianum* where Church and State were two facets of one Christian commonwealth, the very fact of an Established Church, as defined and defended by churchmen of this middle sort, implied a not dissimilar objective. 'A Church of England man', wrote Swift, 'hath a true veneration for the scheme established among us of ecclesiastical government: and though he will not determine whether episcopacy be of divine right, he is sure it is most agreeable to primitive institution and . . . best fitted for our civil state.' What was meant by such a national Church appears clearly in Wake's eirenical correspondence with the leaders of the Gallican Church.

The Church of England as a national church has all that power within herself over her own members which is necessary to enable her to settle her doctrines, government and discipline according to the will of Christ, and the edification of her members. We have no concern for other Christian churches more than that of charity and to keep up the unity of the catholic church in the communion of saints.[5]

I shall always account our church to stand upon an equal footing with theirs: and that we are no more to receive laws from them, than we desire to impose any upon them, in short the Church of England is free, is orthodox: she has a plenary authority within herself . . . we are as much and upon as good ground a free, independent church as they are.[6]

The theological grounds on which a national Church must be adjudged to have 'a plenary authority within herself' were never given, and one would have been interested to know how Wake would have answered the criticisms of the notion in the writings of John Owen. But it is important that all Wake's correspondence about unity is addressed to established Churches, and that as he rigorously excluded the English Dissenters from his hopes and schemes for the recovery of unity, so his Reformed correspondents, like Ostervald in Switzerland, were energetic in their own attempts to root out their Separatists.

The new confidence and self-consciousness of the Church of England in regard to its structure and its liturgy is amply illustrated in the

---

[5] Sykes, *William Wake* i. 260.   [6] Ibid. i. 266.

writings of the small group of eminent clergy who in England sought to further the cause of unity.

ii. Conversations

Most of them—John Sharp is an exception—had become interested in the Continental Churches during their own travels and sojourns abroad, Compton, Burnet, Robinson, and Wake especially having made personal contacts with leading churchmen in France, Germany, and Switzerland. The involvement of the Protestant succession in England with the House of Hanover drew the affair into the realm of high politics.

The terrible events of the Wars of Religion, which had swept great parts of Germany with plague, pestilence, and famine, battle, murder, and sudden death left an exhausted Protestantism in those countries, and one still menaced by a militant and persecuting Catholicism. At the height of the conflict there had been urgent attempts to find a way of unity, by the remarkable group which included Comenius and his friends Samuel Hartlib and John Durie. Durie himself deserves the modern term 'ecumaniac' for he poured out his energies to win adherents to this cause, and there were many others, like Ussher and Bedell in Ireland, who supported him financially as well as with their prayers.

The persecution of Protestants in France, in the Palatinate, in the Savoy, and in Bavaria had led to a flood of refugees, many of them seeking to settle in England, or to pass through it on their way to America, and their very presence kept the peril to Protestantism alive in the hearts of most Englishmen.

There were many reasons why English churchmen at this time should feel drawn to the cause of restoring Christian unity in a network of conversations, negotiations, and correspondence. Catholics, Gallicans, Lutherans, and Reformed—French, German, Swiss, English, formed a network of friendships and ideas which recall the sixteenth-century humanist connection. They too were involved in common enterprises of Biblical and historical learning, had the same perception of great issues, and perhaps the same élitism, bordering on dilettantism, whose imaginative ploys broke down when things had to be earthed in the manœuvres of the politicians and amid the contradiction of theologians.

It was natural that as the Church of England emerged from its inner conflicts, its leaders should regard themselves as the true *via media* between the Catholic and Protestant worlds and should regard their own historic episcopate, within a true succession, and their liturgy as instruments to facilitate a wider union.

William Wake's deep concern for Christian unity had been shown early in his ministry in the remarkable sermon which, as a young royal chaplain, he preached before William and Mary at Hampton Court, 21 May 1689, on the theme 'Mutual Charity and Union among Protestants' and if such sentiments might seem to come a little trippingly off the tongue of a young man on his way up, in the first days of a new regime, when all the talk was of 'Comprehension', there was more than rhetoric or courtly gesture to the occasion, in his peroration.

Who would not wish to see those days, when a general *Reformation* and true *Zeal*, and a *perfect Charity* passing through the World, we should All be united in the same *Faith*, the same *Worship*, the same *Communion* and *Fellowship* with one another? When all *Pride* and *Prejudice*, all *Interests* and *Designs* being submitted to the Honour of God and the discharge of our duty, the Holy Scriptures shall again triumph over the vain Traditions of Men: and Religion no longer take its denomination from little *Sects* and *Factions*, but we shall be content with the same common, primitive Names of *Christians* and *Brethren*, and live together as becomes our Character, in *Brotherly Love* and *Christian Charity* one with another?[7]

Fundamental to Wake's eirenicism, and very much in the air in that day was a distinction, between fundamentals of the faith where unity was essential, and non-fundamentals about which Christian men might differ, while still living in full communion with one another. This view of what we might, after the Second Vatican council, call 'a hierarchy of truths' goes back to the more Erasmian side of the Reformation, and had been expounded in differing ways in many countries. It was a distinction which bound Wake at once with the 'reasonable orthodoxy' of the famous 'Swiss triumvirate' who were among his chief friends and most ardent correspondents. The distinction was important but it was rather a framework of debate than a step towards solution of problems. For there remained the question of the grey area, the borderline between things necessary and things indifferent, and despite Lancelot Andrewes's and William Wake's refusal to unchurch those who had it not, the insistence on the necessity of an episcopate within the apostolic succession, for the integration of church unity, and Wake's desire for a common declaration of faith and a common liturgy, show where the problems might really lie.

Wake's immense correspondence on behalf of Christian unity has been analysed fully, if not definitively, by Norman Sykes, and related to

---

[7] W. Wake, *Sermons and Discourses* (1960), p. 292.

the situations in France, Switzerland, and Germany, but we may adventure a comment upon it without recapitulating an intricate, and like ecumenical narratives generally, often tedious, story.[8]

There were obvious ties between the English and the Gallican Churches. Not only had there been the personal contacts during the exile, but there was a common interest in patristic studies, of which the age witnessed the publication of monumental editions, a learned enterprise to which scholars of both nations contributed. Wake's own sojourn as chaplain to the English ambassador in Paris had brought him into personal contact with distinguished French Catholics, and after the cessation of the wars, the way was open for lively correspondence with French theologians, eminent among them the church historian, Louis du Pin.

In the troubled aftermath of the Jansenist controversy the Gallican Church was sensitive about its liberties, and following the publication of the papal constitution 'Unigenitus' it seemed that it would not take much to provoke the Gallican Church into making what might be called a unilateral declaration of independence from Rome. The frankest exposition of Wake's views was given in his letters to his Swiss correspondent Jean Alphonse Turrettini,[9] from which it is clear that the French were inclined to be obstinate and hoity-toity, while it irked Wake that the Cardinal de Noailles would discuss with Wake only through the intermediary of the Sorbonne. Du Pin's running commentary on the Thirty-nine Articles, his *Commonitorium*, did not much delight Wake, who grumbled that the French would also have to make concessions. The death of Du Pin terminated the more interesting part of the discussions, and with an attempt to demonstrate a French version of the English liturgy in Paris, and a project for the SPCK to infiltrate copies of the same, touched the borders of propriety. Wake of course had to keep the correspondence secret and though, had anything positive transpired, he might have found some distinguished English support, he would have undoubtedly run into a deep anti-Popery, if not anti-Gallican, feeling in England. But in fact the whole project was chimerical.

There is a parallel in a small-scale earlier project, when William Bedell and Sir Nicholas Wootton had encouraged Sarpi to induce the Republic of Venice to break with Rome. For when it came to the crunch, there was all the difference between frustration, resentment, opposition to Papal autocracy and an act of formal schism. The English, who had had

---

[8] Sykes, *William Wake*, i, chs. 4, 5, ii, ch. 6; also R. Rouse and S. C. Neill, *A History of the Ecumenical Movement* (1954), ch. 3.

[9] Sykes, *William Wake*; Rouse and Neill, *History of the Ecumenical Movement*, p. 105.

two centuries to get used to the idea, underestimated the forces necessary to make such a drastic break. A by-blow of Wake's discussions was a renewed investigation into Anglican orders and if the chief contribution was from le Courayer, Wake made an impressive interpolation, powerfully argued and grounded in historical learning of a high order.[10]

Wake's relations with the Swiss Churches[11] were perhaps more intriguing. Not since the days of Henry Bullinger and Theodore Beza had the English been so bombarded with letters from Switzerland. Not since the Edwardian divines and the returned Marian exiles, had so many Swiss students been cordially welcomed and encouraged to study in Britain. And here a basis for negotiation had already been prepared by the relations between the SPCK and the SPG with the Swiss Churches in the previous decades.[12]

In 1700 Robert Hales had gone to Switzerland with the aim of furthering friendship between Protestant nations, and the SPCK invited him and his Swiss ally, Jacob Scherer of Saint-Gall, to become corresponding members of the Society, as their advisers on how best to get in touch with the Swiss churches. J. F. Ostervald was a key figure because of the quality of his own catechetical and liturgical works. His *Traité des sources de la corruption* was translated and published by Burnet, who had his own interest in Switzerland arising from his earlier travels. There was soon a considerable two-way traffic in edifying literature and no work from the English side was more seminal than Woodward's account of the religious societies. But as the two bodies knew more of one another, the Swiss were inclined to bring the English Dissenters into the picture, since manifestly they were many of them firmly in the Reformed tradition of churchmanship. But in 1707 the book by William Nichols, a Latin *Defence of the Doctrine and Discipline of the Church of England* was not only a typical exposition of contemporary Anglican patriotism of the Church, but an attack on the English Dissenters. Woodward published a rather naïve edition of a liturgy by Ostervald in which he tried to show how near it came to the English rite, though in fact most of the similarities go back to medieval liturgies. After the

---

[10] Sykes, *William Wake*, i, ch. 5.

[11] There had been interesting, but abortive, discussions between J. C. Werndley in Switzerland and Bishop Compton: E. F. Carpenter, *The Protestant Bishop* (1956), pp. 439ff.

[12] See the luminous article by E. A. Duffy, '"Correspondence Fraternelle", the SPCK, the SPG, and the churches of Switzerland in the War of the Spanish Succession,' in *Reform and Reformation, Studies in Church History*, ed. D. Baker (Oxford 1979), pp. 251–80.

Treaty of Utrecht the contacts between the SPCK and the Swiss Churches gradually lapsed.

Naturally Wake was drawn to the 'Swiss Triumvirate'—J. A. Turrettini (1671–1737), Professor of Church History in the University of Geneva, Samuel Werenfels (1657–1740), Professor of Theology at Basle, and J. F. Ostervald (1663–1747) pastor and professor at Neuchâtel. He also kept in touch with the Antistes of the Churches of Zurich, Basle, and Berne. What drew him to the Triumvirate was less their 'reasonable orthodoxy' which had perhaps more in common with Tillotson and Burnet, as the fact that for them too, the distinction between fundamentals and non-essentials of the faith was a paramount consideration. Wake emphasized the friendly relations which the Church of England had had with the Reformed Churches on the Continent. Despite his concern for the historic episcopate he was clear that he would not unchurch the Continental Protestants, whose lack of the episcopate and of the succession had been conditioned by historical necessity. He pointed to the communion of Englishmen in Protestant Churches when abroad, and the accepted occasional conformity in England of a Calvinist like William III and the Lutheran George of Denmark. Wake pleaded with Ostervald to restore episcopacy to the Reformed Churches and promised 'It will be our part to provide that if for this reason they come here, they may receive ordination with the minimum of difficulty, and expense from our bishops and presbyters.'[13]

Wake gives a revealing pedigree of the English episcopate. He begins after the time of Whitgift, with the émigrés, Baro and Saravia, and 'divine right' episcopacy, which he finds expressed in the works of Bancroft and Bilson, Andrewes, Overall, Bramhall, and Davenant. The English Reformers who would have given little support for his emphasis on apostolic succession, and the English Puritans (Whittaker is dismissed as one of 'several professors') are ignored.

Wake's friendly overtures to his Swiss friends were interrupted by a crisis in their Church. There was the same tension between conservative and liberal notions among the Swiss Calvinists as divided the English Dissenters, and in each case the conflict erupted in a controversy about compulsory subscription. The Swiss conservatives, anxious to preserve their churches from the infiltration of Amyrautist notions from Saumur and Montpellier, had imposed in 1675 the conservatively Calvinist 'Helvetic Consensus', and a crisis arose in an old place of tension, the Pays de Vaud and the University of Lausanne. Into this controversy Wake plunged, putting forward the example of the Thirty-nine Articles

---

[13] Sykes, *William Wake*, ii. 7.

as a confession of faith deliberately framed to comprehend a wide difference of opinion, though he was a little disconcerted when the argument proved two-edged, or at least was used to justify both subscription and non-subscription. Wake ingenuously asserts that the English Church had not been troubled by the debate about pre-destination, after James I and Charles I had forbidden the discussion in the pulpit of those doctrines.

There must be some allowance for the fact that Wake occasionally tempered his arguments to the supposed predispositions of his various correspondents, but it is a revealing foreshortening which ignored the Calvinists of the Church of England or dismissed them as 'several professors', which did not mention the English participation in the Synod of Dort, or the deliberations and confessional statements of the Westminster Assembly the vast majority of whose English members had been episcopally ordained within the Church of England. But, abortive though it was, it was for Wake a warm and meaningful correspondence, brought out of the field of abstractions by his generous hospitality to those like the Swiss John Ott, and by his invitations to Swiss students to visit England, on some of whom he bestowed Anglican orders, a gesture which, we shall see, is less ecumenically satisfactory than might appear.

More notable, because espoused by a group of important high churchmen, and because more grounded in politically favourable pressures, was the attempt to forward the union between the Lutheran and Reformed Churches in Germany, using the Church of England as a catalytic agent.

The approach to English churchmen came at a time when eirenical discussions were already in progress in Germany, at an intricate and often profound level, between the Catholics Bossuet and Spinola and the Protestants Leibniz and Molanus, the Lutheran abbot of Lokkum. Things began to move when the two Electoral Houses of Brandenburg and Brunswick, the princes of Prussia and Hanover, were involved.

Archbishop Sharp was almost alone in the group of English churchmen in that, unlike Burnet, Compton, Robinson, and Wake he had no firsthand experience of Continental Protestantism. But he had become a regular correspondent of the Electress of Sophia in Hanover who in 1710 seemed to favour the introduction of the English liturgy to the Court of Hanover with a view to its extended use. More important, her son-in-law, Frederick William III, had been declared King of Prussia, and was taken with the idea of uniting the Lutherans and Calvinists of his dominion, on the basis of an English model of episcopacy and of The Book of Common Prayer.

Behind this programme there was the remarkable champion of unity, Daniel Ernst Jablonski (1660–1741). Jablonski's own ancestry was part Polish, part German, but he had the cause of unity in his blood, for he was a grandson of Amos Comenius and his father had been secretary to John Durie. He was a bishop in the Moravian Church and Wake deemed his orders impeccable. He had been converted from a Presbyterian horror of the Church of England to a convert's devotion, and along with his Prussian friend Dr Grabe, was the latest in a long line of foreigners beginning with the Belgian Saravia who became more Anglican than the Anglicans. His somewhat selective reading of the Fathers, and especially of St Cyprian, led him to believe that of all Churches, the Church of England was nearest to the Church of the Fathers. At Jablonski's request, Grabe turned the English liturgy into German, and it was published in Germany in 1704. Two copies had already been sent by Frederick to England: one for the Queen which was graciously acknowledged, the other to Tenison. Why Tenison did not reply is not known, but he may have been enough of a little Englander not to want to get involved, and less sure than the high churchmen that the constitution and liturgy of the Church of England could be potent for the healing of the Lutherans. But the failure to reply gave offence to the impatient Frederick and the matter lapsed.

'It was emphatically a project of high churchmen and Tories' comments Norman Sykes. And it was a plan which they could heartily support, since they would sacrifice nothing whatever, but would instead see their Anglican principles not only defended but made the pillar of a great united Church. Sharp, Grabe, and Smalridge continued to correspond with the Germans and succeeded at length in getting the matter on the agenda of Convocation. With the advent of Wake to the primacy, hopes revived, for Wake and Jablonski had been together at Christ Church, and both in these matters shared the same dedication to the cause of unity.

Again Jablonski commended the Church of England in memoranda to the advisers of his prince. Again it was proposed to demonstrate The Book of Common Prayer in Berlin, and thereafter in Prussia. The thirty-six states represented in the Corpus Evangelicorum which met at Ratisbon were to be kept in the picture. But behind the enthusiasm of Jablonski there were to be heard the murmurings of established rivalries of theologians and pastors which could not be brushed aside. And in the end, the political difficulties were insuperable: the rival interests of the Electoral Houses of Brandenburg and Brunswick, enmities between Hanover and Prussia. The project could never have got off the ground without the initiative of the temporal power, and when Caesar took away what Caesar alone could have given, the whole project was aborted.

Yet perhaps the comment may be adventured that the failure of these ecumenical projects may after all have been for the progress of the gospel. What the results might have been, even on Wake's terms of mutual independence of a union between the Church of England and the Gallican Church, is as conjectural as the desperate offer to unite France and England in 1940.

Wake's gesture towards the Swiss Churches by ordaining Swiss students was well intentioned. And Jablonski speaks of young Germans, doubtful of their orders, who sought ordination in England. But this surely was a private gesture by an Archbishop, completely isolated from any formal scheme of union between Churches. Was it much more than an exchange of gifts and compliments—if not an intolerable isolation of the act of ordination from the Christian communions and ecclesial communities where ministry was to be exercised? John Jewel, Richard Coxe, and Robert Horne among the Elizabethans had delighted to give good gifts to their Swiss brethren—chalices, bales of cloth, books—but they would never have thought of laying hands suddenly on the Swiss students in Oxford, or that by so doing they were contributing to the solidarity of Protestantism, nor would the Swiss leaders, Bullinger, Gualter, and Stumphius have thanked them for their pains. And while the gesture might meet with the approval of Swiss professors, or with the Antistes of the Swiss cities, is it anachronistic to wonder how these ordinands would be regarded by their colleagues, who found a two-tiered ministry in their midst, one within and the other without the historic episcopate?

Wake and his colleagues believed that the Book of Common Prayer was the best of all liturgies and many will sympathize with them. But one wonders about their export form. There is something disquieting about those new versions in French, German, and Spanish. There was happily no notion at that time that what was 'incomparable' about the English liturgy was its fine English, but one wonders if some glory was not rubbed off in the translation from sixteenth-century English to seventeenth-century German?

Nor, to be honest, was the English liturgy beyond criticism, for if we except John Knox and the Puritans, we have to reckon with the critique of the Non-Jurors. In fact many Lutheran liturgies have features superior to The Book of Common Prayer, such as the use of antiphons and the wider range of canticles. And at this time, at the heart of the Lutheran liturgy, something marvellous and creative was emerging— the combination of chorales, sung by the congregation, with the successive wonders, month by month of the cantatas of John Sebastian Bach, perhaps also 'incomparable'?[14]

It was inevitable that in these ecumenical ventures, much should depend on the authority of the godly Prince. But it was a part of Europe which had long accepted the principle of 'cujus regio, ejus religio'. Norman Sykes suggested that an episcopate on the Anglican model might well have been ground between the power of the temporal *summus episcopus* and a clerical consistory. It would be anachronistic therefore to overstress the fact that the theological convictions of the clerical *Pastorenkirchen* could not have been brushed aside, or that the grass root millions of wayfaring Christians—had any views that might properly be considered.

Prussia, where the rulers were Calvinist, but their subjects Lutheran, was indeed a test case, but when at last Prussian unity was imposed a century later it was surely the least satisfactory of all German unions. Those who labour for the cause of Christian unity need the skills of horticulturists rather than those of engineers and too many of these projects were mechanical rather than organic, and had no thought at all for the business of growing together at a congregational level.

Sharp and Wake and Gibson would not have admitted any inconsistency in their double standards with regard to Continental Protestants and English Nonconformists. For they believed the whole onus of schism lay with Dissent, and their hearts' desire for the Nonconformists was simply that they might disappear. When, after 1689, it became plain not only that they would continue to exist, but that they might even grow in strength, their attitude hardened. Wake's speech in 1718 opposing the repeal of the Occasional Conformity and the Schism Acts was cold and hostile towards the separated brethren—The Dissenters [he said] were at present decreasing both in number and interests: no persons of quality left among them, but few gentlemen. 'Even in corporations the richer merchants would rather leave the conventicle than be shut out of the corporation. For indeed nobody can think that this will satisfy either the hopes or expectations of the Dissenters, rather it will make them more importunate and encourage them to expect more'.[15]

And yet in their doctrines of the Church and of the Ministry the Swiss and German Protestants were often nearer the Dissenters than the Church of England, not least in rejecting a *de jure divino* doctrine of the episcopate and of the necessity for strict adherence to an apostolic

---

[14] C. S. Terry, *J. S. Bach Cantata Texts, Sacred and Secular* (1964), Introduction.
[15] Sykes, *William Wake*, ii. 124.

succession. Wake could write with deep sympathy to his Swiss friends when the dissolution of orthodoxy involved a subscription controversy: he had nothing to say by way of comfort or counsel to the Dissenters at Salter's Hall, even though their crisis had been largely fuelled by the writings of Anglican divines. 'Give 'em an inch and they'll take a yard' was the general Anglican reaction to the Nonconformist pleas for relief from their disabilities, and into the mid-eighteenth century the cliché held that if ever the Dissenters got into power, there would be no more talk of toleration from them.

But if Wake, like most of us, had blind spots, they do not detract from the noble vision of a rather lonely spirit who, having begun his ministry by pleading the cause of unity, laboured for it to the end. On that day in 1689 the Lord had opened the eyes of the young man that he saw, and his closing prayer must surely be echoed by all who like him, have given their best energies to realizing hopes of unity which in the end have been denied:

To have contributed, tho' in the least degree, to the healing of those *divisions* we so unhappily labour under, shall be esteemed a greater Honour, than to have *silenced* all the Cavils of our *Enemies*: and even to have pray'd and wish'd for it, and where we could not other wise have contributed ourselves, but to have exhorted others to it, shall be rewarded with *Blessings more than all the Stars in the Firmament for number.*[16]

iii. Burnet

At the end of the seventeenth century the word 'Latitudinarian' changed somewhat in meaning, as 'high churchmen' and 'low churchmen' became involved in controversy of ever increasing bitterness. And though Gilbert Burnet assuredly belongs to the group which had included Tillotson and Patrick, not least in his concern for 'practical theology' and for pastoral care, it is evident that his enemies considered that his aggressive role in the party controversies entitled him to be considered a 'low churchman'.

Thus the egregious Mr Sewell in an acid attack on Burnet refers to 'the Low churchmen among whom your Lordship owns yourself to be ranked'. And he claims to find in Burnet three marks of the low churchmen:

The first . . . that they are cordially and conscientiously zealous for the Church as established by Law: but yet they think no Human Constitution is so perfect but that it may be made better, and that the Church would be both more secure

---

[16] W. Wake, *Sermons*, p. 294.

and more unexceptionable if the Administration of the discipline were put into other hands and into a better method. . . .

Second, they think that in matters declared to be indifferent, no Harm could follow on it if some regard were had to the Scruples of those who divide from Us, in order to the fortifying the whole by Uniting us among ourselves.

The third is that 'great difference they make between the Dissenters and the Papists'—the Dissenters being 'a handful of men not capable of doing us much mischief.'[17]

Gilbert Burnet (1643–1715) lends himself to caricature because he was in some ways a caricature himself, for his high ideals were refracted through his behaviour in a way which led some, unwarrantably, to dismiss him as a humbug. He burst through all labels and was a man of contraries. At one time he contemplated turning hermit, and he praised clerical celibacy, yet he was much married in turn to three remarkable women, and was almost obsessed with the rearing of his children. He was, in Queen Anne's word, 'a meddler' drawn as by a magnet to 'great affairs', a master of backstairs gossip, yet he longed to be away from Court and immersed in pastoral care. A man so partisan that he could infuriate opponents with his biting tongue, yet he showed kindness and generosity to Roman Catholics, Presbyterians, Dissenters, and Non-Jurors. A man who sought earnestly the best gifts, including humility, but who in his great shovel hat, and reeking of tobacco, attracted ridicule as a Great Panjandrum.

Yet the man who dared rebuke Charles II for his private life, and to upbraid William III for his neglect of Mary, had plenty of courage to accompany a complete absence of tact, and he could occasionally, as in November 1688, intervene with wisdom. The expatriate Scot had something not quite couth about him, reflected in the frequent inelegance of his speech and writing.

Something of a child prodigy, he had worked furiously at learning, sometimes studying for fourteen hours a day. He had an immense memory, a large frame, and for most of his life, unlike most of his episcopal colleagues, was in perfect health. Despite the fact that he held a Chair in Theology at Glasgow, his learning was not of a university kind, but he had the wide interests of his time and was more than a dabbler in chemistry and mathematics. More important, and at the heart of his religion, was his attachment to the exponents of 'inward religion' in north-east Scotland, to Nairn and Charteris, to Scougal, and above all to Archbishop Leighton who was his guiding light.

In his quick scamper through the English Universities he was

---

[17] *Mr. Sewell's First Letter to the Bishop of Salisbury*, 1713.

accordingly drawn to the Platonists, More and Cudworth, and to John Wilkins. His involvement in Church and Court in Scotland brought him a wealth of experience, and access to so much of what we should call 'classified material' that it and his talent for indiscretion brought him into conflict, first with Lauderdale and then with James II. It also brought him the friendship of Queen Mary and the ambivalent favour of William III who alternately despised and respected him. A great traveller, his sojourn in France brought him many friends, as did his stay in Holland where he found his second wife, while his account of his travels in Italy and Switzerland was lively and Protestant enough for James II to ban it.[18] He was involved in correspondence with Leibniz about reunion but was more realist and sceptical about results than Sharp or Wake. He had been a member of the influential group of London preachers, for from 1675–84 he was chaplain to the Rolls, and lecturer at St Clement's. He was a fluent preacher, given to extempore sermons, who often had his congregation appreciatively humming. But at this time he was occupied in writing. Some of his best writing was done in small biographies (his thumb-nail sketches in his later histories are often excellent miniatures) and he followed the example of Rushworth in printing documents in full. His *History of the Reformation* may have contained more than ten thousand 'downright mistakes' (Foxcroft) but it was a landmark in historical writing, and he had copied a sound methodology from De Thou and Sarpi. The first volume was a timely success and won him the expressed thanks of Parliament. The more controversial *History of My Own Time* was not published during his life, but its mixture of gossip, history, and autobiography has made it an indispensable source for the history of his age.

He rated most highly his tract *Of Pastoral Care*, which takes high rank among a host of contemporary edifying writings. This was for him the root of his calling. As a young Scots clergyman he had been much beloved by his people, and he threw himself into his work as Bishop of Salisbury with great dedication, much labour, and impressive success. Some reforms he had to give up: the excess of hospitality which he could barely cut down, the inefficiencies of the ecclesiastical courts which baffled him as they had done Matthew Parker. But in the care of his churches, in the examination of ordinands, in administering confirmation, and in the visitation of his clergy he was outstanding, in the limited time at his disposal from attendance at Parliament and the education of that pathetic young *Wasserkopf*, the Duke of Gloucester. For a time he adventured his own theological college, something only a

---

[18] *Some Letters containing an Account of what Seemed more Remarkable in Switzerland, Italy, etc.*, Amsterdam 1686.

non-Oxford/Cambridge man would have attempted, and which their hostility soon brought to an end.

What was intended as a major gift to his Church was a long-planned and meditated *Exposition of the Thirty-nine Articles*, but in its breadth of sympathy it displeased the High Church Party who tried to get it condemned by Convocation, as favouring a 'diversity of opinions which the articles were framed to avoid'. For Burnet, as for Tenison, the Protestant succession was all important for the safety of the Church, but he was equally concerned to defend the Glorious Revolution, in whose encompassing he had played a signal role. It was his dislike of Tories and high churchmen, rather than any deep love for the Whigs, that accounts for the antagonisms he aroused and from time to time warps his historical judgements. One is either for Burnet or against him, but those who are for him cannot escape affection for this invariably disconcerting genius.

iv. Hoadly and the Bangorian Controversy

Benjamin Hoadly (1676–1761) might have sat for the portrait of a low churchman by Henry Sacheverell. His was a Latitudinarianism from which the mystical element had gone, leaving only the rationalism and moralism. If Burnet was of the seventeenth century, Hoadly belongs to the eighteenth. Despite the condemnation heaped upon him, the stars in their courses seemed on his side, and his cool and acid rationalism was of the very temper of the age.

He was of clerical, if Puritan, background and went to St Catharine's College in Cambridge. Here he vied with another bright undergraduate, Thomas Sherlock. Both men were seriously ill during their student days and each had to be allowed seven terms for illness. But Hoadly was left an incipient consumptive and a lifelong cripple, needing always a crutch or a stick and having to kneel in the pulpit. Both men were ambitious, though Sherlock as son of the Dean of St Paul's had the better start. Sherlock followed close on his father's steps, succeeding him as Master of the Temple at an indecently early age, and inheriting from him the makings of the fortune which he increased at each rung of the ladder of preferment. But Hoadly was a Whig, and Sherlock a Tory.

Whig ministries meant that Sherlock had long to wait for episcopal office, though he collected enough high university dignities to console him in the interval. With the advent of George I Hoadly advanced rapidly, but it was not until the 1720s that Sherlock (by favour of Queen Caroline) was able to succeed, and then outstrip his rival, so that in his later years he refused two archbishoprics. In his old age he delivered an astonishing charge on the problem of pluralities, a subject on which he certainly had authority to speak.

Hoadly had been Fellow and Tutor of his College, but left for London on his marriage and ordination. Unlike Sherlock, he was no orator, and soon, as he said, preached his lectureship at St Mildred's, Poultry, 'down to £30'. He then became Rector of St Peter-le-Poer.

Some of his sermons preached during this period (1714–24) were afterwards published.[19] Like William Wake, among many other preachers, he had a sermon on the danger of putting off repentance, and succeeded in turning the story of the dying thief into a cautionary tale. In a later sermon on 'The Good Samaritan' he explained that 'universal charity is not designed to break in upon the duties which we owe to ourselves, our parents, our children, our friends, nay, and our acquaintance . . . it is not in the power of any man to assist everyone in distress . . . nature drives him to prefer these before strangers.[20] The Good Samaritan, one feels, would have done better to have stayed at home.

In his sermon on 'Superstition' which he preached before the King in March 1717 he explained that

Neither our Lord nor his disciples have formed any exact system of morality, explicitly mentioning every particular duty or sin: but have thought it better to appeal . . . to the great and Universal law of reason, which they send every Christian to consult with sincerity and uprightness of heart as he will answer it at the great day of Accounts.[21]

All is in order, he says,

when Christ's authority is once suffered to settle the faith and worship of Christians: when obedience to his commands under the conduct of that faith is sufficient to pass for religion: when the rule of every man's conduct is universally allowed to be his sincere attention to the directions of Christ, and Christians are so upright as to take that for their religion which they find recommended of their Lord and his disciples.[22]

But if Hoadly was a poor preacher, he was an able pamphleteer. This was the great hour of the coffee house, and if books were dear, there was readily available a flood of tracts and pamphlets selling at 6*d.* or 1*s.* It was his pamphlets rather than his sermons which won him the favour of the Whig politicians. He had begun by defending Dissenters in the matter of occasional conformity, but then became involved in a running fight with the eminent Nonconformist, Edmund Calamy, in which he

[19] *The Works of Benjamin Hoadly*, ed. J. Hoadly (3 vols, 1773), vol. iii.
[20] Ibid. iii. 811. [21] Ibid. iii. 704. [22] Ibid. iii. 706.

set forth 'the reasonableness of conformity'. He included an excursus on the theme that 'episcopal ordination was the regular ordination settled in the Church of Christ' which was important enough to be published separately. These tracts were reprinted in the 1720s and afford part of the evidence that he did not dismiss the idea of the 'visible' Church.

But it was high-church doctrine that roused him. He attacked a sermon of Atterbury which, though it had no connection with the high-church doctrines, gave useful practice in sharpening his claws. Next he directly attacked the views of Atterbury and Bishop Blackhall of Exeter on government. With the revival of the doctrines of passive obedience in the reign of Anne he hit out in a notable sermon before the Lord Mayor of London, on Michaelmas Day 1705, taking the darling text of his opponents, Romans 13: 1, and turning it inside out, making it a defence of the Glorious Revolution. This earned him the angry censure of the Lower House of Convocation as 'dishonouring the Church'. But in two notable assize sermons and in a series of tracts he so ably defended the Whig notions of the origin and nature of civil government as to receive the thanks of the House of Commons. Henceforward his appeals were directed towards the laity. His political ideas have been sufficiently analysed by Norman Sykes[23] and we shall concentrate on his theological views which perhaps merit more sympathetic presentation than they have generally received.

Hoadly's important tract *A Preservative against the Principles and Practices of the Non-Jurors* (1716) was the real origin of what was to become famous as the 'Bangorian Controversy'. It was occasioned by the publication in that year of the posthumous papers of George Hickes, in which the extreme views of Hickes were made startlingly plain.[24] Among the papers were draft letters to Robert Nelson warning him against returning to communion with the Church of England, and attacking the Church of England conformists not only for their illegal deprivations, but still more for their heretical doctrines about obedience, and even more, it seems, for the 'damnable prayers' which, he claimed, polluted the entire liturgy. 'God will not hear their petitions but . . . all the offices are polluted by those abominable prayers.' And Nelson, by attending them would bring into dire temptation not only himself, but his servants and his family, a 'temptation indeed in which I think you have no reason to expect that God should support you.'

In his tract Hoadly refers to the attack on Robert Nelson by Hickes,

---

[23] N. Sykes, 'Benjamin Hoadly', in *The Social and Political Ideas of some English Thinkers of the Augustan Age*, ed. F. J. C. Hearnshaw, 1928.

[24] *The Constitution of the Catholic Church and the Nature and Consequences of Schism, set forth in a Collection of Papers written by the late Right Revd George Hickes, D.D.*, 1716.

and it is in this connection that he stresses the importance of 'sincerity' for which he was to be most sharply attacked.

To claim a right to stand in God's stead in such sense that they with all their infirmities and prejudices and mistakes about them can absolutely and certainly bless some and withhold a blessing from others, and that God Almighty hath obliged himself to bless or not to bless also, this is the highest absurdity.

To assume this without first assuming infallibility is nonsense, and to assume infallibility is blasphemy.

This was the work which infuriated the High Church Party, but since it was directed against the Non-Jurors, it was difficult for Convocation to take notice of it without further evidence. This was now forthcoming. Hoadly had been made a royal chaplain, and in 1716 was made Bishop of Bangor. It was a remote and miserably paid see, and most of those who went to it clung to the banner with the strange device, 'Excelsior'! But it gave Hoadly episcopal status, and made him a sizeable target. It was on 31 March 1717 that he preached a fateful sermon before the King on John 18: 36. 'My Kingdom is not of this world', a theme which may have been suggested to him by his monarch.

Within ten years two sermons were to have immense political and ecclesiastical repercussions. The two preachers, Henry Sacheverell and Benjamin Hoadly, could hardly have been more different: Sacheverell with his imposing presence—'tall as a maypole, fine as an archbishop' is how the schoolboy John Wesley saw him; Hoadly, on the other hand, was a little man and a cripple. But they had one thing in common, each was a master of the ambivalent and enigmatic, each had important silences. Atterbury was to charge Hoadly with 'those little shifting equivocal forms of speech—those savings and softenings he throws in everywhere—show that the thistles he was mumbling did not pass easily.'

The beginning of the famous sermon makes the point that words may come, through constant usage and with the passing of time, to acquire meanings which contradict their original significance. The process is to be resisted when it invades 'the most sacred and important subjects' and the cure is to have recourse to the originals of things: 'to the Law of Reason . . . and to the Declarations of *Jesus Christ* and his immediate Followers'.

He then examines the fate of the word 'Kingdom'.

The *Kingdom* of *Christ*, is the same with the *Church* of *Christ*. And the *Notion* of the *Church* of *Christ* which, at first, was only the Number, small or great of those who believed *Him* to be the Messiah: or of those who subjected themselves to *Him* as their King in the Affair of Religion.

In Christ's Kingdom '*He* himself is *King* . . . He is himself the sole *Law-giver* to his Subjects: . . . the sole *Judge* of their *Behaviour*, in the affairs of *Conscience* and *Eternal Salvation*.' The phrase '*Conscience* and *Eternal Salvation*' is vital to the whole exposition and we shall find it repeated several times at key points in the discourse. 'In those Points', that is, 'in the affairs of Conscience and Eternal Salvation' he hath left behind him no visible, humane *Authority*, no *Vice Gerents*, who can be said properly to supply his Place—no *Interpreters*, upon whom his Subjects are absolutely to depend: no *Judges* over the Consciences of Religion of his people.' For 'whoever hath an *absolute Authority* to *interpret* any written or spoken Laws; it is He who is truly the *Law-giver*.'

In human society laws have interpreters, though the original legislators can, if they will, 'resume the *Interpretation* into their own hands.' But Christ himself never interposes in this way 'either to convey *Infallibility* to Such as pretend to handle it over again; or to assert the true *Interpretation* of it.' It is the same with rewards and punishments, for if men alter the number and nature of these in matters of conscience and salvation

they are so far *Kings* in his stead. . . . If therefore the *Church* of *Christ* be the *Kingdom* of *Christ*; it is essential to it, that Christ himself be the Sole *Law-giver* and Sole *Judge* of his Subjects, in all points relating to the favour or displeasure of *Almighty God*, and that all His *Subjects* in what station soever they may be are equally *Subjects* to *Him*.

His second argument concerns rewards and punishments, deriving from the laws of Christ. 'The laws of this Kingdom, as Christ left them, have nothing of this world about them, no Tendency either to the Exaltation of *Some*, in worldly pomp and dignity: or to their absolute Dominion over the Faith and Religious conduct of *Others* of his Subjects: or to the erecting of any sort of *Temporal Kingdom*, under the Covert and Name of a *Spiritual* one.'

Unlike St Paul, however, who wrote that he sought to persuade men, in too many countries, 'it must be in a quite contrary strain; *knowing the terrors of this World, and having them in our power, We do, not persuade men, but force their outward Profession against their inward Persuasion*.'

As soon therefore as you hear 'of any of the *Engines* of *this world* . . . think that then, and so far the *Kingdom of this world* takes place'. For Christ declared that his Kingdom was not 'of the same sort with other Common *Earthly* Kingdoms, in which the Rewards are Worldly Honours, Posts, Offices, Pomp, Attendance, Dominion: and the Punishments are Prisons, Fines, Banishment, Gallies, and Racks.' If these things pertained to the Kingdom, then 'Sincerity and Hypocrisy:

Religion and No Religion: Force and Persuasion: a Willing Choice and a Terrified Heart, are become the same things: truth and falsehood stand in need of the same methods to propagate and support them.'

The sermon concludes with three observations. The grossest mistakes about the Kingdom have come when men have argued from 'Other Visible *Societies*, and Other Visible *Kingdoms of this World* . . . to what ought to be Visible and Sensible *in His Kingdom.*' Second, the Church of Christ consists of 'the *Number* of Persons who are Sincerely and Willingly *Subjects* to *Him*, as *Law-giver* and *Judge* in all matters truly relating to Conscience or Eternal Salvation.'

Finally, he asserts that 'to set up any other *Authority* in *His* Kingdom, to which his Subjects are indispensably and absolutely obliged to Submit their Consciences, or their Conduct, in what is properly called Religion' destroys the authority of Christ. Such pretensions mistake the character of the Kingdom. 'But the *Peace* of *Christ's Kingdom* is a manly and Reasonable *Peace*: built upon Charity and Love and mutual forbearance and receiving one another, as God receives us.'

The conclusion of the matter is that Christ is '*King* in his own Kingdom: he is sole *Law-giver to his Subjects and Sole Judge* in matters relating to salvation.' Those who seek out 'the plain and short declarations of their *King* and *Law-giver* himself' are the most becoming subjects of the Kingdom and not those who

hunt after Them through the infinite contradictions, the numberless perplexities, the endless disputes of *Weak Men*, in several ages, till the Enquirer himself is lost in the Labyrinth and perhaps sits down in Despair or Infidelity.

If Christ be our King, let us show ourselves subject to him alone . . . and live and act as those who wait for the appearance of an all knowing and impartial judge: even that King, whose Kingdom is not of this world.

It is worth noting, before turning to the subsequent uproar, that one of Hoadly's later champions, the Revd A. A. Sykes,[25] the Rector of Dry Drayton, had earlier preached a sermon on this very theme and text in St Michael's, Cambridge, on the occasion of an archidiaconal visitation on 13 December 1716, and that this sermon was published in 1717. There are striking parallels in ideas and in technical vocabulary. We think it likely that Hoadly had read, and indeed, had borrowed from, this sermon.

[25] The Revd Anthony Ashley Sykes, of St Paul's and Corpus Christi College, Cambridge. MA 1708. DD 1726. He was a friend of Samuel Clarke and of Hoadly who helped him with a number of preferments culminating in a Prebend of Winchester, 1740. He was a famous pamphleteer and took on Warburton among others.

A. A. SYKES

B. HOADLY

'The Difference between the Kingdom of Christ and the Kingdom of this World'

Jno. 18. 36

. . . A Sermon preached at the Archdeacon's Visitation in St. Michael's Church, Cambridge, Dec. 13, 1716. [pub. 1717.]

'Christ's Kingdom not of this World' Jno. 18. 36.

Before King George 1, 31 March, 1717

Our Saviour was *born for this End* that he should propose to mankind certain Terms and Conditions on the Acceptance of which . . . Heaven was offered . . .

[Cf. Hoadly's sermons at St Peter-le-Poer on 'The terms of our acceptance with God']

All that would acknowledge him for the Messiah, accept Him as their King and live under the Direction of his Laws . . . who are Sincere and Honest in their Endeavours to find out his Will, and as sincerely endeavour to practise it are . . . the Church.

[p. 250] the number of those . . . who believed Him to be the Messiah . . . subjected to Him as their King . . .

The church is . . . the number of Persons who are sincerely and willingly subjects to Him . . . have recourse to Him in the Gospel . . . resolve to perform what they see he layeth a stress upon.

[p. 7] Force is absolutely *forbid* in the *Kingdom of Christ* . . . to *compel* is repugnant to Scripture, Reason, and to *common Sense* . . . plainly cancelling out all the Boundaries of Virtue and Vice. Force may make men Hypocrites.

We do not (some say) persuade men, but force their outward profession against their inward persuasion . . . a change to the Kingdom of this World . . . then sincerity and hypocrisy force and persuasion are become the same things. [p. 255]

Whoever offends against the laws of *That* Kingdom can be responsible only at *That* tribunal, nay, the *Sincerity and Uprightness* of our hearts being the All required by God.

Christ . . . hath left behind Him, no visible human authority . . . no *interpreters upon whom his subjects are* absolutely to depend—no judges over the consciences or religion of his his people . . either for the making new laws or interpreting old ones . . . Who ever can add new laws . . . is as truly a King as Christ himself . . . He Himself never interposeth. [p. 251]

[p. 9] In the Kingdom of Christ no Men have an absolute Power to determine Controversies . . .

References are to J. M. Creed and J. S. Boys-Smith, *Religious Thought in the Eighteenth Century* (Cambridge 1934), pp. 249–60.

A. A. SYKES   B. HOADLY

[p. 11] (It is an error to suppose) that
God has appointed visible Judges of
Controversies, Or that the Kingdom
of Christ must be managed like the
kingdoms of the earth by *final decisions*
. . and *absolute submission* . . . as if the
Kingdom of Christ could not subsist   . . . no one of them . . . hath authority
unless men authoritatively interposed   to make new laws for Christ's subjects
. . . As if religion were not sufficiently   or to impose a sense upon the old
revealed by Christ himself as he lives   ones, which is the same thing. [p. 253]
now (Rom. 6. 9) . . . there can be no
Occasion of any *Successors*, strictly
speaking who may have Authority to
make New Laws, or change, repeal,
relax the Old Ones . . . those cannot   the church . . . is the number of those
be considered his *Successors* unless they   . . . who are sincerely and willingly
had equal Authority and Power to   subject to him . . . it is a sufficient
make Laws which Christ himself had.   authority that he hath declared the
                                              conditions of their salvation.

[p. 10] honesty in searching out the
Will of Christ and Sincerity in following it is all that is required of us.

Why then doth any Man presume to
make Salvation and the Favour of God   [cf. Hoadly, *Preservative against Non-*
depend upon any *external Regimen* . . .   *Jurors* (1716), p. 98; William Law,
. . . or what more *absolute Necessity* is   *Three Letters*, p. 27.]
is there for any particular *uninterrupted*
Succesion of Men than there is for an
uninterrupted succession of Platonists
to make a man a disciple of *Plato*. . . .
[p. 10]

That Faith and Repentance are not
sufficient for Salvation without *human*   [cf. *Preservative*, pp. 92, 98.]
Absolutions and *Benedictions* from such
or such particular persons.

All arguments drawn from the nature   the grossest mistakes . . . have arisen
of Other Societies to that of the King-   . . . that men have argued from other
dom of Christ are Unconclusive.   visible societies.
[p. 22]

Hoadly's was no doubt a remarkable sermon, but it is doubtful if it would have had such sensational consequences, had it not been for the resentment in the Lower House of Convocation at Hoadly's earlier utterances, and above all for his work against the Non-Jurors, which in effect condemned most of the high-church principles. When the sermon was published the storm broke, and the enemies of Hoadly must have felt he had been delivered into their hands. In an astonishingly short time there was a pile of pamphlets read and discussed in coffee-house debates. Among the first into the fray was Dr Snape, Headmaster of Eton, who charged that the sermon was 'entirely destructive of all order and argument, of all unity, peace and concord in the church' and that 'your lordship appears very unfriendly to anything that is external in the worship of God.' There were minor skirmishes between Thomas Sherlock and the Revd A. A. Sykes, who defended Hoadly—a tedious little scrap of this, of the 'You said', 'Oh, no I didn't', 'Oh yes, you did' variety. Then there was the black comedy about whether Hoadly, on advice, had inserted qualifying phrases, like the word 'absolute', between the preaching and the publication. The result was a series of the most solemn asseverations, printed in the *Post* or *Courant*, from all concerned, the Bishop of Carlisle (Nicolson), the Dean of Peterborough (White Kennett), the Bishop of Bangor, and Mr Childe, the proprietor of Childe's coffee house (and Hoadly's brother-in-law). Hoadly's solemn oath is surely to be believed, for in fact he had used the word 'absolute' in his earlier writing against the Non-Jurors, and a careful examination shows it to be central to the whole argument of the sermon. More important was the attack from Convocation, a committee of which, under Thomas Sherlock's chairmanship and probable authorship, drew up a report which condemned Hoadly, 'nemine contradicente', as 'tending to subvert all government and discipline in the church and to reduce this kingdom to anarchy and chaos.' He was also charged with denying the Royal Supremacy. This provoked Hoadly at least into his fullest defence of his sermon. But it is interesting that Sherlock himself in writing a much acclaimed tract in defence of the Test Act (1718) could claim 'it is now I think agreed on all hands that the design of the Bishop of Bangor's sermon before the King was to make way for the repeal of the Test Act.'

But the one devastating reply to Hoadly was that of William Law in his celebrated *Three Letters to the Bishop of Bangor*. Law was at this time quite unknown. Hoadly did not answer it, not that he was too scared to reply—he was not at all timorous in such matters—but he was needlessly hoity-toity in stressing the prior importance of replying to a dean, and thereafter Law did not pull any punches. As polemical divinity Law's *Three Letters* are near the top of a fairly small class of great theological polemic in our literature. In continually varying, but always lucid and flowing, prose, in ruthless argument, and in drawing more and more outrageously apparent conclusions from statements, conclusions which readers were delighted to see drawn (even though the original author never intended them) and in rapier-like thrusts of irony, they could hardly be equalled. But perhaps this is not all the truth.

For one thing, the quantity and violence of high-church reaction cannot be simply taken at its own face value. The report of Convocation is no theological masterpiece, but a rather muddled document, as is shown by the fact that Sherlock and the rest of the committee were soon divided in public about its meaning. The fact that the Lower House of Convocation condemned Hoadly 'nemine contradicente' is not con-clusive evidence that they were any more just to Hoadly than they had been to Burnet, Wake, or Tenison. Moreover, brilliant as his letters were, Law's methods had some serious weaknesses. These can be best seen in the later controversy between Law and Hoadly about the Sacrament of Holy Communion, but they are noticeable here.

Thus he begins with the statement that 'there is not a Libertine or Loose Thinker in England but he imagines you intend to dissolve the Church of England as a Society'—to which Gilbert Burnet, the Younger, in one of the more lively pamphlets, put the equally apposite point that the Roman Catholics would be mightily pleased with Law.

But the one really serious misrepresentation of Hoadly is Law's citation from Hoadly's *Preservative* (which is the major target rather than the sermon):

That every one may find it in his own Conduct to be true, that his Title to God's favour cannot depend upon his actual being or continuing in any particular method: but upon his *Real Sincerity* in the conduct of his Conscience . . . the favour of God follows *sincerity* considered as such, and consequently follows every *Equal Degree of Sincerity*.[26]

From this Law draws the conclusion that 'Quakers, Ranters, Muggletonians, and the Fifth Monarchy men are as much in favour with God as any of the Apostles;' and 'likewise sincere Jews, Turks and Deists'.[27]

But Law wrenches this from its true context which he does not really consider until his Second Letter (p. 67) nor does he examine the meaning of 'sincerity' in Hoadly's usage until the Third (pp. 187–9).

[26] Hoadly, *A Preservative against the Principles and Practices of Non-Jurors both in Church and State* (1716), p. 90.
[27] William Law, *The Works of the Reverend William Law M.A.* (9 vols., 1762, repr., 1892), i. 4.

But that context is really important. Hoadly had been going back to the Hickes's papers, and their attack on the layman, Robert Nelson, who intended to leave the Non-Jurors and return to the Communion of the Church of England. Hickes uttered dire warnings that Nelson would be imperilling his own soul and those of his family and servants, cutting himself off from the true (non-juring) Church. It is Hoadly who puts a fair question. The Non-Jurors had left the Church of England— or it had left them—on a point of conscience, the refusal to take improper oaths. Their sincere, conscientious disobedience was the nerve of their protest. Now one of their members, also because of his sincerity and in obedience to his conscience, was returning to the Church of England. Surely what mattered most in the sight of God was not his leaving one communion for another, but his sincerity of conscience?

Nor was Hoadly thinking merely of 'sincerity' in the abstract. As Hoadly himself said in his *Answer to Dr Hare*, 'the passage relates expressly to the choice of church communions amongst persons always supposed to be Christians.' He should not have been so warm, says Hoadly,

in charging Me with maintaining that all Heathen, Jews, Turks, Infidels, if *sincere*, were within . . . the rewards of sincere *Christians* . . . my Thoughts did not extend when I was writing that Passage in a Christian Country . . . as if I had thought that All equally sincere Persons should have the same Reward in Heaven.

What he intended 'solely related to the ridding of sincere Christians in the choice of a communion from the . . . thoughts of their being out of God's favour and liable to his wrath upon their involuntary errors . . .'[28]

Yet it was on the basis of this misunderstanding that Law made one of his most devastating points, accusing Hoadly of an argument which put all Churches and religions on one level, and gave rise to the immortal sentence 'Your Lordship is ours, as you fill a Bishopric: but we are at a loss to discover from this Discourse what other interest we have in your Lordship.'[29]

Yet Hoadly's pamphlets were still in circulation and would soon be reprinted, in which he argued against Nonconformists the paramount claims of the episcopal Church of England. And Law himself proceeded

---

[28] Hoadly, *Works*, ii. 875ff. 'Sincerity' was not in that age a tepid word. Evelyn's *Diary* records several major sermons on the theme, and in a notable sermon at Whitehall, 7 March 1679. E. Stillingfleet (*Works*, i. 253, also pub. separately, 1680) expounds sincerity and integrity against the equivocations and mental reservations attributed to Catholic casuistry. It was also an important concept for John Wesley.

[29] Law, *Works*, i. 5.

to expound and defend the most rigorous high-church notions of the authority of the clergy, and of an uninterrupted apostolic succession.

His appeal to history on behalf of an uninterrupted succession is feeble and he is driven back on the argument that it is a 'moral impossibility' that things could have happened otherwise.

If there be no Uninterrupted Succession then there are no Authorised Ministers from Christ: if no such Ministers, then no Christian Sacraments: if no Christian Sacraments, then no Christian Covenant whereof the Sacraments are the Stated and Visible Seals.[30]

There were and no doubt still are many for whom these affirmations were impelling, but there were also others who might be sympathetic to Hoadly's final disclaimer.

I am fully satisfied that, till a Consummate Stupidity and Ignorance can be happily established and universally spread over the face of the Land; there is nothing that tends so much to destroy All Due Respect to the *Clergy* as the Demands of more than can be due to Them, and nothing that has so effectually thrown *Contempt* upon a *Regular Succession* of the Ministry as this calling no Succession *Regular* but what is *Uninterrupted*, and the making the Eternal Salvation of Christians to depend upon that *Uninterrupted Succession*, of which the most *Learned* must have the least Assurance; and the *Unlearned* can have no Notion, but through Ignorance and Credulity.[31]

The Convocation Report had charged Hoadly with taking away all authority from the Church and tending 'to subvert all Government and discipline in the Church of Christ.'[32] It also charged him with contradicting the visibility of the Church as affirmed in Articles 19 and 20 of the Thirty-nine Articles.

Hoadly's answer is that what he had to say about the Church and especially his definitions in his sermon, were not concerned with the characteristics of the particular Churches, but 'no other but the Universal Invisible Church. It is a description not of a Church in our modern way of speaking, but of the Church, the Invisible Church of Christ.'

It does not seem indeed that Hoadly and his friends (e.g. Ashley Sykes) intended to deny visible particular Churches their government, discipline, and sacraments. What they rejected was an authoritarian and clerically dominated Church which claimed absolute obedience in matters concerned with conscience and eternal salvation. They also opposed the use of force, rather than persuasion, in matters of religion. Hoadly could also properly claim that he had not denied, since he had

---

[30] Law, *Works*, i. 9.   [31] Hoadly, *Works*, ii. 485.
[32] Hoadly, *Works*, ii. 477.

not in his sermon discussed, the government, discipline and sacraments of particular and visible Churches, or their claim to obedience in the wider field of 'things indifferent', though he says that the test of those things is not an ecclesiastical 'say so' but their agreement with the revealed commands of God.

It is true that, like the great Erasmus before him and his contemporary friend Samuel Clarke, Hoadly raised the cult of the enigmatic to a fine art, and gave rise to suspicion that he and his friends held a reduced theology, yet Hoadly hardly deserved Law's ascending insinuations that he must be a Deist or an Atheist.

It is also true that Thomas Sherlock had a point when he asked why Hoadly should spend so many thousands of words explaining what he had not meant, when a few hundred words would have made clear what he really intended, and what he really thought of the discipline and government of the Church of England. But while it is true that there was evident in Hoadly an individualist view of salvation which was the mark of the age, there seems no evidence that he believed in 'an unlimited private judgement' (N. Sykes).

Yet Norman Sykes can hardly be gainsaid when he insists that the great majority of those who disagreed with Hoadly—and who included many Whigs, though Wake and Gibson were high church in their views of Church and Ministry—were much more concerned with the empirical situation. 'The volume and vehemence of denunciation which descended on the author afforded convincing proof if that were needed to the Whig administration that their ecclesiastical policy could not be allied with such a veritable kingdom of fairies.'[33]

Yet as we have seen, the virulence came almost entirely from high churchmen. Realists as indeed they were, the Whig politicians do not seem to have thought of Hoadly as in any way an ethereal theoretician. They did not abandon him. On the contrary, they exerted that pressure which suspended indefinitely the sitting of Convocation, while it was Hoadly's opponents who were stripped of their royal chaplaincies. Nor is it proven that Hoadly's doctrines would have made an end of the Establishment. Of a coercive Establishment indeed, for it was a main thrust of the sermon, as Sherlock said, to make an end of the grim and repressive authoritarianism of contemporary Catholicism, and of the sanctions of the Test Act in England which though milder, embodied the same coercive principles. But a thoroughgoing Erastianism was compatible with Hoadly's views, and Thomas Cranmer's view of episcopal commission was nearer to Hoadly than to William Law.

If the Church of England at this time practised the art of the possible,

---

[33] Sykes, *Church and State*, p. 294.

and if a measure of worldliness and political self-interest were inseparable from the 'earthing' of the Church, and so was far removed from any 'kingdom of fairies', was not the Whig alliance itself a little distant from the Kingdom of God as set forth in the New Testament? Was not the theme of Hoadly's sermon (as George I may have hinted when suggesting it) a timely one at the moment when the Church was involved in a new and complex political pattern, and was it not in order, in a sermon and before a Christian prince, to remind men that Christ spoke of his Kingdom in other terms than did the Benefactors of the Gentiles? And in deprecating a clerical authoritarianism which coerced men's consciences, was not the very question raised which would one day be put immortally in the great parable of Dostoevsky's 'Grand Inquisitor'?

Was it not then proper to hold up the mirror of the Gospels—is it not one of the ends of Christian preaching to do this in each changing age—at this time? And what would Paul and Timothy and Titus whose episcopal authority Law stressed, have made of a Church where good archbishops like Sharp and Wake bestowed sacred offices on their friends and poor relations, or where a man like Dr Bisse might be regarded as episcopable because he had married the third daughter of the Duke of Leeds?

In fact neither Hoadly's earlier writings nor his subsequent ecclesiastical career suggest him as addicted to ethereal notions. Perhaps we might allow that he was like the man in *Iolanthe* who was a fairy down to the waist, for he certainly kept his feet on the ground. Of course his sermon was radical, in its return to a *sola scriptura* against Catholic usage and tradition, and in its rejection by implication of all *de jure divino* discipline in the Church, setting all human authority under the sole jurisdiction of Christ.

Yet if such trenchant criticism might have come properly from a Francis of Assisi or even a Martin Luther, or from Thomas Ken and William Law, it came wryly from the man who never visited his sees of Bangor and Hereford and whose record at Salisbury and Winchester bears no comparison with his immediate predecessors, and whose progress was from influence to affluence. He had some human virtues, and was a good father and friend. Nor may we forget the courage which had brought him on his way, remembering the enfeebled and crippled student whose career was wrecked before it had begun, but who struggled grimly to the top as persistently as his equally ambitious rival, Thomas Sherlock. A cynic might suggest that in the low churchman Benjamin Hoadly and in the high churchman Thomas Sherlock the involvement of the historic episcopate in party politics was beginning to show results.

PART II
THE DISSIDENTS

Nor can it be thought unreasonable for us to prize our Liberty yet the more, because it comes to us as the Fruit of the Prayers and Tears, the Sufferings and Hardships, the Conflicts and Vows of our Fathers before us. Some of us I doubt not may well remember that in the Course of our Education, in the Midst of their most sorrowful complaints of their own hard Usage, they to prevent our being disheartened would freely entertain us with the Hopes they had for better things reserved for us. These better things through the great Mercy of God we have in good part lived to reach. And therefore we should take Heart, cheerfully following them as far as they followed Christ: adhering firmly to the cause of Truth and Purity, Liberty and Charity in conjunction and trusting God with the Sequel.

EDMUND CALAMY, *A Continuation of the Account . . . of the Ministers . . . Ejected*, 1727.

THE origins of English Nonconformity lie far back, centuries before the Great Ejectment of 1662. There have been free-church historians who seek their origins in medieval movements of Dissent, or who would simply leap back over the centuries to the primitive Church. Others would mistrust this interpretation as a dissolution of the holy tradition into isolated pockets of purely spiritual religion, and would rather affirm their place within the one continuing life of the Church.

Perhaps we should not press the problem of pedigree, for while there are obvious affinities of ideas between groups of sixteenth-century Anabaptists and seventeenth-century Puritans, the case for a genuine pedigree of contact is much more difficult to prove. It is likely that an anti-clerical, Biblical, and sacramentarian piety was preserved in families and maybe in conventicles between the Lollards and the Puritans. Yet despite the fact that some Baptist families in Buckinghamshire bore surnames familiar among the Lollard trials, there does not seem to have been any claim on the part of the early Dissenters to have belonged to dissident groups going back four or five generations.

The English Lollards, as medieval sects went, were geographically vulnerable. There were no deep ravines, mountains, deserts, and forests for the Lollards of the Chiltern Hills or the East Anglian plain such as would protect the Waldensians or Hussites and it seems likely that Lollards simply melted into the ever widening pattern of English Protestantism.

More important is the growth of separatist doctrines in the reign of Elizabeth and James I, a polemic against a 'mixed' and Established Church, against bishops and against the liturgy. Many of those who expressed such views were ready for their sake to go into exile in Holland or America, but there were others who remained within the Established Church, and that for conscience sake. These were the Presbyterians who accepted the notion of a national Church, though they attacked the medieval discipline which pervaded the diocesan system. When it came to an issue, there were those like William Perkins who would not face final confrontation on a point of church polity, but who in all other ways accepted the Calvinist world view. Calvinism, as refracted through the teachings of Beza and Zanchius, surrounding

England with models of the 'best Reformed Churches' in France, Scotland, and Holland, became for a time a dominating Protestant influence in England.

It may be doubted whether the Nonconformists of the 1660s looked back so far. Most of them had lived through the Civil War (and there was a handful of veterans who had been born in the last years of the sixteenth century) and had shared the fateful experience of wielding political power. But now the majority of Englishmen held them responsible for the ugly years of civil war and for the murder of a Christian prince. After 1660 the violence of the Fifth Monarchy men and rumours of further plotting bred fear and the suspicion that the Dissenters nourished faction and held treasonable ambitions.

Yet during the last half of the century there were still giants among them. George Fox was still a vibrant voice in the land. Bunyan achieved in his *Pilgrim's Progress* a work second only in influence to Foxe's *Book of Martyrs*, while in the reign of Charles II he became a famous preacher attracting great London audiences. Milton produced his mighty epics after the Restoration. And Richard Baxter became a father figure for the Nonconformist cause, the man even more important than his influential writings.

As English political life swung into a division between Whig and Tory, it was inevitable that the Nonconformists, whose patrons among the aristocracy were few and diminishing, should be allied with the party of trade and industry, particularly since they had in common a desire for peace and toleration.

Many of the ejected clergy, like those of the Non-Jurors, retired into other avocations, into teaching or medicine, others accepted early retirement, for there were still among them a number with private means. But others ministered to Nonconformist congregations, and their meeting houses, like Salter's Hall, were thronged by overflowing congregations. There were those among them who were not offended by the liturgy, and who desired for charity's sake to keep open all links with the Established Church. For them Occasional Conformity and intercommunion were no mere opportunistic devices by which to qualify for civic or national office.

And there were those among the Established clergy and laity who recognized and welcomed such gestures, for there were still many ties of personal friendship, and Thomas Ken, George Hickes, and Robert Nelson had their friendly links with individual Dissenters. The diary of that unflagging sermon-taster Ralph Thoresby (even though he moved towards the High Church Party) shows us one who could hear a sermon in the Established Church in the morning and from a Nonconformist in the evening, one who valued the preachings of such Nonconformist divines as Edmund Calamy and Philip and Matthew Henry.

6

ENGLISH PRESBYTERIANS

IN 1660 the English Presbyterians were a formidable body, exceeding all other Nonconformists in learning, numbers, and influence. Their great moment was indeed past and gone for ever, when in the mid-1640s the shape of the National Church seemed within their grasp, and Parliament ready to impose a Presbyterian discipline upon the nation. Thereafter they were more and more displaced by Independents and sectaries, though their authority revived in the last months of the Commonwealth, and their share in the return of Charles II and the promises of the returning monarch raised hopes of a measure of comprehension. There was nothing to suggest that within fifty years their discipline would have collapsed, and that the reformed tradition in theology, which they had championed, would have disintegrated or evolved, whichever verb is preferred, into a liberal unorthodoxy, while many of their churches turned to Calvinist congregationalism or embraced Unitarianism. The reasons for these developments, partly historical, partly theological, are complex, so intricate indeed that the riddles may never be satisfactorily explained.

Richard Baxter makes a useful starting-point. As is well known, he repudiated for himself the label 'Presbyterian'. But then his definition of Presbyterian was a fairly strict one.

I have met with few Presbyterian ministers in England . . . a presbyterian is one that is for the Divine right of Ruling Elders, unordained, having no power to Preach and Administer the sacraments, and for the Government of the church by Presbyteries, Classes and Synods, composed of Teaching Elders, in parity with these Ruling Elders conjunct, so that a General Assembly of them is the true Ecclesiastical Head of a National-Church.[1]

But he admitted that in popular usage the term was more generally defined. 'Of late Presbyterianism is like Puritan of old, a word which hath as many and as bad significations as speakers have diversity of designs or intents' and he says of the situation in 1660:

any man that was for a spiritual, serious way of worship (though he were for a moderate episcopacy and liturgy) . . . was commonly called a Presbyterian that

---

[1] R. Baxter. *Sacrilegious Desertion of the Holy Ministry Rebuked*, 1672, p. 5.

was for episcopacy and Liturgy if he conformed not so far as to subscribe to the English diocesan frame and all their impositions.[2]

But despite his repudiation of labels and his claim to be 'meere catholicke', Baxter himself clearly belongs to the Reformed tradition within which, hitherto, the English Presbyterians had occupied a central place. A hallmark was its concern for discipline. In the Swiss cities in the 1520s there grew up alongside the great twofold Lutheran dimensions of Word and Sacrament, a concern for the 'discipline of Christ' an extensive term which covered pastoral care and ecclesiastical polity. And though Calvin himself put discipline in a subordinate category, a great deal of conflict in which the Reformed Churches were involved in the period 1550–1660 was concerned with discipline.

Most of the fundamental issues concerning discipline had in fact been raised among the Swiss cities in the 1520s. None knew better than Oecolampadius, who had been Penitentiary in Basle, what problems were left in the vacuum made by the abandonment of the Sacrament of Penance and of the Confessional, and some of these he dealt with in a notable synod oration in 1531. The questions raised were discussed in a flurry of correspondence between himself and Ulrich Zwingli in Zurich and Martin Bucer in Strasbourg. Oecolampadius's solutions were like a blueprint, and doctrinaire in comparison with Zwingli's pragmatism, while Zwingli's heavily prophylactic view of discipline was in contrast with what he called Bucer's 'lenity' which relied heavily on patristic authority. But between them they raised ultimate questions, the authority of the clergy over one another and in relation to the laity: the relative powers of the congregation and the godly magistracy. Thus a concern for discipline loomed large in the Reformed programme as it was transmitted to France, Scotland, and Holland, and in England it was elucidated by Cartwright and Travers and expressed in the famous *Book of Discipline* (reissued by Parliament in 1644).

Discipline, then, was the point of sharp conflict with the episcopally administered discipline of the Church of England. Here, weakened by the disuse of the Sacrament of Penance, and generally, of the Confessional, the penitential discipline of the Church seemed to its radical critics to be too rooted in ancient canon law, and in the survival of church courts, not greatly modified at the Reformation, the administration of which seemed to the Puritans slow, cumbrous, often venal, and impersonally remote from the congregations. And though there was more effective discipline exercised and more white sheets and candles persisted than was generally admitted, to many Puritans the lack

---

[2] *The Autobiography of Richard Baxter*, ed. J. M. Lloyd Thomas (Everyman edn. 1931), p. 154.

of discipline in regard to the Eucharist, from which only notorious offenders might be excluded and which all members of the Church were bound to attend, seemed offensive and scandalous. And it may well be that it was their concern for discipline which was a greater stumbling-block to reconciliation between Anglicans and Nonconformists than the old nitpicking objections to the liturgy, to the sign of the Cross, to the use of the ring, etc. It was the fact that safeguards were offered at this very point which made the Worcester House declaration (1660) the most hopeful of all the abortive attempts at reconciliation.

Baxter, we have seen, claimed support from a wider body of opinion than that of the strict Presbyterians, one which was ready to accept a modified episcopacy, though repudiating what it called 'diocesan prelacy'. It may be suggested too, that this in turn was a wider body than that which specifically supported Archbishop Ussher's eirenical blueprint of a collegiate episcopacy in which presbyters shared with bishops in the administration of discipline. Ussher's view, which claimed to be scriptural and primitive, Baxter found congenial and to it he gave his own support, and it became a platform in negotiations between the Nonconformists and the Government.

But 'moderate episcopacy' to many members of Baxter's Worcester Association must have meant something more general than Ussher. Moderate episcopacy had existed in England since the Reformation. It was the episcopacy of those venerated founding fathers, Cranmer, Ridley, Latimer. It was the kind of episcopacy illuminated by Jewell, by Grindal, and by Abbott. It could be claimed that this kind of episcopacy was not incompatible with the 'best Reformed Churches' and of a kind which Calvin and Knox (though not Beza and Melville) might have tolerated.

With the defeat of Cartwright and Travers, and the collapse of the 'classis' movement it seemed to many Protestant and Puritan church leaders that a Presbyterian polity might, after all, be relinquished relatively painlessly. And though they were in a sheltered position in Cambridge, both Laurence Chaderton and William Perkins continued to uphold a Protestant, Puritan, and Calvinist theology, while in the country parishes in East Anglia devoted preachers and pastors like Greenham, Hildersham, and Dodd (whom Richard Baxter could rightly regard as among his own spiritual ancestors) practised a reformed churchmanship within a diocesan framework, and exercised a Puritan discipline, although removed from the synodical apparatus of the Reformed Churches in Scotland and elsewhere.

Alongside the Reformed view of discipline, and its persistence within an episcopal framework (which therefore gave a new emphasis to the importance of the individual congregation) there was a pattern of theology which is roughly and generally labelled 'Calvinism'.

The doctrines of predestination and Election, which had been kept in subordination by Calvin himself, and sensitively related to Scripture, were systematized and, some would say, petrified in the emerging Protestant and Puritan scholasticism, amid the categories first of Covenant and then of Federal theology. Perkins had elaborated the Plan of Salvation in an intricate map based on the *Tabulae* of Theodore Beza, and it is this pattern of salvation which is to be found in the formidable doctrinal sections of the Synod of Dort, of the Westminster Confession, and the Savoy Declaration. It was this doctrine which was most ably expounded later in the century not by a Presbyterian, but by the Congregationalist John Owen.

In its emphasis on the Divine Will or on God's sovereign freedom, Puritan scholasticism recalls the expositions of salvation among the late-medieval schoolmen, as put forward by the Augustinians like Bradwardine and Wyclif, or even by some of the later Nominalists, yet without their counterbalancing emphasis on the human will. But it is noticeable how even moderate Puritans were shocked by Arminianism, and how reluctant they were, despite misgivings about the Antinomian wing among the Calvinists, to repudiate the Calvinist pattern. From the correspondence between William Bedell and Samuel Ward (who did not at the Synod of Dort so much bid John Calvin good-night as good-afternoon!) one can see that the criticisms which Richard Baxter felt constrained to make of the extreme Calvinist or Antinomian position did not begin with himself, but were rooted in a long English Protestant tradition going back at least to the homilies 'Of Salvation', and 'Of Good Works'.

On the other hand, perhaps we ought not simply to think of this Calvinist view of salvation as continuing only in the Presbyterian, Baptist, and Congregational Churches. There was a large body of Anglican clergy who were conformist, and who do not fit into the list of ejected confessors chronicled by Calamy and Walker, who retained their benefices not only during the Commonwealth, but also after the Restoration, and who were neither Trimmers, high-church Tories, nor Latitudinarian Whigs. Was there not a persistence of Calvinism within the Church of England, whose descendants would emerge in the eighteenth century as the non-Wesleyan, anti-Arminian, Calvinist wing of the Evangelical Revival? Is there not a continuous Calvinist, evangelical tradition within the Church of England from the last decades of the sixteenth century onwards? Had not the evangelical Calvinism of the eighteenth century such roots? Be that as it may, the main Calvinist

tradition in the middle of seventeenth-century England was that of the
Presbyterians, and it was strongly learned, and produced a formidable
array of preachers and theologians.

When in the 1640s the Presbyterians seemed within sight of political
power, the Scottish Church was at hand to remind them they had a
massive and coherent theological inheritance. In the debates of the
Westminster Assembly, and in the documents which issued from it,
they achieved, theologically, their finest hour. Themselves the creature
of Parliament and of the civil magistrate (who on one occasion at least
sharply reminded the Assembly of its subordination) they were
assembled to give advice to the Government, and with not always
welcome Scottish advisers breathing down their necks, they none the
less produced one of the last and greatest of Protestant confessions in
their Shorter and Larger Catechisms (but above all in the Shorter
Catechism). Baxter paid them a glowing tribute.

The divines there congregate were men of eminent learning and godliness, and
ministerial abilities and fidelity . . . as far as I am able to judge . . . the Christian
world since the time of the Apostles, had never a Synod of more excellent
divines (taking one thing with another) than this Synod and the Synod of Dort
were.[3]

In Cambridge the Puritan, Calvinist stronghold was attacked from
within, a decade after the departure of the anti-Arminians, Samuel Ward
and William Bedell; and while the Calvinist Anthony Tuckney still
dominated the University Establishment, the Cambridge Platonists
launched a radical attack on Puritan rationalism from Emmanuel
College which had been its heart. The extent of this attack is to be
seen in the splendid oration which Ralph Cudworth delivered before
Parliament in 1647 in which he attacked those who put Predestination at
the forefront of their theology, and directed his hearers away from
intricate controversies to the view of Christianity as a way of life, and a
vision of God. It was an appeal to reason as illuminated by the Spirit, a
return to a Christian Platonism which had perhaps never died out in
Cambridge since the sixteenth century.

Alongside the appeal to reason, there were increasing signs of
scepticism and indeed unbelief, such as the Christian world had not yet
known. It is a mark of the perception of John Tillotson that he seems to
preach with the awareness that there may be atheists in his audience, and
with him there comes defensiveness in the pulpit which it would never
again entirely lose. The writings of Thomas Hobbes, the great
bogyman, were not isolated portents. The philosophy of John Locke,

---

[3] Baxter, *Autobiography*, p. 72.

the new science of Newton and the Royal Society provided a plausible setting for a vigorous critique of orthodoxy and challenged the traditional arguments and apologetic for the Christian religion, and this assault was already well launched before 1680.

As the young men of the Church of England became aggressively high churchmen, so the younger Nonconformists coming from the Dissenting Academies had been many of them psychologically conditioned to be chip-on-the-shoulder rebels. They brusquely denied the labels of ancient heresies among them, for in truth they were not backward-looking, but trying to evaluate the Christian religion in terms of the new learning of the age. Isaac Newton's preoccupation with alchemy, and William Law's 'Behmenism' belong to this search for a new rationale as truly as did the doctrines of Clarke and Whiston. This is part of the background against which the revolt of the younger Nonconformist minds must be seen as it appeared in the confrontation at Salter's Hall.

One may ask if it was accidental that from within a Puritan Calvinist tradition this new rationalism emerged. The emphasis on the Divine Majesty, the divine sovereign freedom, not so much in Calvin himself, but in some Puritan theologians, might not seem immeasurably distant from the new emphasis on a Supreme Being, and a view of the person and work of Christ which was subordinationist.

The gulf between Calvin and Socinus, between the Genevan Reformers, and the Polish rationalists was indeed deep and unbridgeable, but can the same be said of Puritan scholasticism? Did John Owen's intricate expositions represent the rallying round the standards of the Old Guard, where elsewhere on the battlefield ground was being abandoned?

This loosening of orthodoxy has to be set in a wider context which involves the Church of England as much as Nonconformity, and we shall try to look at it as a whole at another stage. Here we may simply add the comment that the battle about subscription which was launched at Salter's Hall in 1719 did not necessarily involve any dissolution of dogma, or the repudiation of confessions. But it did represent a new attitude on the part of a younger generation towards subscription to formulas. Watts and Doddridge were as firm as the most radical among them, that church formularies, whether of ancient councils or recent assemblies could not rank beside Scripture as expressions of true faith.

After 1660 Richard Baxter, together with presbyterians of the older generation led by Calamy, Bates, and Manton, continued to hope for comprehension, but it became more and more evident that those were more realist who, like the Congregationalists led by John Owen, opted for toleration as the only possible way forward. This produced a difference in the Presbyterian ranks, between those older leaders, whom Sir Joseph Williamson in a famous label called the 'Dons', and younger men, led by the firmly Calvinist Samuel Annesley, whom he called the 'Ducklings'. Amid all the fading hopes and possibilities, which were raised, dashed, and raised again during the reign of James II, there were always difficulties between the policy of the Court and the practice of Parliament, where Commons and Lords might often come to different conclusions. And although in the opening months of the reign of William III it seemed that at last Comprehension, the removal of civil disabilities, and toleration might be achieved, in the end the Non-conformists had to be content with the Toleration Act, itself a dangerously one-sided measure once Comprehension had failed.

Obviously the failure of the Nonconformists to agree with one another was a fatal weakness, which perhaps could hardly have been avoided. But it was aggravated by theological controversy which simply bedevilled the situation as, once again, the painful situation arose which has often occurred in Christian history, of one party simply devouring another, to the amused triumph of their opponents. Baxter himself became the centre of attack from his Pinner's Hall lectures, was charged with a crypto-Arminianism and with preaching salvation by works. And there were other differences in the realm of ecclesiology and evangelism.

The Presbyterians, despite their belief in a national Church and a parochial system, were now reduced in practice to a Congregational existence, since their very association together was disallowed in the time of persecution, under the Conventicle and Five Mile Acts. In many places congregations moved from one party to the other. And then came the difficulties about subscription, and the infiltration of Deist and Socinian ideas which came into the open first in the Exeter district and then at the debate in Salter's Hall.

But at least there was some real relief. In 1689 Protestant Dissenters who believed in the Trinity and who swore the oaths of allegiance and supremacy, might obtain licence for their meetings, and so were absolved from the penalties of the Elizabethan Act of 1593, and the Conventicle Act of 1670. Those who accepted thirty-six of the Thirty-nine Articles were exempt from the penalties of the Act of Uniformity and of the Five Mile Act. As Michael Watts comments, 'The Revolution thus marked the victory of the Independent concept of toleration over Presbyterian hopes of comprehension. It also completed the meta-morphosis of Presbyterianism from the religion of a national church to that of a Dissenting sect.'

The pressures of common persecution had indeed brought the two denominations closer together. In 1669 a lecture was set up at Hackney, and a group of merchants financed the notable Pinner's Hall lecture in the City in 1672. By now the two denominations in Yarmouth had composed former differences and in 1675 met together for worship.

In 1678 some City laymen produced an *Essay for the Accommodation betwixt the Ministers of the Presbyterian and the Congregational Way* which was subscribed in June 1690 by ministers from Somerset, Gloucester, Wiltshire, and Dorset. In London, in July, a Common Fund was instituted to finance ministerial training. In March 1691 it seemed that the great step forward was at hand, when between eighty and one hundred ministers signed the 'Heads of Agreement' which had been compiled in the preceding months, a 'happy union' indeed which in London was to break down, but which left a more permanent mark in other parts of the country as far apart as Exeter, Lancashire, and Cheshire.

The Dissenters were naturally inclined to support the Hanoverian kings, and successive governments looked for their support, offering minor concessions which stopped well short of the repeal of the Test and Corporation Acts. Abortive discussions in 1732 led to the formation of a board of 'Dissenting Deputies' who henceforth became the spokesmen for the three denominations in matters of common concern and who acquired the privilege of direct access to the Throne. In 1723 George I made a grant of £500 to the widows of Dissenting ministers. This sum, the so-called 'Regium donum' was increased to £1,000 a year and its distribution placed in the hands of a committee of ministers. It became a formal government grant and was increased until its abolition in 1851. There were those who from its inception suspected it was a bribe on the part of Walpole. It was within this framework of toleration for their beliefs and worship, and grave cultural and political restrictions, that the eighteenth-century Nonconformists lived. Their ills did not any longer demand costly confession, and the liabilities stopped short of major harassment, let alone persecution. They too, suffered from the spirit of the age, and a widespread religious lethargy. They too, needed the blood transfusion of an evangelical revival.

7

CONGREGATIONALISTS

THE word 'Congregationalist'[1] appears in the 1640s. At its heart is the 'gathered Church'. It is perhaps coincidental that the phrase appeared in one of the first Protestant definitions of the Church. In the catechism which the Strasbourg reformer, Wolfgang Capito, composed, and which was translated into English in 1527 by the English exile, William Roye, as a 'Dialogue between a Christian Father and his Stubborn son' there is a question:

SON: What maner a churche is this?

FATHER: It is a company gaddred or assembled together of true and faythfull christen people which as members of one body (by the operation of the wholy ghost) are fastened in one Hed Christ Jesus their Lorde.[2]

Strasbourg was, with Basle, Zurich, and Berne one of the centres from which the Reformed tradition emerged, before it found its habitation and name in Calvin's Geneva. In Strasbourg a group of preachers carried on the work of the reformation in close, if sometimes uneasy, alliance with the godly magistrates. The most eminent of them was Martin Bucer who defined the Church in terms of the company of the 'elect'. In the years 1527–31 the city became a sanctuary for radicals on the run, and both Bucer and Capito were impressed by the more moderate Anabaptist leaders. Bucer was struck by the quality of their lives, and took from them the thought of small Christian cells within the larger community. Capito especially befriended and helped some of the radical exiles. Here then were two differing concepts side by side: on the one hand the theme of a Christian commonwealth, visible as the mixed community of a Christian city, but invisible in so far as within it there existed numbers of the elect. And on the other hand the separatist view of the Church as a disciplined, separated community, in vehement contradiction to the established Churches, keeping unspotted from the world and from the Church.

Both those views of the Church contribute to the doctrine of the

---

[1] M. Watts, *The Dissenters* (Oxford 1978), pp. 108–9; G. Yule, *The Independents in the Civil War* (Cambridge 1955).

[2] E. G. Rupp, *Studies in the Making of the English Protestant Tradition* (Cambridge 1966), p. 55.

'gathered Church' and account for some of the problems of early Congregationalist history. Much as the more conservative among them in the 1640s might disavow connection with the first English separatists, the Brownists, who by then had become a byword for sectarianism, they did in fact owe something to them, to the Brownist insistence on the autonomy and catholicity of each individual Christian congregation, called into existence by God and therefore competent to initiate its own pattern of reform 'without tarrying' for any permission of the magistrate. And it seems too, that the vehement unchurching by the Separatists of the Church of England persisted in some Congregationalist communities, as the first Covenant of the church at Bury St Edmunds testifies (16 August 1646).

We, being convinced in conscience of the evil of the Church of England and of all other states which are contrary to Christ's institution and being . . . fully separated from those who communicate with them either publicly or privately . . . we resolve by the grace of God not to return unto their vain inventions, their human devices, their abominable idolatries, or superstitious high places which were built and dedicated to idolatry.[3]

And at Bristol where the formidable Dorothy Kelly (a grocer's widow) gathered a church of kindred spirits—'it pleased the Lord to stir up some few of the professors of this city to begin to lead the way out of Babylon, the corrupt worship, and to separate from them and not so much as come near any of their superstitions.'[4]

But among the Puritan exiles in Holland there were those, sometimes called semi-separatists, who, like Henry Jacob, Henry Ainsworth, and William Bradshaw also refused to unchurch an established Church and who in their exiled churches worked out a cordial relationship with the established civil and religious authorities of Holland. Future leaders among the Congregationalists, Philip Nye, William Bridge, and Jeremiah Burroughs were members of gathered churches, brought into being by covenant, in Rotterdam and Arnhem. Later, in their *Apologeticall Narration* (1646), they affirmed that the real defects of the Church of England

did never work in any of us any other thought, much less opinion but that multitudes of the assemblies and parochial congregations thereof were the true churches and body of Christ and the ministry thereof a true ministry: much less did it ever enter our hearts to judge them anti-Christian.

A 'gathered Church' must not be supposed to imply a purely voluntary association, coming into being, after the order of Mel-

---

[3] G. F. Nuttall, *Visible Saints* (Oxford 1957), p. 49.   [4] Ibid., p. 46.

chizedek, whenever two or three say 'Go to, let us make a Church.' It is
certainly an authentic Congregationalist stress that God's people are 'of
a willing sort', freely and not compulsorily brought together, but it is of
the essence of it that it is God himself who gathers people together into
fellowship with Himself and with one another. Nor is the Church some
kind of optional afterthought whereby individual Christians, already
converted, decide to enter the fellowship of believers.

On the other hand, there may be separatist implications in the speed
with which 'gathered churches' multiplied in the 1640s, and not least in
the remarkable way in which sundry troops in the New Model Army
could decide to become 'gathered churches', calling such as Richard
Baxter to be their chaplains.

The distaste of some Congregationalists for being associated with the
Brownists may have some origin in their association with bitter
invective against the Church of England. But if the non-separatists
disliked the over-frequent comparison of the Church of England to
Babylon or Sodom, there were obvious affinities, such as their rejection
of the Prayer Book, their continuance of more charismatic usages,
extempore prayer, prophesyings, and the quizzing of preachers at the
end of the sermon.

But at the root of non-separating Congregationalism there is a
problem, which has never been better put or more ably, if un-
convincingly, argued than by J. Perry Miller in his study of *Orthodoxy in
Massachusetts.*[5] 'Did not Congregationalism make separatism imperative?' and 'How could these men justify the glaring inconsistencies of
their position?' He answers that they sought to do so by a splendid and
subtle casuistry, and by an attempt to hold 'the ancient and inviolable
principle of uniformity'. They refused to unchurch the Church of
England, and justified this by the fact that there were always in that
Church numbers of genuine Christians, that, despite episcopacy and
patronage, there was always an element of congregational consent
present, so that a beneficed incumbent might hold the Congregationalist
way, and ignore those features which contradicted it as of only
secondary importance. Perry Miller produces many texts to support this
reading, including those of William Ames, the most redoubtable
theologian of the forerunners of Congregationalism. In this way, oscil-
lating between the doctrinaire and the pragmatic, the non-separatists
were able to obtain a royal charter with the acquiescence of the Church
of England, to institute in Massachusetts Bay a Christian commonwealth where civil magistrates and Congregationalist preachers worked
hand in hand.

[5] Cambridge, Mass. 1932.

Soon, in England too, under the Commonwealth, it proved possible for Congregationalists to work within the framework of the Establishment. We can trace how, in Yarmouth, the Presbyterian attempts to smother gathered churches broke down and they were forced into unwilling accommodation with their fellow Puritans, sometimes literally when, as in Norwich, one congregation occupied the nave, and the other the chancel, of a parish church. It was thought defensible for Congregationalists to hold public preaching posts and lectureships paid for by the civil authorities, while others were able to set up 'gathered churches' in such places as Westminster Abbey and the cathedrals of Winchester and Exeter. More striking was the number of Congregationalists who accepted benefices, and those not always in the gift of congregations. The greater number of these were in East Anglia, where there were twenty-seven so beneficed in Suffolk and Norfolk. Of the 170 or so Congregationalists ejected in 1660–2, 130 were in livings at the time of their removal. And while tithes were a highly disputable subject among all sorts and conditions of Puritans, there were Congregationalists who accepted them and defended their use, not only on grounds of expediency. The sight of a Congregationalist who confessed the doctrine of a 'gathered Church', accepting a parish living and restricting the sacraments only to his own flock living within it, may seem as reprehensible to us after three centuries as it did to Richard Baxter. But we have an uncomfortable feeling that in practice and in Churches of every kind, there does exist within most congregations in many different Churches an inner core of the devoted and committed, to whom necessarily the minister must turn, visible saints, among the majority of half-committed.

Gathered churches often came into being through lay initiative, and a church might be embodied by covenant before a pastor had been called. The ministry therefore was not of the 'essence' of the Church. But the repudiation of their Anglican orders by men like William Bridge and John Owen did not mean that they considered ministry to be irrelevant, as the *Savoy Declaration* makes abundantly clear. In fact, there were always links of fraternity and counsel between the gathered churches, who, like the Baptists, kept the office, which they considered scriptural, of the 'messenger' who might represent the local congregation in relation to other churches, or like those who in 1658 were sent as delegates to the Savoy. 'The celebrated fifteen churches upon the coasts of Suffolk and Norfolk' stood in the relation of daughter churches to the church at Yarmouth under William Bridge. Invariably the counsel of existing churches was sought before the embodiment of new ones, if only because to obtain pastors they must often get the permission to do so from that church in whose covenanted membership the prospective leader was enrolled. It was of course a mark of Congregationalism as distinct from Presbyterianism to reject the outside jurisdiction of other churches, and especially that of synods.

None the less, when discipline and brotherly admonition were taken so seriously, this exterior counsel might not seem to differ greatly from jurisdiction. This is seen in the case of John Ward who was in trouble in the church in Rotterdam respecting 'the matter of prophesy', a dispute into which the ministers and elders of the church of Arnhem were called, and which was later recalled by Nye and his colleagues in their *Apologetical Narration* as an example of the way in which

churches challenged to *offend* or *differ* are to submit themselves . . . to the most full and open trial and examination by other neighbour churches offended thereat . . . and the churches offended may and ought upon the impenitency of those churches persisting in their error and miscarriage, pronounce that heavy sentence upon them of withdrawing and renouncing all Christian communion with them until they do repent and further to declare and protest this, with the causes thereof to all other Churches of Christ, that they may do the like.[6]

In the dangerous political situation into which Owen's Wallingford House 'gathered church' had got itself, it turned to William Bridge and his Yarmouth congregation for moral support and advice. Moral support it got, in the shape of a day of prayer and humiliation. Advice was prudently and noticeably withheld.

This day the church received a letter from the church at Wallingford-House desiring advice from the church, what they apprehended was needful for the Commonwealth: the church considering it ordered the elders to write to them, thanking them for their love and care of them: but considering civil business, the church, as a church desire not to meddle with.

But this mutual counsel between congregations was not all about matters of dispute and friction. There is the pleasing correspondence between the church at Wymondham (Norfolk) and the church of Yarmouth in 1646 when the first of six questions ran: 'Whether we may join comfortably together when as we are divided in our judgments: some looking upon the baptizing of infants the way of God: and others questioning the truth of it therefore suspend it?' To which came the reply 'We think there ought to be on both sides a full knowledge and experience of one another's affections and judgments, how far they can bear in point of practice, lest after differences should be more sad than church fellowship comfortable.' The fine last sentence, 'lest after

---

[6] J. Browne, *The History of Congregationalism in Norfolk and Suffolk* (1877), p. 107.

differences be more sad than church fellowship comfortable' might be the epitaph of the more melancholy side of Nonconformist history.

The happy concelebration between churches is well illustrated in the account of the ordination service in Yarmouth, 31 March 1688.

At the church meeting, with many other friends, Our Elder Mr. John Albertson stood up and declared the cause of our meeting, which was to set up Mr. James Hannot in the pastoral office. He then desired Mr. Finch who was pastor of the church at Norwich, to carry on the work, and then Mr. Finch went to prayer. After prayer he desired the church would declare their unanimous consent which they did by holding up their hands: he then desired Mr. Hannot to declare his acceptation which he did in a few words.

There followed two sermonettes by Finch and Hannot,

and after this he prayed again and he with Mr. Bidbank, Mr. Say and Mr. Albertson laid their hands on Mr. Hannot's head.'

There followed a Charge by Mr. Finch and prayers by those who had participated in the ordination (from neighbouring churches) followed by a speech and prayer by the new minister, the singing of the 23rd Psalm and the dismissal of the Congregation. 'Thus was the day spent'. At the end of it the congregation might have found rueful meaning in the last line of the Psalm about dwelling in the house of the Lord for ever. But they all knew that they could have been put in prison for the day's business which no doubt they thoroughly enjoyed.

Most churches had a pastor and a few teachers as well. The ruling elders had no power to preach or administer the sacraments and for this were criticized by Richard Baxter. But Bridge told his Yarmouth congregation 'that then we were in our beauty when the brethren prophesy according to the proportion of faith, and that one by one: and when we have ruling elders.' They appointed four, but the office seems to have soon lapsed. At Yarmouth they also appointed deaconesses. We are told that at Norwich in 1645 there were 114 members of the congregation and this consisted of thirty-one men and eighty-three women. There are other indications that, as so often in evangelical history, females greatly outnumbered males, and that, as generally in church history, the list of male officers did not preclude much feminine influence, not by any means always in the background, often as the angels, and sometimes the dragons, of the churches.

Whenever the Independents were threatened as a minority, they pleaded the cause of toleration, in which indeed they believed more firmly than many. It is interesting that in their *Savoy Declaration* they interpolated into a section on the duties of the magistrate regarding religion the words:

yet in such differences about the Doctrines of the Gospel, or ways of the worship of God, as may befall men exercising a good conscience, manifesting it in their conversation and holding the foundation, not disturbing others in their ways or worship that differ from them: there is no warrant for the Magistrate under the Gospel to abridge men of their liberty.[7]

The Westminster Assembly (1644–6) showed that the little band of Independents was influential out of all proportion to their numbers. But Bridge, Burroughs, Goodwin, Nye, and Simpson were men of learning and unmatched experience and their stubborn eloquence forced the Assembly again and again to listen to their arguments and on one occasion to appoint a Committee to refute them. But as the *Savoy Declaration* was to confirm, they agreed with the Presbyterians in almost the whole field of Christian doctrine, not least in recognizing the power and duty of the Christian magistrate to suppress blasphemy and heresy. They also shared the long debates about excommunication, the offences for which the ignorant and scandalous were to be barred from Communion. In the next years a new leader emerged. John Owen (1616–83) after some time at Queen's College, Oxford, obtained the living of Fordham in Essex in 1642 and in 1647 became pastor of the church in Coggeshall (a centre of evangelical Puritanism from the time of the Lollards). He was turned from Presbyterianism by reading John Cotton's *Keyes of the Kingdom*. He drew the attention of Cromwell, who showered favours on him, and was made Dean of Christ Church and then Vice-Chancellor of Oxford (1652–7). He cut quite a figure in the city, as Anthony à Wood acidly observed, 'going in quirpo like a young scholar, with powdered hair, snakebone bandstrings, lawn bands, a large set of ribbons pointed and Spanish leather boots with large lawn tops and his hat mostly cocked.' On at least two occasions of political crisis he was to be seen riding at the head of a troop of soldiers, pistols displayed. His renunciation of his Anglican orders may underlie his attempts to dress as a layman, and to enter the House of Commons. He was tolerant or tactful enough to turn a deaf ear to the Episcopalians who worshipped next door, but sadly followed the example of the mayor in Cambridge by ordering the whipping and expulsion of the Quaker prophetesses, Elizabeth Fletcher and Elizabeth Holmes.

The names of William Ames, of Bridge, Nye, Goodwin, and Owen remind us that the Puritan Congregationalist tradition made notable contributions to Puritan divinity, not least in the field of moral and practical theology. Their works (Owen is still much read in conservative evangelical circles) were not all, or even mainly, concerned

[7] *The Savoy Declaration of Faith and Order* (1658), ed. A. G. Matthews, 1959, p. 109.

with ecclesiology, with problems of ministry and discipline, nor even with the Calvinist case against the Arminians and Antinomians, but with the New Testament gospel itself, with grace, and salvation by Jesus Christ. There is a Christocentric devotion, within a soundly Trinitarian frame which is expressed in prose, often of baroque magnificence, as in the writings of Francis Rous and Peter Sterry, and Thomas Goodwin whose sermons on the Heart of Jesus anticipate the Catholic devotion of Paray-le-Monial. Owen was the outstanding theologian, many of his treatises complex and dull, the crown of them a massive exposition of the doctrine of the Holy Spirit. He might be named the Karl Barth of English Calvinism, but he lacked Barth's freshness and originality and his sense of humour.

We must, I think, remember that the eclipse of all Puritan hopes might not have seemed irremediable or final in the years following the Restoration. They had won two wars and lost a long peace, but to have lived through a revolution is to become accustomed to the prospect of change, and there must have been many of Republican beliefs, who hoped for future triumph, and who in the years between Restoration and the Glorious Revolution hoped that at least their civil disabilities might be removed. The practice of some of the teachers in the new Dissenting Academies of encouraging their young men to put down their names at least for Oxford and Cambridge colleges bears witness to this mood. The only impressive thing about Samuel Wesley's two letters regarding those Academies is not his strictures on their teachers or their method, but the witness it bears to the bitterness of defeat among some older Nonconformists, their own myth about the events of their lifetime, to offset the myth of the 'Royal Martyr', and a good deal of understandable underground gossip among the new generation of sons of rebels. Samuel Wesley's own Academy was in Stoke Newington, an almost 'White Russian' colony of former Puritan notabilities.

It is inevitable that any account of the development of Congregationalism during the period 1640–60 should concentrate on a small group of mainly clerical leaders who had in their youth been exiles in Holland. We need to remember Dr Nuttall's wise remark that the majority of Congregational ministers went neither to the Netherlands nor to New England, neither to Westminster nor to the Savoy.

And alas, the many church-meeting records tell us all too little of the Christian manners and life-style of the congregations. One such glimpse we get in Yarmouth. In addition to Sunday worship they had weekday services at 4 o'clock. On Monday there was a meeting 'for brethren to give a taste of their gifts'. On the first Tuesday of the month they held their church meeting for business and also for edification. These were at

2 o'clock in the afternoon, no witching hour for ecclesiastical business.

In our time two luminous discussions of the Congregationalist way, in America and in England, have been entitled *Visible Saints*.[8] And properly, for the expression is much more than jargon. William Bartlet in 1647 defined the Church State as 'a society of fellowship of visible saints'[9] and in the definition of the *Savoy Declaration* membership is defined in these terms.

The members of these Churches are Saints by calling, visibly manifesting and evidencing in and by their profession and walking their obedience unto that Call of Christ, who being further known to one another by their confession of the Faith wrought in them by the power of God, declared themselves or otherwise manifested, do willingly consent to walk together according to the appointment of Christ, giving themselves to the Lord and to one another by the will of God in professed subjection to the Ordinances of the gospel.[10]

If the discipline of visible saints was difficult for separatists, immense problems arose when the ministers of 'gathered' churches found themselves involved in responsibility for parish churches, and for whole communities. For them to preach to a mixed parochial congregation while restricting the seals of Communion to the members of the 'gathered Church' was bound to be seen as an invidious discrimination. Thus the parishioners of Thomas Jollie, curate of Altham in Lancashire, complained that he declined to baptize their children, and refused the Lord's Supper to all save three families. In the church of St Bartholomew, Exchange, in London, the parishioners counterattacked by refusing to pay tithes when John Loder refused the sacraments to the general congregation. Richard Baxter, who had other and better ideas about all this based on his own success as a pastor at Kidderminster, wrote plainly to John Owen:

My Acton neighbour told me that there is but one person (a woman) in all this town and parish that was here admitted to the sacrament, and that the rest were partly by this course (and other reasons) distasted and their dislike increased and partly neglected and left to themselves: that rich families (Mr. Rouse, Major Skippon, Colonel Sely and Mr. Humphreys) were admitted while the rest were refused or neglected.[11]

Congregationalists were richly to contribute to eucharistic worship, but one cannot but be aware that controversies about discipline which have exclusion from the Lord's Table at the heart, must have 'distasted' many from the sacrament itself.

[8] E. S. Morgan, *Visible Saints*, Cornell 1963. G. Nuttall, *Visible Saints*, Oxford 1957.
[9] Nutall, *Visible Saints*, p. 53.   [10] *Savoy Declaration*, p. 122.
[11] J. Owen, *Correspondence*, ed. P. Toon (1970), p. 143.

Congregationalists differed from the Presbyterians, and perhaps from the early Separatists, in demanding not only a profession of faith from candidates for membership or for admission to Holy Communion, but an account of Christian experience.

Christian experience, the awareness of grace in the heart, is a mark of the religion of the Puritans of all kinds from Richard Baxter and Samuel Rutherford to Thomas Goodwin and George Fox. It provides an affective undertone to a great number of sermons, giving a quality of devotion and even of rapture, which in prose often rivals the poetry of Herbert or Crashaw. Dr Nuttall and Professor E. S. Morgan refer to many collections of such evangelical testimonies on both sides of the Atlantic, a reminder, if it were needed, that conversion was not something which began with the Evangelical Revival. It is also true that as a test of membership it was not without its drawbacks. It is not accidental perhaps that the later Methodists did not make conversion the test of membership, or of admission to the Lord's Table. John Cotton admitted that such a test opened a way for hypocrisy. Richard Baxter made a serious point when he commented to John Owen,

while you seem to be for a stricter discipline than others . . . your way (or usual practice) tendeth to extirpate godliness out of the land; by taking a very few that can talk more than the rest, and making them the church, and shutting out more that are as worthy, and by neglecting the souls of all the parish else, except as to some public preaching.[12]

Baxter may have been right that when Christian discipline is wound too high it defeats its own ends and instead of making the Church safe for Mercy and Christiana, enables Mr. Talkative and Mr. By-Ends to rule the roost. There is also evidence, which Professor Morgan cites, of a sapping of missionary zeal.

The references in the Westminster Assembly to excommunication for lovelocks, topless gowns, and the drinking of healths, while an obvious retort to the malignant life-style of the Cavaliers, suggests a scaling down of New Testament standards. There was none of the ethical challenge which, despite eccentricities, was explicit in the Quaker behaviour, and not least in their repudiation of violence. John Owen, with his cocked hat and pistols and his gathered church of Top People, suggests that sometimes what was visible was not so much New Testament holiness as affluence and gentility. The figure cut was not so much of heroic and supernatural virtue as the bourgeois figure of the 'honnête homme', which, to the cool view of the outsider, might seem a

12 Owen, *Correspondence*, p. 142.

true emblem of the typical Nonconformist in the coming mercantile age.

Modern writers, among them Lord Lindsay, have stressed the Congregationalist contribution to what he called 'Christian' as distinct from 'rationalist' democracy. In their churchmanship they demonstrated the truth which modern Christians claim to have rediscovered, that the Biblical word *laos* means the whole People of God. Three centuries before the Second Vatican Council, they insisted that all Christians have an apostolate and share (in a favourite image of Calvin) the threefold office of Christ as Prophet, Priest, and King. And in the concept of a 'willing people' and in the discussion, voting, and agreement of the church meeting there was a device with much wider than religious implication. But we must not forget, either that the Puritans themselves preferred a mixed polity, had no liking for democracy, and that when they had the chance, as in New England, they left little room for the innovations of the despised multitude.

The Congregationalists bore their share of the harassments of the Clarendon Code, sometimes with poignant and heroic suffering, as in the case of Joseph Alleine of Taunton, whose *Directions for Making a Covenant with God* proved a treasured legacy to the Methodists. Under the pressure, above all of the Conventicle Act, some churches nearly ceased to meet or could only come together, as one document quaintly puts it, in 'little parcels' of three or four. John Owen, absent through illness, wrote to his congregation in Leadenhall Street:

I beseech you to hear a word of advice in case the persecution increases . . . I could wish that because you have no ruling elders and your teachers cannot walk about publicly with safety, that you would appoint some among yourselves who may . . . go up and down from house to house . . . by this means you will know what is the frame of the members of the church.[13]

There had been moments during the Commonwealth when it had seemed that Presbyterians and Independents might have agreed at least to live in peace with one another, and the correspondence between John Owen and Richard Baxter shows the possibilities, and also the difficulties, of such union. Had they had any inkling in the hectic months of 1659, of how near at hand was the Restoration of what they called the 'Common Enemy' one wonders if they might not have reached some agreement, but they had got in the way of squabbling in a manner which reminds us a little of the parties in the German Church under the Nazi regime. And so, even during the time of persecution, they continued their perennial dog-fights, theological controversies

---

[13] Owen, *Correspondence*, p. 171.

treated with a disproportionate seriousness, dilemmas such as the revival under Richard Davies in Northampton which revived old prejudices against mechanic preachers. And when at last, in 1691, a 'happy union' was temporarily reached, it soon broke down, though there were co-operative funds established in regard to training the ministry, and in some areas of the country there was an awareness of a common theological tradition, sufficient for ministers, and sometimes for congregations, to change fairly easily from one denomination to the other.

If the Congregationalists were at this time divided in their attitude to Infant Baptism, this was a problem for a wide spectrum of Puritans, including Baxter. At least the English churches seem to have been spared the problems which arose in New England in the admission of the children of believers, which in turn led to the astonishing anomalies of the 'Half Way' Covenant.

According to Michael Watts, who has carefully sifted older statistics, the Congregationalists were strongest 'in those counties which had provided the heart of the Puritan movement in the reign of Elizabeth and which had sustained the parliamentary cause in the Civil War'. They were strongest in East Anglia, Hertfordshire, and Northamptonshire, and strongest of all in parts of South Wales and Monmouthshire where they owed much to the outstanding labours of pastors like Vavasour Powell, William Wroth, and Henry Maurice.

The Congregationalists offered an alternative society to both the Catholic and the Anglican episcopal systems, and to the Presbyterian machinery of government and discipline, and it was one they believed congruous with the New Testament, as other systems were not. They had stressed the importance of toleration (tell it not in New England, whisper it not among the Quakers!). It was their achievement to carry on the Calvinist tradition in theology into the eighteenth century together with a genuine regard for liberty in regard to non-essentials, the fruits of which would not be shown in the dogmatic dissolution which befell the Presbyterians, but rather in an openness of mind, reflected in the teaching and example of the leaders of the next generation like Philip Doddridge. If they were a garden walled around, it was a garden in which the flowers and fruits of the Spirit grew and were nourished in devout companies of good men and women, leavening society with integrities, honesties, and decencies in an age where permissiveness, greed, and callousness unchecked might have brought England to great disaster amid the new wealth and the moral dilemmas of the coming age.

8

BAPTISTS

B Y the beginning of the eighteenth century the Baptists had simmered down. Their springtime came in the first half of the seventeenth century when little groups of sectaries and Puritan congregations multiplied and merged, Presbyterians, Independents, Baptists, Quakers, Seekers—names whose distinctions melted at the edges. With other radicals they lived through the tumultuous period when, drunk with sight of power, they loosed wild tongues. Now Anglican parsons like Samuel Wesley (but he had tangled with Benjamin Keach in the *Athenian Magazine*), John Wesley, or William Cole might continue to refer to them as 'Anabaptists'; but there was about them in this period not the faintest whiff of Münster and the taunt excited them less, perhaps, than it has exercised Baptist historians. But they had faced a genuine identity crisis. Like the Swiss Brethren a century before, they had known the tension between hawks and doves.

A number of Baptist military men infiltrated the higher echelons of the New Model Army, so that soon Baptist conventicles were studded with retired colonels and major-generals much in the way that the bursary departments of modern Oxford and Cambridge colleges draw on the same expertise in efficiency and administration. But great numbers of Baptists were simple and unlearned (but by no means ignorant and unintelligent) in whom an ardent commitment mingled spiritualist theology with a literalist Biblicism (like the Anabaptists in the Pilgrim Marbeck period). They had been infected also with the apocalyptic millenarianism which had swept along a wide spectrum of English Christianity from Anglicans like Joseph Mede and John Worthington to Independents like Peter Sterry and, above all, the Fifth Monarchy men. And there were enough Baptists involved in the Fifth Monarchy risings, in the Rye House Plot, and even in the Monmouth Rebellion to bring the moderate majority into suspicion and danger.

Like the other Nonconformists (though hardly affected by the Great Ejectment, since they had so few trained ministers), they suffered the grim harassment of the Clarendon Code and knew the pain and exultation of a confessing Church 'under the Cross'. They came up for breath during the brief periods of indulgence; and with the Toleration Act, with the end of the censorship, and with the failure of the

Occasional Conformity (the one Baptist who so conformed was excommunicated by his fellows) and Schism Acts, the terms of reference were given for the next century of Baptist existence. Exclusion from the Universities did not perhaps much affect a movement suspicious of learning, but the exclusion from the professions and from civic and governmental office set up serious road-blocks in their path. In the next decades, apart from a few part-time ministers, part-time business men, and a handful of affluent merchants, physicians, and ushers, they produced no leaders with whom Government had to reckon. 'The Baptists and their friends had henceforth a history which rarely touches and scarcely ever influences the course of national history.'[1]

Clearly the Bible was at the heart of Baptist spirituality, and one could wish that Baptist historians would give us a full exposition of their seventeenth-century hermeneutic. How did their literalist Biblicism arise, and how did it relate to their conception of the relation between Gospel and Law? It would seem that it goes back, theologically, to the beginnings of the Reformed tradition, and perhaps more nearly to that of Bullinger's Zurich than to Calvin's Geneva. Against the Anglican view of *adiaphora*, which permitted all that was not 'repugnant' to Holy Scripture, it seems that they followed the Puritan view that God's commands in Scripture are binding even in matters of ceremony. From the attitude of the fringe, the millenarians among them, the small number of Seventh Day Baptists, and those General Baptists who seem to have felt that the apostolic decision of Acts 15 was binding on Christians who must abstain from things strangled, and from blood, it would seem that this was their view of the Law.

The two streams of Augustinian theology which run through the seventeenth century, Arminian and Calvinist, also divided the Baptists. The General Baptists went back to the congregations of John Smyth and Thomas Helwys during their sojourn in Holland at the beginning of the century. They framed a Christian rationale of toleration, and disowned the notion that the scope of redemption was limited and particular to the elect, and though they became increasingly conservative in practice, they were also more sympathetic to the criticism of classical orthodoxy by those who had begun to question the doctrine of the Trinity and the Nicene and Chalcedonian definitions of the person of Christ.

The Particular Baptists held to Puritan Calvinism of which the Five Points of the Synod of Dort are a useful summary, i.e. unconditional election, limited atonement, total depravity, irresistibility of grace, and final perseverance. Both groups of Baptists paid some deference to the

[1] W. T. Whitley, *History of the British Baptists* (1932), p. 166.

Westminster Confession which reappears (with suitable modifications in the realm of ecclesiology) in the extremely interesting Baptist confessions of the seventeenth century. For while eschewing the use of creeds as matters for subscription, they by no means disregarded dogmatic theology. Nor did they succumb to the congregational atomism of some Independents. The seventeenth-century words 'Association' and 'Assembly' were important for them. Some congregations were so closely linked as to resemble the later Methodist circuit, and there were those who walked or rode great distances to meet their fellows, like the family which commuted between Watford and London. The seventeenth century saw the emergence of regional associations of churches which were to endure for centuries, and had something of the robust vigour which comes from being earthed in an English county. Nor were these mere improvised groupings, for the many seventeenth-century Baptist confessions offer a rationale of such solidarity. Thus the General Baptist Creed of 1678 affirmed that 'General councils or assemblies . . . of the several churches of Christ . . . make but one church and have a lawful right in this general assembly to act in the name of Christ.' The first assembly of the Particular Baptists was held in 1689 and to it more than a hundred congregations in England and Wales sent representatives, affirming their intention 'to be helpers together of one another by way of counsel and advice' while disclaiming 'all manner of superiority or superintendency over the churches'.[2]

None the less, though Baptists themselves might complain of languor and decay, they achieved one note of catholicity which is often undervalued: they survived. Their congregations, apart from a few imposing congregations such as Broadmead, Bristol, and St Paul's, Barbican, were mainly small and rural, but they were no mere evanescent ropes of sand. Their continuing existence as communities of committed Christians, feeding on the Word and on the sacred ordinances, and exercising the discipline of Christ, was more important than big names, loud controversies, and theological and party labels.

It was a threefold ministry which they found in the New Testament: messengers, elders, deacons. In the Orthodox Creed (1679) which was intended to stress the orthodoxy and catholicity of the Baptists, the word 'bishop' is used for those who 'have the government of those churches that had suffrage in their election and no other ordinarily: as also to preach the word or gospel to the world or unbelievers.' But their normal word was 'messenger' and they believed they were following the model of the apostolic men of the New Testament who had a roving

[2] C. A. Underwood, *A History of English Baptists* (1932), p. 129.

commission and a responsibility for extending the gospel. The Particular Baptists were more guarded, and in the circular letter sent out after their Assembly of 1689 they affirmed that 'the officers appointed by Christ are Bishops or Elders, and Deacons' and insisted that 'messengers are not entrusted with any church power properly so called, or with any jurisdiction over the churches themselves . . . or to impose their determination on the churches.'[3]

The Elder was the pastor of the local church. To the Deacon fell the administration of charity—for the Baptists generally looked after the needy and unfortunate in their own flock and were not insensitive to wider calls. These ministers were carefully chosen and tested and ordained by the local church, and it was generally the elder who presided at the Lord's Table. For the most part they continued to earn their own living, getting only their travelling expenses from the church. Their inability to sustain a full-time and educated ministry was a grave disability, though it did perhaps preserve them from some of the more intricate theological wrangles of other Nonconformists.

The General Baptists found a convenient summary of practice in the so-called Six Principles of Hebrews 6: 1–2. The fourth principle, that of laying on of hands, was the most controversial, and there was division of opinion whether laying on of hands should be restricted to ordination or whether they should be imposed on each baptized believer.

For a time some of them (possibly drawing on Mennonite precedent) practised foot-washing and anointed the sick with oil. The attempt to confine marriage within the household of their faith might have been disastrous, but was in fact gradually relaxed. We have noticed their practical conservatism, shown by their long-continued opposition to congregational singing.

The Particular Baptists had a strong backbone of Calvinist doctrine, and their vulnerability was in the opposite direction from that of the General Baptists in a hyper-Calvinism which might cut the nerve of missionary effort, and in Antinomianism which, while mercifully more theoretical than practical, gave rise to bitter controversy. If their greater emphasis on the autonomy of the local congregation withdrew them further from the life of the wider community, they were swifter than the General Baptists to recognize the need for a full-time trained and decently paid ministry. They were pioneers in the introduction of congregational hymn singing. Hitherto other Dissenting bodies had, like the Church of England, allowed only the use of the Scriptural Psalms. The Continental Anabaptists had produced an impressive

---

[3] J. F. V. Nicholson, 'The Office of "Messenger" amongst British Baptists in the Seventeenth and Eighteenth Centuries', *BQ* xxii (1957–8), 208, 212, 214.

hymnology, but there was certainly among the Swiss Brethren the view that music should not be allowed in Christian worship, and, as their famous letter to Thomas Müntzer showed, references in Scripture to music and singing were spiritualized away. At first such singing as was permitted was solo singing, either by the minister or by some charismatic layman. But it could not be ignored that the Lord and the disciples had sung a hymn at the Last Supper. Hence it was that the first Nonconformist hymns concerned Holy Communion. Benjamin Keach, a Baptist publicist whose edifying writing and spiritual allegories for a time ran ahead of Bunyan in popularity, became a Particular Baptist and started a congregation at Horsleydown to whom he introduced in 1691 a hymn he had composed for use at the Lord's Supper. Another Baptist, John Stennett, produced in 1697 some *Hymns in Commemoration of the Sufferings of Our Blessed Saviour, Jesus Christ, composed for the celebration of His Holy Supper.* They were not very good hymns and the day of Watts and Wesley was yet to come. There were, of course, no organs and very rarely any musical instruments, and the practice of the minister's 'lining' the hymn with repetition by the congregation did not make, one might think, for fervour or spontaneity. That there should be some time of debate and controversy during which congregational singing might be appended as an optional extra at the end of worship is thoroughly understandable. During the centuries Christians seem to get hot under the collar about such things, and heated arguments, walk-outs, and resignations still attend choirs and the places where they sing, as a pillar of cloud by mattins and a pillar of fire by evensong.

But it was the ordinance of Baptism which gave coherence to the Baptist witness. The practice of Believers' Baptism stressed the inexorably personal character of faith, and tried to do justice to the New Testament teaching about Baptism by returning to primitive Christian practice. With the Swiss Brethren the stress had been on the personal commitment of faith, against a Zwinglian view of Church and community as one mixed body into which one could be both born and baptized, and was therefore a protest against what would be called an Erastian involvement with temporal affairs.

With the English Baptists, the point of attack was not the Zwinglian idea of a Christian commonwealth, but the practice in the 'mixed' Churches of Infant Baptism. There was, however, a considerable divergence about the significance of the rite of Baptism and its relation to the initiation and involvement of Baptists in the congregation. While they rejected an *ex opere operato* doctrine of baptismal regeneration, not many would have gone as far as John Bunyan when he wrote of water baptism as 'shadowish . . . figurative' and of the sacraments as 'helps to our faith . . . but not the fundamentals of Christianity, nor grounds or rule to communion with other Christians'. Nor was it always clear how Baptism was related to membership, since some congregations, like many Independents, came into existence on the basis of an explicit covenant and demanded of the individual a profession of faith and Christian experience. There was the further vexed question whether Communion should be confined to those who had received believers' Baptism, and how this related to opening the Table of the Lord to other Christians of other Churches. 'Open' churches like Bunyan's Bedford congregation were a minority.

In the early eighteenth century few churches had specially constructed baptisteries. The prosperous London church of St Paul's, Barbican, was an exception. Here the meeting-house contained three changing rooms for ministers and candidates for baptism, a water-pump, a stove, two black gowns and a dressing-gown for the minister, eight cinnamon-coloured serge coats for the males, and four serge petticoats for the females. This baptistery was loaned or hired for use by other congregations. But the majority of baptisms were held out of doors, often by the riverside. Robert Robinson's description of such a baptism at Whittlesford, near Cambridge is well known.

the administrator . . . in a long black gown of fine baize, without a hat, with a small New Testament in his hand, came down to the river side accompanied by several Baptist ministers and deacons of their churches, and the persons to be baptized. The men came first, two by two, without hats and dressed as usual, except that instead of coats each had on a long white baize gown tied round the waist with a sash. Such as had no hair wore white cotton or linen caps. The women followed the men, two by two all dressed neat clean and plain and their gowns white linen or dimity. It was said the garments had knobs of lead at the bottom to make them sink. Each had a long light silk cloak hanging loosely over her shoulders, a broad ribband tied over her gown beneath her breast and a hat over her head. They all ranged themselves around the administrator at the water side. A great multitude of spectators stood on the banks of the river on both sides: some had climbed and sat in the trees, many sat on horseback and in carriages, and all behaved with a decent seriousness which did honour to the good sense and good manners of the assembly.[4]

A scene which a William Blake or a Samuel Palmer might have painted.

The Lord's Supper was similarly treated with decent seriousness and at the celebration (usually monthly) it might be a matter for disciplinary comment if a member did not 'fill up his place at the Lord's Table' and

---

[4] Horton Davies, *Worship and Theology in England*, iii. 130.

indeed a membership roll might be read.[5] In rural areas it might take place in the afternoon, and since many came a distance, was often accompanied by a meal, in conscious reminiscence of the New Testament *agapē*, though of a more substantial nature than the later Methodist lovefeast, since it was cooked and brought a nickname 'Leg of Mutton Christians'. There might be church business and a period for catechism, while intervals might be filled with edifying readings, material for which was kept in a long drawer in the Communion Table, which was placed below the pulpit. There is not much sign of instruction in eucharistic doctrine, though it would be oversimplifying to say that it oscillated between a low Zwinglianism and a high Calvinism in its views of a True Presence. In fact the labels 'Zwinglian' and 'Calvinist' as applied to the Eucharist are baffling when one turns to the often complex statements of these two Reformers. Nor does the word 'memorial' necessarily imply a negative view of the True Presence, and certainly need not involve a notion of a 'Real Absence'. The remembrance at the Lord's Table might involve an individual mental reminiscence of the past, but it could as well represent the living *anamnēsis* of the People of God, since all believed that at the Lord's Table they encountered the One who had been crucified, but was now alive for evermore. As in other Protestant churches, there was an inevitable 'fencing' of the Table which became involved in discipline and excommunication, and for the Baptists this led to vexed problems, whether they should communicate only with baptized believers, or should open the Table to other than those baptized as adults, as well as the question of communion with other Christians of other Churches.

The service of the Word in the days before the advent of a congregational 'hymn sandwich', was an amalgam of prayer, Scripture, and sermon. Though we hear of some spiritualists in early days who objected to the physical presence of a Bible in worship, and though for a time there was preference for a running commentary on scriptures, of a spontaneous kind (a relic of 'prophesying'?), exposition came in the end to be confined to the sermon. The so-called 'long prayer' (the phrase has survived into this century) might be very long indeed.

In the exercise of discipline the Baptists retained an important element of the Reformed tradition at a time when it was being abandoned by the English Presbyterians. The records show that discipline was often rigid and narrow, covering a whole range of trespasses from breaches of the

[5] E. A. Payne, *The Fellowship of Believers* (1952), ch. 4; E. P. Winter, 'The Lord's Supper. Admission and Exclusion among the Baptists of the seventeenth century', *BQ* xvii (1957–8); 'The Administration of the Lord's Supper among Baptists in the seventeenth century', *BQ* xviii (1960).

moral law to attendance at parish churches, or even gadding about to other meeting houses, while there was the notorious attempt of Matthew Caffyn to excommunicate a leading layman, Richard Haines, for taking out a patent for his invention of a new technique for cleaning hop clover. They followed the counsels of Matthew 18: 15–19, and if they were, in the general manner of the age, severe, there was a blend of severity and mercy which recalls the Rule of St Benedict.

The order of worship at St Paul's, Barbican, was described in 1695:

That the publick worship in the Congregation on the Lord's Day be thus performed viz. In the morning about half an hour after nine, some Brother be appointed to begin the Exercise in reading a Psalm, and then to spend some time in prayer: and after it to read some other Portion of H. Scripture till the minister comes into the pulpit: and after Preaching and Prayer to conclude with singing a Psalm. The afternoon exercise to begin about half an hour after one and to be carried on and concluded as in the forenoon.[6]

While the Baptists escaped the dog-fights between Independents and Presbyterians, they had their own share of theological controversy.[7] Matthew Caffyn (1628–1715), after an abortive Oxford career, became a General Baptist Messenger at Horsham where he became a leader of influence who threw his theological weight about. He began to expound Christological notions which recall those of the early English Anabaptists and Lollards. There seems no reason to suppose that he had read the works of the sixteenth-century radical Melchior Hofmann, who is often associated with a Gnostic and Docetic view of the person of Christ, as one who did not receive his human nature from the Virgin Mary, but who passed through her as 'water through a conduit'. It is a view which recurs through many centuries and had been put forward by Kentish radicals in the mid-sixteenth century, notably by Joan Bocher who was both a Lollard and an Anabaptist. Caffyn's views, about which, when driven into a corner, he could lapse into a cloudy imprecision, caused a great stir, and there were conferences with those alarmed at such patent unorthodoxy.

In 1673 Thomas Monk, a farmer and Messenger from Bierton, voiced the opposition to heresy of the Baptists of Buckinghamshire, Bedford, Hertford, and all points north, in an impressive defence of the historic creeds, *A Cure for the Cankering Error of the New Eutychians*.[8] No high churchman, no orthodox Anglican, not Daniel Waterland himself

---

[6] Horton Davies, iii. 127.
[7] Whitley, *History of the British Baptists*, pp. 162, 172; Underwood, *History of the English Baptists*, p. 106; A. H. J. Baines, 'Signatories to the Orthodox Confession', *BQ* xvii (1957–8), 35, 74, 122, 170.
[8] T. Monk, *A Cure for the Cankering Error of the New Eutychians*, 1673.

produced an abler defence of catholic doctrine. For the age it is moderate and eirenical and it names no names, keeping only the ancient labels. But it is saturated in Scripture, and in Fathers like Hilary and Augustine, in Reformation divines like Peter Martyr and Zanchius, and in the leading Puritans, Perkins, Goodwin, and Greenham. More astonishing is the knowledge of the great medieval theodicies, the definition of the simplicity of God, of his being as Pure Act, discussion of the analogical uses of the *via negativa* and the *via eminentia* and of the complex medieval hermeneutic, the so-called *quadriga*. For him, as for the Fathers, the person and work of Christ are indivisible, and he is as sure as Luther and Calvin that the unity of the divine and human in Christ is essential to his role as Mediator and so as Saviour.

Monk must surely have been dominant among the company of the fifty-four General Baptists who met on 30 January 1679 to sign fifty theological articles which became known as the Orthodox Confession. The signatories included five gentlemen, two shopkeepers, a bookseller, two grocers, thirteen yeomen, farmers, or husbandmen, a labourer, two carpenters, a currier, a retired naval officer, a barber-surgeon, and an ostler. The suggestion made by A. H. J. Baines in an illuminating series of articles, and repeated by M. R. Watts, is that Buckinghamshire was an old Lollard stronghold, and that Caffyn represents the Continental Anabaptist influence which dominated radicalism in Kent and in the eastern counties. This needs to be treated with some reserve. For one thing it may be that Caffyn got his ideas while he was at Oxford. For another, while it is true that the names of sixteenth-century Lollards of the Chiltern Hills turn up among Baptist families a century later, it is not certain that this is not simply because those family names were always to be found in that area. I do not know one single piece of evidence beyond this, that there were Baptist congregations who knew of, or claimed, a Lollard pedigree. Moreover, there was close association between the Chiltern and the Essex Lollards, by the exchange of such itinerants as Thomas Man. This is not to deny the infiltration of ideas, and of what is known as a 'Melchiorite' Christology, into London and the eastern counties from the mid-1530s. And it is important to note that chronologically the Lollards disappear from the records at the moment when the Continental Anabaptists came into touch with England. Despite the determined stand of the Orthodox Baptists, Caffyn seems to have escaped condemnation and made a series of ambiguous pronouncements of the kind which in another theological stratum were to be made by Samuel Clarke. As the century proceeded, Arian and Socinian ideas certainly permeated the General Baptists on a wider scale than among the Particular Baptists, an important exception being St Paul's, Barbican, under the two outstanding and learned preachers, John Gale and James Foster.

Michael Watts[9] has carefully analysed the available statistics for Nonconformity, and gives maps of the spread of the Baptists which show that only in Wales and in Northamptonshire did the Particular Baptists (in the years 1716–18) attain to 5 per cent of the community, while the General Baptists did not exceed 2 per cent. He gives a total of Baptist congregations in England and Wales at that time as 220 Particular Baptists and 122 General Baptists (with five Seventh Day Baptist congregations). He suggests a total of 40,520 Particular Baptists in England and 4,050 in Wales, with 18,800 General Baptists in England and apparently none in Wales.

A note at the end of Thomas Monk's apologia tells how he had been solicited by friends to append another writing in which he had eirenically attempted to reconcile universal and particular redemption. But he explains that he had intended his book for 'the poorer sort'. (It was in fact sold for a shilling and seems to be an early instance of a subsidized best-seller.) But this is surely a revealing sentence, and one which warns us not to underestimate the theological competence of the average seventeenth-century Baptist. It is more than likely that most of them could wipe the floor with a modern Nonconformist congregation in theological debate. After all, they had most of them chalked up many hundreds of hours of sermon hearing, discourses which were meaty, and, all in all, with more to say about God, about grace and salvation, than about predestination or even Believers' Baptism, and are by no means to be written off as the windy, nasal rantings of high-church satire. We remember how John Bunyan overheard housewives sitting on their doorsteps in Bedford discussing Christian experience in technical theological language, and how Greatheart expounded two pages of intricate Christology to the young woman, Christiana. It was among such people that the towering genius of John Bunyan was earthed, and he was bone of their bone and flesh of their flesh, not only in his religion and his knowledge of the English Bible, but also in his awareness of common, everyday life. Lowly in social status they might be, simple, even sombre, their religious forms. But the history of Christianity, Catholic as well as Protestant, reminds us that penny plain has its own virtue.

[9] Watts, *The Dissenters*, pp. 267ff.

9

QUAKERS

IF the Quakers stand somewhat apart from the other Nonconformist bodies, it has less perhaps to do with a certain corporate introspection than with the historical context from which they emerged, and the normative shape they received during those astonishing middle decades of the seventeenth century. Whereas the proliferating sects of that ferment, the Diggers and the Levellers, the Muggletonians and Ranters, the Fifth Monarchy men and the Seekers, have long since fallen asleep, until summoned by modern historians from the vasty deep of national memory, the Quakers survived, grew, and developed into a movement world-wide in scope and deep in spiritual influence.

George Fox (1624–1791), like that other popular genius, John Bunyan, came from the lower orders of society. He was the son of a Leicestershire weaver, himself emerging as part-time shoemaker, part-time shepherd in the village of Fenny Drayton, literate, but not lettered. A serious youngster, he found no relief from spiritual hunger from either the clergy of the Established Church or the ministers of the gathered churches. His conversion was gradual, not so much like 'once at a crash' Paul, whom he somewhat resembled, as the 'lingering skill' of Augustine whom he resembled only in his deep introspection.

But when all my hopes in . . . all men were gone, so that I had nothing outwardly to help me, nor could I tell what to do, then, oh then, I heard a voice which said 'There is one, even Christ Jesus, that can speak to thy condition!,' and when I heard it my heart did leap for joy . . . and this I knew experimentally . . . without the help of any man, book or writing.[1]

For Fox this 'inner light' or 'divine seed' was no abstract idea, but the personal, living God, the indwelling Christ, guiding, commissioning, leading into ever deepening spiritual truth. In the compelling simplicities of his *Journal*, a whole pedigree of the Johannine view of truth is embodied in the often repeated words 'I saw . . .'.

Now he had a message and a mission, and a continuing sense of divine guidance, which was perhaps a more fallible intuition than he thought it to be. 'I was commanded to turn people to that inward light, spirit and

---

[1] G. Fox, *Journal*, ed. N. Penney, Cambridge, 1911; rev. edn. N. Penney, Everyman edn. 1924.

grace by which all might know their salvation and their way to God: even that divine spirit which would lead them into all truth.' Soon the fame of this young man, with his white hat, his leather breeches, his long hair, his great frame, and his piercing eyes went before him in the villages and the very same story was told to explain his magnetic charm as was told of the Thuringian radical, Hans Huth, a century before, that he carried round with him a magic potion which bemused the drinker into becoming his follower.

Fox's conception of truth bound together inner conviction and outward integrity. Like Christian and Faithful in Vanity Fair, he and his comrades replied to the worldly taunt 'What will ye buy?' with the solemn answer 'We buy the truth.' This involved them in a drastic repudiation, a challenge and protest against many accepted ways of contemporary society.

I was to bring people off from all the world's religions, which are vain, that they might know the pure religion, might visit the fatherless, the widows and the strangers, and keep themselves from the spots of the world . . . and I was to bring them off from all the world's fellowships, and prayings, and singings which stood in forms without power, that their fellowships might be in the Holy Ghost, and in the Eternal Spirit of God.[2]

His refusal of customary courtesies and especially of 'hat honour'—a levelling gesture, this—aroused immediate antagonism from social superiors.

When the Lord sent me forth into the world, he forbade me to put off my hat to any, high or low, and I was required to 'Thee' and 'Thou' all men and women without any respect to rich or poor, great or small. And as I travelled up and down I was not to bid people 'Good Morrow!' [so the hills were not to echo as they had done in Umbria to Francis's joyful 'Buon giorno'—Puritan rapture being in a minor key] or 'good Evening!' neither might I bow or scrape with my leg to any one . . . this made the sects and professors to rage.[3]

It was an age when extravagance of dress was matched by an elaborate pattern of manners resulting in a good deal of humbug, and in overmuch speaking, profanity, and swearing. But Fox took seriously the words of Jesus about the swearing of oaths, costly though this refusal was to prove in those politically unstable years when oaths of allegiance were often in demand. But there was more to it than simply an attack on manners. Fox struck below accumulated traditions of Christian culture, and ways of Christian existence which almost all Christians, Catholic, Protestant, and Puritan, had long accepted. Luther

---

[2] *Journal*, Everyman edn., p. 21.
[3] *Journal*, p. 22. I think the reading 'professors' more likely than 'professions'.

had returned to the view of the Church as a 'communion of saints' that is, the word 'Church' denotes people rather than buildings. Now this was taken further by Fox who not only saw the Church as a society of friends, but called men to leave the 'steeple houses' (and these were the majestic steeples of Wren and Gibbs!) and, as Milton and Baxter had vehemently done, attacked a venal and place-hunting clergy. 'When I heard the bell toll to call people together to the steeple house it struck at my life, for it was just like a market-bell to gather the people together that the priest might set forth his ware to sell.'[4]

As many radicals since the Reformation had long demanded, he insisted that men cease to pay tithes. In that age of violence, amid a ubiquitous soldiery, he reaffirmed the Christian message as one of reconciliation, forgiveness, and peace. And when the soldiers, who generally took to him, recognized him as a man under authority and offered him a commission, perhaps a regiment, 'I told them I lived in the virtue of that life and power that took away the occasion of all wars, and I knew whence all wars did rise, from the lust according to James's doctrine . . . I told them I was come into the covenant of peace which was before wars and strifes were.'[5]

It was of moment when this young man, under divine impulsion, turned northward in his journeys, through Derbyshire and Nottinghamshire towards the open spaces, the lakes and fells of Lancashire, Yorkshire, Durham, and Westmorland. This northern area became the heartland of his movement, almost a portent, a revival in England springing from the north. Perhaps the Christians of the age of Bede and that early Puritan movement, the Cistercian Order, and Rievaulx, Fountains, and Tintern Abbeys, with some help from Wordsworth, Ruskin, and Turner, could help us better to understand why, than some of the guesses of sociologists. And the Quakers drew upon that plainness of speech, blunt to the point of rudeness, which some think still marks off the northern from the southern Englishman.

In the late 1640s Fox won new comrades, some from groups of Baptists and Seekers (young men of a certain temperament might have found that the Baptists in the 1620s, the Quakers in the 1640s, and the Methodists a century later 'spoke to their condition'). In these years he fashioned a pattern of teaching and behaviour which would direct the Quaker way of life for a long time to come. But the movement took new impetus from the happenings of the summer of 1652 when a small mass movement among the Seekers turned towards him, and by a mighty harangue to thousands in Firbank Fell and in subsequent gatherings in the neighbourhood of Preston Patrick he won important

---

[4] *Journal*, p. 23.   [5] *Journal*, p. 11.

followers, the core of the so-called 'Valiant Sixty', such gifted helpers as Richard Hubberthorne and Francis Howgill and the boy John Camm, who in the next years went out two by two (much as the Anabaptists had gone out into Austria after their 'Synod' at Augsburg in 1527).

And at Ulverston, in Swarthmoor Hall, his soul dropped anchor in the home and devotion of Margaret Fell, and under the protection of her husband, Judge Fell, Vice-Chancellor of the Duchy of Lancaster.

Like John Wesley a century later, Fox was now able to count on a band of devoted lay helpers who took the message south, to Bristol and London, to the south and west of England, to France and Holland, to Rome and the Levant until at last a woman Quaker bore witness before the Grand Turk himself and his assembled Court.

The name 'Quaker' is said to have been first bestowed by Justice Bennett at Derby in 1650 when Fox bade him tremble at the Word of the Lord. If the name stuck, it was partly because friends in those early days were given to the shakes, to what are sometimes described, but hardly explained, as 'psycho-physical phenomena' of hysterical origin, such as would recur in the Evangelical Revival and, more relevantly, were a feature of the persecuted religion of the Huguenots of the Cévennes.

And certainly in those days Fox in court was more notable for his fire and earthquake than for his still small voice. There he could not keep silence or refrain from good words, for in full tilt Fox could be a holy terror, his great voice drowning not only a fiddler who had been sent to drown him, but a whole court room which tried to shout him down. His verbal assaults and interruptions would have exasperated any magistrate in any age and we are reminded that in the Old Testament the word 'meek' is applied to Moses, which is the only way in which meekness could be applied to Fox. He had a way (it became a fashion) of summing up men at a glance, a not infallible discernment, and his capacity to address an opponent as 'Filth!' on two or three moments' acquaintance was one of his less endearing traits. But his courage was absolute, and the ranks of Tuscany could sometimes not forbear to cheer. He had a quick wit, irony if little humour, and more than a bit of the sea lawyer in him: again and again he was able to put a finger on some legal defect in a mittimus or writ, at a time when Quakers were vulnerable to legal wiles, from the Elizabethan Act against vagabonds, the oaths of allegiance, the charge of *praemunire* and the Quaker Act of May 1662. Indeed so important was this that one of the first Quaker schools desired to have a book 'for teaching . . . Court hands, lawyers' Latin etc. the better to enable them to read a writ and other law process.'[6]

[6] W. C. Braithwaite, *The Second Period of Quakerism* (1919, rev. edn. 1961), p. 526.

In the early years, to use a perhaps inappropriate image, Fox marched towards the sound of the guns. He could sniff the battle from afar, and would stride into parish churches determined to make his witness in angry dialogue at the end of the sermon. No wonder he was hustled and assaulted and suffered brutalities of which he wrote down a meticulous description, clinical in its details. And there were the prisons and the gaolers, some of them like the hideous Doomsdale at Launceston which seem to fit the lower circles of Dante's *Inferno*. Beatings and bruisings, deprivation of food and fresh air, a minimum of decencies, in the end wore down even his great frame, though never his spirit, and brought about the weakness and ill health of his last years—though they did not stop him from travels to Ireland, the West Indies, and North America.

Yet what Fox himself suffered was only a drop in the ocean of sufferings of all the Quakers, many thousands of whom were imprisoned, and hundreds of whom died directly or indirectly as the result of their confinement. What they endured during the Commonwealth was grim enough, perhaps worse than the multiple harassments suffered with the Restoration and the Clarendon Code. Their confusion in the popular mind with other radicals, Fifth Monarchy men, and Ranters was not allayed by the plainest public statements from the Quakers, and they seem to have roused specially the cruel hostilities of callous, unimaginative opponents which were most aggravated by their own non-violence. And then there was their obstinacy. If some of their notions had parallels in the Family of Love, there was none of that movement's Nicodemism, nor would they hide or run away like other Dissenters. Not for them the back door, the hastily lowered curtain, the *sotto voce* psalm in a back parlour, or the forest glade. And in Bristol in 1682 the very children witnessed their good confession:

on 18th June six boys were taken from the Temple street meeting and put for an hour in the stocks and some thirty children were imprisoned for a time. In July the meetings consisted of hardly any but children. On 23rd the boys' hats were taken away and cast into a neighbour's yard and eight lads were put in the stocks for two hours who behaved themselves soberly and cheerfully.

(The little boys, frightened and abused as they were, may have found those days more exciting than tedious hours of sitting through the long elderly silences of Meeting.) In the early days there was a good deal of violence of the tongue from some Quakers. If in December 1653 two Quaker heroines, Mary Fisher (she who would one day confront the Sultan) and Elizabeth Williams, were stripped and flogged for upbraiding Cambridge theological students, it was possible for their denunciations, not softly spoken, to be mistaken for the railing of common scolds. But since one example must suffice, let Cambridge illustrate the continuance of persecution at the Restoration, in a *Kristallnacht* in Jesus Lane, the sorry work of town and gown.

Yesterday in our meeting-house when we had been together two hours, the soldiers came in and set upon us with swords and their staves, and brake in upon us and gat smith's hammers and brake the windows and doors in pieces, and with shivered boards and window bars fell upon us, and beat and wounded many Friends, that few or none did escape without a wound, and haled every one out, and would not suffer one to stay within the house: only I stayed to see what they would do. And when the house was emptied of Friends, they brake down all the glass windows, the stairs, the forms, benches, chairs etc. whatever could be broken in the house. The soldiers and scholars began, and the rude people in the town made an end. Wm. Allen was much beaten and bruised.[7]

But there they were, there they stayed. Pull down a meeting-house over their heads and the next day they would be back, sitting mum among the ruins, a gesture more devastating than any violent reaction could ever have been. No wonder that one of the most enduring of Quaker committees was to be 'the Meeting for Sufferings'.

Organization was inevitable if Friends were to keep in touch and if the movement were not to disappear Fox, who had a shrewd, practical side to him, guided the development of a simple network of meetings, wheels within wheels, from the local particular meeting, to the area quarterly gatherings and the great annual meetings for edification and mutual counsel.

At the root was the simple formation of a Christian cell. 'We had no settled or appointed meetings,' said one pioneer, 'but on the first day of the week (they rejected as pagan the customary names for weeks and months and days) it was the manner of some of us to go to some town where were friendly people and there sit and sometimes confer with one another of the dealings of the Lord with us.'

'Waiting on the Lord' was the heart of their corporate worship, when in a way reminiscent of earlier Protestant 'prophesyings' members might from time to time be moved to utterance, as has been well said, not breaking silence, but breaking out of silence which became more and more the characteristic of the Quaker meeting. And this could bring its problems in a meeting of several hours on a warm day, when a half-hour's silence might be as soporific in its effect on the elderly and the young as any droning from parish clerk or parson in a steeple house.

Since they had no Eucharist, they had no communion collections such

[7] Alderman James Blackley, 28 May 1660: Braithwaite, *The Beginnings of Quakerism*, p. 296.

as the Church and the Nonconformists held regularly for the poor. But they were no way behind in philanthropy and soon had their own meeting, in which they began with the care of the poor of their own household, being very reluctant to let any distressed Quaker come on the parish. From the first the key role of the women in these matters was recognized, and Margaret Fell was a pioneer, while at the centre in London, at the hall behind the Bull and Mouth two Funds, the Box meeting and the Two Weeks meeting, were early established. Their insistence on intermarriage, and the discipline they exercised over it, gave to Quaker family life a great importance and made possible the maintenance of an amazingly taut tradition of dress, manners, and behaviour. No other Christian Church of that age showed more interest in their children, and this was shown by the early development of Quaker schools. Margaret Fell liked colourful dresses (Fox in one letter tells her he is sending a piece of scarlet cloth) and deprecated (rather prophetically) a nascent 'Jewishness' which might place too high a value on outward customs. But in fact in the eighteenth century the Quaker was most easily recognizable by the shape of his hat, and the cut of his coat, by the absence of revers or stand-up collars, and the ladies by the simplicity and quiet comeliness of their attire.

In the eighteenth century, as seems generally admitted, the Quakers settled down from the fiery evangelism which had swollen their numbers into 30,000 or 40,000 in the first decades, but they continued to bear dignified, and sometimes startling, witness to a way of life which might be regarded as mildly eccentric, but invariably won respect.

The first Quakers were not theologians, and indeed looked askance at educated doctors of the schools. Their thinking was often intuitive, though it was far removed from the modern irrationalism of so-called 'gut thinking'. And Fox's aphorisms and prophetic utterances were sometimes less confused than his own attempts to explain them. In fact their view of 'inward religion' had a more ancient and distinguished pedigree than they knew, and it was perhaps unfortunate that they were not equipped to draw upon the classical exponents of the Johannine traditions of the Spirit and of the Word, the great patristic doctrines of the Logos, or of Hildegard of Bingen with her doctrine of a 'light within a light' in her soul. Nor was this tradition lost at the Reformation. Rufus Jones, in those luminous essays which anticipated the modern rediscovery of the radical Reformation, drew attention to the so-called 'spiritualists' and to Hans Denck, the gifted usher of the Sebaldus Kirche in Nuremberg, with his concentration on the Johannine epistles, his doctrine of the 'inner Word', and his insistence that the living Spirit takes precedence over the written Scriptures. From these rich intuitions the first Quakers were cut off.

Barclay's collection of citations from Christian tradition are the weakest part of his apologetic, and Rufus Jones rightly wishes he had paid attention to the Cambridge Platonists, though he overlooks the fact that Barclay's opening pages contain a fine quotation from John Smith.

From the doctrine of the Word and of the Spirit the first Quakers turned to the more congenial image of a divine seed, implanted and growing within the soul.

True sanctification consists in the growth of the seed, and its spreading like a leaven, over the heart and over the whole man. By faith Christ is formed in the heart: the hidden man in the mystery is formed there; and as this seed, this leaven, this man grows, so he makes the man holy in whom he grows. The seed of life, the Kingdom of Heaven, is an holy thing: and as it grows and spreads it purgeth out the old leaven, and makes the lump new: but now in Christians that have grown up in the apostasy, this seed is not known.[8]

The 'inner light', said Pennington, does not lead to the disparagement of the witness of the Holy Scriptures.

it came from the spirit that gave forth the scriptures; it is of the same nature with the light that shone in them that gave forth scriptures: it speaks the same thing with scriptures, it leads to the same thing, and it opens and witnesses to the words which the scriptures speak: and so it brings the scriptures which have been long abused to their true use.[9]

For them John 1:9 was a seminal text. But what is the nature of that light which lightens every man? Is it indeed a light which shines in all human beings, and how does this view of a universal redemption relate to faith on the one hand, and to conscience and the light of reason? Is it something innate or wholly supernatural? Barclay struggled hardest to give a rationale at this point, and was perhaps aware of the difficulties of tackling such a problem in the age of Descartes and Malebranche. He was driven to draw heavily on his senior comrade George Keith in using the not very happy image of a '*Vehiculum Dei*'.

By this seed, grace and word of God and light, wherewith we say every man is enlightened . . . we understand not the proper essence and nature of God precisely taken, which is not divisible into parts and measures, as being a most pure, simple being void of all composition or division . . . but we understand a spiritual, heavenly and invisible principle in which God, as Father, Son and Spirit dwells: a measure of which divine and glorious life is in all men as a seed,

---

[8] I. Pennington, *The Way of Life and Death*, in *Works* (1681), i. 14.
[9] Ibid. i. 44.

which of its own nature draws, invites, and inclines to God and this we call 'Vehiculum Dei' or the spiritual body of Christ, the flesh and blood of Christ which came down from heaven.[10]

It all raises more questions than it answers. The huge volume which Charles Leslie devoted to writings against the Quakers, beginning with his *Snake in the Grass*, is full of tedious nit-picking, but is not perhaps to be brushed aside, as by Braithwaite and others, as the work of a money-grubbing hack (shades of Dr Johnson's encomium of Leslie!)

The Quakers derided the apparent assumption in the Prayer Book of the persistence of sin throughout the life of a believer, but though they emphasized the victorious power of grace, they stopped short of the 'perfectionism' which had marked some of the writers among the Anabaptists, the Ranters, and the Family of Love. And certainly in the writings of Fox, Penn, Pennington, and Barclay there is an awareness of the corruption of sin to an extent which obviously grates on nineteenth- and twentieth-century Quaker liberal historians. But if Fox is aware of the Old Adam, he also returns to what we might call the Older Adam, Adam before the Fall, man in the state of innocence, so that for redeemed men there may yet be truly a 'Paradise Regained'. Though in respect of Christology and Atonement, Barclay's *Apology* was disarming and reassuring, there were some very confused Christological statements in the first Quaker utterances as well as a deal of rather nasty vituperation. Though the Quakers did not evolve a complex jargon like that of Böhme or Swedenborg, they did produce astonishingly early an 'in' language with its own expressions, and Quakers continued to speak of 'convincement', 'speaking to one's condition', 'concerns', and the 'feeling of the meeting'.

Though many of the ideas of the Quakers can be paralleled in church history, among the Anabaptists, the Family of Love, and the Puritan sects of the Reformation, their gospel had its own coherence, its own dynamic quality. In one way it was a return to prophetic religion, for the Quaker leaders were conscious of their resemblance to the Hebrew prophets, in their dooms and burdens and symbolic actions, and in witnessing to truth and righteousness in an age of apostasy. But the heart of their message was in the New Testament, that the Kingdom of God is within. In an age when Protestant theology stressed 'Christ for us' they returned to the equally indispensable theme of 'Christ in us'. It is noticeable that these doctrines were put forward in the 1640s, that they were not the 'realized eschatology' by which those disillusioned by the collapse of their apocalyptic, spiritualized their political hopes, as

[10] R. Barclay, *Apology* (Glasgow 1886), pp. 96f.

happened with Peter Sterry. If they spoke to the condition of many thousands, it was not to those who were seeking a world turned upside down, but to those whose heart and flesh cried out for the living God.

Of course their story, particularly under the strain of persecution, was not all sweetness and light. As with the Anabaptists, the movement attracted wild men, even crackpots.

The hysteria, megalomania, exhibitionism which had appeared in David Joris and some of the Rhineland Anabaptists appeared among the Quakers. The insistence of George Fox that there is an indwelling of Christ in the human soul, and his use of the thought of 'substance' to describe it, involved statements which sounded like heresy and even blasphemy. There are adulatory letters of the Fell family to Fox so extravagant as to resemble religious Bunthornism, and these traits were fatally apparent in the case of James Naylor. Naylor was a Yorkshire-man of fire and eloquence, a doughty publicist of Quaker doctrines. But he succumbed to the devotion of his female disciples which came to a head in the fantastic spectacle of his triumphal entry into Bristol (in the pouring rain!) while the women strewed garments before him and alternately hummed, cooed, and shouted his praises. This confirmed Fox's growing fears about Naylor, and it outraged the Puritan government into inflicting hideous and barbaric punishment, branding and whippings which broke him and, despite his deep penitence and restoration to grace, soon brought him to a pathetic end.

Nor were the Quakers exempt from schism. The personal authority of Fox himself, the power he exercised over Quakers in all parts, his own device of a machinery of government and discipline which seemed to limit the local meeting in favour of a centralizing authority attracted the vehement opposition of John Story and John Wilkinson, who from the heart of Westmorland had travelled to become a power in the West of England, and this produced the gravest of a small number of schisms, of which the departure of George Keith attracted a good deal of publicity.

In an extraordinary way the Quakers had been able to get their pleas 'right to the top', to Cromwell himself and to Charles II. Soon, in a special sense, they had friends at Court. The 'convincement' of Isaac Pennington (1616–79) son of a former Lord Mayor of London and a Cambridge man, brought them a mind of high quality, one whose meditations have beauty and whose peaceable reasonableness shows Quaker apologetic at its most attractive. Even more momentous was the adherence of the young William Penn (1644–1718), son of a famous Admiral, wealthy and aristocratic, who studied at Christ Church and at Lincoln's Inn. He became a very forthright radical and one of the few traces of aristocratic hauteur was his dismissal of the Dissenters as 'an ill bred pedantick crew, the bane of reason and the pest of the world'.

A vehement attack on Christian orthodoxy landed him in the Tower, where he wrote a minor classic, *No Cross, no Crown*, in a prose so much more polished than the pamphlets of Fox that Leslie says he taught the Quakers to write 'sense and English'. His acquittal by a London jury in 1670 became famous in English law as 'Bushell's Case', since it vindicated the freedom of the English jury. Penn found an ally in another personable young man, Robert Barclay, Laird of Ury, whose father, an earlier convert to Quakerism than himself, had been a famous soldier. Barclay was a kinsman of the Stuarts and had the ear of James II and of the Princess Elizabeth of the Palatinate. He too did not shrink from the more extreme gestures, and once strode down the streets of Aberdeen in sackcloth and ashes, calling on the townsmen to repent, an act which he is said to have regretted—not the Barclay most often presented to the world, which was that of a laird of affluence. But he had a trained mind, a good library, and wrote a *Catechism* (1673), followed by an immensely influential *Apology*, printed first in Latin at Amsterdam as *Theologiae Verae Christianae Apologia*, soon translated into several languages, and published in English as an *Apology for the true Christian religion, as the same is set forth and preached by the People called in Scorn 'Quakers'* (1678). Its learning and its persuasive rationality impressed and reassured and did much to stem contemporary suspicion. He seems to have had help from George Keith who provided some technical terms and much of the great array of gobbets from theologians, Fathers, Reformers, Catholic and Protestant divines. Both Penn and Barclay were often consulted by James II and stood by him in the last hours of his reign, though their political reticences helped little to strengthen his unsteady hands or confirm his feeble knees. For Penn and Barclay this tip-toeing along the corridors of power paid off. When like many before them the Quakers left England for America, they ran into trouble in the Puritan colonies, notably in Massachusetts where some were executed, a fate the Quakers in England had at least been spared. Penn had long dreamed of a colony where toleration and Quaker principles might flourish. He and Barclay were involved in the establishment of New Jersey of which Barclay became Governor in 1683.

Charles II granted to William Penn the land and jurisdiction over a new crown colony, to be called Pennsylvania, though the attempt to enlarge it with a further grant of Delaware failed. Penn and his fellow Quakers pursued policies aimed at peace and understanding, and not the exploitation and cozening of the Indians. But there were inevitable problems for Quakers in relation to politics and to military defence, and tensions in respect of other colonies where good Thomas Bray typified the kind of hostility towards the Quakers of godly churchmen, who if they had done little to instigate persecution had done little enough to help assuage it. Penn ran into difficulties, therefore, and retired to London. None the less, it was a signal achievement. The modern visitor to Philadelphia will not be surprised if its local politics seem no more like a city of brotherly love than most great cities. But if, as his aeroplane circles round the monument of William Penn, his thoughts are cynical, he cannot fail to be moved in downtown Philadelphia in what is now a poor, immigrant section to see the simple plaque which marks Penn's treaty with the Indians.

If the Quakers in the seventeenth century might have echoed the liturgy they despised, they would have prayed 'In all time of our tribulation, Good Lord deliver us', but in the succeeding century they might have turned to the other half of that supplication 'In all time of our wealth'. As so often in Christian history, godliness was profitable, integrity paid dividends, and there was movement up the social escalator. The famous comment of George Fox must be cited at this point:

At the first convincement, when Friends could not put off their hats to people nor say 'you' to a particular, but 'thee' and 'thou'; and could not bow nor use the world's salutations, nor fashions, nor customs, many Friends being tradesmen of several sorts they lost their custom at the first: for the people would not trade with them nor trust them, and for a time Friends that were tradesmen could hardly get enough money to buy bread. But afterwards people came to see Friends' honesty and truthfulness and 'yea' and 'nay' at a word in their dealing and their lives and conversations did preach and reach to the witness of God in all people, and they knew and saw that for conscience sake towards God, they would not cozen and cheat them, and at last that they might send any child and be as well used as themselves, at any of their shops.[11]

As Dissenters the Quakers were confined within a narrow band of social opportunity. They were excluded from the Universities, from Church, Army, Law, and from Parliament, either by law or by their own convictions. The result was that a wealth of intelligence, moral fibre, and personal initiative was channelled into trade and industry, and though other Dissenters had their share, the Quakers almost colonized the early Industrial Revolution.[12] Many of them were involved in the wool trade, but it was in the new industries that Quakers were inventors and pioneers, notably among the ironmasters of the north-west and of Wales, and in the potteries of the Black Country. And in an age when

[11] Fox, *Journal* (Everyman edn.), p. 94; (Cambridge edn.) i. 138.
[12] A. Raistrick, *Quakers in Science and Industry* (Newton Abbott 1950).

finance had become of great importance there were affluent and influential Quaker bankers like the Gurneys, the Barclays, the Hoares, and the family of Lloyd.

It has been plausibly said that the Quakers, with their reverence for truth, found the study of nature and of science particularly congenial. Amid the great happenings of the summer of 1652 there is a trivial, but revealing, incident when a youngster named John Story offered Fox a pipe of tobacco. 'Tobacco I did not take, but it came into my mind that the lad might think I had not unity with the creation . . . so I took his pipe and put it to my mouth and gave it to him to stop him lest his rude tongue should say I had not unity with creation.'[13] It reminds us that the first Thuringian Anabaptists had taught a 'gospel of all creatures'. The Quaker experience taught them that all life is sacramental and all creation a unity. It is no wonder that they were interested, like so many in the age of Ray, in botany and horticulture, and families like the Lawsons and the Millers, and distinguished individual scholars like Peter Collison and John Bartram made important contributions to the development of these sciences.

It has also been said that Quakers have had a participation in the Royal Society which is forty times the natural proportion. Among clock- and instrument-makers were the famous Thomas Tompion, and Daniel Quare, and George Graham. In medicine, alone of the professions, it was possible for Dissenters to engage in training either in Holland or in Scotland and there were a number of eminent Quaker physicians, who included the notable John Fothergill, who put into practice many of the researches and enquiries into epidemics and the like which, years before, the Quaker John Bellars had set as goals of urgency for the medical profession.

By the middle of the eighteenth century, though there were plenty of humble people in their ranks, there were enough who were comfortably off and prosperous to arouse some criticism. As at the Goat Lane meeting-house in Norwich where the Gurney family regularly met, and where that wonderful galaxy of daughters fidgeted and thought their own rebel thoughts through what were for some of them dreary and unprofitable sessions. But even where there was restiveness and a loosening of older restrictions, when the Gurney daughters took to dancing and to friendships with families outside the Quaker world, the girls kept up the Quaker practices of self-examination and of keeping diaries, while inevitably there came the splendid rebellion against rebellion in the return to earlier Quaker austerities of Elizabeth Fry and her brother.

[13] *Journal* (Everyman edn.), p. 63.

Nor did their practical compassion wither. The Quakers were in the van as regards the new philanthropies, prison reform, the attack on the slave trade, and schemes like the manifold projects of John Bellars for the education and training of the poor.

The fact that the Quaker world was to a growing extent self-contained within its families, and a great network of friendships, insulated them a little from a sense of isolation which the disapproval of churchmen and Nonconformists brought to bear. It was not easy for most Christians to accept as authentically Christian a community which rejected the sacraments, the ministries, the liturgies, the observances of most believers over most of the Christian centuries. That the Quakers regarded themselves as the rediscoverers of truth after the long interval of apostasy did not make it easier.

Yet it was of immense significance that in the middle of the seventeenth century and in the succeeding age of the Enlightenment the Quakers should set a question mark against the nature of a Christian culture, and demand the restoration of earlier simplicities and a detachment from the world. The kind of criticism which Kierkegaard by his devastating writings would apply to the Lutheran Establishment was here applied in a living way to the English Church. But it was a modern Lutheran church historian who could write 'if the tree is to be known by its fruits then the Society of Friends is a Christian church, despite the absence of the sacraments and the relatively subordinate part played by the Word.'[14]

And those who murmur 'not a Church, surely, but an ecclesial community' might ponder certain sayings of earlier centuries—that doctrine of 'the Word going forth out of silence', the affirmation that 'God is not bound to His sacraments', and above all the assertion of the sovereign freedom of the Holy Spirit to move, enlighten, and sanctify, 'ubi et quando', when and where and as He wills.

What distinguished Quaker spirituality from the abundant religiosity of that age, is surely its quality of depth. It was the return to the heart of Christian spirituality, at a level which wayfaring men could understand and appropriate and practise which made it the most impressive revival of Johannine Christianity in Protestant history.

[14] E. Molland, *Christendom* (1959), p. 328.

10

ISAAC WATTS

ISAAC WATTS was born in 1674, and the tale that he was suckled on the steps of Southampton Gaol, within which his Nonconformist father was confined, reminds us that he grew up under the shadow of the Great Harassment. But he was in his teens when the advent of William III and the Toleration Act ushered in a more peaceful, if still restricted, period in Nonconformist history. He was a bright, precocious child who tackled the three sacred languages before he was ten and began to dabble in verse as soon as he could read and write. His friends and teachers tried to get him to University, but he was not prepared to conform, and went instead to one of the best Dissenting Academies, under Thomas Rowe, What he learned there was reflected in his classical training and the wide range of his intellectual pursuits.

The pleasant villages of North London, Islington and Stoke Newington, were colonies of the more affluent Dissenters. It was a time, Defoe reminds us, of constant building as villages became suburbs, and he added that the new houses 'are generally belonging to the middle sort of mankind, grown wealthy by trade, and who still taste of London: some of them live both in the city and in the country at the same time: yet many of these are immensely rich.'[1]

Two such well-to-do Dissenting laymen were of great moment in Watts's life. Sir John Hartopp not only was a man of affairs, but cared deeply for things of the mind, and began to learn Hebrew at the age of fifty. Isaac Watts became tutor to his son and a valued member of his household. Sir Thomas Abney, sometime Lord Mayor of London, was an occasional conformist who made no secret of his allegiance to Dissent. He had a house at Theobalds and his second wife brought him a fine dwelling in Stoke Newington. It was to his household that Watts came for a weekend, but remained for thirty-six years, finding the kind of loving patronage which Samuel Johnson describes a little enviously.

His heart and his gifts lay in the ministry, and the obviously 'coming' young man was appointed, on his twenty-fourth birthday, assistant to the notable Dr Chauncey, minister of the most reputable and prosperous of all the London Chapels, which had moved to Mark Lane from

---

[1] Daniel Defoe, *A Tour of England and Wales* (2 vols., Everyman edn. n.d.), ii. 2.

Leadenhall Street, and was later moved to Pinner's Hall (1704) and Bury Street, St Mary Axe (1708). Almost immediately his health broke down and there were tiresome months spent attending spas at Bath and Tunbridge Wells. The welcome refuge in the Abney household took care of almost all his physical problems for the rest of his life, so that he was able to devote one-third of his £100 a year to charity. The congregation soon learned his value, and appointed him minister and provided assistants. They learned to put up with his frequent absences, for when he came among them it was well worth waiting for, as their little minister was transformed in the pulpit, and his restrained, but warm, eloquence never strayed far from the heart of the Christian gospel.

The months and weeks of illness, spread over many years, at least meant that he could spend far more time in his study, reading and writing, and, despite the valetudinarian cast of his existence and occasional hypochondria, he wrote enough to fill seven large volumes, beside some 700 hymns. Samuel Johnson in his perceptive and always sympathetic study of Watts, suggests that he did indeed cast his net too widely: 'perhaps there was nothing in which he could not have excelled, if he had not divided his powers to different pursuits.'

His Latin verse, as Johnson also noted, was far from flawless, and he modelled himself on a Polish poet, Casimir Sarbiewski, whom he overrated much as the sixteenth century overrated Baptista Mantuanus. His religious verse generally places him but a little above Samuel Wesley and a little below Nahum Tate, as a very minor poet.

His prose works were well earthed in his tutorial experiences, and, like those of Erasmus, the most effective were written as text-books for his pupils. One of them, his handbook on *Logic* was effective enough to be used as a textbook at Oxford and Cambridge, Yale and Harvard. It shows his hard-won ability to write simply and it reduced technical terms to a minimum—a little handbook about straight and crooked thinking. Words for him, as poet, divine, and thinker, were tools to which he devoted much care and attention and Johnson imported many of Watts's definitions into his English dictionary.

Of more ephemeral interest was his essay *On the Improvement of the Mind*, which Johnson read with enjoyment, and commended to universal attention. For Sir John Hartopp he wrote two textbooks on Geometry and Astronomy and was able to draw on the learning of the greatest of the Dissenting scientists, John Eames, FRS, who wrote a kindly preface. He was well abreast of the intellectual fashions of the day, in an age when great issues had been raised within a half-century by thinkers as diverse as Descartes and Malebranche, Newton, Leibniz, and

Locke. His *Philosophical Essays* are perhaps slight, though read with undiscriminating rapture by Mrs Thrale, who at one point burst out 'This is like Ajax's prayer in the Iliad. Scarce inferior to Homer in Poetical expression. O admirable Isaac Watts!'

On the Education of Youth shows that Watts was no Milton nor a Comenius, but it does centre attention on the home, and on the responsibilities of parents in an age when there were but few schools for girls. (Watts taught the Abney daughters, and he may have had them in mind.) But there are some interesting sidelights on the changing attitudes of parents to children which have an almost modern ring. Thus he contrasts the strictness and severity of the seventeenth-century home (much as modern parents look back to the Victorian age).

In that day many children were kept in a most servile subjection . . . now they are made familiar companions to their parents, almost from the nursery: and therefore they will hardly bear a check or rebuke at their hand.

In short, the last age taught mankind to believe that they were mere children and treated them as such until they were near thirty years old: but the present gives them leave to fancy themselves complete men and women at twelve or fifteen.

And he pursues this theme with thumb-nail sketches (which he does not manage, generally, as well as did William Law) of Antigone who brought up her children—daughters—agreeable to her own loose notions, with the result that they 'are seized and married before sixteen being tempted away to bind themselves for life to a laced coat and a fashionable wig.' Whereas Phronissa 'used to spend some hours daily in the nursery and taught the young creatures to recite many a pretty passage out of the Bible before they were capable of reading it themselves.' His thought is never radical, but at one point he utters his fears that the education of women is defective and that far more opportunities and activities should be open to the female sex than in his contemporary male-dominated world.

These are the thoughts, arising out of his own teaching experience, which inspired two sets of his most effective writings, his carefully graded catechisms and his children's hymns. He perhaps forgot sometimes that all little children were not as gifted as the infant Watts, but his first catechism, for a child between three and four years of age, is simple, but not banal.

Q. Can you tell me, child, who made you?
A. The Great God who made heaven and earth.

The next, for a child between seven and eight, begins:

Q. Dear child, do you know what you are?
A. I am a creature of God, for he made me both body and soul.

Those between twelve and fourteen can now be safely exposed to the Westminster Catechism, with its sublime opening,

Q. What is the chief end of Man?
A. Man's chief end is to glorify God, and enjoy him forever.

But there are explanatory notes on 'chief end', 'glorify', and 'enjoy'.

If it was an age which treated little boys as though they were old men, at least it produced *The Pilgrim's Progress*, *Robinson Crusoe* and *Gulliver's Travels*, while Watts's *Divine Songs for Children* became a best seller for a hundred years. We who look at them through the eyes of another very bachelorish bachelor who knew how to talk to children, Lewis Carroll, do not perhaps, like Alice, get them 'quite right'. John Mason Neale, brought up after the straitest sect of Evangelicals, had to get them by heart and loathed them nearly as much as he detested Nonconformists. He hated their sombre Calvinism, and produced a set of verses to save children from the 'Yoke of Watts', but his own poems (as distinct from his translations) have no memorable lines, while many of Watts's have become proverbs. And if the sternness in Watts is not to be denied, yet warnings about the consequences of sin were not invented by him.

Thus the unexceptionable counsel of Watts,

> Our tongues were made to bless the Lord
> And not speak ill of men:
> When others give a railing word
> We must not rail again.

is tacked on to the story of the rude boys and Elisha and the awful warnings:

> God quickly stopp'd their wicked breath
> And sent two raging bears
> That tore them limb from limb to death
> With blood, and groans, and tears.
> Great God! how terrible thou art
> To sinners ne'er so young.

But Watts did not invent the story, though he perhaps need not have called attention to it! And an age where little boys are encouraged to throw stones and petrol bombs might consider that the often derided words about dogs barking and biting are followed by the lovely lines

Let love thro' all your actions run
And all your words be mild:
Live like the blessed Virgin's son,
That sweet and lovely child!
His soul was gentle as a Lamb.

And if our generation, when some Christians seem to find the heart of the gospel in the cursing of the fig tree rather than the Sermon on the Mount, hesitates over the word 'gentle' we might reflect that it is not Watts, but the meaning of a noble word which has changed with two centuries, and alas, not just the word itself.

There is much more to Watts than the Calvinist *chiaroscuro*. He shows us a pattern of Christian virtues and decent manners, of truthfulness and honesty, integrity and gentleness not irrelevant to an age of youthful violence, and applauded artful dodgery. And so while we bury in a dictionary of quotations the lines about the dogs who bark and bite, the birds who in their nests agree to differ, and the little bees who improve each shining hour, we may perhaps smile, but have little right to sneer.

Watts, said Johnson, was 'one of the first authors that taught the Dissenters to court attention by the graces of language.' But the modern reader will very likely find his theological treatises solid, but unappetizing. His treatise on the *Ruin and Recovery of Mankind* was heavily and gratefully pillaged by John Wesley in his reply to John Taylor of Norwich on *Original Sin*. In his published sermons he strongly emphasizes the centrality of the person and work of Christ, with a stress on the 'satisfaction' of the Atonement. His sermon on 'Divine Election' is as Augustinian as it is Calvinist, but shows no signs of modification in what might be called a Baxterian direction. And if he got into trouble with his American friends—for the fathers of Salem had noses as sensitive for heresy as for witchcraft—he was perhaps more aware than they that in Newman's phrase 'new questions demand new answers' and that there were special problems for the age of Newton when it came to evaluating the Christological definitions of the early Councils.

In face of the winds of change to which his generation was exposed and the heady freedom of a new liberty of speculation, it was not always easy for theologians to stand upright. It did not occur to eighteenth-century divines, any more than to some modern successors, to wonder if their equipment for tackling Christological questions might be less competent than that of the Fathers of the fourth and fifth centuries, in respect of subtlety and flexibility of language, or that the ancient philosophy of substance, susceptible at least of rational definition, might be more satisfactory than the shifting sand of their own vocabularies about the relation between soul and body, spirit and matter. If Watts fell into mistaken notions about the pre-existence of the human soul of Christ, and if towards the end of his life he was worried about the inward economy of the Holy Trinity, there is no heresy (*pace* J. M. Neale) in his hymns about Christ, Atonement, or the Trinity.

Like most Englishmen of that age, he was a sturdy patriot, and his sermons and his hymns rejoice in the liberties of true-born Englishmen. What is called 'the Whig Interpretation of History' is in fact, the Protestant interpretation of history grafted on a wild olive tree of politics. Before the Whigs were, the Protestants were, acclaiming a coherent view of their history in terms of preservation from Popery in the saving acts of 1588, 1605, and 1688.

For Watts, as for his Puritan forebears and evangelical successors, 'practical theology' was all-important and his lucid tract on prayer has well deserved its modern republication.

But when all is said and done, it is the hymns which had the flashpoint of genius, and were the proper reason for his lasting fame. The success of his *Hymns and Songs* (1707), which ran into sixteen editions in his lifetime, showed that they were swiftly of significance outside the bounds of his own communion. Hitherto, singing in the Protestant churches had been restricted to the singing of psalms. As a concession to the dryness of worship almost entirely centred on the spoken word, metrical psalms were permitted, but the two most notable collections, of Sternhold and Hopkins and Tate and Brady, were generally of poor quality (there are some splendid exceptions) and often not much above jingles. Certainly the young Isaac Watts had writhed under them and determined quite early on to attempt better things.

As his famous prefaces show, he was consciously a rebel and a pioneer, not least in a Reformed tradition which sought to oust the mere human words of men from divine worship. What Isaac Watts attacked was the dullness into which Nonconformist worship had been brought by wooden and indiscriminate use of inferior versions. 'They love the driest translation of the psalm best. They will venture to sing a dull hymn or two at church in tunes of equal dullness.' But his real point was more positive that 'David has left us a richer variety of songs than all that went before him but rich as it is it is still far short of the glorious things that we Christians have to sing before the Lord.'

But despite his vocation, as he conceived it, to Christianize the Psalms, he did not despise them in their original setting, and what is arguably his greatest hymn, is a strict rendering of Psalm 90.

Among the 697 of Watts's hymns there is a great range of quality.

Many poor hymns have fine single lines and single verses. It is ironical that he who laboured hard to avoid the anachronistic, the dated and grotesque, should himself have been so often overtaken by the changes in taste and language of two and a half centuries. We can all amuse ourselves with picking out such lines as 'Well, the Redeemer's gone!' or 'The mischiefs that infect the earth/When the hot dogstar fires the realms on high', as long as we remember that this has nothing to do with the intrinsic quality of the hymns.

What his hymns meant to ordinary Christians can be judged from a letter Philip Doddridge wrote him in April 1731.

On Tuesday last I was preaching to a large assembly of plain country people at a village a few miles off . . . we sang one of your hymns, which if I remember right was the 140th of the 2nd book . . . and in that part of the worship I had the satisfaction to observe tears in the eyes of several of the people: and after the service was over, some of them told me that they were not able to sing, so deeply were their minds affected! and the clerk in particular said he could hardly utter the words as he gave them out. They were most of them poor people who work for their living yet on the mention of your name I found that they had read several of your books with great delight: and that your psalms and hymns were almost their daily entertainment: and when one of the company said 'What if Dr. Watts should come down to Northampton?' another replied with remarkable warmth 'The very sight of him would be as good as an ordinance to me.'[2]

No account of Isaac Watts can omit the all too laconic entry in the *Diary* of John Wesley for 4 October 1738 when apparently both John and Charles Wesley visited Isaac: '1.30 at Dr Watts', conversed: 2.30 walked, singing, conversed.'

There are perhaps two score of Watts's hymns which no decent hymn book dare omit. Let it be granted, to use a crude image, that there are far more oysters and oyster shells than goodly pearls. But splendid those pearls are, though room permits only a comment on two of great price.

Watts shared with his contemporaries in the age of Pascal and Newton an almost modern sense of the surrounding silences of infinite space. 'Watts sees the Cross', said Bernard Manning, 'as Milton had seen it planted on a globe in space, surrounded by the vast distances of the universe.' But, like Augustine, Watts was sensitive to the mystery of time, the transitoriness of our human existence. This was something he seems to have learned in long weary months of illness and convalescence.

---

[2] J. D. Humphreys, *The Correspondence and Diary of Philip Doddridge* (5 vols., 1829), ii. 74. The hymn was 'Give me the wings of faith'.

My watch, the solitary kind companion
Of my imprisonment, my faithful watch
Hangs by, and with a short repeated sound
Beats like the pulse of time, and numbers off
My woes, a long succession, while the finger
Slow moving points out the slow moving minutes,
The slower hand the hours. O thou dear engine!
Thou little brass accountant of my life.
Would but the mighty wheels of heav'n and nature
Once imitate thy movements and whirl away
These clouded wintry suns, these tedious moons
These midnights!

It is a happy accident that in Westminster Abbey the bust of Isaac Watts looks across to where another Nonconformist is commemorated, the great Quaker clock-maker, Thomas Tompion. But it is no accident at all that Isaac Watts came so sensitively to grasp the Hebrew sense of the transitoriness of our existence, that the life of man is as a shadow that falleth. And this is man *coram Deo*, for it is in the presence of the eternal God that man realizes his own frailty. He had not pondered this theme in Job and in the Psalms in vain. And all this is the background of the great hymn. For Watts time is not, as in our usage, the Great Enemy, nor is it a Friend, whom St Francis might have called Brother Time. It is rather something of great solemnity, an awareness that nothing so emphasizes the dignity of man, as the moment of his dying.

Our God, our help in ages past . . .

The busy tribes of flesh and blood
With all their lives and cares
Are carried downwards by the flood
And lost in following years.

Time, like an ever rolling stream
Bears all its sons away,
They fly forgotten as a dream
Dies at the opening day.

Our God, our help in ages past.

And when we have smiled at Watts's sometimes naïve expressions of patriotism, we find that he has the last word, if ever we have stood before the Cenotaph in Whitehall on 11 November in the poignant seconds of national remembrance, a moment to which Watts's hymn is befitting as no other hymn could ever be.

In his day there was a recovery of devotion to the Holy Sacrament. It was so in the Church of England and among Roman Catholics. In

Watts's communion, one cannot but feel that the rigid, high fencing of
the Lord's Table as the focal point of discipline may have contributed to
breeding a distaste towards the Ordinance. If this were so, then the
eucharistic hymns of Isaac Watts were not only signs, but instruments,
of better things. They are not as grand as the eucharistic hymns of
Charles Wesley, nor as joyous as those of Philip Doddridge, but if their
theology is Calvinistic, it is a high Calvinism far removed from a
negative memorialism.

The first thing to note about the great hymn.

> When I survey the wondrous Cross
> Where the young Prince of glory died . . .

is that it was written specifically for use at the Lord's Supper and is an
act of eucharistic devotion. The second is that it expounds a text, Gal.
6: 14, and is entitled 'Crucifixion to the world by the Cross of Christ'. It
is therefore necessarily a blend of 'Christ for us' and 'Christ in us'. It is
not the Cross as Matthias Grünewald and Pieter Breughel have shown
us, but it is near to Fra Angelico.

It is sad that the pivotal, Donne-like existential verse is often omitted

> His dying crimson like a robe
> Hangs o'er his body on the tree,
> Then I am dead to all the globe,
> And all the globe is dead to me.

It is beloved in all English-speaking Churches. On a Good Friday it will
likely be the climax of a service in numerous little village chapels, as well
as at the close of a Three Hours Devotion in some great cathedral. It has
taken its place as a noble expression of Christian devotion. It is also a
work of Christian art, as truly as a fifth-century mosaic, an Anglo-
Saxon rood, a window in Canterbury Cathedral, or an anthem by
Purcell or Elgar. And it lives on, not least for its final recognition that all
the realm of nature (galaxies and all) does not match two ultimate
mysteries, God's broken body, and a humble, contrite heart.

Watts as an old man was known and respected by the nation, admired
by Samuel Johnson, and painted by Kneller. The Scottish Universities,
Edinburgh and Aberdeen, wont to expend uncovenanted mercies on
their reformed fellow Christians across the border, gave him a double
portion of their spirit, in two Doctorates of Divinity. Among the
Nonconformists he had become the great father figure, not least to
younger men like Philip Doddridge. He had become a little querulous,
and the new enthusiasm and pulpit ways of the blossoming Evangelical
Revival, as represented by George Whitefield, seem to have exasperated

and bemused him. There was family trouble, too, a nephew whose disgraceful conduct disturbed his mind and broke his spirit. But the slow flame of his existence, so often nearly quenched, continued to burn into his seventy-fifth year. When he died he was buried in Bunhill Fields, where he lies with other Nonconformist worthies, John Bunyan, Daniel Defoe, and William Blake. At his request, all the Nonconformist Churches were represented by two Congregationalist, two Presbyterian and two Baptist ministers. In Bunhill Fields, unlike Westminster Abbey, the memorials are generally noticeable for their understatements, and none more so than Watts's epitaph which he composed for himself, to the effect that he 'after fifty years of feeble labours, interrupted by four years of tiresome sickness, was at last dismissed to his rest. In uno Jesu omnia.'

11

PHILIP DODDRIDGE

PHILIP DODDRIDGE (1702–51) perfectly illustrates the changing temper of his age, and of the Nonconformist way of life, for in him the great differences between his generation and that of Richard Baxter are apparent. Despite his intensity of spirit, and an austere discipline of time and devotion, the sombre days of Puritanism were over and in its place a much more human attitude to the world than either ·the previous Reformed tradition or the coming evangelicalism would have thought proper. It was not only that Doddridge could smoke his pipe and play at cards, but his amiable and cheerful temperament pervades his religion and his hymns as truly as it does his correspondence and his home life. He himself was the last of twenty children and only he and one sister survived, to be orphaned in their childhood, while a few years later his guardian went bankrupt. There was in him a deep need of affection, not least after the death of his mother, which was partly met by a harmless succession of what the poet calls accomplished female friends, and wholly satisfied by his marvellous marriage and in the quality of his friends and disciples who by the end of his life included members of all ranks of society, from the Royal Family downwards.

He owed most to the love and care of his Father in God, Samuel Clark of St Albans, who saw him through the difficult and penurious years and was always at hand with kindly and wise counsel. He had also contacts with the Duchess of Bedford who was of help in his early career, though he refused offers to send him to University and remained a Nonconformist. Like Isaac Watts, he had the good fortune to be sent to an outstanding Dissenting Academy, that of the learned John Jennings at Kibworth. He provided a very tough and many-sided course into which Philip threw himself with gusto, and he read away at a fierce rate both in classical and French literature. Though very near-sighted, he kept up his reading until the end of his life. At Kibworth it was the slightly bogus discipline of 'Pneumatology' which enthralled him since it introduced students to what would now be called 'modern thought'. Jennings encouraged the freest and widest opinions and led the way by his own example, as Doddridge told his correspondents.

Mr. Jennings encourages the greatest freedom of enquiry, and always inculcates it as a law that the Scriptures are the only genuine standard of faith . . . Mr.

6 December 1729 he accepted the call to Castle Hill church and his solemn ordination followed 19 March 1730 when eight ministers took part, five of them Presbyterians, and Samuel Clark gave the ordination charge. The following December he was married and here the home base of a wide and influential ministry was settled. He was a kind and amiable man who found it difficult to say 'No', to refuse invitations from ever widening circles, involving tiresome and often dangerous journeys in all kinds of weather, in perils from damp beds and cold lodgings.

In Northampton he exercised a careful and conscientious ministry at the heart of which was a guarded and disciplined devotional life. He was not a flashy preacher, but his sermons had always meat in them, and an argument to be followed, and he could at times attain a striking eloquence, so that he was reckoned one of the more notable preachers of his day.

Of the hymns which he specially composed to follow his sermons, we shall have more to say. As it was for Isaac Watts and Philip and Matthew Henry, the Lord's Supper was of immense importance for him, both as an act of private devotion and as a public ordinance. He kept a tally of his sacraments and wrote hundreds of meditations on those occasions. Often the Sacrament marked a high moment in his own experience. He wrote to his wife in March 1743 (she was recovering slowly at Bath from a serious illness):

You knew, my dearest, it [your letter] would arrive on Lord's day night. It was our sacrament day, and indeed it was a most comfortable one to me: my joy at that ordinance was so great I could not well contain it: I had much ado to forbear telling all about me as well as I could for it would have been in a very imperfect way what a divine flame I felt in my soul, which indeed put me in mind of Mr. Howe's 'full-stream of rays'.[4]

An earlier love letter written straight after attendance at the Sacrament beautifully illustrates the wholeness of natural and supernatural in his religion, a facet of eighteenth-century spirituality which the evangelical revival may even have retarded. And it is quite likely that what struck his hearers most was not his preaching, but his prayers.

The time expended in preaching and teaching did not prevent his visitation of the sick and needy and he contrived to look after not only those within Northampton, but also those in the surrounding villages which he visited at least twice a year. He was particularly concerned with family religion, and his printed sermon *The Young Christian invited to Communion* reveals his concern for the young. In later years, his pastoral care was too much interrupted so that, when it ended, he was

---

[4] Ibid. iv. 211.

worried to find his membership had been reduced by almost a third.

In 1730 he began an Academy in his own house, with forty carefully seeded students. He had soon to find larger accommodation and by 1743 had sixty. Its fame led John Wesley to seek him out, and he was invited to address the students, while Wesley sought from him book lists which he might use in the planning of his schools at Kingswood and his 'Christian Library'.

Doddridge was no great manager and no disciplinarian. John Barker again told the truth in love when he wrote:

> You are so entirely devoted to God, to truth, and holiness that it is very easy to impose upon you under the appearance of any of these: and are so made up of candour and good nature that a pious enthusiast or a godly dunce is welcome to your table and heart. You are so good yourself that you think everybody else ten times better than they are.[5]

But he had perforce to deal with bursarial matters: 'as for my terms, they are sixteen pounds a year board and four pounds teaching . . . when pupils enter the academy they pay a guinea each for closet and bring a pair of sheets. They find their own candles, and put out their washing.'

The students rose at 6.00 in summer and 7.00 in winter. They met for an assembly prayer and then retired to their rooms, meeting again for family prayers at 8.00 when a chapter from the Old Testament was read in Hebrew and Doddridge expounded the text.

There were no tests of religious beliefs, and from time to time the Academy included students intending to take orders in the Church of England as well as sons of Anglican laymen. One of the most notable, but a real *Sorgenkind*, was the son of Lord Kilkerran. Even had Doddridge no other calls on his time he would have had to sublet his chores and devolve some administration on his assistant, and he also remitted some of the teaching in Greek to the best of the senior students. The syllabus included not only the blessed theme of Pneumatology, but algebra and geometry, as well as ecclesiastical history and Jewish antiquities. Not only did Doddridge build up a good working library, but he laboured to acquire good scientific apparatus. He knew it was important not only to teach homiletics, but to give his young men practice in preaching, and they were sent out in what was almost the beginning of an evangelical itinerancy.

Naturally Doddridge's Academy attracted notice, and there was ugly opposition. In 1736 there was a savage incident when one of his students taking a cottage service was attacked by a mob, escaping by the window, while his host was pelted with dirt and dragged through a horsepond. It would be interesting to know how early the Church of England developed a social contempt for Nonconformity, perhaps the nastiest disability inflicted by the Establishment on its separated brethren.

But it clearly appears in the great test case which developed in 1732 when an Anglican Chancellor at a diocesan visitation at Northampton said that 'he was informed that there was a fellow in their parish who taught a grammar school, which he had the assurance to call an academy as he supposed without any licence from the bishop',[6] and he ordered an enquiry to be made, that Doddridge might be prosecuted. Fortunately he found a champion in Lord Halifax, and both men realized the importance of the affair as a test case. The Chancellor began to climb down, suggesting that Doddridge might have a licence if he would subscribe the articles, but maintaining his right to examine him. By this time Doddridge had sought help in the highest legal quarters and the matter had been brought to the attention of Sir Robert Walpole. So Doddridge dug his toes in, and at the end of January 1737 was able to write triumphantly to his wife, 'I am just come from Westminster Hall where our cause was gained without any opposition worth naming.'[7]

And when an appeal was threatened, the matter was ended by the personal intervention of the King. In Northampton Doddridge was by now a citizen of renown, involved more and more in town concerns. He took the initiative in starting a charity school (Samuel Clark had founded the first dissenting charity school outside London). Among Doddridge's converts was a wealthy ne'er-do-well, James Stonhouse, who went on to become a very notable clergyman. He and Doddridge formed and executed a great project of founding a General Hospital in Northampton, a hospital which was opened in 1744, Doddridge characteristically retiring into the background for the opening ceremonies where the rector took the leading part. Doddridge had all too much reason to be preoccupied with health and wrote a pioneer tract in defence of inoculations.

Doddridge was not only a citizen, but a patriot, and like most Dissenters firmly on the Hanoverian side. When danger loomed in 1745 it is said that Charles Wesley wrote a hymn and John Wesley talked of raising a regiment. But Doddridge went further in alliance with Lord Halifax, and raised a troop 814 strong. When the panic was over and the rebellion collapsed, Doddridge was able to preach a thanksgiving sermon on the theme 'Deliverance out of the hands of our enemies'.

He was not a polemical divine, though he wrote a forceful and

[6] Ibid. iii. 108ff.   [7] Ibid. iii. 139.

disarming reply to the tract in which Strickland Gough had alleged a decline in the Dissenting interest. It was a time, as we have already seen, when spiritual reading was far more widespread than the alleged lethargy of the contemporary churches can explain. One of the much read 'Lives' had been that written by Matthew Henry about his father, Philip. Now Doddridge wrote a little biography which was even more widely acclaimed; its subject his admired and lamented friend, a Colonel of Hussars, the godly Colonel Gardiner, who fell in the battle at Prestonpans. It was also a time of interest in edifying expositions of the Scriptures, of the kind which in the sixteenth century had made the *Paraphrases* of Erasmus and the *Postills* of Luther so popular. Matthew Henry had produced a series of expositions of Holy Scripture (1708–10) of solid worth and lasting influence, and John Locke's more up-to-date theology attracted attention to his own paraphrases.

Now Doddridge attempted something between the two, and his *Family Expositor* while soon dated, provided what many people, including some members of the Royal Family, most needed. The text was paraphrased verse by verse and section by section, and critical questions and the comments of other Biblical expositors were dealt with in the footnotes. Each section ended with an improving paragraph of a devotional kind, often more a prayer than an exposition, lifting the whole into the realm of 'practical theology' or spirituality. Even more impressive was his minor religious classic in which he developed an idea of Isaac Watts, entitled *The Rise and Progress of Religion in the Soul* (1745). He wrote it when the new Evangelical Revival was in full spate, but, as we have suggested, it belongs in an older tradition of Puritan evangelicalism. Among the many on whose souls it made dramatic impact was William Wilberforce.

Doddridge, like his beloved Baxter, was missionary minded. He was much moved by the life of David Brainerd, the missionary to the Red Indians. Although the SPCK and SPG had already sent missionaries to America and to India, Doddridge was the first Nonconformist to take steps towards founding a missionary society. As Ernest Payne argued in a fine essay on this theme, it is hardly accidental that, after Doddridge's death, the great work of William Carey began in Northampton.[8]

Unlike Isaac Watts, who was just that much older, and who was in any case much more emotionally reserved, Doddridge was actively sympathetic to the new evangelism, and as the religious elements in society hummed with gossip about the controversial figure of George Whitefield, Doddridge became a member of an attracted group which

[8] E. A. Payne, 'Doddridge and the Missionary Enterprise' in *Philip Doddridge*, ed. G. F. Nuttall, 1951.

included John Byrom and the Countess of Huntingdon. Despite the antagonism of his friends, Dr Watts and Bishop Warburton, he went to hear Whitefield and allowed him to preach for him. He had been fascinated by what he had heard of the revived Moravianism now infiltrating England, with its combination of evangelism and missionary zeal and did not rest till he had met Count Zinzendorf, though, like John Wesley, his admiration waned when he saw the results of Moravian quietism and sheep-stealing in the early 1740s.

In the last years of his life, then, he had crammed more and more into a timetable already dangerously overcrowded and ever more extensive. He was by now a courted figure. His honorary doctorate from Aberdeen was but one instance of public recognition and he was greeted with respect by Heads of Houses in Oxford and Cambridge and consulted by an eirenical Archbishop of Canterbury to whom he propounded the novel notion of an occasional exchange of pulpits.

The long, often poignantly anxious, illness of his wife was now succeeded by his own consumption and he became gravely ill. Well-intentioned friends and benefactors thought a warmer climate might help and it was decided to go to Lisbon. There they met, not the hoped-for dry weather, but torrential rains and unpleasant humidity. He would have been much better off had he stayed in England, but he died in a corner of a foreign field and was buried in Lisbon. In him the Nonconformists of the third generation had produced a son of the very highest spiritual stature whose fame is now in all the Churches.

The hymns of Doddridge, far less numerous than those of Watts or Wesley, have a quality which derives from his own attractive character, as much as from his not mean poetic abilities.

We have remarked his special devotion to the Eucharist, and one of the results is the fine hymn, Donne-like, Herbert-like in its beginning

> My God, and is thy Table spread,
> And does thy Cup with Love o'erflow?

There is his lovely hymn for Baptism:

> See Israel's gentle shepherd stand
> With all engaging charms;
> Hark how he calls the tender lambs,
> And folds them in his arms.

And if it trembles on the edge of sentimentalism, so invariably does the whole Church of Christ on these occasions, as every minister knows who ever faced a congregation across a font.

The Doddridge who founded a charity school and was alert to many

new philanthropic enterprises, believed, like Robert Nelson, that when
we meet the poor we do indeed encounter Christ.

> Thy face with reverence and with love
> I in thy poor would see;
> O let me rather beg my bread
> Than hold it back from Thee.

Some of the sermons of Watts had been followed by hymns written
for the occasion, but for Doddridge this was the central reason for hymn
writing. This made their own fresh impact on the congregation. It is no
accident that words like 'cheerful', 'joy', 'rapture', abound. It is this
which gives a gaiety and liveliness to all he writes and there can be few
writers of hymns through whose works there runs such a silver stream
of joy:

> O happy day that fixed my choice
> On Thee my Saviour and my God!
> Well may this glowing heart rejoice,
> And tell its raptures all abroad.

Or his fine Resurrection hymn:

> Ye humble souls that seek the Lord
> Chase all your fears away:
> And bow with rapture down to see
> The place where Jesus lay.

There is a solemn beauty in his development of the theme of the
pilgrim people of God:

> O God of Jacob by whose hand
> Thy people still are fed.

And an exultant cheer, amid the noise of trumpets in

> Hark the glad sound! the Saviour comes,
> The Saviour promised long;
> Let every heart prepare a throne,
> And every voice a song

It is one of the few Advent hymns which echoes the old Puritan whose
comment on the Second Coming was 'Who would not be glad to see
Jesus Christ?' But perhaps finest of all is his thrilling ordination hymn,
which may one day be included in an ecumenical ordinal:

> The Saviour when to heaven he rose
> In splendid triumph o'er his foes,

> Scattered his gifts on men below,
> And wide his royal bounties flow.
>
> From Christ their varied gifts derive,
> And fed by Christ their graces live;
> While guarded by his mighty hand,
> Midst all the rage of hell they stand,
>
> So shall the bright succession run
> Through the last courses of the sun;
> And unborn churches by their care
> Shall rise and flourish large and fair.

Most of his hymns become airborne and move into the heavenly dimension, not least the moving 'God of my life through all my days' with its true premonition of his own good end:

> When death o'er nature shall prevail,
> And all the powers of language fail,
> Joy through my swimming eyes shall break,
> And mean the thanks I cannot speak.

For running through Doddridge's life from its beginnings to the end, there is the ground bass of mortality, the falling shadow of death, the whiff of corruption and disease, and amid all the cheerfulness and kindness, his hymns remind us of that with which husbands and wives, fathers and friends ever had to contend. The seventeenth century knew all about mortality, too, as marbled tombs bear witness; and for one generation the Great Plague had been a traumatic experience, a long-drawn-out Hiroshima. But death in childbirth, death of little children, deaths of young theological students and of ministers just setting out on a promising life's work—here is something which the volumes of funeral sermons preserved in Dr. Williams's Library testify about the Doddridge generation. Many of Doddridge's letters and sermons were concerned to comfort those in grief and in bereavement. There is reason enough why mortality and immortality jostle one another in his hymns, and why, having met the grimmest experiences of the human condition, he could none the less still, as a Christian, sing.

12

THE DISSENTING ACADEMIES

THE Dissenting Academies were the one sweet use which adversity brought the Nonconformists. Not only did they ensure the continuance of an educated Dissenting ministry, but they made a notable contribution to the history of education in England.

They arose directly from the Clarendon Code. It was natural that some of the ejected ministers, save for a handful who could get employment as ushers or tutors in genteel families, should turn to teaching. Their expulsion and exclusion from Oxford and Cambridge meant that the future of their Churches was in jeopardy, not only in respect of ministerial training, but for the sons of the laity. With no central planning, and no carefully thought-out educational theory, Academies sprang up now here, now there, in all parts of the country.

From the beginning the enterprises were hazardous: the more successful, the quicker the envious hostility of churchmen was aroused. The obsolete Stamford Oath (which dated from the restrictive jealousies of medieval Universities—Luther had been in hot water for taking his higher degrees at Wittenberg rather than Erfurt) forbade Oxford alumni to teach elsewhere. Under the Act of Uniformity, soon supported by the heavier sanctions of the Conventicle Act, it was forbidden to teach without licence from a bishop, and even after the Toleration Act it was necessary to subscribe to all but three of the Thirty-nine Articles. The first seminaries had often to go underground and their Principals into hiding, in some resemblance to the Confessing Church under the Nazis and Bonhoeffer's seminary at Finkenwalde.

Three phases have been noted in the development of the movement. First, the vulnerable early period when laws were enforced against them, and when the existence of the seminaries was precarious, often having to move from one place to another or collapsing altogether on the death of their founder. The second phase may be dated from the time of the Toleration Act, though it was not until the abortion of the Schism Act at the end of the reign of Anne that the Dissenters had room to breathe. This was a time when funds and subscriptions were well organized, when Dissent had realized it had somehow acquired crown jewels, and when Academies like those of Philip Doddridge at Northampton could offer a broad education, attractive and competent, with the benefits of a disciplined community life. The third phase, later in the eighteenth century, was marked by the consolidation of fully fledged institutions with their Boards of Trustees. It reached its climax perhaps in the Warrington Academy (the 'Athens of the North') with its learned and versatile staff, coruscating with honorary Scottish doctorates. The removal of the ban on Nonconformist teaching in 1779, and problems of discipline and politics, led to the disappearance of the Academies and their replacement by schools and by theological colleges.

A Dissenting Academy was exactly what a former grateful pupil, Thomas Secker, described as 'an extraordinary place of education'. Its core was a pattern of theological training, but from the first the Academies were open to the laity, and their fame and their sobrieties led some Anglicans to send their sons, as Samuel Wesley observed at Morton's Academy where 'not a few knights' and baronets' sons and one Lord's son were sent to avoid the debauchery of the Universities.'

Nobody can discuss the merits of the Academies without taking note of the rather damp squibs exchanged between Samuel Wesley, who had left the Newington Green Academy for Oxford and conformity, and Samuel Palmer, who stoutly defended them (but also later conformed). In 1703 a *Letter from a Country Divine* was published, written by Samuel Wesley, but published without his knowledge or consent. To this Palmer replied, and when Wesley wrote a rambling and incoherent defence of his original letter, Palmer wrote a second. It is a useful rule to take seriously anything Wesley says on behalf of the Academies and any admission by Palmer of their defects.

What is more important is that both men were looking back, in remembrance of times past, to what they had known twenty years earlier. In fact the debate is coloured by the situation in the first years of the reign of Anne. In 1703 there had appeared the second volume of Clarendon's *History of the Rebellion*. In the Preface there was a waspish reference to the Academies:

It may be consider'd what can be the meaning of the several Seminaries, and as it were, Universities set up in diverse parts of the Kingdom by more than ordinary Industry, supported by large contributions; where the Youth is brought up in Principles directly contrary to Monarchical and Episcopal government.

And the author ominously added, with reference to Nonconformist jollities on 30 January,

whether this does not look like an industrious propagation of the Rebellious principles of the last Age and on that score render it necessary that Your

Majesty should have an eye toward such unaccountable proceedings: is humbly submitted to Your Majesty.

Edmund Calamy's abridgement of Richard Baxter's autobiography had attracted hostile comment, soon to be reinforced by his *Memorials* of the ejected Nonconformists, which in turn gave rise to Walker's *Sufferings of the Clergy*, at a time when the High Church Party was rapidly coalescing under Atterbury and Sacheverell.

So it was that Samuel Wesley's laboured anecdotes stress the sour undercurrent of disloyalty and Republican sentiments kept alive by the 'Calves' Head' clubs which were a counterpoint to the growing myth of Charles the Martyr. And while Palmer successfully defends the loyalty of such men as Morton to the State and their amity towards the Established Church—Philip Henry indeed kept 30 January as a sacred day—Palmer becomes confused and unconvincing about what some of the young men said among themselves and about sundry uproarious demonstrations.

But Wesley himself pays tribute to the character of Charles Morton, who founded the second Academy at Newington Green (1675–1706). Morton, sometime of Wadham College, Oxford, was a noted mathematician who was to end his career as Vice-President of Harvard. Himself a pupil of John Wilkins, he was eager to offer facilities for scientific study, and Wesley tells how the Academy had a fine garden, a bowling green 'and some not inconsiderable rarities with an air pump, thermometers and all sorts of mathematical instruments'.

He drew up his own compendium of logic and a systematic treatment of the arts and sciences included a review of political ideas consonant with the English constitution. We learn of facilities for the study of modern languages; and Morton achieved an educational breakthrough of sorts by carrying on part of the instruction in English rather than in Latin and by taking special care of the training in English.

He had a class for eloquence and his pupils declaim'd weekly in the English tongue, made orations and wrote epistles twice every week upon such subjects as he prescrib'd for them or upon such as they themselves chose to write upon. Sometimes they were ambassadors or agents abroad at foreign courts, and wrote accounts of their negotiations and reception in foreign Courts directed to the Secretary of State and sometimes to the sovereign himself. . . .

Thus he taught his pupils to write a masculine and manly stile, to write the most polite English and at the same time to know how to suit their manner as well to the subject they were to write upon as to the persons or degrees of persons they were to write to: and all equally free and plain, without foolish flourishes and ridiculous flights of jingling bombast in stile, or dull meanness of expression below the dignity of the subject or the character of the writer.[1]

But in the main Latin continued to be, as at the Universities, the ground base of learning and it was generally expected that most Academy students had already had some preliminary grounding in it. One difficulty in changing to English was that the textbooks, while admirably European in range, were in Latin, and heavily pressed tutors had either to write their own or to rely on one another's manuscripts which were passed round and in some cases handed on.

But Latin dominated, and the future bishops Thomas Secker and Joseph Butler owed much to the fact that at Tewkesbury Academy 'We are obliged to rise at five of the clock every morning, and to speak Latin always, except when below stairs among the family.'[2] Richard Frankland (1630–98)[3] was another outstanding character, 'entirely beloved' by his students. In 1695 he had eighty students at his college at Rathmell in Yorkshire. He had constantly to move. In 1690 some Yorkshire clergy prosecuted him, and he was excommunicated by the Consistory Court. The result was a prompt order from the King for his absolution, and on three other occasions the Archbishop of York quashed proceedings against him. Outstanding, too, was the Tewkesbury Academy under the learned Samuel Jones,[4] who had studied at Leyden under Witsius and Spanheim. He seems to have been a kindly man, though at the end he took to tippling and the effect on his temper was such as to impair the quality and good fame of his college.

There was little attempt to break the older educational pattern with its base of logic and rhetoric and the devotion of much time to the study of Latin and Greek classical authors. In the Puritan humanist tradition the sacred languages were still taken seriously. In many seminaries the Greek New Testament was gone through every year. Secker told Isaac Watts: 'I began to learn Hebrew as soon as I came hither . . . we read every day two verses apiece in the Hebrew Bible which we turn into Greek.'[5] At Findern, under Thomas Hill, students had to sing the Psalms 'not merely as rendered in Latin but in Greek too'. A tutor of even more severe stamp made his pupils sing them in the original Hebrew. (How the Puritans of the age of William Bedell would have approved!) On the other hand there were seminaries where Greek was

---

[1] F. Bastian, *Defoe's Early Life* (1981), p. 51.

[2] T. Gibbons, *Memoirs of the Rev. Isaac Watts, D.D.* (1780), p. 351.

[3] H. McLachlan, *English Education under the Test Acts* (Manchester 1941), p. 62; Bennett, *Tory Crisis*, p. 13.

[4] McLachlan, *English Education*, p. 126.   [5] Gibbons, *Memoirs*, p. 349.

taught without accents, and Hebrew without points. Other languages, as in Oxford and Cambridge, came off badly, and Jennings at Kibworth taught French without any idea at all of the way it should be pronounced!

A good teacher with a bad textbook will always be more effective than a poor teacher with a first-rate one, and it is difficult to know if in fact the Latin tomes were as dull as they sound. Many of them had been long in use at Oxford and Cambridge at least from the time when John Milton was an undergraduate. Wesley put into verse what he could remember of their names.

> Stalius & Suarez, Gassendus cum Zabarella,
> Et Keckermannus, tuq, Hereborde Pater!
> Hisce opus immortale tuum, Venerande Cracanthorp!
> Scheibleriq: ingens, Smiglecijq: Labor
> Carolus & Morton; Mortonius inclytus et tu,
>   Carole![6]

If older texts on logic sufficed, there were many teachers who, in philosophy, began with Descartes and went on to Locke and even to Newton. Charles Morton's interest in mathematics and science was paralleled in other Academies, but in John Eames, FRS, they possessed a layman of distinction, so that Thomas Secker was but one of those who migrated south to hear him. In theology the textbooks were those which represented the Reformed tradition, from Ames and Baxter to the grim pair, Wollebius and Turrettini, whose memory was recalled to our time by the *Dogmatik* of Karl Barth.

The most remarkable subject, which seems a premonition of those partly prophetic, partly bogus, subjects which seem to flourish in schools of education, was 'Pneumatologia', on which several handbooks were written, and which might include anatomy and elementary psychology, the relation of mind to spirit, and some natural philosophy.[7]

Doddridge wisely insisted that the students follow his example and learn shorthand. But a good deal of the teaching method continued to be tedious, an unending dictation of notes, the cold porridge of yesterday's lessons warmed up for rehearsal on the following day, and much passing of notebooks tatty and dog-eared, from one generation of students to another. There were many good teachers who got results, and perhaps few were as naïve as the well-meaning lecturer who each day asked the fatal question, 'Gentlemen, have I made myself clear?', opening the door to endless filibustering.

[6] S. Wesley, *A Defence of a Letter* . . . (1704), p. 51.
[7] McLachlan, *English Education*, p. 276.

The course generally was five years for theological students and three for lay students. The theological students had, as well as their Biblical studies, to attend to homiletics and the preparation of sermons which were read and preached in the college and outside in the neighbouring churches.

In the early Academies, when tutors set up school in their own houses, it was not possible for many students to be in residence. Later, when larger buildings could be openly acquired, they became seminaries where students could chum together. Some of the sets of rules about their community life give an attractive picture of small societies where all could know one another and where the students were indeed one family. And the young being what they always are, rules were needed to make explicit the customs of the house. They range from a system of small fines for those who stayed out or turned up late, or cut lectures, down to the vexed questions of making toasted cheese and keeping students away from the kitchen, while Doddridge's own youthful correspondence attests the perils to the more susceptible young men in a predominantly masculine community, of sitting at table with the Principal's daughters.

No doubt there was a flexibility of syllabus and freedom of discussion such as the older Universities lacked, so that a tutor like Jennings could even include a course on drama, which must have run against the grain of contemporary Nonconformist taste.

But it must be remembered that however much the Universities might have ceased to be as good as they never were, this was a period of exciting intellectual ferment and rising cultural standards, and of ever-widening horizons in science and philosophy. To these new currents the Dissenting seminaries were more open, though perhaps more vulnerable to the spirit of the time. Hidebound Oxford and Cambridge might be, but there are times, as superficial fashions sweep along, when there is something to be said for having an extra skin.

It seems likely that the Academies cast their nets too widely. To take in a series of new disciplines while maintaining in large part a rhetorical and classical tradition, meant that something had to go somewhere and that quality might suffer. There was a strangely modern proliferation of subjects and options, and one suspects that what was gained in width might be lost in depth, and that a number of the more mediocre students might go away with little more than the smell of learning.

To compare the Academies with Oxford and Cambridge would be a delicate and perhaps otiose task, though no writers seem to be able to avoid it. The older Universities, we have already suggested, are not to be written down or off, as centres of scholarship, still less as though no good teaching continued. If the half-century following the Restoration encouraged too many sons of the well-to-do to waste their time in lazy pleasures, if not debauchery, there were always poor students like Samuel Wesley and Samuel Johnson, and enough single-minded loners like Isaac Newton and John Byrom for us to believe that those who wanted learning could get it. And always, as Samuel Palmer conceded, the Universities had the advantages of buildings, gardens, and libraries, while Daniel Defoe may have made the most profound comment of all when he thought that where the Academies suffered in comparison with the Universities was in the matter of good conversation.

When in this present century historians began to recognize afresh the educational importance of the Dissenting Academies, claims were made which were perhaps a little too exuberant. The idea that new educational philosophies were at hand, from Bacon and Milton, and above all from Samuel Hartlib and his friend Comenius, and that these notions inspired the founders of the first Academies lacks demonstrative evidence. Hartlib himself was a marvel, but something of an intellectual Autolycus whose myriad ploys included alchemy and a Utopia on the Baltic coast, as well as his hoped-for college of liberal studies in London, and his notions swung from the brilliant to the crackpot. The Academies had, on the contrary, little doctrinaire planning about them, but arose from practical and urgent exigencies. And while the best teaching in the Academies and the learning of their ablest tutors need not fear comparison with that of the Universities, and while for divers reasons wealthy laymen might prefer to send their sons to the more sobering context of the Academies, Samuel Palmer was not alone in admitting that if their disabilities were once removed, the Non-conformists would flock to Oxford and to Cambridge. But if we cannot therefore claim for them as much as some historians have done, or see them in the van of educational studies, still less of modern methods and perspectives, they did have freedoms and flexibilities of their own, were able to make genuine fresh starts. Above all it seems they were able to encourage freedom of enquiry and discussion, more open than that of the Universities, which had come some way from the days when a Joseph Mede could ask his students at the end of each day 'What have you doubted today?'

It has been said that at least 300 names of former students at Nonconformist Academies can be found in the *Dictionary of National Biography*.[8] If the teachers did not make many contributions to learning, it was because a great deal of their energy had perforce to go into

---

[8] Ibid., p. 44.

textbooks and to teaching. A dozen or so bishops, peers like Harley and Bolingbroke, a distinguished company of lawyers and scientists, were profitable by-blows of the Academies into the outside world.

What mattered even more were the rank and file, the great majority of their students, through whom the Nonconformist Churches, Presbyterian, Congregationalist, Baptist, Unitarian, were able to keep alive the tradition of Biblical learning and piety, and be able to stand against the storms of cultural repression from without, and a recurrent anti-intellectualist peril from within. They gave their Churches, and through them contributed to the nation, a backbone of sound education and moral discipline, fitting them to survive and meet the intellectual and moral demands of a century of change.

13

THE ENGLISH CATHOLICS

CATHOLICS have appeared many times in our narrative, and often in invidious roles. We have seen how urgent and bitter was the opposition to them of many even among the Non-Jurors, at a time when the existence of the Church of England seemed at stake. For while the Nonconformist bodies had their own tradition, their own polities and ethos, and would have gone about the business of surviving in their different ways, had James II been able to return England to the Catholic fold, the Church of England, as an established national Church, was more drastically threatened. Neither the historic episcopate nor the liturgy could have prevented its reduction to a sect, perhaps of not much more than non-juring proportions, within a generation. Hence the intensity of the great argument. For if 'No Popery' as a popular outcry merited the terms which modern historians have taken from psychiatry —paranoia, obsession, etc.,—there was none the less a remnant of opposition which was rational and learned.

The refugees who streamed into and through England in the opening decades of the eighteenth century were reminders that there were lively and present events which amounted to something more than a mindless harking back to Marian martyrs, the Armada, and the Gunpowder Plot. G. K. Chesterton once told of a story he would like to write: about a band of pioneers who set sail for unknown lands. Buffeted by storms, and driven out of their way, they were eventually cast up on a distant shore, to find it was Brighton beach and that they had come home. They would have, said Chesterton, two contradictory, but fundamental, experiences: they would know the hazardous adventure of pioneers, but they would also have the experience of coming home to their own land.

Something of that double rhythm was the fate of the English Catholic community from the sixteenth to the nineteenth centuries. Indubitably, England was a *pays de mission*. This was the official verdict on the character of the English mission and determined its administration, and its governance from the office of Propaganda. On the other hand their roots in England were deep and ancient. The family of Bonaventure Giffard had been continuously Catholic in England from before the

Norman Conquest. It was not only the nostalgic ruins of Rievaulx and Fountains which were reminders of 'the old religion'.

Every parish church, every English cathedral bore on its walls the record of incumbents and dignitaries, a large part of whom belonged within a Catholic pedigree. And while perhaps the 'Englishness' of the English Catholics has been a little exaggerated by some historians, yet the old Catholic families among the nobility and landed gentry were so obviously rooted in England that their Protestant peers and neighbours could indeed manage to live peaceably together since they were joined with them by deep spiritual and material ties.

The reign of James II saw changes in the form of the administration of the English Mission which were of permanent importance. In the absence of a diocesan framework with bishops-in-ordinary, which was judged impracticable and undesirable for England, there had been various temporary expedients, Archpriests, one single bishop, and with the exile of Bishop Smith in 1613, the rule of the Chapter, which endured until the appointment in the reign of James I, of first one, then two, and finally four vicars-apostolic.[1] The leaders of the secular clergy had pleaded for bishops-in-ordinary to be appointed, and had persuaded the King that it was in his interest to have such bishops who would have full and inherent authority, instead of clergy who as bishops *in partibus infidelium* had no sees of their own in England and were tied to more direct papal rule. But the decision from Rome was for vicars-apostolic, and it was one of the few hours of sunlight during the troubled months of James's reign that the new bishops were able to be formally appointed, Bonaventure Giffard as Bishop of Madura being solemnly installed in Inigo Jones's splendid Banqueting House in Whitehall. The country was divided into four districts, London, the North, the Midlands, and the West. Save for the exception of Bishop Williams, a Dominican who was appointed to the Northern District in 1725, only the Vicar in the West was from the ranks of the religious. But it soon became clear that there were difficulties, which bade fair to revive the disastrous and bitter disputes between the secular and religious of Elizabeth's time. The religious orders themselves were, they thought, pre-eminently suited for mission. And if some of them in isolated stations lived almost the life of secular priests and were cut off from their communities, still they had their own superiors and 'they asserted that the Pope as head over the whole church' had the right 'to send his missionaries anywhere with faculties from himself.'

A special problem was the question whether the faculty to hear

[1] B. Hemphill, *The Early Vicars Apostolic of England 1685–1750*, 1954.

confessions, according to the disciplinary measures of the Council of Trent, needed the approbation of the secular clergy, or whether this approval was, as the regulars claimed, a mere formality. Also involved were the leading laity, who had been accustomed to choose and to dismiss their own chaplains who were regular clergy, and who now saw their liberties menaced by the authority of the seculars. Both sides appealed to Rome, and in 1696 Pope Innocent XI issued a decree to the effect that all regulars were subject to the vicars-apostolic as regards an approbation for confessions and other offices affecting cure of souls and the administration of the sacraments.[2]

Discord continued, however, and in 1739 the vicars-apostolic formally asked Rome for definite regulations. A papal brief of 1745 confirmed the authority of the secular clergy, but it was not received in England until 1748, and the reception by the regulars was so uneven and so grudging that once again there came pressures from both sides in Rome. The Pope appointed a commission of cardinals from Propaganda who spent two years going thoroughly into the complex question and the result was the document *Apostolicum Ministerium* (30 May 1753) which laid down rules of mission which prevailed for the next century. Benedict XIV was himself a distinguished canonist and had seen to it that his judgement was clear and as far as possible, definitive. It fully supported the jurisdiction of the vicars-apostolic and if some of its recommendations—e.g. the 'six-year' rule which would send regular missioners back to their communities after six years in the world—were the subject of further queries, the main issue was now settled. Bishop Challoner, who had been deeply involved in the controversy in the last years, behaved with tact and wisdom, and when in 1773 disaster overtook the Jesuit order, was able and forward to take measures for their aid and protection.[3]

Some of the vicars-apostolic had no financial problems, for they were, like Bishop Smith, heirs to great estates or, like Witham, possessed of a large annuity. It was very different for others, among them Bonaventure Giffard, who had again and again to face great fines and periods of imprisonment. He bore continual harassments and real sufferings with noble patience though he could not sometimes forbear from speaking of them to his friends, as to Laurence Mayes:

I have had all your letters, though at present cannot set down the dates, being tossed about into different lodgings . . . I had a poor garret at the Venetian ambassador's which served for a lodging, oratory, dining room kitchen, etc. but

---

[2] E. H. Burton, *The Life and Times of Bishop Challoner* (1909), i. 251.
[3] Burton, *Bishop Challoner*, i. 306.

the Ambassador being upon his remove I am forced to seek another habitation
. . . if your great men saw my circumstances they would be much surprised.
However such was the life of our Divine Master.[4]

The vicars-apostolic who came from the religious orders had no sort
of financial backing. Perhaps the most poignant case was the appointment of the Dominican Bishop Williams, unknown and, it seems,
unwanted, to the Northern District, who, after months of difficult and
frustrating journeys across Europe, landed unexpected and unmet on
the Northumbrian coast, alone, penniless, and with nowhere to lay his
head. But friends were soon around him, and he won the hearts of a
northern people who know more about hospitality than most.
Gradually subscriptions were raised, and he lived as a guest in the house
of Sir Edward Gascoigne. It was not an end of his financial difficulties
which persisted for several more years, but these he patiently bore.

Bonaventure Giffard attracts our attention as one of the notable
vicars-apostolic because he was such a great survivor. His long life went
back to the days of Cromwell and he had exercised a precarious
episcopate for forty-five years, imprisoned, in hiding, and often on the
run, and through ninety-one years he had lived Christianly as seeing
Him who is invisible.

On the other hand, in the Northern District Bishop James Smith was
able to conduct his visitations in public as a report from a green-eyed
Vicar of Blackburn to the Archbishop of Canterbury, 3 November 1709
clearly showed.

The number of the papists . . . was very great: Mr. Hull, my curate at
Samlesbury Chapel tells me that he saw multitudes go that way past his house
some on foot, some on horseback, most of them with little children in their
arms. But the greatest concourse of people was on Sunday because the bishop
was to preach that day . . . I think the papists have been a little more reserved
this, than they were the last time the bishop was in this neighbourhood. For
then they made great boasts of their vast numbers.[5]

But if the framework of administration was that of the secular clergy
under the guidance of the vicars-apostolic, the part played by the
religious in the English mission continued to be important. 'Until the
very end of the eighteenth century religious outnumbered secular clergy
on the English mission.' The Jesuits played the major role, but the
second-largest group, the Benedictines, played an important middle
role, though their numbers fell away in the later part of the eighteenth

[4] Hemphill, *The Early Vicars-Apostolic*, p. 47.
[5] G. Anstruther, *The Seminary Priests* (4 vols., Gt. Wakering 1975), iii. 206.

century.[6] The Franciscans and Dominicans exercised smaller missions, but both supplied vicars-apostolic, the Franciscan Bishop Pritchard in the West and Bishop Williams, a Dominican, in the North.

i. Pains and Penalties

In the eyes of the law the English Catholics were gagged, fettered, and bound by a multiplicity of restraints and penalties. In recurrent times of crisis proclamations again and again threatened their enforcement. No doubt a comparative table of the measures against Protestants and Catholics in other parts of Europe needs to be borne in mind. The more outrageous demands by pamphlet or by speech, that all Catholics should be deported, had at least a parallel in the mass expulsions of Protestants in Germany, and the nasty suggestion that Catholics should be forced 'like the Jews at Rome' to wear a mark of distinction on the crowns of their hats, visible to all men, reminds us that invidious discrimination could be practised at the heart of Catholic Christendom. It is not irrelevant, when one considers the peril in which the English Government stood from Jacobite plot, from assassination and invasion, to say that any government in such a crisis, must take measures against a fifth column, with, as in the case of the internment of Germans in England in 1940 and of Japanese by the Americans after Pearl Harbour, an ugly element of intolerance and injustice.

None the less, on paper and only too often in practice it was a pattern of harassment which far outwent the harsh treatment of the Nonconformists. It is true that the most dire of the Elizabethan laws (27 Elizabeth, cap. 2) which imposed the terrible penalties for treason on priests returning from abroad, was still on the statute book, but it was because it was practically unenforceable that the Act of 11 William III substituted life imprisonment.[7] Yet this was no empty gesture. Hurst Castle was set aside for the grim purpose and one priest at least, Father Atkinson, lingered there until his death thirty years on.[8] In 1689 the machinery of law for dealing with recusancy was updated and new oaths of allegiance imposed in such a way that no Catholic could take them. But anybody refusing the oaths could be imprisoned.[9]

After each real or imagined plot and rebellion, in 1696, 1700, 1706,

---

[6] J. H. C. Aveling, 'The Eighteenth Century English Benedictines', in *Challoner and his Church*, ed. E. Duffy (1981), p. 154. 'In 1773 the total of regulars returned by the vicars-apostolic to Propaganda was 217, 121 Jesuits, 44 Benedictines and 52 others' J. Bossy, *The English Catholic Community, 1570–1850* (1975), p. 218.

[7] H. Aveling, *Northern Catholics* (1966), p. 139.

[8] J. A. Williams, *Catholic Recusancy in Wiltshire* (CRS 1968), p. 50.

[9] Aveling, *Northern Catholics*, p. 336.

1715, 1722, new measures were put out, or the enforcement of old ones threatened. The network of fines and financial penalties became more and more intricate. Baptisms, marriages, funerals were subject to penalties. Restrictions were renewed on travel and Catholics forbidden to remain in London.

In the various Jacobite scares searches were made for arms and horses. It had long been an offence to send children abroad to be educated, and efforts were made to stop Catholic money going out of the country. More threatening were the financial measures against the nobility and landed gentry, and though their bark was generally worse than their bite there is no doubt at all they produced alarm, and even panic, among leading Catholic families.[10] In 1692 a double land tax was imposed on Catholics, but after the 1715 rising two new statutes (1 Geo., caps. 50; 55) claimed that two-thirds of Catholic property was due to the State and that they should bear the charges incurred in suppressing the rebellion. In 1714 and 1717 compulsory registration of all property was ordered, as well as of all transactions, settlements, and mortgages. After the Atterbury plot in 1722 a special levy of £100,000 was imposed. Catholics could not in theory exercise the vote or practise as barristers. Their property was at the mercy of Protestant kinsmen who might sue for it.

The difficulties involved for Catholics in swearing oaths of allegiance were complex and would remain until 1791.

But a great many penalties were not enforced. Not by any means all of the Catholic gentry were 'recusant convicts' and class sympathy and tolerance rendered much of the legislation innocuous. It has been estimated that the clergy returning figures of Papists to Archbishop Herring for his Visitation in 1743 could only have reported one in four of the priests practising in their midst. Once the memory of the '45 died away there was growing sympathy for relief for Catholics. When in 1772 the famous case of Anne Fenwick of Hornby whose possessions had been seized by her Protestant brother-in-law, was won, it was the end of such attempts to seize Catholic property, and was hailed by Fox and Burke as well as the boys of Sedgeley College whose President wrote:

I treated ye Masters with a Sneaker of Punch to drink the health of so true and worthy a friend, and gave a play day to the boys ordering them to give 4 Huzzas as loud as their mouths could stretch, with 'A Fenwick for ever!' which was accordingly done with hats flying in the air.[11]

---

[10] E. Duffy, 'Englishmen in Vaine: Roman Catholic Allegiance to George I', in *Studies in Church History*, ed. S. Mews (Oxford 1982), p. 348.

[11] *Anne Fenwick of Hornby* (Lancaster 1977), p. 17.

In the most difficult years, between 1700 and 1715, there are plenty of stories of harassment and impoverishment. Bonaventure Giffard was hounded from pillar to post, in 1714 changing his lodgings fourteen times in five months, 'being under a persecution which obliges me to scamper about and often change lodgings and seek hiding holes.' When the agent, Laurence Mayes, was in financial straits in Rome because the English bishops had not been able to send his money, Giffard sent him £10 with the comment: 'I have been twice stripped of all I had in the world. No less than £600 taken from me at the first time. At the second all my fine ornaments and whatever belonged to my office taken away.'[12]

ii. Richard Challoner (1691–1781)

'Unimaginative . . . unoriginal', 'no poetry', 'conservative', 'doing things by the book'. These are not the adjectives generally applied to great spiritual leaders, and not one of them, for example, would be used of St Francis of Sales. On the strength of them we might suppose that Richard Challoner was a five-talent man whose industry improved his gains to ten. But this would be quite wrong, though it is true that his greatness lies otherwhere than among the more glamorous charismata. Sober, even sombre, might be his temperament, but he was greatly loved and deeply reverenced, and is deservedly reckoned the outstanding English Catholic leader in the period of his long life.[13]

Both Belloc and Kipling might for different reasons have sung the praise of so worthy a son of downland Sussex. But it was in Northamptonshire in his teens that he was trained and received into the Church by John Gother, the chaplain to the Lady Anastasia Holman, in whose service Richard's mother was employed. They sent him to Douai in 1705 and he was ordained in 1716. He was made Vice-President of the College and Professor of Theology, and took his DD in 1727. In 1730 he entered the English mission at a critical time, when on the one hand Catholics were still oppressed by the aftermath of the '15, but also when they were engaged in aggressive and successful mission among the middle and poorer classes, and when their achievements in the towns, and above all in London, more than offset their losses in the countryside. As a true spiritual son of John Gother, Challoner found the London District his true element and he was always more at home with

---

[12] Hemphill, *The Early Vicars-Apostolic*, p. 93.

[13] Burton, *Bishop Challoner*; Duffy (ed.), *Challoner and his Church*; Hemphill, *Early Vicars-Apostolic*, pp. 145ff. Anstruther, *Seminary priests*, iv. 59. E. Duffy, 'Richard Challoner and the Salesian Tradition', *Clergy Review*, lxvi, Dec. 1981.

middle-class merchants like his friend William Mawood than among the aristocracy. Like Gother, he was drawn into controversial divinity, but, like him, turned with relief and pleasure into writing works of devotion and edification.

Discipline, abnegation, commitment to a rigid timetable channelled his energies fruitfully in a devoted and inspiring ministry in the streets and alleys of London, a cure of souls which did not neglect their material, and even medical, needs (there were large charities available which he was glad to administer), while surrounding them all with his prayers. Benjamin Petre, the ineffectual angel of the London District for whom 'Nolo episcopari' was not so much a sentiment as a way of life, knew how to value this man whom he had made his Vicar-General. So that when Douai chose Challoner for its President, for one rare moment Petre was roused to energetic firmness, dug his toes in, and got his way, with the result that Challoner was appointed his coadjutor and consecrated Bishop of Debra on the feast day of his beloved Francis of Sales. Petre's encomium is worth quoting:

he has scarcely reached his 49th year but by his many remarkable gifts of mind, his great humility and gentleness, by his assiduous fidelity in reclaiming sinners . . . by his marvellous power in preaching, in instructing the ignorant and in writing books . . . he has won not only the esteem but the veneration of all who have heard him.[14]

For the next twenty years Challoner served him as his coadjutor and in 1758 succeeded him as vicar-apostolic of the London District. It covered a wide area, roughly within a triangle of Hertfordshire, Kent and Hampshire, and was served by about sixty secular priests and a hundred or so religious, chiefly Jesuits and Franciscans. He was therefore necessarily much occupied with the discipline of his clergy, some of whom, and especially those in the not-so-get-at-able embassy chapels, were certainly in need of oversight. He found that regular conferences of clergy (like the Anglican London clergy in the time of Compton) were an excellent vehicle for teaching, and for re-impressing on their minds the ideals of ministry which he expounded in a series of regulations.

For, in the footsteps of John Gother, Challoner realized that the need of the hour was for a ministry of preaching, teaching, and continuous instruction. The successes of the mission, which were real and growing, demanded that for the new converts there should be ministry in depth. His regular preachments in the Sardinian Chapel and in the Ship in Holborn were vigorous and solid. His edifying writings, especially his

---

[14] Hemphill, *Early Vicars-Apostolic*, p. 148.

Garden of the Soul and his *Meditations* were a seminal influence for generations, as were his version of the Bible, his attention to the lives of the saints and martyrs. He had a special care for the English saints which would have delighted Matthew Parker, but, like Parker, he found it was not easy to get this across to his superiors. Nor were his activities confined to London or to England. He kept an eye on things at Douai and took action to revive the seminaries in Lisbon and in Rome. He was well aware of the importance of education, himself founding the schools at Standon Lordship and Sedgeley Park. Although his devotional writings, in the Salesian spirit, concentrated on the centralities of the Christian faith, he was consciously and determinedly orthodox and had no room for the kind of accommodating Catholicism which had earlier been a mark of Blacklow and Sergeant and was to reappear in the Cisalpine clergy.

He was more than once forced to turn aside to administrative and ecclesiastical crises: the dispute over the claims of secular and regular clergy, the problems caused by the Hardwicke Marriage Act of 1753, and the even more intricate and delicate matters raised by the attempts to secure Catholic relief in 1778. That which came upon him daily was a great correspondence, a ministry of spiritual and practical counsel which touched many people in many walks of life. Like Bonaventure Giffard, his ministry extended into his great age, though he was better able to keep his authority and his wits about him. It was cruel that having achieved so much and seen such a transformation of the English Catholic plight, he should have had to endure the malice and the violence of the Gordon Riots, even though the underlying situation was not much altered, for he had indeed led his people to the edge of a Promised Land. But he had learned amid the fire and earthquake to listen for the voice of gentle stillness, and throughout the hubbub good friends lovingly cared for him on the edge of smoking London, where he died in January 1781.

The English Catholics, as a cross-section of English society, differed greatly from the Nonconformists, who, apart from the Commonwealth period when they had, so to speak, hijacked the Establishment, and apart from the affluent circle around the Countess of Huntingdon, had few noble or gently born within their ranks.

But the Catholics were well rooted in the ancient families of England and something of a crisis arose when in the eighteenth century the upper crust began to crumble. The two words 'apostate' and 'convert' are absolutes, but in fact they cover a wide range of motive, between fear and self-interest and honest conviction. Such conversions and desertions were a two-way traffic, causing little splashes of scandal and a small pamphlet literature on both sides. And we need to remember not to press statistics too hard, for more depended on quality than on numbers.[15]

The weakening of Catholic links with the gentry was serious at a time when as a propertied class they were of pivotal political and social importance, though it was important that trade and industry were a direction into which Catholic missionary effort could be fruitfully turned. There were gains by the Catholics in the new towns and in the enlarging cities, and not least in the mission to the poor which presented opportunities seized with urgency and compassion.

None the less the losses were real. The number of Catholic peers had shrunk from twenty-four to seven by 1791. There is a long list of notable Catholic families lost, 'the Gages and Shelleys of Sussex, the Giffords of Staffordshire, the Swinburnes and Brandlings of Northumberland, the Gascoignes, Tankreds, and Smithsons of Yorkshire, the Chichesters of Devonshire'.[16]

Rich men furnished with ability have always had a part to play in the history of the Church, though they have sometimes been an intolerable nuisance. But the Catholic gentry of England exercised a traditional authority within the Catholic community more than strong enough to offset any signs of a too intrusive clericalism, whether from the secular or religious clerical side. When they chose and appointed their chaplains, their attitude to their spiritual employees was not much different from that of their Anglican neighbours. The famous incident of the chaplain waiting at Mass until his employer should say to him 'Mr . . . you may begin' has its place alongside the even more famous story of the Anglican curate dismissed from table before the jellies were brought in.

The defection of the head of a gentle family invariably meant losses among dependents and employees, the drying up of benevolences which had subsidized mission and education and sustained priests and Mass centres. To the defections caused by straitened finances, and in some cases bankruptcy, and to the effect of the economic pressures of the penal laws, there must be added the relatively small, but continuous, trickle of those conscientiously converted to the Church of England, and much less frequently to Dissent and Methodism.[17] One feature of

---

[15] E. Duffy, '"Over the Wall": Converts from Popery in eighteenth century England', *Downside Review*, xciv, Jan. 1976; E. Duffy, '"Poor Protestant Flies": conversions to Catholicism in early Eighteenth Century England', in *Studies in Church History*, ed. D. Baker, vol. xv, Oxford 1978; E. Duffy, *Peter and Jack: Roman Catholics and Dissent in eighteenth century England*, Friends of Dr. Williams Library, Lecture 36, 1982.

[16] H. Aveling, *The Handle and the Axe* (1976), p. 262.

[17] Duffy, 'Over the Wall'.

the period, which was non-theological (save for the longish line of sons who joined the celibate clergy) was the failure of many Catholic families in the male line.

But if the losses among the upper classes were notable enough to create something of a historical myth for Catholic interpretation between Berington and Newman, there is evidence that the losses were more than made good as the mission penetrated the middle and lower classes, and turned from the country to the towns and to the new industrial undertakings. The statistics are confusing, and have not perhaps been definitively evaluated,[18] but it is likely that in the first seventy years of the century the English Catholic community moved from over 60,000 to under 80,000. After the measures of emancipation, it grew at an ever-increasing rate. Like the Baptists, the Quakers, and the Methodists, there were Catholics who profitably turned to banking and to industry. Sir Henry Lawson of Brough in Yorkshire was a striking example of one who cherished traditional loyalties and pedigree, but who

as his business records—banking transactions, colliery accounts, factory accounts show—was a shrewd man of affairs with an eye to every possible source of profit. He imported coffee from the plantations he had bought in Jamaica: he opened a 'pott and pantile' factory at Byker.[19]

The number of Catholics in London seems to have been about 20,000 and to have increased steadily throughout the century.[20] London was beginning to sprawl, though its core was still surprisingly compact (Challoner's, Johnson's, Wesley's London could be crossed in a stroll). There was a whole range of residences, from the large town houses of the merchants and the aristocracy, many still in the old City, but closing up in the new and impressive squares to the north and west of Holborn. In the East End and in the St Giles area were swarming slums, and here Irish Catholics were compressed. Between the extremes there were the tradesmen, the skilled workmen, and the professional class, and the shops, though these were not so numerous as they would become when the great markets were reduced in number. It was to this field of mission that the vicars-apostolic, Giffard, Petre, and Challoner turned their attention. Recent historians have dismissed the view that the Catholics were driven underground, a Church 'under the Cross' living in the catacombs (even though catacombs in the third century were far from

[18] J. Bossy, *The English Catholic Community*, ch. 8.

[19] Aveling, *The Handle and the Axe*, p. 267.

[20] Burton, *Bishop Challoner*, chs. 5 and 6. Duffy, 'Poor Protestant Flies', pp. 289ff; Duffy (ed.), *Challoner and his Church*, ch. 1; Aveling, *The Handle and the Axe*, ch. 14.

being like the London Underground during the Blitz). In most parts of the country, and for most of the time, Catholics could go about openly, if discreetly. Yet their worship was legally illicit, and there was always the possibility of menace. They were not, after all, less harried than the Non-Jurors who had a good deal to put up with. So we need not play down the old stories: Challoner preaching in the Ship Tavern amid the beer mugs and the pipes; Moxon moving between a dozen inns and garrets; the famous gathering in Shoreditch in 1725 when constables stumbled on what must have looked and smelled like a glorified doss-house, but was in fact a stubborn Irish Mass centre. But it is true enough that, while the authorities had a surprising propensity for counting heads, they generally did nothing more, comforted by the thought that they knew where to lay hands on Catholics if a real crisis came.

Despite the high quality of pastoral care in the Anglican parishes of St Martin's and St Giles (even if it had fallen away from the days of Tenison and Sharp) it was here in the crowded tenements of the poor that the Catholic missioners made their gains. The first two Anglican charity schools in the area seem to have been in response to Jesuit schools in the Savoy and in St Giles. John Gother and Richard Challoner were as assiduous as John Wesley in writing simple tracts for the poor, and in providing medical advice and financial aid. Such devoted and continuous ministry was successful, and there seems to have been a surge forward in the 1730s. Moxon Harvey's diary records some ninety converts in seven years, among which the largest group were 'marriage' converts.

Where Catholics could meet for worship overtly and regularly was in the embassy chapels of the Catholic powers (slightly at the mercy of foreign policy as when for a short time there was an alliance with the Emperor, susceptible to governmental pressure). The large Sardinian Embassy in Duke Street, Lincoln's Inn, has been described as the 'Cathedral' of the London Catholic community, and there was a tendency for affluent Catholics to find their own residences in the area from Lincoln's Inn westward to Soho where the main Catholic embassies were. The building erected for the Sardinian Chapel in 1760 was impressively rococo and its two galleries and spacious interior could accommodate a large congregation, which it invariably did, and which ranged from the seated well-to-do, to the poor who thronged the nave. The Embassy had what has been called 'a handful' of about thirty clergy—but this was far larger than the Sardinian community needed and it had in mind the English Catholic diaspora. But they were appointed and controlled by the Embassy and were often a very mixed bag. But here at least a full range of services and sacraments was

available—Masses, Confessions, Vespers, Complines and Benedictions
—with organists like Arne and Webbe, and the best Italian musicians. It
was frequented by Protestant visitors to London, as one of the places to
which one went. But there were also Anglican churches well worth
seeing, as anybody remembers who has seen Canaletto's *Thames from
Richmond House* with its tiara of lovely new Wren churches on the
horizon. And James Gibbs's (a Catholic) St Mary-le-Strand is a little
baroque marvel which might have hopped Loreto-like straight from
the streets of Italy. And there was after all plenty of fine English
church music available, though some of the best of it, alas, more
accessible outside the churches which looked askance at oratorios.

Though Catholics were kept away from Court, they mingled in the
upper levels of the large and glittering London society. There was a
constant infiltration of artists and craftsmen supporting Catholic interest
in the arts, in singing and instrumental music at a time when public
concerts were becoming numerous. Like the great poets Dryden and
Pope, Gibbs and Arne and J. C. Bach were honoured. There were some
notable temporary conversions, Edward Gibbon, James Boswell,
Christopher Smart, and Charles Wesley's son Samuel (in a community
which perhaps has a high share of 'in and out'ers').

The splendid circle of friends which included Samuel Johnson, the
Burneys, and the Thrales had all their Catholic friends and relatives. As
to Edmund Burke, the champion of their liberties, with his Catholic
background and his throng of Catholic relatives, recent historians have
perhaps done more justice to his Catholic sympathies than to his loyalty
to the Established Church of England.

iii. Spirituality

A comparative study of spirituality in England from 1688 onwards
might have surprising results. For though it would be wrong to speak of
an ecumenical overspill in times when, in worship at least, the Catholics
strove to keep unspotted from the Protestants, there is no doubt of the
wide impact of Catholic devotional material from the Continent, via
France and Holland, which brought the riches of French, Spanish, and
Italian mystical writings into the devotion of English Christians of
many kinds. Nor was this infection a novelty. The convergent interests
in moral theology of Puritans, Jesuits, and Arminian divines had led
Puritans, for example, to make use of Catholic material such as Bunny's
Resolutions. Students of Richard Baxter have perhaps overstressed his

debt to Catholic sources in his insistence on the importance of meditation.

The Imitation of Christ, trailing clouds of glory from the lay spirituality of the modern devotion, appeared in new Protestant, as well as Catholic, translations, and as *The Christian's Pattern*—John Worthington's edition and John Wesley's revision—went into many editions.

Although St Francis of Sales intended his *Introduction to the Devout Life* for a very wide audience, it perhaps had a special appeal for young women of the aristocracy, and it is not surprising to find young ladies at the Court of William and Mary passing round their French copy (his chapters 'Des amourettes' and 'Des vrayes amitiés' perhaps badly needed to be read in the Court of Mary and of Anne). And when we are speaking of the Salesian tradition we cannot possibly ignore Thomas Ken. For the sparkling qualities of Francis match Thomas Ken, as perhaps they do not at all fit Gother and Challoner—poetry, imagination, irony. When Ken turned ordinary catechetical material into a marvellous treatise on the Love of God,[21] his introduction, like the preface of St Francis, emphasized the peculiar responsibility of a bishop for the care of devotion. And if it was a great point of St Francis that he extended the scope of devotion from beyond the cloister to 'la compagnie des soldats . . . la boutique des artisans . . . la cour des princes, du ménage des gens mariés'. Thomas Ken went further and took thought for schoolboys in his hymns and in his *Manual of Prayers for Winchester Scholars* (which are addressed throughout, in the exact Salesian idiom, to 'Philotheus').[22] The specific Catholic writings of Gother and Challoner do not lose, but gain in interest, when we remember that an emphasis on devout study of Scripture, on catechisms, on manuals of prayer, above all on 'practical theology' was common to Anglican and Nonconformist spirituality.

Dr Duffy suggests that the main stream of English secular spirituality was an 'Anglicized Salesianism'. There has never been a work quite the equal of the *Introduction to the Devout Life* in the attractiveness of its appeal, its poetry and imagination, its tenderness and irony, and within the velvet glove an iron quality which underlies the whole in its demand for sacrifice and for commitment. And it is set in the chiaroscuro of the early seventeenth century, of heaven and hell and judgement and the direness and ultimacy of the decision for or against God. It provided for the secular clergy a counterpart of the Ignatian method, which could be directed to Christians of all kinds living in the world. Gother extended Francis's range when he wrote 'The Tradesman may find him in his

[21] Ken, *Prose Works*, ed. Benham, 'Exposition of the Church Catechism'.
[22] St Francis of Sales, *Oevres* (Annécy 1893), p. 20; Ken, *Prose Works*, pp. 211ff.

shop, the labourer at his work, the porter in the streets . . . the servant in the kitchen . . . and the afflicted in their distress.'[23]

There were a number of devotional works in the seventeenth century like those from Lisbon, of Edward Danniell and William Clifford, which continued the Salesian method. John Gother (1654–1704)[24] laid the foundation of the new kind of ministry in which the teacher should play an important role. Like his successor, Richard Challoner, his writings were plain and practical, and austere and demanding. His enemies mistook his austerity for Jansenism. But it is true that he laid stress on the careful preparation for Confession, and of careful examination of the soul, and he criticizes those who think they can run from Confession straight to Communion when they should rather begin a solemn preparation for Communion, which on the whole he thinks should be received once a month.[25] But it was Challoner whose writings provided an abiding pattern. His *Garden of the Soul* is, like most of his writings, an unoriginal compilation, and one wonders if there is more than its title to link it with the 'hortuli animae' of the early sixteenth century (the imagery seems to be taken from the Song of Songs, and it got into Protestant spirituality in sermons by Oecolampadius and the writings of Thomas Becon). It was plain and straightforward and superseded the customary 'Manual of Devotion' for many Catholic congregations. The structure was threefold: doctrine, faith, and morals.[26] 'What every Christian must believe—and do'. Prayers are mingled with instructions and there are devotions for hearing Mass. Near the beginning there are ten meditations translated from St Francis of Sales. The meditations have a threefold scheme: preparation, consideration, and practical resolutions. But they are what the age called 'inward religion', 'practical theology'. 'These considerations are not designed to be a matter of barren study or speculation of the brain: but to be the seeds of pious affections in the heart: which affections are looked upon by the spiritual writers as the principal part of mental prayer.'

[23] J. Gother, *Works* (16 vols. 1708), i. 108. It may perhaps not be too mean-minded to point out that Protestant spirituality had from the first been concerned with the devotion of the common man. Luther's letter to Peter the Barber, *A Simple Way to Pray*, in *Works* (Philadelphia 1968), p. 43.18, is such a work, and he uses the image so often used by St Francis, of weaving one's prayers into a spiritual nosegay, though I suspect it is a medieval image.

[24] Duffy, 'Richard Challoner and the English Salesian Tradition', p. 450; R. Luckett, 'Bishop Challoner the Devotionary Writer' in *Challoner and his Church*, ed. Duffy, ch. 4. Burton, *Life of Challoner*, 127–36. Duffy, 'Poor Protestant Flies', p. 294. Bossy, *English Catholic Community*, ch. 15.

[25] J. Gother, *Instructions and Devotions for Confession, Communion and Confirmation*, n.d.

[26] Duffy, 'Richard Challoner and the English Salesian Tradition', p. 453.

Hardly less seminal were Challoner's *Meditations for Every Day of the Year* and his powerful, meaty, but never flamboyant, preaching.

The phrase 'Garden of the Soul Catholics' shows how deep was the imprint of Challoner's devotional writings. Both Anglicans and Catholics talked about 'reformed devotions' in the sense of re-forming, and most manuals of prayer changed between editions, with additions and excisions. It seems interesting to look at one Catholic manual which, though not in the same class of influence, must have been widely read, and may represent a slightly different tradition, since it was sponsored by John Sergeant whom modern Catholic historians do not seem to like very much, but about whose later years we could bear to know more.

This work was called *Devotions in the Ancient Way of Offices, with Psalms, Hymns and Prayers for Every Day in the Week and Every Holiday in the Year.*[27] They are the impressive work of an English Catholic lawyer-layman (shades of Thomas More!) John Austin (1603–69). A Norfolk man, he was at St John's College, Cambridge, with John Sergeant, when they were both converted. He then went to Lincoln's Inn with which his name was associated. He travelled extensively and knew many languages. His prayers go back to the pattern of the primitive Church and there are offices for every day of the week, Mattins and Lauds, Vespers and Compline. There are also offices for 'Our Saviour's office', for the Holy Ghost and the Communion of Saints, and for preparation for death. There are some fine antiphons, and a series of psalms written by Austin which are in the main Scriptural meditations written with imagination and beauty. The hymns which are interspersed are not of high quality, and it is thought that one of his group of friends, a Mr Keightley, wrote most of the prayers.[28] It may be used, said the author, by individuals, but could even more appropriately be used by two people or by a Christian society. The first edition rapidly sold out, as Sergeant reported in his preface to the second, posthumous edition, which had an office for the Virgin. There were at least four further editions for Catholics, when the fine work was given a deservedly wider audience. It was 're-formed' by Mrs Susannah Hopton, an accomplished Anglican who had been converted to the Roman Church, but had been won back to the Church of England. She was probably a Non-Juror, for it was George Hickes who issued the eleventh edition, which became known rather unjustifiably as 'Hickes's Devotions' going through several more editions. Hickes commended it especially to the London Religious Societies, and John Wesley not only

[27] Paris 1668. There is a first edition in the Cambridge University Library.
[28] *DNB* s.v. J. Austin and J. Sergeant.

used it a great deal in Georgia, but included a drastically abbreviated version of the original *Austin's Devotions* in his Christian Library (shorn of its antiphons—one sometimes thinks John Wesley was liturgically tone deaf).[29] Although the Catholic material had been trimmed (especially the office for preparation for death), most of it remained, and as Hickes's eirenical preface shows, it is a welcome relief from the general repudiation of all things from the Catholic side.

Both Gother and Challoner were preachers and were much heard in what was still an age for sermon-crawling. Some Catholics, even Challoner's friend Mawood, seem to have gone to hear Protestants too, and it is certain that Protestants both heard and read the preachments of the outstanding Catholic preacher of the 1780s, James Archer, whose themes were those central to all Christians. The achievements of this group of Catholic leaders in the field of instruction, edification, and devotion can hardly be overestimated in a growing, missionary Church. It ensured that the converts were grounded in the doctrines, privileges, and duties of the Christian religion, where regained souls could be safely anchored.

iv. Relief

In the 1770s the English Catholics found themselves more able than for a long time to reconcile their loyalties. The Jacobite cause was dead, and George III was the first of the Hanoverians who by reason of his character and Englishness could attract the respect, and even the affection, of his subjects. The rash of attempts by common informers to harass Catholics had proved in the end almost counter-productive. But it was from a quite unexpected source that the impulse came which was to lead to the relief of Catholics by Act of Parliament. The American war forced the Government to seek Irish and Scottish Catholic warriors and in 1775 the Irish Parliament enacted that 'any person professing the Popish religion' might take a relatively simple oath of allegiance. Bishop Hay in Scotland thought the need for Scottish troops might be the opportunity to press, in return, for the end of all the penal laws. The Government in its turn initiated conversations through Sir John Dalrymple. He found that Bishop Challoner was most reluctant to become involved in such pressure on the Government, was sceptical of the goodwill of the politicians, and even more fearful of what might be the consequences in a popular backlash. The initiative was left therefore

---

[29] *Devotions in the Ancient way of Offices*, Reformed by a Person of Quality and published by George Hickes, DD (2nd edn.) 1701: R. Green, *Wesley Bibliography* (1896), p. 93.

to the laity, under the energetic leadership of the young lawyer William Sheldon. He insisted that this was a temporal matter, between the Government and the Catholic laity—for 'the English Roman Catholic Gentlemen could act for themselves.' A lay committee was formed and its authority came from the landed gentry, as was reasonable, since it was upon this class that the penal legislation bore hardest, and the point at which they might most hopefully look for relief. It was also a great point of contact with Edmund Burke for whose view of the nature of society in these years the importance of the landed, propertied class was central. Challoner would have wanted, provided that the issue was to go forward, an appeal for complete relief from all penal legislation and complete liberty given to Catholics for the private exercise of their religion. But it became plain that nothing like this wholesale emancipation would be possible. Yet, with a more limited demand, matters went ahead with astonishing speed and an amazing absence of last-minute difficulties. This was not only because of the ability and sense of the Catholic committee, but because such legislation reflected a weight of public opinion which felt that the days of persecution were, and ought to be, numbered. It was the committee under Lord Petre that drew up the preliminaries of an address to the King, which was to precede the presentation of new laws to Parliament. The address was in the end largely the work of Edmund Burke who was to lend the full force of his authority and oratory to the cause. On 1 May it was presented to the King who was pleased with it. At one time it seemed that the Dissenters might ruin the business, but in the event they stood aside. The Bill was introduced by Sir George Savile and supported by the eminent lawyer John Dunning. It went to the Lords on 22 May, where it had its third reading on 1 June, went back to the Commons and received Royal Assent on 3 June. There had been minor amendments, but nothing that emasculated the Bill.

The evil work of the common informer was at an end. The Acts of William III, which had carried the penalty of life imprisonment for Catholic priests, were repealed. Catholics could now buy and sell and inherit property. The benefits of the new Act applied to those who took the oath, about which there was still some difficulty, as the next decade was to show. On the day after the Act was passed Bishop Challoner issued a pastoral letter to his clergy recommending Catholics to pray for the King, Queen, and Royal Family.

If Georgian London might have preened itself on having behaved in an up-to-date, civilized manner, in relieving its Catholic fellow citizens, the satisfaction was swiftly wiped away by the explosion of malice and violence of the Gordon Riots. There was not unexpected disturbance in

Scotland at the prospect of new liberties for Scottish Catholics, but in London the trouble brewed in the forming of the Protestant Association, which chose as its leader Lord George Gordon, a philanthropic crackpot such as the British aristocracy throws up from time to time. Long-faced, red-haired, wildly blue-eyed, he might have been left over from one of the more improbable parts of Aubrey's *Lives*.[30]

Gordon organized a huge petition, and summoned a mass demonstration on Parliament for 2 June 1780. It was rough, noisy, and abusive, and members were jostled and a few roughed up, while Gordon clucked his way between the House and his demonstrators like an agitated hen. Only later that day did real violence erupt in an attack upon the Bavarian and Sardinian chapels which were looted, fired, and wrecked. These were followed on subsequent days by attacks on chapels at Moorfields and Wapping. At Wapping the chapel was the centre of a community of thousands of Irish workmen, and to 'No Popery' there was added the enmity against foreign workers which had been a feature of so many demonstrations from the time of Evil May Day 1517. The houses of two eminent protagonists of Catholic relief, Sir George Savile and Lord Mansfield, were given the dire treatment. The mob now took over, and the Protestant association more and more lost control, though there seems to have been an underlying direction against Catholics. Many Catholic houses near the chapels were set on fire, and a climax came when the great distillery of the Catholic Langdale was looted and set on fire.

One extraordinary feature was the reluctance of the civil magistrates, from the Lord Mayor downwards, to take forthright action and to command the troops to fire, with the result that what soldiery there was was reduced to being futile and ridiculed spectators. Nor was the House of Commons more energetic, where the more liberal members made it plain that while they feared the mob, they hated a standing army much more. It was in the end the first initiative of the King which resulted in the military action which brought the affair to an end. One spectacular feature had been the opening of the prisons, beginning with Newgate and the Fleet, but involving half a dozen other gaols from

---

[30] John Wesley wrote two letters to the Press opposing further concessions to Catholics on the ground that they already had complete(!) toleration. But he raised the question, which also exercised Pitt, of the claims of Popes to dispense from oaths. The account of Wesley's writings and views in Burton *Challoner*, ii. 216–18, is inaccurate and misleading. Wesley never, as is stated there, wrote a pamphlet supporting the Protestant Association. The quotation about the 'purple power of Rome' is from a spurious pamphlet which Wesley repudiated. It is a pity that these misstatements are repeated in M. D. R. Leys, *Catholics in England 1559–1892* (1961), p. 134, and C. Hibbert, *King Mob* (1958), p. 20. See Wesley, *Works* (1856), vol. X; Green, *Wesley Bibliography*, pp. 201, 207.

which hundreds of debtors and a greater number of really violent criminals were loosed upon the streets. At last there were enough troops to dominate the situation and volleys were fired, causing many casualties. Some 285 people had been killed, and large numbers were arrested. But most of them were small fry, and though some sixty-two were condemned to death, only twenty-five were executed. Lord George Gordon, who had spent the last days of the riots in a frenzied dash hither and thither, and finally, appalled by the bloodshed and ignored by the rioters, had been sent to the Tower. But after a brilliant defence he was acquitted of high treason. His later agitations were isolated and lonely and landed him in Newgate, where he died in 1793, having some time before become a Jew.

Johnson and his friends, Walpole and his, had gone out at night to see 'the glare of the conflagration fill the sky'—as Londoners had done in 1666 and would again in 1940. That the rioters should have assaulted the better houses and the well-to-do are what one would expect. Tenements and hutments are not in the same class as new mansions and fine libraries for those caught up in the vandal fever for smashing the beautiful. I have some reservation about the assertion (Rudé, Hibbert) that it was the dispossessed getting their own back on the rich. Certainly to have a go at the Archbishop of Canterbury was almost a mob tradition in English history. Nor does there seem to have been much in the rumours of French and American *agents provocateurs*, still less that it was a cunning ploy of His Majesty's Opposition, since the effect was to strengthen the Government and to enhance the prestige of the King, the only notable to come out of it with much credit. Boswell's commonsense comment seems sound: 'Whatever some may maintain, I am satisfied there was no combination or plan, either domestick or foreign: but that the mischief spread by a gradual contagion of frenzy, augmented by the qualities of fermented liquors.'[31]

For Richard Challoner it must have been the confirmation of his worst fears. But it was soon over and despite the immense shock, the damage done was less than might have been feared. In the end it may even have helped the cause of Catholic relief, for it strengthened the Government and Burke made a mighty speech in Bristol in September, though it cost him votes.

The cause of relief went forward in 1782 when a Catholic committee was re-formed with an able lawyer, Charles Butler as its secretary. Its chairman, Lord Petre, saw William Pitt who sought reassurance from the Government that the Pope would not claim to absolve Catholics

---

[31] Boswell's *Life of Johnson*, ed. G. B. Hill (1934), iii, 431; G. Rudé, 'The Gordon Riots', *TRHS* 5th series, 1956, vi. 93.

from any oaths they might have to swear. The committee then drew up a Protestation of their loyalty which sat much more loosely to Papal authority than Challoner or his predecessors could have done, a sign of the strength of a new spirit. At this time, since the death of Challoner, there was no outstanding vicar-apostolic, and all four vicars-apostolic now signed the Protestation, together with 240 priests and 1,500 laymen. By this time the Catholics were beginning to be sharply divided among themselves, and the complex and difficult matter of the oaths became a focus for the wider controversy. The first draft of a new bill contained a form of oath which to many seemed to deny even the spiritual authority of the Pope, and limited its benefits to 'Protesting Catholic Dissenters'—a silly phrase which outraged many of the clergy and which was in the event withdrawn. The Bishop of St David's got the offending phrase withdrawn in the House of Lords, and it was replaced by the less complex, if ambivalent, oath which had appeared in the Irish Act of 1774. Now at last Catholics could worship openly, if in duly registered chapels. The registration of wills, the double land-tax were abolished. Important disabilities, most of which they shared with the Dissenters, remained, but the Act of 1791 even more than that of 1778 had important and lasting social effects. And with ancient disabilities removed, the mission was set free to grow and prosper.

v. The Cisalpines

The doors which now opened for the English Catholics led to a very different world from that on which they had closed a century before. During that century they had been excluded from important social and political roles within the establishment. Now, as the very effort to begin a dialogue with Government revealed, there were new issues, about which Catholics were to be sharply divided, but which, new as they were, reflected older tensions going right back through recusant history.

It was a world in which the winds of change were blowing to gale force. Not simply the world of the Enlightenment, of Locke and Newton, of the Deists and the philosophers, but the pragmatic realm of government and politics. The authoritarian despots, the emergence of the modern state with its claims to omnicompetence, its bureaucracy, its power structures gave new form to the ancient dilemma of the relation between temporal and spiritual power, and this not only meant unfolding problems for Protestant countries, but bore with special force upon those paying allegiance to the Church of Rome.

In the heartland of the Holy Roman Empire, in the Austria of Kaunitz, Maria Theresa, and Joseph II, and in the Italy of Leopold of

Tuscany, Ricci, and the Synod of Pistoja, the scaling down of the powers of Rome and the reassertion of the secular authority became vehement, and this was not old Gallicanism writ large, but geared to a new age.

But there were other, headier currents of European thought. In the English Civil War a doctrine of human rights had emerged which turned natural law inside out and made it the basis of revolutionary claims, and which appeared in ever more articulate libertarian forms in eighteenth-century radical agitations, more explicitly still in the Americans' War of Independence, and found its climax in the French Revolution. The new liberal ideas, dynamic, optimistic, aggressive, attracted not only the underdogs and the dispossessed, but all who wished for reform of the established order. Greatly over-simplifying, it might be said that in the sixteenth and seventeenth centuries the Christian Churches had lost control of two powerful traditions of the human spirit, one in letters, philosophy, and science which we may roughly call humanism, and the other, a tradition of social justice, of the rights and liberties of men. Both of these were now returning in confrontation with the Church, one-sided, anti-clerical, even atheistic, refracted and bent indeed, but to them by reason of its own failure, the Church could not reply with an unqualified 'No' while equally unable to give an unequivocal 'Yes'.

Recent historians[1] have properly related what now emerged within English Catholicism as the 'Cisalpine' movement not only to a wider Catholic Enlightenment, but to the whole ferment of thought which would find a new peak in the Second Vatican Council. And certainly for those English Catholics who stepped out from a 'Garden of the soul' piety, a garden walled around by the conservatism of a Witham, a Challoner, or a Butler, into an unsheltered contact with the contemporary world it was an exhilarating, as well as a dangerous, experience. It involved problems of relating faith to culture as subtle as those which had faced Matthew Ricci or Roberto Nobili as they sought to communicate the gospel to the ancient and alien civilizations of the Far East.

One senses that the Cisalpines now receive a more kindly judgement from historians than they were wont to receive, though one feels that if that is so, some reconsideration might be sympathetically given to the young Stonor, to Sergeant, and to Blacklow of the preceding generation.

By the 1770s there were a number of English Catholics who were

---

[1] J. P. Chinnici, *The English Catholic Enlightenment*, 1980; O. Chadwick, *The Popes and European Revolution*, Oxford 1981, ch. 6.

eminent and distinguished in the secular field. The Benedictine Bishop
Charles Walmesley was a mathematician of European fame, and John
Needham and the Abbé Mann were honoured by the Royal Society in
England and by many learned societies abroad. Matthew Norton, the
Dominican, brought his learning in political economy and agriculture to
bear in practical experiments which were rightly acclaimed. Although
they were a small minority, there were men of the new, more liberal,
outlook in all the upper levels of Catholic society, and if there was only
Bishop James Talbot among the vicars-apostolic, there was a formidable
group of gentry headed by Lord Petre and Sir John Throckmorton who
took an important lead in the negotiations for Catholic relief. There was
a notable group of lawyers, for it seems that the pressure points of penal
frustration were where in the 1770s the new attitude appeared.[2]

Joseph Berington (1743–1827) was the angel who troubled the
waters. This he began to do when he gave sensational lectures at Douai
which attacked the previous tradition of philosophical and scholàstic
teaching. He brought down the swift wrath of Alban Butler, the learned
and conservatively minded hagiographer who secured his dismissal.
Berington spent the next years going to and fro upon the earth and
walking up and down in England making contacts with liberals of all
kinds, encouraged by a large and sympathetic correspondence, and
finding a notable ally in the ex-Jesuit John Carroll in America. In 1780
he published the *State and Behaviour of the English Catholics from the
Reformation to the Year 1780*. He found a dichotomy going back through
recusant history to the Reformation period, and while this was no new
theme, since it had been embodied in the histories of Charles Dodd, he
now drew more radical lessons from the story. One of the objectives of
his group was to demonstrate to Protestants that their notion of
Catholicism was untrue and unfair, though it was a myth which a one-
sided view of Catholic actions might have supported. He intended to
demonstrate that what mattered supremely for Catholics was the core of
the one essential Christian faith, and not what he regarded as peripheral
rites and usages. More important was the minimizing of Papal
authority, the view which earned the title 'Cisalpine' in contrast to the
'Ultramontanes' beyond the Alps. 'I am no Papist,' said Berington, 'the
Pope is the first magistrate in a well-regulated state.'

In a decade which had begun with the suppression of the Jesuits, and
at a time when in Austria measures had been taken against other
religious orders, Berington attacked the religious with sharpness. The

---

[2] H. Aveling, *The Handle and the Axe*, pp. 326ff. E. Duffy, 'Ecclesiastical Democracy
detected', I: '1779–87', II: '1787–96', *Recusant History* x, Jan.–Oct. 1970, pp. 193ff. and
309ff.

book outraged the authorities, who looked with loathing at a view of history which bypassed the very Church of martyrs and confessors who had suffered to uphold Catholic faith and loyalties. But if the President of Douai could consign Berington's volume to the 'hell' to which Protestant books were devoted, Berington received from other quarters a heady volume of praise. In the new situation after 1778 it was possible for Catholics to hold public meetings, and the novelty was popular. They drew large audiences and at some of them the most reckless ideas were propagated. Berington and Carroll discussed the advantages of a vernacular liturgy and of married clergy.

Nor did he neglect a wider audience. His Gothic romance, *Abellard and Heloise* (1787), conveyed his notions satirically and readably, with St Bernard in the background as the very model of the arch-conservative. The liberal cause was now joined by the ebullient Scottish priest Alexander Geddes, Lord Petre's chaplain, and an enthusiastic defender of the French Revolution whose praises he sang. Bliss was it in that dawn to be mentally intoxicated, while even Sir John Throckmorton became President of the rather pinkly radical 'Friends of the People'. The conservative Catholics seem to have been stunned and carried along, and at least allowed the London committee under Lord Petre and the young lawyers to negotiate with William Pitt and to pursue further legal measures of Catholic relief on their behalf. They signed the controversial 'Protestation'.

There was less success for the attempt to bring the rule of vicars-apostolic to an end and to replace it with elected bishops in ordinary. But somewhere about here the movement halted and its proud waves were stayed.

As the decade proceeded, and the excesses of revolution appeared, and as war with France followed, most Englishmen found Edmund Burke's alternative society more convincing than the brave new world of Tom Paine. By 1800 the Cisalpines were running out of steam, and there was a new and energetic conservative group doughtily led by John Milner. But the conflict was far from over, and the Cisalpines found new leaders, prominent among them John Lingard. The splendid, tragic, poignant, and glorious events of the nineteenth-century Catholic expansion are immensely intricate variations on our theme and the whole story perhaps reads differently when viewed from the end of the twentieth, than from the end of the eighteenth, century.

PART III

MYSTICS, RATIONALISTS, AND MORALISTS

How much better to know, more to abhor, the Evil that is in my *own Nature*, and how to obtain a *Supernatural Birth* of the Divine Life brought forth within me. All besides this is *Pushpin*.

WILLIAM LAW, *To a Clergyman in the North of England*, 1753

The very old gentleman said, Clarke was very wicked, for going so much into the Arian system. 'I will not say he was wicked', said Dr. Johnson: 'he might be mistaken.' McLean: 'He was wicked, to shut his eyes against the Scriptures: and worthy men in England have since confuted him to all intents and purposes.' Johnson: 'I know not who has confuted him to all intents and purposes.

J. BOSWELL, *Journal of a Tour to the Hebrides*

14

'INWARD RELIGION'

THE wholeness of faith, under the immense pressures of a century of theological conflict and religious war, seemed in England to split into three disparate strands, mysticism, moralism, and rationalism. The terms are inadequate and the categories overlap, for there is a moralism of mysticism, with its insistence on the call to Christian perfection, as there is a rationalist moralism stressing the profitableness of godliness and the danger of being righteous overmuch. The word 'mysticism' is itself a dangerous complexity and we much prefer to use the eighteenth-century term 'inward religion' to cover not only the contemplative lives and devotion of a few gifted individuals, but movements in religion which might include the French Prophets, the Philadelphians, the Pietists, and assuredly also the Moravians and the beginnings of the Evangelical Revival.

The seventeenth century was as remarkable for spiritual depth as the succeeding century for breadth and at the end of it there was in circulation a remarkable number of books representing new and ancient spiritual traditions. Thomas Ken, Anthony Horneck, George Hickes, John Byrom, and William Law were able to draw upon an astonishing number of new and old editions of works reflecting the devotion of many centuries. There were indeed some ominous gaps. Ignorance and contempt for the Middle Ages was not compensated for by the high-church attention to the Fathers and to the primitive Church. Anglican rigorists like William Law knew little of the 'discretion' of St Benedict, or the joy in creation of St Francis, while the great Bernardine tradition, with its fine German inheritance through Hildegard of Bingen and the sisters of Helfta, to say nothing of the great Victorines, was little known. There is in fact something faintly off centre, exotic, about the mystic devotees at the beginning of the eighteenth century. They overvalued women like Antoinette de Bourignon and Mme Guyon, and saintly ascetics like Gregory Lopez and M. de Renty counted for more with them than St John of the Cross or St Theresa.

None the less the disparate strands of devotion were weighty and important. There was the continuance of Platonism among the Scottish mystics, Leighton, Scougal, the Garden brothers, and the Chevalier Ramsay,[1] and of course the full-blooded Platonism of the Cambridge divines, deeply indebted as they were to the Florentine Platonists of the previous century, reading their Ficino and their Mirandola, and through them Plotinus and Porphyry, the Hermetic writings, the Cabbala, and the writings of the pseudo-Dionysius the Areopagite. It is very possible that this was no sudden importation, but something that had never entirely disappeared from the time of John Colet. Then there was a radical Protestantism from the Continental Reformation, the tradition stemming from Andrew Karlstadt, Thomas Müntzer, Sebastian Franck, through Hans Denck, Schwenckfeld, Paracelsus, and Weigel to Jacob Boehme, writings and ideas which had entered England through Anabaptist writers and the Family of Love, and some of those translated into English during the Puritan period by writers like John Everard.

There were also available the works of the German mystical writings of Tauler, Suso, and Ruysbroeck and two smaller, but deeply influential, classics, the *Theologia Germanica* and the *Imitation of Christ*. There were also works of Catholic spirituality from Spain, Italy, and France. From Spain John of Avila and Molinos, St John of the Cross and St Theresa. From France, the many volumes of Antoinette de Bourignon, edited by her indefatigable disciple Pierre Poiret,[2] and the writings of Fénelon and his protégée Mme Guyon, and smaller writings of a less controversial character from St Francis of Sales, Brother Lawrence, Nicola Armelle, and what Samuel Wesley called 'the amazing thoughts of M. Pascal'. Much of this literature found a clearing house in Holland, where it mingled with a quite different stream, the writings of J. Boehme and the movement of Pietism, which beginning with Arndt's *True Christianity*, introduced into England the work of A. H. Francke, Philip Spener, and a new generation of German hymns and hymn writers. Those who cared for such things, who gave time and attention to their study, were indeed swimming against the in-coming rationalist tide. But if they were a minority, they were by no means insignificant and they have to be taken seriously as a characteristic of English religion between 1660 and 1750. Certainly without them the religion of John Wesley, and in consequence that of the Evangelical Revival, would have taken another shape.

---

[1] G. D. Henderson, *The Mystics of the North East*, Aberdeen 1934; *The Burning Bush*, Edinburgh 1957; D. P. Walker, *The Ancient Theology*, Edinburgh 1972.

[2] G. A. Krieg, *Der mystische Kreis*, Göttingen 1979; E. Hirsch, *Geschichte der neueren evangelischen Theologie*, Gütersloh 1975, i. 196ff.

i. *John Byrom (1692–1761)*[3]

Two Manchester men, John Worthington and John Byrom, are among the most endearing of our English diarists. Neither of them is in the Pepys, Evelyn, or Parson Woodforde class, but their attractive characters come through the often laconic and ingenuous narrative. 'Inward religion' mattered to both men. Worthington does not rank with his Platonist colleagues as a thinker, but he was Biblically learned and widely read and, like Byrom, had a never satisfied appetite for books. He produced little beyond a monumental edition of the works of his teacher Joseph Mede, but his little edition of the *Imitation of Christ* as *The Christian's Pattern* was an influence on later versions. He was much interested in Nicholas Ferrar's community at Little Gidding. The clutch of sermons on 'Resignation' which he preached at St Bene't Fink, at the time of the Plague and Fire were about that *Gelassenheit* which was as important to the German mystical tradition as 'Faith' in Luther's.

Both men spent much of their lives in Cambridge and in London, but had their roots in Manchester. Both were devoted to their wives and children, though neither of them—it may be a mark of that age—felt it necessary to return home on the death or birth of an infant. But Byrom had no abiding lodging in the south, and the little group of dark stone buildings at the heart of the great overgrown village of Manchester—the collegiate church (now the Cathedral) and the adjacent Chetham's School and Library—still seem reminiscent of the kindly stooping giant. Above all is this true of the reading room in Chetham's Library with its fine seventeenth-century chairs, and the alcove where Byrom and his high-church friends studied and discussed the Christian Fathers, unaware that one day Marx and Engels would sit where they sat, brooding revolution.

John Byrom came of an old Manchester family which bore arms. From the Merchant Taylors' school he went to Trinity College, Cambridge, where he became Scholar and Fellow, taking his BA in 1712, and his MA in 1715. There he became a protégé of the formidable Master, Richard Bentley, and was liked by the family for his honesty. A pastoral poem, featuring Bentley's astonishing and splendid daughter Jug, was considered good enough for the *Spectator* which also published two or three other pieces by the young man who might have seemed set for a career in letters. But there was something in him of the dilettante and he only produced a mass of rather inferior verse which perhaps his

[3] R. Parkinson (ed.), *The Private Journals and Literary Remains of John Byrom*, Chetham Society, 2 vols. 1854–7; H. Talon, *Selections from the Journals and Papers of John Byrom*, 1950.

contemporaries and at least one later editor—Sir Adolphus Ward—took too seriously.[4] In fact two hymns, one of them the superb hymn 'Christians, awake! salute the happy morn', and a couple of epigrams are his chief claim to literary remembrance. He was too prone to turn into verse the more abstruse mysteries of Law and Boehme, which often fitted ill the rather jiggety-jog measures he employed. He was probably right to refuse to take orders, though this meant abandoning his fellowship. He was a slightly cautious Jacobite, but not it seems a Non-Juror, though it may be that politics had something to do with his leaving England for France where he studied medicine at Montpellier. It was a severe and grinding course which he did not pursue as far as the degree. His title 'Dr.' was honorific and he was always reluctant to practise what he could not in conscience make his career. He had married a cousin with no dowry, and had somehow to earn his living.

Byrom was a gifted linguist, interested in words, and he invented a method of shorthand, which proved most timely in an age of public discussion and debate, with the obvious advantages of conciseness and privacy. He found more and more takers at 5 guineas a lesson, and his method became something of a rage, attracting peers like the Duke of Devonshire and scientists like the members of the Royal Society who enrolled him among their members on its account, while among the parsons none made better use of him than Charles and John Wesley. Although as a system his shorthand had drawbacks and came to be superseded, it was guarded by Act of Parliament and brought him a living. He did his touting in the most genteel way, among the dons at high tables in the universities, and among an ever widening circle of learned contacts in the coffee houses and taverns of London. Despite some comic rows with his rival Weston, Byrom's method became famous. In 1740 family legacies enabled him to abandon a strenuous and wearing way of life. For he tramped incessantly the lanes and streets of London and was a familiar figure at scores of coffee houses. His many friends were cultured and some of them distinguished, and included eminent members of the professions and of the Royal Society, such as Dr Jurin and David Hartley. He wined and dined and took innumerable dishes of coffee, chocolate, and tea with an impressive collection of learned men, so numerous indeed as to put yet another question mark against the view that the Universities which bred most of them were in complete decay.

It was the heyday of what we have called 'coffee-house Christianity', a popularized discussion and debate about religion which bears some

    [4] *The Poems of John Byrom*, ed. A. Ward, Chetham Society, 3 vols. 1894, 1895, 1912.

resemblance to BBC religion and the media of our day, not least in its preference for the discussion of the latest books and novel ideas, the most surprising, and if possible slightly shocking, theories, preferably those which 'knocked' the Christian Establishment. For at this time corrosive satire was more active than at any time since the beginning of the sixteenth century. It was therefore of some significance that among the wits, the sceptics, and the atheists there should be a few Christian laymen, like John Byrom, Samuel Johnson, and Dr Cheyne who could outwit their opponents, put them down, and turn the laugh against them.

It was all perhaps a little facile.

We had a supper below of turbot, turkey, sweetbreads, rabbit and dessert of cherries, strawberries, raspberries, a great custard—a mighty fine supper in short: . . . we stayed till past twelve and then came away: we talked about persecution and prosecution, believing Christianity, original sin and they all sang a song, but I did not, because I could not.[5]

And there is something almost Pickwickian about the following:

At Richard's there was Pits, and Strut, who desired me to come to the Jack and Grapes in the Strand, and I did so and had much talk with Strut, Pits etc. about Christianity which I defended as well as I could, Pits talking in favour of reason by which only we could find out whether God was God: I said reason was the gift of this very God and therefore we could hardly find him out to be not God by it . . . I exhorted Struts to lay aside a little vanity and embrace Christianity, he was for necessity and I for free will: there were twelve of us in all . . . they seemed to whisper about me when I came to them, but were very civil and desired I would favour them with my company. Sit anima mea cum Christianis.[6]

We may be sure that Byrom caught the cacophony of Pits and Struts, who perhaps did the cause of Deism no good by keeping such close company, but Byrom had an ear for words, and some of the best moments in his diary are when he records the very accents of an irate Scottish MP or the exact words of a panicky Enfield highwayman. We find him leading little groups of learned friends on excursions and expeditions, to Greenwich or up the Thames, sometimes reading to them, and generally talking most of the time until the day wore away with himself tired, pleased, and as always penitent about his own much speaking. And there were more serious discussions with Hoadly and Clarke and Joseph Butler.

But beyond doubt the most important person in his life, his family

[5] Talon, Selections, p. 112 (27 May 1729).   [6] Ibid., p. 127 (1731).

apart, was William Law. The two men have often been compared with Boswell and Johnson, but perhaps Dr Watson and Sherlock Holmes would be a better comparison, for Byrom knew his mentor's methods, and his own word for his attitude to Law was 'veneration'. Their congruence was inevitable. Both rummaged all the bookstalls and went for the same kind of books, though Byrom the linguist had a wider-ranging taste and could never resist a bargain. Before they met both men had begun to collect mystical writings, which were to an astonishing extent cheaply available—Tauler, Suso, Ruysbroeck, Walter Hilton, the *Theologia Germanica*, and of course the works and editions and biographies of Pierre Poiret. Byrom had a large collection of editions of the *Imitation of Christ* and perhaps drew from Law a sharp remark that it was more important to practise than to collect mystical writings.

Both belonged to a group of high churchmen who valued and indeed over-valued the philosophy of the French Oratorian Malebranche—who offered a congenial and religious answer to the philosophic problems of the age, but who perhaps represented the same kind of specious short cuts as the writings of Ramus had offered the early Puritans.

The initiative was always with Byrom. He made the first of many treks to Putney after reading the *Serious Call*. He waited on the Oracle with diffidence, and was content to be greeted with laconic irony, until, as with another devotee, John Wesley, the moment came when Law would let loose his rare eloquence. He always deferred to Law's decisive judgements on people and books, with some reluctance in the case of Antoinette de Bourignon, though both men shuddered at the thought of Mme Guyon playing cards with the Chevalier Ramsay. Byrom and Wesley had the habit of bringing other young men to Putney, generally rather unsettled, and sometimes rather foolish, ones, and the sage, who did not suffer fools gladly, would sometimes chew them up as he did the almost stutteringly admiring John Gambold. Law was a dab hand at detecting the voice of nature where his hearers claimed the experience of grace.

In the mid 1730s Byrom became caught in a tug of war between the non-juring family of a young woman, Fanny Henshaw, and the Quakers. Byrom was too kindly to be of much use, but he did manage to involve Law, who agreed to correspond with her on his own strict conditions, and wrote a series of letters, learned, often beautifully written, but psychologically disastrous, with a sort of bullying undertone which, like the tactics of her relatives, was completely counter-productive. So she went to the Quakers to become a notable prophetess, and when the two men next met, Law's brusque 'Well, have you made any more Quakers?' would have affronted one less deferential. They corresponded, examined books, swapped manuscripts, and walked and talked together in Somerset Gardens. But after Law's withdrawal to King's Cliffe and Byrom's to Manchester, there was only one visit. One of Law's last letters to Byrom breathes affection, and perhaps some guilt, at his neglect of a friend whose unswerving loyalty and whose intellect might have given a critical whetstone which the two maiden ladies and the bank clerk Langcake could never provide.

But in public, for Byrom, Law could do no wrong. He defended Law's absolute repudiation of all stage entertainments—this though he himself was head over heels with delight at having written an epilogue to the rumbustious Haymarket farce *Hurlothrumbo* and obviously enjoyed attending one of those masquerades which Law conceived to be an even worse fate than death. In the breach between Law and Wesley he was on Law's side and withstood John Wesley whom he addressed as 'Pope John' to his face. Even more remarkably, though it left him out of his depth, he defended, and to some extent shared, Law's infatuation with the theosophical speculations of Jacob Boehme.

During a visit in 1743 Law made some remark about the danger of 'building spirituality upon an unmortified life'. It may have been a dig at his friend, for between Law's rigorism and Byrom's cheerful happy-go-lucky existence there was an obvious gulf. Byrom was after all a layman and a good-natured man, whose friendships were not doctrinaire and who could hob-nob, if not with the great heretics, at least with the sons of Hoadly or of Wollaston. But Byrom is not really to be ranked among the English mystics and, like Robert Nelson and Samuel Johnson, found a staple Christian diet in the City churches, in prayers and sermons and sacraments. In the matter of self-examination he took only a pass degree in mortification. His attempts at frugality were intermittent, but his determined attempts to be a vegetarian might be shattered at any moment by the smell of mutton chops. Law insisted on the vital importance of early rising, but Byrom generally stayed up too late anyway, and was often in bed late in the morning, so that there is a *semper peccator* ground bass to his devotional life reminiscent of Samuel Johnson. As for innocent diversions which Law repudiated as misspent 'holes' in time, Byrom enjoyed chess and backgammon, drinks and a pipe, and obviously delighted in great argument. We think of Byrom typically as talking loudly in a group of friends: but of Law as mooching solitary in Somerset Gardens or sitting alone, eyeing with sharp penetration the manners of the passers-by, material for those marvellous thumbnail character sketches that suggest—how he would have hated the thought—that he might have been a great playwright and novelist.

Weaknesses, foibles, Byrom candidly records. Forgetful and absent-minded, he once wrote his wife asking her to remind him of anything she thinks he might have forgotten. One wonders why he stayed in Cambridge on the death of his daughter Nelly, and we are dismayed by the cold charity with which he wrote to his wife, bereft as she was, a carefully and beautifully written letter:

I am very well satisfied with your care and management of her: and though I do not expect that you can divest yourself of all grief upon so tender an occasion, yet I persuade myself that you will be so moderate in it as not to prejudice your own health: such excess being very useless and very irrational.

Obviously the voice that was heard in Rama was not overheard at the High Table in Trinity where Byrom got the news. How different from Martin Luther and his poignant comments on the death of his daughter Magdalene.

He kept his friendships in repair with Clayton and Deacon and old friends, but he was also intrigued, if puzzled and a little dismayed, by the nascent Evangelical Revival, and there are new names in his Journals: Philip Doddridge, the Countess of Huntingdon, George Whitefield, the Moravians, Count Zinzendorf, the Huttons and the mechanic Mr Bray of Little Britain and of course the Wesleys ('Mr Charles Wesley came while I was shaving') and their egregious friend James Stonehouse, the Vicar of Islington, who averred that the air of his parish was filled with devils.

John Byrom was no mere Autolycus of mystic writings. Rather he was a godly Christian layman, one whose kindliness and tolerance offset the austerity of his great and always rather daunting friend, the one perhaps too human, the other slightly inhuman. At any rate, wherever John Byrom companied among the practitioners of inward religion, cheerfulness broke in.

ii. The Philadelphians

At the end of the seventeenth century the influence of the writings of Jacob Boehme was seen in a small charismatic movement among educated lay men and women. Just as in France and Holland his teachings had been reflected and refracted through the visionary experiences of Antoinette de Bourignon, and her interpreter Pierre Poiret, so in England the prophetess Jane Leade was closely linked with her coadjutor Dr John Pordage, and her amanuensis son-in-law, Francis Lee.[7]

[7] N. Thune, *The Behmenists and the Philadelphians*, Uppsala 1948; S. Hutin, *Les Disciples anglais de Jacob Boehme*, Paris 1960; *DNB*, s.vv. 'Pordage', 'Leade', 'Lee'.

Boehme's writings bowled over Dr John Pordage (1607–81), a Berkshire rector, who in 1649 began to have visionary experiences in the light of which he interpreted the German seer. A powerful university sermon at Oxford gained him the adherence of two Fellows of All Souls, the writer Thomas Bromley and Edmund Brice, who joined the circle meeting in Pordage's house, which also included the Earl of Pembroke. Pordage soon got into trouble for spreading unorthodox opinions, was hauled before two Cromwellian commissions, and was extruded from his living on theological and moral grounds. In 1663 he was a minister of a London congregation where he was joined by Mrs Jane Leade (1624–1704). She came of a good Norfolk family, but at a Christmas party, at the age of fifteen, she heard a voice during the festivities: 'Cease from this, I have another Dance to lead thee in, for this is vanity.' In Dr Pordage she found an ally who could add a learned and theological dimension to her intuitions, and in residence together they prayed and waited on the revelations which were soon vouchsafed to them. To his Behmenism she added her own apocalyptic notions, chiliasm, and her favourite theme of a final *apocatastasis*. She wrote a number of tracts which made little impact in England, but found congenial soil among the illuminati in Holland and Germany. Her writings were translated, and among their fruits was a solid pension from a Baron Knyphausen which greatly eased her penurious situation. After the death of Pordage she leaned heavily on the help and advice of Francis Lee (1649–1728). He became her son-in-law, and when she became blind, her guide and amanuensis. In him the movement found its most distinguished adherent. A Doctor of Medicine, a former Fellow of St John's College, Oxford, an orientalist nicknamed 'Rabbi', he had been an eminent Non-Juror. In 1694–7 when the Philadelphian Society was formed, they were joined by another former Fellow of St John's, Richard Roach, who also began to receive divine 'communications'. The core of this sodality was therefore a strange blend of the charismatic and the intellectual, with some admixture of hysteria, and as the society grew in numbers, moving and moving again to ever larger premises, they aroused public antagonism. The rules they drew up have a stress on liberty of prophesying, on silent prayer, on waiting on 'the sweet internal breathings of the divine spirit', and on the Kiss of Peace.

The little movement spread to the Continent, and while, as in the case of the older Family of Love, it is not easy to distinguish calumny from fact, it seems that hysteria led in the case of some German Philadelphians to genuine scandals. But they did stress practical charity, and sought to be a leaven within the Churches rather than a new sect. In England the movement, which at first had been compared with the Quakers, never got off the ground, having from the first attracted a much more esoteric clientele among slightly eccentric highbrows. Mrs Leade herself was a strong character and bore her last illnesses bravely and with an unselfish charity to all who came to her. At the age of eighty she was buried in Bunhill Fields. Her experiences and writings raise questions we cannot probe in these pages. That other tough prophetess and mystic, Hildegard of Bingen, also had her experiences and her claims to divine illumination. What are the criteria to be applied, and why is it that in the end the difference between the spirituality of the two women is like that between genuine and sham Gothic?

Certainly Francis Lee, after the death of his mother-in-law and after many doughty writings in defence of her, in correspondence with Dodwell and in writings which William Law constantly pondered in his last days at King's Cliffe, repented of his own 'enthusiasm' at the end of his life. But some of his most brave projects of practical philanthropy were published by the Philadelphia Society. They include not only a very early prospectus for charity schools, but also a set of proposals for 'cultural, religious, mercantile and jurisprudential work in Russia' presented to Peter the Great, at his own request. Francis Lee was without doubt a noble character, the much loved and close friend of Robert Nelson.

On the fringe of these societies was the expatriate German, Andreas Dionysius Freher,[8] a learned man who devoted all his energies to editing and expounding and in a sense extending, the doctrines of Jacob Boehme. He got a skilled draughtsman to produce the extraordinary illustrations, charts, and emblems which were printed in the eighteenth-century reprint of the works of Boehme in English. His extensive writings remained in manuscript, some in the British Museum, while others, which William Law got hold of and which he also studied intensively in his last years, are now in Dr Williams's Library.

In 1707 the movement received a brief stimulus from the incursion into England of the charismatic movement of the French Prophets. They had their origins among the Camisards, the French Protestants of the Cevennes. Under the cruel pressures of savage persecution, the Huguenot resistance movement became fiercely militant. It also produced a remarkable 'Liturgy of the Desert', and developed into a charismatic movement complete with visionaries, ecstasies, and mass hysteria which made it a perfect embodiment of what the age called 'enthusiasm'. In England the French refugees, torn from their poignant context, retained the less happy and more sensational characteristics of

---

[8] C. A. Muses, *Illumination on Jacob Boehme, The Work of Dionysius Andreas Freher*, New York 1951. The title is unjustifiably optimistic.

the movement. Lord Shaftesbury, in a completely insensitive paragraph, mocked them and suggested that those who made a puppet show in St Bartholomew's, which held them up to ridicule, had perhaps found the best way of treating such extravagances. The movement grew, but reached its peak when it was claimed that one of their number, Thomas Emes, would rise again from the dead in Bunhill Fields on 25 May 1708. But when the expectation was not fulfilled, interest dwindled and the movement died.

15

WILLIAM LAW

i. Life

WILLIAM LAW (1686–1761) was born in the Northamptonshire village of King's Cliffe, where also he died. He was a son of a grocer and went up to Emmanuel College, Cambridge, as a sizar in 1706, took his BA in 1708, his MA in 1712, and became a Fellow of the College. Emmanuel had been transformed under the influence of William Sancroft and had turned its back on its Puritan, and indeed its Platonist, past. There was therefore nothing out of the way in Law becoming a truculent Jacobite. A wittily offensive speech in that subversive vein at his Tripos led to him being set back from his MA status. John Byrom, to whom he was then unknown, commented: 'he is much blamed by some, defended by others, has the character of a vain, conceited fellow.'[1]

There are gaps in our knowledge of the career of this reticent man. He was ordained deacon (23 September 1710) but was not priested until persuaded to it by his non-juring superiors (27 January 1728). He was probably curate at Haslingfield near Cambridge, under John Heylyn. Heylyn was quite a character and was later known as 'the mystic divine'. Curiously, two Easter sermons have survived, one by Heylyn, the other by Law from this time. Heylyn's sermon[2] (printed thirty years later) contains the phrase 'all saving knowledge is experimental' and compares the triumph of the New Man in Christ over the Old Adam in a way so reminiscent of the *Theologia Germanica* that one wonders if he pointed Law towards mystical writings. Law's sermon is floridly old-fashioned, contrasting guilt and penitence with the joy of Easter.

He had become a Fellow of Emmanuel College in 1711. After the 1715 rebellion, oaths of loyalty were reimposed and in 1716 Law resigned his fellowship at Emmanuel College, the only Fellow to become a Non-Juror. He seems to have remained at the College until 1723.[3] Church-outed by his own deliberate choice, he gave up hopes of

---

[1] J. Byrom, *Remains* i, pt. 1, p. 20.

[2] J. Heylyn, *Sermon on the Resurrection of Our Lord*, 1732. The manuscript of Law's sermon is in Dr Williams's Library and seems to be conjecturally dated by Walton.

[3] College documents, Order Book Col. 14. 1 and the Commons Account Book, STE 15. 6, show that he resigned in 1716, and that Samuel Fletcher was appointed in his stead from 31 August, though Law remains among the Fellows until the end of November. But his name appears then under 'Collegium' and he seems to have remained in residence until 1723, when he went to Putney.

an ecclesiastical or academic career. His later attacks on ecclesiastical climbers and academic luminaries have a bitter taste. One who cherished, and perhaps carried about with him, a miniature of the Pretender was also at odds with the political Establishment.

There are some indications that this brilliant young divine, whose letters to the Bishop of Bangor in 1717 brought him out of complete obscurity, had not yet himself answered the call to a devout and holy life.

Byrom records lunching with Mrs Cecilia Collier (wife of Jeremy and mother of Thomas Deacon) who said that Mr Law 'had been a great beau, that he was very sweet upon the ladies, that he had promised to marry one and that his great change was in 1720.' Overton and Inge dismiss this as gossip, but if it was, it was top gossip, for the formidable Mrs Collier was a mother-in-law in Israel, and knew very much about the little community of Non-Jurors. There is moreover the statement of Rivington the publisher that John Heylyn had said of his erstwhile curate's *Serious Call* that he would have been more impressed with it had its author himself travelled that way.

This might mean no more than that Heylyn had lost touch with his former curate who had not been heavenly minded at Haslingfield, but, rather like Ouranios in the *Serious Call*, who in his first parish was a fish out of water, taking refuge in his study with his books.

If, as for his beloved Desert Fathers, conversion meant for Law a life of renunciation and discipline, then an early love of fine linen gives point to his later insistence of wearing only coarse shirts, and for a deliberate carelessness about dress in later life when he was criticized for going about 'in a pair of stockings that a ploughman would not have picked off a dunghill'.[4]

If there was some crisis, some turning-point (and a line in Law's epitaph seems to confirm the indications we have given), Law never spoke of it, though there are prayers among what may be his early writings which suggest he shared Bunyan's experience of a 'bruised conscience'. And I should place later rather than earlier in his academic days the rule of life which he drew up, and which is similar to other rules suggested by Taylor, Ken, and Horneck. Law's rule has a revealing sentence: 'no condition of life is for enjoyment, but for trial.'

He became tutor and chaplain in the family of an affluent army contractor, Edward Gibbon of Putney, and taught his not very bright or very diligent son Edward. Edward was twice entered at Emmanuel College as Pensioner in 1723 and as Fellow Commoner in 1727 and in

---

[4] Byrom, i. 2. 114.

the second period Law accompanied his pupil to Cambridge, though the young man could hardly master Byrom's shorthand, let alone his academic chores, and was to reach his ceiling as MP and an Alderman.

Law lived at Putney in moderate comfort and with no remarkable austerity. The good impression he made on the family elicited the testimony of Edward Gibbon the third, the historian: 'In our family William Law left the reputation of a worthy and pious man who believed all that he professed and practised all that he enjoined.' But his greatest influence was on the daughter, Hester, who was completely devoted to him. Correspondence shows her going many errands for him, bringing books and manuscripts to London (he gave her strict instructions not to enter his room further than the table on which the papers lay, and not to take anybody else in with her). And at one point he signs himself in French: 'Entièrement à toi, en J.C.'

If the Bangor controversy made Law known, fame came to him with two outstanding works, his treatise on *Christian Perfection* (1726) and his *Serious Call to a Devout and Holy Life* (1729).

As an undergraduate, like other high churchmen, he had found satisfaction in the writings of Malebranche, whose saying, 'We see all things in God', he had taken as a theme for his degree disputation. Since then he had read more and more mystical literature, the fruit of which in these two books showed a masterly capacity for writing about 'inward religion' and brought him a flood of correspondence and a number of young disciples, including John Byrom and John Wesley. To them and to their friends he became the Oracle of Putney, and they had a way of turning up with friends, whom, rather like dogs with bones, they laid expectantly at their master's feet. Byrom brought his always dithering friend Mr Walker. John Wesley consulted him about a reluctant member of the Holy Club and got the wise, but disconcerting, counsel 'Let him alone'. Some of these young men were as preoccupied with themselves as they had been before they got religion and Law did not take kindly to being their guru. He treated their long-winded spiritual testimonies with scepticism, especially when, after their return from America, the Wesleys brought him new German friends, this time, one feels, not so much to see what Law would make of them as to try what they would make of William Law. There was a cool audience with Peter Böhler, each taking the other with a large pinch of salt. Law was probably quite unfair to another evangelical specimen, the mechanic Mr Bray of Little Britain, who won John Byrom's heart when he advised him about a kettle, and whom Charles Wesley treated as a father-in-God. In the end John Wesley upbraided his former adviser in a tactless and exasperating letter, to which Law wrote a reply so withering as effectually to end their friendship. At the end of his life Law revealed how little to his taste had been this kind of spiritual counselling, advised his correspondents against it, and discouraged this kind of visitation.

It is at this time that we glimpse him from a different angle, as a participator in the irate in-fighting among the Non-Jurors, at the height of the Essentialist dispute and schism, and in the attempts to make peace. Law, it seems, was not simply a passive signatory of manifestos, but is plausibly conjectured to have been the author of a long and rebellious memorandum from the right-wing presbyters, in which they severely attacked their bishops, including Dr Brett.[5] George Smith, who could be venomous, complained:

'I understand Mr. Law is the penman of this paper whom I don't take to be that meek and humble man that he would make people believe he is: his conduct in this whole affair shows him to be one of the proudest men living.'[6]

There were many comings and goings, and for one of them, a heated interview with Dr Richard Rawlinson, Law was constrained to write an apology. But he seems to have had a change of heart and we finally hear of him as composing a more eirenical document which was the basis of the eventual peace. We hear no more of Law among the Non-Jurors, save for their laments that he had followed Francis Lee and succumbed to mystical enthusiasm. It looks as though Law was not good at public relations, still less intrigues, and it was a mercy all round that he refused to be made a non-juring bishop.

He had kept in touch with King's Cliffe, where his brother George was steward to the Earl of Westmorland's estates. An anonymous gift of £1,000 from an admiring reader enabled him to found a charity school in 1727 for fourteen girls, the first of a whole complex of charitable foundations. The rules he drew up were not very different from those in many similar foundations, but strict they certainly were. Apart from the daily chores of learning, there were ever-recurring prayers and Scripture readings, attendances at church, including all funerals, while their comings and goings were punctuated by so many bobs and curtseyings that one feels that the poor darlings spent a great deal of time between the vertical and horizontal positions. For such offences as lying, swearing, and stealing, the child would be chained to a pillar for half a day, after which public confession and absolution would follow. After a third offence Mr George Law would be summoned and the delinquent turned away.

In 1740 Law himself had retired to King's Cliffe. It would have been

---

[5] H. Broxap, *The Later Non-Jurors*, p. 154. [6] Ibid., p. 159.

improper for Hester to have joined him, but a sanctified *ménage à trois* became possible when the widow Hutcheson, whom her husband had commended to Law's care, joined them in 1743. The two well-to-do ladies appointed Law as their chaplain, almoner, and spiritual director, and allowed him to dispose of their considerable income.

In 1745 Mrs Hutcheson founded a school for the education and clothing of eighteen boys (extended to twenty in 1756), and paid the salary of a master. She built a schoolhouse and had tenements erected for four old and poor widows. In 1756 Law built a schoolhouse and school and tenements for ten old and poor widows or spinsters. In 1752 he founded a library for the circulation of 'Books of Piety'.

When it came to the contemporary much discussed question, whether charity should be discriminating or unrestricted, Law came down entirely on the side of refusing none. Each day he saw that the milk from his four cows was distributed, and there was soup on the hob. He seems to have been always accessible to those in need, who now descended on the village from all quarters. If we may discount the stories of the not-so-needy importunate changing into rags behind the bushes, there is no doubt that this charitable Liberty Hall became a village scandal, was the subject of protest by the rector in the pulpit, and in the end of a public remonstrance from parishioners who relished the quieter days before the advent of this colony of do-gooders. This in turn brought a very angry reply from Law and his no less offended if less articulate companions, who threatened to pull out altogether. Whereupon peace was made and benevolences continued. Law had a study bedroom with a little alcove. He rose early, and spent much time in prayer, study, and writing. He had his horse and Mrs Hutcheson her chaise, and there were servants. They went riding and had a few female regular guests. It was satisfyingly off the beaten track, and John Byrom visited him only once again, in 1743. His female charges were kept busy and employed much time, as did Law himself, copying out long passages from good books. Their way of life was frugal, but not ascetic—it was a landmark when Law ordered cheesecakes to be made to celebrate the fact that Mrs Hutcheson had bought the house in King's Cliffe. There are references to gifts of chocolate, to which he was partial. He found some family comfort in the nearness of his nieces and nephews and there is one pleasant picture of him dandling them and giving them 'rides' on his feet. A. W. Hopkinson drily comments that the thing about children is not whether we like them, but whether they like us, and I suspect that many found Law, for all his kindness, a little daunting. The pleasing story is told that he liked to release birds from their cages, and it is a little hard of Dean Inge to have suggested that this showed more kindness to cats than to canaries. His books brought him a wide correspondence, including letters from young people—a young lawyer in Philadelphia, and an Oxford undergraduate—who felt they owed their souls to him. In his last years he made much of a son in the gospel, the London bank clerk Edward Langcake to whom he wrote letters a little dismaying in their sentiment.

The idea that in his age he mellowed into a mild amiability is not borne out by his writings, for some of his saltiest and fiercest judgements on men and books come from the last years, and he could still disconcert his disciples, as when he wrote of a book which Langcake had sent, by a prophetic numerologist 'your friend Clark's piece will have its place among those books which at certain times help to kindle my fire'! Meekness still struggled with asperity, and there was often fire behind the kindly eyes.

He died triumphantly on 9 April 1761. In due season Mrs Hutcheson was buried at his feet. Many years later the aged Hester Gibbon was interred by his side.

ii. The Master Pieces

Law's Treatise on *Christian Perfection* was overshadowed by the immense popular success of his *Serious Call*. But as an exposition of the absolute demands of Christ upon men, and a call to religious men not to stop short of perfection, it probably surpasses the more celebrated work. Far from perfection being something not demanded of the generality of Christians, there is, says Law, only one common Christianity which does not rest in any state or condition of life but is 'that height of Holiness and Purity to which Christianity calls all its members.'

When Law turns to the theme of the vanity and transience of this world he uses the kind of language about the body which Plotinus might have used:

The divine image . . . this spirit is now in a fallen corrupt Condition, that the Body in which it is placed is its Grave or Sepulchre where it is enslaved to fleshly Thoughts, blinded with false notions of Good and Evil, and dead to all Taste and Relish of its true happiness.[7]

There is a sombre beauty about his description of the dream-like quality of our existence: 'A mere wilderness, state of darkness, a vale of

---

[7] *The Works of the Reverend William Law, M.A.* (9 vols., 1892), iii. 12.

misery, where vice and madness, dreams and shadows variously please, agitate and torment the short, miserable lives of men.'[8]

There follows a running commentary on those New Testament passages which demand absolute renunciation. Every now and then there is some sparkling Law-ism: 'A Christian . . . that wants to add a worldly joy and pleasure to the great things of religion is more senseless than the man who should think he had hard usage to be saved from shipwreck unless he were carried off upon a cedar plank.'[9]

If a person was to walk upon a *Rope* across some great River, and he was bid to deny himself the Pleasure of walking in *silver shoes*, or looking about at the Beauty of the Waves, or listening to the Noise of Sailors, if he was commanded to deny himself the advantage of *fishing* by the Way, would there be any Hardship in such Self-denial?[10]

Half-way through we are introduced to Law's most brilliant and successful rhetorical device, his little, satirical thumb-nail character sketches.

Titius is temperate and regular, but then he is so great a *Mathematician* that he does not know when *Sunday* comes . . . *Philo* . . . is a *Virtuoso* devoted to polite literature . . . and thinks all Time to be lost that is not spent in search of *Shells, Urns, Inscriptions and broken pieces of Pavements. Patronus* is fond of a *Clergyman* who understands *Music, Painting, Statuary, and Architecture* . . . he never comes to the Sacrament but will go forty miles to see a fine *Altar-piece.*[11]

There is a rigorous definition of what constitutes gluttony, which would disconcert a Byrom and a Johnson, to say nothing of Parson Woodforde. In the ninth and tenth chapters there is an all-out attack on play-reading, and on the stage.

The most innocent diversions are for Law literally a waste of time, and the idea that God intends any part of our human existence for beauty and delight or that the pursuit of learning might itself be the goal of a dedicated life seems quite excluded. Yet, despite the seers of Koheleth and Putney, all that is human is not vanity nor human joys empty.

We turn with relief to his positive teaching.

We are true members of the Kingdom of God when the Kingdom of God is within us, when the Spirit of religion is the Spirit of our Lives, when seated in our Hearts, it diffuses itself into all our Notions, when we are wise by its Wisdom, sober by its Sobriety, and humble by its Humility: when it is the Principle of all our Thoughts and Desires, the Spring of all our Hopes and Fears:

---

[8] Ibid. iii. 12.   [9] Ibid. iii. 98.   [10] Ibid. iii. 104.
[11] Ibid. iii. 139.

when we like and dislike, seek and avoid, mourn and rejoice as becomes those who are born again of God.[12]

The work closes with a chapter on the imitation of Christ, and it includes this fine exhortation to the study of the gospels:

nothing is so likely a Means to fill us with His Spirit and Temper as to be frequent in reading the *Gospels* which contain the History of his Life and Conversation in the world. We are apt to think that we have sufficiently read a book, when we have so read it as to know what it contains, this reading may be sufficient as to many books, but as to the Gospels, we are not to think that we have ever read them enough because we have often read and heard what they contain. But we must read them as we do our *Prayers*, not to know what they contain but to fill our Hearts with the Spirit of them . . . by thus conversing with our Blessed Lord looking into his actions and manner of life, hearing his Divine Sayings, his Heavenly Instructions, his accounts of the Terrors of the Damned, his Descriptions of the Glory of the Righteous, we should find our hearts formed and disposed to *Hunger and Thirst after Righteousness*.[13]

What Law knew, but what the Dr Trapps of this world forget, is that young men find no challenge in a call to mediocrity. But through the centuries there has been a succession of young men, like the Rich Young Ruler, in that they have had great material or spiritual possessions, but who, instead of turning away from Christ, have gladly and joyfully left all to follow him, and obeyed the drastic call—a Benedict, a Francis, an Ignatius, a Wesley—and amid the trivialities of our own age, a Thomas Merton. No wonder that John Wesley recommended these two treatises to his followers, while the *Perfection* was perhaps even more beloved by Charles Wesley, for some of its phrases got into his hymns, and at least one of them turns sentences of Law into verse.[14] And if it be true, as it seems to be true, that one grateful reader sent his servant to seek out the author, to hand him a note for £1,000, it seems that at least one rich young ruler may have got the message.

Law's *Serious Call to a Devout and Holy Life* (1729) has become a classic, sure to be reprinted in any collection of devotional writings, still speaking to the condition of men and women, rooted though it is in a transient social context of a genteel society. Law writes mainly for the well-to-do, and for those with leisure, and he has little use for trade, while he is completely silent about the splendid army of skilled craftsmen in that age, whose furniture, pottery, silver, and clocks might illustrate the theme that in the handiwork of their craft is their prayer.

[12] Ibid. iii. 142.   [13] Ibid. iii. 231.
[14] Ibid. iii. 29–30. The Hymn is 'Lord that I may learn of thee, give me true simplicity.'

But on his chosen audience his impact was direct. 'When I was at Oxford', said Dr Johnson in the most famous of all tributes to the book, 'I took up Law's *Serious Call to a Devout and Holy Life*, expecting to find it a dull book (as such books generally are) and perhaps to laugh at it. But I found Law quite an overmatch for me, and this was the first occasion of my thinking in earnest about religion.' 'By means of it God worked powerfully upon my soul', said George Whitefield, and John Wesley was exactly right when he praised it as a work 'which will hardly be excelled either for beauty of expression, or for justness and depth of thought . . . an almost unequalled standard of the strength and purity of our language as well as of sound divinity.'

What had been a minor feature of his earlier treatise now becomes a central feature of this work, the little thumb-nail character sketches become carefully and meticulously thought-out miniature portraits, the like of which had not perhaps appeared since the characters in *Pilgrim's Progress*, though a small literature of character sketches lay between. They appear between the passages of exhortation and counsel, always riveting attention and engaging the imagination. Law's gallery has a range and variety, with shrewd delineation of recognizable types of men and women very much in the world. There is Calidus, the wealthy tradesman: 'he is now so rich that he would leave off his business and amuse his old age with building, and furnishing a fine house in the country, but that he is afraid he should grow melancholy if he were to quit his business.'[15]

It is of course a retelling of the parable of the man who rebuilt his barns, but Law on the whole takes a poor view of trade and considers that men devote more than ten times the proper amount of time to it. He knows nothing of that world which Defoe knew so well, and there would have been no prosperous Britain had men carried out his precepts. Some of his characters make splendid satire, none better than Flatus, that Mr Toad of Toad Hall always turning from one project to another, and Flavia, who,

if she lives ten years longer . . . will have spent about *fifteen hundred and sixty Sundays* after this manner. She will have worn out *two hundred* different suits of clothes. Out of this *thirty* years of her life, *fifteen* of them will have been disposed of in bed: and of the remaining fifteen, about *fourteen* of them will have been consumed in eating, drinking, dressing, visiting, conversation, reading and hearing Plays and Romances, at Operas, Assemblies, Balls and Diversions.[16]

It is notoriously easier to depict sinners than saints and Law's ideal women, Miranda and Eusebia, are perhaps too severe, and fail to make

[15] *Works*, iv. 36.   [16] Ibid. iv. 59.

their goodness charming or attractive. Miranda lacks the appeal of Thomas Ken's Lady Mainard, and Eusebia cannot delight us as does Bunyan's Mercy. Isaac Watts's ladies may be clumsily drawn in comparison, but they are more human, and one sighs for a little of the humanity of Sir Thomas More's daughters before him or the ladies of Jane Austen yet to come.

There are moments which border on the grotesque as witness the dreadful fate, worthy of Belloc's *Cautionary Tales*, of Matilda's daughter who

died in the twentieth year of her age. When her body was opened it appeared that her *ribs* had grown into her *liver*, and that her other *entrails* were much hurt, by being *crushed* together with her *stays*, which her mother had ordered to be twitched so strait.[17]

There is of course an adulation of virginity, and an abhorrence of any kind of delight in dress and ornamentation. One feels that the stately homes of Hanoverian England, had Law had his way, would have overflowed with dowdy spinsters. His schools, where there must be no competition, no ambition, in the paramount interests of inculcating humility, must have been crawling with little Uriah Heeps.

He has one or two harmless bees in his bonnet: six pages on the need to rise early in the morning (no doubt rueful reading for Byrom and Johnson) and a curious insistence on the benefit of singing aloud at one's prayers. This was fine for Thomas Ken, and perhaps for Law himself, but when he recommends it for those who have no privacy one shudders at the context of barking dogs and howling infants in the humbler dwellings.

None the less there are some unforgettable portraits, Susurrus, the evil gossiper, Ouranios, the parson who gradually learns more excellent ways, and old Paternus speaking for an earlier generation, out of a store of traditional Christian wisdom, for some of it may go back to Thomas Becon's catechism.

And here and there are splendid images:

if you should see a man that had a large *pond* of water, yet living in *continual thirst*, not suffering himself to drink *half a draught* for fear of lessening his pond: if you should see him wasting his time and strength, in *fetching more* water to his pond, always *thirsty*, yet always carrying a *bucket* of water in his hand, watching early and late to catch the *drops* of rain, gaping after every cloud and running greedily into every *mire* and *mud* in hopes of water, and always studying how to make every *ditch* empty itself into his *pond*. If you should see him grow *grey* and *old* in these anxious labours, and at last end a *careful, thirsty* life by falling into his

[17] Ibid. iv. 195.

own *pond* would you not say that such a one . . . was foolish enough to be reckoned amongst *idiots* and *madmen*?[18]

But this, Law adds is only half the folly of the covetous man.

The last part of the book is about prayer. He considered suitable themes for prayer at intervals during every day: humility at 9 a.m., at noon universal love (John Wesley's emphasis on universal love owed more to Law than to Arminius). This is expanded into some fine passages about intercession: 'For there is nothing that makes us love a man so much as praying for him: and when you once do this sincerely for any man you have fitted your soul for the performance of everything that is kind and civil towards him.'[19] At 3 o'clock the theme is resignation and conformity to the will of God, that *Gelassenheit* which Law had learned from Tauler, Suso, and the *Theologia Germanica*. At night we are to confess our sins 'particularly' and to meditate on death. And although this is in the mode of Ken's great evening hymn, we may need Charles Wesley's hymns about the surrounding presence of Christ and his angels as a corrective. And always there are plain and fluent sentences, engaging and attractive:

God loves us not because we are wise and good, and holy, but in pity to us, because we want this happiness. He loves us in order to make us good. Our love therefore must take this course; not looking for, or requiring the merit of our brethren, but pitying their disorders, and wishing them all the good that they want, and are capable of receiving.[20]

It would be wrong to make these two treatises the dividing line between Law as moralist and Law as mystic. For this is not simply morality, but that without which morality becomes impossible and meaningless, the new life which God pours into the hearts of those who unreservedly commit themselves to him.

iii. Law's Rigorism

No appraisal of William Law can ignore his rigorism. It was something deeper than the austerity of the high-church tradition as we find it in Andrewes and Ken. In part it may have been temperamental, but it stemmed also from his conviction of the absolute demands of the gospel for renunciation, mortification, and resignation, his sense of the transitoriness of human life and the peril and vanity of its pleasures. He found support for it in the Gospels, and in a rather one-sided reading of the primitive Church, which he expounded more in the spirit of

---

[18] *Works*, iv. 96.   [19] Ibid. iv. 228.   [20] Ibid. iv. 223.

Tertullian than that of Clement. With Boehme he seems to come to the edge of Gnosticism and to a disparagement of the flesh, and of the relations between the sexes such as the Manichaeans and Cathari embraced, though he draws back just in time in his discussion about marriage. While he acknowledges the divine light shining on all creatures, what he has to say is far more sombre than the delight and joy in creation of a Francis, a Vaughan, or a Traherne.

This appears in startling form in his answer to the sermons of Dr Trapp on 'The Folly and Danger of being Righteous overmuch'.[21]

To this he was provoked by the fact that Trapp cited his *Christian Perfection* as an example of Enthusiasm. He was also outraged that in a dissolute and worldly age, the gospel should be used to encourage complacent worldliness and self-indulgence, substituting conventional usages and manners for the absolute demands of the Christian ethic.

He was angered when Trapp suggested that the miracle of turning water into wine at Cana showed Jesus seeking to give men pleasure, affirming that 'it is plain there had been more drunk than was absolutely necessary for the support of nature and consequently something indulged to pleasure and to cheerfulness.'[22]

It is a typical ploy of Law's polemic to turn 'pleasure and cheerfulness' into 'indulgence' and thereafter to assume that his adversary was condoning 'indulgence'.

Overton dismisses Law's exegesis as whimsical, but its implications are surely serious. For Law says that the wine into which the water was miraculously turned

> was not *common Wine*, and therefore has not the *least Relation* to our *common drinking* . . . it was not wine from the *Juice* of the *Grape* . . . it had nothing in it but what came from a heavenly Hand . . . it was water . . . only so altered and endued with *such Qualities* as he pleased to put into it: . . . to allay the Heat and Disorder of drinking.[23]

And he later refers to common wine as 'that which has the curse of the earth in it . . . the wine that is squeezed from the grape under the curse of sin.'[24] (One would like to ask Law how such wine could fitly be used in the Eucharist.) 'Wine so created could not possibly be *just the same sort of Wine as if it had been from the Juice of the Grape* . . . because the Grape and every earthly thing stands in a state of Evil, Corruption, and Curse through . . . Sin . . .'[25]

---

[21] Joseph Trapp DD (b. 1697) was the first Professor of Poetry at Oxford. He held two city livings and was chaplain to Bolingbroke.

[22] Quoted *Works*, vi. 27.   [23] Ibid. vi. 28.   [24] Ibid. vi. 158.

[25] Ibid. vi. 159.

In his later 'Animadversions' against Trapp's reply, Law goes even further. Jesus, he says, did order a number of jars to be filled to the brim with water, but not with any intention of turning them into 'wine'. Only that one cup, which he had given to the steward was in fact made the subject of the miracle and the other jars of water were there to increase the awe of the guests. The object of the miracle was not to bring happiness and pleasure, but 'to put an astonishing end to their drinking'.[26] Law was very pleased with this, his very own explanation, but one would not find it out of place in some Gnostic apocryphal gospel. At this point Law eulogizes St John the Baptist, and conforms Jesus to the image of his cousin. Jesus, he says did indeed dine with publicans and sinners, but only in order to convert them. One wonders why in the teaching of Jesus so many parables are concerned with feasting and even with dancing, and why in fact the Gospels mention so many festive meals where he was the invited guest.

In the same treatise Law attacks clerical marriage. He does not deny that the institution of marriage is honourable, even though it is a concession to sinful man in a fallen world.[27] But he asserts that from the first the Church has discouraged clerical marriage. 'St Paul has done everything to hinder a minister of Christ from entering into marriage except calling it a sinful state.'[28] The lesson of St John the Baptist to ministers is that 'they should look upon love addresses to the sex as unbecoming and foreign to their characters as to the Baptist's.[29]

In the early Church 'need anyone be told it must have been highly shameful . . . for a priest . . . to be looking out for a wife?'[30] When one thinks of the love between Matthew Parker and his wife, or of Richard and Margaret Baxter, examples which could be multiplied many thousandfold, there is something rather like an obscene Hogarth cartoon in Law's shuddering comment: 'If a Christian of those days were to come into the world . . . he must needs be more shocked at seeing Reverend Doctors in sacerdotal robes making love to women than at seeing a monk in his cell kissing a crucifix.'[31]

For Law sex and human birth are seen as part of the fallen human condition. Only a bachelor could have written as Law does about human birth.

Look at the human infant just come out of the Womb, you can hardly bear the sight; it is a Picture of such Deformity, Nakedness, Weakness and helpless Distress, as is not seen among the home-born Animals of this World. The *Chicken* has its Birth from no Sin, and therefore it comes forth in beauty: it runs

---

[26] Ibid. vi. 160–1.　　　[27] *Works*, vii. 90.　　　[28] Ibid., vi. 176.
[29] Ibid. vi. 176.　　　[30] Ibid. vi. 177.　　　[31] Ibid. vi. 175.

and pecks as soon as its Shell is broken: the *Pig* and the *Calf* go both to play, as soon as their Dam is delivered of them; they are pleased with themselves, and please the Eye that beholds their frolic State and beauteous Clothing; while the new born Babe of a Woman that is to have an upright form, that is to view the heavens and worship the God that made them, lies for Months in gross Ignorance, Weakness and Impurity; as sad a Spectacle when he first begins to breathe the Life of this World as when in the Agonies of Death he breathes his last.[32]

Man, he adds 'had been born of a bestial womb, like the wild asses' colt.'

And though Law admits, within its limits, the value of secular employment, there are moments when he is as savage as Swift about human nature.

Man gives himself up to a Wisdom that is Foolishness, a Greatness that is all Meanness, and a Happiness that begins and ends in Torment and Delusion. Would you see all his Greatness, Wisdom and Happiness united, the Sum total of earthly Glory! It is, when he has in his Cap the Feathers of some Birds, wears a painted Riband, laced Clothes, is called by some new Name and drawn from Place to Place by Number of beasts.[33]

The highest good of this world 'is a bestial life . . . it has no other happiness for a man than for a beast.'[34]

It has to be admitted that in his denunciation of contemporary worldliness and in his distrust of marriage his views were shared by the young men he influenced. George Whitefield accepted his absolute denunciation of the stage, and not only believed that no Christian could be an actor, but denied that the office of an attorney was possible for good Christians. John Wesley's rules about dress and his tracts on the subject keep close to those of Law, as do Wesley's own tracts about celibacy which he recommended strongly for his preachers, though not, perhaps unhappily, for himself.

Law's attack on the stage includes a stern denunciation of the evil of painting—the use of cosmetics—and he constantly emphasized the grievous consequences to young women of taking pride in their personal appearance or delighting in nice clothes. In one of his oddly peremptory notes to Hester Gibbon he complains about her maid, Betty:

Her dress was not much according to my mind—she is too fine and seems too

---

[32] *Works*, vii. 165.

[33] Ibid. vii. 248. Elsewhere Law uses this imagery about Haman in the Book of Esther. But it might be George I!

[34] *Works*, vii. 248, also vi. 166: 'our natural life in this world is a corrupt, disorderly, bestial, diabolical life brought forth by the Fall.'

much pleased with it—had she come down as plain and unhooped as she went up, it had been better for herself and more suitable to ye mistress she comes from and to ye mother she comes to—when a girl is once pleased with her dress she is exposed to every folly—I have often been afraid that I gave too good cloths in ye school, but to prevent all thoughts of finery I never allowed a white apron, or a bit of rippon [*sic*] on ye head.[35]

He might have learned from Hildegard of Bingen, who encouraged her nuns to celebrate Easter by adorning their habits with flowers.

The most devastating comment on Law's rigorism came from his own household, when soon after his death Hester Gibbon appeared in yellow stockings, and his niece announced that in future she would wear a new dress a month.

iv. Law and Boehme

Jacob Boehme (1575–1624),[36] the seer, stands well above a number of lesser luminaries who emerged under the shadow of the Reformation. His reputation is high in his native Germany, where he is seen as a seminal influence on the great idealist philosophers. A small Behmenist[37] sect has survived into recent times. He profoundly influenced a number of thinkers, Pierre Poiret, William Law, and C. F. Oetinger in the eighteenth, and the Scandinavian H. L. Martensen in the nineteenth, centuries.

Boehme, who was in turn shepherd, shoemaker, and linen draper, like our John Bunyan and George Fox, came from a lettered, but not highly educated, class, and lived at Görlitz in Silesia, a part of Germany much influenced by the radical reformation and where there were groups adherent to the teachings of Paracelsus, Schwenckfeld, and Weigel. Here he underwent experiences which he believed were a direct communication from God. His first work, the '*Aurora*', circulated in manuscript, but got into the hands of the local Lutheran pastor, Richter, who became a relentless enemy. But he found friends among educated

---

[35] Walton MS (Dr Williams's Library) 186.5.22, 10 Sept. 1742.

[36] Difficult though his writings are, he is easier to understand than his commentators. A good book is A. Koyré, *La Philosophie de J. Boehme*, 1929. Also P. Hankamer, *J. Boehme*, 1924. On his relation with Luther, H. Bornkamm, *Böhme und Luther*, 1920, and *Luther Jahrbuch*, 1927, ix. 156–98; also A. A. Muller, 'The theologies of Luther and Boehme in the light of their Genesis commentaries', *Harvard Theological Review*, 63 (1970), 261–303. For a not very satisfactory version of Martensen's *Studies*, S. Hobhouse, 1959.

[37] We have generally used Boehme for his name and the old fashioned 'Behmenist' for his ideas and disciples.

groups of medical men and scholars, who sometimes tried to exploit his writings in their alchemical pursuits.

His writing *Der Weg zu Christo*[38] expounds the evangelical core of his message, the need for repentance, for the New Birth, and the divine life within the redeemed soul. Much more complex were his cosmological myths, which he believed to be revealed descriptions of ultimate realities, and these he treated in *Die drei Prinzipien*, *Signatura Rerum*, and the *Mysterium Magnum*, an exposition of the story of Adam in Genesis. His writings are highly original, but often confused and obscure. But he had no traditional metaphysical framework and was driven to rely on a vocabulary and symbolism derived from Paracelsus, and from the astrologers and alchemists, though it seems that his debts to an earlier mystical tradition were unconscious.

A drowsy numbness seems to steal over the critical sense of their admirers when they touch this side of Boehme and of Law. But we do not serve either of them, still less the truth, if we walk round the problems involved. No doubt we are not to evaluate Boehme's teachings as though he were St Anselm or Martin Luther or Karl Barth, but rather as we should judge the *Two Ways* of St Hildegard (who got her natural science much better than Boehme) or the *Shewings* of the Lady Julian. And it may be true that his symbolism is like poetry or a superior science fiction rather than philosophy. At his best we glimpse what is beautiful and profound, albeit as through a glass, darkly. But at its worst we have the imagery of a Jerome Bosch expressed in the language of Jabberwocky. 'We must not blame him', says Rufus Jones, 'for his obscurities and for his large regions of rubbish and confusion, but be thankful for the luminous patches.' But we may not pass by with a wink and a pat on the head what Boehme and Law believed to be vital elements in their teaching. At the end of the day the questions must be asked.

Does this description of the universe correspond to any real truth? Does this complex myth of creation and redemption not involve serious errors about God and about the human condition, which more than invalidate their genuine insights? And at the very least we must understand why a Hoadly, a Trapp, a Warburton, and a Wesley could make nothing of the great wodges of Boehme suddenly intruded into a rational debate, and which seemed to them but gibberish and 'enthusiasm'.

We are not directly concerned to expound Boehme, and in what follows shall concentrate on that part of his teaching which was anglicized by Law. In his answer to Dr Trapp, Law acknowledged his

[38] A recent modern translation by P. Erb has been published in the series *Classics of Western Spirituality*, New York 1978.

debt to the whole mystic tradition as well as to Boehme and claimed, 'I never wrote upon any subject till I could call it my own, till I was so possessed of the truth of it, that I could sufficiently prove it in my own way, without borrowed arguments.'[39] But whether assimilated or borrowed, the main teachings of Boehme become central to the exposition of salvation by the later Law. He seems to have been put on to Boehme by a reference by Dr Cheyne to a German writing *Fides et ratio* in the period 1733–5, though the first real indication of his new preoccuption comes in a startling digression in the middle of his eucharistic debate with Hoadly.[40]

In William Law Boehme found what Kierkegaard would have called 'his lover'.[41] The books which influence us most deeply are very often not those which tell us something new, but those which confirm and make articulate what we have always known. Law did not need to alter deep convictions already arrived at, and he says he does not always agree with Boehme. It is sad that it was the more dubious parts of Boehme that he swallowed, hook, line, and sinker.

He did not need to be told by Boehme of the supreme importance of 'inward religion'. The stress on 'Christ in us', the need for resignation and conformity to the will of God, the need to mortify the old Adam—those he knew already from his reading of Tauler, Suso, Ruysbroeck, the *Theologia Germanica*, and the *Imitation of Christ*, and he had already found support for his view of religion in his reading of the Early Church and of the Desert Fathers, notably Macarius.

Law accepts, but does not expound, Boehme's doctrine of God in himself as the 'Abyss'[42] or *Urgrund*, the 'ground of all things'. But he refers often to the 'Abyssal all'.[43] He also accepts Boehme's teaching about Eternal Nature which precedes the created world,[44] and so, with Boehme, fiercely attacks the traditional doctrine of a *creatio ex nihilo*.[45]

Further, he accepts Boehme's vital doctrine of the Seven Properties of this Eternal Nature.[46] They are almost untranslatable, and when turned into such English terms as 'whirling' seemed gibberish to John Wesley. They are fundamental dynamic energies, in conflict and polarity, dividing the universe between darkness and light but bringing all things

---

[39] *Works*, vi. 204.   [40] Ibid. v. 70–112.

[41] For Law's references to Boehme see *Works*, vi. 205; vii. 47, 76, 148, 188, 195; viii. 13; ix. 153.

[42] *Works*, viii. 37.   [43] Ibid. vii. 199; viii. 11.

[44] Ibid. vi. 108; viii. 90, 147.   [45] Ibid. vi. 60, 108.

[46] They are: 'Herbigkeit, Bitterkeit, Angst-Rad ("Wirrung") Feuerschrack, Liebe-essenz, Schall, Gehaüse.'

to eventual harmony. Fallen creation belongs to an underworld of fire and wrath, but the divine light and love also shine upon it.[47]

There are in Boehme many subsidiary themes, some of which are highly complex and which perhaps are not always harmonized with one another. There is the important doctrine of the Virginal Wisdom, which within the framework of the creative work of the Holy Trinity, touches the relation between Creator and creation. There is the doctrine of what he calls 'the Centre', and an insistence on the freedom of the will. Throughout, the physical universe is endowed with moral, and even human, attributes, and plants and vegetables 'hunger' and 'desire', while the wrath of a storm and the wrath of a human being are not so described in terms of mere analogy, but really represent characteristics of the fallen world. He even uses the category of magic. The somewhat bizarre tables and figures which Freher uses to illustrate these doctrines link the whole with astrological, alchemical, and numerological symbols (seven, two, three) and to tables relating the fate of man, under the stars and the elements, to salt and mercury and sulphur. Law never disagrees with any of this though these things are often implicit rather than explicit in his arguments.

In the process Law's language is Teutonized into such grisly phrases as 'The Eternal will in the Deity is a desiring or generating the Son from whence the Holy Spirit of God proceeds. And therefore attraction which is an Out-birth of the divine desire stands in a perpetual desiring.'[48] Both thinkers make much of Trinitarian imagery, in the doctrine of God and in their doctrine of Adam.[49]

Perhaps the idea of wrath is more complex in Boehme than in Law, but the image of fire is one that appeals to Law and he returns to it constantly, backing it up with quotations from the Pseudo-Dionysius which had thrilled John Colet two centuries before.[50] Important for both is the positive character of darkness, in opposition to light.[51]

The fall of the angels is very important for the salvation myth. One result was the creation of a fallen world, even before the fall of Adam.[52] Boehme and Law's central Adamic myth has a Gnostic character, and Law's preoccupation with apocryphal gospels and his acceptance of apostolic authority for Pseudo-Dionysius may have strengthened a spiritualism, the origins of which are in Hellenistic thought. All that is heavenly is spiritual, from Adam himself to the fruits and vegetables which existed before the Fall, even though he speaks of a 'heavenly' or

[47] *Works*, vi. 709; vii. 237; viii. 61, 118, 120.   [48] *Works*, vi. 86.
[49] Ibid. v. 138; vi. 16, 77, 86; ix. 147.
[50] Ibid. vi. 132; also v. 140, 150; vi. 112; vii. 45, 57; viii. 37, 39, 55, 66.
[51] Ibid. vii. 72; viii. 111.   [52] Ibid. vi. 16.

'spiritual materiality'. Only after the Fall did man receive a 'gross, heavy, fleshly body'.[53] Before the Fall Adam had a 'pearly paradisiacal body'.[54] And if he admits the Incarnation, what are we to make out of his doctrine that 'our Blessed Lord had a heavenly humanity which clothed itself with the Flesh and Blood in the Womb of the Virgin?[55] . . . if our Lord Christ had not had a heavenly humanity consisting of such flesh and blood as is not of this world he had not been so perfect as Adam was.'[56] It is this heavenly flesh and blood on which Christians feed in the Eucharist.

Boehme's myth of Adam and the Fall is much more complex than that of the main Christian tradition. For him, the eating of the forbidden fruit is trivial. The real fall of Adam was a gradual process which began with Adam's roving eye: 'his first *longing look* towards the Knowledge of the Life of this World—was the first *loosening* of the Reins of Evil—it began to have Life, and a Power of stirring, as soon as his Desire began to be earthly.'[57]

Adam was androgynous—as Kipling said of the marine, 'a kind of a giddy harumfrodite'—male and female in one person. Adam had in fact already 'lost much of his perfection before Eve was taken out of him'[58] as a lesser evil to prevent a worse.[59] 'His first virginity was lost by an *adulterate* Love which had turned its desire into this World. This state of *Inability* is that which is called his falling into a deep sleep: And in this sleep, God divides this overcome humanity . . .'[60] Eve was created as a lesser evil, 'for it was a less degree of falling . . . to love the female part of his own divided nature . . . than to . . . love that . . . which was so much lower.'[61] This, Law explains, does not disparage the female sex or the honourable estate of matrimony. And of course the pivot of this whole myth is the famous Protevangelium of Genesis 3: 15 which speaks of redemption coming from the seed of woman.[62] For it is central to this myth that 'mankind were redeemed as soon as they were lost',[63] and the promise to Adam that the Seed of the woman shall bruise the serpent's head was accomplished, then and there, in the garden of Eden. This declaration of pardon was as creative as when God said 'Let there be light.' Instead of the particularity of the incarnation and the Cross, the history of salvation now becomes a timeless myth for it was 'then' that God gave to fallen man and woman a divine seed, a spark, a principle of holiness, the pearl of the Gospel, the hidden Kingdom of God.[64]

And though Law speaks again and again of our incorporation into

[53] Ibid. v. 138.   [54] Ibid. vi. 19.   [55] Ibid. vi. 150–1.
[56] Ibid. vi. 150.   [57] Ibid. vii. 93.   [58] Ibid. vii. 80.
[59] Ibid. vii. 84.   [60] Ibid. vii. 84.   [61] Ibid. vii. 85.
[62] Ibid. v. 72–3.   [63] Ibid. v. 71.   [64] Ibid. v. 73–4.

Christ, the second Adam,[65] and would have been shocked at the suggestion that he in any way disparaged the part played by the Son of God in our redemption, when he expounds this myth he pays little attention to the true humanity of Christ, and it is perhaps not accidental that in his later writings he refers more and more often to the 'Christ process'.[66]

The great myth, for all its talk of two humanities, is almost entirely concerned with individual souls. Though Law read and annotated St Irenaeus, with his powerful doctrine of a *recapitulatio*, Law is not interested in history nor does he expound the Two Adams in terms of the 'mystical body'. In fact the busy tribes of flesh and blood, man in his cities and nations and societies, hardly feature in Law's later writings. He has less to say about what Wesley called 'social holiness' than about the nature of heavenly and earthly vegetables.[67]

Both Boehme and Law believe that the real confirmation of their view is to be found in the human heart and man's condition. He knows the Two Adams in his own life. He himself is under the stars and the elements, knows the struggle of wrath within himself, finds that in no way, by his own efforts, can he turn himself from this fallen state not even with the aid of reason, or by the effort of his will. All he can do in freedom is to turn towards the divine communication of new life, which enables him to experience the New Birth,[68] an event which, like the Fall, is not a once-for-all happening, but a process.

We have seen that for doctrinaire reasons Boehme and Law oppose the *creatio ex nihilo*. And no doubt one of the easements which Boehme brought to Law was that it gave him an answer to the Calvinist scheme of predestination, to the traditional Protestant doctrine of the work of Christ 'for us', with its forensic and 'objective' view of the Atonement.[69] For both Law and Boehme believed that the heart of God is pure love, and that in the heart of the Divine Being there is no wrath. They both attack fiercely the doctrine of imputation, and the analogy of debts and debtors. It is interesting to find that Pierre Poiret used the same arguments to the same end.[70]

No doubt Lutheran orthodoxy in Silesia and Protestant doctrine in England had a wooden and vulnerable doctrine of atonement. But it was perhaps a pity that the black-out of medieval thought in his age kept

[65] Ibid. v. 74.
[66] Ibid. vi. 149; vii. 200; viii. 83; viii. 145, 251, ix. 139.
[67] Ibid. vi. 93, 85; vii. 164, 117.
[68] Ibid. v. 168; vi. 77; vii. 23, 71; ix. 153, 155.
[69] Ibid. vi. 140; vii. 14; viii. 70, 74, 78, 82; ix. 141.
[70] Krieg, *Der mystische Kreis*, pp. 168ff.

Law from at least pondering the questions profoundly raised if not answered in Anselm's *Cur Deus Homo?*.

Law continues and even extends the range of Boehme's polemic against what he called 'Babel', which for him arose out of his own bitter persecution by learned obscurantists. Reason for both men is part of fallen human nature, and becomes the text for a continuing onslaught by Law against Christian scholarship, Biblical critics and commentators, and all Christians who devote their energies to the study of the pagan classics. There is in fact one moment of partial disclaimer. In one of his *Dialogues* Law says:

> I am no more an Enemy to Learning than I am to that Art which builds Mills to grind our Corn . . . I esteem the liberal Arts and Sciences as the noblest of human Things; I desire no Man to dislike or renounce his Skill in ancient or modern languages: his Knowledge of Medals, Pictures, Paintings, History, Geography or Chronology: I have no more Dislike of these Things in themselves than the art of Throwing silk or making Lace.[71]

It must be admitted that there was some learning in the Church of Law's day which was a little top-heavy. Hervey spoke disdainfully of 'Greek and Hebrew blockheads' among the bishops, and there were plenty of antiquarians about, among them Archbishops Sharp and Wake, with their coins and medals. And no doubt the Biblical commentaries of a Patrick, a Doddridge, a Clarke, a Prideaux, a Heylyn, a Warburton abounded in pedantries and inaccuracies in what was an infant stage of Biblical criticism. But these things do not justify Law's fierce polemic.[72] Yet throughout these writings, through the most tedious repetitions of his later works, there are wonderfully luminous passages about the love of God.

> The universal God is universal love: all is Love, but that which is hellish and earthly. All religion is the Spirit of Love: all its Gifts and Graces are the Gifts and Graces of Love: it has no Breath, no Life but the Life of Love. Nothing exalts, nothing purifies, but the Fire of Love: nothing changes Death into Life, Earth into Heaven, Men into Angels, but Love alone.[73]

A passage worthy of Peter Sterry. Or this, of the order of Nature:

> Eternal Nature is the invisible God, the incomprehensible Trinity *eternally breaking* forth, and manifesting itself in a boundless Height and Depth of blissful Wonders, opening and displaying itself to all its Creatures as in an infinite Variation and endless Multiplicity of its Powers, Beauties, Joys and Glories. So

---

[71] *Works*, vii. 189.

[72] Among many other passages: *Works* v. 91, 117, 168; vi. 20, 183; vii. 150, 152, 157, 162, 182, 192–3, 221, 256; viii. 90, 125, 189; ix. 23.

[73] *Works*, vii. 108.

that all the Inhabitants of Heaven are for ever Knowing, Seeing, Hearing, Feeling and variously enjoying all that is great, amiable, infinite and glorious in the divine nature.[74]

Law's theme of the divine life within us as a seed, or as a hidden pearl, or as a grain of mustard seed, came nearer than perhaps he knew to the teaching of the Quakers whom he had earlier withstood. But in his last years he was more and more aware of the affinities, and judged the writings of Isaac Pennington to be fit for his little lending library. In Law's last writings, he almost out-Quakers the Quakers, in his denunciation of oath taking and of war—this last the most eloquent condemnation perhaps since the *Colloquies* of Erasmus.

How far William Law came to abandon his high-church doctrines about the visible Church cannot be known, but certainly he came to a new conception of the meaning of a catholic spirit, and to think of the Church as supremely a 'communion of saints'.

There is therefore a *Catholic Spirit*, a *Communion of Saints* in the Love of God and all Goodness, which no one can learn from that which is called *Orthodoxy* in particular churches . . . uniting in heart and spirit with all that is *holy* and *good* in all Churches we enter into the true *Communion of Saints*, and become real Members of the holy *Catholic Church*, though we are confined to the outward Worship of only one particular Part of it.[75]

Law's blind spot, perhaps, was a failure to recognize that even if Boehme's teachings were, as he believed, divine communications, they were none the less notions expressed in words, and were in fact speculative philosophy. They were not only descriptions of salvation, but claimed to describe the whole universe and its relation to its divine maker. They gave Law himself something of a rationale of nature in an age when all men felt the need to make sense of it. The point of his claim that Sir Isaac Newton himself had 'ploughed with Boehme's heifer' and owed to him his doctrine of gravity, is not that it was true (Newton at most included Boehme in his great collection of 175 alchemical writings) but that Law believed it to be so and that what Boehme said was not mystic symbolism but a true description of the nature of things. Nor did he consider that it was all a century late: that a vocabulary possible in 1624 was antiquated in 1734, when the whole philosophy of alchemy was on its way out. On the other hand, Boehme's teaching was an immense relief for Law as an apologist. He had long despaired at the endless attempt to meet the Socinians, the Deists and the infidels on rational and scientifically critical grounds. Boehme's way short-

[74] Ibid. vi. 125. See also viii. 35.   [75] *Works*, vi. 184.

circuited all this controversy in the simple demand, 'You must be born again'.

It has sometimes been said that Law's prose improved in his later writings. There seems more evidence that it was spoiled by being Teutonized, and one cannot discover the early commender of simplicity in such sentences as the following:

Darkness is so far from being . . . only an Absence of Light that it is . . . the ground of all the possible Substantiality in Nature and the substantial Manifestor of Light itself . . . this Darkness, Thickness, or Substantiality is not co-existent with God . . . but is the *compressing, astringing thickening* work of the first Property of Desire: Which Desire comes eternally from God, only as a magic Birth from the Will of the Deity.[76]

In his last years, Law tells us, he read little other than the works of Boehme in German and the writings of Freher and Francis Lee. This almost obsessive fascination with Boehme must surely be regarded as a last infirmity of his noble mind. For despite their beautiful ascriptions to the love of God and their stress on the work of God within the soul, the myth of the two Adams seems to be more anthropocentric than Christocentric, and the theme of the 'Christ Process' suggests that Christ's humanity meant for Boehme and Law much less than it had done for St Bernard, for Martin Luther and St Ignatius, for Donne and Herbert and Thomas Ken. And when one reads Law's latter writings with their endless repetition of a blend of nature and redemption much of which has no relation to genuine description, most of it in language which can hardly be called technical, so idiosyncratic is its vocabulary, one sighs to find it so far removed from the luminous clarities of the earlier Law, who had once told John Wesley: 'you would have a philosophical religion, but there can be no such thing. Religion is the most plain, simple thing in the world. It is only "We love him, because he first loved us."'

v. *'A celebrated enthusiast'*[77]

The indwelling Christ, 'God within us', is at the heart of Law's religion. In an age when men stressed the divine transcendence and thought of God as remote from the machinery of creation, and when Protestant orthodoxy stressed 'Christ for us' to the neglect of 'Christ in us', Law followed in the succession of the Cambridge Platonists and the Scottish mystical divines, in returning to the view of Christianity as a divine life communicated to men. At a time when reason was considered to be an

---

[76] *Works*, vii. 241.   [77] Archives, Emmanuel College, Cambridge.

almost flawless tool, Law drew attention to the hidden, irrational, forces in man and in the universe, the conflicts and eruptions in the hidden depths of our being, which distort and deceive our judgements. And if he gives plenty of space and much repetition to the dark side, to the fire and wrath of things, he is in no more doubt than Boehme that the end of all is to be blessedness, harmony, and joy.

It is always perilous to disagree with the judgements of Alexander Whyte, but to call Law the greatest of the English mystics is to beg questions which cannot be answered. Jacob Boehme was a seer, but Law himself disclaimed any such illumination, and he cannot therefore properly be compared with the Lady Julian of Norwich, or with the author of *The Cloud of Unknowing*. About the claims of others to have such experiences, Law was always sceptical and his judgement was shrewd enough about Antoinette de Bourignon and Mme Guyon. He had a good ear for a false note, which he detected in the would-be Quaker, Fanny Henshaw, and in the young men who came to Putney. But about his own inner life he was deliberately reticent, and he left no prayers of the quality of Thomas Ken's. Since he himself vehemently warned of the distinction between mystical writings and mystical experience, we cannot tell from his writings how far he himself had advanced towards perfect resignation and conformity to the divine will.

It is tempting to make Law too modern. For ours, too, is an age which has reacted against a too remote, transcendent God, who is 'out there'. But it is doubtful whether in him we can find premonitions of Tillich or Berdyaev, still less of 'panentheism' or 'process theology'. What is really relevant, surely, is his appeal to a great tradition of Christian spirituality.

Of these Mystical Divines, I thank God, I have been a diligent reader, through all the Ages of the Church from the Apostolical *Dionysius the Areopagite* down to the great *Fenelon . . . St. Cassian . . . The Holy Fathers of the Deserts . . .* the Divine *Rusbrochius, Thaulerus, Suso . . . Johannes de Cruce,* etc. . . . . You will perhaps say, 'Do I then call all the World to these Spiritual Books? No, by no means. But I call all those whom our Saviour called to Himself in these words, "Come unto me all ye that labour and are heavy laden and I will refresh you." '[78]

In our age, when so many have turned away from this and other Christian traditions, to wizards that chirp and mutter, compassing land and sea to sit at the feet of any plausible guru, or turning to schemes, often bogus, of transcendental meditation, Law points us to a great succession of saints and seers and a rich tradition of spiritual wisdom.

Modern Christians, immersed in the world's problems, feeling the

[78] *Works*, vi. 203–5.

strain of a strident activism, are beginning to feel a need to recover the dimension of spiritual depth. It is no disparagement of the insights of the great eastern religions to draw attention to the mystical heritage of the Christian West. From the little Northamptonshire village Law reminds us of a great consensus, over many generations, that the life of God is our eternal home.

Books about William Law

A difficult but indispensible compilation is that of the well-to-do Methodist layman, A. C. Walton: *Materials for an Adequate Biography of William Law* (privately printed 1854). A copy, corrected in his own hand, is in the University Library, Cambridge. He deposited his collection of Law MSS in Dr. Williams's Library. Rather untidy, too, are the compilations of S. Hobhouse: *Selected Mystical Writings of William Law* (1948), and his version, with notes of H. L. Martensen's *Studies in Jacob Boehme* (1949). His *William Law and Eighteenth Century Quakerism* (1929) is a more concentrated study with documents not easily accessible elsewhere. The nine volumes of Law's *Works* published by G. Moreton in 1893 is the best tool. Law seems to be treated rather uncritically by those who have 'rediscovered' his importance—J. H. Overton and Alexander Whyte. Of modern studies A. K. Walker *William Law, his Life and Thought* (1973) is not very perceptive, whereas the less scholarly *About William Law* by A. W. Hopkinson (1948) is full of good things.

16

RATIONALISTS

i. Heresy—and Half Belief?

IT was the modest image of the Middle Ages which protested that its thinkers were, in relation to their forebears, but as dwarfs sitting on the shoulders of giants. The theologians of the eighteenth century suffered from no such inhibitions. They were the giants, and the previous thousand years of thought and devotion was for them a map of darkest Europe, bearing the intermittent labels 'Here be pygmies'. A Stillingfleet, a Tillotson, a Samuel Clarke, a Lavington, a 'John Smith' wrote off the medieval saints and doctors with contempt.[1] Of this the most grotesque illustration is Archbishop Herring when confronted with the request from the Sardinian ambassador that his master, King Charles Emmanuel I, might be given the relics of St Anselm, from Canterbury Cathedral. He wrote to the Dean:

You will believe that I have no great scruples on this head, but if I had I would get rid of them all, if the parting with the rotten remains of a Rebel to his King, a Slave to the Popedom, and an enemy to the married clergy (all this Anselm was) would purchase Ease and Indulgence to one living Protestant . . . really for this, I would make no conscience of palming off on the Simpletons any other old bishop of the name of Anselm.[2]

It is a good question whether this smug barbarism was rooted in the English Protestant tradition, a result of the long hatred of Popery and an Erastian view of English history, and how much it owed to the new Latitudinarianism of the age of Newton. It encouraged eighteenth-century divines to think more highly of their theological originality and competence than they had any right to do. At the moment when the Church had to face an intellectual assault of power and gravity, it abandoned an impressive armament of medieval rationality. After all, it was not their readiness to give away the bones of St Anselm which mattered, but that they had painlessly, and almost without noticing it, given away his mind, the argument of one of the finest theologians ever to tread our shores. They were like that most foolish of the foolish

---

[1] See below, pp. 247, 383, 386.
[2] *Archbishop Herring's Visitation Returns*, York Diocese (1743), ed. S. L. Ollard. vol. v. app. D, Dec. 23, 1752.

virgins shown on the wall of Strasbourg Cathedral, the one who is smiling, with her oil flask upside down, with no idea that she is missing anything. In the debate with Deism, there was no treatise with the profundities of the *Monologium* and the *Proslogion*, and in the argument with Socinianism nothing to match the *Cur Deus Homo?*. In our time Karl Barth could willingly devote much time and attention to a critical discussion of Anselm. He had perhaps hardly heard of Samuel Clarke.

In a well-known essay, Paul Hasard[3] described the age which began with Bossuet and ended with Voltaire as the crisis of European conscience. In England we might delimit it as the century which began with Thomas Hobbes and ended with David Hume. During the interval an apparently monolithic Christian society became divided into those, still the great majority, who took it for granted that Christianity was true, and those who took it for granted that it was false. For such a crisis the English Churches were unprepared, in military jargon, caught off balance. We may trace the growing unease at the signs of unbelief, an awareness that behind noisy coffee-house discussion and printed debate there was a continuing silent apostasy, not to be shrugged off or debated away, a dimension of national life which had come to stay. Like the French army, the Church always seemed ready for the previous war. Its belief in the plenary inspiration of the whole of Scripture—more rigidly conceived than by the Reformers of the sixteenth century which treated it not as a collection of historical documents, but as an arsenal of proof texts—gave little room for manœuvre and none for retreat. Thus both believers and unbelievers accepted that the Christian case stood or fell by the 'proofs' from miracle and prophecy. Only slowly and reluctantly did Christians re-examine their assumptions and come to understand that their massive fortifications—bastions and ravelins and all—were as out of date and irrelevant as those of My Uncle Toby.

Beginning with the Italian humanists, and radicals like the 'godless painters of Nuremberg' it is not easy to trace the growth of overt unbelief in the sixteenth and seventeenth centuries, so many were the prudential considerations which led to dissimulation in a society with savage sanctions against unbelief and blasphemy. It may be that explicit atheism was rare, though Hobbes and Spinoza were bogymen for preachers to tilt at as 'atheistic' and there was obviously a cynical and flamboyant scepticism among the 'Witts' at Restoration Court. But I do not think that Tenison and Tillotson would have devoted so much attention to atheism had there not been some real menace, and it is

[3] *The European Mind*, Eng. Tr. 1964.

perhaps significant that Richard Bentley should devote the first Boyle lectures to the atheistic theme.

Socinianism was the one sustained and heretical creed. It took its name from Lelio Sozini (1525–62) and Fausto Sozzini (1539–1604). Its evangelical rationalism was spread by a group of Italian humanists who moved in exile from Switzerland to Poland. There, like many radicals of the Reformation, they found aristocratic patronage, were allowed to settle, and produced in 1605 the Racovian Catechism, a handy summary of their doctrine which infiltrated western Europe, entering England by Holland. They rejected orthodox Christology, and denied the pre-existence and the deity of Christ, though they invoked him in prayer and gave him honour. Almost as important, they rejected the orthodox doctrines of Atonement and would have nothing to do with a vicarious sacrifice or satisfaction for sin. What attracted many to them was their appeal to reason and Scripture, their rejection of scholasticism, for all these were congenial to the mood of seventeenth-century England.

A few isolated scholars seem to have held Socinian views during the Commonwealth, among them two Royalist divines, John Webberley and Thomas Lushington.[4] But it was another Oxford man, John Biddle (1615–62), an usher at Gloucester, who put Socinianism on the English map, and who for his writings and his obstinacy was imprisoned and sent to exile in the Isles of Scilly. He made a notable convert in the wealthy London merchant and philanthropist, Thomas Firmin (1632–97), who financed the spread of Socinian literature while remaining a faithful pillar of St Mary Woolnoth and an honoured friend of Tillotson and Nelson.

Stephen Nye (1648–1715), who stuck faithfully to his tiny parish of Little Hormead, Hertfordshire, disclaimed the title of Socinian, but accepted that of being a Unitarian, the name which appeared on the title-page of his tract *A Brief History of the Unitarians, Called also Socinians* (1687). He seems to have talked Firmin out of some of Biddle's more exotic beliefs, his anthropomorphic notion that God had a body, and his reduction of the Holy Spirit to the status of a divine emissary. Socinian writings and the growing ferment of discussion in pamphlets and coffee houses, and in many a stately home, raised questions about the person of Christ and the doctrine of the Holy Trinity which could not be ignored.

ii. Tillotson and the Rule of Faith

'There are some who do not stick to brand him with the mark of Heresie, though (to tell the truth), I verily think the only reason is

[4] H. McLachlan, *Socinianism in Seventeenth-Century England*, Oxford 1951; J. H. Colligan, *The Arian Movement in England*, Manchester 1936.

because they imagine he doth believe whatsoever he doth not fiercely oppose.' Simon Patrick's description of the Guide in his *Parable of the Pilgrim* is an apt description of John Tillotson, whose Latitudinarian temper caused him to be charged with teaching the heresies of Hobbes, Socinus, and Arius. But in fact Tillotson's services as a defender of the faith have been generally underestimated, or perhaps obscured, by his fame as a moralist.

But though he wrote only one short treatise—significantly *The Rule of Faith*—his sermons[5] show that he by no means neglected Christian doctrine and worship. His sermons on 'Frequent Communion' and on 'Transubstantiation' were reprinted in the great symposium against Popery. His sermon 'On the Wisdom of Being Religious' is an admirable and forceful attack on atheism, and shows that he was aware that the strength of the argument from Design appears most clearly when opposed to the view that all that exists is a matter of chance. Hence the impressive and unusually extended illustration.

Will chance fit means to ends and that in ten thousand instances and not fail in any one? How often might a man after he had jumbled a set of letters in a bag, fling them out upon the ground before they would fall into an exact poem, yea, or so much as make a good discourse in Prose? And may not a little *Book* be as easily made by chance as this great *Volume* of the world? How long might a man be in sprinkling colours upon Canvas with a careless hand, before they could happen to make the exact Picture of a man? . . . How long might twenty thousand *blind men*, which should be sent out from the several remote parts of *England*, wander up and down before they would all meet upon *Salisbury Plains*, and fall into rank and file in the exact order of an Army? . . . . A man that sees *Henry* the *Seventh*'s Chapel at *Westminster*, might with as good reason maintain . . . that it was never contrived or built by any man, but that the stones did by chance grow into those curious figures into which they seem to have been cut and graven: and that *upon a time* (as tales usually begin) the materials of that building, the stone, mortar, timber, iron, lead and glass, happily met together and very fortunately ranged themselves into that delicate order in which we see them now so close compacted that it must be a very great chance that parts them again.[6]

In 1679 he preached against Socinianism in a series of Christmas sermons in St Lawrence Jewry, on the Incarnation. He was able to quote and to refute such Socinian authors as Johannes Crellius. He deals brusquely with one of the Socinian fringe doctrines which supposed that Jesus was taken up to heaven at the time of his Temptations, to be briefed about his mission—'So sorry and pitiful a shift'.[7]

[5] J. Tillotson, *Works*, 1704.   [6] *Works*, p. 15.
[7] Ibid., Sermons 43 and 47.

Tillotson was well aware of the connection between the person and the work of Christ. His sermon (47) *On the Sacrifice and Satisfaction of Christ* is a powerful discourse sensitive to the Socinian case but uncompromising (despite the complaints of the Non-Jurors Hickes and Leslie) in its orthodoxy. Nor did he shrink from defending the doctrine of the Trinity which he expounded in a sermon (48) on 'The Unity of the Divine Nature and the Blessed Trinity'.

For him the Trinity in Unity is a mystery to be accepted by the faithful, albeit 'so imperfectly revealed as to be in great measure incomprehensible by human reason.' He himself dare not attempt an explanation: 'all that I ever designed upon this argument was to make out the credibility of the thing from the authority of Holy Scripture without descending to a more particular explanation of it than Scripture hath given us.'[8]

Yet Tillotson had been born into the revolt against all kinds of scholasticism, so that the following sentences were to have powerful effect on the mind of Samuel Clarke.

It is not to be deny'd but that the *Schoolmen*, who abounded in wit and leisure, though very few among them had either exact skill in the *H. Scriptures*, or in *Ecclesiastical Antiquity*, and the writings of the *ancient Fathers* of the *Christian church*: I say it cannot be deny'd but that these *Speculative* and very acute men, who wrought a great part of their divinity out of their own brains, as *Spiders* do *Cobwebs* out of their own bowels, have started a thousand subtleties about this mystery, such as no Christian is bound to trouble his head withal.[9]

He probably included the Athanasian Creed among the examples of such scholasticism (Clarke dated its reception in the eleventh century) and he certainly objected to the damnatory clauses, supporting the rubric of the 1689 Commission on the Liturgy which said that they related 'only to those who obstinately deny the substance of the Christian Faith.'[10]

Moreover, Tillotson's is an attractive gospel, in contrast to his low-church successors. The God of Hoadly is a kind of glorified Dr Busby. The Christian religion is distinguished, says Tillotson, for its 'more amiable and lovely character of the Divine Nature.' No religion in the world 'does so fully represent the goodness of God and his tender love to mankind which is the best and most powerful argument to the love of God.'[11]

That there should be such a Being in the world as takes care of the frame of it

---

[8] Ibid., pp. 572–3.   [9] Ibid., pp. 572–3.
[10] D. Waterland, *A Critical History of the Athanasian Creed*, 2nd edn. 1727, Preface.
[11] *Works*, Sermon 5, The Excellency of the Christian religion, p. 60.

. . . such a Being as takes particular care of us and loves us and delights to do us good: as understands all our wants and is able and willing to relieve us in our greatest straits when nothing else can: to preserve us in our greatest dangers, to assist us against our worst enemies and to comfort us under our sharpest sufferings?

Anthony Collins might sneer at this as 'Charming!'[12] But if the next generation after Tillotson had laid as much stress on the love of God, the unbelievers and half believers would not have won so much sympathy.

iii. The Trinitarian Debate

Controversy about the Trinity erupted in 1690 when a number of the more voluble divines rushed into the defence of the faith, blissfully unaware of the pitfalls ahead, or of the difficulty, in a public controversy on so intricate a theme, of avoiding the language of Tritheism or Modalism. Thus what happened was less like a marriage of true minds than a pile-up on a modern motorway as one theologian after another crashed into the other.

A nasty, but not untypical, university row enshrouded the Rector of Exeter College, Oxford, the Revd Dr Arthur Bury, whose *Naked Gospel*, a plea for a minimal Rule of Faith, was condemned by the Convocation and burned. The great mathematical divine, John Wallis, published a massive compilation of proof texts, and was followed by Daniel Whitby, who at this time was orthodox. But they were eclipsed by the ebullient William Sherlock and his *Vindication of the Holy and Ever Blessed Trinity*. In his turn he was attacked by the mordant Robert South as teaching sheer Tritheism, to which Sherlock retorted by charging South as a Sabellian, at the same time running foul of the university authorities. Stephen Nye scattered his fire, charging South as a Socinian, Wallis as a Sabellian, Sherlock as a Tritheist, and even including Cudworth and Hooker among the heretics.

Here was more heat than light, and in 1695 Tenison got the King to forbid lay discussion of the Trinity, while in 1695 an Act imposed sanctions on all who denied the doctrine. Against this background the Boyle Lectures were a portent. The Christian and scientist, Robert Boyle had founded a series of lectures in 1691, 'to prove the truth of the Christian religion against infidels'. They were given as a series of sermons, in churches like St Paul's, or St Martin-in-the-Fields. Anthony

---

[12] On this, with comments, see N. Sykes, 'The Sermons of Archbishop Tillotson', *Theology*, 422 (1955), 301.

Collins gibed that the lectures raised more questions than they answered: 'the existence of God is often made a question, which otherwise would be with few any question at all.' And some of the lecturers, like Francis Gastrell, made rather grandiose claims about what they could demonstrate and prove. The debates of the 1690s were in an older framework. But now, with the new day of Locke and Newton there came a new dimension of enquiry.[13]

iv. *William Whiston*

Locke's *Reasonableness of Christianity* and his reduced Christian creed, together with his philosophy regarding 'substance', convinced Stilling-fleet that he was less than orthodox. And among his associates were to be two eminent Deists, Toland and Collins. But it was in Sir Isaac Newton's Cambridge that the new learning engendered a remarkable euphoria, an excited awareness that the recent discoveries were opening new methods and new truths, with the prospect that in philosophy and theology, in philology and historical criticism, there might be equally radical advances. Until Newton's massive manuscripts on early church history and doctrine have been assessed by theologians nobody can confidently pronounce on the extent to which Newton himself departed from orthodoxy.[14] He remained within the Church of England and became one of the commissioners for building new churches. On the other hand his insistence on the Unity of the one God, the Governor of the Universe, may have led him to adopt what is loosely called an 'Arian' view. But there can be no doubt of his effect on the minds of two of his friends and pupils, William Whiston and Samuel Clarke.

William Whiston (1667–1752) was an eccentric, a perennial Cambridge type, of immense and many-sided learning, combined with feeble judgement, and complete faith in his own opinions. He resembles the White Knight in *Alice* in his irregular procession from one kind of lop-sidedness to another and the oddity of his never-ceasing stream of projects. But he is like the White Knight, too, in that we are drawn to him, by a disarming and honest simplicity, an inner kindliness which shines through his prolix memoirs, through which also we catch the shrill, plaintive, and generally accusing voice. A son of the Manse,

---

[13] Milton's 'Christian Doctrine' had remained in manuscript, an unexploded shell from a previous war.

[14] F. E. Manuel, *The Religion of Isaac Newton*, Oxford 1974 sheds little light on the problem. R. S. Westfall, *Never at Rest: A Biography of Isaac Newton*, Cambridge, 1980.

cooped up for too long with his father as his tutor, a lifelong
neurasthenic, he went up to Clare College, Cambridge, where he
became a Fellow. In 1696 he produced a *New Theory of the Earth*, an
explanation of the Deluge on Newtonian lines, which foundered on a
howler about hydrostatics. He then went off to Lowestoft where for a
space he was its Dr Primrose, a devoted pastor and an admirable cleric.
But he returned to Cambridge to succeed Newton in the Lucasian chair
of mathematics. In 1708 he gave the Boyle Lectures on the validity of
Biblical prophecies. Almost, but not quite, a Non-Juror, he shared their
devotion to the study of the primitive Church, but went beyond them in
acclaiming the fourth-century *Apostolic Constitutions* as an Apostolic
authority of canonical status. More disconcerting, he discovered that the
true Christology of the fourth-century Church was not that of the
rascally Athanasius—but if not that of Arius, at least that of Eusebius,
who had the truth of it. As he proclaimed these views 'urbi et orbi' he
was banished the university, and deprived of his chair on 30 October
1710. For further writings giving this unwelcome view of the nature of
the primitive Church, he was in trouble from Convocation, though it
did not come to a final issue. He now moved to London, making a
precarious living from fees and pensions and from lecturing. He sought
by a 'dipping needle' to find the much needed means of determining
longitude at sea. He founded a Society for Promoting Primitive
Christianity, the members of which, some thought, were only as
primitive as Alexander the Coppersmith and Diotrephes. *Tristram
Shandy* reminds us that he was famous for his lectures on comets and
earthquakes, and he was one of the first to lecture with experiments,
which he did at Button's Coffee House. His friendships were as
precarious as his income, and that with Samuel Clarke, originally very
close, became rather worn, but Clarke introduced him into the
intellectual circle surrounding the Princess Caroline, and later of her
friend Lady Sundon, where he amused her by his habit of ticking off the
highest in the land when their morals, or lack of them, provoked him.
He became a London 'character' though he got across two other
celebrated figures, 'Orator' Henley and Henry Sacheverell, who turned
him out of St Andrew's Holborn. In his later years he became more and
more intrigued by apocalyptic, discovering among other things that the
Tartars were the Lost Tribes of Israel. But he had the courage to suffer
for his convictions, and he had a rare quality of integrity in a venal age.
It is perhaps the belated apology of history that of all the learned editions
which were produced by contemporary clergy, his of the works of
Josephus should have the longest survival value.

v. Samuel Clarke

Samuel Clarke[15] (1675–1729) is dismissed by Sir Leslie Stephen as a second-rater, of no originality. But if he did not attain to the first three, Locke, Newton, and Leibniz, he was regarded in his day, even by his opponents, as an outstanding churchman and philosopher, esteemed alike for the propriety of his character and his intellectual distinction. He was by far the most formidable of the Latitudinarians, and but for his lapse into heresy, might have reached the highest preferment.

A Norfolk man, he went up to Gonville and Caius College, of which he became a Fellow. Through Whiston, who took him and befriended him, he became a chaplain to Bishop Moore who became his friend and patron. Clarke had a splendid university training, in mathematics, and science, in philosophy and classical learning. As a classical scholar he was the friend of Richard Bentley and in 1713 produced a beautiful edition of Caesar's *Commentaries*, a discipline to which he returned at the end of his life, for when he died he was engaged upon a learned edition of Homer.

In 1699, at the age of twenty-four, he produced *Three Practical Essays on Baptism, Confirmation and Repentance*. It is perhaps rather a young man's book, over-learned and sententious, but it shows how close he was to Whiston at this time. The sub-title is revealing—'Instructions for a Holy Life—a consideration of the severity of the discipline of the Primitive Church'. Severity is the operative word.

What he says about Baptism is taken mostly from Tertullian, Clement and Justin Martyr. The section on Repentance (and this delighted Whiston) is mainly supported from the *Shepherd of Hermas*. Clarke admits that in the early days of the Church Baptism was often accompanied by a radical transformation of character, but wistfully admits that nowadays men become religious by gradual progress. We are not to sit down he says (against the Calvinists) 'in expectation of being converted suddenly by an irresistible grace—but we must persevere in well doing.'[16]

In a curious digression Clarke squares the circle of St Paul and St James on the relation between Faith and Works. He comes down heavily on the side of St James, for his definition of Faith is 'a declaration of firm belief in the great doctrines of the Christian religion' (p. 3) and his discussion is illustrated by long quotations on the theme of duty from

---

[15] Ferguson, *Dr. Samuel Clarke*; L. Stephen, *English Thought in the Eighteenth Century* (2 vols. 1963), i. 119ff.

[16] S. Clarke, *Three Practical Essays*, 1699, p. 145.

the Stoic Seneca. For Clarke 'the essence and end of all true religion is obedience to the moral and eternal law of God.'

But the influence of a greater than Whiston was soon evident—that of Isaac Newton. Clarke's edition of the Cartesian *Traité de physique* of Rohault became a university textbook and was accompanied by critical notes on Newtonian lines. Later, he was to defend Newton against Leibniz, prompted by Newton in the background. The men were friends, and no doubt continued to meet when Newton lived in Leicester Square and Clarke in Piccadilly. This may account for the curious offer to Clarke of the office of Master of the Mint when Newton vacated it.

In 1704 and 1705 he was paid the signal compliment (denied to Richard Bentley) of being asked to give a double series of Boyle Lectures, which he gave in St Paul's.[17] The first series was concerned with the existence and attributes of God, the second with natural and revealed religion, against the Deists. In the first he refurbished older arguments from Design and from ontology, with some Newtonian animadversions on the relation of Deity to time and space. These last did not convince a young student at a Dissenting Academy, Joseph Butler, whose subsequent correspondence with Clarke on the subject Clarke judged important enough to include in later editions. Clarke devoted a large amount of space to the notion of the divine self-existence, which to him necessarily implied the unity of God, and this was to have a bearing on his Trinitarian views.[18] He seems to have kept suspect company in the house of Lady Calverly, where he and Whiston argued with Tindal and Collins, and he may have been on visiting terms with Collins. He was always ready to help those radicals who suffered harassment for their opinions. When he returned to Cambridge to take his DD, his skill in disputation confounded and abashed the Regius Professor, and his famous victory was talked of for years in senior commonrooms. He became involved in minor controversies, including one with the Non-Juror Dodwell and Anthony Collins about the immortality of the soul.[19]

Through Bishop Moore he obtained in 1706 the City living of St Benet, Paul's Wharf, its building an elegant box wherein Inigo Jones lay buried, and in 1709 he pulled out a plum, the splendid Church of St James, Piccadilly. It was a living worth £600 a year with many perquisites, but Clarke had a large family. He had assistants, the most

---

[17] *A Discourse concerning the Being and Attributes of God, the obligations of Natural Religion and the Truth and Certainty of the Christian revelation*, 10th edn. 1766.

[18] *A Discourse concerning the Being and Attributes etc.*, props. III–VII.

[19] O'Higgins, *Anthony Collins*, pp. 27, 109.

notable of whom was his friend and protégé Ashley Sykes. Defoe described the congregation as a 'fine assembly of beauties and quality' among whom it was difficult to get a seat. The good story is told of one 'eminent man' who told the genteel assembly 'If you do not repent, you will go to a place which I shall not name before this audience.' Unexciting and moralistic as Clarke's preaching might be, Samuel Johnson replied to the question 'Whose sermons are the best?' with 'Why, sir, bating a little heresy, those of Dr Samuel Clarke', and it was one of his sermons *On the Shortness of life* which he made Boswell read to him in the last days of his life. St James's was in Piccadilly at the heart of society, and Clarke became an eminent member of the collection of tame theologians which Queen Caroline and the Lady Sundon collected.

Then, in 1712, came the fateful volume, *The Scripture Doctrine of the Trinity*. It was a subject, he said, that he had long pondered, and he must have followed closely the recent debates. He must also have been aware that this work would be a sensation, but he may have thought he could ride out this storm without damaging his career. In any case, he firmly believed that he had recovered the true Scriptural doctrine of the Trinity, and removed the confusions and perversions of later centuries. It was not intended in any way to expound the Newtonian world view, though, more than he seemed aware, this moulded his conclusions. Rather he would eschew all metaphysics, all the unintelligibilities of essence and substance, and return to the plain text of Holy Writ. In the first part of the work he educed some 1,251 texts, divided between the Three Persons, and concluded that 'it appears beyond contradiction that the words God and Father, not God and Three Persons, are synonymous terms.'

The second part of the work propounded fifty-five theses, each proposition supported by citations from the Fathers, but as illustrative not demonstrative testimonies. The third was devoted to the Liturgy and those places which supported or denied his conclusions. He had argued in his Boyle Lectures that the unity and self-existence of God were inseparable, and he now concluded that it is only God the Father who is supreme over all and who governs the Universe. The Son and the Spirit are truly divine, but there cannot be two self-existent beings, and both the Son and the Spirit derive their existence from the will of the Father. They are neither coequal nor coeternal with Him. The stress on the supremacy of the divine governance gave a new accentuation to the traditional teaching of the subordination of the Son, though Clarke never refers to either Son or Spirit as a creature, and fiercely repudiated the title of 'Arian'. But it is easy to see why his opponents, and notably Daniel Waterland, insisted that his teaching was within the Arian circle of ideas, and was in any case a radical departure from the main Christian tradition, as expressed in the Nicene and Athanasian Creeds.

Clarke on the other hand insisted that those who rejected his solution, must inevitably become either Tritheist or Sabellian. One or two of his friends were delighted—William Whiston and the Irishman, Thomas Emlyn. Others were horrified and alarmed and one of them, Dr Smalridge, tried to talk him out of it in a learned conference at Aynho in Northamptonshire, but as usual, Clarke was invincible in spoken debate. On the next Trinity Sunday Clarke obviated the difficulty of reading the Collect and Preface, by cancelling the Communion service, an act which cost him his royal chaplaincy.

The pamphlet war began anew, but not until 1714 was complaint made from the Lower to the Upper House of Convocation. On 26 June Clarke submitted a paper in which he counterattacked with vigour. Then, on 2 July he submitted another statement, which read like a recantation, in which he conceded that 'The Son of God was eternally begotten by the eternal, incomprehensible will of the Father', promised that he would preach no more on the doctrine of the Trinity and announced 'I do not intend to write any more concerning the Trinity.' Like his friend Hoadly, he could take refuge in the enigmatic.

Whiston was dismayed and then disgusted by such craven behaviour, and shared Waterland's indignation when Clarke put forward a view of subscription to the Thirty-nine Articles which would allow any interpretation which the subscriber might reasonably suppose to agree with Scripture. Clarke never again put himself in the position where he must subscribe, so that the only preferment which he received thereafter was the Mastership of the Wigston Hospital, Leicester.

Those who disliked theological witch-hunts were sympathetic. Francis Hare, in his satirical *Letter to a Young Clergyman on the difficulties and discouragements which attend the study of the Scriptures*, referred to Clarke as one in whom 'all good qualities meet together, wide and profound learning in the ancient languages, in philosophy, in science and divinity . . . to this are added a happy temper and a modest, obliging behaviour', and concluded 'he who has such shining qualities must not be insulted by a worthless wretch.'

But Clarke's opponents were by no means worthless wretches, and the ensuing debate was probably more perceptive and learned than the argumentation of the nineties. This was not a war of slight tracts, but of treatises. They came from all directions: from Oxford, Dr Wells (*Remarks . . .*, 1713) and Dr Welchman (*Dr Clarke . . . examined*, 1714) and from Cambridge, and from a very sick man, Dr Edward Potter of Emmanuel (*A Vindication . . .* 1713), from the layman Robert Nelson, and from City divines like Dr Knight of St Sepulchre's (*True Scripture Doctrine*, 1713) and from Dr Bennet, of St Giles, Cripplegate, from John Edwards the Calvinist and Stephen Nye the Unitarian, and from two of Clarke's disciples, John Jackson of Rossington, and Ashley Sykes of Dry Drayton.[20] Veterans from the earlier debate were Daniel Whitby and Francis Gastrell. But it was in Daniel Waterland that Clarke met his match in learning.

Daniel Waterland (1683–1740) became Master of Magdalene College, Cambridge, in 1713 and then Regius Professor of Divinity. He seems to have followed an older and very decent Cambridge custom of circulating memoranda rather than rushing into print, after the ways of the earlier generation of Mede and Bedell and Ward. But such a set of 'Queries' about Clarke's doctrines was seized upon by John Jackson, who with Clarke's connivance, printed them with his own reply. Waterland's subsequent treatises, with the exception of his Lady Moyer Lectures, are a series of concentric circles around those original queries. They began with his *Vindication of Christ's Divinity* and elicited a series of writings from Jackson, culminating in a work of more than 500 pages, to which Waterland replied with a *Second Defence* also of 500 pages. In 1719 Waterland delivered in St Paul's the Lady Moyer Lectures, a positive statement of the orthodox position which was widely acclaimed.[21]

Yet Waterland seems to have been content to conform to his opponent's pattern in concentration on a succession of texts, and above all on the theme of God as the Creator and Governor of the Universe. But in the fourth-century Christological debates redemption, rather than revelation, had been the heart of the matter, and the nerve of the case against the Arians was the conviction that only one who was truly God could be the Saviour of the world. The doctrine of the Trinity, after all, was not something thought up by Christians who wanted to be abstruse, but it emerged against the Jewish background of a deep belief in the unity of God. It was out of the experience of redemption of the first Christians and the first Christian community that the thought of God as Trinity emerged. It was not nearly as obscurantist as Collins asserted when Francis Gastrell said 'God must be one and three in some way and manner not conceivable to understanding.' Here, rather than in hundreds of proof texts, lay the real appeal to Holy Scripture. 'You might be ashamed', wrote Waterland in his final summing up, 'to mention metaphysics when everybody knows you have little else to rely

[20] The debate is admirably summarized in Ferguson, *Samuel Clarke*. chs. 5–11.
[21] D. Waterland, *Works* (Oxford 1823), vol. ii.

upon . . . a false notion of the self-existence of the Father . . . that the three persons must be three intelligent agents . . . that three agents cannot be one being, one substance . . .'[22] Sadly a debate which began as an appeal to the plain text of Scripture petered out in intricate arguments about the authenticity of Greek particles in an obscure treatise of Athenagoras.

Although Clarke said that the doctrine of the Trinity was 'the great foundation and main economy of the Christian religion', it is doubtful whether the long debate had much enriched Christian truth. It was ironical that a Latitudinarian who stood for minimal intellectual demands on the faithful, and whose view of Christianity was moralistic, should himself become the centre of such an intricate and at times abstruse debate. And this at a time when the laity were more and more exposed to the icy winds of unbelief, and an anti-clerical propaganda which could mockingly cry, 'See how these theologians devour one another.'[23]

Whiston, Emlyn, Whitby renounced orthodox Christology for their own reasons, not perhaps much influenced by Clarke. Clarke's own friends, like Hoadly, who was to edit his works, and Arthur Ashley Sykes stuck to the Church of England, though Sykes's house at Rayleigh was one where Anthony Collins was a welcome visitor. It was upon the younger Dissenters that Clarke's words fell with power, and reinforced existing tendencies in a rationalist and Unitarian direction, and his writings must be seen among the influences leading to the Salter's Hall debate. Clarke's arguments fell into abeyance, but Daniel Waterland, by his learning, if not by his arguments, had rallied the clergy to the Nicene and Athanasian Creeds and had continued to expound an ancient rationale, the long tradition of many centuries which confessed God as Trinity in Unity.

---

[22] Ibid. iii. 4.

[23] It might seem there is some resemblance to modern and recent Christological and Trinitarian discussion, where there has been a similar rejection of the fourth-century doctrines and vocabulary and an attempt at radical revision of orthodox tradition. But in fact Clarke's doctrine is imbedded in the Newtonian world view. The parallel seems to lie in the fact that it is easier to demythologize the early Church than to recognize the conditioning effect of the world view of one's own age, whether the eighteenth or the twentieth century.

17

DEISTS

i. How Defined?

In his classic, luminous essay,[1] Mark Pattison remarked that 'the church and the world to-day are what they are as a result of the whole of their history'. Yet the whole past does not bear equally on the Church at any one time. It is important to notice the discontinuities, the excommunications self-inflicted, so to speak, by which a Church may become cut off from parts of its own history, the myths that are then created to plug the gap, and above all those times when catastrophic events interrupt the stream of tradition, like some great cataract. Such a time was that of the Civil War, the Restoration, and the Glorious Revolution.

As in Germany in 1945, defeat in war led to the disappearance almost overnight of a coherent world view, that of National Socialism, so in 1660 the Puritan way of life was discredited, and the period 1640–60 became a kind of black hole. The repudiation of Calvinism involved also the comparative isolation of the beginning of the English Protestant tradition, from William Tyndale and Hugh Latimer and Thomas Cranmer to John Jewel. 'Ancient sermons' is the disparaging comment of that middle-of-the-road Church of England man 'John Smith' when John Wesley appealed to the teaching about Justification by Faith alone, in Article XI and the Homily of Salvation.[2] Moreover in revulsion against 'enthusiasm' it was not only fanaticism and illuminism which was rejected, but elements of that 'theology of the Cross' and devotion to Jesus Christ which is so apparent in the greatest Caroline and Puritan divinity, clearly marked in both Richard Baxter and Thomas Ken, and indeed Tillotson and Patrick, one which seemed to have been overlaid by the end of the century by a religion of duty, in which the practice of virtue rather than the vision of God became the true end of man.

Under the influence of the Cambridge Platonists who had assaulted Puritan rationalism, the Latitudinarians, in the new methodology of Locke and Newton, rejected a priori thinking and metaphysical speculation. One result of this was a curious mental 'black-out' of the Middle Ages, a contempt for those medieval theologians who had

[1] M. Pattison, 'Tendencies of Religious Thought in England 1688–1750', *Essays and Reviews*, 1860.
[2] *The Works of John Wesley* (OE), vol. 26, Letters II, ed. F. Baker (Oxford 1982), p. 143.

formed a tradition of Christian rationality perhaps more impressive, had they known it, than their own. The debates between Archbishop King and Anthony Collins, and the theodicies of Samuel Clarke and the Boyle Lecturers generally, not least about the meaning of natural law, are simplistic and confused compared with the expositions of St Thomas, Scotus, and William of Occam.

The oblivion of the medieval tradition—a thousand years of Christian thought and spirituality—would not have mattered so much in the light of the Anglican appeal to primitive Christianity and to the Fathers. After all, the seventeenth century had produced, in Italy, France, and England a massive patristic scholarship with new learned and critical editions of the Fathers. But now these began to be regarded with suspicion. Those very critical methods by which the humanists had exposed the un-authentic character of the *Donation of Constantine*, of Pseudo-Dionysius, and of the Hermetic writings, were now turned on the Fathers. One side-effect of the long controversy with the Roman Catholics had been the evidence that many Papist rites and usages were to be found in the early centuries. The new texts and editions, and the new histories like those of Daillé, Leclerc, and Tillemont, suggested that far from there being a patristic consensus in favour of Nicene orthodoxy, there were many variations, not least between the Christology of the pre-Nicene and post-Nicene Fathers. There followed Whiston's portrayal of Athanasius as a heretic and a rascal, which was to be out-done in 1749 by Conyers Middleton for whom the Fathers, the whole lot of them, from Clement of Rome to Gregory the Great, were either noodles or frauds, and probably both.

Those who lived in the age of Grotius and Locke could not think of natural law in medieval terms, but at least in Nathaniel Culverwell's beautiful treatise *The Light of Nature* (1652) there had been a deliberate return to Suarez and St Thomas and to the thought of the natural order as infiltrated and interpenetrated at all levels by the supernatural, and where grace and redemption, rather than propositional revelation were the true polarity of nature and of reason.

The medieval world had been curtained off from heathendom, save for a few tip-and-run raids by Marco Polo and the Saracens. Now two centuries of voyages, explorations, and the ever widening contacts of trade, had amassed a great body of new information about those who lived outside the Christian world, new evidence about natural religion.

This was not entirely new in the sixteenth century. One of the clues to the Utopia of Sir Thomas More is that it represents the kind of society which natural man, apart from revelation, might achieve. And this enhanced his satire on contemporary English society. Luther and his colleagues, faced with the imminence of Turkish invasion, published an edition of the Koran, and studied the narratives of Christians captured among the Saracens, and he too does not refrain from moralizing, and showing where Turks behave better than the Christians.

But in the next century a whole new world was opened up, and a great literature of travellers' tales became available. Christian missions had made contact with ancient cultures and religions in India, China, and Japan and seventy-three volumes of Jesuit records bore witness to them. We in England have domesticated two such volumes, *Robinson Crusoe* and *Gulliver's Travels*, which were written by Christians for Christians. But in France the 'imaginary voyage', like the genuine travel narrative, was used for the cause of Deism.[3] It is notable that the imaginary and the true blended together (there has been a long debate whether the *Voyage* of François Léguat was fiction or genuine science), and indeed for propaganda purposes either would have done equally well. Some of the imaginary voyages were in fact science fiction about trips to the moon or into outer space. But the accounts of how primitive peoples live and worship, and of the rites and philosophies of other religions were used to show that unspoiled man (the return to the 'noble savage' was much older than Rousseau) and philosophers like Confucius were far superior to the decadent, priest-ridden faith of the Christians.

The range of this new popular literature is startling, for it included descriptions of the Tartars and the American Indians, about the inhabitants of Greenland and the Antarctica, Chinese cities, and Polynesian islands. The books describing them were generally very readable, well documented, plausible, though in fact there was a great deal of exaggeration, much that was bogus and far from critically digested.

Thus the Deists conjured up a new world to upset the balance of the old. The one people, the one religion which really got under their skins, was Judaism. This impersonal antisemitism was directed at the Old Testament, which was seen as a repulsive blend of ritual and superstition, the story of a people led astray by tales of wonders, imposed upon by tricksters, in the name of a cruel and savage Deity whose own behaviour frequently dropped below that of normal decent human beings. But if they side-stepped the great Hebraic traditions of mercy and of righteousness—which Luther had sensitively understood —it was quite other with the world of Greece and Rome.

Long before Matthew Arnold, the Deists had shown the preference

[3] G. Atkinson, *The Extraordinary Voyage in French Literature, 1700–1720*, (Paris 1922); D. A. Pailin, *Attitudes to Other Religions, Comparative Religion in Seventeenth and Eighteenth Century Britain*, Manchester, 1984.

for Hellenic sweetness and light compared with the fire of Hebraism. Every now and again through the Christian centuries, there have been important revivals of Hellenism, and such a movement played its part in the crisis of European conscience. But it was not the Deists who contributed to the classical revival. The basis of education in the Dissenting Academies as in the older Universities, was the classics, and no candidate for ordination could be accepted without some smattering of the sacred languages. The leading Anglican divines from Bentley to Warburton and including Clarke, Wake, Gibson, and Waterland, were classical scholars. If the Deists quoted the classics it was very often from editions edited by clergymen. Thus, in the endpaper of Waterland's *History of the Athanasian Creed* the Cambridge bookseller Cornelius Crownfield advertised, as might be expected, the anti-Socinian writings of Waterland and Bentley. But on the same page he offered new editions of the works of Horace and Terence by Bentley, and of Julius Caesar by John Davis. Yet these were the works which commended classical antiquity to the generation of Edward Gibbon. Here, in a pre-Christian world was a belief in rationality and freedom, a splendid culture in prose and verse, the bearers of which were cultivated and liberal-minded men, who saw beneath the façade of ritual and superstition of their age.[4] For everyone who could read about the supposed simplicities of the thinkers of Persia and China, there were ten who were familiar with the life style of the classical, pagan world.

While main features of Deism may be found in France earlier than in England, Stillingfleet's *Letter to a Deist* (1677) seems to be the first attack on the movement. In 1675 Matthew Clifford had printed a *Treatise of Human reason*, described by Mossner as 'a mild semi-Deistic' plea for rational religion. But Charles Blount (1654–93) in his *Anima Mundi* (1697) had attacked the doctrine of immortality, and shown sympathy for the teaching of Hobbes, and attacked priestcraft. Though the chief figures in the movement knew one another, they were not a close-knit body, despite the fact that there were clubs and coffee houses, like the Grecian and the Jack and Grapes where they were known to meet. In his second series of Boyle Lectures, Samuel Clarke had distinguished four kinds of Deists. There are those who accept the existence of God, but 'fancy God does not at all concern himself in the government of the world'. Others believe in God and in Providence but suppose that He 'takes no notice of the morally good or evil actions of men: these things depending, they imagine on the arbitrary constitution of human laws.' Another sort accept the moral perfections of God, his infinite justice,

---

[4] P. Gay, *The Enlightenment* (1967), Book I, ch. 2.

goodness, and truth, but they believe that 'men perish entirely at death . . . without any future restoration or renovation of things.'[5]

The fourth kind have 'just and right notions of God . . . and believe that all created rational beings are bound to adore, worship and obey him. . . . They believe there must be a future state of rewards and punishments in the world to come.' But all this, they think, is 'discoverable by the light of nature alone, without believing any Divine Revelation.' These last, Clarke suggested, were the true Deists and alone worth arguing with but 'alas, there are very few . . .' Such men would not be far from the Kingdom of God. But the majority, with 'their trivial and vain cavils: their mocking and ridiculing . . . their objections against particular customs . . . without at all considering the main body of religion: . . . and above all, their vicious and immoral lives, show plainly that they are not really deists, but mere Atheists.'[6]

The common bond between the four groups of Deists was their rejection of revelation. It is easy to see why many suggest that the true originator of the movement was Lord Herbert of Cherbury (1583–1648) and the five primary beliefs which he suggested are attested by natural religion. They were:

> There is a supreme Deity.
> He ought to be worshipped.
> That virtue with piety is . . . the chief part of divine worship.
> That men have always known that vice and crimes should be expiated
>   by repentance.
> That after this life there are rewards and punishments.

It seems best to follow the development of the movement chronologically in terms of the half a dozen seminal writings, and their authors.

ii. Toland—'not mysterious'

John Toland's (1670–1722) *Christianity not Mysterious* (1696)[7] denied revelation, and was directed against clerical pretensions that believers must 'adore where they cannot comprehend' the divine mysteries, which he defines as esoteric, arcane doctrines which the priests claim to guard and which they put forward for the acceptance of the faithful.

Toland himself was born an Irish Catholic, but became a Protestant at the age of sixteen, studied at Glasgow and Leyden, returning to Oxford in 1696 where he wrote *Christianity not Mysterious*, a work which was publicly burned in Ireland and led him to reside henceforward in

---

[5] Clarke, *A Discourse*, Part II, pp. 12–22.   [6] Ibid., p. 26.

[7] J. Toland, *Christianity not Mysterious*, ed. G. Gawlick, Facsimile edn., Stuttgart 1964.

England. But a writing on behalf of the Act of Succession got him some favour in Hanover and Berlin and for a time he was patronized by the Electress Sophia and the Prussian Queen Charlotte. He wrote many pamphlets, but perhaps was not quite the mountebank which he seemed to Sir Leslie Stephen. Of the Deists he was the one most influenced by the teachings of Spinoza, and he seems to have come near to pantheism. His attack on the authenticity of sub-apostolic documents, which was widely taken to be an attack on the New Testament itself, got him into further trouble. Here we may consider his most famous work which indeed focused the general attitude of the Deists towards revelation, and that clerical control of religion which they most detested.

The heart of his matter was expounded on the title-page: 'Showing that there is nothing in the Gospel contrary to Reason, nor above it: and that no Christian Doctrine can be properly called a Mystery.'

The criterion of truth is reason. 'We hold that Reason is the only foundation of all Certitude: and that nothing revealed, whether as to its *Manner* or *Existence* is more exempted from its Disquisitions than the ordinary Phenomena of Nature.'[8] The argument of the work is somewhat rambling, but it does include a close examination of the meaning of the word 'mystery' in the heathen mystery religions and in the Bible, concluding that '*Mystery* in the whole *New Testament* is never put for *any thing inconceivable in itself, or not to be judg'd by our ordinary Notions and Faculties, however clearly revealed.*'[9]

Men are not therefore endued with new faculties with which to receive revelation, for what God says must be agreeable to and perceptible by our common notions. And in the best-known sentence of the work he adds: 'Could that person justly value himself upon being wiser than his Neighbours, who having infallible Assurance that something called *Blictri* had a Being in Nature, in the mean time knew not what this *Blictri* was?'[10] Throughout there is pungent anti-clericalism and towards the end of the work an indictment of the Christian Church which after the first two centuries wrapped the plain Christian religion in a vast array of ceremonies, notably surrounding the Eucharist, as well as in a great elaboration of the offices and ministries of the clergy. 'There is nothing so naturally opposite as ceremony and Christianity—in short, there's no degree of enthusiasm higher than placing religion in such fooleries.'

Like his acquaintance Anthony Collins, who posited a univocal relation between the attributes of man and God, Toland will not admit a

---

[8] Toland, *Christianity not Mysterious*, p. 6.
[9] Ibid., p. 111.
[10] Ibid., p. 133.

mystery in God's being beyond the understanding and comprehension of human reason. In this he partly shared the world view of contemporary Christianity. The splendid churches of Wren and Gibbs, and the Dissenting chapels like that of John Taylor at Norwich, had no dark corners, but are plain and light. 'In Him is no darkness at all', might be the motto of it all. Yet the shadowy immensities of the great Gothic cathedrals had also their Scriptural point. It was one which the seventeenth century had better understood, as in Henry Vaughan's great poem, 'Night':

> There is in God (some say)
> A deep, but dazzling darkness; as men here
> Say it is late and dusky, because they
>   See not all clear;
>   O for that night! where I in him
>   Might live invisible and dim.

The note of awe in the presence of God who is a *mysterium tremendum* is as lacking from the abstract theism of the Deists, as the note of wonder at the love of God is from the sermons of a Trapp or Hoadly.

But there were others for whom our finite ignorance left room for mystery, in a quite other sense than some secret intelligences locked up by the priests and kept from the laity. There is the image of George Berkeley:

As I was the other day taking a solitary walk in St. Paul's, I indulged my thoughts in the pursuit of a certain analogy between the fabrick and the Christian church in the largest sense. The divine order and economy of the one seemed to me to be emblematically set forth by the just, plain and majestic architecture of the other. And as the one consists of a great variety of parts united in the same regular design, according to the truest art and most exact proportion: so the other contains a decent subordination of members, various sacred institutions, sublime doctrines and solid precepts of morality digested into the same design, and with an admirable concurrence tending to one view, the happiness and exaltation of human nature.

In the midst of my contemplation, I beheld a fly upon one of the pillars: and it straightway came into my head, that this same fly was a Free Thinker. For it required some comprehension in the eye of the spectator to take in at one view the various parts of the building in order to observe their symmetry and design. But to the fly whose prospect was confined to a little part of one of the stones of a single pillar, the joint beauty of the whole or the distinct use of its parts were inconspicuous, and nothing could appear but small inequalities in the surface of the hewn stone, which in the view of that insect seemed to be deformed rocks and precipices. The thoughts of a Free Thinker are employed on certain minute particularities of religion, the difficulty of a single text, or the unaccountableness of some step of Providence or point of doctrine to his narrow faculties, without comprehending the scope and design of Christianity. . . .[11]

William Law, in his answer to Matthew Tindal, says that our relations to God are at once 'very plain and very mysterious'.

That which is *plain and certain* . . . plainly shews our obligations to every instance of *duty, homage, adoration, love and gratitude*. And that which is *mysterious* and *inconceivable* in them, is a just and solid foundation of that *profound humility, awful reverence, internal piety* and *tremendous sense* of the Divine Majesty.[12]

It is the central point of Joseph Butler's powerful argument that not only God, but 'the little scene of human life' is surrounded by mystery, that we live, as a modern scientist put it in a 'Mysterious Universe'.

Whether we are in any way related to the more distant parts of the boundless universe into which we are brought, is altogether uncertain. But it is evident that the course of things which comes within our view is connected with somewhat past, present and future beyond it. So that we are placed, as one may speak, in the middle of a scheme, not a fixed one but a progressive one, every way incomprehensible: incomprehensible in a manner equally with respect to what has been, what now is, and what shall be hereafter. And this scheme cannot but contain in it somewhat as wonderful and as much beyond our thought and conception, as anything in that of religion.[13]

iii.   Collins—'Free Thought'

Anthony Collins (1676–1729) was a wealthy layman. He went from Eton to King's College, Cambridge, where his tutor was Francis Hare, but neither there nor at the Middle Temple did he finish his course, and his polemic was to suffer because he was technically not quite scholarly enough. He married well, and as a landed proprietor and magistrate was a notable in the County of Essex. He acquired a fine library of some 7,000 volumes. Like Toland, whom he knew, he began as a friend and disciple of Locke, and in his thinking owed much to the liberal tradition of Chillingworth and Tillotson. From 1704 he became a prominent member of Deist circles in London where they met in the Grecian Club. The discussions there and the arguments of the company underlay his most famous, though not his most impressive, writing, the *Discourse of Free Thinking*.[14] At a time when 'Free Thinker' was becoming a term of

---

[11] *Guardian Essays*, vol. VII. *The Works of George Berkeley*, edited by A. A. Luce and T. E. Jessop (1955), vii. 206.

[12] W. Law, 'The case of Reason or Natural Religion Stated', *Works*, ii. 71.

[13] J. Butler, *The Analogy of Religion* (Everyman edn. 1906), p. 110.

[14] *A Discourse of Free Thinking* (1713), ed. G. Gawlick (Stuttgart 1965), p. 6.

disparagement he raised it as a banner, the emblem of rationality, toleration, and free enquiry. Since knowledge of any truth is not forbidden by God, we have a right 'to think freely or to use our understandings, in endeavouring to find out the meaning of any proposition whatsoever in considering the evidence for or against it, and in judging of it according to the seeming force or weakness of the evidence.'

The treatise is in three parts. The first defines Free Thought and gives five arguments in its favour. The second adds another six considerations, and turns into a violent attack on the clergy. In the third he answers possible objections and gives a long catena of the views of a succession of Free Thinkers, beginning with Socrates and ending with Tillotson. The work was trenchant, readable, and not too long, and appeared at a time of political crisis. Though Collins had prudently withdrawn to Holland, there was no serious outcry despite the fact that Richard Steele said that the author deserved to be denied 'the common benefits of air and water'. There were many replies, the most famous being from Berkeley, Bentley, and Swift. Berkeley wrote elegant pieces in the *Guardian*. Richard Bentley's was an outstanding piece of polemical writing.[15] The first part was brilliant, the second bogged down in the examination of gobbets, while the third withered away as its author became involved in the great struggle with the Fellows of Trinity. Bentley pretended to be a Professor from Leipzig, and his essay was addressed to Collins's old tutor, Francis Hare. He attacks Collins first for the looseness of his definitions, and for saying that Free Thinking consisted of 'the use of the understanding to find out the meaning of any proposition whatsoever', commenting, ''Tis really no more than think and judge as you find.' But if this freedom is defined by the word 'Whatsoever',

then . . . the soberer part of Mankind, who judge for themselves no further than their Education has fitted them, are wholly excluded: and the *Crackbrain'd* and *Bedlamites* are taken in. *Oliver*'s porter, as I have been told, would determine daily *de omni re scibili*: and if he had been now alive might have had the first chair in the club.[16]

The great classical scholar exposed Collins's carelessness and ignorance. Beginning with the famous howler in which Collins had rendered 'idiotis evangelistis' as 'unlettered evangelists', he exposed the mistranslations. And indeed Collins cannot be acquitted of having

[15] *Remarks upon a late Discourse of Free Thinking: in a letter to F. H., D. D. by Phileleutherus Lipsiensis* (1713).
[16] *Discourse of Free Thinking*, pp. 10–11.

fudged when he gives classical lines an anti-Christian turn, making Socrates speak of 'the Gods' getting women with child', and Varro of Gods 'begotten and proceeding'. At one point Collins used a favourite Deist argument, the unreliability of the Christian scriptures, as is shown by the variations in the text—30,000 he claims, citing John Mills—and proceeds to allege that Christian divines disagree about every major doctrine. Bentley replied with a splendid exposition of the meaning of textual criticism, and the inevitability of textual variations, the vast majority of which were trivial and of a kind to be found in all ancient writings.

Collins was known to have Whig sympathies so that Jonathan Swift had an added cause for attacking him. *Mr C——'s Discourse of Free Thinking* is a small masterpiece.[17] Surely this is the best four pennyworth ever published in our language, and in it Swift uses the Deist weapon of ridicule with deadly effect. His sub-title 'Put into plain English, by way of Abstract for the Use of the Poor' is an obvious dig at the wealthy leader of the well-to-do members of the Grecian Club. With immense skill he compresses Collins's arguments using many of Collins's phrases but making them utterly ridiculous.

Now the *Bible*, which contains the Precepts of the Priest's religion, is the most difficult Book in the World to be understood: it requires a thorow Knowledge in Natural, Civil, Ecclesiastical History, Law, Husbandry, Sailing, Physick, Pharmacy, Mathematicks, Metaphysicks, Ethicks, and everything else that can be named.[18]

The word 'Sailing' in the middle of the list explodes the whole. Swift deals in a similar way with the Deist argument, to be powerful in the hands of Matthew Tindal, that a historical revelation, beginning with the Jews, is absurd and irrational.

The *Bible* says, the *Jews* were a Nation favoured by God: but I, who am a *Free Thinker* say, that cannot be, because the Jews lived in a Corner of the earth, and *Free Thinking* makes it clear that those who live in *Corners* cannot be the Favourites of God.[19]

In a subtle sentence he counters Collins's claim that all the great luminaries of human thought belong to the succession of Free Thinkers.

The *Free Thinkers* use their Understanding, but those who have Religion do not, therefore the first have more understanding than the others. Witness *Toland, Tindal, Gildon, Clendon, Coward* and myself.[20]

---

[17] *The Prose Works of Jonathan Swift*, ed. H. Davies, Oxford 1957, vol. iv.
[18] Ibid. iv. 29.   [19] Ibid. iv. 30.   [20] Ibid. iv. 41.

From the cloudy glories of Socrates and Cicero we come down to reality, a ragtag and bobtail of contemporary Deists, Old Uncle Tom Cobleigh and all.

How much of traditional Christianity remained in Collins cannot be known. He certainly lived and died a member of the Church of England, in friendly relationship with neighbouring low churchmen like Ashley Sykes. His *Discourse of Free Thinking* was not a profound treatise, but it was in its way a kind of manifesto, and some of his main arguments and instances were to be useful ammunition for the much weightier treatises of Matthew Tindal.

The doctrine of Natural Law had received much attention throughout the seventeenth century. On the Continent two thinkers were of seminal influence. The Dutch Arminian, Hugo Grotius (1583–1645) wrote a massive defence of Christianity, the *De Veritate Religionis Christianae*, which while it expounded Christianity as a revealed religion kept a careful substructure of Natural Theology. His great treatise *De Jure Belli et Pacis* fixed the principle of justice in Natural Law. The German Samuel Pufendorf (1632–94) in his *De Jure Naturae et Gentium* (1672) stressed the rational basis of Natural Law.

iv. Wollaston

Nobody had set out more firmly the significance of natural theology than Samuel Clarke in his first series of Boyle Lectures, and his intellectual moralism was taken up by one of the most notable Deist writers, William Wollaston (1660–1724). After a troublesome undergraduate existence at Sidney Sussex College, Cambridge, Wollaston became an usher, and finally took priest's orders. Some years of intermingled family and financial troubles ended with his marriage in 1689 to the daughter of a wealthy London merchant. Thereafter he lived in Charterhouse Square, from which he never emerged, leading a quasi-eremitical existence, as far, as Leslie Stephen comments, as that is possible for a man with eleven children. In 1724 he published *The Religion of Nature Delineated*, a closely argued treatise which went through many editions and is perhaps the most impressive intellectual performance of the Deist movement.

v. Tindal—'old as the creation'

Wollaston's defence of natural religion was eclipsed by the work which was called 'the Bible of the Deists', Matthew Tindal's *Christianity as Old as the Creation* (1730). Tindal (1655–1733) was educated at Lincoln and

Exeter Colleges at Oxford, where he became a Fellow of All Souls and a DCL. He had been brought up in high–church circles, and for a short spell had been a Roman Catholic. In 1706 he attracted attention by a work *The Rights of the Christian Church*, which he followed in 1709 with a 'Defence' of his former book, and this was burned by the common hangman. At the age of seventy-five he published *Christianity as Old as the Creation, or the Gospel a Republication of the Religion of Nature.*

One main feature of his work and from which it drew a good deal of strength, was a massive collection of passages from Anglican divines supporting his contention of the fundamental importance of natural theology. He did not twist them out of their proper context nor did he need to. Nor did he need to confine himself to Latitudinarian or low-church divines. The very title of the book was taken from a sermon by the high churchman Thomas Sherlock, and he finds confirmatory evidence in other sermons from South, Scott, and John Sharp. Joseph Butler was to quote his phrase that 'Christianity is the republican of natural religion.'[21]

The work is written in dialogue form, between speakers A and B. Like the two characters in *The Mikado*, A is the self-satisfied, while wretched, meritorious B puts up arguments only to be knocked down. At the outset Tindal affirms that 'natural and revealed religion differ in nothing, but the manner of their being conveyed to us.'[22] In fact they 'exactly answer one another', like two tallies. But it is plain that natural religion is what counts. God who loves all men, must have made the terms of their salvation able to be known and understood by all. He has made himself known in the human soul, in reason. Revelation, on the other hand depends on tradition, and is an external thing. This religion of Nature, 'is absolutely perfect; . . . and external revelation can neither add to it nor take from its perfection.'[23] He thus defines true religion as 'a constant disposition of mind to do all the good we can: and thereby render ourselves acceptable to God in answering the End of his creation.' This may be very close to Clarke and Hoadly, Sherlock and Butler. But it is very far, despite medieval moral theology and the doctrines of scintilla and synteresis, from the gospel according to St Thomas, and the late-medieval theologians including Luther for whom the question of our 'acceptance' by God was a spiritual agony. It misses altogether that Augustinian dimension of which the Shorter Catechism speaks when it claims that 'Man's chief end is to glorify God and to enjoy him for ever.'

[21] J. Butler, *The Analogy of Religion*, p. 121.
[22] M. Tindal, *Christianity as Old as the Creation* (1730), Facsimile edn. 1967, p. 2.
[23] Ibid., p. 58.

And though Tindal properly sums up natural duties in the commandment to love God and our neighbour, and depicts God as one whose perfections are to be loved, he soon begins to attack revelation for its externality.

No Person is ever the more known to Posterity, because his Name is transferred to them: when we say, *Caesar* conquered *Pompey*, we having no idea of either can only mean, Some-body conquered some-body: and have we more distinct ideas of Jesus and Pilate?[24]

Far from the simplicity and clarity of natural religion, revealed religion had from the first been complicated by superstition, and by the bigotry and fraud of the clergy. Like Collins, he veils an attack on Christian doctrine by attacking the heathen with their gods who were 'mediators' or who have thought 'that an unlimited Being could have appeared under the limited form of a man.' But it is when he turns to customs, rites, and ceremonies that he really lets himself go, citing all the manifold ills that are associated with cruel superstition and bigoted fraud. He had plenty of evidence to go upon, and those who visit the Anti-God museum in Leningrad will find the various showcases comment on many of Tindal's historical examples and his assertion that 'all church history is full of the vilest and most pernicious Things perpetrated by Christian priests.'[25]

Borrowing Collins's methodology, he turns to the obscurity of Holy Scripture. Here again, he has contemporary churchmen at a disadvantage. In England since the Restoration a great emphasis had been placed on the Bible and its exposition. A number of divines, Patrick, Prideaux, Heylyn, Clarke, had published paraphrases of the text of Scripture. Problems of authenticity, and of textual criticism had arisen, first with the study of the Fathers and then with Holy Scripture itself. On the Continent the work of scholars like Le Clerc, Daillé, Bayle, and Simon had turned a critical eye on the Scriptural narratives and begun to ask questions out of which modern Biblical and historical criticism would one day arise.

Orthodox divines, accepting the plenary inspiration of Scripture, were brought face to face with questions which they met with wooden defensiveness. Tindal, who had made reason the criterion, not only of Scripture, but of divine behaviour, raises a formidable array of problems which the Christians old and new had generally evaded—Adam and Eve, Rahab the harlot, the sacrifices of Isaac and of Jephthah's daughter, patriarchal lies, the symbolic acts of the prophets, the unfulfilled prophecies. He scorns the flight to allegory and typology of the Biblical

---

[24] Ibid., p. 48.   [25] Ibid., p. 108.

commentators. In two pages he gives a list of their excuses. Here indeed he over reaches himself, for in fact there are among them genuine considerations—'Allusion to custom . . . want of exactness . . . complying with the opinions prevailing in their times . . . using such ideas as prevailed in a religion . . . the Hebrew tongue . . . its idioms . . . the want of certain expressions used in other tongues'—which would be embodied in later historical criticism. Towards the end of the work he devotes much space to Clarke's Boyle Lectures, using the first set to discredit the arguments of the second.

There was no real, devastating reply to Tindal, for he had in fact cut right across the presuppositions of contemporary Christian moralism. Waterland's attempt in his anonymous *Scripture Vindicated*[26] is a learned attempt to demonstrate from a great range of modern and patristic Biblical learning that the God who is depicted in the Old Testament, and in orthodox doctrines of the Atonement is indeed perfect in truth, justice, and mercy. But as Leslie Stephen said, it shows itself at its feeblest in defending Elisha and the Bears: 'A good lesson of instruction to parents, to educate their children better . . . it was kind of God to take them out of the world . . .' The text, he explains, does not say that the bears devoured the children, but only that they 'tare them'.[27]

Much more impressive, though perhaps too intricate was William Law's reply, *The Case of Religion and Reason or Natural Religion fairly and fully stated* (1731).[28] It was written before Law had succumbed to 'Behmenism' and defends both natural religion and, within limits, the use of reason. His text is the claim by Tindal, 'if the relations between things and the fitness resulting from thence be not the sole rule of God's actions must not God be an arbitrary being?' His impressive and very closely argued work defends God from the charge of caprice and arbitrariness, and revealed religion in its doctrine of God and our redemption in Christ, and especially in the doctrines of a vicarious atonement and sacrifice. It sets forth the capacity of reason and marks out its limitations, and attacks Tindal's arguments at their most vulnerable spot, his failure to take account of the irrationality of much human behaviour, and of the corruptions in the human heart.

And in truth, Tindal's faith of a moralist is that of an élite. The vast majority of mankind did not behave as though they were Fellows of All Souls. There was more truth in Luther's saying that those who really lived by the light of reason were 'rare birds'. Tindal has his own *chiaroscuro*, for though he rejects the division of mankind into elect and reprobate, or Christian and heathen, the dark shadows across human

---

[26] *Scripture Vindicated*, 1731.   [27] Ibid., p. 126.   [28] *Works*, ii. 55ff.

history are the priests and clergy, complicating what was originally simple, manipulating and forging the sacred records, holding men in thrall to superstition and fear in a vast cloud of customs and ceremonies. He does not explain how God could allow such a perverted race to arise, nor does he consider that if church history is full of the sins of the clergy, history itself is much concerned with the sins of the laity. To Tindal forgiveness is no problem, and perhaps he deserves the comment of St Anselm to Boso in the *Cur Deus Homo?*: 'Thou hast not considered the gravity of sin.' On his moralistic terms, revelation is indeed hardly necessary, God having so loved the world that he gave his only-begotten Son to remind men that, after all, honesty is the best policy.

Both Christians and Deists laid stress on the importance of the Biblical prophecies, which seemed to the former one of the grand demonstrations of the truth of Christianity, and which the latter attacked with vehemence. Whiston had delivered his Boyle Lectures on the subject, and in his attempt to make sense of the Biblical tradition had been driven to drastic and eccentric emendations of the text. In 1724 Anthony Collins produced his most impressive writing, the *Discourse of the Grounds and Reasons of the Christian religion*. During the seventeenth century Protestant divines had stressed the inerrancy of the sacred text, and now they were called upon to face some of the problems involved. At the heart of the controversy lay the disposition to treat prophecy, as has been said, as fore-telling rather than forth-telling, and therefore to think of the prophecies as facts to be historically pin-pointed, in the manner of *Old Moore's Almanack*. There was recourse also to allegorizing and to typology, while the commentators wrestled with the question whether a prophecy might have two references, one in the immediate context and the other a further, spiritual reference fulfilled in Christ.

In the uneven beginnings of historical criticism, discussions of, say, the authenticity of prophecies in Isaiah or in Daniel became bedevilled by intricate disputations about the date of the writings and the historical context in which their authors wrote. Deist attacks on prophecy in the Bible were launched in the 1690s and William Nicholls attacked the use of allegory claiming 'if we should once allow this typical or allegorical way of explaining Scripture, one might prove the history of Guy of Warwick out of the first chapters of Genesis.'[29]

Collins asserted that the belief in Jesus Christ as the promised Messiah was central to the Christian position, and he began with the assertion that 'Christianity is founded on Judaism or the New Testament upon

---

[29] O'Higgins, *Anthony Collins*, p. 160.

the Old.' He would not have understood St Ignatius's statement that Judaism was founded on Christianity or Luther's that the key to the Old Testament is 'was Christus treibt'.

Collins claimed that a prophecy has only one immediate historical fulfilment, and the idea of a further and ulterior fulfilment is absurd. Relying heavily on Continental works by Surenhusius and Le Clerc he asserted that while the Apostles took prophecies literally, the early Fathers took over the Jewish method of allegory which began after the Captivity. Collins's tract was too solid to be ignored, and he himself counted some thirty-five replies. Of them the most considerable was that of Edward Chandler, Bishop of Lichfield and Coventry, who provoked Collins into writing an even longer work, *The Scheme of Literal Prophecy considered*. The strength of Chandler, who was not the simpleton that Leslie Stephen supposed, was his knowledge of the Targums and Jewish writers and his consequent discussion of the Messianic hope among the Jews. A great deal of the controversy expended ammunition on individual texts and prophecies about which neither scholar was impeccable, nor did the then state of scholarship permit a complete answer. But the best Christian reply to Collins came from Thomas Sherlock, who stressed that in fact the prophets were not simply fortune-tellers. For he showed that the prophecies had not to be isolated from the divine purpose running through the sacred history.

The argument from the prophecy is not to be formed in this manner: all the ancient prophecies have expressly pointed out and characterized Jesus Christ, but it must be formed in this manner, all the notices which God gave to the Fathers of his intended salvation are perfectly answered in the coming of Christ.[30]

It was all to the good that the whole question of the nature and significance of the Old Testament prophecies relating to the Messiah should be thoroughly, if roughly debated and that their relevance as 'proofs' of Christianity should be reduced to true proportions. But it was a defect of much of this, as of other controversy with the Deists, that both sides were legalistic in their arguments and rabbinical in their methods. For at the end of the day it remained true that it was in the Old Testament that Jesus of Nazareth had found the clues for his ministry and mission and that the prophetic testimonies have an undying value for Christians, since poetry and music have their own certainties and not only schools of logic and the courts of law.

Those who, on 1 May 1749 in the great Chapel of the Foundling

---

[30] O'Higgins, p. 176, has an excellent critical résumé.

Hospital, listened to Handel's *Messiah* heard a whole array of these controverted testimonies, underlined in music of majesty: 'Unto us a son is born'; 'He was despisèd, despisèd and rejected'; 'thou didst not leave his soul in Hell'; 'I know that my Redeemer liveth'. A few yards away, tucked up in their beds in the long dormitories, the little foundlings were yet another testimony that the hope of a Shepherd who should carry the young lambs in his bosom were that day fulfilled. The heart, too, has its reasons.

vi. Woolston and Miracles

The belief that the truth of Christianity could be proved by miracles, was one that was to persist beyond the eighteenth century. But once it was seriously assaulted, it was hard to disguise the fact that it was a circular argument, since these miracles depended on the authenticity of the sacred narratives in which they were recorded. In this long debate the most astonishing document was the *Six Discourses on Miracles* by Thomas Woolston (1669–1733), which appeared from 1727 to 1730. Woolston, like William Woolaston, was a member of Sidney Sussex College, Cambridge, where he became a Fellow, took orders and graduated BD in 1699. From his study of Origen he became interested in the allegorical interpretation of Scripture, and developed his own views in sermons in the College Chapel on the Old Testament. He was in frequent controversy and was deprived of his fellowship. His *Discourses on the Miracles* were sensational and ran quickly into several editions. For them he was put on trial in Guildhall on 4 March 1729, fined £100 and put in the King's Bench prison. There he stayed until his death despite the efforts of Whiston and Clarke on his behalf.

His sufferings weakened a mind already on the verge of mental disorder, and the vitriolic abuse of the various prefaces of his discourses aimed at the Bishops, and the general tone of his later works, show that his writing was pathologically affected. He professed to believe that all the miracles of the New Testament were to be interpreted allegorically, but his main argument, which was to show the absurdity of taking them literally, must have been a sceptical ploy in which he could attack the New Testament and indeed the integrity of Jesus himself. To misquote a famous nineteenth-century saying, where other people might have a bump of reverence, he had a crater. But it has to be admitted that there is more humour in his writing than in all the rest of the Deists put together, and he was a master of the kind of scurrilous anti-Christian knockabout which can be heard nowadays on any Sunday in Hyde Park. Like Collins and Tindal, he goes for the weak spots.

First, the Gadarene Swine: 'not a jury in England would have acquitted anyone arraigned and accused in the like case'; then the 'ridiculous' gifts of the Magi: 'if they had brought sugar, soap and candles they had acted like wise men.' Why should Jesus raise from the dead 'a boy and a girl who were of no consequence to the public—when he might have saved a useful magistrate—an industrious merchant?' But he goes to town on the barren fig tree. Why was Jesus so peevish in an act

as foolishly and passionately done as for another man to throw chairs and stool about the house because his dinner is not ready at a certain time or before it could be got ready for him—what if a Yeoman of Kent should go to look for Pippins in his orchard at Easter . . . and because of a disappointment cut down all the trees?

So he began with these incidents and worked up to the exposure of the greatest 'miracle' of all, the Resurrection. The most famous and popular defence of the authenticity of the Resurrection came from Thomas Sherlock, who used his acquaintance with the lawyers of the Temple to good effect in his *Tryal of the Witnesses of the Resurrection of Jesus* (1729), in which the Resurrection is made the subject of an investigative trial, with a counsel for Thomas Woolston and another for the Apostles. The conclusion was foregone.

Foreman: My Lord, we are ready to give our Verdict.
Judge: Are you all agreed?
Jury: Yes.
Judge: Who shall speak for you?
Jury: Our Foreman.
Judge: What say you? are the apostles guilty of giving false evidence in the case of the resurrection of Jesus or not guilty?
Foreman: Not guilty.
Judge: Very well, and now, Gentlemen, I resign my commission and am your humble servant.

What Dr Johnson called the 'Old Bailey' apologetic might dispose of poor Woolston, but there were still serious questions to be asked and answered, as they soon were at a more competent level, by Conyers Middleton and David Hume.

It was now that the question of testimonies became central. Charles Leslie in his *Short and Easie Method with the Deists* (1698) had laid down the following rules of evidence:

1st That the Matter of Fact be such as Men's outward senses their Eyes and Ears, may be Judges of it. 2. That it be done Publickly in the Face of the World. 3. That not only Public Monuments be kept up in memory of it, but some outward Actions to be performed. 4. That such Monuments and such Actions or Observances be Instituted and do Commence from the Time that the matter of Fact was done.[31]

The trouble with this was that, like many other arguments in this matter, the rules are evidently grounded in what it is attempted to prove.

vii. Middleton and Hume

Conyers Middleton (1683–1750) was that tiresome, but endemic, character, a don with a chip on his shoulder, a good classical scholar and a leader of the Fellows of Trinity, of whom he was one, against Richard Bentley. He became University Librarian but suffered all his days from a sense of grievance at not having received the recognition he thought he deserved. He addressed himself to the much debated question of when miraculous powers ceased to operate in the early Church, rejecting the view of Whiston that they ceased about the time of the Council of Constantinople as a divine reprisal for the Athanasian heresy. Middleton wrote a preliminary essay in which he raised the question, and then in 1748 published *A Free Enquiry into the Miraculous Powers which are supposed to have subsisted in the Christian Church . . . by which it is shewn that we have no sufficient Reason to believe upon the authority of the Primitive Fathers that any such powers were continued to the Church after the Days of the Apostles*. Middleton had a fluent and cogent pen and pursued his argument with a withering denunciation of almost all the Fathers of the early Church, from Clement and Justin Martyr to Gregory the Great, suggesting that they were all either fools or knaves, and insinuating that most of them were both. Not only was it a devastating indictment, but as John Wesley perceived in a not insignificant reply, Middleton's arguments could only too plainly be applied to the Apostles and to the New Testament itself. Beginning with an attack on Popery he had shown that many of the most hated features of it, were to be found in the Church of the first centuries.

Leslie Stephen suggests implausibly that in Middleton we have a recognizable appeal to history and to historical method, and in this way he heralds the appearance of a new and even more deadly criticism of Christianity and the early Church which would emerge in the writings of Edward Gibbon. In the same year as Middleton's *Free Enquiry* there appeared the much shorter, but devastating, essay on miracles by the Scottish philosopher David Hume. Hume laid down two principles,

[31] J. M. Creed and J. S. Boys-Smith, *Religious Thought* (Cambridge 1934), p. 54.

that a miracle was a violation of laws of nature which cannot in effect be violated, and that no evidence from human testimonies can be demonstrative or conclusive of the fact that miracles have taken place. And he ended with a famous paragraph full of enigmatic irony.

So that upon the whole, we may conclude that the Christian religion not only was at first attended with miracles, but even at this day cannot be believed by any reasonable person without one. Mere reason is insufficient to convince us of its veracity: and whoever is moved by faith to assent to it, is conscious of a continued miracle in his own person, which subverts all the principles of his understanding, and gives him a determination to believe what is most contrary to custom and experience.[32]

By the 1740s Deist writings were no longer sensational, and the cause seems to have withered about the middle of the century. This does not mean that their ideas ceased to count, but they mingled with other forces of the century and new and more socially radical forms of scepticism and unbelief. The direct influence of their writings was less to be seen in England than in France and in Germany where they supported a much more powerful movement, the scepticism of Diderot and Voltaire and Frederick the Great, the secularization of the Enlightenment.

The truth is that Deism was a half-way house, and history deals hardly with half-way houses. It was not only Deism that languished in the 1750s, but a pattern of Anglican religion from which it emerged and from which it could never be completely dissociated. It had taken its roots in Lord Herbert, Chillingworth, the Cambridge Platonists, and the Latitudinarians, and its writers shared with their orthodox opponents a moralistic interpretation of religion.

Nobody could say that the Christian counter-attack was ineffective when its champions were Bentley, Berkeley, Swift, and Joseph Butler. Nor was the apologetic of Sherlock unimpressive, or the scholarship of Waterland, which was always better read and better informed than that of those he opposed. But a great deal of its apologetic, it must be admitted, was woodenly defensive and rabbinical in method, always too eager to assume that anybody who dissented from orthodoxy must be immoral, and that the appeal of unbelief lay in the licence it gave to immorality. And though they were not intended as great theological manifestos, Bishop Gibson's best-selling *Pastoral Addresses* deserve attention. For to the conscientious clergy Deism and scepticism were

---

[32] D. Hume, *Dialogues*, ed. N. Kemp-Smith (Oxford 1935), pp. 57ff; *Enquiries concerning Human Understanding*, ed. L. A. Selby-Bigges, 3rd edn. rev. F. H. Nidditch (Oxford 1982), ch. x: see 'Miracles', p. 131.

cause of deep pastoral concern. Ordinary Christians incapable of following abstruse arguments or weighing historical evidence, might be led astray, might miss salvation, and go to hell. So that the intolerance of Gibson, like that of Thomas More two centuries before, had its root in a deep concern for souls in danger.

The Deists made no great positive contributions to thought, either about natural theology, or about its relation to revelation. But they did raise very important questions in a way which could not be ignored, they focused a long pent-up antagonism to clerical bigotry, and they provoked the regular clergy to jealousy at least in one important respect, that they had in the end to find a revised apologetic, with very different theological priorities. They themselves were a self-conscious élite, and, with the exception of Thomas Chubb, the tallow chandler of Salisbury, upper class; aristocrats like Shaftesbury and Bolingbroke, and the landed gentleman Anthony Collins, dons like Wollaston, Woolston, and Tindal, and the medical man, Thomas Morgan. They found their true vehicle for publicity in the heyday of the clubs and coffee houses, but they were never a movement, and in time interest languished and died, while more virile and extreme forms of scepticism and unbelief began to rise.

To a remarkable extent, western unbelief had always been conditioned by the Christian world to which it has been opposed. Tindal's conception of the true religion of nature, his doctrine of God and his view of human duty, had in fact been transmitted and preserved in and by Christian thinkers and theologians in the previous thousand years. Some of the Deists were nearer than others to Christian orthodoxy. Most of them believed in God, as supreme governor of the universe, and accepted a moral law, while some of them as Wollaston and Chubb believed in an afterlife and final judgement. They rejected miracles, and the 'proofs' from prophecy, and particular providences. To a man they were anti-clerical. Their strength was their belief in toleration and the right of free enquiry, and this was the more admirable because Christian intolerance could still make itself felt in nasty and physical ways. And though it is true that they did not answer, as was said, the question how to use liberty of thought once it was gained, their protest was influential. Perhaps from their time the erroneous idea has been generally plausible that somehow honest doubt is more honest than honest faith.

18

MORALISTS

i. The Moralists

THE emphasis on practical Christianity, on the practice of virtue as the end of religion, which became the hallmark of preaching in the period 1688–1750, needs to be seen in its context, a permissive society in which the decline and fall from Christian standards in all classes of society was universally lamented, and not only by the clergy who might be suspected of over-darkening the shadows. The determined effort of the Church to do something about this, and the remarkable, if limited, success of attempts at the amendment of society, will be outlined in the next chapter. Here we have to take note how the very nature of morality and of moral obligations came under scrutiny.

Moral theology had been important in the seventeenth century. The great Puritan moralists like William Perkins and William Ames returned gratefully to the later Middle Ages, to William of Paris and to Gerson.

Cases of conscience were of great importance for Puritans, Jesuits, and Anglicans like Jeremy Taylor, who discussed the same problems, though their resolutions varied from the Puritan subjective doctrines of assurance to the Catholic emphasis on the sacrament of penance. Moreover, the importance of catechetical teaching was generally insisted upon, though the very reiteration of its importance suggests it was often neglected. But, at least in the age following the Restoration, tools were provided, in the catechisms like those of Horneck and of Ken, and in such a staple handbook as the ever popular *The Whole Duty of Man*. From the autobiography of Simon Patrick to the diaries of Parson Woodforde there is evidence that conscientious clergy devoted time and attention to the edification of their flock, and there was not an eminent preacher who did not devote some, and in many cases, most of his sermons to the exposition of the ethical passages of the New Testament, and to the Christian virtues, or to the much discussed problems of the importance of sincerity, and the scope and importance of compassion.

One feature of the Deist controversies was that both sides were convinced of the importance of the moral law. For Samuel Clarke as for Joseph Butler this was part of the very nature of things, and though in his Boyle Lectures Clarke attempts to safeguard the liberty of God, he is clear that the moral law is binding upon God himself. Clarke himself is generally regarded as having been in the tradition of Cudworth and Cumberland, in the 'rationalist' or 'intellectualist' school of moral philosophy, accepting an immutable criterion of right and wrong.

The exponent of the alternative 'moral sense' doctrine was Anthony Ashley Cooper, Third Earl of Shaftesbury (1671–1713). Shaftesbury was of great influence on his own and upon the following generation by reason of his essays published in 1711 as *Characteristics of Men, Manners, Opionions, Times*. Later in the century he ceased to be highly regarded and there seem to be no popular modern republications of his works in the nineteenth and twentieth centuries. A great cosmopolitan and European, he had more influence on the Continent. Emmanuel Hirsch, while disclaiming the view that he represented a 'Gentlemanmoral', sees him as a pioneer of that ideal of *Humanität* which became important in German poetry and philosophy in the age of Goethe. In Shaftesbury's essays on the use of wit and ridicule as the best way of dealing with bigotry or fanaticism he provided the Deists with a rationale for their most effective polemical method, against which Warburton ineffectually protested in a preface to his *Divine Legation*. He has been compared with Matthew Arnold; like him he was an intellectual snob, and like him an exponent of sweetness and light. He finds the seat of virtue in the moral sense which is innate in man (though brought up by Locke, he was spiritually a child of the Cambridge Platonists).

Man is naturally attracted towards moral virtue. And his love of virtue is for its own sake, its blend of what is *pulchrum* and *honestum*. He does not need to be cajoled or blackmailed by the rewards or punishments after this life, though the vulgar may perhaps need this kind of moral reinforcement. Self-love and benevolence are not incompatible and are part of the great fundamental harmony of all nature, in the care of a benevolent creator. His optimism about the human condition may not be quite Panglossian but it seems close to that of Pope's view, in his *Essay on Man* that all must be well,

> All discord, harmony not understood,
> All partial evil, universal good.

His views were in complete contrast with the almost cynical realism of Mandeville in his *Fable of the Bees* with its significant sub-title 'Private Vices, Public Benefits'. Mandeville thought that virtue was an empty sham.

There is not a quarter of the wisdom, solid knowledge or intrinsic worth in the world that men talk of and compliment one another with; and of virtue and religion there is not an hundredth part in reality of what there is in appearance.[1]

ii. Joseph Butler

Authors generally regard critical correspondence about their writings as
something of a penance, but when Samuel Clarke on a November day
in the year 1713 received such a letter from one who signed himself a
'Gentleman in Gloucestershire', its serious courtesy moved him to reply
in kind. The correspondence continued, and Clarke must have been
surprised to learn that the enquirer was a theological student of the age
of twenty-one, at a Dissenting Academy. He would have been still more
surprised to know that this young man's fame would far eclipse his
own, and that Joseph Butler would become one of the glories of
Anglican divinity.

Butler was the son of a Presbyterian linen draper, but at Samuel
Jones's very notable Academy, where the future Archbishop Secker was
a fellow student, he decided, perhaps because he was more than most
men 'anima naturaliter Anglicana', to take Holy Orders. He went to
Oriel College, Oxford, where the triviality and superficiality of the
schools depressed him, though he did not pursue the thought of going
on to Cambridge to take a degree in Law. He was now a friend of
Clarke and was priested in his church of St James. At Oxford he had
found more promising patronage in his friendship with Edward Talbot,
son of the Bishop, and nephew of a future Lord Chancellor. Through
the interest of Clarke and Talbot he was in 1718 appointed Preacher to
the Rolls Chapel. The sermons he preached there became famous, and
some modern philosophers rate them more highly and of more lasting
interest than his more famous *Analogy*. In 1726 he was appointed to the
wealthy benefice of 'the golden Rectory' of Stanhope in Weardale, Co.
Durham. There he remained 'not dead, but buried', as one of his friends
remarked to the Queen. But his friends, who now included an archbishop, drew him south, to a prebend at Rochester, and he became
known to Queen Caroline, who prized him above the other members of
her theological collection, and tried hard to master the difficult,
compressed thought of his great work *The Analogy of Religion, Natural
and Revealed, to the Constitution and Course of Nature* (1736). She made
him Clerk of the Closet, received Communion at his hands on her
death-bed, where she charged the distraught King to see to his preferment. In 1738 he was appointed to the ill-paid see of Bristol which Butler
bluntly complained of as 'not very suitable either to the condition of my
fortune or the circumstances of my preferment', though he was given

---

[1] *The Fable of the Bees* (1725), p. 205; Stephen, *English Thought in the Eighteenth
Century*, ii. 34.

the deanery of St Paul's as a makeweight. But he took his duties with serious responsibility and developed a passion for reconstructing and rebuilding. There is the nice story from his Bristol days of his habit of walking up and down in his garden in the darkness of the night, meditating, or talking with Dr Tucker, his chaplain. In 1750 he was nominated to the great see of Durham, on which he entered with trepidation. He had been the subject of gossip when he put a plain white Cross on his chapel altar at Bristol, and the reproach of Popery revived when, in a remarkable charge he impressed on the Durham clergy the importance of external religion. He conscientiously made the major treks to London and the House of Lords, where he sat mum, so that Horace Walpole gibed that 'the Bishop of Durham had been wafted to that see in a cloud of metaphysics and remained absorbed in it.' He never married and was almost prodigal in the generosity of his charities. A shy man, he was at the opposite extreme of the superficial coffee-house theologians. He died in Bath in June 1752 at the age of sixty. A man so orderly in mind could not but be offended by John Wesley's itinerancy, and he tried in vain to warn him away from the Bristol diocese.

Butler's *Fifteen Sermons Preached at Rolls Chapel*, and his discourse on 'The Nature of Virtue', which is generally printed as an appendix to the *Analogy*, have attracted the attention of modern philosophers, because they deal with fundamental problems in which philosophers are still interested, and they have recently been reprinted.[2]

The question whether Butler is to be classed among the 'intellectual' or 'moral sense' philosophers is not easy to answer. His debt to Clarke was real and lasting, and he seems to accept that there is an immutable moral law. But he was also clearly influenced by Shaftesbury to whom he comes near in his discussions about the motives of human action. More important, perhaps, and something which deeply influenced Newman, is his affirmation of the primacy of conscience.

A superior principle or reflection or conscience in every man, which distinguishes between the internal principles of his heart, as well as his external actions: which passes judgment upon himself and them: pronounces determinately some actions to be in themselves just, right, good: others to be in themselves evil, wrong, unjust: which without being consulted, without being advised with, magisterially exerts itself and approves or condemns the doer of them accordingly.[3]

Butler's analysis of human psychology has been diversely criticized

---

[2] Butler's *Fifteen Sermons*, ed. T. A. Roberts, 1970.
[3] *Sermon* 2. 8 (Roberts, p. 14).

by modern writers, but if it is not always clear how he differentiates 'passions, affections and appetites', there is little ambiguity about the three principles, of self-love, of benevolence and conscience. It is important for Butler that self-love does not conflict with benevolence, and that in his view conscience and 'reasonable' and 'cool self-love' are closely related. 'Conscience and self-love, if we understand our true happiness, always lead us the same way. Duty and interest are perfectly coincident.'[4]

The sermons are packed and compressed in thought, difficult even for a distinguished legal congregation. But there is subtlety and profundity whenever he comes to the analysis of the springs of human action, as may be seen in the sermons on 'Compassion' and on 'Resentment' while the fine sermon on the 'Ignorance of Man' underlines a most powerful argument of the great *Analogy*.

The *Analogy of Religion* is generally taken to be an answer to the Deists, and though Butler never mentions them by name, it is easy to pick out arguments made famous by Collins and by Tindal. But perhaps the true description of his intentions may be found in that first letter to Samuel Clarke where he speaks of his search for a demonstrative proof of the existence of God 'not only more fully to satisfy my own mind, but also in order to defend the great truths of Natural religion, and those of the Christian revelation which follow from them, against all opposers.'

The underlying principle of his great argument, that 'probability is the very guide of life' has sometimes been charged with an implicit scepticism. But this is to misunderstand the truth that there is a scepticism which is inseparably bound with Christian faith. When Joseph Mede used to ask his Puritan students at the end of each day, 'What did you doubt today?' this was not an eccentric anomaly at odds with Christian faith, but something which Augustine and Luther, Kierkegaard and John Henry Newman very well understood.

His chief design was to satisfy his own mind and conscience, and this he attempted with immense and solemn honesty. It was because he had argued it all out with himself that his arguments with Deism were impressive, and even in some sense an anticlimax. Not that he was indifferent to the menace of unbelief, as a thinker and a pastor. It haunted him all his days and affected all his public utterances. In the most famous of all his sayings with which he prefaced his work, he acknowledged that 'It is come, I know not how, to be taken for granted

---

[4] *Sermon* 3.9 (Roberts, pp. 20–1).

by many persons, that Christianity is not so much as a subject of enquiry: but that it is now at length discovered to be fictitious.'

It is easy to see why modern philosophers prefer the sermons. Some of his arguments, and notably the appeal to prophecy and miracles, and his exposition of the content of revelation, are the stock arguments of his age, of Sherlock and of Waterland.

Sir Leslie Stephen rattles off a list of fallacies and unsatisfactory arguments which are cumulative and damaging.[5] But he seems completely to miss the grandeur of this work, and a wayfaring Christian who is no philosopher may only rashly venture to suggest what seems to us to be a classic feature.

The Deists had abolished mystery: they had swept and garnished the very corners of Nature. Toland and Collins and Tindal rejected the ancient arguments of analogy. They knew very well the nature of the Creator and the rules of His behaviour. The light of nature left no darkness at all. Now Butler turns their argument upside down and inside out and he finds the text for a new argument from analogy in a profound saying of Origen: 'He who believes the Scripture to have proceeded from him who is the author of Nature, may well expect to find the same sort of difficulties in it, as are to be found in the constitution of Nature.'

That there is a God, and that He is the author of Nature, Butler takes for granted as outside the scope of his demonstration. That this God is a moral governor, is the theme of the carefully cumulative argument of the opening chapters, and from this he proceeds to draw implications, probable consequences, for a life after death. Far from Scripture alone being dark, and revelation mysterious, these are shown to be the characteristics of all human existence. Butler draws attention to facts. If it seems strange that he begins with a future life, and that he moves on to an assertion of future rewards and punishments, it must be remembered that from Lord Herbert onwards, these were truths which many Deists accepted as provable by reason. In fact Butler goes at once to a fundamental and primary fact of human experience, the fact of death, the mystery of the dissolution of our bodies, the query whether man is as the beasts that perish. He begins with the immediate experience of all men, with their own bodies, still more full of secrets than physical science. The argument continues to keep close to the facts of human behaviour, our capacity for happiness and misery.[6] Pleasure and pain, virtue and vice, we know, though we cannot know why these things are, since 'the end for which God made and thus governs the world may

[5] Stephen, *English Thought*, i, ch. 9, section iv.
[6] *The Analogy of Religion* (Everyman edn.), p. 22.

be utterly beyond the reach of our faculties: there may be somewhat in it
as impossible for us to have any conception of as for a blind man to have a
conception of colours.'[7] Butler next develops the theme of the moral
government of God as it is reflected in the reward of virtue and the
punishment of vice, a moral law at work despite all the hazards and
uncertainties and inequalities of human existence. Moreover it can be
seen that this life is one in which men may be improved by discipline
and trained in habits of virtue, and if these things are true, it may be
further and probably suggested that they are intended to prepare us
for a future state in which the rewards and punishments will be
consummated.

In the second part of the work, Butler turns to revelation.
'Christianity is a republication of Natural Religion' he says, quoting the
Deists, but 'though natural Religion is the foundation and principal part
of Christianity, it is not in any sense the whole of it.'[8] Here, naturally,
he simply explains traditional Christian arguments, the necessity for a
Church, the argument from miracles and prophecies. But in this second
part he constantly reverts to the analogy of nature. Although he asserts
that objections to Christianity itself are, in great measure frivolous, he
adds: 'I express myself with caution, lest I should be mistaken to vilify
reason: which is indeed the only faculty we have wherewith to judge
concerning anything, even revelation itself.'[9]

And here again the man who delighted to walk and meditate at night,
under the darkest of skies, returns to his theme of 'this little scene of
human life' as it touches the vast mysteries which surround it.

Whether this scheme of nature be, in the strictest sense, infinite or not, it is
evidently vast, even beyond all possible imagination. And doubtless that part of
it which is opened to our view is but as a point, in comparison of the whole plan
of Providence, reaching throughout eternity, past and future: in comparison of
what is even now going on in the remote parts of the boundless universe: nay,
in comparison of the whole scheme of this world.[10]

Fallacies, unequal demonstrations there are, and arguments often used
which might be turned easily in favour of unbelief, or at least the
suspension of belief. But the immense and careful honesty is impressive.
Whereas William Law shows a similar genius in argument, but presses
on with evident fire and emotion, the word 'cool' is perhaps a clue to
Butler's reasoning. No wonder that his hobby was building, for such is
his theodicy, brick upon brick, stone upon stone, each carefully aligned.
Those who simply read the *Analogy* or even the sermons on moral

---

[7] Ibid., p. 24.   [8] Ibid., p. 121.   [9] Ibid., p. 142.
[10] Ibid., p. 136.

themes, might suppose that Butler's religion was a severe moralism, his God one who rewards and punishes, in no sense a Saviour or a God of Grace. But this would be entirely to misunderstand him, as may be seen at once in his fine sermon on 'The Love of God', and by the testimonies to his character and his devotion, who consciously braved public disapproval to put the emblem of divine suffering before his eyes, in his private chapel.

Like that of Richard Hooker, the stature of his work was not seen at once, in his own generation, and he too, has been more generally admired than read. But, like Hooker, he had done something of immense importance for his Church. Amid much that was fussily second rate, ineffectual, even slightly bogus, in contemporary Christian apologetic, here was one of imperturbable and impressive integrity.

PART IV
INCREASE OF CHARITY

'You and I,' said Peter, 'have different notions of charity. I own, as it is generally used, I do not like the word, nor do I think it becomes one of us gentlemen: it is a mean, Parson-like quality: tho' I would not infer many Parsons have it neither.' 'Sir,' said Adams, 'my definition of Charity is a generous Disposition to relieve the Distressed.'

H. FIELDING, The Adventures of Joseph Andrews, Bk. iii. ch. 13.

In other countries the giver is generally influenced by the immediate impulse of pity: his generosity is exerted as much to relieve his own uneasy sensations as to comfort the object in distress: in England benefactions are of a more general nature: some men of fortune and universal benevolence propose the proper objects: the wants and the merits of the petitioners are canvassed by the people: neither passion nor pity find a place in the cool discussion: and charity is then only exerted when it has received the approbation of reason.

OLIVER GOLDSMITH, The Citizen of the World, Letter xxiii.

19

THE NEW BENEVOLENCE

GENERALIZATIONS about the health of the Church have in every age to be taken with caution: saint and cynic, moralist and sceptic turn to one side of the picture, one part of the evidence. The historian has to allow for the immense silences of the unassuming and unpublicized, the multitude of the inarticulate, the unremembered acts of kindness, the cup of cold water. The records and the registers, the diaries and sermons, satirists and publicists may add up to something impressive in the way of evidence, but may miss altogether those authentic standards by which, according to the New Testament, the Christian quality of life is to be judged.

Perhaps less than justice has been done to the state of religion in the last decades of the seventeenth century. While the testimony is overwhelming and from all sides, that the permissive society which took its example from the Court of Charles II and his brother James was a time of overtly loosening standards, it is not the whole story. It was a period when the seeds were sown and when the first fruits appeared of a genuine and deep renewal of devotion, of sustained attempts to secure public amendment, and an impressive increase of philanthropy.

There were those in the highest ranks of society who in the old phrase 'swam against the tide'. Lady Margaret Blagge might be a ridiculed and isolated figure as she sat reading a good book a little ostentatiously while the royal ladies decked themselves with jewels for the slightly silly court masque *Calysto*, but there is evidence that within the Royal Family the teaching of the chaplains Compton, Hooper, and Ken were not without effect. We find the Princess Mary, during her very sticky friendship with the Lady Frances Apsley, discussing the *Introduction to the Devout Life of St Francis of Sales* (which they may have read in the French); while at the height of a tempestuous quarrel the Duchess of Marlborough could remind Queen Anne of what *The Whole Duty of Man* says about Holy Communion.

That was no mean half-century which witnessed the appearance of *Paradise Lost* and *Samson Agonistes*, of *Pilgrim's Progress* and the works of John Owen and Richard Baxter, which launched on their century of success the sermons of John Tillotson, amid a swelling flood of printed sermons and works of devotion, and a perhaps unparalleled spate of collections of prayers. While the reports of the decay of morals and teaching in the universities are too well attested to be brushed aside, the age of Bentley and Newton and a splendid array of antiquarians and historians, to say nothing of learned divines, is not to be written off as decadent. In the field of polemic divinity the debate between orthodoxy and the new scepticism, and with the Deists and Socinians was not uninformed debate. Impressive, too, were the writings of the eminent clergy of the City of London and Westminster which in the 1680s countered the claims of Rome with sermons later printed in three massive volumes of *A Preservative against Popery* and, on the side, the composite volume *Cases against Dissent.*

The notion of a Church sick, languishing, and corrupt, only saved at the last moment by the irruption of the Evangelical Revival ignores the fact that the revival itself had roots, and that it would have been impossible apart from the several converging movements of a renewal which had already begun.

i. The Religious Societies (1)

The Christian cell, the small, dedicated company of Christians who know one another by name, have even when in retreat from or even in rebellion against the wider community, again and again been a seed of renewal of the greater whole. That they so constantly appealed to the primitive Church reminds us that their ultimate authority was the example of Christ and the Apostles. Throughout the following centuries the great religious orders, embodied what we might call the *koinōnia* principle: at the end of the Middle Ages the lay spirituality of the Brothers of the Common Life, and on the Christian fringe the Hussite, Waldensian, and Lollard groups, derived their strength from their simple, cell-like structure. Luther himself laid stress on the importance of the 'mutual counsel of the brethren', and in the Preface to his German Mass tentatively outlined the possibility of such groups of 'earnest Christians' within the wider parish congregational *Gemeinde*, though it was among the Anabaptist sects that this came to a new form of life. It seems that Martin Bucer, impressed by the spiritual calibre of some of the more moderate Anabaptists, began to introduce such lay companies within the Strasburg framework, and if the pedigree be uncertain, this was at least a clue taken up a century later by the *collegia pietatis* of the German Pietists.

As with other religious movements, it is difficult to pinpoint the emergence in the 1670s of the Religious Societies. But it seems right to associate them with the striking and attractive figure of Anthony Horneck, though his biographer, Bishop Kidder, admitted that 'whether he did move them, or he only gave them their rules, I am not able to determine.' Certainly the quality of Horneck as a scholar, pastor, and divine was worthy of a sponsor of this small renewal. (In the history of the Church there have been many thousands of small renewals where one man, touching only a few score of souls, has contributed to a wider regeneration.) An immigrant from the Palatinate (his father had been a civic official at Bacharach), he came to England at the age of nineteen. There seems to be no convincing evidence that he was influenced by Pietism, and his university career at Heidelberg and Wittenberg would have brought him into contact with orthodoxy, Calvinist and Lutheran. It is more likely that at Oxford he came to love the Church of England, in which he took orders, and that his love of the Fathers and of the primitive Church, and above all the writings of St Augustine, gave him his interest in 'practical theology' of a kind not greatly differing from that of Simon Patrick in Cambridge.[1]

In 1671 he went to the Chapel of the Savoy in London, financially an ill-rewarded post, where there was no manse for himself and his large family. But he set himself against all pluralities, and his courage in rebuking dignities cost him higher preferment to St Paul's Covent Garden (Tillotson seems at one point to have been impressed by Horneck's opponents.) But he had overflowing congregations, despite, or because of, his German accent, and the poor flocked to hear him. Kidder had access to his diaries in which he kept strict account of his use of time, and commented that 'he was one of the kindest men to others who ever lived and one of the strictest to himself.' At the centre of his ministry were the monthly Communion services and an anonymous donor paid for his lectures at them to be printed in 1700 as *The Crucified Jesus*.

His sermons were direct, his learning not obtrusive, and it is interesting to find him paying attention to the lay Christian community of Nicholas Ferrar at Little Gidding.

He was of primitive zeal and practice in his devotion [wrote Burnet], his preaching most florid but all upon the mystic way which did take much with the common sort of serious people who are many times wrought upon by zealous raptures of communion with God . . . indwelling in Christ . . . the joy of the Holy Spirit which they fancy rather than feel or understand.

---

[1] The statement in A. W. Nagler, *Pietism and Methodism* (Nashville 1918), p. 140, that he was a young Pietist rests on no evidence or is a misreading of the sources quoted. M. Schmidt's suggestion that he had been influenced by disciples of De Labadie seems also unlikely: Rouse-Neill, *History of the Ecumenical Movement*, p. 105.

This is not quite the impression given by his printed works, but it is supported by the fine Christocentric prayers which intersperse his sermons and by such sentences as appear in his *Happy Ascetic, or the Best Exercise* (1724).

The Furniture God likes, is good Works and Devotion to the *happiness* he delights to look upon. No Jewels are so amiable in his eyes as the Graces of a holy Soul and her Virtues are the only Embroidery he is pleased with. Her breathings and Pantings after a Crucified Redeemer are the fine Linnen he loves to see her in. (Preface)

His devotion to the Fathers and to the Eucharist might seem to place him with the Caroline divines, though it was not high churchmen, but Burnet, Kidder, and Woodward who sang his praises. And indeed, while untouched by the Platonists, he has something in common with John Worthington (similarly drawn to Little Gidding), and his insistence on the advantages of a private covenant with God is strikingly akin to the tone of the Puritan Joseph Alleine.

London at this time swarmed with small companies, inns, chocolate and coffee houses, gossiping and arguing groups of all kinds, among them sceptics, Deists, and Socinians. It is against this background that Josiah Woodward, twenty years on, set his *Account of the Rise and Progress of the Religious Societies* (1701), in which he described how a band of young men came together under the direction of Horneck and framed their rules, which were in turn copied by others, as may be seen in their expanded form in the rules for the society of St Giles, Cripplegate.

There are some interesting lists of the occupations from which the young men came (in some of them apprentices were excluded). The societies of St Giles included a 'joiner, perfumer, leatherdresser, taylor, perukemaker, barber, cooper, taylor, shoemaker, clockmaker, druggist, distiller, silk man, buttonseller, needle-maker, turner, ironmonger, plumber, glover, jeweller, cook, schoolmaster, plaisterer'.

They were therefore in the main skilled mechanics from the artisan class, not, it seems, from the professions, still less from the young gentlemen who came down from the Universities. They were young men, literate and only able to anticipate moderate livelihood, but they were also intelligent and articulate Christian laymen, dissatisfied for whatever reason with their spiritual condition, and now given an instrument for their own discipline and enabled to make their own contribution in an active way, to the life of the Church.

The first of the Horneck rules enjoins

that all that entered into such a society should resolve upon a holy and serious life, that the sole design of this society [that of St Giles] being to promote real holiness of heart and life, it is absolutely necessary that the persons who enter into it do seriously resolve to apply themselves in good earnest to all means proper to make them wise unto salvation.

They were open only to confirmed members of the Church of England, apprentices being excluded, and each society was to be under the direction of a Church of England clergyman, while devotions were to be taken from the Liturgy, though a psalm might be sung and readings given from works of 'practical theology'. They paid 6*d*. a week and fines for non-attendance, and these funds were annually disbursed for charitable causes. They were to keep off 'controverted points of divinity . . . neither shall they discourse of the Government of Church and State'—St Giles's adding 'or the concerns of trade and worldly things'!

They may discuss with one another about their spiritual concerns, but this shall not be a standing exercise which any shall be obliged to attend to.

Their rule of life is to love one another, to pray if possible seven times a day, to keep close to the Church of England, to obey superiors both spiritual and temporal.

When, at the end of the reign of James II, the societies were suspect and suffered harassment, they turned themselves into clubs and met in more public places., But the confrontation with Roman Catholicism sharpened their zeal and they held daily prayers in St Clement Danes where also a lecture was given in preparation for the monthly communion. The Horneck societies held an annual audit dinner on Whit Tuesday where the accumulated funds were disposed of to various charities. There was a more slap-up affair at St Giles on Easter Monday where they were regaled in almost Pickwickian fashion with veal cutlets and marrow pies, washed down with the delectable Bumbo. It is difficult to speak of numbers, though a document of 1694 speaks of some sixteen societies in London and Westminster. Of course they aroused criticism, from some high churchmen who did not look kindly on anything resembling a conventicle, and who probably felt that what was most needed was the revival of the ancient Anglican discipline rather than innovations of this kind. But Robert Nelson, in the preface to his *Festivals and Fasts* stoutly defended them:

They distinguish themselves by their regular conformity and obedience to the laws of the church . . . they embrace the opportunities provided, there being two churches in London employed for that purpose, where they duly receive the Blessed sacrament upon all festivals how . . . they spend their Vigils in preparing their minds for a due celebration of the ensuing solemnity is more private but not less commendable . . . the great care they take to suppress the dawnings of enthusiasm, and to discountenance the first appearance of any vicious practices amongst their members, and the methods they impose before delinquents are entirely reconciled or totally rejected is . . . a preparation of the minds of the laity for their reception of that discipline which is wanted in the church.

And with a forthright blow at critics he added:

I see no reason why men may not meet and consult together, to improve one another in Christian knowledge, and by mutual advice . . . to further their own salvation, as well as promote their neighbours: when the same liberty is taken for the Improvement of trade: and for carrying on the Pleasures and Diversions of life. And if at such meetings they shall voluntarily subscribe any certain sums to be disposed of in such charities, as shall seem most proper to the majority of their members, I cannot imagine how this can deserve censure, when the liberal contributions of Gentlemen to support a Horse race or a Musick meeting have never been taxed with the least illegality.

Of great interest is Samuel Wesley's formation of a religious society in the depths of Lincolnshire, which he described as a corresponding member of the newly formed SPCK. 'I had an earnest desire for some years to see a religious society form'd among my people having hopes of assistance from thence in time to reform others . . . this I proposed to my Reverend Diocesan who gave me liberty to attempt it.'

Encouraged by Josiah Woodward's book, Samuel Wesley began with the young men in his choir and

We met for the first time at my own house, the 7th Feb. Present 8 persons beside myself, the Rules and orders were distinctly and deliberately read over . . . it was objected that their affairs of husbandry would sometimes unavoidably take them off from Family prayers in the mornings . . . then the orders were subscribed as they have been since then by several others (one of them the son of an anabaptist) and near twenty besides, several of whom have been occasionally present at our meetings which are every Saturday evening: in order to prepare for the Lord's Day.

They are most of them remarkably altered since we began: they forbear public houses unless when their necessary occasions calls them thither: are much more careful of their lives and conversations, communicate monthly with great devotion and appear very zealous for the glory of God and the welfare of their own and others' souls.

I cannot say that they yet increase much in knowledge, having been formerly very ignorant, but I verily think they do in piety and humility.

Like the London religious societies, the company at Epworth was not introverted.

Their first care is to set schools for the poor, wherein children (and if need be, adult persons) may be instructed in the fundamentals of Christianity . . .

their second design is to procure little practical treatises from Holland and Germany . . . to translate them into the vulgar tongue . . .

the third is to establish a correspondence with such societies in England, Germany etc. so that they may mutually edify one another

the fourth to take care of the sick and poor and to afford them spiritual as well as corporal helps.

Wesley claimed that there were thirty or forty other sober persons in the town who would be glad to join ('but we are not hasty in admitting them till we are very well acquainted with them'). Admissions, he says were done by the consent of all, 'when they have twelve members they admit no more'. Characteristically he adds 'they do not take in any women into their societies in order to avoid scandal and all other abuses. . . . Women may hear their husbands at home, and girls their parents.'[2]

No doubt these Church of England societies were not the only religious sodalities in London, where more exotic companies like those of the French Prophets or the Philadelphian Society and soon the Moravian societies would meet. The Wesleys' Holy Club had its independent origin, since we find John Wesley at one time seriously contemplating turning it into a formal Religious Society on the earlier and orthodox pattern.

ii. The Reformation of Manners

A decline in public manners and morals in the last half of the seventeenth century is attested by public documents and by private testimonies from Christians of all parties. Repeated proclamations from Charles II, Mary II, and Queen Anne had been elicited by public opinion. Defoe spoke of 'the present torrent of vice', and Josiah Woodward drew attention to the evils in the metropolis, 'horrid enormities which have for some years abounded in this great city'. The high churchmen who drafted the *Representation of the Present State of Religion* (1711) affirmed that 'we cannot without unspeakable grief reflect on that deluge of impiety and licentiousness which hath broken in upon us and overspread the face of this church and kingdom'.[3]

The Dissenter Isaac Watts confirmed this diagnosis in a sermon preached in 1707.

Though perhaps some particular sins were not so much talked of before, yet

---

[2] W. O. B. Allen and E. McClure, *Two Hundred Years: the History of the SPCK* (1898), pp. 87ff.

[3] *A Representation of the Present State of Religion*; p. 000.

sinners of various kinds were much more numerous, more public and more shameless. The streets rung with oaths and blasphemy: the taverns were nightly witnesses of lust and drunkenness: open houses of abomination were maintained with many inhabitants, and the fields were polluted with lewdness in the very face of heaven in the sight of the sun or stars . . . you may most effectually convince yourselves that crimes will grow numerous and shameless again, if you forbear the prosecution.[4]

If it be true that men cannot be made good by Act of Parliament, still less by royal proclamation, the function of law in protecting and moulding at least public and overt behaviour and in abolishing offensive disorder belongs to the very notion of a just State. What were lacking were not new laws, but the carrying out of a body of legislation which existed. But, as G. V. Portus says, 'laws . . . would do little towards checking vice and immorality without the presence either of a strong police-executive or a high moral tone in the nation. Unfortunately in the Restoration period neither of these things was present.' But in the 1690s there was a feeling in the air that something more needed to be done for the reformation of manners, a phrase generally in use before the formation of specific societies. In 1690 the constables and the inhabitants of Tower Hamlets entered into an agreement to clean up their immediate neighbourhood and the idea spread quickly to the other end of town where Edward Stephens claimed, probably truthfully, to have set in motion a society to promote reformation of manners. Important too, and perhaps more efficacious than the more general royal proclamations, was the letter from Queen Mary to the Justices of Middlesex in July 1691 bidding them put the laws in better execution. The new society had the patronage of the civic authorities and there were soon sub-societies, including one of constables who met weekly at Hamlin's Coffee house. Lawyers were needed, so that from the first these societies drew upon a higher social order than the young tradesmen of the Religious Societies, though it seems that these too became involved, and there is an evident overlapping, and more and more earnest young men were involved who were prepared to 'have a go'. At the heart of the movement, and in the end its fatal weakness was the need to lay information, and thus the unsavoury occupation of common informer, for long and perhaps for ever leaving a nasty taste in the public mouth, became the chief legal instrument in enabling the magistrates themselves, who were not always incorrupt, to do their work. In that age when profanity and swearing were as shocking as vicious crime, the range of abuses attacked was wide, covering drunkenness, immorality, gaming, and sabbath breaking.

[4] I. Watts, *Works*, i. 629.

Some of the easiest illegalities to spot, and again attracting note out of proportion to the sacrilege involved, were the laws regarding the sabbath. By the beginning of the eighteenth century the English Sunday was well established, and this was much more than a mere hangover from the Puritan sabbath. The setting apart of Sunday, the day of the Lord's resurrection, for devotion and for rest, was something recommended and endorsed by the Church of England as vehemently as by the Dissenters, who might be supposed in this to be the immediate heirs of Puritanism. There is a long section upon it in *The Whole Duty of Man*, in the sermons of Horneck and Archbishop Sharp, and in the *Festivals and Fasts* of Robert Nelson. Margaret Blagge wrote to John Evelyn about her qualms after playing cards on Sunday. John Locke surmised (wrongly) in November 1688 that Queen Mary would not set sail from Holland on a Sunday. The proclamation of Queen Anne about public morals 'enjoin and prohibit all our subjects of what degree and quality so ever from playing on the Lord's day at dice, cards or any other game whatsoever.'

Half a century later Parson Woodforde entered the astonishing memorandum (12 March 1769):

As I was going to shave myself this morning as usual on Sundays, my razor broke in my hand as I was setting it on the strop without any violence. May it always be a warning to me not to shave on the Lord's day or do any work or profane it 'pro futuro'.[5]

The vigilantes therefore were on the watch for 'Bakers appearing in the Streets with their baskets, or barbers with their Pot, Bason or Periwig box, shoe makers, taylors, hatters or other tradesmen carrying out their work and ware'.

Eminent bishops, not least those like Compton, Tenison, and Wake, who knew their London, patronized their efforts, which were commended publicly in a series of sermons by eminent divines, by the Church of England at St Mary-le-Bow, and by the Dissenters in Salter's Hall. These discourses were usually printed. It has been reasonably estimated that for a time, perhaps until 1714, these societies administered a short sharp shock, to a profligate section of society, and resulted in obvious and in some directions startling amendment.

This was perhaps not entirely due to these societies, for there is some evidence of a discernible raising of the tone and standards of society to which many elements contributed, among them the essays of Steele and Addison in the *Spectator*.

On the other hand, they were under continual assault; Archbishop

---

[5] *The Diary of a Country Parson*, ed. J. Beresford (5 vols, Oxford 1968), i. 85.

Sharp was critical, as were other high churchmen who were offended by
the co-operation with the Dissenters. Defoe and Swift were powerful
critics, pointing out the defects of a reform which touched only the
lower orders of society and left untouched the leaders of the nation, and
the misbehaviour of the Court. And Defoe showed a lively sense of
inefficacy of law to achieve moral reform: 'these are all cobweb laws, in
which the small flies are catch'd and the great ones break through . . . we
do not find a Rich drunkard carried before my Lord Mayor nor a
swearing lewd merchant.'[6]

Swift's *Project for the Advancement of Religion, and the Reformation of
Manners* (1709) was intended for the eyes of the Queen and she may well
have read it. After a sombre review of the evils of contemporary society,
he made it plain that in his view the best means of amendment would be
for the Court to set a good example: 'it is in the power of the Prince to
make piety and virtue become the fashion of the age.' If only good men
and women were chosen as leaders of the nation, as statesmen, civil
servants, and ecclesiastics, then integrity might prove infectious.
Despite his practical plea for the building of more churches, the projects
of the essay hang in the air, and perhaps take insufficient account of the
difficulties of the situation, too complex for an elderly royal invalid to
overcome. In the end it was no good putting a programme before
Queen Anne which would have been unrealizable under Queen
Victoria.

The Societies for the Reformation of Manners, however distasteful
their instruments might seem to those obsessed with civil liberties,
which then, as now, often meant licence for irresponsibility, did achieve
something, and had real impact. They represent an essential element in
the renewal of a sick society, the maintenance of moral standards, even
though the tendency of the age was to be more faithful to law than to
gospel in its programme of reform.

iii. Thomas Bray

What the Society for the Reformation of Manners could not do, indeed
never attempted to do, was to touch the mind and consciences of men.
This was done by new instruments of faith and charity in a growing
alliance between clergy and laymen, despite all the fuss of clericalism
and anticlericalism which raged on the surface and in which all too much
publicity centred.

'Projects' were an 'in' word of the age, and Defoe, Swift, and Robert

---

[6] Daniel Defoe, *The Poor Man's Plea* (1698), p. 10.

Nelson were among the dreamers of practical dreams. But his friends called Thomas Bray (1656–1730) the 'Great Projector'. His imagination teemed with ideas, many of which never came off, or were only to be realized in time to come, such as his hope of renewing the Church through rural deaneries and what would now be called 'fraternals'— regular gatherings of clergy for theological conversation, at the 'grass-root level'. The call from the Bishop of London for Bray to become the Commissary for the Church of England in the colony of Maryland brought him face to face with a range of problems.

Much that he tried to do was frustrated by powerful opposition from the Quakers, who saw their own precarious and hard-won liberties threatened by this churchman who had little room for Dissent. He never was able to exercise the needful authority of a Commissary, over a not very high-quality clergy. Still sadder, his hopes that the bishops so sorely needed might be appointed for the Americas were frustrated. But he himself was fully seized of the need for decent stipends for the clergy, and even more of the urgency to provide for them the tools for pastoral care and instruction, books for their own reading and for catechetical purposes. He became a pioneer in the establishment of parish libraries, and at the time of his death at least eighty owed their existence to him. But the crown of his achievements was the formation, in 1698, of the Society for the Promotion of Christian Knowledge. This aimed at the 'improvement' (another 'in' word of the age) of the Church through the education of its ministers and by means of their teaching of the laity. Of the founding members, four out of five were laymen and the society soon counted among its supporters bishops, clergy, gentry, and eminent lay Christians. Its purpose was defined as:

To promote and encourage the erection of charity schools in all parts of England and Wales: to disperse both at home and abroad Bibles and Tracts of religion and in general to advance the honour of God and the good of mankind, by promoting Christian knowledge both at home and in the other parts of the world by the best methods that should offer.

It became evident that the missionary purposes of the SPCK needed its own instrument and this was provided in 1701 by the formation of the 'Society for the Propagation of the Gospel in foreign parts to minister to British Christians overseas and to evangelise the non-Christian races of the world'. The SPCK kept in touch with happenings overseas and in distant parts of England and Wales by means of its Corresponding Members, among whom Samuel and John Wesley were numbered, and they gratefully received, read from and instructed out of the portable libraries of Christian classics and manuals of instruction

such as *The Whole Duty of Man*, Ken's *Catechism*, Tillotson's *Sermons*,
and half a dozen commentaries on the Catechism or the Creed: there
were Nelson's *Festivals and Fasts* and pastoral treatises from Burnet and
Spincke, while Bray himself wrote a four-volume commentary on the
Catechism. Among their chief publications was the provision of Bibles,
notably in Wales where they supplemented the work already begun
by the exiled Nonconformist Thomas Gouge.

iv. The Charity Schools

But the most important achievement of the SPCK in its beginnings, was
its support of the establishment and multiplication of charity schools. It
did not start them, but its leaders saw with immediate insight that this
was an imperative call of the day. At the eleventh hour, society was
about to remember the poor. A social condition could be made to touch
the conscience, and fire the imagination of good people, in effectual
action.

Common opinion divided the poor into two classes. There were the
formerly affluent, who had become victims of the poverty trap, with the
increasing oscillation of the economic see-saw in the expansion of trade
and industry. Isaac Watts spoke of those who had formerly enjoyed
'plentiful circumstances', but who 'by the wise providence of God have
been reduced to great degrees of poverty, and hardly able to provide
food and clothing for their own offspring and much less bestow a good
education upon them.'[7] Swift admitted that

sometimes honest, endeavouring men are reduced to extreme Want, even to the
Begging of Alms, by Losses, by Accidents, by Diseases and old Age, without
any Fault of their own . . . these indeed are properly and justly called the Poor,
by whom it should be our Study to find out and distinguish, by making them
partake of our Superfluity and Abundance.

But Swift had little patience for the mass of the poor:

Among . . . those who beg in our streets or are half starved at home, or languish
in Prison for Debt, there is hardly one in a hundred who doth not owe his
Misfortunes to his own laziness, or Drunkenness or worse Vices. To these he
owes those very Diseases which often disable him from getting his Bread. Such
Wretches are deservedly unhappy: they can only blame themselves: and when
we are commanded to have pity on the Poor, these are not understood to be of
the number.[8]

He did not face the question, 'But what of their children?'

---

[7] Watts, *Works*, iv. 528.
[8] Sermon, 'On the Poor man's Contentment', *Works*, ix. 191.

It was a callous and insensitive age, where people enjoyed public executions, and where a visit to watch the antics of the demented in Bedlam was as great an attraction as the lions in the Tower of London. There were to be seen sights of suffering and need in the streets of cities and in country lanes, the more sharp in contrast to the rising national prosperity, while in the slums of London and Westminster, in Spitalfields and St Giles there were masses of ignorant and depraved human beings in foetid tenements, cripples, beggars, and destitute children running wild, such as may still be seen in some parts of Asia, but here on the doorstep of the Church and in a nation which had had the Christian gospel for a thousand years.

Specific instances are best. Here is one witnessed by that impoverished undergraduate Samuel Wesley, in a pleasant village outside Oxford.

It being the height of winter and a very severe one, I walked out in the morning alone and as I went musing along in an unfrequented path near the riverside I saw a little boy about some seven or eight years old, lying under a hedge and crying bitterly, I went up to him and asked the reason. He told me that two days before his Father died, his mother having been dead several years and left none in the house but himself and a little sister about ten years old, without any victuals or money, that they had stayed at home all the next day but none took care of them nor brought them any relief. That they resolved in the morning she should go a-begging in their own parish about a mile or two from Oxford, and he would go to the city and try what they could get to keep themselves alive; accordingly he told me he got up as soon as it was day and walked towards Oxford but being weak through a long ague and want of meat was forced to lie down there and could go no further. I confess I was touched with the boy's story, I raised him from the ground to which his clothes were almost frozen and rubbed his limbs, benumbed and almost dead with the cold till he could make a shift to go, then I pulled out my twopence—all the stock I had in the world—and gave it him seeing him in greater extremity than I was myself with which he went overjoyed into the town and bought a twopenny loaf which he carried home to his sister.[9]

A century later John Wesley said in one of his sermons:

That the people suffer none can deny . . . thousands of people in the West of England, throughout Cornwall in particular, in the north and even in the midland counties are totally unemployed. . . . I have seen not a few of these wretched creatures . . . standing in the streets with pale looks and hollow eyes and meager limbs: or creeping up and down like walking shadows. I have

[9] H. A. Beecham, 'Samuel Wesley, Senior: new biographical evidence'. App. Letter, 22 Aug. 1692, in *Renaissance and Modern Studies*, University of Nottingham, vii (1963), 104.

known families who a few years ago lived in an easy, genteel manner reduced to just as much raiment as they had on, and as much food as they could gather in the field. To this one or other of them repaired once a day, to pick up the turnips which the cattle had left: which they boiled, if they could get a few sticks, or, otherwise, ate them raw.[10]

In London scores died weekly either from starvation or its side-effects. The exposure of unwanted infants was something the cumbrous parish machinery failed to cope with. Dr Thomas Coram, the redoubtable sea captain, was appalled in his trips to and from London, by the sight of children lying dead or abandoned in the gutters and he and a few allies did not rest until they had opened the famous hospital for foundlings. On the first day when it was opened to all comers, 117 unwanted babies were put in the basket which was hung on the gate in Guildford Street, while the first month brought in 425 infants.[11]

Bands of violent and vicious orphans the so-called 'blackguards' roamed the streets

Without shoes and stockings, perhaps half naked, or in tattered rags, cursing and swearing at one another almost before he can speak, or he shall find them with the like blackguard to themselves, rolling in the dirt and kennels or pilfering on the wharfs . . . devoid of all breeding and good manners.[12]

And of this number, which may have been as many as 10,000, a proportion were immigrants 'altogether friendless and who by being born in Flanders or Spain are strictly of no parish in Great Britain, such whose parents have been knocked in the head in the service of Her Majesty.'[13]

The scope of the charity-school movement was immediate and empirical. None of the bishops had the same enthusiasm for educating the poor as had Cranmer and Latimer at the beginning of their small sixteenth-century educational revolution, behind it an Erasmian view of learning. Here there was the compulsive threat of the evident consequences of poverty for society and the belief that the stability of society as a whole demanded some reform of morals and manners as the base of the pyramid of knowledge and faith. There was also the belief that Popery and ignorance were allies, a theme which is perhaps more prominent in the formal charity-school sermons, than in the minds of those who made the new schools. But it does seem that such schools had begun to appear before the SPCK was formed, though that rapidly

[10] J. Wesley, Sermon on 'National Sins and Miseries' (1775), *Works*, vii. 384.
[11] D. Owen, *English Philanthropy, 1660–1960* (1964), p. 55.
[12] George, *London Life in the Eighteenth Century*, p. 219.
[13] L. Cowie, *Henry Newman, an American in London, 1708–43* (1956), p. 76.

became the clearing-house for the movement. It may be that it was a Jesuit school in the Strand which provoked Simon Patrick and William Tenison to begin schools in 1687 at St Margaret's, Westminster, and St Martin-in-the-Fields.[14] From the first, the schools depended on a new kind of associated, lay philanthropy, on subscribed or endowed schools behind which groups of trustees and governors planned and executed this relatively simple and relatively cheap new form of educational philanthropy.

Mandeville might after his manner deride and ascribe the worst motives to these people and suggest they were young tradesmen irked by their inability to count for anything in their local vestry, but, as M. G. Jones notes, the evidence from St Margaret's, Westminster, alone refutes the charge. Here six tradesmen—a cheesemonger, a draper, a bookseller, and three dealers in soap, candles, brooms, and leather— contributed freely to the charges of the new schools and induced others to join them. They proposed to teach forty poor children 'in sober and virtuous principles and in the Christian religion', to clothe them and to put them out as apprentices 'to get an honest livelihood'.

The trustees of St. Margaret's were unsparing of their time and care. They met every week to supervise the charity they had set up. They ordered the new gray coats for the children and were present when the tailor tried them on. They supplied the mothers with gray yarn to make stockings for the children and prevailed on their own wives and daughters to make the caps and stitch the bands which constituted the boys' uniforms. . . . they evolved schemes for testing the children's progress in learning.[15]

Like many other governing bodies, they realized how important was the quality of the teachers they chose and paid.

But if the butcher, the baker, the candlestick-maker found a field for lay Christian initiative, it was part of the work of the SPCK to bring together men and women of all classes.[16] The movement took on and acquired momentum so that Mandeville grumbled that it was as much a fashion as hooped petticoats.

The London parish churches were in the van. The rich congregation of fashionable St James's, Piccadilly, which under the incumbency of William Wake disbursed large sums monthly for coals, clothing, and gifts to the poor; St Giles-in-the-Fields, on the edge of some of the worst slums in London; St Andrew's, Holborn, a centre of high churchmanship, while St Botolph's, Aldgate, which had its school in

[14] A. Shallet funded a Dissenting charity school in Gravel Lane, Southwark, in opposition to another Jesuit venture: A. P. Davis, *Isaac Watts* (1943), p. 93.

[15] Jones, *The Charity School Movement*, pp. 44–6.

[16] Cowie, *Henry Newman*, p. 73.

1689, owed much to the vigorous championship of White Kennett.[17]
The society published regular statements about their progress. In 1704
fifty-four schools had been established in and about London, with 2,131
children. By 1714 there were more than 1,000 schools in the country
which had bound apprentice over 2,000 children.

One of the features which no doubt assisted the growth of the
movement was that it was comparatively cheap, or rather the outward
and visible results seemed out of proportion to the money expended.
Robert Nelson's estimate for the cost of a school for young blackguards,
for providing a room and a master, uniform for thirty boys, and a daily
loaf of bread, was under £100 a year, a figure supported by other
statistics.

In the many printed accounts of the schools the clothing of the
children is an important item. They were of plain stuff, not calculated to
give the poor ideas above their station. But the bands for the boys and
their stockings, and the coifs for the girls and their gloves, and the grey
or red or blue coats had a comeliness which is evident from their statues
which still appear outside St Botolph's, Bishopsgate, and St Andrew's,
Holborn, and in those schools which are their descendants, now many
rungs further up the social ladder. They are a pleasant contrast to the
modern school uniforms of a thousand Greyfriars and St Trinian's, and
scruffier breeds without the law. There is evidence that for most of the
children, the badge and numbers they wore were no 'Star of David'
discrimination, and that they were not ashamed of the uniform.

They were seen to most advantage in the annual services where, as in
the town of Cambridge or the London churches, the children marched
in procession to hear sermons which were intended to open purses and
to advertise the good cause. Charity-school sermons were preached
by eminent clergy, and by some, like Parson Woodforde, rather
reluctantly.

The sermons were invariably printed, a rarefied art form which often
included much good sense, a reminder to the children of their good
fortune and to the congregation of the rewards of doing good, much
that was mealy-mouthed, and perhaps very little trace of honest
indignation or compassion. In 1704 a joint procession of 2,000 children
was held in St Andrew's, Holborn, and John Strype described it as
'wondrous surprising as well as a pleasing sight . . . when all the boys
and girls in their habits walked two by two with their masters and
mistresses.' But Robert Nelson organized the Society of Patrons of
Charity Schools, which arranged a service on an even greater scale.

---

[17] Bennett, *White Kennett*, pp. 188ff.

While Sir Christopher Wren refused to endanger the new fabric of St Paul's with the wooden galleries to hold up to 12,000 'little Elymosynaries', such great occasions touched the public imagination, as for instance the immense gathering of children on embanked seating along the Strand at the National Thanksgiving for the Peace of Utrecht in 1713: and after 1780, when they had at last got the use of St Paul's, there were impressive services in the presence of Royalty. We need not forbear to quote William Blake's 'Holy Thursday'

> 'Twas on a Holy Thursday, their innocent faces clean,
> The children walking two and two, in red and blue and green,
> Grey-headed beadles walk'd before, with wands as white as snow,
> Till into the high dome of Paul's they like Thames' waters flow.
>
> O what a multitude they seem'd, these flowers of London town!
> Seated in companies they sit with radiance all their own.
> The hum of multitudes was there, but multitudes of lambs,
> Thousands of little boys and girls raising their innocent hands.
>
> Now like a mighty wind they raise to heaven the voice of song,
> Or like harmonious thunderings the seats of Heaven among.
> Beneath them sit the aged men, wise guardians of the poor;
> Then cherish pity, lest you drive an angel from your door.

Nor may we forget, beneath the neat and comely uniforms, the pale, pock-marked faces of the semi-invalid, the handicapped, the defective, and the half-starved.

Bishop Nicolson describes an evening service at the Gray Coat Hospital, Tothill Fields, Westminster (30 December 1704):

We were present with great numbers of ye neighborhood at their usual Sunday nights exercise: which began with two Collects (Prevent us O Lord etc. and O God, who has caused all holy scriptures etc.) and a chapter read by one of the boyes. This was followed by a psalm sung. Then ye Master examin'd twelve of ye girls throughout ye church catechism and six of the boyes in an Introductory Explanation of ye English liturgy. This done, there was another psalm sung and an Anthem: and then, (concluding with an evening Ditty in verse, and two or three Collects) ye children sat down to their suppers of bak'd Pudding.[18]

The charity schools were an experiment in Christian education, designed to turn young savages into decent, God-fearing men and women. They were therefore to be washed and clothed, as well as trained in the doctrines, privileges, and duties of the Christian religion, according to the principles of the Church of England. We may not simply focus attention on the demerits of the educational elements in

---

[18] 'Bishop Nicolson's Diaries', p. 38.

their programme, unless it is recognized that there is everything to be said for setting education against a background of community, where morals and manners are seen as contributing to the training of the whole man. It is understandable, too, that the literature used should be Biblical and catechetical: not *Sir Bevis of Hampton* nor *The Seven Champions of Christendom*, such as lit the imaginations of John Bunyan and Samuel Johnson, nor the lurid contemporary tales and ballads. It would not have occurred to them that *Robinson Crusoe* and *Gulliver's Travels* could be read as children's books! There were, however, many books for children published at this time, many by Baptist authors. But then the Bible is, as has been said, a book full of stories, some of them calculated to thrill the most blood-thirsty teenager. And some may consider that the pattern of behaviour inculcated in the Prayer Book Catechism is not without relevance to the adolescent violence of our own day.

To hurt no body by word nor deed: To be true and just in all my dealing: To bear no malice nor hatred in my heart: To keep my hands from picking and stealing, and my tongue from evil speaking, lying, and slandering: To keep my body in temperance, soberness, and chastity: Not to covet nor desire other men's goods; but to learn and labour truly to get mine own living, and to do my duty in that state of life, unto which it shall please God to call me.

That the children should be taught to read, was, after all, the main exercise of the charity schools' programme. Only thereafter were they to be taught to write and only after that, and not by any means in all schools, was there to be instruction in casting simple accounts. The girls learned to sew and darn, to execute household chores, and in some cases to spin, in order to be fitted for the more menial household tasks to which they might one day profitably aspire. Many of the boys were apprenticed, and a proportion fitted for the Navy or the Merchant Service. Of the three Rs, it was the second and third about which there was most argument, and the fear of their effect on competitive labour with the more privileged ranks of society was most often expressed.

A movement so public, and indeed so spectacular in the speed of its development, could not fail to attract criticism and it was inevitable that it should be affected by the intense party passions of the day, partisan emotions which filtered down from trustees and clergy, through the ushers to the children. Those schools which were patronized by the high churchmen, and especially the Non-Jurors, were suspect to the Whigs as nurseries of Jacobitism, where disobedience to lawful Government was taught, and where funds were raised for dubious purposes. There was a notorious case when the managers of St Anne's, Aldersgate, sent a group of children under the aegis of a high churchman, the Revd Mr

Hendley (Atterbury was his diocesan), who was to preach in the pleasant country village of Chislehurst in Kent. There on a sunny Sunday in August 1718 the congregation observed the children and gazed out at the lovely surrounding common. Uproar came with the offertory, and an unseemly fight centred on the collection plate. The Rector, lecturer, and trustees were taken into custody, charged with unlawfully strolling up and down, and with conspiracy to extract unlawful charity. The Rector collapsed and died within hours of his return from the Assizes.

Defoe wrote a tract about the incident, ironically entitled *Charity still a Christian Virtue*. In fact there had been sufficient truth in the charges of disaffection and sedition, and small boys had been encouraged to take to the streets wearing coloured bows and crying 'High church and Ormonde'. An enquiry among the Committee of London Charity Schools led to the dismissal of a number of teachers, and it may be a good deal of hushing-up about others.

The most bitter literary onslaught, in Bernard Mandeville's essay on *Charity and Charity Schools*, attained great publicity, not least because it was published bound together with the author's celebrated *Fable of the Bees*. Mandeville at his worst had a nasty tongue as well as a nasty mind, and his Hobbesian ethics led him to believe the worst about the motives of philanthropy, while he had nothing but contempt for pity and compassion as womanish traits. He attacked the schools for breeding sloth and idleness which he took to be endemic vices of the poor. In an almost modern passage he claims that it is parents, and not schools, which should be the object of concern: 'as soon as school is over they are as much at liberty as other poor children. It is the precept and example of parents and home, those they eat drink and converse with that have an influence on the minds of children.' The schools, he concludes are auxiliaries to mischief to the forming of habits 'of sloth and idleness and strong aversion to labour'.

In some ways more depressing than Mandeville's blast, which perhaps did blow away a lot of sanctimonious humbug, is the defence of the schools by some of the more illustrious clergy. The Revd Dr R. Moss, preaching at St Sepulchre's on 27 May 1706 entitled his discourse, 'The Providential Division of Men into Rich and Poor and the respective duties thence arising', and his sermon echoes the sentiments of Swift's sermon on 'The Poor Man's Contentment'. Bishop Edmund Gibson was concerned lest the simple, basic teaching of the schools might become dangerously elaborate.

If charity schools should grow by degrees into a more polite art of education, if the boys should be taught fine writing, and the girls fine working and both of them fine singing . . . this would have a natural tendency to set them above the meaner and more laborious stations and offices of life.

The Dissenters came into the new field on a smaller scale, and started their own schools in 1678. But in his *Essay on Charity Schools* (1728) Isaac Watts leaned over backwards to meet contemporary criticism.

The great God, he wrote, has wisely ordained in the course of his providence in all ages that among mankind there should be some rich and some poor. And the same providence hath allotted to the poor the meaner services and hath given to the right the superior and more honourable businesses of life: nor is it possible according to the present course of nature and human affairs to alter this constitution of things, nor is it our design to attempt anything so unreasonable.[19]

None the less he vigorously defends the benefits of reading, even for the lowly poor, and to be able to write and add simple sums of money is, he suggests, what any employer would value in his meanest servants.

All that is pleaded . . . is that they may be taught to add and subtract little parcels of money such as may come within their possession or be entrusted to them—let it be considered that it is the custom of the nation in our day to run much deeper into debt, and deal more generally upon trust and credit than was done in the days of our fathers: and even poor labourers are seldom paid every night, nor perhaps every week nowadays. And is it not a hard case if they may not have leave to learn to help their memories by short accounts of the money that is due to them, that in their demands they may neither do injury to their masters or themselves?[20]

And yet Watts put in a plea for the occasional lad of bright genius endowed 'with more sprightly talents of nature . . . let him not be thrust out of the schools sooner than his neighbours, out of a mere caution that he may learn too much.' This is perhaps the measure of the strength and weakness of the movement, that it was an eminently practical, and as we have seen a relatively cheap way of remedying a crying evil, but it was financed and advertised by moderate men on rational grounds, and with the approval of many Biblical texts, but with very rare instances of burning compassion, and no vision at all of the benefits of an extending culture, or of the transformation of an advancing society, not even the vigorous belief in the capacities of 'poor men's children' which Cranmer had put roughly before the gentlemen of Canterbury, and Latimer defiantly expounded in his sermons before the Court.

There were ups and downs, especially among the subscription

---

[19] Watts, *Works*, iv. 528.   [20] Ibid. iv. 542.

schools, many of which flourished for a short while and then disappeared, despite the support of the SPCK. The total figures can hardly be determined, but it seems certain that it is an understatement to say that, by 1729, 1,419 schools existed in England with 22,503 pupils (5,225 in London and Westminster) and that in the middle of the century the charity-school movement dwindled and faded, to be replaced with the Sunday School movement. In Wales, where the movement was even more significant, it could claim nearly 3,500 schools, with more than 150,000 pupils, between 1727 and 1761.

v. Rational Philanthropy

Christian philanthropy has taken many forms during the centuries, though it has always been rooted in the Bible, in the Hebrew traditions of righteousness and mercy, and in the teaching and example, in the New Testament, of Him who went about doing good. Sometimes it has been expressed in an intricate world view. Byzantine philanthropy had great achievements to its credit, not least in its provision for the sick and aged, though set against a vast background of poverty and destitution. But here was a coherent Neo-platonic world view, which saw the Emperor at the head of a social pyramid and philanthropy as a necessary imperial attribute.

In our time action to relieve the social ills tends to be visionary—a kind of realized apocalyptic, a determination to 'build Jerusalem': 'I have a dream!' In the eighteenth century the philanthropy which brought into existence the new societies for doing good, the charity schools and the hospitals, was much more limited in scope, its doctrine of charity expressed without emotional fuss, commended by rational argument and set at practicable and immediate objectives.

None the less, it was a movement which acquired momentum in the half-century from 1688 onwards. There were those who took a cynical view of the possibilities of social amendment. The Augustinian view of man in the state of nature, after the Fall, spoke of total depravity, but only in the context of total grace. Now publicists arose who believed only in original sin and the view of man in Hobbes, Mandeville, and to some extent, Swift, showed little optimism about the possibilities of human action. We can understand how William Law called Mandeville a 'missioner from the kingdom of darkness', since he dissolved the virtues into utilities, expediences, and hypocrisy, seeing only a desire for self-advertisement in the good deeds of the rich.

We have noticed already how philanthropy by association was the mark of the new age, and this is nowhere better seen than in the growth and multiplication of hospitals. Before 1700 there were only St Bartholomew's and St Thomas's in London, but both were in financial difficulties, since the Great Fire had demolished areas from which they drew their incomes in the City. Now, between 1719 and 1750, five general hospitals came into being, along with nine in the country, reaching thirty-one by 1800.

Some of them, the Radcliffe in Oxford, and Addenbrooke's in Cambridge, owed much to eminent physicians who saw in the new institutions a machinery for the advancement of medical science. The London Hospital owed much to its first surgeon, John Harrison, while St George's Hospital was aided by the defection of some of the doctors at Westminster Hospital, dissatisfied with the facilities offered there. Westminster Hospital was indebted to the wealthy banker, Henry Hoare, an eminent layman from St Dunstan's-in-the-West. St George's was in a commanding position at Hyde Park Corner, and here, unlike some other hospitals, the governing body was limited to those who subscribed more than £5. In the East End, the London Hospital (1740) was the one general hospital ministering to that crowded and poverty-stricken area. In the Middlesex Hospital for the first time, provision was made for women lying in. Guy's owed its existence almost entirely to the benevolence of the flourishing bookseller and publisher, Thomas Guy. Other hospitals began to appear in different parts of the country, two notable establishments being at Bristol and Norwich, and a lovely Fishermen's Hospital at Great Yarmouth (1702).

Despite the manifold shortcomings in medicine and in nursing and medical attention, a high proportion of successes was plausibly claimed. In 1734 Guy's discharged 1,524 patients and buried 277, while in 1747 Westminster cured 705 and buried only 48. The figures for Bridewell were more grim.[21]

The Lock Hospital and the Magdalen were for unfortunate women, and their money-raising public services were thronged by the same kind of spiritual voyeurs who got a kick out of trips to Bedlam. At the Magdalen they provided an outlet for the performances of William Dodd, the 'macaroni preacher', grimacing from the pulpit with a posy in his hand. Shortly before his downfall and execution he preached on behalf of the curious New Society for the Rescuing of Drowning Persons, part of whose recommended resuscitation was the insufflation of tobacco fumes into the 'Grand Intestine'. Dodd annually addressed a parade of these reluctant Lazaruses. It was generally agreed that the state of the prisons, in London especially, was appalling, and Hogarth and

---

[21] Rudé, *Hanoverian London*, pp. 84–6.

others drew terrible pictures of their manifold horrors. General Oglethorpe took action in respect of the debtors' prisons, above all in attempting to find them a new life in the new colony of Georgia.

A careful, if smooth, rationale for Christian philanthropy was given by Isaac Barrow in his well-known 'Spital Sermon' at Eastertide 1671.

The pious man giveth, that is with a free heart and pure intention bestoweth his goods on the indigent without designing any benefit or hoping for any requital to himself: except for God in conscience, respect and love to whom he doth it. God lendeth the poor man his own name and alloweth him to crave our succour for his sake.[22]

Prominent among the subscription lists were the names of members of Court and society, bishops and local gentry. Rich men furnished with ability played their part, and those who then, as now, denigrate the 'anonymous donor' often forget how easily such men might, like the majority of their class, have spent their fortunes on stately homes or not so stately pleasures or on the welfare of their own kin. Among such Christian philanthropists were Samuel Wright, in London, commemorated in a pamphlet as *London's Wonder: or the Chaste Old Bachelor*; Edward Colston at Bristol, a high churchman who barred Dissenters from his school, and refused to apprentice the children of Nonconformists; John Bellars and Richard Reynolds, the Quakers; Daniel Williams, the Presbyterian; and Richard Taunton, the mayor of Southampton.

Their motives ranged from local patriotism and self-advertisement to human pity and Christian conviction. Thomas Firmin, the most famous philanthropist at the end of the seventeenth century, was addicted to Socinian innovations in theology. But in Robert Nelson (1656–1715), philanthropy was grounded in Christian conviction, in the ancient Catholic notion that in the poor we encounter not only human beings, but Christ himself.

Nelson, like Bunyan's Mr. Honest, did not go in for abstractions, but was a great 'projector' of what could and should, and one day would be done. Brought up by Bishop Bull, that champion of Nicene Orthodoxy, always an uncompromising high churchman, and for a time a Non-Juror, his friendships went across party barriers and John Tillotson died in his arms. Son of a wealthy Turkey merchant (the Middle Eastern trade was of growing importance in his day) he took care to be abroad on a Grand Tour in 1688, and married the well-to-do niece of the Earl of Berkeley—whose conversion to Roman Catholicism did not disturb his own rugged high church Protestantism. Though a

---

[22] I. Barrow, *The Duty and Reward of Bounty to the Poor*, 1671.

Non-Juror, he was glad to return with the Shottesbrooke group to the Church of England. We have seen how in word and deed he supported all the new movements recorded in this chapter, the Religious Societies, the Society for the Reformation of Manners, the SPCK. In the charity-school movement he was here there and everywhere, on the boards of half a dozen schools, organizing patrons and subscribers. His prominence and his example dispose of the notion, put forward by M. G. Jones, and followed by others, that eighteenth-century philanthropy was a kind of Puritanism, left as a hangover from the Puritans of the preceding century rather like the grin on the face of the Cheshire cat in *Alice*. The truth is that an austere Christian ethic is a general mark of seventeenth-century Christians—Roman Catholics and the Caroline divines as truly as the Puritans—and in the new movements the Church of England was more prominent than the Dissenters, who were the Puritan heirs. Nelson was no mean theologian, (we need not add 'for a layman'!) and his devotional writings included one minor classic, the *Festivals and Fasts*, lucid, sound, and grounded in the Biblical tradition. Perhaps his most remarkable writing, prescient in its anticipation of things to come was his *Address to Persons of Quality*. The first part does not try to say anything new, but is addressed to the minority of committed Christians minded to do good with their time and money. But at the end of the tract there are practical proposals of what needs to be done. 'The chief end which he kept constantly in his eye was to revive the life and spirit of genuine Christianity', for he shared with his Non-Juror friends the belief that primitive Christianity should not only be understood, but imitated.

The list, we shall see, is perhaps not in order of priorities, though they are in some kind of order.

The building of new churches and chapels of ease. [He printed as an appendix the proposed new act to build fifty new churches, of which in fact only a few were built.]

The dispersal of Bibles, Prayer books and other 'practical treatises'.

The support of the Society for the Propagation of the Gospel in Foreign Parts.

Setting up colleges and seminaries for candidates in Holy Orders and providing for the ministry in the Americas and other remote parts.

Providing for the propagation of the Christian faith in parts of the world not covered by the SPG, i.e. Asia, Africa and India.

The fostering of Christian life in the home.

The furthering of schemes like the Queen Anne's Bounty for the maintenance of the poorer clergy.

The Society for the Reformation of Manners 'by which the laws are put in execution'.

The erection of Charity schools.

A school for training school masters and school mistresses.

The erection of parochial libraries.

He laid no claim to originality, though the man who could advocate theological colleges and a college for the training of teachers was well abreast of the time.

Thus far, the proposals concern the spiritual needs of men. He now attends to their bodily needs.

Relieving the orphans and widows of clergymen.

Providing for the able poor in the way of industry as in those charity schools where the young are 'brought up to honest labour under a good discipline'.

Relieving poor, distressed housekeepers.

Relieving decayed tradesmen—'What a great number.'

Relieving poor prisoners.

Hospitals.

Here Nelson really looks ahead.

There might also be hospitals for every capital distemper of the body—in like manner as that at Bethlehem is for lunacy and diseases of the brain, there might be a hospital for the blind, for all diseases of the eye: for arthritis and stone and gout and rheumatism: a fourth for the dropsy, a fifth for the arthrose, and a sixth for consumption and a seventh for the palsy and some other nervous cases . . .

We have not a house of charity for poor exposed infants—for young women, for decayed gentlemen, and for converts from Popery—we have neither school nor hospital for the distressed children called 'Blackguards' and many of the parish children become vagrants.

Nelson's originality might be questioned at this point, for in 1714 a year before his own treatise, the Quaker John Bellars (1654–1725) had issued one of his many social and political appeals to Parliament in his *Essay towards the Improvement of Physick*. In this he similarly pleaded 'that there should be built at or near London, Hospitals for the poor: if not one hospital for every particular distemper: for the entertaining of such poor patients whose conditions may want it' and he devotes more attention than Nelson to the needs and training of physicians. But the wording of the two tracts is so different that we may suppose them to be independent. One consideration must be taken into account, however, that both Bellars and Nelson were friends of Sir Hans Sloane, the eminent physician and scientist, and may have discussed with him some of the needs and possibilities of the hospitals to which, when founded, he generously subscribed.

vi. The Foundling Hospital

The exposure of infants had been an endemic social evil from classical times, a long-drawn-out massacre of innocents, a crime against humanity which stands over and against the Christian centuries. At the turn of the eighteenth century, it was a sharper challenge to the new philanthropy than the education of the poor or the care of the sick. The whole business of illegitimacy, the stigma of bastardy, visiting the sins of the mothers upon their children, involved an incalculable amount of human misery of the most terrible kind. It was, alas, a problem which the moralists were loath to handle, lest they seem to encourage immorality, and this may account for the but slight clerical involvement in the noble project of a foundling hospital. In provision for abandoned children other nations—France, Spain, and Italy—were far in advance of England. By English law each parish was responsible for its own poor and its officers had many excuses for their grudging dispensation of charity towards foundlings. It was to take many decades for Thomas Coram and his allies, to obtain their charter.[23]

Thomas Coram (1668–1751) was a retired sea captain and shipbuilder. He was also a compulsive do-gooder, especially where needy children were concerned. He went down to visit the Salzburg refugees, sitting among the German children who could not understand a word he said to them, but comprehended well enough the plums and sweets and the smiles. But what he saw on his daily trips to and from the City, of infants dead or dying, left in the gutters, outraged and appalled him and he spent most of his energies between the age of fifty-four and seventy in a consuming passion to build a foundling hospital. He enlisted the aid and advice of Thomas Bray and Henry Newman of the SPCK, and they found a valuable precedent in the work of St Vincent de Paul in France who had mobilized noble women into societies of charity. Now Coram enlisted aristocratic ladies to be his Petitioners to the Crown, until he had twenty-one of them, ranging from the young Duchess of Portland, aged twenty, to the elderly Baroness Trevor, aged sixty-four. In 1739 they were granted a royal charter for a 'Hospital for the Maintenance and education of Exposed and Deserted Young Children'. A fine set of

---

[23] R. McClure, *Coram's Children*, Yale 1981. This is an admirable study, but I wonder if the author is correct in claiming Coram's as the first philanthropic corporation. Tillotson, in a sermon in the 1690s, refers to the 'Sons of the Clergy' as a corporation.

buildings was erected on a parcel of land, beginning in 1742, in Lamb's Conduit Fields.

Meanwhile, a house was bought in Hatton Garden and it was opened on Lady Day, 25 March 1741. A number of the Governors, including the Duke of Richmond and the artist William Hogarth, stood on one side of the doors, while outside a crowd milled around, amid the cries of anguished mothers and some coarse ribaldry from the insensitive London crowd. A museum case still contains some of the pathetic notes and tokens pinned to the forsaken children.

It was realized from the first that it would be impossible to take all the children offered, and the Governors acted Solomon, devising a lottery of white, black, and red balls, which accepted, refused, or deferred receiving the children. It seems that, as in similar institutions abroad, there was a wheel which, when turned, could whisk the infant in its basket within the hospital, preserving parental anonymity. No infected children were taken in, and it was arranged from the first to send the babies out into the surrounding villages, to be cared for by wet and dry nurses who became, in some sort, foster parents.

But there were always more children than could be accepted, and the officers of adjoining parishes, at first alarmed lest the rejected children be dumped on their doorstep, began in time to look upon the hospital as a means of evading their own responsibilities.

Thomas Coram was a bluff seaman who all his life had been in trouble for speaking his mind, and he never learned not to speak to the wealthy patrons as though they were lob-lolly boys or powder monkeys. Sad to tell, once the hospital was launched, they took him off their committees and finally excluded him from the Governing Body. And so, while the infants said their daily prayers before Hogarth's splendid portrait of their Founder, more than a little confused in their tiny minds with their Father in Heaven, Coram himself might be seen sitting in the grounds, poor, weeping, but with an unfailing supply of gingerbread. A later cartoonist than Hogarth had a famous cartoon 'Dropping the Pilot'. It would have been an appropriate comment on their treatment of Thomas Coram. They gave him a grand funeral.

None the less, eminent was the assistance with which the project got off the ground. It was as though the good fairies thronged to the belated christenings. Hogarth raffled his best picture and got distinguished fellow artists to adorn the walls with their works, a premonition of the modern exhibition. Handel had known of the German Pietist A. H. Francke's great Orphan House in his native Halle, and was a great friend, writing the fine *Foundling Hospital Anthem* and ensuring that the English performances of *Messiah* were given in its impressive chapel,

while he left the best manuscript of the great oratorio to the Hospital in
his will. It was a pity that Dr Burney's project of making the Hospital
the centre of a great musical academy was aborted. Two of the most
eminent physicians of the day, Richard Mede and Sir Hans Sloane were
Governors and gave their services free, so that the Governors were
generally forward looking in medical matters and were one of the first
institutions to practise inoculation. So successful was the venture that at
last Parliament took it under its wing, giving £10,000 on the fateful
condition that in future no child should be refused admittance.

Ominously the numbers grew, brought from greater and greater
distances, until the intake was over 300 a month. Soon grisly practices
began, as venal carriers brought the babies down from the north, stuffed
in their panniers, and thrown out on the road, when, as often happened,
the children died. So it came about that in 1756 Parliament withdrew its
financial backing, and the first spark of a Welfare State was snuffed, the
Hospital thrown back upon voluntary support. Among the Governors
were many who merely lent their names or gave their money, but
always at the heart of this institution was a core of good and devoted
men, from Coram in the first generation to Jonas Hanway in the next.
They were not sentimentalists and they grappled with great practical
problems as well as questions of discipline and control, of the staff, of
the children, and of the great nursing diaspora. Problems there were,
but no major scandals. The children in their neat brown serge trimmed
with red were decently clothed, and probably better fed than many
children in the charity schools and in the homes of the labouring poor.
Many of the boys went to sea and the girls into domestic service, one or
two to return in later years as wealthy merchants and governors.

It was a drab and foul evil which the Foundling Hospital combated. It
would take a Dante, a Doré, or a John Martin to comment on the deserts
of those who caused or tolerated such suffering, an enormous vista of
millstones in an abyss. Yet, despite Mandeville's sneers at philanthropy,
here were missioners from a kingdom of light, practical compassion
getting into its stride. Well and wisely did Handel choose when he took
the text of his anthem from Psalm 41, 'Blessed is the man that
considereth the poor and needy . . . keep them alive, let them be blessed
upon the earth'.

vii. Almsgiving

Every man ought, of such things as he possesseth, liberally to give alms to the
poor, according to his ability. (The Thirty-Nine Articles, Article 38).

While it is not to be supposed that many in the early eighteenth century were much moved by simple perusal of the Thirty-nine Articles to any kind of action, the duty of almsgiving was impressed upon the contemporary conscience. And indeed the candidates for such charity were all too visible, swarming the lanes and besieging the porches and interiors of churches in a manner not seen any more in England, though still to be observed in some parts of Europe. The churches themselves took this duty seriously, and the increasing devotion to the Eucharist, and the more frequent celebrations added to the occasions when the collections could be distributed to the poor. William Wake's farewell sermon included in its printed form evidence of how a wealthy and fashionable church like St James's, Piccadilly, could set aside money for coals and clothes and for direct gifts of money, and his sermons, as those earlier by Anthony Horneck, suggest that the Communion days brought a thronging number of unfortunates.

The churchmen of the age, bishops like Tenison, Sharp, and Compton, gave generously and unstintingly from their own substance for the relief of the poor and for the succour of refugees. And such giving was recognized as a duty of all lay Christians of substance. Thomas Ken tells of his beloved Lady Mainard that

her charity made her sympathize with all in misery, and besides her private alms, wherein her left hand was not conscious to her right, she was a common patroness to the poor and needy, and a common physician to her sick neighbours and would often with her own hands dress their most loathsome sores, and sometimes keep them in her family and would give them diet and lodging till they were cured and then clothe them and send them home.[24]

The great man of charity among the Nonconformists, Thomas Gouge, asked Richard Baxter what proportion of one's goods should be devoted to others, and elicited some interesting pages in Baxter's *Christian Directory*, while Gouge expressed his own views in a tract on *The Way to Grow Rich*. Both men felt that something more drastic even than tithing was called for. Half a century later William Law at King's Cliffe was to make such giving the very heart of his household. Baxter, in his last compassionate tract, told how

there dwelleth in London a man that liveth by selling rags and glass bottles, that, besides finding works for abundance of the poor, payeth for the teaching of thirty poor children: though he had not five shillings to set up and his nearest friends trouble him with the accusations of imprudent excess of charity. For the more he giveth . . . the more he thriveth . . . I will instance but in one man, my deceased friend, Mr Thomas Foley who . . . was always liberal to the poor and managed all his busyness with multitudes with ease and cheerfulness: and hath

[24] Ken, *Prose Works*, p. 69.

settled an hospital with a governor to teach children to read and write and fit them for trades and then bind them apprentices: and settled in land £500 a year to maintain it.[25]

Sir Isaac Newton believed that charity begins at home and was painstaking in assisting poor but distant relations. When, in 1716, one of them wrote from the Marshalsea, begging Newton to add to a gift already made of £3 4s. 6d. he explained:

I could not live on air, and my bedroom tho' God knows very bad, paymt for 6 weeks, twenty shillings . . . God knows it is a very dismal thing to perish for hunger. Dear Sir, pray pardon my importunities, my life being in danger such a weakness I have upon me that my health is much impair'd. If I dye I must end my life here miserably God knows.

But Newton's benevolence extended far beyond his own family.

Then, as in every age, Christians gave in the way in which in our time flag days touch and relieve uneasy consciences, though not only a sense of guilt was, and is, a dominant motive for such giving. Anybody who followed two Christian laymen, Samuel Johnson and John Byrom, through the narrow, darkened streets of the London they loved, could not fail to remark their benefactions.

Of Johnson it was said, 'He frequently gave all the silver in his pocket to the poor who watched him between his house and the tavern where he dined.' 'He loved the poor', said Mrs Thrale 'as I never yet saw anyone do, with an earnest desire to make them happy.' And when moralists like Fielding wrote against an indiscriminate charity which might do more harm than good, Johnson had his answer. 'What signifies, says someone, giving halfpence to common beggars? they only lay it out in gin or tobacco.' 'And why should they be denied such sweeteners of their existence?'[26]

And what happened when Johnson's shambling figure lurched along the London lanes, occurred also with the tall, stooping, leaner figure of John Byrom.

There was a poor woman sat upon a stone in Chancery Lane with a child. I gave her 1½d and being very thankful, 6d at which she seemed mightily affected, and said that God had inspired a gentleman to give her 6d: I asked the watchman if he knew her, he went to her and brought her to the upper end of the lane where he got her ¾ of beer and I gave him about 4d in farthings to see her safe home in Drury Lane, and I followed them and he brought her part of the way, and then gave her a piece of candle and she went on and through a dark lane with her

[25] R. Baxter, 'The Poor Husbandman's Advocate to Rich Racking Landlords', *The Reverend Richard Baxter's Last Treatise*, ed. F. J. Powicke (Manchester 1926), p. 42.

[26] Boswell's *Life of Johnson*, ed. G. B. Hill and L. F. Powell (Oxford 1971), ii. 119.

candle out at the other end of which I saw her again, having gone round about and gave her a 1s here and the watchman 1d to see her home: she was much moved, and still talked of the gentleman that had given her 6d. I have had many thoughts of this poor creature who cried 'What will my end be?'[27]

I went to St. Clement's, gave a poor woman a halfpenny and she saying that I could not give it to one that wanted it more, that she had a child a-dying, I gave her a shilling, and bid her remember what Christ had suffered for us, and she was so thankful and blessed me forever so heartily that seemed to be so real that I came out of the church again to look for her, but I could not find her.[28]

Johnson would have been the first to admit the comparative triviality of such giving, in relation to the immensity of the problem: 'one might give away five hundred pounds in a year to those that importune in the streets and it would not do any good.' None the less, it is worth noting that in a callous age there were many who inherited that blessing invoked on those who considered the poor and needy.

viii. Christian Aid

Those who have known nothing but the Welfare State, and are accustomed to contribute to international funds distributing millions of pounds across the entire globe, may shudder at the disorganized and haphazard philanthropies of earlier centuries. But, callous though the age might be, and its sympathies narrowed by grim conditions of existence, we should not underestimate the genuine compassion, the touched conscience and imagination of which there is plenty of evidence. A little country church in Dorset could take up collections for distressed Christians in Lithuania, and a great sum be raised in London for the inundated town of Bobbio in Piedmont. The difficulties of such collection and distribution are strangely modern: the fact that the sums raised were often sidetracked and did not reach their proper destination, the draining off from gifts of expenses to such an extent that some appeals might actually end in money lost. And there were the abuses and the frauds, and unscrupulous 'rake-offs'.

The care of vagabonds and of crippled soldiers and distressed mariners had long been put upon the parishes, but there were all-too-frequent personal disasters. These included changes of fortune among the worthy and respectable—there seems to have been a whip-round on behalf of Samuel Wesley at the nadir of his fortunes, in which Robert Nelson was involved. There were innumerable cases of losses by fire, and perhaps the one really important monument to the Great Fire of

---

[27] John Byrom, *Journal*, 2 May 1735.　　[28] Ibid., 28 Mar. 1736.

London is not the stone pillar in Thames Street or even the new St Paul's, but the fact that in 1681 the first regular fire insurance office was opened at the back of the Royal Exchange.

But the main channel of fund-raising and of what would now be called 'Christian Aid' was the 'Brief' which has been defined as 'a Royal Warrant authorizing a collection in places of worship and sometimes from house to house, for a specified charitable object'.[29]

These were officially drawn up and signed and printed on authorized forms. The normal brief was read from the pulpit to the congregation and on great and special emergencies might be sent to the congregations of the Dissenters and the Quakers. As has been said, losses by fire and flood, and the little personal tragedies connected with sudden calamities for which there was no insurance and no compensation, take up the great majority of these appeals, though there is a regular occurrence of appeals to rescue or redeem those who have been captured and sold into slavery among the Turks. There seems to have been a stepping up of such briefs at the Restoration, and Samuel Pepys spoke for many citizens when he complained: '30 June 1661. To church, where we observe the trade of briefs is come up now to so constant a course every Sunday that we resolve to give no more to them.'

Fraud and inefficiency led to great abuses, which came to a crisis in the reign of Anne when the formidable and persistent Margaret Mortimer, one of those stubborn Mothers in Israel who in every generation have scared the daylights out of lethargic and careless officialdom, brought such evidence to light and pressures to bear as led to an Act of Parliament, 4 Anne, cap. 14.

But the great appeals touched not only compassion, but religious zeal and political interest, the causes of persecuted Protestants and of the refugees. And here monarchs as diverse in their sympathy as Charles II and William III were agreed, and high churchmen like Bishops Ken and Sharp with Compton and Tenison. One of the great and most successful appeals had been for the Vaudois during the Commonwealth. But in the 1680s a whole series of harassments and persecutions brought refugees who moved the pity and the indignation of Christian clergy, laity, and ordinary people.

Great sums of money were raised, and William III even contrived a large grant from the Civil List. Money was granted to refugee pastors and their congregations settling in England or in transit, and gifts were even sent into their places of refuge on the Continent. One of the few successful apocalyptic prophecies of Bishop Lloyd occurred when he took back the money given to two Waldensian pastors and packed them

---

[29] W. A. Bewes, *Church Briefs* (1896), p. 6.

off home, assuring them that they would find that policy would be changed and persecution cease by the time they got home, which it had! The Huguenot refugees brought with them great skills, and the people of Ipswich in Suffolk and of Rye in Kent were soon aware that their philanthropy brought dividends. Among them were the splendid Huguenot silver-smiths who settled in St. Giles. But in other places and in times of unemployment the old suspicion of foreigners, with resentment at competition, raised its head, as it had done in the reign of Elizabeth I. In some places, as in Norwich, there were riots. A more difficult situation arose in connection with the German refugees from the Palatinate in the reign of Anne, a motley band of men and women of differing religious affinities and political notions.

The first trickle of refugees had met with a warm and sympathetic reception, but the result was an invasion of great numbers, who camped out in the East End of London and soon brought all kinds of resentments, from the poorer citizens robbed of what they regarded as their own proper charity, and from the warring policies between Whigs and Tories. It was decided to pack as many off as possible to Ireland and to the Plantations. But the official briefs for these great refugee collections are impressive, and issued in the names of all the great notables of Church and State and City. In fact great sums were raised and distributed to many thousands, not only in England, but overseas. Nor was it overlaid with impersonal bureaucracy. Indeed probably as much, if not more, kindly and personal direction went on as in our time, while Bishop Compton at his best was a kind of premonition of Bishop George Bell, and the continuing flow of sympathetic and practical giving recalls the increasing wave of such philanthropy which began in 1945 when the small fund called 'Christian Reconstruction in Europe' swelled in the next decades into the multinational, transcontinental organization, Christian Aid.

Towards the end of his life, John Wesley commented on the philanthropic achievements of his century,

while luxury and profaneness have been increasing on one hand, on the other benevolence and compassion towards all forms of human woe have increased in a manner not known before, from the earliest ages of the world. In proof of this we see more hospitals, infirmaries and other places of public charity have been created at least in or near London within this century than in five hundred years before.

Behind all this were a few thousand men and women, giving of their substance, time, and energy to raise moral standards and better the condition of the less fortunate, and to raise the quality of life for society as a whole. With no conscious overall planning, these benevolences strikingly converged: the religious societies, the Societies for the Reformation of Manners, the charity schools, and the SPCK. They had succeeded in touching the consciences, minds, and wills of men, and they had also reached their pockets. All in all, it was a notable increase of charity, an impressive part of what we have called 'A Small Awakening'.

PART V

EVANGELICAL REVIVAL

See how great a flame aspires,
Kindled by a spark of grace!

C. WESLEY

20

BEGINNINGS

THE causes of the Evangelical Revival will always be mysterious and disputable. 'Mightier than an army is the power of an idea whose time has come.' Who can say why ideas which have been inert and dormant suddenly became alive, operative idealisms moving the emotions and the wills of men; and why later, they seem to have lost their dynamic power and may end up in some ideological museum? What in America was known as the Great Awakening and in Britain as the Evangelical Revival appears startlingly, like a forest fire, or the flowers after some desert drought. And when we have set these firmly in European and American religious history and culture, what do we say when a century later, the same happenings occur on the other side of the world in the entirely different cultural setting of the islands of the Pacific, in Tonga, Fiji, and Samoa?

There are moments in history when things seem to happen at the same time in very different settings. The rediscovery of 'justification by faith' in the 1520s is an example, or what is loosely called the 'splitting of the atom' in our own age. And we can see that this is partly because men were reacting against a similar set of circumstances, asking the same sort of questions, using the same sort of methods.

Something of that background we can surely see. It can be no accident that in America, and Wales, and Scotland there was a background of Puritanism, mainly in its Calvinist form, for in the Revival Wesley's Arminianism is the odd one out. It is true that religious and intellectual influences from Europe were important, from both Lutheran and Reformed Pietism and from the Moravians.[1] But it should be noted that this was also a two-way traffic. If Baily's *Practice of Piety* was well known on the Continent, so Arndt's *True Christendom* and Francke's *Nicodemus* were circulated in America, while it was the Englishman Woodward's account of the Religious Societies which stimulated their growth in America as well as in Germany, Holland, and Switzerland.

It would be foolish to suppose that experimental religion originated in

[1] E. E. Stoeffler, *The Rise of Evangelical Pietism*, Leiden 1971; W. R. Ward, 'Relations of the Enlightenment and religious Revival in Central Europe and in the English-speaking world', in *Reform and Reformation* (*Studies in Church History*, ed. D. Baker, Subsidia 2), Oxford 1979.

Protestantism in the seventeenth century. Without delving into medieval Catholic sources, it is plain within the English Protestant tradition from its beginning. The conversion of the Cambridge scholars Thomas Bilney and Hugh Latimer came after their Pauline experience of being 'under the law' and Latimer's convert, John Bradford, is in this same evangelical succession. We hear in the time of Elizabeth of the Puritan leader Laurence Chaderton converting over forty Cambridge divines, many of eminence, and his influence on Preston and Perkins and their impact on the next generation is well known.

The writings of such Puritan divines as Robert Bolton and Richard Sibbes are full of 'inward religion', while the treatise of Isaac Ambrose on *The New Birth* and Marshall's tract on *Sanctification* were still prized by the eighteenth-century Evangelicals. In England itself the Anglo-Calvinist tradition persisted at a depth and to an extent which has probably been underestimated. Anglican historians (this is very evident in Wake) played down the importance of the Calvinist tradition within the Church of England, but the attempt to confine it to the radical Nonconformists or the Presbyterians is far from convincing, when there were such Calvinists among the Caroline bishops as Davenant and Morley. Although by the turn of the century John Edwards of Cambridge was the only noted Calvinist writer, there were more Calvinist dons at Oxford and Cambridge and (we may surmise) in country parishes than has been recognized.

Nor may we ignore the contrary stream, the influence of the Cambridge Platonists and the first Latitudinarians. Still less may we leave out of account the high-church spirituality of Ken, Nelson, and William Law without which there might have been no Wesleyan movement.

Of course, conversion was at the heart of the Revival. In 1678 Dr Increase Mather had lamented: 'conversions are become rare in this age of the world . . . in the last age, in the days of our fathers, in other parts of the world, scarce a sermon preached but some evidently converted and sometimes hundreds in a sermon.'[2] But perhaps we should be careful about the word 'conversion' which the eighteenth century did not use nearly as much as did the nineteenth century, and if we think that Sankey and Moody or Dr Billy Graham were saying and doing what Whitefield and Wesley were saying and doing we may run into serious misconceptions. The unending debate as to what happened to John Wesley on 24 May 1738 has been blurred by reading back into it nineteenth-century ideas. Drastic it was, but I think John Wesley never

---

[2] J. Gillies, *Historical Collections of accounts of Revival* (Philadelphia, repr. 1981), p. 279.

talked of it as his 'conversion', and in fact what nineteenth-century Evangelicals described as one experience of 'conversion' was for the Methodists a complexity in which at least three of what they called 'our doctrines': justification by faith, the new birth, and the witness of the Spirit, were all involved.

There are two movements which seem to have acted as catalysts, the Religious Societies and the Moravians.

i. The Religious Societies (2)

Religious Societies were the soil in which the Evangelical Revival was rooted. We have already noted the rise of the movement in the 1680s[3] and its progress in the reign of Anne. It has often been assumed that the societies were languishing by the 1730s. But the main evidence seems to be a heavily biased statement by James Hutton (now caught up in the euphoric experiences of the Moravians and Methodists) to the effect that they had become pleasant Sunday evenings for the unco' guid, 'slumbering or dead souls who cared for nothing but their comfort in the world'. But it seems likely that in the 1730s, far from being moribund, the societies were proliferating. The Rules for the Cripplegate Society date from 1718 and show little change from those of Horneck's societies a generation earlier. There are references in the 1720s to other such groups in different parts of the country, in Gloucestershire, Yorkshire, and Lincolnshire. The *Journals* of Whitefield, of Hutton, and of Wesley show a whole series of societies operating in London at the end of 1738, many of which must have existed before the new movement. We know that Whitefield discovered two societies among the garrison at Gibraltar, one called the 'New Lights' composed of members of the Church of England, and a Society of the Scots Kirk called the 'Dark Lanthorns'.[4] It was natural that these associations of earnest young men should turn eagerly to one of their own generation, George Whitefield, that they should invite him to their societies, ask him to preach and administer the Sacrament at their City Communions, while on at least two occasions he was asked to preach their Quarterly Sermon at St Mary-le-Bow. This he did, repeating his ordination sermon on *The Nature and Necessity of Society in General and of Religious Society in Particular*, and with a second on *The Benefits of an Early Piety* (28 September 1737).[5] On his return from America in the

---

[3] See above, p. 290.
[4] G. Whitefield, *Journals* (repr. 1978), p. 131.
[5] A. A. Dallimore, *G. Whitefield*, (2 vols., Edinburgh 1970–80), i. 120–2.

following year he immediately visited a succession of societies within the City.[6]

These societies, which sought means of edification to supplement the liturgy (Hickes and Nelson had them directly in mind with their books of devotion), but were composed of loyal members of the Church of England, offered an opportunity for the new evangelical idealism of the Moravians and the Wesleys, an ideal form in which those awakened by Whitefield's preaching could be built up in the faith (we do not know when women were first admitted to such gatherings). Moreover, such societies were protected from the sanctions of the Conventicle Act. It was therefore a very pertinent question which John and Charles Wesley put to Bishop Gibson in October 1738 when they asked him 'Whether reading in a religious society made it a conventicle?' And when they further pressed the question 'Are religious societies conventicles?', the wary Dr Codex hedged: 'No, I think not—however you can read the acts and laws as well as I: I determine nothing.'[7]

Whitefield's two sermons[8] before the Religious Societies at St Mary-le-Bow suggest that the wind of change was blowing through them. His references elsewhere to singing societies suggests that song was becoming a more prominent feature of their meetings, for he concludes his list of their profitable activities with, 'lastly the commendable, pious zeal you exert by providing and encouraging Divine Psalmody.' In one of the sermons he urges the societies, the staple of whose earlier diet had been prayers and readings, to enlarge the scope of mutual exhortation. And in a letter written to the societies while on his voyage to America, he thinks it good that instead of meeting, as most of them seem to have done, in parish vestries, they should meet in private houses, 'as is the practice of some of the societies who are under the government of those called the Twelve Stewards', while to those who wish to stick close to what they call 'Dr Woodward's form of prayer' he urges the importance of praying 'in the Spirit'. He concludes this forthright letter with the counsel: 'Be not afraid to make innovations in the Church.'

By 1743 the Bishop and his associates had come down against the Methodists and the Moravians. Gibson published his moderate *Pastoral Letter against Lukewarmness and Enthusiasm.* An anonymous pamphlet of

[6] Whitefield, *Journals*, p. 194, where he mentions societies in Fetter Lane, Crooked Lane, Redcross St., and Crutched Friars—all within two days.

[7] J. Wesley, *Journal*, ed. N. Curnock (8 vols., 1931), ii. 93.

[8] *Mr. Whitefield's sermon at Bow Church, before the Religious Societies at one of their Quarterly Meetings, on Youthful Piety*; and *The Nature and Necessity of Society in General and of Religious Societies in Particular, preached before the Religious Societies at one of their Quarterly Meetings*, 1737. *A Letter to the Religious Societies of England, written during a voyage to Philadelphia*, Whitefield, *Works* (1771-2), iv. 23ff.

Observations . . . on the Methodists and Moravians was attributed to Gibson himself, though Benham suggests it was the work of Thomas Broughton of the SPCK and that the intention at first was not to publish, but to circulate it as a warning to the Religious Societies. He says that at this time Mr Hapson, one of the twelve Stewards of the City societies, warned members that they would be excommunicated if they associated with Whitefield or the Moravians.[9]

This seems confirmed by a letter from Howell Harris to Griffith Jones (2 February 1743), which speaks of an attack on the Moravians, Mr Wesley and Mr Whitefield, and their followers,

representing them as dangerous to State and Church: it is supposed to have been connected [concocted?] by the Bishop of London and his clergy, the papers have come out weekly this three months and printed but not published: they have been privately read in the Religious Societies of London and Westminster and handed about amongst all the Bishops and likely to the Parliament of Commons with an intention to have an Act of Parliament against us . . . such severity has been enjoined on all that have them that they dare not lend them to be perused and answered.[10]

The sermon to the societies by the Revd Leonard Twells at St Mary-le-Bow echoes the strictures of the *Pastoral Letter* and is full of warning.

. . . by the original plan of these Societies and also by present standing orders—no addition or alteration is to be made in your methods without the consent of some pious or learned divine of the Church of England, especially of the President for the time being, now as always to be taken out of the clergy of the Establishment: and I take it for granted that hereby were intended such clergymen only as live orderly under the direction of the bishops their superiors and have a stated residence in which they discharge the offices of their sacred function.

. . . if these circumstances are not expressly set down by those who drew up the orders of your societies, it was because those pious men did not imagine the time would come when those who call themselves priests or presbyters of the church of England would break through the laws of church and state . . . and cast perpetual reproach upon all their brethren who are friends to order . . . and who dislike their tumultuous and itinerant assemblies.[11]

He particularly attacked the new practice of commenting extempore on Scripture instead of the old, regular custom of simply reading to the

[9] J. Wickham Legg, *English Church Life from the Restoration to the Tractarian Movement*, 1914; D. Benham, *Memoirs of James Hutton*, 1856; D. Pike, 'The Religious Societies 1678–1738', *PWHS* March 1965; L. Twells, *Twenty-Four Sermons*, 2 vols. 1743; T. Secker, *Sermon at the Yearly Meeting of the Religious Societies, 4 Dec. 1754*.

[10] G. M. Roberts, *Selected Trevecca Letters* (Caernarvon 1956), i. 124.

[11] Twells, *Twenty-Four Sermons*, ii. 363.

society from the works of established Biblical commentators like Hammond and Burnet, and this extempore commenting seems to have annoyed the authorities even more than the practice (which in any case the Dissenters had made notorious) of extempore prayer.

It seems that the older and the new societies drew apart and went their own separate ways. They certainly continued to exist, and when Thomas Secker preached their annual sermon in 1754 he delivered an edifying discourse entirely free from polemic.

Certainly the cell, the *koinōnia*, the society, was at the heart of the Revival. The little groups of M. de Renty in France, the 'collegia pietatis' of the Pietists, the Religious Societies, the Moravian bands, without these and the use made of their precedent, the converts of the Revival might have been, in Wesley's words, 'a rope of sand'. The strategic importance of the societies had been quite clearly seen by Whitefield. And John Wesley too, came to a fundamental conclusion about their relevance to the Christian religion. In that preface to his first hymn books in which he attacked the Mystics, he complained that their manner of building up souls

is quite opposite to that prescribed by Christ. . . . They advise, To the desert! to the desert! and God will build you up . . . whereas according to the judgment of our Lord and the writings of the Apostles, it is only when we are knit together that we have nourishment from him . . . the religion these authors would edify us in is a solitary religion. . . . Directly opposite to this is the gospel of Christ. . . . Solitary religion is not found there. . . . The Gospel of Christ knows of no religion, but social: no holiness, but social holiness.[12]

ii. *The Moravian Brethren*

The settlement (in 1722) of Moravian refugees on the estate of the young Count Zinzendorf at Berthelsdorf in Saxony was a turning point in the history of the Moravian Brethren, but it was also of significance in the history of Christian missions, and influenced the course of the Evangelical Revival in England.

Indeed, so drastic was the change that historians have tended to emphasize the new developments in a historic movement. But despite the sharp discontinuity and the religious and practical influence of Zinzendorf himself, there were underlying elements of continuity.

For groups of radical refugees to seek and find protection on the estates of an aristocrat was no novelty in post-Reformation history. The

---

[12] Wesley, *Works*, xiv. 304–5.

first Anabaptist radicals of the Reformation movement and the Italian reformers had found such protection, from German and Polish aristocracy. The parts of Germany which bordered Poland and Bohemia had been for a century and a half an area where all manner of radical groups might be found, Schwenckfeldians, Anabaptists, Paracelsans, the disciples of Weigel and of Jacob Böhme—with these the Lutheran authorities in Church and State in Lusatia and Silesia lived sometimes at peace, but often in tension. And though the influence of Lutheranism on the refugee settlement is important, and is evident in Zinzendorf himself, who considered himself a Lutheran, we must allow for some sort of influence from the side of the refugees themselves. It was no doubt mistaken to suggest that Zinzendorf himself was affected by theological doctrines which derived from Lukas of Prague, but there may well have been subtler ways in which the persecuted underground movement had protected itself. The Unitas Fratrum naturally was concerned for toleration, and showed an unusual openness towards both Lutheran and Reformed Confessions. But like other late medieval sects, the Waldensians and the Lollards, the Brethren may have developed their own smokescreen methods of evasion, casuistry, and a certain Nicodemitism which turned away from trouble. This may account in part for their reservation in language, and for reticences about their doctrines which not only John Wesley noticed among them. Even the attempt of Benjamin Ingham to silence his exhorters for a time when persecution began in Yorkshire, which brought him into confrontation with the far from Nicodemite John Nelson, may owe something to this background.

Caught between the upper and nether millstones of a persecuting Catholicism and militant Hussitism, the Brethren managed to survive the sixteenth centry, as scattered and sometimes isolated groups.

Among their early confessional documents is one which has received little attention, *Die Guldene Himmelpforte: das ist, Bekenntnis des Glaubens der Christlichen Brüder in Behemen und Merhern.*[13] which in 1586 was offered to another protecting aristocrat, Count Conrad von Kreyck, who had been requested by his overlord, the Margrave of Brandenburg, for some account of the faith and worship of his refugees. It is an able document, and although the authors disclaim any university education, they go out of their way to emphasize their respect for learning. There seems no reminiscence in the document of earlier teachings of Huss (and Wyclif) though they have a general reference to believers as 'the elect'. Interesting in relation to what we shall note about Zinzendorf's

---

[13] Newenstadt 1568.

presentation of the gospel, and the Pietist emphasis on the New Birth, is its description of the work of the Holy Spirit in renewing the redeemed soul.

The Holy Spirit indeed out of the Grace of the Father through the merits of Christ makes new, betters and makes alive not the flesh but the spirits of the elect. But how and when God does this no man knows, not even the man to whom this happens. For just as he hears the wind roaring and knows not whence it comes or whither it goes: and even when he likewise feels an inner transformation [*Verenderung*] yet he does not know from whence it comes, whether it is for good or evil, or how he shall make use of it, and indeed he cannot know this unless the Holy Ghost makes it known to him through the Minister with the word of God and the gospel.[14]

Here indeed is a pattern of inward religion, of the kind which both Luther and Calvin would have endorsed, with a strong emphasis on the Word of God and its mediation through the sacraments. In the second half of the seventeenth century it was the great Comenius and his grandson Jablonski who put the movement on the ecumenical map.

Between 1568 and 1722 the wandering groups of Brethren undoubtedly underwent changes. But the little group who came to Herrnhut from Bohemia and Poland did not derive their understanding of the gospel solely through Pietist contacts, or even from Zinzendorf. In the early days of their settlement the influence upon them of the Lutheran pastor J. A. Rothe was important, but it was when Nicholas Zinzendorf turned to them and identified himself with them that the tensions and differences were smoothed out, and he brought them to a reformed way of life, which he later marvelled to find was congruous with the earlier ideals of the Unitas Fratrum as they had been set out by Comenius.

Nicholas, Graf von Zinzendorf (1700–60) was born in Dresden, of a noble and ancient family. He was brought up by his grandmother, a devout and learned Pietist and a friend of Spener. The boy was religiously precocious and claimed in later life to have known his Saviour from his earliest years. He was sent (1710–16) to Francke's Adelspaedagogium at Halle where his precocities brought him a mixed reception, and he became critical of some aspects of Pietism in its second generation. As a schoolboy he founded the 'Order of the Grain of Mustard Seed' the members of which were pledged to love all mankind and act as an eirenical leaven within the Churches. The adolescent society matured with its originator, and its later members included notabilities from many nations and communions, including the Car-

---

[14] Ibid., b.i–b.ii.

dinal de Noailles, Archbishop Potter, and Bishop Wilson. He now moved from the citadel of Pietism to the heart of Lutheran orthodoxy, to Wittenberg (1716–19) and nearly brought off an astonishing *rapprochement* between the two suspicious and hostile camps. His guardians intended him for the higher civil service of the Saxon state, and he was sent on the Grand Tour, to Holland, France, and Switzerland where he met eminences in Church and society and made fruitful contact with contemporary Catholic mysticism and with Pietism in its Reformed, non-Lutheran form. To his indebtedness to Pietism and its religion of the heart must be added a short-lived rationalist phase expressed in his life-long enthusiasm for Bayle, and in some 'Socratic' writings penned on his return to Dresden. But it was in the refugee community at Herrnhut that he realized his vocation, and found ever deeper confirmation of his central intuitions, the catholicity of the Church, the centrality of fellowship (*koinōnia*) and, above all, the Saviourhood of the Crucified Lamb of God. He rejoiced to find within the Moravian traditions a similar emphasis on Christ as the victorious Lamb and a devotion to the 'Wounds of Jesus' with deep and ancient roots in medieval spirituality.

In a few marvellous months in the summer of 1727 Zinzendorf in conference, and with incessant pastoral care, transformed the community and harmonized its inevitable tensions. He gave them a leadership and a constitution, a 'Brotherly Agreement' to which all would subscribe. It blended the artisan leadership of the core of devoted Moravians, David Christian, the Nitschmann brothers, John Töltschig, with the leading roles of himself and his fellow grandee, De Watteville. It was a time of growing fervour which reached a euphoric climax on 13 August 1727 which Zinzendorf described as the 'Pentecost' of the new community. From then on, to the close of his life, his own influence was paramount. The little huddles of needy refugees became a great community, impressively housed. Within, the members lived according to a strict pattern of disciplined worship which gave ample room for spontaneity: from the little bands of a few who met for confession and consultation, to the choirs, divided and subdivided into houses according to sex, age, and marital status. Over all, there was a network of pastoral care from Warden, elders (male and female), and exhorters, and there were devotions at all hours, culminating in vigils, communions, and love feasts. They took great care of the very young, paid particular attention to funerals, and arranged the marriages. Many of their gravest decisions were determined by lot. Their devotion to hymns and to the Scriptures resulted in one of the most famous and beneficent of all their devices, the Text for the Day, the *Losungswort*, an enduring gift to the Church, as was proved by many members of the German Confessing Church in prison in our time.

Inevitably there were questions raised by the Saxon authorities, since the Herrnhut community had hitherto existed within a Lutheran setting. Zinzendorf took steps to refute the idea that he himself lacked theological competence and in 1734 submitted to a Lutheran theological examination at Stralsund, and was thereafter recognized by the Theological Faculty at Tübingen. But more important matters of ecclesiastical status now arose, and on 13 March 1735 David Nitschmann was consecrated as a bishop of the Unitas Fratrum by Jablonski in Berlin. Finally, on 20 May 1737, Zinzendorf was himself consecrated bishop by Jablonski and Nitschmann.

We are concerned with Zinzendorf only as he touches the English story, and are not able to appraise his theology, still less his character. But his thought appears to have undergone changes[15] and retractations and does not always seem to cohere. His luminous idea of the 'Tropus' which, while recognizing the treasure within each denomination, fastened on the eirenical core of a common Christianity, was, and still is, of ecumenical significance. But it was not always clearly understood, least of all by his English Brethren, and perhaps he never fully reconciled this with the existence of the Unitas Fratrum as an empirical, historical institution, claiming to be in a true episcopal succession. It seems hyperbolical to suggest, as some have done, that he is the greatest German theologian between Luther and Schleiermacher (Chemnitz—Gerhardt—Leibniz—Böhme—Oetinger—Hamann—Herder??). Karl Barth's deep interest in him may tell us more about the twentieth than the eighteenth-century theological scene. His 'Christocentric' or 'Christomonistic' teaching, his overemphasis on the roles of the Second and Third Persons of the Trinity, are on the borders of unorthodoxy, while his Bride mysticism was to land his movement in serious trouble. That he rejected extreme doctrines of predestination was to be important in England and he seems to have held a doctrine of double election, of those predestined and chosen in Christ before the foundation of the world, and others who might respond to the offer of the gospel (a doctrine which John Wesley held for a time but which he came to reject as unscriptural). His preaching was fervent, evangelical, compassionate, though he was too prone to garnish it with ill-considered *obiter dicta*, and

---

[15] L. Aalen, 'Die Theologie des Grafen von Zinzendorf', in *Gedenkschrift für W. Elert*, Berlin 1955; M. Schmidt, *Luther und Zinzendorf*, *Luther JB*, 1951; G. W. Forell, *Zinzendorf: Nine Lectures* (Fetter Lane), Iowa 1973; E. Beyreuther, *Studien zur Theologie Zinzendorfs*, Neukirchen 1962.

his own free translations from Holy Scripture. Perhaps his fine hymns do him most justice, above all the noble 'Christi Blut und Gerechtigkeit' ('Jesus, thy Blood and Righteousness') and the lovely 'Jesu, geh' voran' ('Jesus still lead on').

It is even less easy to appraise his character. That his person was charming and appealing is evident, though his strenuous and unceasing effort to take upon himself the form of a servant never quite broke through the aristocratic and autocratic mould. His admirers, from James Hutton to the Revd A. J. Lewis, thought him beyond reproach, a very perfect, gentle Graf, and though they mention faults and foibles they are never discussed. But the antagonism of many Lutheran leaders to him and his ways is not altogether due to the defects of Pietism or those theological nuances which the Germans take with such deadly seriousness. Ziegenhagen had something to complain of when Zinzendorf turned up under an incognito in Philadelphia, and had himself declared Lutheran Pastor. The set-to when Ziegenhagen's nominee arrived is not pleasant reading, and it includes the brusque dismissal of the young man by Zinzendorf as a 'mere country parson'—but the young man was in fact Mühlenberg, the patriarch-to-be of American Lutheranism.

John Wesley, like Philip Doddridge, had second thoughts about him, again, not entirely due to jealousy or theological disagreement. Zinzendorf evidently thought he had put Wesley down in a twenty-minute stroll in Lincoln's Inn Fields. Between the product of Epworth Rectory and the Court of Augustus the Virile there was a cultural gulf, and Wesley, who never had £100 of his own to play with, could not take to the wealthy nobleman whose cloak-and-dagger devices affronted his own plainness. And it is true that there was about both men a touch of the 'prima donna assoluta'. None the less, despite his wraths and his irritabilities, there were many gestures of penitence and compassion, and he won and kept the unbounded love and admiration of many thousands of good Christian men and women. The quality of Christian life of his scattered communities, in their devotion and simplicity, courage and hope, owed a great deal, humanly speaking, to Nicholas Zinzendorf.

An astonishing missionary impetus followed the Renewal. The Pietist missions to Tranquebar and Georgia were the immediate precedent, but there are few parallels to the speed with which devoted young men took the Pilgrim Church within a few years to the West Indies, to Greenland, to the Baltic states, and to South Africa. Among Zinzendorf's fertile ideas was this conception of a Pilgrim Church, a body of committed 'labourers', living in community where possible, but always on the move, answering the call to minister. This was the heart of the missionary enterprise.

England,[16] it seems, was at first significant as a place of transit where German missionaries might pause en route to Georgia or Pennsylvania. One result was that some of the ablest Moravian leaders sojourned in England, including Spangenberg, Böhler, Töltschig, and Molther. As a result of visits in 1728 and 1735 a group of Germans met in London and made contact with the Church of England societies, especially the one in Fetter Lane. Here on 1 May 1738 Peter Böhler and John Wesley framed the rules which introduced a Moravian discipline. Eventually, after the departure of John Wesley and his followers in 1741, the Fetter Lane Society became a Moravian society, and indeed the site of a fully fledged congregation, a Church of the Unitas Fratrum. This congregation was very much a 'closed shop', quite distinct from the larger Fetter Lane Society, and its members were known only to one another.[17] The opposition to Methodists and Moravians of Bishop Gibson and some of his London clergy, and his suggestion that as a foreign group they were not covered by either the Act of Uniformity or the Toleration Act, led the Brethren to seek legal safeguards. The warm patronage of Archbishop Potter and his endorsement of their orders did not quite meet the new need and the English members, encouraged by Spangenberg, finally sought a licence under the Toleration Act. This incensed Zinzendorf, whose catholicity did not include the designation of the Brethren as Dissenters, and who disliked the overt declaration that the society in London was part of the episcopal Unitas Fratrum. He suggested as an alternative phrase 'Lutheran Protestants'.[18] But the English Brethren found this meaningless, and persisted in the original terms of their licence.

Meanwhile the Pilgrim Church had moved into Red Lion Square where Spangenberg took a house from which the English work might be directed. Here there was founded their 'Society for the Furtherance of the Gospel', of which the very missionary-minded Philip Doddridge became a Corresponding Member, and which raised funds, received and read reports from the new mission fields. In September 1741 an important Synod was held here. Zinzendorf had resigned as Warden, intending to reappear in Philadelphia as a Lutheran pastor under one of his incognitos, and so the Synod declared that 'Our Saviour Himself would be and remain the Chief Elder and Guide of His People.'

[16] J. Pinnington, 'Moravian and Anglican', BJRL lii, no. 1, Manchester 1969; W. G. Addison, The Renewed Church of the United Brethren, 1932.

[17] Benham, Memoirs of James Hutton, p. 133.

[18] Ibid., p. 74. The Lutherans had a Charter from Charles II.

Soon the Brethren moved to fine buildings at Lindsey House, Chelsea (Sir Thomas More would have been shocked to know that one day there would be Lutherans at the bottom of his garden). But perhaps London was ill suited to the ethos of a movement which flourished in green pastures. There was a lodgement at Bedford where they took over the revival under Rogers and Okely, but it was fatefully agreed to move north when Benjamin Ingham offered to turn over to their discipline the group of Yorkshire societies which he had fashioned. The result was that in the north-west, in Yorkshire and Lancashire, there were established fully fledged communities after the pattern of Herrnhut at Fulneck, Grace Hall, and Fairfield, which with their choir houses, schools, and bake-houses flourished enough to rouse the envy of John Wesley. They were the kind of devout community of which John Worthington had dreamed in the 1660s as he pondered the records of Little Gidding. The lovely needlework of the ladies of Fairfield is not the only similarity with the earlier Arminian nunnery.

The problem of legal vulnerability remained, not least in America. In 1749, after skilful enlistment of patrons, the Brethren secured official recognition by Act of Parliament of the Unitas Fratrum as a true, episcopal Church.[19]

The leadership in England was from Germany by Germans. Far from resenting this, the English brethren at Fetter Lane repeatedly asked that Spangenberg or Böhler or Molther might be permanently stationed in England. The very un-Englishness of much of it may have been an attraction to some. And while the House of Hanover ruled, nobody could complain that these men spoke what was in a special sense the King's English. Despite John Nelson's gibe at 'one that had got into the poor sinnership, who held his head to one side, and talked as if he had been brought up in the borders of Bohemia',[20] a magnetic attraction seemed to come upon many Methodists. It was as though inside every Methodist there was a Moravian trying to get out. Although they disclaimed proselytizing, they infiltrated societies. It is easy to understand how John Wesley should come to look askance at a movement which won over such eminent members of the Holy Club as Ingham, Kinchin, Simpson, and Gambold; William Hammond and Francis Okeley from the Cambridge Methodists,[21] key families like the

[19] A. J. Lewis, *Zinzendorf, the Ecumenical Pioneer* (1962), p. 155; Benham, *Memoirs of James Hutton*, p. 215.

[20] J. Nelson, in *Wesley's Veterans*, ed. J. Telford (7 vols. 1912), iii. 59.

[21] J. Walsh, 'The Cambridge Methodists' in *Christian Spirituality, Essays in Honour of Gordon Rupp*, 1975.

Claggetts and Delamottes, the Stonehouses and the Huttons, Whitefield's secretary John Sims, the evangelist John Cennick.

John Walsh has finely expounded some of the reasons for the attraction of a spirituality more introverted than that of the Methodists,[22]
whose hymns and devotions, disciplined community life, and the
simple goodness of the societies of 'poor sinners' seemed to offer a
quieter way than the aggressive fervour of the noisy Methodists. And
though the 'labourers' among the Brethren were in fact as fully
committed to dynamic evangelism as the Methodists, the demands on
the ordinary believer were perhaps less strenuous. That mystical
element in religion which Wesley now tried to purge from his societies
had after all had a genuine place in the pattern of devotion of the first
days of the Holy Club.

Not that it was all plain sailing. Zinzendorf's frequent absences and
travels could not but affect the overall stability of the wide-ranging
movement. In the so-called 'sifting years' of the mid-1740s a number of
alarming and dangerous features appeared which cannot be dissociated
from the words and methods of Zinzendorf himself. Simplicity is one
thing, naïveté another, and the devotion to the Blood of Christ and to
the Wounds of Jesus began to dissolve into a vapid sentimentalism; and
if they still sang the great hymns, there were too many inferior and
occasional ditties and some doggerel, which must, alas, include the
verse of James Hutton. The theme of Christ as Bridegroom was
pervaded by an unsavoury eroticism of language. The attempt to
level up the social mores of societies with a large prosperous upper crust
led to trivial customs of Gemüthlichkeit bordering on the extravagant and
ridiculous. Above all, their contempt for pietist and methodist legalism
led them to liberties of dubious edification. And there was soon a
grievous financial mess. Bold vision, reliance on faith and prayer, are
sound marks of missionary movements, but prudence also is a virtue,
and some of the Moravian projects tried to do too much too soon and
some were grandiose. There followed financial crises which nearly
wrecked the movement. But they repented. They amended. They
survived.

On the death of Zinzendorf the movement passed into the leadership
of the less exotic Spangenberg, and a series of constitutional reforms
gave a new stability and renewed momentum to the Moravian
Church. There were reasons why they should be vastly outnumbered by
the Methodists, but their influence was out of all proportion to their
numbers, not least in their missionary fervour and what we may call
their ecumenism.

[22] Ibid., pp. 262ff.

iii. George Whitefield

That the latest Sanctorale of the Church of England[23] would include John and Charles Wesley, quaintly described as 'Priests, Poets and Teachers of the Faith', but should not include George Whitefield, tells us no doubt more about contemporary Anglicanism than about the Evangelical Revival. But it gives colour to those evangelical historians who have long protested that the pioneer role of Whitefield has been obscured by the two Wesleys and the potent mythology of Methodism. Yet he was the first who ever burst into that silent sea, and was converted while the two Wesleys were still fast bound in sin and nature's night, and he was the one great evangelist to share in the Revival as it embraced America, Wales, Scotland, and England. The rather odd tract in which Whitefield was compared with John Wyclif had its point. He was the Morning Star of the Evangelical Revival.

Yet John Wesley was right in beginning his oft-told tale of the story of Methodism with the year 1729, when his brother Charles and a few fellow students formed what became known as the 'Holy Club'. These young men adopted a Rule, a pattern of self-examination, mutual oversight, and good works far more demanding than that of the Religious Societies, which won for them the abiding name of 'Methodists'. Many of these young men were to have notable careers, but George Whitefield was a late-comer and very much the ugly duckling. One morning in September 1732 Charles Wesley got a message, passed on by an old apple woman, and invited the sender to breakfast. He recognized him as one he had seen mooching about Oxford by himself, but the thin young man with a cast in his eye, woollen gloves, patched gown, was not prepossessing. Rightly suspecting that fear of ridicule had kept him away, he lent him Francke's *Nicodemus: or the Fear of Man* and the much praised *Country Parson's Advice to his Parishioners*, and promised to keep an eye on him. Whitefield seems to have met John Wesley a few days later, and to have been slightly in awe of him.

George Whitefield (1714–70) was the youngest son of the proprietor of the Bell Inn, Gloucester. At school he had been unremarkable, save for a talent for acting which made him at one time contemplate the stage as a career. But he left school early, and when his brother took over the inn, became a hewer of wood and a drawer of porter. But his mother had immortal longings for her son. Her persistence and the kindness of friends enabled him, in December 1732, to enter Pembroke College, Oxford, as a servitor. Here his publican experience enabled him to make

---

[23] *The Alternative Service Book*, 1980.

the chores profitable that were unavailable to that other impoverished member of the same college, Samuel Johnson. After a slightly wild adolescence, he had begun to take religion seriously, and went up to Oxford grimly resolved not to be led astray, which meant keeping himself to himself. The Holy Club was therefore a godsend, but its austere pattern of devotion and works of mercy increased, rather than lessened, the spiritual strain, and he began to practise foolish and extravagant austerities which brought him to the edge of complete breakdown in health. His college tutor and doctor did what they could, and a worried Charles Wesley (one founding member of the Holy Club had died raving) put him in touch with John Wesley, who loved nothing more than to bestow medical advice. They all blamed 'the Oxford air'.

A turning-point was when Charles Wesley lent him Henry Scougal's *Life of God in the Soul of Man* which spoke of true religion as the indwelling Christ, and of the need for a change so drastic from the Old Adam to the New that it could only be described as a 'New Birth'. The liberating experience came to him some time in 1735, and his original account of it is so reticent as to be convincingly authentic. 'The spirit of mourning was taken from me, and I knew what it was truly to rejoice in God my Saviour.' Where and how this took place he never said, though the spot became for him a place of recurrent pilgrimage. It is one of the least melodramatic of all conversion stories of the Revival. But when he went home to convalesce he began to write and speak of the New Birth, and he formed not only a small religious society, but also a group of '6 or 7 female disciples'—one of the earliest references to females in a religious society.[24]

His doings attracted the kindly attention of Bishop Benson, who sent for him and offered to ordain him, confirming his growing conviction that he was called to the ministry. So he returned to Oxford to take his degree but found that, in the way of universities, a generation had gone down, the Wesleys gone abroad and other members of the Holy Club to country livings. But Sir John Phillips provided him with funds which would enable him to stay in Oxford and nourish a new generation of the languishing Holy Club. On 20 June 1736 he was ordained deacon in the noble cathedral of his home town, and a week later, in St Mary de Crypt, he preached his first sermon on Eccles. 4:9–12, a sermon later re-preached and printed as *The Nature and necessity of Society in General and Religious Society in Particular*. His friends were delighted, but its contents do not seem to be likely to convert anybody, and none that day could have realized that the greatest popular preacher since Hugh

---

[24] Dallimore, *Whitefield*, i. 83.

Latimer, and perhaps of all time, had raised his voice among them.

But soon, and indeed with incredible swiftness, the slim young man, long arms raised to heaven, with his streaming eloquence and vibrant voice, was caught up in a growing demand for sermons in Gloucester, Stonehouse, Oxford, Bristol, and London and became in a few months a cult figure. The young men of the Religious Societies turned eagerly to one of their own age and he responded eagerly, for with the Holy Club behind him, he was deeply convinced that in such religious societies lay the secret of renewal. So he preached twice during 1727 at the Quarterly Service of the London Societies at St Mary-le-Bow and preached and administered the Sacrament at the lectures and prayers which the Religious Societies financially sustained within the City. But it was not only the young who flocked to hear him.

The congregations continually increased, and generally on a Lord's Day I used to preach four times to very large and affected auditories, besides reading prayers twice or thrice, and walking perhaps twelve miles in going backwards and forwards.

These were heady experiences and many might have been thrown off balance. But there was a deep simplicity in this young man, and if he was not unmarked by the excitement, there was no venality in him and no thought of personal advantage. It took something different to call forth the mettle of his pasture. It came when in December 1737 Charles Wesley returned to England seeking reinforcements for the Georgia mission, and a letter followed from John asking 'What if thou art the Man, Mr. Whitefield?' This was the kind of thing which spoke to his condition. 'Do you ask what you shall have? Why, all you desire,' wrote John, 'food to eat, raiment to put on, a place where to lay your head (such as your Lord had not) and a crown of glory that fadeth not away.'[25]

The wheels of bureaucracy ground slowly, and between them the SPG and the Georgia Trustees caused delays that kept him nine months more in England. But what tumultuous months they became. By now the 'New Birth' was at the centre of his preaching and already beginning to offend the City clergy. But opposition at this stage only increased the number of his hearers: 'constables were obliged to be placed at the door, to keep the people in order. The sight of the congregation was awful. One might as it were walk upon the peoples' heads: and thousands went away from the largest churches for want of room.'[26]

Cheapside had then a kind of Piazza Navona dignity, and there on a Sunday morning, long before daylight, could be seen hundreds of little

[25] Dallimore, *Whitefield*, i. 107.   [26] Whitefield, *Journals*, p. 79.

lights, bobbing up and down like fireflies, as people made their way to hear George Whitefield preach the gospel, lanthorns in their hands, talking earnestly as they went.[27]

'The tide of popularity', he admitted, 'now began to run very high. In a short time I could no longer walk on foot, but was constrained to go in a coach from place to place.' He was made aware of advantageous openings, and was pressed to remain in England. But he determined to sail at the first opportunity. At last, after the usual weeks spent in the journey from Gravesend and in waiting for a favourable wind, the *Whitaker* set sail on 1 February.

John Wesley wrote in his *Journal*: 'The day before, Mr. Whitefield had sailed out, neither of us then knowing anything of the other.' Whether he really did not know that Whitefield was still accessible is not certain from this statement. But it is sure that Wesley landed at Deal on 1 February, and preached there before going on to London by way of the Delamottes at Blendon. It also seems clear that he had been exercised about whether Whitefield should in fact have gone to Georgia.[28]

How much he had heard of the Whitefield furore we do not know, but he sent him a note in which he said 'When I saw that God, by the wind which was carrying you out, brought me in, I asked counsel of God. His answer you have enclosed.' It was a slip of paper and on it the words: 'Let him return to London.'[29] But not all the casuistries of Urim and of Thummim could divert Whitefield at this stage. And yet, though no evangelical American is likely to believe it, John Wesley had a point. For Whitefield's American connection, glorious as it was, was to draw him away from England again and again at critical moments, leaving the care of the converts and the nurture of his societies either to John Wesley's Arminianism, or to assistants like Howell Harris or John Cennick who, despite their great gifts, had no flair for administration. Had George Whitefield returned to London that day, the history of the Evangelical Revival in England must have been greatly altered, if not certainly for the better.

iv. John Wesley

Samuel (1690–1739), John (1703–91), and Charles (1707–88), and their seven sisters, were the survivors of the nineteen children born to Susanna and Samuel Wesley. Their home was in the Rectory of Epworth amid the upland men of the Lincolnshire Fens, augmented at a

[27] Ibid., p. 88.
[28] The footnote in *Wesley Letters* (OE), i. 527, seems unhelpful and unlikely.
[29] Dallimore, *Whitefield*, i. 150.

later stage with the living of Wroot, and its bleak parsonage. It was desolate in winter, and access was often only by waterways fraught with the possibilities of accident, as Samuel found more than once. And though Samuel Wesley fulfilled his pastoral duties with stubborn persistence, founding one of the first rural Religious Societies, he was glad to be off to Convocation or among the hacks of Grub Street where he contributed a quiz page to Dunton's *Athenian Gazette*. But he got across many of his parishioners, mismanaged his affairs, landed in gaol for debt, and had to be helped out more than once by friends, from Archbishop Sharp to Robert Nelson. His learning and his reading were wide and deep, to judge from the immense prospectus of reading which he set before his curate,[30] but he belonged to a generation which was immersed in texts and in Biblical linguistics, which in his case resulted in an abortive project to produce a new polyglot Bible and the great Latin dissertations on the Book of Job, which he did not live to see published, and which was read by very few—an all-time Worst Seller.

His was the kind of philological learning against which William Law was furiously to protest, and Susanna made no bones about her preference for practical theology. But in this field both parents were well read and when their sons excitedly discovered à Kempis or Jeremy Taylor they were swiftly reminded that their parents had been familiar with them thirty years before. Susanna, poor woman, stayed at home, worn out by successive child-bearing, the care of the drab home, and constant disagreements with her overbearing spouse. She devoted what energies remained to the education of the children, devoting one evening to each child (Thursday was 'Jacky's night'), but did not go out much after the birth of John. She had been the youngest of the twenty-five children of the eminent Nonconformist Samuel Annesley and, like her husband, had turned from Dissent, she to become a member of the non-juring sect. And although attempts have been made to discern Puritan traits in her thought, it is better to drop the labels and admit that there was much overall consensus about the essentials of the Christian religion—not only Susanna Wesley, but Hoadly and Clarke as well as William Law could talk about the 'covenanted terms of salvation'. But she had a clear, shrewd mind, was a better theologian than her undergraduate son, and gave him good counsel from a middle-of-the-road high-church theology which was none the worse for being that.

A clannish lot, the Wesleys, and conscious of it, but if their mother's first rule in their education had been to break their infant wills, the result was a lively little tribe who said their own say, even though ill fortune

---

[30] S. Wesley's *Advice to a Young Clergyman* is a revealing document printed in T. Jackson, *Life of Charles Wesley* (1841), ii. 499ff.

prevented the girls at least from 'doing their own thing'. Though there was constant affection, there was nothing starry-eyed about the way they regarded one another, so that the family correspondence is of great importance for a study of John Wesley. Although Samuel Wesley honestly claimed to love all his children, it was for the boys that he and the rest of the family scraped and suffered. They had the best that could be given them: Samuel and Charles went to Westminster, and John to Charterhouse and, in due season, all three to Christ Church, Oxford.

No such opportunities were open to the girls, and it was, we have seen, an eighteenth (and perhaps not only an eighteenth) century way, for men to take for granted the disabilities of the female estate. No wonder if the drably clad girls paid the price a little bitterly, and that some of them became what Charles called 'Grumbletonians'. Samuel wrote to John in 1726: 'You have had better luck than I if you have not been upbraided with the disproportioned charge of the boys and of the girls.'[31]

With no money and a dowdy background they had no chance of making good marriages and most of the girls went to oafs below their own cultural capacity, one to a villain and to poignant tragedy.

Samuel did well at Westminster, to which he returned, to become head usher, after his Oxford studies, and was much befriended by Harley and Atterbury who could, however, do little for him. He settled down at last as headmaster of Blundell's School, Tiverton. Like his father, he wrote a good deal of rather inferior poetry. Relations with his younger brothers were not as close as one feels he wished, and he was irked by John's dominance of Charles. But at least he took his responsibilities to his parents and family conscientiously. In the last exchanges of letters with John, one's sympathies must be very much on his side.

John Wesley went up to Oxford with a sound classical training, and from the first took himself, as well as his religion, seriously. The family poked fun at his rationality, but he took to the study of logic and returned to it at intervals, and it gave a strength to him in public controversy. His letters to his mother and father were often long, and there may have been a slight and unacknowledged tug-of-war between his parents as to who was his real mentor. John recounted at great length improbable ghost stories, betraying an interest in the occult and in the relation between things spiritual and material which would reappear in the disproportion of old wives' tales in his later *Journals*. But he was also on to important problems, which he discussed at length with his

[31] Wesley, *Letters* (OE), i. 207.

parents—whether Thomas à Kempis[32] did not champion an intolerable other worldliness and the whole business of Predestination, on which he and his mother agreed and about which he soon reached abiding convictions fateful for his future career.

Like a good many theological students, John Wesley read contemporary divinity with the usual leapfrog over the previous generation, and he tended to enthuse, as students do, overrating those like Bishop Peter Browne whose vulnerable arguments about the limitations of reason impressed him, falling in and out with Bishop Berkeley in a week or two. He took over uncritically the definition of Richard Fiddes about faith as an 'assent upon rational grounds',[33] but was soon won over by his mother's views ('the matter is fully and accurately explained by Bishop Pearson')[34] of it as 'an assent to what God has revealed because he has revealed it'.[35] Both definitions fell far short of what he would later find to be a true definition in the *Homily of Salvation*.

When, in 1725, he spoke of taking orders, his father counselled caution, but his mother encouraged him to go ahead. There followed a succession of events which together were the turning-point of his career. On 19 September 1725 he was ordained deacon by Bishop Potter. Then there opened up the possibility of a fellowship at Lincoln College, and his brother Samuel and his father pulled out all the stops and used all their influence. There were other candidates, and the usual lobbying, so that it was with devout thankfulness that he learned on 17 March 1726 that he was elected Fellow of Lincoln, with a secure living until he obtained preferment or until he married. His father, whose financial affairs were again desperate and who had to face the need to supply Charles, also up at Christ Church, wrote jubilantly: 'What will be my own fate God only knows. Sed passi graviora. Wherever I am, my Jack is Fellow of Lincoln.' On 14 February 1727 he took his degree of MA and in September 1728 was ordained priest by Bishop Potter, not upon a title, but on his fellowship, which he later interpreted as a roving commission which justified his itinerancy.

John and Charles got home when they could, and once they walked, and to their mother's indignation, fasted all the way. But their father had had one or two nasty tumbles, and needed help, so John consented to act as curate and spent most of the period between 1727 and 1729 at Epworth. While he was there, his brother Charles founded the Holy Club, in the beginnings of which John was very much in the background, a kind of Mycroft Holmes to the deferential Charles's

---

[32] From Susanna, June 1725. Wesley, *Letters* (OE), i. 164. From Samuel, 14 July, ibid. i. 171.

[33] Ibid. 175.   [34] Ibid. i. 179.   [35] Ibid. i. 188.

Sherlock. He had begun to live by rule, and, following the counsel of Jeremy Taylor (echoed in many other contemporary works), he decided on a pattern of devotion and self-examination, taking and writing down his spiritual temperature as often as possible and praying at regular intervals, later culminating in ejaculatory prayer every hour on the hour. In Taylor and even more in à Kempis, he found a call to inward holiness, a resolve strengthened when he read Law's *Serious Call* and *Christian Perfection*, probably in that order. He began to keep tightly written and encoded diaries which provide priceless evidence about his thought and behaviour in the next years.

Like many another theological student, he went through phases. He began as a young high churchman, interested in the sacred languages, and in the writings of the Fathers, though it was very important for him when 1729–30 he decided to make the Bible the centre of his studies. But he still was much concerned with the primitive Church, and shared in the patristic studies which not only Clarke and Whiston, but Deacon and Hickes, felt to be important. The advent of the gifted John Clayton, of Brasenose College, to the Holy Club led to a deeper and more sympathetic interest in non-juring theology, and John adhered to the radical practices and ideas of the 'essentialist' Non-Jurors, and assisted Thomas Deacon in the preparation of his *Complete Devotions* while for a time George Hickes's *Reformed Devotions* became his tool and handbook. But he moved from this position, and the People Called Methodist at least may be grateful that he was early freed from the liturgiological virus. At the same time, and partly under the influence of the William Law circle, he explored the mystical writers, Molinos, Mme Guyon, Antoinette de Bourignon, though he was soon to turn very sharply against a tradition which, as Martin Schmidt suggests, did in fact leave a mark upon him.

One result of his return to Oxford and his presence in the Holy Club was to extend their little circulating library of edifying works, such as Castaniza's *Spiritual Combat*, Francke's *Nicodemus* and the inevitable *Country Parson's Advice to his Parishioners*. William Morgan had begun prison visiting and this soon became a primary concern of the Club, preaching, pastoral care, devotions, and setting up a school, and an active philanthropy which attracted attention and got a subscription from the sympathetic Sir John Phillips. By now they had become the butt of common-room gossip and growing antagonism. This centred at first on their attendance at the Eucharist at Christ Church, was strengthened after the death of William Morgan, and found public expression in 1732 in a famous article in Fogg's *Weekly Journal*, against the Methodists. But they had their defenders, as an answering broadsheet showed,[36] while from Epworth and from Samuel Wesley came a resounding 'Valde probo' and a claim to be the spiritual grandfather of the Holy Club.

About the Wesley brothers at this time, there was no grim asceticism, nor any attempt to imitate the absolutist rejection of worldly pastimes demanded by William Law. John Wesley continued to enjoy reading poetry and plays, visited the theatre, drank, and played cards, while Charles hovered on the edge of involvement with an actress. Through the least unworldly member of the Holy Club, Robert Kirkham, John Wesley was introduced to a circle of friends in a cluster of Cotswold villages, centring on Stanton Harcourt. They included a glamorous group of genteel young ladies who were interested in religion and in devout young men. Their amusements were innocent, and they spent much time talking about religion and edifying books. They not only met, but corresponded. As with Doddridge at the same age, this took place under cover of classical pseudonyms—Sally Kirkham became Varanese, Anne Granville, Selina, Mary Pendarves, Aspasia (how different from the home life of the Epworth 'Patty', 'Suky', 'Hetty', 'Martha', and 'Molly'!) and John Wesley became Cyrus and Charles Araspes. The trim, long-haired, serious John was one at whom they might occasionally smile as 'Little Primitive Christianity' but he had a presence and when he read or talked to them, commanded willing attention.

John seems to have been in love with Sally Kirkham and continued to correspond with her (to his mother's dismay and sarcastic comments from his sister) after her marriage with John Chapone. He may also have had romantic aspirations towards Mary Pendarves, who, as Mary Delany, was to become one of the great charmers of the century, the cherished friend of Royalty, who died at a great age and whose memorial is in the pantheon of genteel society, St James's, Piccadilly. But she was a pearl of great price, well beyond John Wesley's charm or affluence. John made many visits, and spent a Christmas vacation with these friends, but the correspondence lapsed and the relationships ceased as John himself withdrew more and more from worldly pastimes and friendships. It was all very harmless, at a time when young divines are wont to be silly, and it probably had a civilizing and humanizing effect on the Wesley brothers.

John had become an earnest preacher on themes which involved inward holiness, and some of his sermons he never afterwards had reason to repudiate. In the manner of the day, he and Charles preached

[36] It is highly unlikely that this was written by William Law, but the possibility cannot entirely be ruled out.

one another's sermons, and on occasion read out other people's as well. This was true of the sermons of William Tilly, an unremarkable Oxford divine, whose doctrine of sin and of prevenient grace, along Augustinian lines, Wesley found congenial and important, but whose significance ought not to be overestimated.[37] More important were sermons preached before the University, his sermons preached before the University, his sermon on 1 January 1733 on 'Circumcision of the heart'—a sermon which he still affirmed as sound doctrine forty years after: and the following year what Charles called a 'Jacobite sermon', but which seems to have survived examination by the Vice-Chancellor, and of which nothing which could plausibly be called 'Jacobite' has survived.

He began to publish, in 1733, a *Collection of Forms of Prayer* and in the next year an abridgment of a tract he valued highly, John Norris on *Christian Prudence*, and a titivated, rather than retranslated, version of à Kempis, borrowing at least the title from John Worthington's translation *The Christian's Pattern*.

In October 1734 Samuel was seriously ill and, though his health mended, it warned the family to face the crisis which his death must bring, not least the break-up of the family home. It seemed to all but John that the obvious solution would be for him to succeed his father as Rector of Epworth (the living was in the gift of the Crown, and the presentation liable to be governed by politics and interest). But when Samuel put the question to John, he received an extraordinary reply. John spent a week over the letter and sent a copy to his brother Samuel. Since he later published an abridged version of it in his *Journal* it seems to have pleased him. But it obviously dismayed his father and it shocked his brother. Although couched in respectful and affectionate terms, it is an insensitive document, and shows how his rigorous introspective practices had made him preoccupied with himself. He is above all, he says, concerned with the glory of God, but this is interpreted in terms of where he could best find improvement of his own holiness. There are paragraphs of sermonizing, laments about the surrounding worldliness of half-hearted Christians at Oxford, which he might have spared his old father. There is no mention at all of the family plight, though he is delighted to say that the Holy Club has raised over £80 to give to the poor (£40 would have much increased the quality of life of his mother and sisters!) and he ends with the cold comfort to his father: 'He that took care of those poor sheep before you was born will not forget them

---

[37] See C. A. Roberts, 'John Wesley and William Tilly', *PWHS* xxxv (June 1966), 136ff.

when you are dead.'[38] If there is such a thing as sincere humbug, there was a good deal of it in this letter.

His brother Samuel was as usual forthright and perceptive and tore through the balanced sentences. He put his finger on the two vulnerabilities: 'I see your love to yourself, but your love to your neighbour I do not see. This was not the spirit of St. Paul.' And second, it was contrary to John's ordination vows. 'It is not a college, not an University, it is the order of the Church to which you are called.' That the latter point touched a nerve is plain from the haste with which John appealed to Bishop Potter about the moral theology. The truth seems to be that John had an almost claustrophobic aversion to being cooped up in the Lincolnshire parish, was determined that whatever ministry lay ahead of him, it would not be an 'action replay' of his father's. And yet, however weak his arguments and dubious his motives, the verdict of history seems to be that he was right.

At Eastertide John and Charles walked home from Oxford for the last time, to be with their father who died on 25 April. He made a good end, and among his last sayings, which John would forcefully recall, was 'the inward witness, the inward witness'. He had died with his commentary on Job finished, but not published, and it fell to John to present the copy to the Queen, who did not much regard it. In some ways his career had been one of frustration and of failure, but there was goodness and kindness in him, and he was a great character.

And many of his abortive dreams were to be fulfilled by his sons. He had thought of becoming a missionary to the East Indies. They were pioneer missionaries in a new field. He wrote a mass of generally undistinguished poetry, but his sons were decisively to contribute to what has been called a 'century of Divine Songs'. He had done his duty in his parish, though the results could not be called awakening. His sons were among the champions of a great revival.

John stayed on after the funeral to look after the parish and seems to have relented about becoming Rector of Epworth. But it was too late, and the busy good offices of Thomas Broughton (a former member of the Holy Club, soon to be Secretary of the SPCK) were of no avail. So Oxford it was to be. But not for long. Among those who cast a friendly, and not uncritical, eye on the university Methodists was Dr John Burton, of Corpus Christi College, one of the trustees for the infant colony of Georgia.

Georgia was on the edge of empire where Spaniards and British rattled sabres at one another. Its inhabitants were a mixed bag. There

---

[38] Wesley, *Works* (OE), i. 409.

were some dour Scots moving up from Darien, some released ex-debtors whose emigration owed much to the philanthropic intervention of General Oglethorpe, groups of Moravian and German refugees, and a few settlers who had Martin Chuzzlewit dreams about a new life in a new world. It was a polyglot community where English, French, German, and Spanish could be heard. And around and beyond were the Indians. The poor quality of the clergy going out to America exercised Burton when he thought of the Church in Georgia, and he turned to the group of dedicated and disciplined young men whose zeal had provoked such lively opposition and ridicule. He got John Wesley to meet Oglethorpe, and after seeing a number of people, his mother and brother, John Clayton and William Law, he decided this was a divine call. It seems certain that he thought of it primarily as a call to evangelize the Indians, but it does not seem that he had any missionary thoughts much different from other supporters of the SPG.

There was an interesting correspondence between Burton and Wesley about motives and missionary tactics. A friendly warning can be read between the lines: 'The motive to your pious undertaking is the desire of doing good to the souls of others.' What would be wrong would be a legalistic insistence on non-essentials: 'here is a nice trial of Christian prudence . . . in every case you would distinguish between what is essential and what is variable.'[39]

But John's ideas about going to Georgia were similar to those for not going to Epworth. 'My chief motive, to which all the rest is subordinate is the hope of saving my own soul. I hope to learn the true sense of the gospel of Christ, by preaching it to the heathen.' There follows a statement of the spiritual advantages of living among simple, innocent people, a naïve and ironical utterance since almost every sentence was to be brutally contradicted by reality. Soon a small team was recruited. The twenty-three-year-old Benjamin Ingham, a valued member of the Holy Club, something of an expert catechist, and a rather un-Yorkshire Yorkshireman, a charmer not very good at blunt speech and tough decisions; the twenty-one-year-old Charles Delamotte: and Charles Wesley, twenty-seven, and for all his evangelical breakfasts, still wet behind the ears and hastily ordained. The terms of reference were vague, but Charles was designated as secretary to General Oglethorpe in Indian affairs, a post for which by gifts and temperament he was quite unsuited, while John and Benjamin were hoping to evangelize the Indians, but became more and more immersed in the pastoral care of the parish of Savannah and the outpost settlement of Frederica.

[39] Burton to Wesley, 28 Sept. 1735. Wesley, *Journal*, viii. 288.

On 14 October 1735 they set out from Gravesend, but there were the usual delays and they stuck at the Isle of Wight. Not till 10 December did the emigrant convoy, guarded by HMS *Hawk* and composed of the *Simmonds* and the *London Merchant*, set sail, plunged almost at once into the winter gales.

Before they left England, the little team was working to rule on board ship. 'We began to be a little regular' was Wesley's understatement. From half past five in the morning an exact timetable focused the immense energy which he displayed in every part of his new ministry. The theology behind it was high church, if not non-juring. Before they left Gravesend, he had re-baptized a layman who had had lay baptism and he continued to re-baptize such laymen and Dissenters (thoroughly bad theology and rightly deprecated by Bishop Gibson). Like the Non-Jurors, he stuck to the first Prayer Book of Edward VI, baptizing with immersion. But most fateful of all, he met the Germans. There were twenty-six on board and he began to learn German, three hours a day, in order to converse with them. He admired their simplicity, their patience, and their fervour. And when, during a storm, a great wave overflowed the ship, he marked their courage, for they calmly went on singing psalms, while the English screamed and John Wesley, to his chagrin, found himself afraid to die.

Beside their own prayers and Bible study, the group held public services and constant visitation of passengers who were not all delighted by the practice, carried over from the Holy Club, of having long passages read aloud to them from edifying books. John Wesley was always liable to take people at their face value and listened agog to the self-revelations of some of the women, and notably the doctor's wife, Mrs Hawkins, with a deference which even at this stage, Charles and Benjamin Ingham found disconcerting.

But the voyage was safely accomplished and the landing made off Tybee island, which John Wesley celebrated by staving in the casks of rum. The passengers went their ways, Charles Wesley accompanying General Oglethorpe with a group of settlers to the outposts of Frederica, an embryo township, John Wesley and Ingham to Savannah, Ingham already preparing an Indian dictionary.

There were two German settlements. At Ebenezer were the Lutheran refugees from Salzburg, under two ministers, Bolzius and Gronau, who had been trained by the Pietists at Halle. There were tensions between them and the Moravians. For though Zinzendorf had been educated at Halle and Spangenberg at Jena, and despite Zinzendorf's attachment to the Lutherans, they had both criticized the Pietist views and practices and had run into trouble with the Saxon authorities, while in London they had roused the sharp distrust of the German court chaplain Dr Ziegenhagen. Since the Moravians possessed an episcopal ministry in the true succession, John Wesley would communicate with them, but not with the Lutherans.

Although August Gottlieb Spangenberg was of his own age, John Wesley treated him with great deference and there was a memorable conversation two days after his arrival.

I asked [Mr Spangenberg's] advice with regard to my own conduct. He told me he could say nothing till he had asked me two or three questions, 'Do you know yourself? Have you the witness within yourself? Does the Spirit of God bear witness with your spirit that you are a child of God?' I was surprised, and knew not what to answer. He observed it, and asked, 'Do you know Jesus Christ?' I paused, and said 'I know he is the Saviour of the world.' 'True,' replied he. 'But do you know He has saved you?' I answered, 'I hope he has died to save me.' He only added, 'Do you know yourself?' I said, 'I do'. But I fear they were vain words.

Spanish moss and alligators apart, there were resemblances between the marshes of Savannah and the Lincolnshire fens. And the pastoral problems of an English village where squire, doctor, and parson, to say nothing of gossipy women, might get across one another, were soon to reappear in Frederica. Isaac Watts's busy bee and industrious ant had nothing on John Wesley, who now scurried hither and thither to all corners of his large parish, between little villages with nostalgic English names, like Hampstead and Highgate, mixed with unpronounceable Indian names, and some of more immediate inspiration, like Cowpen and Thunderbolt. But he took long journeys to attend the sick, often got lost, and on one occasion ended by running into Savannah in fear of being late.

Wesley had persuaded the team to turn vegetarian and even induced young Delamotte to explore whether man might not live by bread alone. He rearranged the time of the public prayers, and perhaps not only the sluggards were annoyed to find that Mattins and the Litany would be at 6.00 in the morning on Sunday. There were little rows about immersing babies, about refusing the Sacrament to Dissenters, until an exasperated critic spoke for his friends. 'They say they are Protestants. But as for you, they cannot tell what religion you are of . . . they do not know what to make of it.' It was neither Anglican flesh nor Presbyterian fowl nor Quaker good red herring, though it was perhaps the Methodist egg. The situation was not clarified by Wesley's continual hob-nobbing with the Moravians in conversation, groups and in shared devotions.

Yet all the time Wesley went about doing good, and there was a core of faithful families who loved and respected him. Soon he had little societies which met for edification and prayer. He took a refresher course in German, and learned Spanish for the sake of Spanish Jews within the parish. His linguistic studies paid remarkable dividends. He had been much impressed by the singing of the Germans, and by their hymns which struck him by their beauty and depth. He selected a few of the best, a mixed bag, from Lutheran Orthodoxy, Reformed and Lutheran Pietism, and the Moravians, adding one Spanish hymn. These he turned into English verse, hymns as fine as anything his brother would ever write. They were the core of his first hymn book, published at Charlestown in 1737. Books from time to time bowled Wesley over. One such was the life of M. de Renty, which he read to all and sundry. The Presbyterian minister at Darien introduced him to the *Life* of a Scottish professor, Thomas Haliburton, which moved him to exclaim, 'I cannot but value it above any other human compositions except *The Christian Pattern* and the small remains of Clemens Romanus, Polycarp and Ignatius' (his brother Samuel gave it short sharp shrift in one withering sentence). John published an abridgement of the *Life* in 1739.

He was also busy with correspondence: a *Journal* of his voyage for the authorities at home, letters to SPCK about books, and the family. A letter from Samuel spoke some home truths. 'My time is never worth a Journal . . . you must therefore be content with . . . letters.' But Samuel's main concern is for his mother who had been arrested for debt.

. . . my mother has met with abundance of troubles. . . . I heartily wish . . . that you may have provided for my mother's subsistence, if I should die . . . if you have not taken any care for her, if surviving me, 'tis a guilty, a very guilty omission which I would not willingly have been stained with—no, not to convert a Continent.

I don't blame you upon the whole for not taking my sister Ellison along with you, but I should have commended you exceedingly had you taken three or four of her children.[40]

A not pleasant letter, that one, but perhaps not undeserved.

He had now come through another of his phases from which, as from the others, he had learned more than he knew. This was the mystical teaching about which he now dispatched an astonishing memorandum dressed up as a letter to his brother Samuel.[41] It seems to be a compound of his reading and his conversation, of Molinos and the *Theologia Germanica*, Tauler, and perhaps Poiret and Mme Guyon and Antoinette de Bourignon, and almost certainly a saying of William Law which had

[40] *Letters* (OE), i. 459–60. [41] Ibid. i. 487, 23 Nov. 1736.

rankled when he consulted him about a member of the Holy Club: 'Let him alone!' What he now distrusted was a depreciation of the means of grace, of spiritual discipline, and of good works. It was a battle he had now fought, and it was to be important four years later when he thought to find the same dangerous fallacies among the Moravians.

Meanwhile Charles was in deep trouble. There was no soul the brothers were more anxious to save than Mrs Hawkins, but she and her friends posed problems beyond the ken of one whose pastoral experience was confined to exhorting gaol birds and teaching earnest undergraduates. She and her friend Mrs Welch now wove a tissue of malice and lies about him. They 'confessed' to adulteries with Oglethorpe, and then went to Oglethorpe with the accusation that Charles Wesley was telling fearful lies about him. Both men swallowed the stories. Disaster lay close at hand, and Ingham went post haste to Savannah to fetch John to the rescue. John, too, believed the tales, and only slowly did he unravel the truth and patch things up, after a period when a sick Charles had been sent to Coventry by Oglethorpe. But Charles was done for. He wrote a miserable letter on 1 May: 'I am heartily weary of my fellow creatures . . . when a way is made for me to escape, escape I shall, for my life, and not look behind.'[42] In July he resigned his secretaryship, and soon left for England, which he reached after long delays in Boston. But when Wesley went to Frederica in August, and to the doctor for medicine, it all broke out again, and a hysterical Mrs Hawkins pointed a pistol at John Wesley, lashed out with a pair of scissors, and finally tore his hair and bit his cassock. There was inevitably a flood of contradictory gossip.

But now John himself was to be caught up in scandal. His diary records that he was spending more and more time with one of his female parishioners, an attractive eighteen-year-old girl, Sophy Hopkey, niece of the Chief Magistrate of Savannah, Thomas Causton. John was thirty-four years of age, and there was nothing in the least discreditable in his falling in love. But he was in conflict with his natural human feelings and his theological principles, the disparagement of the married estate and the demand for clerical celibacy which he and William Law claimed to find in primitive Christianity. As he read early church history to her on a boat in the waterways between Frederica and Savannah, he found it difficult to concentrate, and surprised himself as well as her into something like 'a declaration'. Whether she was anything more than flattered by the romantic devotion of her minister cannot be known, but she had other suitors, and just when Wesley had decided to marry her, she wed a Mr Williamson.

---

[42] Ibid. i. 460.

John Wesley interpreted her embarrassed ambiguities as wilful deceit, and refused to give her and her husband Holy Communion. It was a public affront, and Causton had some cause to complain: 'I am the person that am injured . . . the affront is offered to me . . . it will be the worst thing Mr Wesley ever did in his life, to fix upon my family.'[43] Now all Wesley's critics came together. He was arrested, and true bills were brought on ten indictments (the Bishop's Commissary was later to declare them 'impertinent, false or frivolous').[44] As the affair dragged on between September and November 1737, John Wesley took counsel with his friends and decided that his powers were now so straitened he had better go. Though the magistrates had warned him not to leave, under a bond for £50, he posted a notice in the Great Square of Savannah announcing his imminent departure. He set out for Carolina and reached Purrysburg easily, but this was followed by a nightmare journey to Port Royal. The little party got lost, tormented by thirst, and torn by brambles, and the trim Mr Wesley arrived dirty, weary, and dishevelled. The venture which he had begun with such high hopes had ended in near disaster. Dr Burton had warned that it would be a 'nice trial of Christian prudence'. But at this stage of their lives it was a virtue which for the Wesley brothers was in short supply.

On the voyage home John Wesley wrote the poignant words: 'I went to America to convert the Indians: but oh, who shall convert me?' The Indian mission had never got off the ground, beyond a few set-piece conversations with chiefs which he wrote down and dispatched to London. Yet he had not laboured in vain in Georgia, and it was perhaps more than politeness when George Whitefield declared that John Wesley had done 'inexpressible good'. Curnock's summary is worth attention:

The crowning achievement was the slow moulding of the Methodist system. The circuit, the society, the itinerant ministry: the class meeting, the band meeting, the lovefeast: leaders and lay assistants: extempore prayer and preaching: and even the building of a meeting house—all this and much more in the form and spirit of early Methodism came to Wesley in Georgia, and was transplanted.[45]

'God has poured out his spirit . . . the whole nation is in an uproar . . . we see all about us an amazing ferment. Surely Christianity is once more lifting up its head.'[46] So wrote Charles of the effect of Whitefield's ministry. But though John Wesley had no part in these doings, it was a new John Wesley who re-entered the English scene. After his first service at Millbank on 5 February he was told 'I was not to preach there

[43] Ibid. i. 518.   [44] Ibid. ii. 520 n.   [45] *Journal*, i. 426.
[46] *Letters* (OE), i. 526.

any more.' Ten days later he was in Manchester and his old friends, Clayton and Byrom, were shocked and shaken. Clayton wrote a few weeks later a friendly warning in which he complained 'your using no notes, and so very much action . . . has established your reputation for . . . ostentation' and 'prodigious singularities'. Byrom seemed to think all would be well if this fiery Samson would cut his hair and bade him curb 'your action and vehement emphasis'.[47]

But for John Wesley his contact with the Germans was more important. On 7 February he met the Moravian minister, Peter Böhler, who was to be Evangelist in his pilgrim's progress. And what Böhler had to say was not on the margin between Pietist and Moravian theology, but from the heart of the original Protestant Reformation. It is not accidental that the writings of Martin Luther now appear at the centre of the story. Wesley professed not to understand when Böhler told him, 'My brother, that philosophy of yours must be purged away.' He took his new friend to see William Law at Putney, but the interview was not a success. Wesley was now sure that what he himself lacked was saving faith, and Böhler counselled him. 'Preach faith till you have it, and then because you have faith you will preach faith.' On 2 April Böhler convinced Wesley that instantaneous conversion was Scriptural and brought other witnesses to attest it.

The young James Hutton (he was twenty-one years old) was a family friend, and might be called a 'fan' of John Wesley. He had gone into publishing, and now organized a number of religious societies, one of which was in Fetter Lane. Though this was for some time a Religious Society within the Church of England, Moravian infiltration became increasingly important and on 1 May Peter Böhler and John Wesley revised its rules, in terms of Moravian discipline, with bands, love feasts, and days of general intercession.[48]

It is important to note that well before 24 May John Wesley's preaching was such that he was banned from several City churches. Meanwhile Charles, whose health had been poor for months, consulted Böhler on his own account, and then found spiritual help from the brazier Mr Bray, with whom he took lodgings in Little Britain.[49] There his friend William Holland introduced him to Luther on the Galatians: 'We . . . found him nobly full of faith.'[50] 'I spent some hours this evening in private with Martin Luther, who was greatly blessed to me. . . . I laboured waited and prayed to feel "who loved ME, and gave

[47] Ibid. i. 539.   [48] *Journal*, i. 458. Benham, *Memoirs*, p. 29.
[49] *The Life of the Rev. Charles Wesley, M.A.* by Thomas Jackson, 2 vols. 1841. vol. i. p. 129.
[50] Jackson, *Life of Charles Wesley*, i. 131.

himself for ME".' The festival of Whitsuntide was the crisis for both brothers. At last, on Whit Sunday, 21 May, Charles Wesley could say, 'I now found myself at peace with God, and rejoiced in hope of loving Christ.'[51] For John, 24 May was the great day of the feast and we may not here omit the passage from his *Journal* which has become a point of *anamnēsis* for a great communion.

He had opened the Scriptures in the early morning on a text (2 Pet. 1: 4) of great significance for the Pietists and Moravians. At an afternoon service in St Paul's he had been comforted by the anthem, perhaps Purcell's rendering of Psalm 130. Then:

In the evening I went very unwillingly to a society in Aldersgate St. where one was reading Luther's preface to the 'Epistle to the Romans'. About a quarter before nine, while he was describing the change which God works in the heart through faith in Christ, I felt my heart strangely warmed. I felt I did trust in Christ, Christ alone for salvation: and an assurance was given me that He had taken away *my* sins, even *mine* and saved *me* from the law of sin and death. I began to pray with all my might for those who had in a more especial manner despitefully used me and persecuted me. I then testified openly to all there what I now first felt in my heart.[52]

Charles in his diary told how 'towards ten my brother was brought in triumph by a troop of friends: and declared "I believe!" We sang the hymn with great joy and parted with prayer.' If that was indeed, as has been often claimed, the hymn that begins, 'Where shall my wondering soul begin?',[53] it is the most appropriate comment on what is sometimes called 'the Aldersgate Street experience', for wonder was the missing note in contemporary Anglican spirituality. And if we may bypass the controversies between those who would 'play up' or 'play down' the significance of it, it was certainly no flash in the pan. It is noteworthy that at this point in his *Journal*, John Wesley paused and recapitulated the story of his religious development. Even more striking is the evidence of what happened on the following Sunday in the house of the Revd John Hutton in Westminster.

Here the Non-Juror kept a superior lodging-house where the Wesleys were always welcome, and here on Sundays a Religious Society (or was it a non-juring congregation?) worshipped. John Wesley attended and Mr Hutton read a sermon of the high-church Bishop Blackall. But at its close (as a horrified Mr Hutton wrote to Samuel Wesley) John stood up and 'told the people that five days before he was not a Christian . . . and the way for them all to be Christians was to believe and own that they

---

[51] Ibid. i. 135.   [52] *Journal*, i. 476.
[53] The argument against in P. W. Grant, 'The Wesleys' Conversion Hymn', *PWHS* xxxv, Sept. 1966, and in favour of a Pentecost hymn is quite unconvincing.

were not now Christians.' An argument followed, during which Hutton said, 'If you was not a Christian ever since I knew you, you was a great hypocrite, for you made us all believe you was one.' Mrs Hutton was angry and distressed, for, as she told Samuel, John Wesley 'is my son's Pope'. She was convinced that he was mad and begged Samuel 'either to confine or convert Mr John when he is with you.' Her letter and Samuel's reply are confirmation that what happened on 24 May was indeed deeply significant.[54]

Wesley now proceeded with a plan, formed in Georgia, to visit the Moravians in Germany and see for himself 'where the Christians live'. He said goodbye to his mother at Salisbury, and left with Benjamin Ingham, an even greater admirer of the Moravians than himself. They travelled through Holland, a country for which John Wesley found an affinity. He had written deferential letters to Count Zinzendorf whom he thought of as a kind of Count de Renty writ German. But Zinzendorf had been exiled by the Saxons, and had formed a new community in Reformed territory at Herrenhaag, Marienborn, near Frankfurt. Here they went and had conversations with the Count, and then went on via Dresden to Herrnhut. To him all was marvel, and Wesley was lost in admiration at the buildings, the economy, the Religious Societies, married, single, male, female, a close community in which marriages were carefully arranged, and where the rites of passage were conducted with public solemnity and decorum. He admired the fervour of their singing, though perhaps was less moved by the Teutonic addiction to sounding brass, for when they passed over all the trombones sounded on every side.

It seems that the submissive Ingham was even admitted to the Lord's Table, which was fairly carefully fenced, but that Wesley was refused as 'homo perturbatus', an enigmatic phrase which may be bound up with an intricate Zinzendorfian analysis of salvation. He had long talks with leading members of the community and took down their spiritual autobiographies in detail. On their return they met the Pietists at the famous Orphan House at Halle. All in all, it was a moving experience, though when he wrote it up, Charles Wesley wrote on the back of it 'Panegyric on Germans'. Other members of the family were more caustic. Sister Emily had a point when she complained,

For God's sake tell me how a distressed woman who daily expects to have the very bed taken from her for rent can consider the state of the churches in Germany.

If you had come to me, instead of going to Germany, and laid out your money

[54] Benham, *Memoirs*, pp. 33ff.

in travelling hither instead of visiting Count Zinzendorf, you would have been, I dare say, as acceptable to our common Master.[55]

Nor was Samuel better pleased. John Wesley had shown signs in recent weeks of a not unknown evangelical trait of thinking he had a divine call to tick people off. This he had done in two unpleasant letters to William Law, to which reference has already been made.[56] From Marienborn he had written a very nasty letter to Samuel and his wife about the sin of detraction, and spreading harmful gossip: 'I doubt you sometimes and my sister often, have been under this condemnation.' And he pins on his sister-in-law that most scathing of all Law's character sketches, Susurrus, the gossiper: 'Yes, my sister, the character of Susurrus is your own.' Now though Ursula Wesley's sharp tongue was a family byword, Samuel was marvellous in his dignified reply, not least in its close: 'My wife joins with love . . . I am, dear Jack, your sincere and affectionate friend and brother.'[57]

John Wesley wrote on 17 September:

I began again to declare in my own country the glad tidings of salvation, preaching three times, and afterwards expounding the Holy Scripture to a large company in the Minories. On Monday I rejoiced to meet with our little society which now consisted of thirty-two persons. The next day I went to the condemned felons in Newgate and offered them free salvation.[58]

Preaching, meeting societies, visiting—Wesley had begun a ceaseless round of evangelical activity which would not cease until his death and which now began to acquire momentum. As he wrote to Herrnhut in October:

Fourteen were added to us since our return, so that we have now eight bands of men, consisting of fifty-six persons, all of whom seek salvation only in the blood of Christ. As yet we have only two small bands of women . . . but here are many others who only wait till we have leisure to instruct them.[59]

Samuel Wesley died suddenly in November 1739, but he had been in ill health and John had never visited Tiverton since his return from Germany. Instead he had alarmed his brother by hints of his own impending death (a defence mechanism he had used in his younger days, and which recurred at intervals all through his life), and it seems he did not relish a confrontation about recent events with so rigorous, if affectionate, a critic. When he had reported Whitefield's forebodings, after encounters with the Bishops of Gloucester and Bristol, that excommunication lay ahead, Samuel had made the canny comment

[55] *Letters* (OE), i. 589–90. [56] See above, p. 000.
[57] *Letters* (OE), i. 578–9. [58] *Journal*, ii. 70. [59] *Letters* (OE), i. 572.

'there is no fear of being cast out of our synagogue for any tenets whatsoever. Did not Clarke die preferred? Were not Collins and Coward free from anathema?'[60]

The death of Samuel was perhaps a more grievous blow to the Methodist movement than anybody realized. Wesley had lost the one person capable of standing right up to him, within a bond of affection. Nobody among his friends and followers, certainly not even Charles, had the same quality of a critical cutting edge, and one consequence perhaps was to increase John Wesley's isolation as a thinker, the results of which we shall examine later on.

Oxford and London were now the two limits of Wesley's activity. On 9 October 1738 he walked to Oxford. On the road (both brothers were accustomed to reading while walking or on horseback) he read Jonathan Edwards's account of the American awakening. 'I read the surprising narrative of the conversions lately wrought in and about the town of Northampton in New England. "Surely this is the Lord's doing and is marvellous in our eyes."' He made another visit to Oxford in November.

On 11 December Wesley hastened to London to greet the returned George Whitefield. Whitefield's first visit to America was the least spectacular of his journeys. He had gone there in order to take up the work of the Wesleys and had been warmly received. He began to work on a project already mooted, to establish an orphan house on the lines, but on a much smaller scale, of the famous Orphan House at Halle. It was to raise money for the project, and also to be ordained priest, that Whitefield returned to England. The next few months were to be fateful for the movement, at a time when the leaders were still in harmony. On 1 January 1739 there was a splendid love feast at Fetter Lane, a reunion of the Holy Club, the Wesleys and Whitefield, Wesley Hall, Kinchin, Ingham, Hutchins, with some sixty members of the society, 'about three in the morning as we were continuing instant in prayer the power of God came mightily upon us insomuch that many cried out with exceeding joy and many fell to the ground.'[61]

Whitefield was still the adventurous pioneer. On his return to England he had been disconcerted to find that he could not take on where he had left off, on a wave of public excitement, for now, as with the Wesleys, there were churches closed to him. The publication of his sermon On the New Birth and the damaging effect on critical minds of the publication of his Journals were not without effect. But he soon got into his stride and once again the congregations overflowed. He wished to return to America quite soon, and felt that John Wesley's gift for 'confirming' those awakened by his preaching might now be of critical importance. For in a few weeks he had set alight his old stamping ground, the area between Bristol and Gloucester, and in March he sent a call to London for John Wesley to come over and help him. Despite fervent opposition from Charles and the ever dubious mechanism of *sortes scripturae*, Wesley decided to go to Bristol, which would now become a vital centre of the Methodist revival. And if Whitefield ran into trouble with his bishops and their chancellors, he now had further support, not least from the leaders of the Revival in Wales, an awakening which had preceded that of the English Methodists. He was able to take counsel with Griffith Jones of Llanddowror, a pioneer, not only in evangelism, but in his association of evangelism with education. Even more important was the opening of correspondence with Howell Harris, who wrote excitedly of the happenings in Wales:

I have some good news to send you from Wales. There is a great revival in Cardiganshire, through Mr. D. Rowlands, a Church minister . . . there is another of the same character in Montgomeryshire . . . there are two or three young curates in Glamorganshire . . . and we have an exceedingly valuable clergyman in Breconshire.[62]

The result was a growing friendship between Harris and Whitefield, and a short visit to Wales by Whitefield (who could not fail to notice the Calvinist theological background) which was followed some months later by John Wesley's first visit to the Principality. At this time, too, Whitefield won two staunch followers in the stockbroker William Seward (1711–40) and the deeply gifted John Cennick (1718–55). Now Whitefield took the most fateful of all his adventurous initiatives, and in order to preach to the largely unchurched miners at Kingswood, outside Bristol, he turned to preach in the open air. The precedents of Howell Harris and Richard Morgan are probably not very relevant. Whitefield's description is reticent: 'I went upon a mount, and spake to as many people as came unto me. They were upwards of two hundred.'[63] But he added 'Blessed be God that I have now broken the ice! I believe I was never more acceptable to my master than when I was standing to teach those hearers in the open fields.'

What began on 17 February 1739 on a hill outside Bristol was to change completely the scope of the Revival, and was the feature which roused to the fury the opposition and captured the imagination of the nation. Swiftly the audiences swelled from hundreds to thousands. On

---

[62] Dallimore, *Whitefield*, i. 234.
[63] Whitefield, *Journals*, p. 216; Dallimore, *Whitefield*, i. 256.

31 March John Wesley arrived in Bristol and was at first taken aback:

I could scarce reconcile myself at first to this strange way of preaching in the
fields of which he set me an example on Sunday: having been all my life (till
very lately) tenacious of every point relating to decency and order, that I should
have thought the saving of souls almost a sin if it had not been done in a
church.[64]

Then, on Monday,

at four in the afternoon, I submitted to be more vile and proclaimed in the
highways the glad tidings of salvation. . . . The scripture on which I spoke
was this (is it possible anyone should be ignorant that it is fulfilled in every true
Minister of Christ?) 'The Spirit of the Lord is upon me, because he hath
anointed me to preach the gospel to the poor . . .'[65]

Whitefield, in the short time remaining to him in England, took steps
towards building a school for the children of the colliers of Kingswood.
Then he moved to London and a great preaching campaign. It is
notoriously difficult to count heads in crowds, as the divergent
estimates of police and demonstrators show in our own day, and no
doubt there was exaggeration in the statistics which Whitefield and
Wesley henceforward record. But that there were immense crowds
cannot be questioned, and of the impact of the preaching there are
such disinterested testimonies as the famous comments of Benjamin
Franklin, Horace Walpole, and Lord Chesterfield. But now the revival
in Bristol and London had really taken off. Wesley himself began to
speak and act with a new clarity and authority, and for the first time
perhaps his true greatness emerges. And never more clearly than in the
splendid utterance of one of his most famous letters (March 1739):

Suffer me now to tell you my principles in this matter. I look upon all the world
as my parish: thus far, I mean, that in whatever part of it I am, I judge it meet,
right and my bounden duty to declare unto all that are willing to hear the glad
tidings of salvation. This is the work I know God has called me to. And sure I
am that his blessing attends it. Great encouragement have I therefore to be
faithful in fulfilling the work he hath given me to do.[66]

Whitefield's greatest occasions were in Moorfields, where once again
the hundreds of little lanterns bobbed before dawn, and in Kennington.

Sunday, May 6th. Preached this morning in Moorfields to about twenty
thousand people who were very quiet and attentive and much affected. Went to
public worship morning and evening and at six, preached at Kennington. Such

---

[64] Wesley, *Journal*, ii. 167.   [65] Ibid., i. 173.

[66] *Letters* (OE), i. 616. the ascription of J. Clayton as the one to whom the letter was
addressed is unconvincing, and indeed improbable.

a sight I never saw before. I believe there were no less than fifty thousand people, and near fourscore coaches, besides great numbers of horses.[67]

The poor heard him gladly and gave of their little to the Orphan House.

Sunday May 13th. Preached this morning to a prodigious number of people in Moorfields and collected for the orphans £52. 19s. 6d. above £20 of which was in half-pence. Indeed, they almost wearied me in receiving their mites and they were more than one man could carry home.[68]

The most vivid accounts of these scenes were written in letters by Whitefield on an amazing London public holiday in May 1742. It was later painted by Eyre Crowe, but rather deserved a Hogarth, a Frith, or a John Martin. The scene was Moorfields where for 'many years past booths of all kinds have been erected for mountebanks, players, puppet shows and such like'. The early sermon was fairly quietly received, but by midday the fair was in full swing: 'drummers, trumpeters, Merry Andrews, masters of puppet shows, exhibitors of wild beasts . . . I was honoured with having a few stones, dirt, rotten eggs, and pieces of dead cats thrown at me.' There were demonstrations against him: a recruiting sergeant and his drummers, and the Merry Andrew with a whip. Similar scenes occurred next day at Marylebone, where a band of boys and girls sat at the preacher's feet, passing to him little notes, cries for help, and joyful testimonies, and these appeals soon stuffed and overflowed his pockets. Nor was it all noise. 'Three hundred and fifty awakened souls were received in one day, and I believe the number of notes exceeded a thousand.'[69] It was not all noise with John Wesley, either. In the end it is not the crying and emotion which impresses, but the thousands of occasions in all corners of England where the great crowds were abashed to silence, hanging on his words.

Wesley's visit to Bristol had done what Whitefield had hoped, and more. And not only were the converts now cared for in the societies of Nicholas and Baldwin Streets, but the building was put in hand of the commodious premises of the famous 'New Room'.

v. The 'Stillness' Controversy

The first reference to what became known as the 'Stillness' controversy is in Wesley's *Journal* for 1 November 1739, where he tells how on his return to London,

---

[67] Whitefield, *Journals*, p. 262.   [68] Dallimore, *Whitefield*, i. 291.

[69] Whitefield, *Letters* (1771, repr. 1776), ccccxi, ccccxii, 11 and 15 May 1742, pp. 384–8. There is a problem about the date, as Whit Monday was on 7 June 1742. It seems possible that he intended Eastertide. 1741 is ruled out by the second letter.

the first person I met was [Mrs Turner] whom I had left strong in the faith and in good works: but now she told me Mr. Molther had fully convinced her she never had any faith at all: and had advised her until she received faith, to be "still," ceasing from outward works.

Wesley saw in this the very mystical fallacies to which he himself had once been attracted, and now had to face the serious effects of such teaching on his converts and those of Whitefield. Philip Molther was an Alsatian, a people not given to emotionalism, and he had been deeply shocked by the noisy goings on at Fetter Lane. 'The very first time I entered their meeting, I was alarmed and almost terror stricken at hearing their sighing and groaning, their whinings and howlings which strange proceeding they called the demonstration of spirit and power.'[70] To Molther this seemed to be due to an erroneous conception of the experience of salvation. He saw in it the fruit of the Pietist insistence on a long struggle for true penitence. The joyous testimonies to the fruits of conversion he was inclined (like William Law) to put down to animal spirits. The remedy was to insist on the passivity with which the soul must await Christ, and the need, if be, to cease from outward good works, from what Wesley unscripturally (but with the Prayer Book) called 'the means of grace'.

Now Wesley had taken his doctrine of conversion from Peter Böhler (though he found confirmation of it in Article XI and the *Homily of Salvation*), both in regard to the nature of saving faith, and in the instantaneous conversion of sinners. But the 'Stillness' teaching is not to be written off, as is generally done, as an aberration of Molther. Its implications are to be found in Zinzendorf. Nor did Zinzendorf get it from the teaching of Luther, even the young Luther. It is true that Luther's *Galatians* stresses the passivity with which the soul receives grace, that he depreciates reason in comparison with faith, and says little (at this time) of the relevance of the law for Christians, so that one can understand how Wesley was shocked when he read it at this time and thought it the root of the Moravian errors. But there are some very un-Luther-like doctrines in Zinzendorf. Though he has a doctrine of the Word, and gives a high value to Holy Communion, the doctrine of the Word has not for him the centrality it has for Luther, nor are the sacraments for him mediated through the Word. His teaching about the coming of Christ to the soul and the role of the Holy Spirit is much nearer to the doctrine of the 'inner word'—not balanced as it is in Augustine's *Spirit and Letter*, or in Luther by association with the 'outer word', but more like the spiritualism of radicals such as Hans Denck and

---

[70] Benham, *Memoirs*, p. 53.

Sebastian Franck.[71] This appears plainly in the sermons which Zinzendorf would preach at Fetter Lane in 1746.

When a man is begotten again, it is just as if a wind should come (John 3. 7)—the immediate begetting of God is such a secret, sudden, unknown reality, hidden from the eyes of all mankind, that it can never be described.[72]

It is never the responsibility of the preacher that one is awakened, but rather the Holy Spirit acted at least a minute, an instant before the word touched me . . . the Holy Spirit has done everything beforehand: everything invisible, everything inexpressible, everything that happens in the spirit of the mind, everything that takes place in the soul, out of which faith may arise—the Holy Spirit has inspired all this . . . the word is nothing other than the explanation of the truth which already lies in the heart . . . The Word of God is the food The eternal Word is Christ.[73]

. . . they ought not drive away their consternation, their perplexity, their restlessness, with something else or escape by some strange means. Rather they must hold still for the Holy Spirit who always keeps his eye on them until He can note his time . . . consternation, perplexity and restlessness must remain. Whoever gets rid of them on his own, be it through a spiritual or a temporal or any other circumstance, through a spiritual hymn or book, and although it were the Bible itself, for this man at this time it is poison.[74]

His frequent absences from London did not enable Wesley to control the situation, or even to realize that he was facing a takeover bid from the Moravians which had every chance of being successful. Fetter Lane had been the centre of Wesley's work in London, and since 1 May 1738 he was naturally regarded as one of the leaders of the renewed Society. He had sent regular reports to Fetter Lane on his travels, by his right-hand man, James Hutton. But now Hutton turned from John Wesley—whom his mother had described as 'my son's Pope'—and gave even more unbounded commitment to Zinzendorf. He went to Germany (where soon the Moravians would choose him a Swiss wife) and was thereafter the leading English Moravian. There must have been some small personal crisis in his change of affection and it colours his description of the ensuing troubles, which he blamed on Wesley's ambition to dominate.[75]

It was evident that Moravian influence was gaining ground, not only

[71] E. G. Rupp, 'Word and Spirit in the First Years of the Reformation', *ARG* 1958, pp. 13ff.

[72] Zinzendorf, *Nine Lectures*, p. 28.   [73] Ibid., p. 51.   [74] Ibid., p. 57.

[75] There are waspish comments in his letters to Zinzendorf: '"J. W. and C. W." are dangerous snares to many young women: several are in love with them: I wish they were once married to some good sisters, but I would not give them one of my sisters if I had any.'

in London, but in Bristol. Although the Brethren made a great point of never proselytizing, this applied to other Churches, and not to Religious Societies, and it was now evident that the Moravian leaders had come to the conclusion that the Wesleys were not fitted for the direction of souls. In London there was a group of leading English members of the Fetter Lane Society which was restive about the connection with the Church of England talking about 'raising a church'. To John Wesley the Moravians were now a menace, rather like the Triffids in the science-fiction story, a shapeless mass ever advancing, infiltrating, engulfing, swallowing his converts.

He had indeed a foothold elsewhere, for he had begun a society in the ruins of the old cannon 'Foundery' near Moorfields, at the end of 1739, which by June 1740 had 300 members. But by then Wesley felt that a crisis had come and he took steps to bring matters to a head.

First, he made clear to his followers (and to himself) just what the issues were. This he did in a series of early morning sermons at the Foundery. They were generally extempore, based on notes, but he robed for these early services at 5.30 or 6 a.m. It might seem over-dramatic to compare them with the sermons which Luther preached in Wittenberg in March 1522 when his movement, too, was faced with a takeover, but it is arguable that just as much was now at stake, the future of a great communion. And in both cases it could be said that it was a personal crisis, as important as the matter of the sermons.

He began with the words of Jeremiah, 'Stand ye in the way, ask for the old paths', and described the old way as the proclamation of salvation by faith alone.

But eight or nine months ago, certain men arose, speaking contrary to the doctrines we had received. They affirmed that we were in the wrong way still: that we had no faith at all . . . they affirmed also that there is no commandment in the New Testament but 'to believe': that no other duty lies upon us: that when a man does believe . . . he is not subject to ordinances . . . indeed there is no such thing as any 'means of grace'.[76]

In his second address he affirmed that there are commandments in the New Testament. In the third he spoke of Christian, as distinct from Jewish, ordinances, and in the next talks stressed the importance of prayer, reading the Scriptures, and finally Holy Communion, which he declared to be (appealing to the experience of people present) a converting, as well as a confirming, ordinance. But it seemed that Wesley was losing this battle. On 2 July he went to Fetter Lane, 'but I found their hearts quite estranged.' Finally, on 20 July he attended the

[76] *Journal*, ii. 354ff.

Fetter Lane Love Feast and read a short paper declaring the 'Stillness' doctrines to be 'flatly contradictory to the Word of God', after which he walked out saying 'Ye that are of the same judgment follow me!' Only eighteen did so, but three days later he noted:

Our little company met at the Foundery instead of Fetter Lane. About twenty-five of our Brethren, God hath given us already all of whom think and speak the same: seven or eight and forty likewise of the fifty women that were in band desired to cast in their lot with us.[77]

The walk-out shook the Moravians, who got in touch with Zinzendorf. He told them to apologize. They seemed to think of the affair in personal terms of a hurt and offended Wesley, but he disregarded what seemed to him an offhand and formal apology. Henceforward the two communities went their separate ways. Fetter Lane became a wholly Moravian society and eventually a congregation of the Unitas Fratrum. Wesley joined together the little remnant from Fetter Lane with his Foundery Society, and with those in Bristol they became the 'United Societies' for which he drew up significant rules. But it had been a close-run thing and it left its mark on Wesley's future dealings with the Moravians.

For those dealings continued, if only because in Bristol, in the Midlands, and in Yorkshire there was still the overlap of Methodists and Moravians. Wesley now wrote a long letter to Herrnhut, explaining the grounds of his dissent from the Moravians, to which a reply was sent defending their position.[78]

It confirmed, rather than satisfied, Wesley's fears and criticisms. These he was to repeat at some vehemence in a letter to George Stonehouse, who had turned Moravian and whose wealthy wife became an adopted daughter of Zinzendorf.[79] But in public Wesley was more restrained. In May 1741 he had talks with his former friends, Böhler and Spangenberg, and this paved the way for the Latin conversation with Zinzendorf which took place in Lincoln's Inn on 3 September 1741.[80] But Wesley was taken aback by the consequences which Zinzendorf drew from the Lutheran view that all the righteousness of the Christian derives from the *justitia aliena* of Christ. Moreover Zinzendorf denied that renewal in grace of the new man involved a growth in sanctification, and he repudiated the idea that the law stood

---

[77] *Journal*, ii. 371. He had been accompanied to the confrontation by William Seward and by the Countess of Huntingdon.

[78] *Journal*, ii. 496. For the reply, see the summary in M. Schmidt, *John Wesley* (Zurich 1966), ii. 1. 45.

[79] 27 Nov. 1750: *Letters* (OE), ii. 441.

[80] *Journal*, ii. 487; *Schmidt*, ii. 1. 56.

over and against Christians as duty and demand. But what angered
Zinzendorf was what Wesley began to expound as Christian perfection,
the possibility that Christians might in this life attain the goal of perfect
love of God and man. Had the two men been able and willing to
continue the conversation for a fortnight, or had there ever been serious
conversations over a period between all the leaders on both sides,
misunderstandings might have been removed. As it was they hardened,
and when Wesley published the fourth part of the *Journal* in June 1744 he
did so with a preface addressed to the Moravians which gave great
offence to them. Yet neither side wished entirely to repudiate the other,
and in 1745 there was an abortive attempt to bring all the leaders
together.

Henceforth the leaders kept clear of one another, while the comments
of the rank and file, on both sides, to judge from Hutton and John
Nelson, were acid and hostile. Zinzendorf had now written Wesley off
as an exponent of legalistic Pietism, quite underestimating the strength
of the English religious tradition in which Wesley's idea of holiness was
steeped. The Moravians prided themselves on not answering back when
attacked from outside, but they twice printed advertisements dissociating themselves from the Methodists. The only witty remark in the
whole affair came when Hutton was asked by Lord Shelburne, 'What is
your footing with the Methodists?', to which he replied 'They kick us
whenever they can.' But in his last years Wesley was delighted to
resume relations with Hutton and Gambold. The discussions conducted
by the Moravian, La Trobe, and Coke and Charles Wesley in 1784 about
the possibility of union between the two bodies, had, as we shall see, an
ulterior motive in the crisis in which the Methodists were placed in
relation to the Church of England. In one letter La Trobe, who steered
clear of John Wesley, made the remark, which no doubt derived from
the Zinzendorfian tradition, that John Wesley did not understand
salvation and had never been converted.

vi.   Predestination

Before Whitefield's departure from America, after his astonishing eight
months' mission, there were ominous tensions between the two leaders.
For one thing Whitefield was at first puzzled and then offended by the
extraordinary emotional manifestations which attended the preaching
and speaking of John Wesley. These, which are sometimes called,
though hardly explained, psycho-physical phenomena, happened
most frequently with John's preaching at the beginning of the Revival,
though they never completely ceased, and were also to be found in the

Revivals in America and Wales, and in Scotland at Cambuslang and Kilsyth. One such scene he vividly described in a report to the Fetter Lane Society.

The power of God fell upon us. One, and another, and another sunk to the earth. You might seem the dropping on all sides as thunderstruck. One cried out aloud. I went and prayed over her and she received joy in the Holy Ghost. A second falling into the same agony, we turned to her . . . a young woman was seized with such pangs as I never saw before. And in a quarter of an hour she had a new song in her mouth.[81]

Wesley always allowed for the fact that there were natural and physical causes at work, though he thought the proportion much higher in the case of the French Prophets who had made such happenings into the hallmark of 'enthusiasm'. But he also admitted that some seemed to be the work of the Devil (and he records cases which in many centuries would have been thought to demand exorcism). He was still more convinced that behind it all was the work of God himself, bringing men and women to agonized self-recognition and, through the distress of repentance, to the joy of conversion and the peace of sins forgiven. For a time at least he seems to have looked on these things as 'signs' which did not embarrass him. He loved nothing better than to take down and record such case histories in his *Journal* and there are hundreds of pages about them which the modern reader tends to skip, but which provided ammunition for his critics. Charles Wesley was much more sceptical. He kept a bucket of water in plain view and put the noisier ladies at the back, preferably out of sight, with evident results.

In the same letter (25 June 1739) in which Whitefield, had raised with Wesley the problem of these emotional happenings, he had raised another matter and one which was fatefully to divide the Methodists, and for a time to estrange the two leaders—Predestination.

The doctrine had been intermittently the theme of detailed controversy. The debates between the time of Augustine and the Council of Orange (529), and the medieval debates of the fourteenth and fifteenth centuries are probably more intricate and profound than those of the seventeenth and eighteenth centuries. It was the final edition of Calvin's *Institutes* (1559) which made the doctrine once again a divisive theme and it was further systematized by Beza and Zanchius. The doctrine became central to English Puritanism, and was given a normative expression in the writings of William Perkins. Nearly all evangelical Puritans regarded it as an integral part of the doctrine of salvation, and there were eminent Calvinists among the bishops, such as Davenant and Morley.

---

[81] *Letters*, i. 640.

On the positive side there were many Christians who, like Luther, found the notion of 'Election' very full of comfort. Those who believed and proclaimed it felt it to be of the essence of the truth of free grace, namely, salvation does not depend on a human, but upon a divine, initiative: that when a man responds to the grace of God the divine promises are irrevocably at work within him. God will not let him go. And it seemed to those who thought this way that Wesley's doctrine of assurance—that a man may only know by faith that he is at that moment in a state of salvation—under-valued the certainty of the divine promises, since such an assurance must rest upon an unchanging divine will to accept the sinner, which could not stop short of his final perseverance. To those who associated Arminianism with the kind of rationalist, half-way houses of Anglican Establishment, low-church, and incipiently Socinian, the notion of an evangelical Arminianism seemed a strange innovation, against the grain of a formidable and long-established Protestant tradition. Neither Whitefield nor his young disciple, John Cennick, had read much Calvin. But in the west of England and Wales and in the Dissenting tradition (to which Whitefield was more open than Wesley) it is evident that there were aggressive predestinarians who were offended by the Wesleys. And in the next months Whitefield's susceptibility to this interpretation of the gospel was reinforced by the Calvinist background of the Awakening in Wales, in Scotland, and in America.

Wesley, from his youth up, had believed that the offer of salvation was for all mankind. He and his parents were agreed in repudiating the doctrine of Predestination. But in 1739[82] he found that his teaching was arousing opposition from within his societies, and it seems indeed that this was a ground swell, independent of the teaching of the leaders. At the end of April 1739 Wesley began to read and write about the problem. And he recorded how, before he left London for Bristol, 'our brother Whitefield here, and our Brother Chapman since, had conjured me to enter into no disputes, least of all concerning Predestination, because this people was so deeply prejudiced for it.'[83]

But when he got to Bristol, he found that a letter had been circulating in which Wesley was charged with 'resisting and perverting the truth', while in another the writer warned against Wesley as a false teacher.[84]

Wesley had not begun to stir up the issue, but in his letter of 30 April he told the London brethren how 'I was led, I know not how, to speak strongly and explicitly of predestination.'[85]

---

[82] A. Coppedge, 'John Wesley and the Doctrine of Predestination' (Cambridge University Dissertation 1976), pp. 20ff.

[83] *Letters* (OE), i. 639.   [84] Ibid. i. 639.   [85] Ibid. i. 640.

On 28 April he wrote and soon after preached his famous sermon on 'Free Grace' and in the next weeks, when preparing it for publication, he seems to have read the hyper-Calvinist works of the Particular Baptist Dr John Gill.[86] It was certainly the hyper-Calvinist view which Wesley attacked in the sermon. With ruthless logic Wesley tore into the implications of it for the character of God himself and for the mixture of fatalism and Antinomianism which it must involve to those who believed it. The sermon is full of savage irony and towards the end there is a flamboyant dialogue between God and the Devil, who expresses his delight at such doctrines. It was what we might call the Screwtape portion of the sermon which gave most offence. The sermon was not numbered among the normative 'Forty-Four' sermons, but in its contents and in their effect is one of the most important of his utterances.[87]

Whitefield wrote to Wesley from America and he begged Wesley 'for Christ's sake, Sir, if possible, never speak against election in your sermons.'[88]

In a letter of 9 August 1740 Wesley tried to find some providential meaning in their dispute.

The case is quite plain. There are bigots both for Predestination and against it. God is sending a message to those on either side; but neither will receive it unless from one of their own opinion. Therefore for a time, you are suffered to be of one opinion and I of another. But when his time is come, God will do what man cannot, make us both of one mind. Then persecution will flame out and it will be seen whether we count our lives dear unto ourselves, so that we may finish our course with joy.[89]

On Whitefield's return from America the two men met face to face and there was plain speaking (28 March 1741). The affair was complicated by a row about the young John Cennick whom Wesley had first met at his home in Reading and who had been appointed to teach at the colliers' school at Kingswood. Cennick held the doctrine of election firmly and made no bones about his dislike of Wesley's doctrine of perfection, which he described as Popery. The result was a grievous division within the Kingswood Society, from which it never quite recovered. On 6 March Wesley bade the people choose between them, and fifty-two seceded with Cennick, ninety remaining with Wesley. Wesley based his action, not on the doctrinal differences between them, but on the intrigue which had led Cennick to denounce the Wesleys to

---

[86] 'Free Grace', Sermon cxxviii; Wesley, *Works*, vii. 356ff.
[87] *Journal*, ii. 184 n.   [88] Whitefield, *Letters*, cxix, 25 June 1740.
[89] Wesley, *Letters* (OE), i. 31.

Whitefield in a letter seen by many, and for his equivocal behaviour when challenged. Meanwhile Whitefield had himself published a counterblast to the Wesley sermon and appended to it the Articles of the Church of England and a mildly predestinarian hymn of Isaac Watts.

Plainly, and sometimes very emotionally, Whitefield might upbraid John Wesley, but there was never any discourtesy, and always the undertone of deference going back to his undergraduate days. But Whitefield and the Wesleys (Charles was the fiercer about Calvinism) were deeply divided on a point of conscience. Wesley had needed to act vigorously to save his societies for the evangelicalism which he could claim to have been their original gospel. There had therefore to be a separation and a division of the work, and a price paid for the divided front and inevitable recriminations, which were perhaps more bitter among the rank and file than among the leaders. Eventually the personal friendship would be resumed. Wesley himself was willing to make doctrinal concessions of a surprising kind and later was to come to an accommodating silence about predestination, not least when he went to Scotland. But, we shall see, this was not the end of the Predestination controversy, which was to be still more vehement after Whitefield's death. There were now two camps in London and in Bristol, and Whitefield's friends had established a temporary 'Tabernacle' a few hundred yards from Wesley's Foundery in 1741. In 1742 Whitefield, had a paper, the *Weekly History*, which carried news of the Revival in America and England.

vii. Opposition to the Methodists

(a) 'The Lamb that Troubles the Waters'

Between 1739 and 1743 the Methodists spread across the nation with astonishing speed and tenacity. Newcastle was the apex of the great triangle, Bristol, London, the north. Wherever they went, they aroused opposition, and there were major incidents of violence. Among these the chief were: in the west St Ives, Falmouth, Exeter, Plymouth, Devizes; in the Midlands Wednesbury, Darlaston, Walsall, Dudley, Derby, and Newark; in the north Rochdale, Bolton, Sheffield, Manchester, and Grimsby; in Norwich, Evesham, and Shoreham, Kent. Such violence was sporadic, and unco-ordinated, rarely spontaneous, and might often have been stopped in its tracks by the clergy and magistrates, who too often connived at, and in many cases engineered, what happened, which often got out of hand and beyond control. 'September 22nd (1740) Mr. C. Wesley was informed that the colliers had risen: and riding out from Bristol, he met about a thousand of them at Lawrence Hill. The occasion of their rising was, the dearness of Corn.'[90]

The historian will find much to ponder in this confrontation where the recently converted colliers argued with their demonstrating fellow workers. But it is a reminder that in all countries of Europe there was a ground swell of sporadic rioting. And within living memory the Dissenters and the Quakers had been the subject of such violence as led the latter to record poignantly their 'Book of Sufferings'.

There were obvious reasons why such violence should be turned against the Methodists.[91] In the isolated communities of north and west, amid the hills and dales, or in the *bocage* country of Cornwall and Devonshire, the advent of fiery young preachers, with unfamiliar accents, affronted the natural conservatism of village people and easily roused the passions of the rougher new industrial communities at a time when there was no public press nor organized police force, and when rumours could run wild.

In the tense months before the '45, there were those who readily believed that the Methodist preachers were Papists, Jesuits in disguise, or at the very least Jacobites (there were more Jacobites in cathedral stalls than among the Methodists), while in Ireland their vehement and obvious Protestantism brought vicious reprisal for an opposite reason.

Every Sunday [said Charles Wesley], damnation is denounced by some of the clergy against all who hear us: for we are Papists, Jesuits, seducers and bringers in of the Pretender . . . yet will not the world bear, that we should talk of persecution: No: for the world now is Christian . . . some lose their bread, some, their habitations: one suffers stripes another confinement: yet we must not call this persecution! Doubtless they will find some other name for it . . . it is always the lamb that troubles the waters.[92]

The modern historian seems to have found that other word. It is 'culture shock' which describes the natural reaction of eighteenth-century communities to the intrusion of a disturbing alien element. But this seems to throw the onus for violence upon the victims rather than the aggressors. It is a useful word, and it draws attention to genuine elements in the situation. But it can also be applied to the Nazi holocausts, to apartheid and the Klu Klux Klan, and to soccer hooligans. It tells us nothing of the point at which resentment breaks out into violence, nor does any list of rational underlying causes touch the root

[90] H. Moore, *Life of the Revd John Wesley* (2 vols. 1824), i. 527.
[91] J. Walsh, 'Methodism and the Mob in the Eighteenth Century', *Studies in Church History*, ed. D. Baker (1972), 213ff.; L. F. Church, *More about the Early Methodist People* (1949), ch. 11, D. D. Wilson, *Many Waters Cannot Quench*, 1969.
[92] Moore, *Life*, i. 517.

of the problem, the fundamental irrationality of group misbehaviour.

It is true that there were a handful of cases (Wesley admitted it) where the Methodists asked for trouble, when they hit back or even fired shots. More often their real offence was when tactless young preachers inveighed against the local clergy, setting up their pitch within yards of the parish church. It is also suggested that the accounts of their harassments were exaggerated by preachers to the Methodist audiences— though little evidence is given, and one is driven to the 'Name Three!' response. For the leaders were aware of the danger, even of talking of what was going on.

I might advise you [said John Wesley] not to talk much of what you suffer . . . do it as seldom as you can with a safe conscience. For beside its tendency to inflame them, it has the appearance of evil, of ostentation, of magnifying yourselves . . . to make you think yourselves some great ones . . . it is at best, loss of time: for instead of the wickedness of men, you might be talking of the goodness of God.[93]

And in fact no list of reasonable causes for the outbreak of violence dare ignore the sad fact to which all centuries, not least our own, bear witness, that it is the innocent and the vulnerable who seem somehow to stir up what is most evil in group violence. How right was Charles Wesley: 'It is always the lamb that troubles the waters.'

But the Methodists did not grow in such numbers simply because they denounced the Establishment. At the height of the very ugly troubles at Devizes when the least harmful element was water from the fire engines which was played on the cowering Methodists, breaking their windows, spoiling their goods, Charles Wesley tells us how

The Mayor's maid came, and told us her mistress was in tears about me: and begged me to disguise myself in women's clothes . . . her heart had been turned towards us by the conversion of her son, just on the brink of ruin . . . instead of running away to sea, he entered the Society.[94]

The troubles were soon over in Bristol and in London, where the magistrates were susceptible to pressure from a Government at whose head was a King known to be an enemy to persecution. The London mob which, from the time of the Sacheverell Case to the later Gordon Riots, could rage like a roaring lion, was kindlier to the Methodists than to the Dissenters, save for the connived disturbances against Whitefield in Long Acre, and the abuses and pelting in Moorfields. In the more remote and isolated parts of England and Wales it was another story.

Inevitably, the leaders attracted violence. Whitefield had his share of

---

[93] Moore, *Life*, ii. 91.   [94] Ibid. ii. 78.

it. He was not naturally brave and on one occasion it was his wife's encouragement that made him stand his ground. Howell Harris suffered again and again from mindless brutalities, which shattered his health, and his fellow traveller, William Seward, lost his eye and then his life, to become the proto-martyr of the movement. John Wesley himself had that apostolic quality which the New Testament calls *parrēsia*. When he heard of the riots in Wednesbury, he went directly there, and a few days later his brother followed him.

We cannot forbear to quote the famous incident, when the mobs of Darlaston and Walsall came together in October 1743 and Wesley, who a few moments before had been quietly writing in a Methodist home, was dragged out into a frightening scene.

To attempt speaking was in vain, for the noise on every side was like the roaring of the sea. So they dragged me along till we came to the town where, seeing the door of a large house open, I attempted to go in: but a man, catching me by the hair pulled me back into the middle of the mob. . . . At the west end of the town, seeing a door open I made toward it and would have gone in, but a gentleman in the shop would not suffer me, saying they would pull the house to the ground. However I stood at the door and asked 'Are you willing to hear me speak?' Man cried out 'No! No! knock his brains out, down with him: kill him at once.' Others said 'Nay but we will hear him first.' I began asking 'What evil have I done? Which of you all have I wronged in word and deed?' and continued speaking for above a quarter of an hour, till my voice suddenly failed. Then the floods began to lift up their voice again, many crying out 'Bring him away! Bring him away!'[95]

Charles Wesley had a habit of steering for the sound of the guns, making up fine hymns on his way hither and thither. His experiences varied from comedy to near disaster: sick comedy, as when a parish clerk advanced on him as he came forward to take Communion, and thrusting a huge Prayer Book in his face cried, 'Avaunt Satan!'[96]

At Birstall, in the time of the '45, Charles Wesley was told there was a warrant out against him for treason. He at once demanded a hearing before the magistrates (one of them a clergyman). But the witnesses melted away and the only evidence was that Wesley had prayed that God would bring home 'his banished ones'. He demanded to be given the oaths of allegiance, but was excused by the now embarrassed authorities. But it was one thing to be Charles Wesley, a Student of Christ Church who at Birstall handed over copies of his university sermons, and who on another occasion in Ireland found the magistrate to have been a contemporary of his at the House. It was quite another

---

[95] *Journal*, iii. 99.   [96] Moore, *Life*, ii. 21.

thing for some of the lay preachers, of little affluence and no standing at all. And it was another thing for the good Methodist people, who had sought and found God, to have their windows smashed, their meeting-house razed to the ground, their shops spoiled, and their women assaulted or insulted.[97] For the mobs were not decent citizens on the spree, but included an element of vicious bullies, brave with alcohol, but often preferring to act in cowardly isolation as when they waylaid 'Swaddler John' Smith in Ireland and left him by the roadside to die of a fearful pitchfork wound.

There were the inevitable lesser harassments, as when farm labourers lost their jobs, or servants were dismissed, and there is a long list of Methodist preachers who were impressed into the forces. Not all of these gave soft answers, though none was a greater trouble to the authorities than the non-violent John Nelson. Sometimes the Methodist women showed their mettle, like the large and godly lady who stood between a mob and the preacher brandishing a large poker—or the band of Methodist women who scared the daylights out of a group of drunken dragoons and put to flight the army of aliens.

At first the Methodist preachers, as members of the Church of England, seemed beyond the protection of the law, and when Wesley, who was reluctant to have them licensed as Dissenters under the Toleration Act, saw this as the only remedy, he sometimes managed to get the terms of the licence to bear an equivocal description. When the Methodists sought redress at law, and especially when they pressed as far as the King's Bench, they were often successful, but these affairs were long drawn out and expensive. Sometimes the magistrates were helpful, but a minority were actively hostile, especially when allied with the small number of 'rent-a-mob' parsons, and were at the heart of some of the ugliest scenes. At Devizes the Curate, Mr Innys, stood in the street with the mob. He had been about the town several days, stirring up the people, and canvassing the gentry for their vote and interest. At Dudley one of the Justices said

it was the best thing the mob ever did, so to treat the Methodists: and he would give five pounds to drive them from the country.

Another, when our brother Ward begged his protection, delivered him up to the mercy of the mob who had half murdered him before, and throwing his hat round his head, cried 'Huzza, boys. Well done! Stand up for the Church!'

And there was the notorious George White of Colne who issued a proclamation in military terms enlisting men for 'the defence of the

[97] J. Wesley, *A Farther Appeal to Men of Reason and Religion, Works* (OE), ed. G. R. Cragg, ii. 282.

Church of England' and bidding them to repair to the drumhead at the Cross, 'where each man shall have a pint of ale for advance'.[98] These disturbances were at their liveliest during the 1740s, but were liable to blow up at any time, as in the curious affray at Perronet's Shoreham, in Kent. They happened when the Methodists advanced into new areas, as Adam Clarke found when he took the cause of Methodism to the Channel Islands later in the century. The Methodists of Gibraltar have in their museum a cat-o'-nine-tails commemorating how a Methodist sergeant, a private, and a drummer boy were sentenced to 500 lashes for attending a Methodist class meeting.

Modern Methodists decorously singing, would be astonished to know that some of the most joyful, and indeed peaceful, of their hymns were written in the midst of riots, that the splendid

> Angels our servants are,
> And keep in all our ways,
> And in their watchful hands they bear
> The sacred sons of grace

emerged from the exceptionally vicious riots in Dublin, that 'Ye servants of God, your Master proclaim' was part of a special collection of hymns to be sung 'in times of tumult', and that

> Worship, and thanks, and blessing,
> And strength ascribe to Jesus!
> Jesus alone defends his own,
> When earth and hell oppress us

came to Charles Wesley on horseback as he rode away from an ugly scene where mob and gentry had literally unloosed the dogs of war and set a pack of hounds at them. Sometimes, it seems, a culture needs a shock.

(b) 'Great Argument'

'Sticks and stones may break my bones, but words never hurt me.' But for the first Methodists it is true that but for the words there might have been fewer sticks and stones. It was from the pulpit and in print that the incentive came. John Wesley could plausibly say, 'Nor have I known any considerable riot in any part of England for which such preaching did not pave the way.'[99]

There was, after all, a case against the Methodists. It is not our purpose to try to disentangle what was true and plausible from what is

---

[98] Moore, *Life*, ii. 25; L. F. Church, *More about the Early Methodist People*, 1949.

[99] J. Wesley, 'A Second Letter to the author of *The Enthusiasm of the Methodists . . .*', *Works*, (OE), xi. 383.

obviously false and malicious. But it is important to realize why good
and conscientious English churchmen, like Bishop Gibson and 'John
Smith', were shocked and affronted by what they understood to be the
message and the methods of the leaders of the Evangelical Revival.[100]

The pamphlet war began with the publication in 1739 of Whitefield's
first *Journal*.[101] When this was followed by John Wesley's *Journal* there
was ample material for critical minds to feed upon. And while the desire
to be open and honest, and to edify their own followers, had to be
admitted, the early apologias gave hostages to fortune and may have
done their movements as much harm as good. Whitefield himself came
deeply to regret many of the things in his first writings. There was a
preoccupation with his mission and his sense of divine impulsion, and
attacks upon the faith and morals of the clergy which could not but give
offence, even to those given to lamenting the poor state of religion.
More dubious, and in fact stupid, were letters in which Whitefield
attacked two of the staples of contemporary theological diet, Tillotson's
sermons and *The Whole Duty of Man*. For the saying that the saintly
Archbishop 'knew no more of Christ than did Mahomet', Whitefield
blamed, probably correctly, an off-the-cuff remark of John Wesley in a
society meeting. But he had not needed to enlarge the subject. It should
be said that the depreciation of Tillotson as a Latitudinarian was part of
the high-church tradition which the Holy Club inherited, and that in the
eighteenth century it was the moralistic parts of Tillotson's sermons that
most people read, so that even Bishop Gibson seemed to feel that the
charge of moralism lay against him. But Whitefield's extracts ignored so
much evidence to the contrary that he almost forfeited the right to
complain when others meted out to him the same one-sided treatment.
It has to be said that he retracted, and that Wesley included not only *The
Whole Duty of Man* in his Christian Library, but (a little reluctantly) also
extracts from Tillotson. It was a foolish attack which at one blow
alienated friends, especially readers of the SPCK who rated both
authors highly.

In that year too there appeared the first anti-Methodist satirical poem,
and a farce, *The Mock Preacher*. This was a vein of literature which varied
much from misplaced humour to downright obscenity.

Although William Law and Edmund Gibson had attacked the stage

---

[100] R. Green, *Anti-Methodist Publications issued during the Eighteenth Century*, 1902;
D. H. Kirkham, 'Pamphlets Opposing the Methodists', Duke University Dissertation,
1973. One of the excellencies of Tyerman's biographies of Wesley and of Whitefield is
that he summarized the arguments of many pamphlets.

[101] The religious weekly, the *Weekly Miscellany*, kept up a continuous running fire of
criticism of the Revival.

and masquerades, Whitefield and Wesley seemed to have got across the acting profession and Whitefield was in serious trouble when he tried to preach in the heart of 'theatre land' in Long Acre. An extremity of abuse was reached with the salacious buffoonery of Samuel Foote's plays *The Minor* (1760) and *The Methodist*, in which Whitefield was ridiculed as 'Dr. Squintum'. In this middle period, too, there were many ballads and songs against the Methodists, good ammunition for the ridiculing mob. The many tracts by divines attacking the doctrines of Salvation by Faith, and the New Birth, and the supposed superior airs of the Methodists, were in the traditions of a century of clerical polemic, and generally undistinguished. And there was the almost universal cry that it was all 'Enthusiasm'.

It seems well to concentrate on one or two which John Wesley took so seriously that he spent much time and energy replying to them.[102] These were the obviously seriously and honourably intended works of divines like Thomas Church and John Smith, while he dared not ignore the influential writings of the Bishops, of Smalridge, Lavington, Gibson, and Warburton.

John Wesley shows a certain reticence in what he says in his printed *Journal* about his dealings with the Bishops. Thus he only gives the first part of his interview with Bishop Butler in August 1739, with the famous remark about Whitefield: 'Sir, the pretending to extraordinary revelations and gifts of the Holy Ghost is a horrid thing, a very horrid thing.' Wesley did not print what happened the next day when he was brought to book by the Bishop for traducing Dr Tucker, the Bishop's chaplain, for heresy. The Bishop told him that he had been guilty of 'great want of candour and Christian charity', and there are signs that Wesley felt he deserved the reprimand and took it to heart. In January 1758 he wrote a letter to a 'Gentleman at Bristol' in which he said:

one would not desire to hear any private person, of no great note in the Church or world, speak as it were *ex cathedra*, on a point wherein men of eminence, both for piety, learning and office have been so greatly divided. Though my judgment is nothing altered, yet I often condemn myself for my past manner of speaking on this head.[103]

Bishop Gibson dealt kindly with the Wesleys when they called on him, though he was understandably impatient at their insistence on re-baptizing laymen and Dissenters. It seems likely that it was the publication of Whitefield's *Journals* which first turned him against the

---

[102] *Works* (OE), vol. xi.
[103] Wesley, *Letters* (ed. Telford), iii. 245; F. Baker, 'John Wesley and Joseph Butler', *PWHS* xlii. 4 (May 1980), 94–100.

new movement, and this was aggravated by the increasing complaints of numbers of his clergy.

He had published a quite remarkable Pastoral Letter, *Against Luke-warmness on the one hand and Enthusiasm on the other*.[104] He attacked the moralists, those who 'are not likely to think of growing better . . . if they are not going forward, they are certainly going backwards.' And he made an admission which he perhaps would not have made a few years later: 'God forbid that in this profane and degenerate age everything that has an appearance of piety should not be considered in the most favourable light that it is capable of.'

He stressed that 'We are Christian preachers and not merely preachers of Morality.' He recommended preachers therefore to pay much attention to the doctrines of redemption, to what he calls 'The Mediatorial scheme—the whole work of our Redemption in Christ, particularly the two doctrines of Justification by Faith and our Sanctification by the Spirit'. He gave a list of those passages in the liturgy, in prayers and collects, where the inward role of the Holy Spirit is mentioned, and begged preachers to warn their hearers 'not to rest in a moral heathenism, but to aspire to Christian Perfections.' There is much in this to suggest that Gibson's was a slightly old-fashioned religion which dated back to the days of Patrick, Sharp, and Tenison rather than to the more arid and moralistic high and low church doctrines of the 1730s. And it helps us to understand how, when Wesley explained to him what he meant by Christian perfection, Gibson approved.

But the second half of the Pastoral Letter is ominously different. It is true that the extracts he gives from Whitefield's *Journals* are torn from their context, but it is also true that there is much that, on Whitefield's own admission, was brash and offensive. We had better admit that there was a good deal in the young Whitefield and in the mature Wesley which merited condemnation as irrationalist and imprudent enthusiasm. Gibson's Letter was deservedly well read and approved by his friend Isaac Watts. He followed it with a Fourth Pastoral Letter in which he repeated his earlier reproach, for he had not been appeased by the moderation of Whitefield's reply to him. Then in 1744 came the anonymous *Observations Upon the Conduct and Behaviour of a Certain Sect, usually distinguished by the name of Methodist*, which was generally ascribed to the Bishop, and which was distributed to the Religious Societies and to the clergy of more than one diocese. It now included an even longer catena of passages from the writings of Whitefield, Wesley, and Howell Harris. It included also an attack upon the Moravians,

---

[104] 1739.

whom it panicked. Finally, Gibson devoted his last charge to his clergy in 1747 to the Methodists, retracting nothing of his earlier indictments.

John Wesley's open *Letter to the Right Reverend the Lord Bishop of London* (1747) is therefore important for more than one reason. For he singles out from Gibson's attacks the really damaging charges—for example that they must be regarded as enemies who 'give shameful disturbances to the parochial clergy and use very unwarrantable methods to prejudice their people against them and to seduce their flocks from them.'[105] Wesley has little difficulty in refuting the charge that his doctrine of assurance involved the certainty of Final Perseverance, or that he taught 'sinless perfection'. Gibson, who stressed more and more the sufficiency of the regular worship of the Church, blamed the Methodists because 'they persuade the people that the established worship, with a regular attendance upon it, is not sufficient to answer the ends of devotion.' But why, then, did he patronize the Religious Societies, and why were there so many books like Nelson's and Hickes's books of extra-Prayer Book devotions? The Bishop had closed his letter with the words: 'Reverend Brothers, I charge you all, lift up your voice like a trumpet! And warn and arm and fortify all mankind—against a People called Methodists.'[106]

It gave Wesley a marvellous opening and the opportunity to write some of the most moving paragraphs he ever penned. 'Could your lordship discern no other enemies of the gospel of Christ? . . . are there no Papists, no Deists left in the land? . . . have the Methodists (so called) monopolized all the sins, as well as all the errors of the nation?'

Here are, in and near Moorfields, ten thousand poor souls for whom Christ died, rushing head-long into hell. Is Dr Bulkeley the parochial minister, both willing and able to stop them? If so let it be done, and I have no place in these parts . . . but if after all he has done and all he can do, they are still in the broad way to destruction, let me see if God will put a word even in my mouth.

He closed with the moving lines:

My Lord, the time is short. I am past the noon of life, and my remaining years flee away as a shadow. Your lordship is old and full of days, having passed the usual age of man. It cannot be long therefore before we shall both drop this house of earth, and stand naked before God; no, nor before we shall see 'the great white throne coming down from heaven and him that sitteth thereon.' On his left hand shall be those who are shortly to dwell in 'everlasting fire prepared for the devil and his angels'. In that number will be all who died in their sins.

---

[105] Wesley, *Works* (OE), xi. 336.
[106] Ibid. xi. 346–7.

And among the rest those whom you preserved from repentance. Will you then rejoice in your success?[107]

This was one of Wesley's most effective writings, and made a great impression. Rumour had it that it had deeply moved the old man. And Wesley later said that he had very good reason to believe that it had done so.

John Wesley's *An Earnest Appeal to Men of Reason and Religion* (1743) and the three parts of his *A Farther Appeal . . .* (1745)[108] were carefully written replies to most of the contemporary objections to the Methodists, their doctrines, and their methods. They persuaded many readers, not least by a reasonableness which more than offset the irrationalism, as it appeared to many to be, of some of the narratives in his *Journal*.

Among those who read them and were impressed by them was the clergyman who conducted a correspondence under the name 'John Smith'.[109]

The letters are the most interesting of all Wesley's encounters and dialogues, for they are between two Church of England men, rivals in learning, modest and courteous, not so much a confrontation as a continuing conversation. True, Smith thought Wesley mistaken, if sincere, and at the end he does not seem to have been reassured about the subjective doctrines of the Witness of the Spirit and the assurance of forgiveness, nor can he believe that the irregularities of John Wesley's itinerancy, still less the ministry of his lay preachers, can outbalance the harm they have done, by opening the door to even more grievous disorders. But if Wesley, too, has his obstinacies and perhaps obtuseness, in not really comprehending how shocking and abstruse some of his arguments really seemed, he does increasingly score points and in the course of it pens some of his finest apologetic.

What interests about 'Smith's' theological approach is what we might call its 'modernism'. He speaks for a generation which rated contemporary Anglican divinity much more highly than the thought of the past. Wesley appealed conscientiously to the Articles and Homilies of the Church of England, which he had subscribed according to their plain meaning. For Smith those old controversies about 'Calvinistical points' had been settled in the seventeenth century.[110] 'I know no divines of the

    [107] *Works* (OE), vol. xi. 351.   [108] Ibid.

    [109] H. Moore, *Life*, vol. ii, Appendix. The letters are printed in Wesley, *Works* (OE), vol. xxvi, Letters II, ed. F. Baker, pp. 138ff. and further refs. ad loc. There seems to be no evidence, and little likelihood, that 'John Smith' was Secker, at that time Bishop of Oxford.

    [110] Ibid., p. 143.

Church of England from Barrow, Sharp and Tillotson, to Smalridge, Clarke and Waterland and quite to this very day, who have gone back into the old and exploded expositions except yourself and Mr. Whitefield.'[111]

If there were a difference between the present Church and the Church of the Reformation, 'the presumption would lie in favour of the modern Church, for it would be much more probable that some truths might be brought to light, and some first hasty errors rectified, upon the increase of learning and growth of criticism.'[112] If one had to choose between Bishop Jewell and Archbishop Sharp, 'the reasonable presumption would have been in favour of that latter who had abundantly the best means of being accurate.'[113] He draws from this the conclusion that 'whatever partiality you, as a subscribing clergyman may have to ancient sermons published formerly under the name of Homilies, others free from all bias must be allowed to judge quite impartially between the more ancient and more modern sermons.' It is evident that he is uneasy with Article XI, with its clear reference both to the *Homily of Salvation* and to the doctrine of 'sola fide' and he tries to pin St Paul and the Reformers down to a narrow interpretation of the conflicts of their times, the inference being that Paul was attacking the Jewish law, and the Reformers the doctrine of merit, robbing both arguments of their relevance to the eighteenth-century Church. His definition of faith as 'a rational assent and moral virtue'[114] is a rationalist one which belongs to the age of Samuel Clarke, and it is plain that John Wesley here is much nearer to the definition of the *Homily of Salvation*. But Wesley, too, has some trouble in finding all he wants for his definition in Hebrews 11:1 and has to stand some battering for his own suggestion that it is 'a supernatural conviction of the things of God, with a filial confidence in His love.'[115]

Smith, in the contemporary manner, would distinguish sharply between the ordinary and extraordinary gifts of the Spirit, and this is apparent when he comes to the eighth chapter of Romans, and especially 8:16 concerning the witness of the Spirit. He will only allow an 'imperceptible witness' for Christians since the apostolic age, and Wesley has him at this point when he asks how such a witness can be imperceptible? When Wesley cites the *Confessions* of St Augustine,[116] Smith dismisses Augustine as a 'flighty and injudicious' author, 'flighty and Rapturous', while he similarly shrugs off a plain testimony from St Bernard that he 'was somewhat enthusiastically given'.[117]

[111] Ibid., p. 169. [112] Ibid., p. 143. [113] Ibid., p. 143.
[114] Ibid., p. 139. [115] Ibid., p. 159. [116] Ibid., p. 186.
[117] Ibid., p. 240.

It is plain that the great Christian tradition of inwardness means nothing to him: 'almost every error that has crept into the church has owed its true rise more or less to rhetorical heightening.'[118] He elicits from Wesley the good story of how his dying father had spoken to him of the importance of the inward witness, while about his own attainment of perfect love Wesley makes the very significant admission 'I no more imagine that I have already attained, that I already love God with all my heart, soul and strength, than that I am in the third heaven.'[119]

Deeply convinced is 'John Smith' of the paramount evil of irregularity.

If we cast up the account at a hundred years' end we shall find the loss exceed the profit . . . whoever should be suffered to look out of his grave the middle of next century will find, I believe that the orderly preaching at St. Luke's and St. Giles' Church . . . has done more good and abundant less harm than the disorderly preaching at Kennington and Moorfields.[120]

Neither he nor Wesley could know that in fact in 1850 there would be in existence a third and a fourth generation of Methodist descendants of men who had plucked up stones to cast at Wesley, or that by that time many millions of men and women in many lands and continents would give thanks, under God, for him.

But Wesley's own answer was not a bad one. 'I am not careful for what may be a hundred years hence. He who governed the world before I was born shall take care of it likewise when I am dead. My part is to improve the present moment.'[121] Rather than admit that Wesley might be an instrument of grace, for the conversion of souls, 'Smith' in Wesley's word 'wriggles' to suggest other reasons, the novelty and sensation of field preaching, and in the end he weakly suggests that the Revival is due to 'your natural knack of persuasion, that you speak with much awakening warmth and earnestness, that God has blessed you with a strength of constitution equal to the indefatigable industry of your mind.'[122]

Wesley's final reply is: 'it is only the gospel of Jesus Christ which is the power of God to salvation. Human wisdom, as human laws may restrain from outward sin: but they cannot avail to the saving of the soul.'[123]

You know no call I have to preach up and down, to play the part of an itinerant evangelist. Perhaps you do not. But I do: I know God hath required this at my

---

[118] Ibid., p. 187. [119] Ibid., p. 294. [120] Ibid., p. 212.
[121] Ibid., p. 235. [122] Ibid., p. 213. [123] Ibid., p. 289.

hands . . . I know and feel that the spring of this is a deep conviction that it is the will of God.[124]

In an ironical passage John Smith suggested that Wesley felt called to the 'apostolate of England'. But one hundred years thence men would think that something rather like that had indeed been going on.

Gibson and 'John Smith' are a far cry from the writings of Lavington and Warburton. George Lavington (1684–1762) was a Fellow of New College who had, like so many, come there from Winchester and had held several livings and dignities before being appointed Bishop of Exeter. His public enmity towards the Methodists dated from the moment when somebody printed what purported to be an extract from his charge to his clergy, which attacked moralist preaching and commended the preaching of Christ 'and him crucified'. It is sometimes said that this was a Methodist practical joke, but Methodists (alas!) were not given to jokes of any kind. But it was printed and then disclaimed by Whitefield and by the Stewards of the Foundery. Its authenticity was furiously denied by Lavington himself, whose ill manners caused the Countess of Huntingdon to intervene and extract from him an unwilling apology.[125]

What does not seem to have been noticed is that the sentiments of the extract, though certainly not from Lavington, are very similar to the Pastoral Letter of Bishop Gibson against Lukewarmness, in which he similarly attacks moralism and stresses the need to preach Christ crucified. In order to buttress his attacks on the Methodists, Lavington began to collect evidence and testimony from hostile witnesses, some of which he kept up his lawn sleeves and produced as surmises, but of which the most controversial part proved to be allegations about the misbehaviour of Wesley and his preachers at the Plume of Feathers in the village of Mitchell. It was a tiresome and fairly discreditable libel which Wesley easily disposed of.[126]

Meanwhile Lavington entered the lists in the field of theological argument with the three parts of his *Enthusiasm of Methodists and Papists compar'd* (1749–54). This is a work of somewhat garbled learning. Much of it could only have appealed to people with an invincible opposition to Popery, including the entire history of Catholic spirituality from the beginning. He had enough classical learning to know where to go to in ancient history, and what modern works he should consult, to enable

---

[124] Ibid., p. 237.

[125] See O. Beckerlegge, 'The Lavington Correspondence', *PWHS* xlii (May 1980), 101ff.; Wesley, *Works* (OE), vol. xi.

[126] See Wesley, *A Second Letter to the Author of the 'Enthusiasm of Methodists and Papists compared'*, 1751: Wesley, *Works* (OE), xi. 377ff.

him to bring extended comparisons between the Methodists, the
mystery religions, and the Montanists. Anything in Wesley that
savoured of devotion or of strictness of life was flanked with citations
from a whole gallery of Roman saints, whom he held in abysmal
contempt. Typical is his reference to 'the most nasty, ridiculous, crack
brained, nay wicked saints, Murtherers, Traytors and Rebels, such as
the saints Francis, Dominic, Ignatius, Thomas à Becket, Hildebrand . . .
this Hildebrand, one of the most wicked of mankind (and most
infamous of Popes).'[127] He makes use of other collections of excerpts
from the *Journals* of Whitefield and Wesley, though he has also
scavenged them on his own account. They are torn from context and
generally abused, while Antoinette de Bourignon is raked in as of the
same company. There are a good many unsubstantiated rumours and
highly suspect 'testimonies'. None the less he succeeds in building up an
overall picture of Methodist enthusiasm, for some of which the leaders
of Methodism had only themselves to blame. There were too many
unconvincing case histories which seemed to claim miraculous cures,
and a number of foolish, if earnestly intended, stories which could only
distract from the main issue, which was the conversion of men and
women from depravity and unbelief into soberness and godliness of life.
But this ill-mannered controversy had at least a happy ending. On 29
August 1762 Wesley was pleased in Exeter Cathedral 'to partake of the
Lord's Supper with my old opponent, Bishop Lavington. O may we sit
down together in the Kingdom of our Father.'

William Warburton (1698–1779), Bishop of Gloucester, was the best
known, if by no means the most distinguished, of those who wrote
against Wesley. From grammar school he had gone to an attorney's
office, and the technical grounding he missed by not going to a
university was compensated for by an immense and devouring capacity
for reading incessantly and at all hours of day and night. The result was
that in his classical learning he was inferior to a Bentley, or even to a
Gibson. He got into so many dog fights, for which his downright
dogmatism and fierce humour fitted him, that he reminds us of Giant
Despair in *Pilgrim's Progress*, whose weapon was a club and whose
courtyard was littered with the bones and skulls of those he had
dispatched, both theologians and men of letters. His friendship with
Alexander Pope led him to fame and fortune, for he was made Pope's
literary heir, and he went on to produce an edition of Shakespeare of
ephemeral value, but sufficiently praised by Dr Johnson to enable him to
be acclaimed as a foremost critic in the world of letters. His angry and

[127] Bishop Lavington, *The Enthusiasm of Methodists and Papists Compar'd* (2 vols. 1745),
Pt. II, p. 213.

pretentious bluster hid a more kindly side, which is shown by his affection for his old mother, and the warm and generous friendship for the Nonconformist Philip Doddridge. His close friendship with his crony, Bishop Hurd, and the latter's unqualified admiration, did not perhaps quite merit the contempt which Leslie Stephen poured upon it.[128]

His best work was his *Alliance of Church and State* (1736), a lucid exposition of the two powers and a summary of views about a national Church such as had been stated by Gibson and Wake. His *Divine Legation* (1737–41) was a *tour de force*, and a vast compilation of not always accurate learning to prove that Moses and the Jewish people did not believe in immortality and must therefore have a divine vocation. In 1763 he attacked both the Deist Conyers Middleton and John Wesley in *The Doctrine of Grace: or the Office and Operations of the Holy Spirit Vindicated from the Insults of Infidelity and the Abuses of Fanaticism.* In this he sought to expose Wesley not only as a fanatic, but as a gifted fraud. 'Methodism', he said, 'is modern saintship: Mr. Law begat it: Count Zinzendorf rocked the cradle: and the devil himself was midwife to their new Birth.' But the nub of his argument was the contemporary distinction between the work of the Holy Spirit in the apostolic age, and the signs of his presence thereafter in the Church. In a series of garbled extracts from Wesley's *Journal*, he tried to show that Wesley himself laid claim to all the extraordinary gifts of the Holy Ghost, and above all that he claimed to cast out devils and perform miracles. In so doing he so played down the subjective work of the Holy Spirit, that Wesley needed only to give a lengthy quotation from Bishop Pearson and quote the Collects and Prayers of the Liturgy to show that his opponent had overshot the mark. None the less, Wesley did not get it all his own way, for this wily and much battered warrior of a hundred fights knew how to pick on weak arguments and useful quotations. And once again an opponent was able to exploit the scores of case histories, of which Wesley made so much, and which were so interlarded with Scriptural allusions and particular and providential answers to prayer, as to distract from the real heart of the Revival to which they were by no means essential, and even in the long run, irrelevant. But many thought that Warburton had slain yet another dragon. Hurd uttered the silliest tribute of all when he prophesied that it was 'the singular merit of this discourse that it will be read when the sect that gave occasion to it is forgotten: or rather the sect will find in it a sort of immortality.'[129] Even so, it was to

---

[128] Stephen, *English Thought in the Eighteenth Century*, i, ch. 7; and *DNB*, art. 'Warburton'.

[129] C. J. Abbey, *The English Church and its Bishops 1700–1880*, (1887) ii. 229.

be Warburton's last triumph. A few months later, in 1765, he took on one too many, and Robert Lowth gave him his come-uppance.

There was therefore a mass of misunderstanding and misrepresentation from even the more fair-minded and distinguished of those who opposed the Methodists. But, especially in the beginning, there was a good deal of veritable and rightly deprecated Methodist 'enthusiasm' of which the first published Journals contained too much evidence. One is bound to conclude that Gibson's *First Pastoral Letter against Lukewarmness and Enthusiasm* is a sane, balanced, and valid argument (whatever one may think of his later statements). It is interesting that Lavington and 'John Smith' sometimes agree. Both fasten on Wesley's oft-repeated statement that all that Methodism is about is love of God and man. But this ideal character of a Methodist (which Wesley intended as an ideal) was in obvious contrast to that sorry Fourth Part of Wesley's *Journal* which details all the contumely and angry controversy, rows, walk-outs, expulsions, between the Methodists and the Moravians on the one hand, and the Calvinists on the other. The modern reader of Wesley's *Journal* is inclined to skip the hundreds of little case histories, about unbalanced, hysterical, psychotic, or emotionally disturbed people, and the ill proportion which gave their first readers an untrue picture of what was really happening under the surface. The modern reader smiles at the way in which these stories are encrusted with Scriptural allusion, and the ever recurring particular providences and judgements which befell opponents (of which a generation later Sydney Smith would make much), or the way clouds appeared or disappeared and rain ceased as though under an angelic umbrella. And though Wesley claimed that nine out of ten of his words were about the love of God and Man, 'John Smith' pointed out that this was just not true about his sermons, where the Methodist 'special doctrines' loomed large. The sad fact seems to be that these things distracted attention from the one really effective answer, the appeal to facts.

What have been the consequences . . . of the doctrines I have preached for nine years? . . . By the fruits shall ye know those of whom I speak . . . the habitual drunkard that was, is now temperate in all things. The whoremonger now flees fornication. . . . He that cursed and swore, perhaps at every sentence, has now learned to serve the Lord with fear, and rejoice unto him with reverence. Those formerly enslaved to various habits of sin are now brought to uniform habits of holiness. These are demonstrable facts. I can name the men, with their places of abode.[130]

---

[130] *A Letter to the Bishop of London*, Works (OE), xi. 350.

21

'THE PEOPLE CALLED METHODISTS'

i. Societies

WE may wonder what those who walked out from Fetter Lane with John Wesley on 20 July 1740 made of their new companions at the Foundery. There seems not to have been a considerable overlap in the London societies, and it may be that they found familiar faces in the new company. If they had been members of a Fetter Lane 'band', they would have found those same rules operative which Wesley had drawn up on Christmas Day 1738.[1] But the larger society which awaited them at the Foundery rested on a different basis from that of Fetter Lane. It was, on the surface at least, a much more 'open' affair.

In the latter end of the year 1739 [wrote Wesley] eight or ten persons came to me in London, who appeared to be deeply convinced of sin and earnestly groaning for redemption. They desired (as did two or three more the next day) that I would spend some time with them in prayer and advise them how to flee from the wrath to come. That we might have more time for this great work, I appointed a day when they might all come together . . . this was the rise of the United Society.[2]

There was, Wesley said, only one condition of membership 'a desire to flee from the wrath to come, to be saved from their sins'. This openness of his society was something in which Wesley always gloried.

There is no other religious society under heaven [he wrote in 1788] which requires nothing of men in order to their admission into it but a desire to save their souls . . . the Methodists alone do not insist on your holding this or that opinion: but they think and let think. Neither do they impose any particular form of worship: but you may continue to worship in your former manner, be it what it may.[3]

But within this openness there was a 'closed shop'. The 'open' invitation was almost immediately glossed with the corollary that the members would meet in 'order to pray together, to receive the word of exhortation, and to watch over one another in love, that they might help each other to work out their salvation.'[4]

Between the openness of the society and the strictness of the bands

[1] Wesley, *Works*, viii. 262.   [2] Ibid. viii. 259.   [3] Wesley, *Journal*, vii. 389.
[4] *A Plain Account of the People called Methodists*; Wesley, *Works*, viii. 241.

there was a gap. It was bridged by one of Wesley's happiest improvisations.

Mr. Wesley met the chief of the society in Bristol, and inquired 'How shall we pay the debt upon the preaching house?' Captain Foy stood up and said 'Let every one in the society give a penny a week, and it will easily be done'. 'But many of them' said one 'have not a penny to give' 'True' said the Captain 'then put ten or twelve of them to me. Let each of these give what they can weekly, and I will supply what is wanting'. Many others made the same offer. So Mr. Wesley divided the societies among them: assigning a class of about twelve persons to each of these, who were termed Leaders.[5]

Thus began the class meeting which became the heart of the Methodist *koinōnia* for a century and a half to come.[6] For the visits to collect money involved conversation, and this revealed spiritual problems, so that here was a useful instrument for pastoral care. Under the supreme direction of Wesley and his Assistants, the men and women class leaders watched over those committed to their care as those who must 'give an account'. Soon their visiting lists became class books and the quarterly class ticket a kind of passport. Its withdrawal was the sign of exclusion from membership. The discipline was strict, though it must always be remembered that what was involved was removal from the membership of a society, and not excommunication from the Catholic Church. The class meeting did not mean a watering down of the quality of membership, for the Bands and Select Societies in which members pressed on to perfection, were an integral part of the whole. Wesley himself devoted a great deal of time to visiting the societies and going over membership lists, especially in London and Bristol.[7] The Methodists had borrowed much from the Moravians, but it looks as though the Moravians took from them the 'class', as a long letter of Hutton to Zinzendorf explained.

The union of the two main Bristol Societies, and the conjunction of the Foundery Society with the Fetter Lane rump, made the title 'United Societies' appropriate. On 1 May 1743, five years to the day after the making of the Fetter Lane rules, Wesley compiled the Rules for his United Societies. The original 'open' condition of membership re-mained, but the 'closed shop' aspect now prevailed. 'It is expected of all who continue in these societies that they should continue to evidence their desire of salvation.' They would show this by negatively avoiding evil, and positively by doing good, and attending the ordinances. The

---

[5] *Thoughts upon Methodism*; Wesley, *Works*, xiii. 245.

[6] Thus the Methodist Polity was rooted in what Burke called 'platoon loyalty'.

[7] See J. Kent, 'Wesleyan Membership in Bristol 1783', *An Ecclesiastical Miscellany*, Publications of the Bristol and Gloucestershire Archaeological Society, 1976.

prohibitions were down to earth: there must be 'no buying or selling of spirituous liquors, or of uncustomed goods', and 'no putting on of gold or costly apparel'.[8]

The Methodists had evolved a simple and flexible machine, like a watch, wheels within wheels, and as throughout the land societies grew and multiplied, it was often in informal, almost haphazard, ways.

Mary Bosanquet in her journal tells how the membership grew in the little 'family' at Leytonstone.

We agreed to spend an hour every night together in spiritual reading and prayer. A poor woman . . . came to ask if she might come in when we made prayer? . . . she soon brought two or three more and they others till in a short time our little company increased to twenty-five.[9]

Only at this stage did they apply to Mr Wesley for a preacher.

In 1773 she was in Yorkshire:

. . . we stopped at a public inn . . . in a few minutes a woman came in who had observed us; she said 'Here are two or three of us who are seeking the Lord, just going to meet together at a house hard by, pray will you come in? . . . when the meeting was concluded R. Taylor (the preacher) said 'If any of you who have a larger house will open the door we will spend half an hour with you . . . several offered . . . the house was fixed on and in the morning we had a good meeting . . . about ten we set off for the coal pit at R. Here I saw a little of what the Methodist preachers see much—deep poverty, dirt and cold—but the Lord gave me freedom of speech and some seemed to have ears to hear. Lord, let me not be a delicate disciple![10]

Under God and John Wesley, the Methodist people were held together by the Methodist preachers.

ii. Preachers

The relations between Wesley's movement and the Church of England might have been different, had the original members of the Holy Club or the new evangelical clergy been prepared to share in the itinerancy. In default of such a company of ordained clergy, John Wesley had no option but to rely on laymen. In his plain way he gave them functional names. They were 'Helpers' and those of their number who took charge of the 'Rounds' or 'Circuits' he called 'Assistants'. The first generation of preachers were a kind of 'Old Contemptibles', reverenced by their

[8] Wesley, *Works*, viii. 259.
[9] Henry Moore, *The Life of Mrs. Mary Fletcher* (2 vols., 1818), p. 50.
[10] Moore, *The Life of Mrs Mary Fletcher*, p. 126.

successors for their faith and for their courage under persecution. They were cut from a coarser social fabric than the clergy of the Church of England. John Nelson and Thomas Mitchell were masons, Haime and Wright were soldiers, Taylor and Hopper apprentices, Thomas Walsh and Silas Told were schoolteachers. It was the social stratum from which in the next age would come the great missionary figures of William Carey the shoemaker, Robert Moffat the jobbing gardener, and David Livingstone. Not officer class, but assuredly officer material. It is no accident that a number of them were in fact soldiers and ex-soldiers who knew how to endure hardness. They were sneered at for their mechanic status, and denounced for their lack of letters. But if many of them had few educational advantages, they made the most of their opportunities, under Wesley's prompting and using tools which he provided. He took this matter very seriously, and in the Conference of 1766 there are brusque answers to the question 'Why are we not more knowing?'

A. because we are idle . . . which of you spends as many hours a day in God's work, as you formerly did in man's work?

Read the most useful books and that regularly and constantly. Steadily spend all the morning in this employ, or at least five hours in twenty four.

'But I have no taste for reading.' Contract a taste for it or return to your trade.[11]

A number of preachers became proficient in Latin, Greek, and Hebrew, while Duncan Wright learned the Gaelic to converse with his people. Wesley's geese were too often swans in his eyes, and he was perhaps exuberant in declaring that John Downes had a mind equal to that of Sir Isaac Newton, or that Thomas Walsh was 'such a master of Biblical knowledge as I never saw before.' But Samuel Drew and Adam Clarke were nationally known as scholars. And learning was not the final yardstick. Rather one would single out such preachers as John Nelson, the non-violent stonemason, a noble character, and Silas Told, who became schoolmaster at the Foundery, but whose life's work was spent with utter devotion among the prisons and prisoners of London, of which he became a kind of honorary, and certainly an honoured, chaplain. What they lacked in learning and manners, they more than made up for in guts. Though they took no formal vows, they came close to the classic commitments of obedience, poverty, and chastity. In the original form of the 'Twelve Rules for a Helper' this was roughly explicit:

[11] W. L. Doughty, *John Wesley, His Conferences and his preachers*, Wesley Historical Society Lectures 10 (1944), p. 49.

Act in all things, not according to your own will, but as a son in the gospel . . . it is needful that you should do that part of the work which we direct at those times and places which we judge most meet for his glory.

Take no money of any one. If they give you food when you are hungry, or clothes when you need them, it is good. But not silver or gold. Let there be no pretence to say, we grow rich by the gospel.

Do nothing as a gentleman: you have no more to do with this character than with that of a dancing master. You are the servant of all, therefore be ashamed of nothing but sin: not of fetching wood or drawing water, if time permit: not of cleaning your own shoes, or your neighbour's.[12]

The preachers roamed the length and breadth of circuits which included Ireland, Scotland, and Wales. They were moved from year to year, at the direction of Wesley and the Conference. 'In 1766', said Thomas Hanby, 'I laboured in the Birstall circuit: in 1767 in Staffordshire: in 1768 in Bedfordshire: in 1769 and 1770 in Newcastle: in 1771 in Edinburgh and Glasgow.'[13] 'I now began to be more employed in and about London', wrote Sampson Staniforth. 'Every Sunday morning I walked thither to meet the preachers and keep my appointments. I had six miles to walk all weathers and in the winter to go and come in the dark.'[14]

Hardly any of them had private means and John Valton, who had a government pension of £40, was a solitary exception. He took no money from his brethren.

In those days [wrote Christopher Hopper—1749] we had no provision made for preachers' wives, no funds, no stewards. He that had a staff might take it, go without, or stay at home. I then set out (from the Dales) for Bristol. I called at Chester, Durham, Stockton, Thirsk and Knaresborough and found the Lord in every place.[15]

What I did was gratis [said Thomas Taylor—1761] not even having a penny for the turnpikes: except that the steward of the Bradford circuit gave me once half a guinea: and when I set out for the Conference, the steward of Leeds circuit gave me fourteen shillings.[16]

A preacher at Bristol said to me. You seem pretty well dressed and will hold out well for a year: but you must expect nothing to buy any more clothes with when these are worn out.[17]

But Wesley did not ask from his followers hardships he would not

[12] 'The "Bennet Minutes, 1744"', PWHS i (1896), 15.
[13] The Lives of the Early Methodist Preachers, republished as Wesley's Veterans, ed. J. Telford (7 vols., 1912), ii. 67.
[14] Ibid. i. 99.
[15] Ibid. i. 131.
[16] Ibid. vii. 99.   [17] Ibid. vii. 26.

share. There is a Franciscan-like quality about this 'little flower' of John Wesley, as reported by John Nelson.

Mr. Wesley and I lay on the floor: he had my great coat for a pillow: and I had Burkitt's Notes on the New Testament for mine: After being here near three weeks, one morning about three o'clock Mr. Wesley turned over and finding me awake, clapped me on the side, saying 'Brother Nelson, let us be of good cheer: I have one whole side yet, for the skin is off but on one side . . . as we returned Mr. Wesley stopped his horse, to pick the blackberries saying 'Brother Nelson, we ought to be thankful that there are plenty of blackberries: for this is the best country I ever saw for getting a stomach, but the worst that ever I saw for getting food.'[18]

When John Jane died, after travelling four years, 'all his clothes, linen and woollen, stockings, hat and wig were not sufficient to answer his funeral expenses, which amount to one pound seventeen shillings and three pence. All the money he had was one shilling and fourpence.' Wesley's comment was 'it was enough for an unmarried preacher of the gospel to leave to his executors.'[19]

If Wesley showed a grim disregard of the hardships of himself and his men, he was even less sensitive about their wives and families. His own views on marriage were those of a mixed-up high churchman, and owed more to William Law than to the New Testament. A fortnight before his own marriage he harangued the single men in London on the virtue and desirability of celibacy, and his *Thoughts on a Single Life* and *Thoughts on Marriage*, several times revised, are a contrast to the sanity of, say, Martin Luther.[20]

One of the saddest stories of what might be involved for the preachers' wives is that told by John Furz. He fell in love with a trim housemaid in the service of the Earl of Pembroke. 'She was fond of dress, and loved to walk for pleasure on the Lord's day.' The discovery that such worldliness lurked in the heart of his bride appalled him, and there were a series of angry incidents which came to blows, until her conversion, after which

I believe she never lost His love from that hour. . . . When I set out as a travelling preacher, leaving my children in her care, she never once asked me when I should come home. . . . When I was informed that she was very ill, I rode seventy miles in one of the shortest days to see her.

But she was dying and to his horror he found that under her meagre bed-covering she wore no clothes for 'her clothes had been sold to

---

[18] Ibid. iii. 80.   [19] Wesley, *Journal*, iii. 494.
[20] Wesley, *Works*, xi. 439–6.

procure her necessaries in time of affliction. . . . So that naked as she came into the world, naked did she return'.[21]

It is perhaps a comment on eighteenth-century males rather than on John Furz himself that he could be earnestly galumphing about over England while at home his wife and children were destitute. One cannot help remembering the smiling girl who liked neat clothes and to go little walks on Sunday.

The rule that preachers should take no money soon proved impracticable as the number of preachers and the extent of their ministries increased.[22] A few had been driven to 'moonlighting', to selling books or medicine on the side, though Conference soon forbade this. At last, in 1752, the Conference decided that each preacher should receive £12 a year. They eventually also decided that wives should also receive £12, but this was often paid to them from three or four disparate circuits by sometimes reluctant or tardy stewards. Children were allotted £4 a year and every use was made of the school at Kingswood for their education.

At the Conference of 1763 some of the preachers pressed for provision to be made for the needs of older preachers who would soon be 'worn out' and for their wives and families. They succeeded in launching a Preachers' Fund. But one of the young men present, John Pawson, thought this showed a shocking lack of trust in Providence and was happy to note that John Wesley agreed with him. Wesley gave little encouragement to schemes for the material relief of preachers or a superannuation fund.[23]

The preachers were encouraged to send Wesley their spiritual autobiographies. The seven volumes of their *Lives*[24] give some indication of the great variety of gifts and temperament among them. One or two, like Thomas Olivers and Samuel Bradburn, were 'rough sticks' but others, like Bennet, Valton, and Adam Clarke, were more mannered.

But there were always preachers who could not travel, and others who ceased to itinerate, and these became 'local preachers' who pursued their own livelihood. They became as essential as the itinerants, but being rooted in their own homes and circuits were that much removed from Wesley's personal control, and once or twice we hear him talking about the need to 'clip the wings' of some of the local preachers.

---

[21] *Wesley's Veterans*, v. 224.

[22] A. K. Lloyd, 'The Labourer's Hire: the Payment and Deployment of the early Methodist preachers' (unpublished MS).

[23] Telford, J. Wesley's veterans, 7 vols. 1912.

[24] Ibid.

iii. Methodist Women

John Wesley was reluctant to allow women to preach. In 1780 he wrote desiring the Assistant at Grimsby 'to put a final stop to the preaching of women in his circuit. If it were suffered, it would grow and we know not where it would end.'[25] This sounds forthright enough. But in fact Wesley had already been forced to admit that women class leaders, from praying and giving their testimony, i.e. reciting their own experiences, might proceed to exhortation and so to preaching. In the case of Sarah Crosby,[26] Wesley did not do much more than attempt to put the brakes on. In 1761 he told her to 'Go on calmly and steadily. If you have time you may read to them the Notes on any chapter before you speak a few words.' In 1769 he told her she might 'properly enough intermix short exhortations with prayer: but keep as far from what is called preaching as you can.' But Sarah's own diary, under the date 31 December 1777, says: 'thou hast enabled me from the first of last January to the fourth of this month, to ride 960 miles, to keep 220 public meetings at many of which some hundreds of precious souls were present, about 600 private meetings and to write 116 letters.'

By the end of the century women preachers were making their own distinctive contribution to the revival, and at least one of the leaders of the next generation, Thomas Jackson, was converted by a woman preacher, Mary Barrett.

As in the first days of the Christian religion, a devout band of godly women were at the heart of the Methodist movement. John Wesley's lady correspondents have been the subject of engaging essays in recent years.[27] But, as usual, it is Alexander Knox who has the perceptive comment.

It is certain that Mr. Wesley had a predilection for the female character: partly because he had a mind ever alive to amiability and partly from his generally finding in females a quicker and fuller responsiveness to his own ideas of interior piety and affectionate devotion.[28]

Wesley perhaps exemplifies the saying of Jean Guitton that writing to ladies lessens the pain of writing. But in having what the poet called accomplished female friends, Wesley was in a succession which includes John Knox and John Bradford, Thomas Ken and William Law, Francis

[25] Wesley, *Letters*, (ed. Telford) vii. 9.
[26] F. Baker, 'John Wesley and Sarah Crosby', *PWHS*, xxvii, (1949), 78–9.
[27] W. F. Lofthouse, 'Wesley and his Women Correspondents', *Wesley's Chapel Magazine*, Jan–April 1959; M. Edwards, *My Dear Sister*, Manchester 1980; J. Banks, *Nancy, Nancy!*, Manchester 1984.
[28] R. Southey, *The Life of Wesley*, ed. C. Southey (1864), p. 295.

of Sales and Fénelon. But, although 'compared with the number of men to whom he wrote his women correspondents were few',[29] they were a spiritual élite. He did not initiate such correspondence, but if they sought his counsel, he did not fail to reply. To about a dozen of them Wesley wrote streams of letters over many years, letters of practical and spiritual counsel, stuffed inevitably with medical advice which they often (wisely) did not heed. The obvious affection of many of them inevitably roused the worst suspicions from his wife. But there is nothing sentimental or offensive about them, and on this Alexander Knox had the wise words.[30]

One group deserves special notice. It began with Sarah Ryan, Sarah Crosby, and Mary Bosanquet. The first two had known distressing marriages, and Mary Bosanquet was something of an invalid. They moved from Moorfields to Leytonstone in 1763 where they formed a 'family', like the smaller Moravian settlements, and still more like Howell Harris's 'family' at Trevecka, and Wesley's own institutions at Newcastle and Kingswood. We should today perhaps call it a 'Centre', for the Leytonstone experiment in community included a school and an orphanage, while at its heart was the small company of godly women, who more than once remind us of the thirteenth-century Gertrudes and Mechtilds of Helfta, or the seventeeth-century ladies of Little Gidding (as Wesley noted) and Thomas Ken's friends at Naish. Sarah Ryan and Sarah Crosby were remarkable ladies, but Mary Bosanquet was a marvellous woman, well fitted to become the wife of the great saint, Fletcher of Madeley. To Leytonstone she devoted her limited financial resources, though they were supplemented when, on her death, the much loved Miss Lewin left them money, and when she benefitted from family legacies. Sarah Ryan perhaps was a little of a problem case, but she had the courage to tell Wesley, in March 1764, 'Honoured and dear Sir, I have often heard you do not take those persons to be real friends who reprove you or tell you what they think wrong: but cleave to those who give you praise and respect, though sometimes only from the teeth outward.' And though John totally, if placidly, rejected the aspersion, she may have been nearly right.

Sarah Ryan lost her health and did not long survive, and the group moved to Otley in Yorkshire where it later split up. In the very last years of his life Wesley had the help of two young women of the same calibre, but over fifty years his junior, the splendid pair, Hester Anne Rogers and Elizabeth Ritchie, who nursed him in his last illness.

---

[29] Lofthouse, 'Wesley and his Women Correspondents'.
[30] Southey, *Life of Wesley*, pp. 296–7.

There was another group of correspondents, between London and Oxford, the schoolmistresses the Misses Owen at Publow (which nearly became a female Kingswood), and Miss Bishop who took on when they left the area, and Hannah Ball who was a pioneer of the Sunday Schools before Robert Raikes brought them fame. Other ladies in this region he regarded as linchpins of the congregations, and commended his preachers to take counsel of them. But his longest series of letters was to Anne ('Nancy! Nancy!') Bolton of Witney for whom he had an abiding affection, though the letters themselves are perhaps disappointing.

But there were many letters to other ladies in many parts of the country and a notable series to Lady Maxwell, his one devotee among the aristocracy. These are the people who explored the Methodist spirituality in depth, whom he would on occasion warn against Mlle de Bourignon and Mme Guyon, and to whom he would extol the inevitable M. de Renty and Gregory Lopez, trying to shield them from Quakers and Anabaptists. Dr Lofthouse has a wise comment when he says 'several wrote to him . . . about the Trinity, perfection, mysticism and quietism, and Wesley's terse comments cannot be thought to have thrown much light on any of these difficult subjects.' If he generally counselled some of them against marrying, and if his advice more than once had unfortunate results, it was not perhaps only because he was jealous of their attention, but because of his predilection for early patristic counsels and his inability in fact to reconcile the claims of the love of God and human love. It is significant that the hymn by Antoinette de Bourignon which he included in his hymn-book contained the lines.

> Empty my heart of earthly love,
> And for thyself prepare a place.

It is generally recognized that the strength of the Methodists lay in what were called the middle and lower orders of society, though such loose descriptions of 'middle' and 'lower' classes over-simplify an extremely complex beehive-like social structure differing in the agricultural and the industrial areas, and differing again in the cities. The list of vocations of the young men in the Religious Societies at the beginning of the century does not seem dissimilar from that of the class leaders in the Foundery Society, while lists of trustees show, as we should expect, the callings of the more prosperous members.[31]

It is a pity that, at least in the present stage of research, we know so little about the rank and file, and have to concentrate on the diaries and

---

[31] C. J. Stevenson, *History of City Road Chapel* (1872), p. 250; Legg, *English Church Life*, p. 295.

spiritual autobiographies, numerous as these are, of the more eminent preachers and leaders among them. There were greater numbers by far of the less articulate and less cultured, who were none the less good and faithful Christians. Of those many thousands who have no memorial, perhaps one story may suffice, and once again we are indebted to the artless simplicity of John Furz.

A poor woman that lived about ten miles from Manchester, hearing some say 'We have been there and have found the Lord' told it to a neighbour and said 'I wish I could go to Manchester and find the Lord'. Her neighbour said 'Then why do you not go?' She said 'O! dear child, I have no shoes'. Her neighbour said, 'I will lend you mine'. She said, 'Then I will go'. She came to Manchester on a Sunday: but knew not where to go. Seeing a gentleman walking in the market place, she went to him and asked 'Where is it that people go to find the Lord?' He said 'Among the Methodists as far as I know'. She asked 'Where are they?' He answered, 'Come, and I will show you'. He brought her to the passage that leads to the preaching house and said 'Go in there'. Thomas Wolfenden came to her and asked what she wanted. She said, 'Is this the place where people find the Lord?' He went and called John Morris one of the leaders: to whom she told all that had happened. He took her in and placed her near the middle of the room, and advised her to look at none but the preacher. She took his advice, and about the middle of the sermon cried out 'Glory be to God, I have found the Lord!' which she repeated over and over, being filled with joy unspeakable.[32]

iv. Change and Development

To say that the years 1750–70 were a time of growth and consolidation for the Methodists, suggests something far too staid. What went on is better described by the image of the volcanic region of Rotorua in New Zealand. Below the surface is unceasing ferment. Today a hot spring or a pool of boiling mud may appear at your door, tomorrow others arise half a mile away, and always there is steam in the air and an acrid smell about the place. The Evangelical Revival was still in ferment, coming to the boil in sundry places and in divers manners, now in Dublin, now in Cornwall, in Berridge's Everton and Grimshaw's Haworth, while at Otley in Yorkshire a small company experienced what Wesley described as 'sanctification'.[33]

Each society was ever-changing. New members came in, new classes and bands were formed. And there were tensions and arguments, backsliders and apostates.

[32] J. Furz, in Telford (ed.), *Wesley's Veterans*, v. 221.
[33] J. S. Simon, *John Wesley the Master Builder* (1927), pp. 68–70; Wesley, *Journal*, iv. 365–6.

A number of preachers withdrew, some disgruntled, others because they found the pace too hard, and sometimes they took a few with them, while now and then a whole group went over to the Baptists, Moravians, or Quakers.

Events in the private lives of the two brothers had public repercussions. In April 1749 Charles Wesley married Sarah Gwynne, daughter of a well-to-do Welsh magistrate. From then on he began to settle down and was less and less inclined to travel. But it was not only because he had married a wife that he began to turn from itinerancy. A severe illness and a heavy fall led him to turn more and more to his poetry and hymns, and, like Luther, he could claim to be evangelizing by his writings. But in the mid-1750s a serious crisis arose when some of the preachers who, Charles thought, were admitted too easily to the work, began to demand the right to administer the Sacraments and to press for separation from the Church of England. Charles Wesley was outraged. John, who had no less love for the Church of England than his brother, was more sympathetic to the pressures working on his preachers, and knew what some of them had to put up with. Charles turned to Grimshaw for support, and not in vain, for Grimshaw declared that he would have nothing to do with a dissenting sect. In his *Journal*[34] at this time Charles has some touching *obiter dicta*—some of which read oddly in the light of his own behaviour—about the double blessing which God gives when a service is held inside a church rather than in the open fields. He records how one man was converted during the Litany and another during the Lord's Prayer. He asked 'Should we not at least shut the stable door?' But his solution, that the Bishops would ordain the loyal preachers and the others become Dissenting ministers, was completely impracticable. Had it taken place, it would have been more than the end of the itinerancy, for it would have stopped the revival in its tracks, disbanded the 'Connexion', leaving John Wesley as an owl in the desert or a sparrow on a housetop. But the crisis passed, the few preachers who had begun to administer the Sacrament refrained. Yet the problem had only been postponed.

Six months after his own happy marriage, Charles Wesley was horrified to learn that his brother was about to succumb to holy matrimony. The object of his affection was Grace Murray, the charming housekeeper of the Newcastle Orphan House, who had nursed him in a recent illness. She was the widow of a seaman, and Charles Wesley may have shared the opinion of some of the ladies at the London Foundery where she had been a class leader, that as John

---

[34] *Journals of the Rev. C. Wesley*, ed. T. Jackson (n.d.), ii. 133, 137.

Wesley's wife she would not do at all. For John Wesley, it was Sophy Hopkey all over again, an eminently marriageable woman, dithering between two suitors, and in the case of one of them, as much flattered as in love. For another of her patients was the presentable itinerant, John Bennet, and happy was she with either, when the other was away. John Wesley twice succeeded in getting a promise from her, before witnesses, when they read bits of the marriage service, but she also had with John Bennet what he interpreted as a firm understanding. At this juncture, Charles Wesley intervened.

There was a good deal of his father in Charles Wesley (as there was a good deal of his mother in John) and it was surely the Old Sam in him which made him blunder violently into the matter and get Grace Murray married to John Bennet before an emotional confrontation with his distraught brother. John Wesley had been involved in a case years before at Oxford when he had acted as go-between in such a breach of promise or contract, and he knew something of the complexity of such cases.[35] Before the Marriage Act of 1753 there was an intricacy and confusion about such private engagements, which had caused controversy for centuries. The lawyers would have had an expensive field day which would have dragged on and on, and there would have been an appalling upset for the peace of the inner circle of his movement. John had to accept it. Like Philip Doddridge, he had an inner loneliness which craved affection and had he, like Doddridge, made a happy marriage and had a happy home, his work and the revival might not have suffered as his brother feared. One by-product of the affair was that when in February 1751 Wesley married an affluent widow Mrs Vazeille, who also had nursed him through an illness, he did not consult his brother, who soon found himself on the worst of terms with his new sister-in-law.

The marriage was a disaster. One must grieve for John Wesley and pity his wife. She made valiant attempts to share his ministry, going with him on the long, uncomfortable journeys, trailing her daughter with them. But whereas John Wesley rather enjoyed roughing it, treating the little mishaps as the chastening will of God, his wife found more human reasons for damp sheets and half cooked meals and often uncouth, if well-meaning, hospitality. For her each resting place was as the house of Simon the Leper, and she saw discourtesy and lack of due respect where it was not intended. In short, she complained more and more, becoming what the young Charles had called a 'Grumbletonian', getting on her husband's nerves and draining the happiness of travel

[35] See F. Baker, 'John Wesley's First Marriage', *LQHR* 1967; F. E. Maser, 'Wesley's Only Marriage', *Methodist History*, 1977.

which was among his chief joys. And he was a stickler for punctuality, waiting at the foot of the stairs, watch in hand, and on one occasion at least going off to his appointment, abandoning his wife to that last-minute titivating, which, as most husbands know, tends to be prolonged. But she was a good business woman, and gave him help with the book affairs, badly needed.

What wrecked the marriage was her suspicion and jealousy, and not least her husband's correspondence with godly women. She herself had no such immortal longings—or if she had, was inarticulate about them—and her distrust turned to hysteria. She stole his letters and traduced him in public before friend and foe. Finally, she left him, returned to him, departed again, returned again, until all affection had been drained away and the breach became irreparable. When she died in 1781 John Wesley did not learn of her death until after she had been buried.

In 1763 the Foundery Society was plunged into deep trouble, the most serious since the disputes with the Moravians and the Calvinists, but this time not from without, but from within, and connected with Wesley's own darling theme of Perfect Love. It centred in two men for whom Wesley had personal friendship, with the result that he was reluctant to take steps to re-establish discipline, with almost fatal results.

John Wesley had from the first admitted that the claim to be entirely sanctified was open to abuse and had already met examples of this, all over the country. But perhaps he did not admit to himself how readily this opened the way to that Antinomianism which he hated, and that in more than one place it led to a veritable enthusiasm which justified his critics, and to parallel which one would have to go back to the wilder Puritan sectaries and the first Anabaptists.

The chief offender was George Bell. He was a sometime Life Guardsman, and though one of the least, must be numbered with the ex-corporals who have disturbed history. From 1761 onwards he claimed to have been sanctified and began to attract wild followers and to make more and more extravagant claims, that he possessed gifts of healing, and was immortal. John Wesley's absences from London may have led him to underestimate the dangers of the situation, which were revealed when Bell announced that the world would come to an end on 28 February 1762.

John Wesley wrote two letters to the *Morning Chronicle*, dissociating himself and his Methodists from George Bell and his views, but as in the earthquake panics of the previous decade, numbers of people were alarmed and the tale seems to have spread with extraordinary swiftness. The young preacher George Story was just entering his first Circuit.

When I got to Darlington, the town was in an uproar occasioned by George Bell's prophecy . . . many people were much frightened. . . . Providentially I found in the Newcastle paper a paragraph wherein Mr. Wesley disavowed all connection with Mr. Bell and all credit to his prophesy. This I read to the people which instantly quieted them.[36]

In the area close to the Foundery, between Moorfields and City Road, inner-city charnel-houses had been emptied, and their contents left in great Boffin-esque mounds, on three of which windmills had been erected. On 27 February George Bell and a bevy of avid fellow doomwatchers perched themselves on one of these grisly eminences and contemplated with relish the surrounding valley of dry bones. They were excellently placed, they must have thought, to view the end of civilization as they knew it, though what excited them most was not the perishing world, but the general resurrection which would follow. This they no doubt envisaged simply, as about to happen in the manner of Stanley Spencer's *Resurrection in Glasgow Cemetery*.[37]

John Wesley went peacefully to bed at 10 o'clock. But a doleful band of his followers, Mr Fearings, Mr Despondencys, and Mistress Much Afraids, sat up fearfully awaiting an anxious dawn. When it came, George Bell was no longer among those present, for the constables had pre-empted the apocalypse and carried him from gaol to gaol, ending up in the Borough. He soon abandoned religion for radical politics, a more dubious eschatology.

More damaging was the disaffection of one of the most eminent preachers, Thomas Maxfield.[38] This highly gifted man had deeply impressed both Susanna Wesley and the Countess of Huntingdon. He took holy orders in order to assist Wesley, who left him in charge when he was absent from London. But he soon had his own devotees, and his doctrines became extreme, as though he would out-Wesley Wesley. He began to preach a 'high' doctrine of Perfection, and to encourage reliance on dreams and visions.

A glance at some of the early Methodist diaries (e.g. that of Mary Bosanquet) and letters show that in fact dreams were a more prominent feature of early Methodist spirituality than one would judge from Wesley's *Journal* or later Methodist historians. Wesley himself had innocently encouraged Maxfield to form a Select Band with two or three 'sanctified' laymen who began to rule the roost, to the annoyance of some of the class leaders and preachers. There was a series of interviews between Wesley and a completely unrepentant Maxfield,

[36] Telford (ed.), *Wesley's Veterans*, ii. 251.
[37] Simon, *John Wesley the Master Builder*, p. 126.
[38] Wesley, *Journal*, v. 4–10.

while a vociferous minority expressed their preference for Maxfield. One woman returned her class ticket with the comment, 'Sir, we will have no more to do with you. Mr. Maxfield is our teacher.' Another said, 'Blind John is not capable of teaching us: we will keep to Mr. Maxfield.' Wesley, deeply wounded in the house of his friends, was reluctant to bring matters to a head, but in the end Maxfield went to form his own Chapel not far away. It was a grievous, though far from mortal, blow to the Foundery Society when a hundred members left with Maxfield. In future Wesley was more ruthless about such matters, and went to Dublin or Colchester when trouble occurred, intervening energetically, while he told one preacher that it would be better to cut off forty members from his small society rather than that 'our discipline' should be impaired.

After the fateful Conferences of 1770 and 1771 and the revival of the Calvinist controversy which ensued, the pamphlet war continued. While the Countess of Huntingdon, Walter Shirley, and Thomas Haweis accepted the complete integrity of John Wesley, which Whitefield had never doubted, the brothers Hill and Toplady now thought of him as an evil and corrupt man. The limit was reached when Mrs Wesley handed over some letters (probably with interpolations) from Wesley, to his Calvinist traducers who intended to send them to the *Morning Post*. It is doubtful whether they were published, and this may have been stopped by more honourable Calvinist pressure.[39] It came at a moment in the year 1775 when Wesley had delighted his niece Sarah with the promise of a trip to Canterbury. But her agitated father turned up at the Foundery, with news of the impending scandal, and begged him to forestall the accusations and reply to them. John Wesley calmly replied, in one of the finest of his utterances—'Brother, when I devoted to God my ease, my time, my life, did I except my reputation? Tell Sally, I will take her to Canterbury tomorrow!'[40]

The growing coherence of Wesley's movement, from a loose conglomeration of disparate societies, linked only by the Wesleys and their helpers into a 'Connexion' is reflected in the growing importance of the Annual Conference. It still consisted only of those preachers and visitors whom Wesley called together for consultation, but more and more of its time was taken up with practical problems and the framing of discipline. As more and more preaching-houses were built, problems of finance had to be met. The Conference of 1767 was the first at which statistics were discussed and published and thereafter the 'Minutes of Conference' provided a sort of temperature reading of the health of

[39] *Works of the Rev. R. Watson* (1848), v. 203–4.
[40] J. S. Simon, *John Wesley, the Last Phase* (1934), p. 78.

Methodism. In that year it appeared that Methodism was now divided into forty-one circuits and employed over 100 itinerant preachers, and the total of a carefully scrutinized membership was 25,911 members. London, Bristol, and Newcastle were still the chief cities, but a fourth of the overall membership was now in the north, in Yorkshire and the surrounding area.[41]

The tensions within his movement, and his worries about the future, were not the dominating features of the last years of Wesley's life. His journeys never let up, though he spent more time in London. But he still travelled through England and over to Ireland, and he knew the length and breadth of our green and pleasant land better than any of his contemporaries. Not for nothing was the verse often on his lips:

> Ye mountains and vales, in praises abound,
> Ye hills and ye dales, continue the sound
> Break forth into singing ye trees of the wood,
> For Jesus is bringing lost sinners to God.

The time came when he had to ride by chaise, but this only increased his time for prayer and reading. It was the old Wesley who said, 'I generally travel alone in my carriage and so consequently am as retired ten hours a day as if I were in a wilderness.' The correspondence of his last years is remarkable. They remind us that his sermons and his conferences were but part of his ministry. He spent many thousands of hours listening to people. One must marvel at the meticulous care and marvellous memory which underlay the long periods devoted simply to going over the lists of names of his members, and not only in London and Bristol. He can discuss in depth the spiritual condition of a member in Manchester or Otley or St Ives and contrive to put one of his young ladies into touch with likely spiritual counsellors in half a dozen widely separated places. If there was a great multitude whom he did not know by face and name, there were none the less thousands of men and women known and dear to him. And there were scores of families among whom he could rest and relax like the Brackenburys, the Blackwells, or the Boltons. Two trips to Holland were all the holiday he ever took.

He kept up his reading to the end. It was an obtuse remark of Ronald Knox in an often imperceptive essay to call Wesley a Philistine, for his mental interests were wide. Medicine was for him, in an ancient clerical tradition, part of pastoral care, and the author of the best-selling *Primitive Physic* read what he could—the books of Dr Cheyne, Cadogan

---

[41] Wesley, *Journal*, v. 227; L. Tyerman, *The Life and Times of John Wesley* (3 vols., 1878), ii. 608–16.

on the gout, and the treatise of Dr Wilson on the *Circulation of the Blood*, which led him to exclaim 'What are we sure of but the Bible?'

About books of travel and of geography he varied between credulity and unbelief, while he showed a salutary scepticism about the latest science. 'I read Mr. Huygen's *Conjectures on the Planetary world*. He surprised me. I think he clearly proves the moon is not habitable . . . I know the earth is, of the rest I know nothing.'

His reading of history was a little exotic. He had a 'chip on the shoulder' delight in going against the received views, accepting the innocence of Mary Queen of Scots and Richard III and reading his own situation back into Montanus and Pelagius. Indeed the enjoyment with which he makes provocative judgements makes one rather wonder about some of his theological *obiter dicta*. He made notes on Shakespeare, knew reams of Milton, and could come up with apposite quotations from Pope and Prior and Thompson. But a sound classical education lay at the root of his learning and he could always quote Horace or Virgil, while in 1768 he attended the performance given by the Westminster boys of the *Adelphi* of Terence, with the comment that it was 'an entertainment not unworthy of a Christian'.

He sometimes made time to hear a concert or an oratorio, and if he did not much enjoy the musical entertainments arranged by his two nephews, Charles and Samuel, it was the fine company, rather than the music, which gave him unease.

In his last years he mellowed. Earlier severities were forgotten. He took up with Gambold and Hutton again: George Bull became once more 'a glory of the Church'. And though for him M. de Renty's name still led all the rest, he republished parts of William Law, and even had kind words about Mme Guyon (though he thought she knew less about God than the young Methodist Channel Islander, Jeanne Bisson).

He had never looked strong and in his early days had been threatened with consumption. Some seventy illnesses and minor mishaps punctuated the long years and he had serious illnesses in 1748, 1753 (when he wrote out his own obituary), 1775, and 1783. Many of the medical remedies he lavished on his friends were nonsensical, but he was not far wrong in recommending exercise and change of air, and, despite the snow and the rain and the damp beds, his own 250,000 miles of travel may have sustained, rather than harmed, him. In these last years he had become a respected figure. 'The tide has turned', he noted when he was received with courtesy where once he had been abused, and when a bishop dined alongside him, or the clergy bade him come up higher at some cathedral Eucharist, his eyes twinkled. And there was that last visit to Falmouth:

The last time I was here, above forty years ago [at eighty-six he had forgotten that he had been there twice since] I was taken prisoner by an immense mob, gaping and roaring like lions. But how the tide is turned! High and low lined the street, from one end to the other, out of stark love and kindness, gaping and staring as if the King were going by.[42]

In his great age, the small frame seemed to shrink. There is a lovely engraving of him walking in Edinburgh, supported on each side by two more robust brethren. John Hampson's recollection of him is memorable.

His face, for an old man, was one of the finest we have seen. A clear, smooth forehead, an aquiline nose, an eye the brightest and most piercing that can be conceived: and a freshness of complexion scarcely ever to be found at his years. . . . In dress he was a pattern of neatness and simplicity. A narrow plaited stock: a coat with a small upright collar: no buckles at his knees: no silk or velvet in any part of his apparel, and a head as white as snow.[43]

In his last years, other great philanthropists turned aside to do him honour. Old General Oglethorpe stooped to kiss his hand. John Howard and William Wilberforce sought his door. It was fitting that his last letter should be to Wilberforce, encouraging him in his great fight for the abolition of slavery: 'O be not weary in well doing. Go on, in the name of God.'

Charles Wesley died in 1788, and when John Wesley a little later gave out his brother's great hymn, 'My company before is gone and I am left alone', the old man broke down. But the last months of his life, when his sight was failing and his voice feeble, found him surrounded by loving attendants, and he died in his bed in the house next to his fine chapel on 2 March 1791. By his instructions the funeral was plain and unpretentious. His coffin, like Thomas Ken's, was borne by six poor men, and he was buried early in the morning, while it was yet dark.

v. Charles Wesley and 'Our Hymns'

Charles Wesley was in no way a mere copy of his elder brother. Though he often leaned on him, especially in his younger days, he was his own man throughout his life. The two brothers were dissimilar in temperament. 'I have much constitutional enthusiasm', John confessed, 'but you have much more.' Certainly Charles had a mercurial temper, and his letters and hymns suggest many ups and downs, so that he was more ready than John to believe that the agony of a 'wilderness' experience was for the progress of the gospel. But he was not as easily taken in as

---

[42] Wesley, *Journal*, viii. 3.   [43] Quoted in Wesley, *Journal*, viii. 63.

his brother, and a bucket of water seemed to him the better cure for hysteria than his brother's deference. If he lacked his brother's wider intellectual interests, save in regard to music, his humanity was warmer, as his friendship with John Byrom and his correspondence with John Fletcher show.

In the first decade of the Revival Charles was not a whit behind his brother and George Whitefield as an untiring evangelist. He was vehement in his denunciation of hyper-Calvinism, and Robert Hill had some justification for bringing his earlier verse against him in the 1770s—such lines as:

> God damned them from the womb,
> For what they could not do,
> For not believing the report
> Of that which was not true.

In the persecutions of the 1740s Charles Wesley showed equal courage to that of his brother, making for the trouble spots, riding with his fellow preachers, singing his hymns with such roaring confidence as to bring, on one occasion at least, a protest from local inhabitants in a world as yet unintimidated by noise pollution. After his marriage, a home life which was precious to him took more and more of his attention, and in the sad manner of that age, he and his wife bore the loss of little children. But the advent of Sally, and of the two musical prodigies, Charles and Samuel, took a good deal of his time, especially after his removal to London. He continued an effective preaching ministry and to the end was an evangelist, but a plain letter from his blunt friend, Ebenezer Blackwell, is a reminder that it was not always upon the mountains that he trod. Blackwell wrote him at the end of a week in which, according to Charles's own diary, he thought he had done rather well. But his friend said that Charles's manner of conducting the preliminary Mattins had kept him from the Lord's Table.

You did indeed read the prayers, but alas, it was more like a priest of the world, who had been up all night, and was not half asleep on the desk. Sir, I say that neither myself nor many that were about me could understand one half of what you said, and pray, how do you think we could say Amen or beseech the Lord to hear us when we knew not what petition you asked? And as for the first lesson in particular you read it so very low that I dare say not one in ten throughout the chapel could hear or perfectly understand what you read.[44]

---

[44] E. Blackwell to Charles Wesley, 18 March 1749; J. C. Bowmer, 'Four Letters from Ebenezer Blackwell', *Proc. Wesley Hist. Soc.* vol. xxxvi, Oct. 1967, pp. 74ff.

It would be difficult to exaggerate the importance for the Wesleyan revival of 'our hymns', and therefore of Charles Wesley. Hymns and hymn-singing we have seen to have been at the centre of the revival as a whole, in Wales and among the Anglican evangelicals. The fervour of their singing was a saner outlet for emotion than the near hysteria of the beginnings, and it continued to be a hallmark of Methodist worship when those transitory manifestations had ceased. There is a famous testimony from Mr Williams of Kidderminster who attended a service of Charles Wesley at Bristol.

Never did I hear such praying or such singing . . . as in that society. At the close of every single petition, a serious Amen like a rushing sound of waters, ran through the whole society: and their singing was not only the most harmonious and delightful I ever heard . . . they sang lustily and with good courage, I never so well understood the meaning of that expression before. Indeed they seemed to sing with melody in their hearts . . . I will venture to say such evident marks of a lively, genuine devotion I never was witness to in any place or on any occasion. If there be such a thing as heavenly music upon earth I heard it there.[45]

Writing religious poetry was a family habit of the Wesleys. The girls dabbled in it. Their father wrote a *Life of Christ* in unmemorable verse and followed it with two volumes which versified the Old Testament to illustrate some 180 inferior woodcuts. But two of his hymns, 'Eupolis's hymn to the Creator' and 'Behold the Saviour of mankind', were deservedly included in his sons' collections. Samuel the younger was better known as the author of the *Battle of the Sexes* than for his religious poetry.

The first collections to be printed by the Wesleys,[46] in Carolina and in London, contain religious poetry rather than hymns. But they include John Wesley's superb translations from the German, some poems by John Gambold, and many verses from George Herbert—but so topped and tailed as to make the later complaint of the Wesleys about those who altered their hymns seem ironical. They published some fifty-seven collections of hymns during fifty-three years, culminating in the famous hymn-book of 1780.

John Wesley undoubtedly wrote some of the hymns, but not all have been identified, and the full extent of his authorship may remain a

---

[45] T. Jackson, *Charles Wesley*, vol. i, p. 196.
[46] *The Poetical Works of J. and Ch. Wesley in Thirteen Volumes*, (ed. G. Osborn), 1872; B. L. Manning, *The Hymns of Wesley and Watts*, 1942; H. Bett, *The Hymns of Methodism in their Literary Relations*, 1913; J. E. Rattenbury, *The Evangelical Doctrines of Charles Wesley's Hymns*, 1941; id., *The Eucharistic Hymns of Charles Wesley*, 1948; R. N. Flew, *The Hymns of Charles Wesley*, 1953; *A Collection of Hymns*, ed. F. Hildebrandt and O. Beckerlegge (Wesley's *Works*, OE 1983), vol. 7.

mystery. Dr Rattenbury estimated that Charles Wesley wrote at least 7,300 hymns, of which nearly 3,000 remained in manuscript.[47] It goes without saying that there are plenty of dry bones. An invidious comparison might suggest that Isaac Watts can be feebler, but that he has many fine single lines and verses even in poor hymns, whereas Charles, like the little girl in the rhyme, is either very very good or horrid. The most pedestrian are many of his obituary verses, and some of his more off-the-cuff comments on national events, like his address to the City of London in 1780:

> Ye Londoners with smiles regard
> The homage of a nameless bard
>
> Who reads you with a lover's eye,
> Exalts your virtues to the sky
>
> And with astonish'd Europe sees
> Your truly wonderful police.[48]

He seems almost to have thought in rhyme. There is a story of how he leaped from his battered old grey pony at City Road, dashed into the house, demanded ink and paper, and only thereafter greeted his friends. This astonishing facility had its defects. There are a great number of Scriptural words which rhyme easily, like 'worth' and 'birth', and he perhaps found it all too easy to string such words together, in verses which are often banal. Partly because of contemporary rationality, but even more as the result of his classical training, there is not much that is ragged, and almost nothing sentimental, though the same background accounts for the often intruded 'plenitudes' and 'panoplies' which may have puzzled the miners of Kingswood, or the humbler Methodists who snapped up the latest hymns at a halfpenny or a penny a time.

Ronald Knox accused the Wesley brothers of talking an unattractive Scriptural argot. We know what he means, though it is uneasy and disjointed mainly in their early writings. Certainly in Charles Wesley's better hymns it is a pleasing and skilful allusiveness, theologically significant.

Many writers have put individual hymns under the microscope and demonstrated the extent to which they are saturated in Scripture, with sometimes half a dozen allusions from very diverse portions in a single verse.[49] It is a modern Roman Catholic scholar, in such a detailed study

---

[47] Rattenbury, *The Evangelical Doctrine of Charles Wesley's Hymns*, p. 20.

[48] Wesley, *Poetical Works*, viii. 475.

[49] e.g. Rattenbury, *The Evangelical Doctrines of Charles Wesley's Hymns*, p. 50; Bett, *Hymns of the Methodists*, p. 16; Flew, *Hymns of Charles Wesley*, p. 76; Hildebrandt and Beckerlegge, *A Collection of Hymns*.

of a single hymn ('See, sinners in the gospel glass'), who explains the importance of this Scriptural reference.

Must we then conclude that Wesley's art of harmoniously ordering the Biblical images has its source in a religious experience which is subjectivity? Certainly not. This is not subjectivism but the life of intense faith. And this personal faith is totally dependent on the 'givenness' of Biblical objectivity which his profound intuitions have made his own.[50]

The commentators have stressed Wesley's flexibility in his choice of metre.[51] On the whole his choices of metre seem as intuitive as contrived. We need to remember that hymns are divine songs, songs with music in the air. One can learn less from the learned autopsies of the prosodists than one would by comparing his choices of metre with those of W. S. Gilbert.[52]

At a time when the Church of England and Dissent were infiltrated by Socinian, Unitarian, and Deist notions it was of great importance for the Methodists that the hymns of the Wesleys, like their sermons, proclaimed the Nicene faith. This was impressively shown in the collection of *Hymns on the Trinity* written on texts purloined from Jones of Nayland's *Catholic Doctrine of the Trinity*.[53] Charles Wesley's Christological hymns, some of the finest of which were written for the Eucharist, flexibly employ the *communicatio idiomatum* for the paradox of incarnation:

> Faith cries out, 'Tis He, 'Tis He,
> My God that suffers there.

Of his hymns on the Nativity, 'Hark how all the welkin rings'[54] is the best known and most sung. John Wesley thought the best of the Nativity hymns was 'All Glory to God in the sky'. But he was shrewd in striking out some verses in these hymns as 'namby pambical' (a recent word) such as the lines

---

[50] F. Frost, 'Poésie biblique et expérience religieuse chez les frères Wesley', in *Pluralisme religieux en Grande Bretagne*, ed. C. d'Haussy, Paris 1980.

[51] Rattenbury, *The Evangelical Doctrines of Charles Wesley's Hymns*, 33; E. H. Hodgson, 'Poetry in the hymns of John and Charles Wesley', PWHS xxxviii, Aug.–Dec. 1972; W. F. Lofthouse, 'Charles Wesley', in *A History of the Methodist Church in Great Britain*, ed. R. Davies and G. Rupp, i. (1965), 131.

[52] The suggestion is seriously intended! One would begin with *Ruddigore*, the plot of which is conditioned by the Evangelical Revival: ancestral curse, repentance, conversion, and hysterical 'enthusiasm' (Mad Margaret).

[53] *Poetical Works*, vol. vii.

[54] Sadly altered to 'Hark, the herald angels sing'.

> The heavenly child
> In innocence smiles,
> No wonder the mother should worship the child.[55]

'Christ the Lord is risen today' is the finest of his Easter hymns, but he invariably links Resurrection and Ascension, as in the sonorous trumpet tones of 'Rejoice, the Lord is King'.

The work of the Holy Spirit is such an important dimension in Wesley's view of salvation that it is no surprise to find dozens of hymns devoted to Him, including the joyous

> Away with our fears
> Our troubles and tears;
> The spirit is come,
> The witness of Jesus returned to His home.

The hymns for the Lord's Supper (1745) are of special interest. The neglect of this Sacrament in the Church of England at this time has perhaps been rather over-stressed. We have seen contrary evidence among the London churches, and the religious societies. But for the Wesleys the Eucharist was an integral part of the Evangelical Revival, the point where the Methodists were most strongly attached to the Church of England.

John Wesley tells how at the opening of his West Street Chapel—in the slums of Seven Dials, within sight of Hogarth's 'Gin Lane'—there were many hundreds of communicants at services which went on, hour after hour, until in the following week he had to divide the congregation into three parts, 'that we might not have above six hundred at once'.[56] Nor was this just London, and early days. Dr Rattenbury quotes figures for Yorkshire and Manchester at which throughout the 1780s sacramental attendances were rarely below 600 and often over 1,000.[57]

Charles Wesley had a knack of turning other men's prose into verse, and this he did with Daniel Brevint's *Christian Sacrament and Sacrifice*. Brevint was a Channel Islander and a high churchman who returned from exile to become the Dean of Lincoln. He was a firm Protestant and had written against the mass, but he expounded a doctrine of eucharistic sacrifice which was in line with the teaching of John Johnson and some of the Non-Jurors, and derived from their study of the Fathers and the Scriptures.

For Charles Wesley the 'memorial' aspect of the Sacrament is no reduced doctrine, but the focus of some of his richest, and most finely expressed, hymns about the person and the work of Christ. The

---

[55] Wesley, *Letters*, iv., 166, Dec. 1761.   [56] *Journal*, iii. 78.
[57] Rattenbury, *Eucharistic Hymns*, p. 5.

'memorial', like the Passover, is a true *anamnēsis* of the people of God[58] and in no way a 'mere' historical reminiscence of a dead, past event. For Wesley the doctrine of a eucharistic sacrifice is anchored in the 1662 rite, and so in a 'theology of the Cross'. There can be no question of a repetition of what was done once for all, in the death of Christ, or of that event as being lacking in sufficiency. None the less, he insists, there is a eucharistic sacrifice, distinct from the offering of our souls and bodies.

> With solemn faith we offer up,
> And spread before thy glorious eyes,
> That solemn ground of all our hope
> That precious, bleeding sacrifice,
> Which brings thy grace on sinners down,
> And perfects all our souls in one.

As with Luther and Cranmer, a theology of the Cross includes both the Sacrament of the Lord's Supper and a view of salvation *sola fide*.

The role of the Holy Spirit is equally important, as lines which suggest an *epiclēsis*:

> Come, Holy Ghost thine influence shed,
> And realize the sign;
> Thy life infuse into the bread,
> And power into the wine.

Like George Herbert and William Laud, Wesley will have nothing to do with a doctrine of the Real Presence defined in Lutheran or Roman terms, but though the mode be undefined, a true presence of Christ is declared.

> Sure and real is the grace,
> The manner be unknown.

Doubtless the average Methodist communicant knew little of the finer points of divinity, and for him the 'doing' of the Sacrament was the important thing; but one or two eminent preachers were converted at the Lord's Table, while it was there that the aged Susanna Wesley received an assurance of faith, that her sins were forgiven.

The variety of themes of Wesley's hymns has something to do with their uneven quality. They range from the cutting of a child's teeth to the Gordon Riots, and from the English earthquakes to the Second Coming. There are hymns to the colliers of Kingswood and Newcastle and to the King and Prince of Wales. And as in the similar hymns of

---

[58] E. G. Rupp, 'The Finished Work of Christ in Word and Sacrament', in *The Finality of Christ*, ed. D. Kirkpatrick (New York 1966), p. 177.

Isaac Watts, the obituary hymns are remote from modern use, so that it is difficult for us to be solemn, as her relatives were, when reading verses on the death of Mrs Popkins.

There are lovely hymns of quiet contemplation. The few words of a verse in Deuteronomy (6: 7) become 'When quiet in my house I sit', and there is a beautiful evening hymn, 'How do thy mercies close me round'. 'Open Lord, my inward ear' is a prayer about prayer, and 'Thou Shepherd of Israel and mine' is about contemplation:

> Ah! show me the happiest place,
> The place of thy people's abode,
> Where saints in an ecstasy gaze,
> And hang on a crucified God.

The roots of any form of Christian spirituality are generally in the preceding century, and there is something seventeenth century about the intimate

> O disclose thy lovely face!
> Quicken all my drooping powers;
> Gasps my fainting soul for grace,
> As a thirsty land for showers;
> Haste, my lord, no more delay,
> Come, my Saviour, come away.

W. F. Lofthouse speaks of the variety of mood and theme. 'The poet is in turn convert, preacher, pastor, controversialist, expositor, divine. It is as if we were to think of the one hundred and fifty poems in the Psalter as composed by one and the same writer.'[59] So there are hymns which mark the inexorable loneliness of the Christian encounter with God, whether in his masterpiece, 'Wrestling Jacob' or in those hymns of penitence which remind us of Augustine's 'abyss of the human conscience'. But there are many hymns about Christian comradeship and about the travelling pilgrim Church:

> That palace of our glorious King,
> We find it nearer while we sing.

'Come let us join our friends above' is one of the very greatest hymns about the Communion of Saints, though only one line seems to have survived the emendations of successive Anglican hymn books. Nor was the company of preachers forgotten. Like Nelson's captains, they were a band of brothers, as is expressed in powerful lines in the hymn 'Rejoice, for a brother deceased':

---

[59] Davies and Rupp, *History of Methodism*, i. 135.

There all the ship's company meet
Who sailed with their Saviour beneath.
With shouting each other they greet,
And triumph o'er trouble and death.

Though the practice of 'lining out' the hymns, which were generally unaccompanied, may have slowed the momentum of their song, the first Methodists found plenty of good tunes, secular and sacred, with which they speedily became familiar and briskly sang. For most of them the words were plain enough. Many thousands of humble people, singing them, found that they had added a cubit to their spiritual stature, realized their true dignity. That quality of 'cheekiness' which D. H. Lawrence detected in the Methodists he knew in his youth he attributed to the Apocalypse, though in fact it is Pauline, and indeed New Testament, and an expression of the fact that, like Luther before them, the Methodists had rediscovered the liberties of Christian men.

Angels our servants are,
And keep in all our ways,
And in their watchful hands they bear
The sacred sons of grace . . .
On all the grovelling kings of earth
With pity we look down:
And claim the virtue of our birth,
A never fading crown.

The so-called 'Large' hymn book of 1780 was for the Methodists at worship what the 'Large Minutes' were for their discipline, and they sum up forty years of the Revival. The book had a notable preface by John Wesley, and the division of the book was theologically conceived with the splendid hammer-like blows 'For Believers Fighting, Watching, Suffering, Groaning for Full Redemption . . .' Bernard Manning's encomium is too well known not to be quoted.

This little book . . . ranks in Christian literature with the Psalms, the Book of Common Prayer and the Canon of the Mass. In its own way it is perfect, unapproachable, elemental in its perfection. You cannot alter it except to mar it: it is a work of supreme devotional art by a religious genius.[60]

The reader who turns the pages of the thirteen volumes of the hymns and poems of Charles Wesley will not be surprised to find in them, on almost every page, evidence of a writer in almost all respects conditioned by the time and culture in which he thought and wrote, and

---

[60] Manning, *The Hymns of Wesley and Watts*, p. 14. *A Collection of Hymns*, ed. Hildebrandt and Beckerlegge, and an admirable reprint of the 1780 Hymn Book.

the limitations imposed by an age which lacked the depth of the preceding century, or the heights of the coming Romantic age. What will astonish him, and may well move him, will be to discover again and again divine songs which seem to escape such limitations altogether, a Christian devotion which is beyond the centuries, full of beauty, grace, and truth.

vi. 'Our Doctrines'

What is Methodism? . . . Methodism, so called is the old religion, the religion of the Bible, the religion of the Primitive Church, the religion of the Church of England. This old religion . . . is no other than love, the love of God and all mankind.

So John Wesley continuously and consistently affirmed. But as 'John Smith' and Bishop Lavington pointed out, a study of the Sermons and the *Journals* of John Wesley presented a more complex picture, and show that in fact Wesley concentrated on a group of doctrines about which there was often sharp conflict among his own followers and between them and other wings of the Evangelical Revival, doctrines which at some points ran sharply counter to the prevailing theological temper of the Church of England.

The point was in fact conceded when the Methodist Conference began to talk about 'our doctrines'.[61] Wesley was no systematizer. Protestant and Puritan orthodoxies arranged the Plan of Salvation in an *ordo salutis*. Following Theodore Beza, William Perkins had a chart which begins and ends with the 'Glory of God' but which has as many intermediate states of the soul as a map of the London Underground has stations. The mystics, from Protestants like Thomas Müntzer, Valentin Weigel, and Jacob Böhme to Catholics like St John of the Cross and St Theresa marked off the states of the soul on its way to union with God. But John Wesley's doctrines are not successive, but more like concentric circles, at the heart of which is God, Father, Son, and Holy Spirit. And four central doctrines are perhaps like the instruments of a quartet, the melodies of which support and interpenetrate one another.

We shall comment briefly on those four doctrines: Justification by Faith, the New Birth, the Witness of the Spirit, and Perfect Love.[62]

---

[61] There is a useful summary in R. E. Davies, 'Our doctrines', in *A History of the Methodist Church in Great Britain*, ed. Rupp and Davies, i, ch. 5.

[62] Of course Wesley's doctrines covered the whole range of what he called 'Scriptural Holiness'.

(a) Justification by Faith

John Wesley experienced for himself that 'we are justified by faith only' and that this was indeed a wholesome doctrine and very full of comfort. But it was an afterthought that told him that this was the teaching of his Church in her articles and homilies. He learned it in the first place from the descendants of the Lutheran Reformers, the Lutherans and Moravians whom he met in Georgia and with whom he sang some of the great hymns of Lutheran and of Reformed Pietism. Above all, it had been the Moravian Peter Böhler who had drawn his attention to the importance of saving faith, as something much more existential than the intellectual and moral assent to revealed truth of contemporary Anglican definition. He advised Wesley not to cease seeking until he had found this living faith. It was not accidental that at this point Martin Luther entered the Methodist story, and that his *Preface to the Epistle to the Romans* and *Commentary on the Epistle to the Galatians* were directly associated with the conversion of himself and of his brother Charles in May 1738. It was this doctrine and this experience which they rejoiced to find in Article XI and in the *Homily of Salvation*. At least two of the sermons which Charles Wesley preached in 1739, to judge by his notes, were a selection of passages from Cranmer's two Homilies, 'Of Salvation by Faith', and 'of Good Works', of which Wesley published an abridgement in that year.[63]

Between Luther and Cranmer, and Wesley there had intervened two centuries of Protestant controversy, and the questions asked and answered from St Paul by Luther in 1521 were not quite the same as those asked and answered by Wesley in 1738. Luther had developed the thought of the marvellous exchange, like that of two souls in marriage, by which Christ, with all his righteousness, becomes one with the sinner with all his sins. And if the forensic verses in Paul, together with the notion of 'imputation' had been behind the definition of the Augsburg Confession (1530), Luther made it plain in a letter to John Brenz that he still thought of faith as the indwelling Christ. Wesley, on the other hand, was opposing a hyper-Calvinism, in which 'imputation' had become jargon, and in his zeal against the heresy of antinomianism had come near to breaking the link between 'Christ for us' and 'Christ in us'.

This criticism cannot be levelled at his major sermons on 'Salvation by faith' (I), on 'Justification by Faith' (V), and on 'The Lord our Righteousness' (XLIX).

---

[63] T. Albin, 'Charles Wesley's Early Evangelical Sermons' (MS); R. Green, *Wesley Bibliography* (1896), p. 12; Wesley's *Abridgement of the Homilies* went into thirteen editions.

Christian faith is then, not only an assent to the whole gospel of Christ but also a full reliance on the blood of Christ: a trust in the merits of his life, death and resurrection; a recumbency upon him as our atonement and our life, as given 'for us' and living 'in us'.[64]

Justification, taken in the largest sense, implies a deliverance from guilt and punishment by the atonement of Christ actually applied to the soul of the sinner now believing on him and a deliverance from the whole body of sin through Christ formed in his heart.[65]

Despite the 'Minutes' of 1770, Wesley never abandoned this insistence on 'only faith' as is shown in his sermon on 'The Lord our Righteousness'.

All believers are forgiven and accepted not for the sake of anything in them, or of anything that ever was, that is, or ever can be done by them but wholly and solely for the sake of what Christ has done and suffered for them . . . and this is not only the means of our obtaining the favour of God, but of our continuing therein. It is thus we come to God at first, it is by the same way that we come unto him ever after. We walk in one and the same new and living way until our spirit returns to God.[66]

These major sermons of John Wesley had been preached many times, carefully worked over and rewritten, so that they are admirably balanced expressions of the doctrine they expound. The same thing cannot perhaps be said of the discussions on the theme of 'justification' in the 'Minutes' of the Conferences 1744–6. The views of the little group of clerics and laymen who attended them were treated seriously by Wesley. At one point they agreed to read together 'Mr. Baxter's aphorisms' concerning justification and 'it was desired that each person present would in the afternoon consult the Scriptures cited therein, and bring what objections might occur the next morning'.[67] They were what would today be called a theological 'workshop', yet in the main we may believe that John Wesley's views dominated. But the language is now looser. Faith is defined as 'a spiritual sight of God, and the things of God'—'seeing God being the essence of faith'.[68]

Moreover there is now much talk about believers being in a 'justified state' and going on to a 'sanctified state' and about 'the moment we are justified'.[69] And we can see from the *Journals* that this had become part of the jargon current among the societies, who spoke about those who

---

[64] *Wesley's Standard Sermons*, ed. E. H. Sugden (2 vols., 1921), i. 40.

[65] Sugden, i. 45. Wesley generally distinguishes between justification and regeneration, but in this 'largest sense' comes nearer to Luther.

[66] Sugden, ii. 430

[67] 'Bennet Minutes', p. 20.   [68] Ibid., pp. 8–9.   [69] Ibid., pp. 22–3.

were 'justified'. The complex doctrine of Scripture in which objectivity and subjective experience were united, the union between Christ 'for us' and 'in us' seems to have been upset, and justification thought of more and more as a once for all experience, instantaneously given. When Pusey later accused the Methodists of teaching 'justification by feeling' they were understandably outraged, but it is easy to see how the misapprehension could have arisen.

When we come to the controversy arising from the 'Minutes of 1770' (themselves a reaction to the Antinomian situation), attention goes further and further from the mystery of divine forgiveness to the relation between faith and good works. Biblical criticism in the eighteenth century could not do justice to the eschatological element in Pauline doctrine, in particular to the eschatological point in justification ('a final act brought into the present' V. Taylor)—that God's verdict upon sinners in the Cross of His Son must be in some sense a final verdict. To this extent the Calvinist emphasis on final perseverance had preserved a true insistence on the unchangeable character of the love of God and the irrevocable once-for-all-ness of the Cross. Now Wesley began to insist that he was talking about our 'first justification' and refused to elaborate on its implications for the final judgement at the Last Day. But Fletcher, in defending Wesley, was driven to the desperate device of postulating a double justification, one by faith, in this present order, the other by works, at the Last Judgement. A more subtle doctrine of double justification had arisen in the 1540s in debates between Bucer and Melanchthon and the Rhineland theologians, but was dropped when it was seen to raise more problems than it resolved. None the less Wesley never let go of the doctrine of justification by faith alone. For if there be a 'heart of the gospel' this would seem to enshrine it. It was as the Methodist preachers 'offered Christ, in all his offices, justifying us by His grace, and sanctifying us by His Spirit' that multitudes of the weary and heavy laden moved towards those who proclaimed God's mercy to lost sinners. They knew what they wanted.

> Gasps my fainting soul for grace,
> As a thirsty land for showers.

For many humble, wayfaring Englishmen, it had been a long drought.

(b) The New Birth

Wesley never ceased to draw attention to the fact that the Articles and Homilies of the Church of England attested the doctrine of justification by faith alone. He did not find it so necessary to point out that there is no Homily on the New Birth, or that what he has to say about it might run contrary to Article 15 and perhaps Article 25. One might suppose that Wesley drew this doctrine from German Pietism, of which, according to Martin Schmidt, it was a central theme.[70] But in fact the first Methodist to stress this doctrine seems to have been George Whitefield, the least affected by the Germans. And it would not be hard to construct an English pedigree from writers who extended the doctrine of regeneration beyond the consideration of Baptism. 'From its union with God by the uniting ray of grace the soul is born again and has a new existence', wrote the Platonist John Colet. The old women sitting on their doorstep in Bedford whom John Bunyan overheard were talking about 'a new birth'. In the seventeenth century Isaac Ambrose wrote a long treatise on *Regeneration* (1650), which Wesley later published, though this is concerned with the whole process whereby the old Adam dies and the new man in Christ is born. The view of the new birth as the continuing transformation of the soul was expounded by Böhme and in consequence by William Law in *The Grounds and Reasons of Christian Regeneration* (1739). In opposition to this Charles Wesley stressed the immediacy of it as an experience, and as a power to overcome sin, which brought it close to the doctrine of Christian Perfection. John Wesley treated the subject in three sermons, 'The Marks of the New Birth' (Sermon XIV), 'The Great Privilege of those that are born of God' (Sermon XV), and a third sermon on 'The New Birth' (XXXIX), which drew the former argument together and qualified earlier statements which might seem to concede too much to baptismal regeneration. Wesley insisted that there were two fundamental doctrines: 'Justification' and the 'New Birth'. In his funeral sermon on George Whitefield he incensed some Calvinists by reaffirming this view, that these were the two 'fundamental' doctrines which he and Whitefield held in common. The two doctrines, he insisted, were very close together. 'In order of time neither of these is before the other: in the moment we are justified by the grace of God through the redemption that is in Jesus, we are also "born of the Spirit" but in order of thinking, justification precedes the new birth.'[71]

Though . . . justification and the new birth are in point of time, inseparable from each other . . . justification implies only a relative, the new birth a real, change. God in justifying us does something 'for us'; in begetting us again he

---

[70] This has been questioned. E. Hirsch would lay equal stress on justification and the new birth. See J. Wallmann, 'Pietismus und Orthodoxie', in *Geist und Geschichte der Reformation* (*Festgabe für Hanns Rückert*) (Berlin 1966), pp. 418ff.

[71] Sugden, ii. 227.

does the work 'in us'—our inmost souls are changed, so that of sinners we become saints.[72]

Wesley recurs (as does Fletcher of Madeley) to a favourite image, which may be Christian Platonist in derivation, that of the unborn infant whose senses only begin to operate when he is born. He rejects the view of William Law that regeneration is a long-continuing process 'carried on in the soul by slow degrees'. This, he says, is true of our sanctification, but 'a child is born of a woman in a moment, or at least in a very short time . . . in like manner a child of God is born in a short time, if not in a moment. But it is by slow degrees that he afterwards grows up to the measure of the full stature of Christ.'

Wesley obviously thought of the New Birth, as he came more and more to speak of justification, as a once-for-all and immediate experience. But he learned from his pastoral experience that it could not in fact be entirely explained in this way, since some of his people knew no such drastic and immediate experience. John Wesley's exegesis of the Johannine literature is perhaps more subjective than his exposition of Romans, and perhaps this doctrine is the least coherent of his doctrines.

(c) The Witness of the Spirit

In his correspondence with 'John Smith' Wesley told how his dying father had said to him, 'The inward witness, son, the inward witness—that is the proof, the strongest proof, of Christianity.'[73] For 'John Smith', as for Lavington and Warburton, the notion of a 'perceptible' inward witness was one of the extraordinary *charismata* of the apostolic age and in no sense an ordinary privilege of believers in subsequent centuries. Their deepest revulsion against Puritan enthusiasm was caused by this claim to be moved and guided by the Spirit. But Wesley had allies. He quoted a plain statement from the impeccable Bishop Pearson and the supporting evidence from the Fathers. He quoted with effect the Collects of the Prayer Book. And nowhere does he show his talents as an exegete so well as in his exposition of Romans 8. In his printed sermons on the subject[74], Wesley distinguished between the witness of the Spirit, and the witness of our own spirits. The latter is the testimony of a good conscience, the awareness of the fruits of the spirit, not only in our behaviour but in the emotions of joy and peace and he gives a variation of what the Puritans had called the 'practical syllogism'

He that now loves God, that delights and rejoices in him . . . is a child of God.

---

[72] Sugden, i. 299.   [73] Wesley, *Letters*, ii. 288.
[74] Sugden, i. X and XI; ii. XLV.

But I thus love, delight and rejoice in God,

Therefore I am a child of God.

But the witness of the Spirit, as distinct from our own inward testimony, is God's own direct encounter with the soul. 'Such a testimony of his adoption that while it is present to the soul, he can no more doubt the reality of his sonship than he can doubt of the shining of the sun, while he stands in the full blaze of his beams.'[75]

His definition of this witness echoes his description of what befell him at Aldersgate Street.

An inward impression on the soul, whereby the Spirit of God directly witnesses to my spirit that I am a child of God; that Jesus Christ hath loved me and given himself for me: and that all my sins are blotted out and I, even I am reconciled to God.[76]

A doctrine of assurance lay deep within the Puritan evangelical tradition. The Calvinist Plan of Salvation, especially when Supra-lapsarian, turned upon the divine freedom and sovereignty and might have become a complex rationalist scheme (it was against this that the Cambridge Platonists protested). It was saved from this by two points, the Christocentric doctrine of election which stressed that the elect were chosen 'in Christ' (Eph. 1:4), and the doctrine of assurance. Both these doctrines are important in the theology of William Perkins. But Samuel Wesley was no Calvinist Puritan, and drew his doctrine from another tradition of 'inward religion' within the Church of England.

It can be seen that to discuss the experience of John Wesley on 24 May 1738 in terms of the word 'conversion' is simplistic, since it obviously has elements in it of all these three doctrines, Justification by Faith, the Witness of the Spirit, and the New Birth.

(d) *The Preaching of the Law to Believers*

Wesley's teaching on this subject is an important bridge between the first three doctrines and his doctrine of Christian Perfection. It has some affinity with Melanchthon's *Third Use of the Law* and with Calvin's teaching on the relevance of the law to believers, but it has its own place in the coherence of Wesley's teaching. He devotes an important part of his published sermons (XVI–XXVIII) to expounding the Law of Christ, not in terms of the Ten Commandments (as in *The Whole Duty of Man* and the general catechetical tradition), but (following Bishop Bull) in terms of the Sermon on the Mount, so that at every point outward Christian behaviour is traced back to purity of intention and

---

[75] Ibid. i. 210.   [76] Ibid. i. 208.

inward motives. But his most striking exposition comes not in the sermons, but in a letter to one of his friends in December 1751.[77]

He fully accepts the Protestant dialectic of preaching the Law to bring men to conviction of sin, and to the point where they despair of saving themselves. But he believes that when converts begin to grow in grace 'a wise builder would preach the law to them again: only taking particular care to place every part of it in a gospel light, as not only a command but a privilege also, as a branch of the glorious liberty of the children of God.' And in what follows there is a blend of the Christian imperative with the Christian indicative.

Whenever [God] gives a new degree of light, He gives likewise a new degree of strength. Now I see He that loves me bids me do this. And now I feel I can do it through Christ strengthening me.[78]

God loves you: therefore love and obey Him. Christ died for you: therefore die to sin. Christ is risen: therefore rise in the image of God. Christ liveth evermore: therefore live to God, till you live with him in glory.[79]

(e) Christian Perfection[80]

The thousands of young people who choose Charles Wesley's 'Love divine, all loves excelling' as their wedding hymn, might be startled to know that according to the meaning and intention of the author, the lines

> Finish then, thy new creation
> Pure and spotless let us be,
> Let us see thy great Salvation . . .

are quite specifically a prayer that they may enter then and there into an experience of entire sanctification and attain the goal of the Christian life, so far as it is realizable here on earth.

The doctrine of Christian Perfection or Perfect Love is one of the most important of Wesley's doctrines, and he claimed it was the 'Grand Depositum' which God had entrusted to the Methodists.

It was also one of his most controversial teachings and in the first years of the Revival was more offensive to the Calvinists (e.g. John Cennick) than the doctrine of Universal Redemption. Yet it was a

---

[77] Wesley, *Letters* (ed. Telford) iii. 78 ff.   [78] Ibid. iii. 81.

[79] Ibid. iii. 85.

[80] R. N. Flew, *The Idea of Perfection in Christian Theology*, Oxford 1934; H. Lindström, *Wesley and Sanctification*, Stockholm 1946; J. Kent, 'Christian Theology in the eighteenth to twentieth centuries', in *A History of Christian Doctrine*, ed. H. Cunliffe-Jones and W. B. Drewery, Edinburgh 1980; *ERE* s.v. 'Perfection' (F. Platt); *RGG* s.v. 'Vollkommenheit' (H. Barion); *DTC* s.v. 'Perfection'.

doctrine about which he had intermittent hesitations, and many discussions with his brother Charles whose poetic absolutes about it were free from John's careful qualifications.

John Wesley expounded the doctrine in one of his sermons (XXXV) and in a number of shorter writings, which culminated in his *Plain Account of Christian Perfection,* a long and rambling document which incorporated almost all his earlier statements on the subject.[81]

Wesley was sensible of the call to evangelical perfection early in his career. In 1725 he read Jeremy Taylor's *Holy Living* and *Holy Dying* and realized the importance of purity of motive and intention. In the next year *The Imitation of Christ* fastened his attention on Christ as the embodiment of perfection, and he set himself to follow in the footsteps of that most holy life. In the next years William Law's *Christian Perfection* and his *Serious Call* set before him the absolute demands of the Sermon on the Mount, and the call to complete commitment to God. This conviction was strengthened when in 1730 he made the Bible the centre of all his study. Henceforth what he sought was 'Scriptural holiness'. In 1733 he preached perhaps the best of his university sermons (Sermon XIII) on 'The Circumcision of the heart', which he defined as 'being endued with those virtues which were also in Christ Jesus'.

It seems important that he held these convictions and preached them before he had any contact with the Germans, and that he did not think of perfection in a Pelagian way, but saw it as the supreme work of grace. Indeed in 1778 he said: 'I know not that I can write a better sermon on the circumcision of the heart that I did five and forty years ago.' There is a hint in his correspondence with 'John Smith' that it was his preaching about perfection which led to his exclusion from some pulpits in the months before May 1738.

It was a suspect doctrine, for it had reappeared at intervals in Christian history among such sects as the Cathari, the Spiritual Franciscans, the Anabaptists, and the Puritan sectaries, often in an Antinomian form. But in his statement of the nature of Christian Perfection Wesley was admirably faithful to the main Christian tradition. For he defined the goal of the Christian life as enshrined in the great commandment—love of God and neighbour. For him as for the first Christians this was no abstraction, a kind of 'Identikit' assembly of virtues, but something which Christ himself embodied, and which he illustrated in the Sermon on the Mount. And from the New Testament Epistles, Wesley again and again portrays an attractive mosaic of Christian virtue, warmly expressed in love, joy, peace, in thankful and praying hearts. When he

---

[81] Wesley, *Works,* xi. (1764, but reprinted unaltered in 1777).

wrote his *Character of a Methodist,* which is really a picture of the perfect Christian, he took as his model the famous portrait of a Christian Gnostic in Clement of Alexandria. In the fourth century the Desert Fathers answered the call to evangelical perfection in complete renunciation of the world and a life of discipline and prayer. Wesley also learned from this tradition in such writings as those of 'Macarius' and Ephrem Syrus. But if the study of the primitive Church enriched his thought, there were also Stoic and Neoplatonic influences which may perhaps be reflected in his and William Law's attitude to marriage and to celibacy.

There is a sadly revealing question in the 'Minutes' of 1745 which asks whether an entirely sanctified man 'would be capable of marriage?' and which gives the extraordinary answer 'We cannot well judge. But supposing he were not, the number of those in that state is so small, that it would produce no inconvenience.'[82]

John Wesley's description of Christian Perfection is admirable and it is no wonder that Bishop Gibson, who is his Charge against Lukewarmness had called on Christians to seek perfection, should have said, 'Mr. Wesley, if this be all you mean, publish it to the world.' Alas, it was not all that Wesley did mean, for it is when we ask how this goal is to be attained and when it may be realized, that difficulties begin.

Although St Ambrose seems to have discussed the possibility that in this life a man might be without sin, this was not the consensus of the early Church. The Protestant reformers held that in this life, though we are to seek perfection, we continue to be sinners (Thirty-nine Articles, 15). In 1583 the Dutch humanist Coornhert attacked the fourth and fifth questions of the Heidelberg Catechism at this point, and in debate with Adrian Saravia affirmed a doctrine of perfection as the result of a long process of growth in which grace and the human will co-operate.[83] Spener, among the German Pietists, urged Christians to seek perfection but did not think of it as an instantaneously given experience.

The view of Protestant orthodoxy was that perfection might be attained 'in articulo mortis', at the moment of death, and Wesley himself admitted that it was 'not ordinarily given till a little before death'.

What then, did Wesley believe might be attained by the Christian in this life? His clearest definition is:

1. Christian perfection is that love of God and our neighbour which implies deliverance from all sin.

2. That this is merely received by faith.

---

[82] 'Bennet Minutes', p. 23.
[83] W. Nijenhuis, *Adrianus Saravia* (Leiden 1980), p. 180.

3. That it is given instantaneously, in one moment.

4. That we are to expect it, not at death but every moment: that now is the accepted time, now is the day of our salvation.

Wesley does not believe, or at least he has never met an example of it, that this is given to Christians when they are first justified, and he thinks of it as a further experience given to those growing in grace and seeking and praying for it. He has, however, important qualifications. The Christian does not possess a love which is free from all the imperfections of infirmity and ignorance, from mistakes and inelegancies of behaviour. (Even M. de Renty mistakenly thought it right to wear an iron girdle). Wesley himself disliked the phrase 'sinless perfection', and he defined sin as the 'voluntary transgression of a known law', so that he denied that involuntary transgressions could be described as sins. Nor did he believe that this perfection could not be lost. Nor did he believe that it was more than a relative perfection, for the believer is to go on to higher and higher forms of love, 'changed from glory into glory' in this life and that which is to come.

These were important qualifications and there are moments when we might almost think that saintly Methodists loving God to the best of their ability (he even discusses the word 'sincerity' in this connection) might have what Wesley means by 'perfect love'. But there are other statements which put its meaning much higher, as a clean heart, a mind into which temptation does not come, and where sin has vanished away.

He never claimed the experience for himself, nor did his brother, though he seems to have thought that Thomas Walsh, John Fletcher, Jane Cooper, and, of course, M. de Renty attained the mark. He was only too well aware that there were false claimants, and his Calvinist friends pointed out how easily the doctrine of Perfect Love might encourage Antinomianism. In the time of the Maxfield–Bell crisis of 1763 there was evident conflict among his own followers. And indeed some of his most perceptive disciples, like Mary Bosanquet, were sometimes puzzled as to what he did mean. Part of the object of the Plain Account was therefore to explain the doctrine to his followers.

Wesley did not believe that testimonies to having attained perfection should be unexamined. He believed that he knew above 500 brethren (and sisters) at once who had the experience, and he and his assistants quizzed them to the best of their ability. But one is bound to ask how deep the probe could go and whether simple, inarticulate, and elderly people could really discriminate between what were sins of infirmity and involuntary transgressions.

Wesley's doctrine has properly been criticized by a number of scholars, some of them Methodists.[84] Perhaps the most serious error is to suppose that on the analogy of conversion, there must be a second experience, when instantaneously sin is taken away. It is a doctrine which nineteenth-century 'holiness' movements often claimed to have taken from Wesley, though it is a simplistic reading of part of his teaching. For Wesley, we have seen, did not think of the soul as being rapt by the Spirit, thought of in charismatic, and even impersonal, terms. He thought of perfect love within the New Testament spectrum, its virtues like the flowers of some splendid garden, differing from one another in shape and colour, but always attractive. And in his *Christian Library* he illustrated the doctrine from the lives of eminent Christians in all the centuries and from schools of sanctity as various as the Fathers, the Reformers, the Puritans and Caroline divines, the Cambridge Platonists, the high churchmen, Non-Jurors, and the Dissenters.

For his movement the doctrine was important. To have preached Christian perfection only in terms of law, rather than gospel, as something to be attained and achieved rather than as a gift, might have landed the Methodists in the kind of legalistic moralism that Zinzendorf had prophesied would be their end. And even though sanctity cannot be quantified, and there are no thermometers by which we can read the temperature of our love of God, it is the saints who pose the question, 'What is the highest kind of spiritual experience attainable by men here on earth?' How near can mortal men come to union with God? Sir Herbert Butterfield suggested that here is the greatest contribution which Christianity has made to European culture, a great succession of men and women who have touched the heights of religious experiences.

And, finally, does not Wesley call all our bluff when he ends his *Plain Account* with the Collect for Purity? What do Christians mean when, at the altar, they pray that their hearts may be cleansed by the Holy Spirit, that they may perfectly love God, and worthily magnify his Holy Name? It would be blasphemy to suppose they mean nothing at all, that it is just a pious hope, a kind of pseudo-Augustinian 'Give me to love thee perfectly — but not yet!' Better surely to say with Wesley, in the words of a modern saint, Temple Gairdner, 'Let us believe the maximum!'

Archbishop Herring had no love for Methodists, and he wrote John Wesley off as a 'dark, saturnine figure' but he confessed in 1748 that 'religion has lost its power over the heart'. And whether we think of the heart as the seat of emotion, or in a wider Biblical or Pascalian sense, it is here that the secret lay of the power of the Evangelical Revival. Wesley

---

[84] e.g. R. N. Flew, H. Lindström, W. E. Sangster.

sought, rationally, scripturally, and from his wide pastoral experience of
men and women to explain this, and show how what God has done 'for
us' is continued and consummated 'in us'. There were other contemporary
patterns of inward religion, but, unlike William Law, unlike the
mystics, Wesley wrote for wayfaring Christians and not just a spiritual
élite.

Those who concede that John Wesley was a great man may not so
easily be convinced that he was a great theologian. (Whether eighteenth-
century England was capable of producing a great theologian is another
thing.) And it may be confessed that sometimes he was not even a very
good one. There were times when, as he said of his brother, he was in a
'contrary mood' and when a sharp reaction against dangerous error
could lead him to make *obiter dicta,* especially when talking to his
preachers, which were imprecise and open to misunderstanding — as in
part were the *Minutes* of 1770 and indeed, of 1745. Nor had he the leisure
for continuous theological study and reflection. Nobody would have
been more scornful of the idea that he needed what would now be called
a 'sabbatical'; nobody needed one more. Marvellous indeed was the
disciplined timetable which enabled him to get through a programme
which would have sufficed half a dozen men. But though he kept time
in it for prayer, meditation, and Bible study and used to the full the
lonely hours on horseback or in his chaise, he was immersed in a great
mass of commitments, and the travel which came upon him daily.
When he did retire for a few days, to Lewisham or Raithby Hall, it was
to catch up with his writing. It is also true that he had a candid mind,
was genuinely ready to be convinced by the arguments of others, and to
the end of his long life gave no signs of mental ossification.

But after the death of his brother Samuel (and not forgetting Charles)
there was nobody near enough to stand up to him in a really critical
way, within the essential bond of affection. Certainly not his preachers,
or even Fletcher of Madeley who rarely differed from his revered friend.

His place in the history of eighteenth-century doctrine does not seem
to lie in any one doctrine — say, Christian Perfection — but rather in a
balance and proportion, what might be called a 'package deal' in which
'our doctrines' explain and supplement one another and which describe
the work of grace within the soul.

It is plausible to suggest that he was too isolated a thinker to
accomplish such a task. He had cut himself off in turn from coherent
traditions, high church, non-juring, mystical, and from the deeply
Augustinian theology of the Calvinists. Though he read the works of
Arminius and valued the Puritan Arminian John Goodwin, he had no
deep roots in the Continental Arminian tradition, while the Arminian

high-church divines had not much in common with Wesley's 'Evangelical Arminianism'. There were reasons, therefore, why his theological achievement should have been imperfect. But he himself did not think of himself more highly than he should have done, in this regard (unlike some of his modern descendants in whom a 'Mr. Wesley' romanticism intermittently takes over).[85] He might have been very content to know that for generations to come his preachers and his people would regard 'our doctrines' as a safeguard and a witness to the gospel of grace.

vii. John Fletcher of Madeley

John Wesley was no man of destiny, no Napoleon who would rough-hew history his own way, nor was he like Luther, who said 'God has led me like an old blind horse'. There was little doctrinaire in him, and much practical empiricism. He responded to events, like a chess player, always having to take into account the state of the board. It was of great importance that in this period two outstanding younger men, clergy of the Church of England, became his partners, John Fletcher (1729–85) and Thomas Coke (1747–1814).

Fletcher of Madeley[86] was the embodiment of what Wesley meant by 'scriptural holiness', a flesh-and-blood image of that Christian perfection described by William Law (with some of the defects of that ethical pattern).

He was born at Nyon in French-speaking Switzerland. His family was affluent and propertied, his father a professional soldier. When at the University of Geneva he found the dogmatic requirements of Reformed Confessionalism offensive, he turned to the profession of arms, but was foiled by the coming of peace. In 1750 he came to England and became tutor to the sons of a Shropshire gentleman, Thomas Hill. In the mid-50s he was drawn to religion, and among those who turned his attention to the Methodists was 'a poor old woman who talked so sweetly of Jesus Christ that I know not how the time passed away.' He joined a Methodist class and read Wesley's writings, and was converted by a series of experiences over several days, culminating in what the old Puritans would have called 'a sight of the Cross'. He was ordained in 1757 and on the day of his ordination as priest, he rushed to West Street to assist Wesley in the administration of the Sacrament. In

---

[85] The notion that Wesley was a 'folk theologian' seems to raise more questions than it answers.

[86] L. Tyerman, *Wesley's Designated Successor*, 1882; G. Lawton, *Shropshire Saints*, 1960; J. Wesley, *Life of Mr. Fletcher, Works*, xi. 262; P. P. Streiff, *John William Fletcher*, Frankfurt 1984, an admirable and perhaps definitive study.

him John Wesley found an ideal helper, one who in genuine humility would do anything he was asked to do without argument or complaint. Charles Wesley, with whom Fletcher's relationship was warmer, thought that beneath the gentle manner there was the stubbornness of a mule.

When Wesley learned that Fletcher had been offered and had accepted the living of Madeley, he was horrified that he would be immersed in the narrow confines of parochial cure. But despite his 'fly from it at the peril of your soul!' and 'others may do well in a living: you cannot! it is not your calling', Fletcher happily settled as vicar in a parish which he served for twenty-five years and left the little town inseparably associated with his name. It was a market town, but though agricultural, it was a focus of nascent industries, with coal mines, iron works, and limestone quarries, and a high proportion of rough and poor inhabitants. The Quakers were influential and there was an unwontedly aggressive Roman Catholic community. Fletcher's utter devotion to God and his people, the strict demands on the morals, manners, and habits of his people soon roused inevitable opposition. And as he roamed through the lanes, ringing his handbell to call them to service (or to some special treat, like a sermon from a young man Charles Simeon, from Cambridge) he was many times threatened with violence.

Alone in his large house, he fed intermittently on scraps, prayed and studied far into the night, his clothes unmended, talking to himself, a very bachelorish bachelor who badly needed looking after. His health began to suffer and soon the fatal signs of tuberculosis began to appear. In 1763 he met the incomparable Mary Bosanquet, who bowled him over, as he told Charles Wesley in a panicky letter:[87] 'her image pursued me for some hours the last day', but it made him 'fly to Jesus who delivered me at the same moment from her image, and the idea of marriage.' It was a strange rigorism which could turn that delectable woman into a roaring lion, seeking whom she might devour, and when he concluded (amid a rabble of bachelor arguments) 'the love of Jesus ought to be my whole felicity', one wonders if Puritanism, with its roots in the Old Testament attitude to the family and to marriage, was not more humane than a so-called primitive, high-church Christianity which so impoverished the lives of William Law, John Wesley, and John Fletcher. The postponement of Fletcher's marriage to her for eighteen years deprived them of half a lifetime's honourable joy, and shortened the life of Fletcher himself, that kind man to whom little children were endearingly drawn.

---

[87] Tyerman, *Wesley's Designated Successor,* p. 91.

In 1773 Wesley solemnly faced the problem of finding somebody who might succeed him in the leadership of his people. He wrote a moving appeal to Fletcher to accept such a responsibility. He listed the formidable qualifications for such a post. He ended with a ringing 'Thou art the Man!' and the invitation 'come, while I am able, God assisting to build you up in the faith, to ripen your gifts and to introduce you to the people . . . come and strengthen the hands, comfort the heart and share the labour of your affectionate friend and brother, John Wesley.'

Fletcher did not, as he might well have done, demur to the notion of himself as passive clay to be moulded by John Wesley. He admitted that he had sometimes wondered whether

it would not be expedient that I should resume my office as your deacon, not with any view to presiding over the Methodists after you: but to care for you in your old age . . . nevertheless I would not leave this place without a fuller persuasion that the time is quite come.[88]

In these years Fletcher had become immersed in even more demanding assistance to John Wesley, sustaining the main defence of his doctrines in the Shirley controversy, and the subsequent pamphlet war with the Hills and Toplady. His *Checks to Antinomianism* were hailed by the Methodists as a great victory, not only in the matter of Anti-nomianism, but in the whole range of issues at stake between them and the Calvinists, though Jabez Bunting in the next generation was right in having reservations about them. He had a clear mind, humour, a gift for illustration, and a thin vein of poetry, but perhaps little originality, and in the main loyally defended Wesley's ideas, as was shown even more clearly in his few political pamphlets.[89]

His health continued to alarm his friends and those who had not seen him for some time were shaken by his sick and ageing appearance. Fifty years on, David Lloyd remembered how he had suddenly appeared before the Conference of 1777. 'The whole assembly stood up as if moved by an electric shock. . . I never saw such an instantaneous effect produced in a religious assembly either before or since . . . he had scarcely pronounced a dozen sentences before a . . . hundred preachers were immersed in tears.' Wesley knelt beside him and the Conference felt they had prayed him back to health. But it was a very temporary remission, and he returned to Switzerland where the high lands and the cold, pure air could not avail, not least because he would not abate his Master's business, as he preached and talked his own brand of edifying conversation, which had a Franciscan and Bunyanesque quality, finding

---

[88] Ibid., p. 1. Wesley, *Letters* (ed. Telford), vi. 10.
[89] Fletcher, *Works* (9 vols. 1877), vol. vii.

spiritual lessons in every little daily incident. There was a morning when he came upon some children 'in my wood, gathering strawberries'. He invited them to his home, and they gleefully fell in behind this strange Pied Piper, yodelling ('such melody as you know is commonly made in these parts'). After that they came back, again and again. 'I make them little hymns which they sing'. He returned home, but all the contrary advice of the most eminent physicians could not mend his condition. In 1781 he married Mary Bosanquet, (Wesley wrote a miserable note, but turned up at the wedding.) Now, if he did not heal, it would not be for lack of loving care, and there were smiles and quiet humour, for they were of one mind in that house. They both had private means and gave beyond them to feed the poor.

He had for years kept a school in Madeley, where he taught, but he was swift to realize the immense opportunities of the new Sunday School movement. Soon he had gathered more than 300 children, whom he regularly met. He gave them 'little hymn books'. So many accounts of Fletcher are stuffed with piety that we prefer to take our leave of him, on that Thursday before his last, fatal seizure, surrounded by clamouring bands of dirty, scruffy, cheerful children.

'Three years, nine months, and two days', so Mary Fletcher retold the hours when she 'possessed my heavenly minded husband'. There was within him a flame of sacred fire which never dimmed, a devotion to Jesus, more Christocentric than the piety of the Wesleys, which links him with Thomas Ken on one side and John Newton on the other. He belongs equally to the Methodist and to the Anglican Evangelical roll of honour, but even more perhaps he is to be seen within the great tradition of pastoral care. It was finely said of another parish priest, the Curé d'Ars, that 'in heaven, where they know the value of men, his century is known as the "century of the Curé d'Ars".' On such a reckoning, too, the great name of the eighteenth-century map might not be Blenheim, Plassey, or Quebec, Bunker's Hill or Quiberon Bay, but little Madeley.

viii. Thomas Coke

John Wesley could not have picked two more dissimilar right-hand men than John Fletcher and Thomas Coke. Fletcher was a humble country parson, 'glebae adscriptus', Coke the ebullient Welshman hopping from place to place like an ecumenical flea (the image is John Wesley's). In Fletcher Wesley thought he had found an *alter ego,* but he, who could take a refresher course in logic in his eighties, had much to put up with from Coke who was for ever 'jumping the gun'. Yet Coke was to end his life in a blaze of glory, and it is perhaps enough to suggest that in the school of Christian sanctity he was a late developer.

The son of a well-to-do apothecary (and always possessed of private means) Thomas Coke[90] was a native of Brecon and became a bailiff of his town at the age of twenty-three. He went to Jesus College, Oxford, where the status of Gentleman Commoner was ill conducive to learning. But he took his arts degrees and some years later (on the say-so of Lord North) was granted the DCL by accumulation; so that one must have reservations about the extent of his legal competence, however useful his doctorate was for him in ecclesiastico-legal negotiations. As a curate at South Petherton in Somerset, he was energetic and evangelical, and tactless enough to invest church funds in new doors and a weathercock without the agreement of his congregation. When, on an Easter Sunday, the new incumbent dismissed him in the middle of the service, and the church bells rang, nobody needed to send to ask for whom the bell tolled.

In August 1776 he met John Wesley and soon afterwards threw in his lot with him, and at last an evangelical and Oxford cleric was prepared to take on the itinerancy. If at his first Conference some of the less couth and anti-clerical preachers looked askance at the tubby little Welshman with his choirboy looks, and an Oxford Doctor and a' and a', he threw himself whole heartedly into the new jargon, talking of 'Brother X' and 'Brother Y' with the best of them. But he did not go in a 'Round' or Circuit, and began to travel on his own, defraying his own expenses. But soon Wesley found urgent use for him as what we should call a 'trouble shooter'. The Methodist polity was having growing pains, and the relations between the Wesleys and their preachers, the Conference and the local trustees, were under evident strain. So Coke went off to Bath and Bristol and Norwich and the north, pouring oil on troubled waters. Serious issues were raised at Birstall and Dewsbury about the rights of the local trustees and class leaders 'to place or displace' the preachers. If the 'Connexion' were not to dissolve into independency it was urgent that some legal definition be given to the Methodist Conference, and the result of this, at which Wesley and Coke laboured hard with the help of the attorney Clulow, and the lawyer Maddox, was the 'Deed of Declaration' of 1784 by which the hundred preachers named by John Wesley in the deed were declared to be the legal conference, and this deed was enrolled in Chancery.

Unwittingly, Wesley had taken the most important step possible to

---

[90] J. Vickers, *Thomas Coke, Apostle of Methodism,* 1969; J. W. Etheridge, *The Life of the Revd. Thomas Coke DCL,* 1860; *PWHS,* xxxi, pts. 2,3; xxxiv, pts 4,5,6; xxxv, pts 2,8; xli, pt. 6.

ensure the persistence of the Methodist connection after his death. But if it solved the Engish problem, it did not touch the even more desperate situation of the Methodists beyond the Atlantic. Here the growing band of Methodists and some scores of their preachers, in the aftermath of independence, were bereft of sacraments, in a situation where the Establishment had come to an end, and where many of the clergy had returned to England. The lamentable consequences were now plain to be seen of the failure of the Church of England to provide bishops for the Plantations, even though, as Norman Sykes has shown, the main responsibility rests upon the secular power. John Wesley now pleaded with Dr Lowth, Bishop of London, to ordain a suitable preacher in order that the Methodists might have the sacraments. When this was refused, he was faced with an urgent situation and was driven after much thought and prayer to what some will believe were desperate and dubious devices, even though thereby he made possible the emergence of one of the greatest of Protestant Churches.

So Coke went to America, endued with Wesley's plenitude of power, and with his fellow preachers, Whatcoat and Vasey, ordained (with the consent of the American Conference) Francis Asbury as joint Superin-tendent. Some may feel that in fact Providence had already made superior arrangements for the care of the American Methodists in Francis Asbury, a man of heroic gifts, sterling character, and free from the self-consciousness which seemed to possess Coke from time to time, and which was not so much personal ambition as identification with all opening opportunities to be 'of use'. And, Coke as a British loyalist, was bound to be caught in the inevitable clash of loyalties (his part in the address offered to Washington was an embarrassment), whereas Asbury was completely identified with his American flock. (No English preacher could have referred to John Wesley as 'Old Daddy!')

As the Pilgrim Fathers had taken immediate care for learning, so the leaders of this new American Episcopal Methodist Church began to plan a college. And though the word 'Cokesbury College', like the word 'bishop', stuck in John Wesley's gullet, and though he perhaps had a point in rebuking them for it, it was plain that the American Methodists had found a life of their own, and were by no means minded to be controlled from beyond the Atlantic, even by the ever-revered John Wesley. Coke was able to do a great work in his eighteen incursions into the American Church, but he could not settle there. Inevitably his authority dwindled in comparison with that of Asbury, who was entirely one with his people. In the end, and after his marriage, Coke's visits ceased.

For the demands made upon him in Europe were always growing, and he seemed to have the makings of an ecumenical patriarch among the Methodists of the world. With Ireland his relations were especially close, and again and again they made him the Secretary of the Irish Conference. On the death of Wesley he scurried back to England, getting off the boat at Cornwall and speeding overland to London. If he expected to become the leader of an episcopal Methodist Church in England he was soon disillusioned, but took calmly the resolve of the preachers not to have another king in Israel, and was content to fill the office of Secretary of the Conference, save for one year, when, fearful they would lose him to America, they made him President. Nor were his services confined to administration, for he produced a Biblical commentary, useful, if very much a compilation, and he stoutly defended the Wesleyan polity and what he judged were its true political implications, against the doctrinaire liberalism which the turbulent Alexander Kilham had derived from the teachings of Drs Priestley and Price.

Between John Wesley and Thomas Coke there was a generation gap of forty years. John Wesley had been brought up by his father to share the missionary concern of the SPCK and SPG and had been a pioneer. Now a more powerful missionary impulse was to seize the churches, an impulse already shown in the Moravian missions, and in the initiatives of Thomas Haweis and the Countess of Huntingdon, and soon to be displayed by the Baptist William Carey. Thomas Coke caught this heavenly vision and it took hold of his best qualities, his imagination and compassion, and his zeal for the gospel. His own blueprint of a missionary society did not get off the ground in 1786, and when he began to take collections he was rapped on the knuckles by John Wesley who knew how hard pressed his people were in so many worthy causes. But there was no holding him. He had been consulted about the situation in Scotland and gave a new impetus to the Wesleyan work in Wales. He went to the Shetlands in the north and the Channel Islands in the south. He planned for Nova Scotia and Newfoundland, and went four times to the West Indies. He pursued a mission to Africa. And if we smile at him for renting a chapel in revolutionary Paris and preaching in French (after the school of Oxford-atte-Brecon) to a thin congregation, it was not an unseemly gesture to tackle revolutionary France, nor was the whole project unfruitful.

But it was the Far East that held his imagination, and with something of the magnetic impulse of Roberto Nobili and Francis Xavier he would not rest until he was able to sail for Ceylon and India. In all these things the Methodist Conference, and indeed the Methodist people, were behind him, though the Missionary committee were more aware of the scarceness of the resources, in men and money, at their command. For Coke had an exasperating way of taking no heed to them and blandly offering to make up any deficit from his own pocket. This showed at its worst in petty wrangles about the cost of long underwear for his missionaries in Nova Scotia, or pewter vessels of dishonour for his Indian team. But just as his care for their ordination (and ordination certificates) shows his realist appraisal of their needs when faced with magistrates in the new fields, so there was a concern for their material welfare which is in refreshing contrast to John Wesley's attitude to his preachers.

When he died at sea, perishing, like Francis Xavier, on the threshold of his desired haven, he had laid upon the heart and conscience of the Methodists a missionary vocation they would never lose.

ix. Separation

'I will not leave the Church of England as by law established, while the breath of God is in my nostrils.' So John Wesley solemnly declared in June 1789. Yet five years before this, he had ordained three men for ministry in America, and had followed this by ordinations for the work in Scotland. In the last months he had set apart Alexander Mather as Superintendent and ordained Henry Moore and Thomas Rankin for England. 'Ordination means separation', said Lord Mansfield, but it seems that John Wesley did not think so, and these ordinations have to be seen in the context of his complex notion of what separation involved.[91]

The possibility of separation from the Church of England was early seen as an option. 'Why don't they leave us?' grumbled Bishop Gibson. But as early as the first Conference of 1744 the question was asked 'Do we separate from the Church?' and answered, 'We conceive not. We hold communion therewith for conscience sake, by constantly attending both the word preached and the sacraments administered.'

When the matter became urgent at the end of Wesley's life, it was sadly enough at a time when he himself was an accepted national figure, and when so far from doors being slammed in his face, he now had more invitations to preach in parish churches than he could accept. Those last years however saw a new kind of trouble for the Methodists. After the Countess of Huntingdon had lost her legal actions at Spa Fields, it was plain that the Methodists were also vulnerable. If the Acts of Toleration and the Conventicle Act offered protection only to

[91] Wesley, Letters (ed. Telford) viii. 143, to the Editor of the Dublin Chronicle.

Dissenters, the Methodists who claimed to be within the Church of England had no redress. They were now subject to attacks which in effect were pushing them into schism. There was a series of harassments and fines, beginning in Lincolnshire. The aged Wesley protested vehemently to the Bishops of Lincoln and London, while he also appealed to William Wilberforce to intervene.[92]

In fact the Methodist societies had developed their own way of religion, long before, and some would date the moment of separation from the time when Wesley appointed his first lay preachers. Wesley did not see it this way, for he believed on Scriptural grounds, and from the example of the Jewish dispensation that there was a clear distinction between the prophetic and preaching, and the pastoral and priestly office.[93]

Certainly by 1780 the Methodist pattern of discipline and worship made prime demands upon their members' time and loyalties. The Methodist was a member of a society and a class meeting, and perhaps a band or a select society as well. If he were a class leader he had demanding pastoral duties. If he were a preacher, the demands on him were even greater. Then there were the extra-liturgical services: the early morning sermon with extempore prayer: the fasts and watchnights and days of intercession: the love feasts and the Covenant service. The whole informal atmosphere of homely fellowship, the fervent song, might be an evident contrast to the parish church. As on moonlight nights the Methodists made their way home, along roads prepared no doubt by many a rolling English drunkard, the stillness might be rent by an intoxication independent of any alcoholic stimulus:

> Our concert of praise
> To Jesus we raise;
> And all the night long,
> Continue the new evangelical song.

A last-minute attempt by Charles Wesley and Thomas Coke to discuss union with the Moravians must be seen against growing tensions. For the Moravians had been a movement with dual member-ship within their own societies and within the Church of England, their status recognized by Act of Parliament. Might not union with them keep the Methodists in some kind of recognized relationship with the Church of England? So Wesley and Coke sought out the Moravian

---

[92] Wesley, *Letters* (ed. Telford), viii. 224, 230.
[93] He expounded this in his statement to the Conference in 1755 (Baker, p. 332) and in his sermon on 'The Ministerial Office' (Sermon CXV, *Works*, vii. 261).

leader, Benjamin La Trobe.[94] But, like two former lovers trying to patch things up, forty years on the estrangement had become too long and damaging. John Wesley said sharp things about Moravians and La Trobe believed the gossip that Wesley was under the thumb of Thomas Coke and that he had never been converted. There were conversations but they never got as far as an interview between La Trobe and Wesley himself. The Moravians were not minded to make concessions, nor did they relish being swallowed within a much larger body, despite the alarmingly good intentions of the Walrus-and-Carpenter-like Charles Wesley and Thomas Coke.

Much has been and will be written about Wesley's ordinations.[95] He had begun with a high-church view of episcopacy and of apostolic succession, as he explained to Westley Hall, in December 1745:

We believe it would not be right for us to administer either baptism or the Lord's supper unless we had a commission to do so from those bishops whom we apprehend to be in a succession from the apostles.[96]

But in his *Journal* for 20 January 1746 he noted:

I set out for Bristol. On the road I read over Lord King's 'Account of the Primitive Church'. In spite of the vehement prejudice of my education, I was ready to believe this was a fair and impartial draught: but if so, it would follow that bishops and presbyters are (essentially) of one order.[97]

In 1784 he told the American Methodists: 'Lord King's account of the primitive Church convinced me many years ago that bishops and presbyters are the same order and consequently have the same right to ordain.'[98] In 1755 he wrote to James Clark,

As to my own judgement, I still believe 'the episcopal form of church government to be both scriptural and apostolic'; I mean, well agreeing with the practice and writings of the Apostles. But that it is prescribed in Scripture I do not believe. This opinion (which I once heartily espoused) I have been heartily

---

[94] W. G. Addison, *The Renewed Church of the United Brethren*, 1932; C. W. Towlson, *Moravian and Methodist*, 1957.

[95] A. R. George, 'Ordination', in *History of the Methodist Church in Great Britain* (ed. Davies and Rupp), ii, ch. 4; G. F. Moede, *The Office of a Bishop in Methodism*, Zurich 1964; A. B. Lawson, *John Wesley and the Christian Ministry*, 1963; F. Baker, *John Wesley and the Church of England*, 1970; J. Vickers, *Thomas Coke, Apostle of Methodism*, 1969; E. W. Thompson, *Wesley, Apostolic Man*, 1957; A. W. Harrison, *The Separation of Methodism from the Church of England*, 1945; PWHS xxx. 72, 162–70, 188; xxxi. 18–19, 21–4, 27–31, 65–70, 102–3, 147–8; xxxii. 63, 86–7, 169, 190–2; xxxiii. 118–21, 178; xxxiv. 99, 141–7, 167–9; xxxv. 78–9, 88–93, 125; xxxvi. 159; xxxviii. 81–7, 97–102; xxxix. 121–7, 153–7; xl. 91.

[96] Wesley, *Letters* (ed. Telford), ii. 55.

[97] *Journal*, iii. 232.

[98] *Letters* (ed. Telford), vii. 238.

ashamed of since I read Dr. Stillingfleet's 'Irenicon'. I think he has unanswerably proved that neither Christ nor his Apostles prescribed any particular form of Church Government, and that the plea for the divine right of episcopacy was never heard of in the Primitive Church.[99]

Peter King's *An Enquiry into the Constitution, Discipline, Unity and Worship of the Primitive Church* was published anonymously in 1692 when the author was a Presbyterian. Edward Stillingfleet's *Irenicum: a Weapon-Salve for the Churches wounds, or the Divine Right of Particular Forms of Church Government* was published in 1661. Both treatises were written with eirenical intention to the situations in 1660 and 1689 when there was an attempt to reconcile Dissent.

They resemble modern prize essays by young men (one was twenty-one, the other twenty-four) brilliant, rather over-impressive in learning, provocative in judgements. Both authors later moved from their early liberalism. King became a member of the Church of England, which opened the way to the glittering prizes of the legal profession, becoming Baron and Lord Chancellor. Stillingfleet became a caustic opponent of the Dissenters. Neither repudiated the patristic evidence of their books, though it may be that King was shaken by the temperate and learned answer to his book by William Sclater.[100]

In his work, which is confined to the evidence of the pre-Nicene fathers, King asserted that bishops and presbyters, though of differing degree, were of the same fundamental *gradus* of ministry, and he defined a presbyter as 'a person in holy orders having thereby an inherent right to perform the whole office of a bishop'.[101] He believed that this included the power to ordain, and offered some evidence, though he stressed that the presbyter must act only at the request, or with the permission, of his bishop, and indeed likened their relationship to that between a curate and his rector. It gives no kind of support to a presbyter like John Wesley 'going it alone'.

Stillingfleet's is a more massive treatise, using post-Nicene evidence and so able to cite the evidence that the presbyteral college of Alexandria had appointed their bishop. He attacked the notion of a 'divine right' church polity in concentric arguments from natural and positive law and Christian tradition, ending with an impressive catena of judgements from Continental Reformers and Anglican divines. He asserted that in case of necessity a presbyter might ordain.

---

[99] *Letters* (ed. Telford) iii. 182. Other references to Stillingfleet: ibid. iii. 135 (Wesley's reference to 'I am the fifteenth' seems to be a misreading of 'John 15th'); iv. 150; vii. 21.
[100] *Original Draught of the Primitive Church,* 1717. It does in fact succeed in blurring at least the effect of King's citations and it is a pity that John Wesley does not seem to have read it.   [101] *An Enquiry* (1692), p. 53.

The convictions Wesley derived from such works underlie his statements

I firmly believe I am a scriptural "episcopos" as much as any man in England or in Europe: for the uninterrupted succession I know to be a fable which no man ever did or can prove.[102]

I know myself to be as real a Christian bishop as the Archbishop of Canterbury.[103]

We do not know what other books helped to make up his mind. He refers to Hooker and Baxter, and it may be that the debate between Law and Hoadly helped him to abandon faith in an uninterrupted apostolic succession. But considering the immense practical consequences which might and did ensue, it seems a pity that Wesley relied so much on King and Stillingfleet. For there was a great debate about these things from the time of the Reformation, and indeed that between Beza and Saravia in the Elizabethan Church argued the whole issue of *de jure divino* polity with more profundity and learning. Wesley must have known that many did not accept King's or Stillingfleet's findings and that there were replies to them. About presbyteral ordination he could find nothing conclusive in Scripture, but it was a pity to lean so heavily on disputable anomalies in the early church when a much greater consensus attested episcopal authority.

He must often have pondered over the possibility that he might act on his conviction, but it was the critical situation of the American Methodists in 1784 which forced him to do so. Above all, he was concerned that the American Methodists were deprived of the Sacraments. Had they, like the Quakers, been prepared to go without the Lord's Supper, this crisis would not have arisen. The refusal of Bishop Lowth to ordain a Methodist preacher was a last straw.

Driven by what Norman Sykes called 'ineluctable necessity', John Wesley ordained the three preachers whom the Conference of 1784 had decided to send to America, setting apart one of them, Dr Coke, as Superintendent. He sent with them a revised and abridged liturgy, *The Sunday Service,* and an open letter to the American Methodists telling them what he had done, and adding that 'if any one will point out a more rational and scriptural way of feeding and guiding those poor sheep in the wilderness, I will gladly embrace it.'[104]

Wesley may have raised the subject at his small inner cabinet in February 1784. Fletcher knew what was in the wind, but it was kept from Charles Wesley. It would be wrong to suppose that Wesley was

---

[102] *Letters* (ed. Telford) vii. 284. [103] Ibid. vii. 262. [104] Ibid. vii. 239.

badgered into it by Thomas Coke, like an aged Lear at the mercy of an ill counsellor. Yet Coke is important. In April he wrote to Wesley suggesting that he might visit America, to report back on the situation. More important was his letter of 9 August which began,

. . . the more maturely I consider this subject the more expedient it appears to me that the power of ordaining others should be received by me from you by the imposition of hands, and that you should lay hands on Brother Whatcoat and Brother Vasey.

The reason given is: 'I may want all the influence in America which you can throw into the scale'.

Coke was evidently unsure of his reception, how the Americans would take his coming among them and ordaining, if he had not evidently behind him the full authority of Wesley himself. So he concludes that the necessary acts should take place 'this side of the water'.

He then made detailed suggestions, all of which in fact Wesley carried out. The ordination could take place 'In Mr. C——'s house, in your chamber' and he would see that a third presbyter, the Revd James Creighton, would also be present. Hence the Nag's Head aura of Wesley's ordinations, and the absence of any assent or representation of the body of the faithful. What was done was entirely directed towards America and had no connection with the English situation. The little room in Bristol seems to have been almost a little bit of America, a kind of spiritual embassy with theological immunity.

As to what happened, the main evidence is Wesley at his most laconic. On 1 September he 'appointed' (Journal) 'Ordained' (Diary) Mr Whatcoat and Mr Vasey. On 2 September 'I added to them three more' — this means in fact that he ordained Whatcoat and Vasey as deacons and elders and 'ordained' (the word consecrated was not used) Thomas Coke as Superintendent.[105]

That Wesley had reconciled himself to the idea of a new and separate Methodist Church in America may be seen from his preparation of an abridged, revised liturgy, which concentrated on the main worship for Sunday.[106] Perhaps one of its sad features was not so much Wesley's 'mangled Mattins' but his eviscerated Evensong — it is no wonder that an Evensong from which the Magnificat and the Nunc Dimittis had been abstracted did not long survive. He also rooted up what he

---

[105] Wesley, *Journal*, vii. 15.
[106] A. R. George, *The Sunday Service of 1784*; Friends of Wesley's Chapel, Annual Lecture 2, 1983; and see above p. 831.

considered the liturgical tares of about a sixth of the Psalms. But he kept the Communion Service little altered and most of the Ordinal, save that 'Superintendent' took the place of 'Bishop'. Wesley deliberately avoided the word 'Bishop' and was affronted when the American Conference made Coke and Asbury the 'Bishops' of their new Methodist Episcopal Church. In this connection Wesley's omission of the service of Confirmation[107] is interesting. The word 'Bishop' had a 'mystique' for Coke and the Americans, whereas for Wesley it was a word, like 'Basingstoke' in *Ruddigore*, teeming with hidden meaning.

Granted that bishops and presbyters were the same essential order of ministry, and that in a case of necessity he had the power to ordain, his ordinations of Whatcoat and Vasey become explicable. But what did it mean that he ordained Coke? For Coke, too, on Wesley's principles was a true *episcopos,* as truly as any Archbishop of Canterbury. Yet Dr Whitehead, Wesley's friend and one of his earliest biographers, did not quite settle the matter when he said 'Dr. Coke had the same right to ordain Mr. Wesley, that Mr. Wesley had to ordain Dr. Coke'.[108]

For therein lies a confusion which perhaps could not be resolved. Wesley had the authority of a presbyter of the Church of England, and Coke had the same authority. But Wesley had something much more important in the American Methodist context. He had an authority over the Methodist people which they themselves freely acknowledged, as the one who over forty years had under God, been chiefly instrumental in fashioning them into a living, disciplined entity. No other human being had or deserved such authority. It was this plenary authority of Wesley over the Methodists which Coke desired to have at his back. But this was something quite different from Wesley's authority as a presbyter, or even a presbyter *episcopos.* Wesley realized this when he stressed the 'extraordinary' mission which he and his preachers had in an 'extraordinary' situation. The difficulty arose when he tried to express this within the ordinary rites and rubrics of the historic Church. At the end of the day, the great American Methodist Church which was thus

---

[107] Wesley's negative attitude to Confirmation deserves examination in one who reverenced the Primitive Church (there is a full section on it in Peter King). For to administer Confirmation was an important part of the office and work of a Bishop. As Norman Sykes has fully demonstrated, it cannot be dismissed on the grounds that in the eighteenth century it was neglected or slovenly performed. From the time of Ken and Kidder an increasing number of bishops took their duties seriously in this matter. One wonders if it is this pastoral conjunction of the Sacrament with the Bishop which offended Wesley. Did the whole theology of the rite, with its fine collects, with the emphasis on the sanctifying by the spirit of the baptized believer really conflict with 'our doctrines': conversion, justification, the new birth?

[108] J. Whitehead, *The Life of the Revd. John Wesley, M. A.* (1796), ii. 423.

enabled to grow is a not unimportant part of the evidence that Wesley had indeed been called and commissioned 'out of the common way'.

Ordination means separation, Lord Mansfield had said to Charles Wesley, who was outraged by his act of schism. And though there is some slight evidence that John Wesley himself was not altogether happy, yet like Father William in the ballad, having in his age stood on his head, so to speak, 'he did it again and again'. When he died he had ordained some twenty-seven preachers for Scotland and the mission field, with two poised for such ministry in England.

That Wesley did not accept that his ordinations were a final act of separation is not due to his obstinacy in old age. He had consistently, for nearly thirty years, believed that the ties which bound him to the Church of England were deeper than those of church order and lawful obedience to the Bishops. He really did believe that it was much more important that he and his Methodists continued to attend the prayers and sacraments of the Established Church. The Methodist timetable had always been very carefully adjusted so as not to conflict with attendance at the ordinances in the parish church. And here the law was on his side, for such attendance and such participation marked off the churchmen from Dissenters, and was fenced by Acts of Parliament.

It is true there was growing pressure to abandon this timetable. There was a great set-to in Dublin in 1789 when Coke connived at such a withdrawal, but he was promptly countered by Wesley who admitted mitigating circumstances, but insisted that the Methodists should take the Sacrament at St Patrick's Cathedral once a month.[109] For Wesley, such attendance was no mere matter of the law of the land.

According to Adam Clarke, John Wesley described to the Conference of 1788 the difference between his methods and those of Thomas Coke:[110] 'He would tear all from top to bottom, I will not tear, but unstitch.' And therein lay great, if unconscious wisdom. Had Wesley 'torn out' the Methodists in 1742 or 1755, the Methodists might have shrunk to a small sect. But the changes Wesley made he made slowly, reluctantly, as he said, 'stitch by stitch', keeping, as he repeatedly affirmed, his love for the Church of England. By drawing things out so long, he contributed powerfully to the stability and growth of the Methodist movement, an inner strength such as enabled it to survive the tensions after his death, the divided forces within, the pressures of the industrial revolution and the revolutionary age.[111]

The Church of England did nothing to prevent the separation. As Newman said, 'it had no one clear consistent view of Methodism as a

[109] Wesley, *Journal*, vii. 482.   [110] Vickers, *Thomas Coke*, p. 46.

[111] The Membership in Great Britain in 1791 was 132,097; in 1814 162,003.

phenomenon: it did not take it as a whole — it did not meet it — it gave out no authoritative judgement on it — it formed no definition of it — it had no line of policy towards it.'[112] Had Convocation been in session, the results might have been happier — or unhappier, who can say? No doubt the Bishops often discussed the Methodists in their meetings in London, but nothing was proposed or done to keep the movement within the Church. In a famous essay Macaulay contrasted the flexibility of the Church of Rome. 'Place Ignatius Loyola at Oxford, he is certain to become the head of a formidable secession. Place John Wesley at Rome, he is certain to become the first General of a new society.'[113] Whether in fact the eighteenth-century Roman Church would have proved so amenable to such a revival might be questioned. But if modern historians have seen obvious similarities between the Methodists and the Franciscans or the Jesuits, such a parallel did not enter into the consideration of Protestant Englishmen, Methodist or Church of England men. Nor is it easy to see what might have been done. A Church which needed a new Act of Parliament for each new parish, which had seen the State baffle each attempt to send a bishop to America for three-quarters of a century, was not able to produce creative and revolutionary measures, nor was its leadership of a calibre likely to promote them. The vague idea that Wesley might have been made a bishop might have raised more difficulties than it solved. The more plausible notion that 'a part' (Wesley at his most optimistic never envisaged the ordination of all his preachers) 'of the preachers might be ordained', would have seemed fantastic to bishops already conscious that there were too many clergy already.[114]

It would perhaps have been something, if any leaders of the Church had expressed in public deep concern or alarm at the prospect of such separation, and made any gesture to prevent it. And Wesley, though he rendered lip service to the Bishops and obeyed them in all things lawful and honest, does not seem to have consulted any one of them, as a Father in God, who might have given him counsel. Thus the overwhelming pressure of events, the religious and psychological, moved towards separation. The leaders of the Church of England, as with the Nonconformists a century before, were content to absolve themselves with an untroubled conscience, from the doleful schism.

We have not felt able to dissent from the common view that the

---

[112] J. H. Newman, *Essays Critical and Historical* (1910) i. 404.

[113] T. B. Macaulay, *Critical and Historical Essays* (1946), ii. 63.

[114] N. Sykes, in *Conversations between the Church of England and the Methodist Church, an Interim Statement*, ch. 3, p. 11.

separation of the Methodists from the Church of England became inevitable once the movement developed its own framework of religious practices and that it was 'natural that the majority of Methodist converts, drawn from the ranks of the dissenters or the classes of those neglected by the administrations of the Church of England should sit loose to the practices of the Church of England.'[115] But at least there are questions to be asked.

The attempt of a handful of Methodist preachers in the 1750s to administer the sacraments and to gain the endorsement of their actions by the Conference of preachers did indeed raise the question of separation. It is often implied that only the personal authority of the Wesleys resolved, or rather postponed, the crisis. But is it really the case that this minority of preachers represented the *communis sensus fidelium?* May not John Wesley have understood his people better than a group of men with strong psychological reasons for enhancing their role? A glance at Wesley's *Journal* for any one year will show that he, and he alone, had his finger on the pulse of the whole movement, north, south, east, west.

As for converts from Dissent, George Whitefield and Howell Harris were more hospitable towards the Nonconformists than Wesley, whom they in turn treated with suspicion. Converts indeed there were, and we hear occasionally of parts of an Independent congregation joining the Methodists. But had there been large-scale defections we should have heard very much more about them. Nor can we assume that the ex-Dissenters kept their anti-Anglican, anti-liturgical predjudices. Converts often undergo a sea change — like those ex-Dissenters Bishop Joseph Butler and Archbishop Secker. We know of Quakers whom the Wesleys baptized and they would not have been the first or the last ex-Quakers to find new meaning in the Eucharist. May not others have been impressed by the example and teaching of John Wesley?

How little the ex-Dissenters among them affected the general temper of the Methodists became clear when the older Nonconformists supported the American colonists and the first stages of the French Revolution. The attempt of Alexander Kilham to swing the Conference behind the doctrinaire liberalism of Price and Priestley was decisively rejected by the Methodists. The sharp distinction which they drew between themselves and the older Dissenting bodies lasted another half a century and would have lasted longer had not the Oxford Movement drawn the non-Anglican bodies together.

As for 'the classes neglected by the administrations of the church', it is

---

[115] Sykes, *Church and State*, p. 394.

true that among the miners of Bristol and Cornwall and the workmen of the Potteries and Black Country there must have been many who, before their conversion, had little to do with religion. But they did not mould the temper of Methodism. A list of the occupations of the class leaders, if not the trustees, shows those who made the movement 'tick'.

In fact it is likely that the largest class of Methodist converts were not ex-Nonconformists or those with minimal contact with the Church, but were members of the Church of England who were no more 'in' or 'out', and alas, neither more nor less neglected than the majority of members of the Church of England. That is, they had been baptized in the Church of England. Like George Whitefield — and Samuel Johnson — they had learned at their mother's knee the elements of doctrine and morality. If they were fortunate, for the administration of the rite was far from universal, they had been confirmed, and if they were luckier still, this had been preceded by instruction. How many of them regularly worshipped in their parish church we cannot tell, any more than we can tell the percentage of regular worshippers in the Church of England throughout the century.

When, in 1782, the Methodist Conference pleaded with the Methodists not to walk out of parish services (which they must have been attending, or the injunction had no point), this was because of the offensive attacks upon them by hyper-Calvinists and not at all in criticism of the liturgy.

It was not the example of the Wesleys alone, still less was it something the Methodists thought up on their own after the death of their founders, which led Methodists to retain the Prayer Book service of Morning Prayer in some churches until within living memory, or to use a hardly altered 1662 rite until the present day.

The Methodists whom we meet in all parts of the land in Wesley's *Journal*, the good people who in Preston, Darlaston, Exeter, and St Ives had their furniture smashed, their windows broken, their shop goods spoiled, were law-abiding citizens and, in the old sense of the word, respectable Christians. The *onus probandi* is on those who assert that they sat loose to the 'practices of the Church of England'.

I do not wish to exaggerate. One must accept the fact that from 1760 onwards there was a growing estrangement. For one thing, there was now a second generation within the Revival itself, and the families of those converted during the 1740s had grown up within a Methodist-centred spiritual environment. Not only did they have their own pattern of disciplined community life, but more and more of them worshipped within their own preaching houses. The second generation of Methodist preachers had matured within this Methodist framework, and some of the leaders now emerging would be those who would direct Methodism after Wesley's death. They had many of them taken hard knocks from hostile clergy, and they did not discourage their people when affronted by the worldliness — very widely defined — of the clergy of the Established Church, at whose hands they received the Sacrament. But to the extent to which the Evangelical Revival was a eucharistic revival, and to which this continued (as statistics attest) during Wesley's lifetime, the identity of the Methodists with the Church of England was real.

We have also to recognize that although the more spectacular anti-Methodist demonstrations had occurred in the 1740s, there was evident from the 1770s onwards a hardening hostility on the part of the Church of England. The Revd William Cole complained to his friend Mrs Barton at his new cure at Waterbeach (1767) partly from chagrin that he had to beg garage space from the Methodists for his beloved chaise with its painted escutcheon.

The grief of grief is yet behind: the parish swarms with Methodists: my two neighbours on each side are such, and opposite to me the same: and indeed, look where I will, the same heresy looks me in the face. . . I am forced to go cap in hand to a little pert teacher among them, by profession a collar maker: this brother preacher accommodates me with his barn for my chaise to stand in . . . I can't cross the yard but this mechanical teacher with the usual puritanical assurance and forwardness must needs greets me every time with 'Good Morrow', or 'How d'ye Neighbour'.[116]

At the end of our period, when a young Painite radical shot and killed that finest of Methodist craftsmen, Enoch Wood, for forbidding him to see his daughter, Samuel Parr wrote to Sheridan that, after all, the murder was a very venial offence, but warned him that the Methodists stick together.

The Methodists unite the language of saints with the temper of fiends. They are not social but gregarious and as they wage war against the common sense and common feelings of mankind, they make common cause among themselves upon all occasions. Monkeys imitate men, and in the same way sectarian tribes imitate that form of commonwealth which one of the seven Greek sages recommended and in which the leading rule was — wrong done to one citizen should be punished and resented by all.[117]

Not that the Tory, William Cole, and the Whig, Samuel Parr, were run-of-the-mill clerical types, but the bitter, angry and contemptuous hostility was there, and played its part in ensuring the separation.

All in all, these considerations help us to understand why Wesley laid more stress on this community in worship than on his ordinations. As

[116] William Cole, *The Blecheley Diary*, ed. F. G. Stokes (1931), pp. 310–11.
[117] W. Derry, *Dr. Parr* (Oxford 1966), p. 194.

far as England was concerned, his ordinations were quite ineffectual and were to be disregarded by the Methodists themselves. And though it is understandable that to contemporary churchmen, as to later generations, the ordinations marked the beginning of overt schism, they were also to some extent a smoke-screen hiding from the Church of England its own share of responsibility for the separation.

None the less, as long as John Wesley lived, his Methodists were able to share in worship with the other members of the Church of England, and as long as great numbers continued to partake of the Eucharist, we may believe that they did so not grudgingly or of necessity, but for conscience sake. They were, in our ecumenical jargon, in full communion *in sacris*. Not as a concession, but as a right and as a bounden duty they kneeled before the Lord's Table, they made their prayers from the Book of Common Prayer, and they received the Body and Blood of Christ at the hands of those authorized to administer them. While Wesley lived, this was not only a sign, but the expression of unity.

x. Kindled by . . .?

The side-effects of great religious movements are not easy to diagnose or to prove, and in the case of the Evangelical Revival, historians have used generalizations which outrun the evidence, in which there are great gaps not yet filled by the rapidly growing number of dissertations and local histories. Great claims have been made, probably rightly, for the effects of the Franciscan movement in the thirteenth century: for its influence on Italian art in Giotto and his successors; for the change of mood from an earlier world pessimism to a new appreciation of nature; and a new learning, and affective spirituality in the writings of Occam, Scotus, and St Bonaventure. Less dramatic but large, claims have been made about the Evangelical Revival, but there must always be an element of uncertainty how far such movements reflect, and how far they really change, the environment.

That the whole manner of existence of individuals and the character of local communities were changed is beyond dispute. Without exaggeration of the number of converted boozers, men and women were turned from disordered characters into sober, decent people into whose homes there came new stabilities and joys. As with the first Quakers, thrift and diligence, the absence of profanity, trustworthiness, put such men on a social escalator which moved. Some of them learned to read first, for the sake of their Bible and hymn books, but thereafter pamphlets, books, and newspapers. Class leaders and preachers became articulate, even eloquent, for most of them were not the noisy windbags they seemed to a Cole, a Sydney Smith, a Cobbett. They became used to handling group relationships, money, and affairs, to caring for one another and to ministering to the poor, though the novelty of this is not to be exaggerated, for the older Nonconformist bodies knew all about these things, and they too taught little people to look out for, and look after, their communities. The more distant side-effects were not observable for a generation, and it is in the interesting period 1791–1815 (when prophets had foretold the Methodists would dwindle and disappear) that an accelerating Methodism became closely involved with the accelerating Industrial Revolution.

It is perhaps high time for historians to escape from what might be called the 'Halévy syndrome'. The eminent French historian, Élie Halévy suggested that it was Methodism which saved England from revolution,[118] by creating among the working people a body of men who were conservative and passive towards social change. Why, in fact, there was no revolution in England in 1789 or 1830 or 1848 is indeed an intriguing question on which others have pondered besides Friedrich Engels (who looked for it to break out in Manchester). But to resolve it one might need to go very far back, to consider the consequences of the Saxon Heptarchy and the Norman Conquest, Magna Carta, Simon de Montfort, Henry VIII and the monasteries, the Civil War and the Glorious Revolution, the growing prosperity and, if the word may still be used, the 'stability' of the Hanoverian age, and the colonial and military adventures of the eighteenth century.

Certainly Halévy exaggerated the extent to which in Wesley's lifetime the Methodists were made up of workers in industry, and the extent to which they 'inundated' such areas as Yorkshire. Without minimizing the significance of the Kingswood colliers, the Staffordshire potters, the keelmen of Newcastle, or the miners of Cornwall, they were not the majority or the influential part of the Methodists. There seem to have been about 54,000 Methodists in England at Wesley's death and it is hard to see how such a body, far removed from the corridors of power, could have 'saved', still less threatened, the nation. Shopkeepers, tradesmen, skilled artisans, and an even higher proportion of young, middle-aged, and elderly women could not have stormed any barricades, had they been so minded. There were more Mary Bosanquets than Madeleines, and even Mrs Sarah Ryan was no Mme Defarge. Unlike the first Anabaptists, the Methodists of that day were short on female viragos. But some Methodists took Halévy's judgement as a compli-

---

[118] É. Halévy, *A History of the English People in the Nineteenth Century* (Eng. Tr. 1949), pp. 387, 590–1.

ment and laid themselves wide open to the retort that they had simply fostered an other-worldly pietism, diverting men from their true business — the amendment of the condition of the working class.

More interesting, because more plausible, was another essay of Halévy, the result of a scamper through the Bodleian Library in 1905, on *The Birth of Methodism*.[119] Halévy saw the Evangelical Revival as a further explosion of the spirit of seventeenth-century Puritanism, and one which finally established the fundamental Puritanism of the English people. 'The English', he declared, 'are a nation of Puritans.' A great field of research since Halévy's death has shown the complex and many-sided character of the Puritan movement, in the light of which Halévy's explanation seems simplistic and indeed naïve.

He thought the Puritans were rather like the 'Muslims of Africa' — 'solemn, proud, silent'. Well, proud they may have been and perhaps needed to be to keep up with the prelates and the courtiers. Silent they certainly were not. Never in the field of human history can so many millions of words have been uttered by so few people. But it was 'solemn' which counted for most. Napoleon called us a nation of shopkeepers, but on Halévy's reading of our national character we seem rather to have been a nation of undertakers, interspersed here and there by little groups of jolly atheists.[120] Halévy thought he found evidence of the Puritan hangover in contemporary references to melancholy as 'the English Malady' (they came mainly from France, and Halévy was perhaps more influenced by Voltaire and de la Rochefoucald than by the English evidence.)[121] He found confirmation in the famous book with that title by Dr George Cheyne. But as Dr Walsh comments, it is not possible to say whether the nervous disorders with which the book deals were not simply the 'hypochondria of a bored and leisured class'. And in fact Dr Cheyne put it down to luxuries ('french cooking' and 'oriental pickles') and laziness — 'the inactivity and sedentary occupations of the better sort (among whom the evil mostly reigns)'.[122] Halévy singled out that part of Cheyne's work in which he told of his own struggles with melancholy (weighing 32 stone he had his problems), but he does not

[119] *The Birth of Methodism in England*, tr. and ed. B. Semmell, Chicago 1971. For a critique, J. D. Walsh, 'Élie Halévy and the Birth of Methodism', *TRHS* (5th series) xxv, 1975. On Halévy's defective knowledge of Methodist history, J. Kent, 'M. Élie Halévy on Methodism', *PWHS* xxix. 4 (Dec. 1953), 84.

[120] 'The temperament of the Free Thinker is quite different . . . souls less accessible to worry and doubt . . . more carefree and if you like more frivolous temperaments are needed', *The Birth of Methodism,* p. 39. One might have thought that doubting was the very *raison d'être* of scepticism.

[121] But see J. McManners, *Death and the Enlightenment* (Oxford, 1981), pp. 428 ff.

[122] G. Cheyne, *The English Malady or a Treatise of Nervous diseases,* 1735.

mention that, far from being a Puritan, Cheyne was a high churchman, as was that other famous melancholic, Samuel Johnson. The high incidence of suicide which Halévy also mentions did indeed trouble men, including John Wesley and William Pitt, but it has to be demonstrated that this had any relation to the side-effects of Puritanism.[123] When we look at examples — as when Sir Wolstan Dixie assaulted his neighbour and then tried in vain and three times to cut his own throat, when the poet Chatterton died in poverty, and when Hannah More and friends rescued a young woman who tried to kill herself at a Masquerade from jealousy — the kind of high- and low-life pictures in Hogarth, in novels and plays, point in the more likely direction. And one may reserve judgement as to whether at any time the English have ever been more melancholic than Goethe's Germans, Catherine the Great's Russians, or Kierkegaard's Scandinavians! The solemnity of the Puritans and the sombreness of the Evangelicals can be exaggerated. There is more music and laughter in *Pilgrim's Progress* than in the writings of John Donne or William Law. Joy was a hallmark of the evangelical experience, and 'dour' the least apposite of all adjectives applied to Methodist spirituality.

A serious moralism was indeed part of the background of the Revival, as it had been of the preceding age. But Halévy, like some modern historians, used the word 'puritan' when he should have written 'Protestant', or simply 'Christian'. From the time of the English Reformers there had been a great emphasis on catechism, on teaching in home and church of the basic elements of Christian doctrine and morality. A succession of churchmen, Puritan and Caroline, had continued this tradition in the next age and it was reinforced in the period after the Restoration by churchmen of all kinds, including Ken and Kidder, Burnet and Samuel Clarke.

One of the few reassuring features of the eighteenth-century Visitation returns is the evidence that such moral instruction was taken seriously, and the number of parishes where it was, at least intermittently, given. It was, after all, not in the conventicles, but in the parish churches that the Ten Commandments were publicly displayed. *The Whole Duty of Man* (written by a high churchman) was read and taught at all levels of society and reinforced by a spate of publications by the (high-church) SPCK. The supreme moralists of the age were the Anglicans Joseph Butler and Samuel Johnson. Not even in Wales was the Evangelical Revival the sole and direct product of the Nonconformists the true heirs of the Puritans.

---

[123] McManners, *Death and the Enlightenment,* p. 429.

Halévy's closing paragraph had a further point. The 'grand accident' that the Evangelical Revival in England broke out in the years 1739–41 was because at that time

England experienced a crisis of industrial over-production of extreme gravity which reduced the lower orders of the manufactories to poverty and made them accessible to all forms of collective emotion, at a time when scientific rationalism had not yet been disseminated.[124]

One might ask why the Welsh Revival, which was already in full spate, and the 'Awakening' in America, which had preceded it, was not rooted in industrial crisis? But if modern economic historians would revise much of Halévy's diagnosis,[125] it may be granted that in those formative years for the English Revival there were bitter winters, poor harvests, high prices, deep poverty. Nor should we deny that extreme physical need, grinding poverty, distress and pain, open the minds and hearts of men to any kind of good news, true or false (any parson knows these things can have the opposite effect, of closing minds and hearts in bitterness and resentment against religion, especially when allied with a comfortable Establishment). And, as Halévy failed to explain, such conditions had nothing to do with the conversions of the Wesleys, Whitefield, and Howell Harris. One may conclude, with a recent Welsh historian, that these things were a fine thread in the stuff of the Revival.

Of course, religious experience does not take place in a vacuum, and we have to do with men in the whole context of their existence. The social and psychological factors are to be treated seriously. Dr Walsh points out how 'the conversion experiences of the first Methodists show many anxiety-producing features — spiritual yearning, religious doubts, sexual difficulty, social and geographical mobility, pain and bereavement', though this is a list of ills to which most young people are heir and it does not explain why such things made *A* conversion-prone and *B* conditioned against it. (Samuel Johnson had every one of the symptoms mentioned.) But when an atheist historian attempts to dispose of the whole Evangelical Revival in psychological terms, one can only say with the lady, 'Well, he would, wouldn't he?' and ask for really convincing evidence. To concentrate on sexual repression not only fudges the evidence, but ignores the fact that the eighteenth century was much more open and relaxed about such things than the nineteenth century. It is similar with the attempt to explain all in terms of fear and 'hell-fire preaching'. It is true that fear was an element in eighteenth-century religion (but not to the degree of say, the later Middle Ages?). A glance at the savage penal code reminds us that in

[124] *Birth of Methodism,* p. 77.
[125] T. E. Ashton, *Economic Fluctuations in England, 1700–1800,* Oxford 1969.

secular society too, fear was the Great Deterrent. The reality of hell, the threat of judgement to come, was an element in all orthodox Christian teaching (it was what Samuel Johnson's mother talked to him about when he was aged two). But there are grimmer passages about it in *The Whole Duty of Man* and in the sermons of St Francis of Sales than in the sermons of John Wesley. Hell fire was not the dominant preaching of the Evangelical Revival.

And if the social historians and the psychologists deserve attention, so do the theologians. Paul and Augustine, Luther, Bunyan, Pascal have something to say about what Augustine called 'the abyss of human conscience'. For in the Evangelical Revival it was not the accepted moralism of the age, not the exposition of the moral law as teaching, as *didachē* but the preaching of the Law as part of the *kērugma* which mattered, not what Freud calls *Angst,* but what Luther called *Anfechtung.*

In 1746 the Conference of Methodist Preachers checked up on their preaching and asked: 'Do we empty men of their own righteousness as we did at first? Do we sufficiently labour when they begin to be convinced of sin, to take away all they lean upon?'

Did we not then purposely throw them into conviction? Into strong sorrow and fear? Nay, did we not strive to make them inconsolable? . . . We did, and so we should do still. For the stronger the conviction, and speedier is the deliverance; and none so soon received the peace of God as those who steadily refuse all other comfort.

This was not something improvised by the Methodists, but a view of salvation going back through the Christian centuries to the New Testament. When God confronts men in their consciences as an 'ought' which stands over and against them, and when they become aware of the seriousness of their own plight, they are at the point when for the first time they can recognize and accept from God forgiveness and reconciliation and a new energy of life.

The historian may not be concerned with such imponderables, but he cannot fail to notice that in the eighteenth century many thousands of men and women believed this to be a true description of the most important encounter in their lives, whose changed content and direction seemed to be compelling evidence that it was no dream. The story of the Evangelical Revival as described by its most authentic witnesses makes neither rhyme nor reason if the possibility is excluded that it was indeed 'kindled by a spark of grace'.

22

CALVINISTS AND EVANGELICALS

i. The Welsh Revival

THE revivals in Wales and in Scotland, the emergence of a Calvinistic Methodist Church, and of the Countess of Huntingdon's Connexion, and of an Evangelical Movement within the Church of England have a common basis in Calvinist (as distinct from Wesley's) theology. All owed something to the inspiration and labours of George Whitefield. To consider only his work in England is to see the smaller part of his achievement in America and in Britain. He was the supreme evangelist, the great reaper, moving instinctively to where the fields were white to harvest. This is in no way to minimize the importance of the forerunners, Freylinghausen, the Tennants, and Jonathan Edwards in America; Griffith Jones, Howell Harris, and Daniel Rowlands in Wales; the Erskine brothers and McCulloch and Robe in Scotland. But in each area he made an indispensable contribution. Where a revival had begun to languish, he brought fresh inspiration; where it was in progress, he raised it to new fervour and fruition. Nor did he believe in isolated tip-and-run raids, but he went again and again to the same places, with an untiring spate of effectual speech. For wherever he went, in America, England, Scotland, and Wales, the crowds came round him and hung upon his words. If his work as a young man had been sensational, it had obviously been flawed by immaturity, but in the 1740s we see him at the full stretch of his powers.

The Welsh Revival was one of the most remarkable of the disparate movements of the Evangelical Revival.[1] It took place within a compact area, of Welsh language and culture (John Wesley's Methodists were chiefly in the English-speaking parts of Wales).[2] Its impact on the life of the country was deep and lasting. Although the leaders and much of the movement had close links with the Established Church, it drew also on the tough, deep roots of Welsh Nonconformity which itself had been nurtured in one of the richest spiritual and theological traditions of Puritanism, and had produced great preachers and leaders and an important edifying literature. The first name to be mentioned must be

---

[1] D. Llwyd Morgan, *Y Diwygiad Mawr*, (Cardiff 1981) (an admirable study).

[2] Wesley made thirty-five visits to Wales, and passed through the country on another eighteen occasions. A. H. Williams, *John Wesley in Wales*, Cardiff 1971; G. H. Jenkins, *Literature, Religion and Society in Wales 1660–1730* (Cardiff 1980).

that of Griffith Jones (1683–1761), the Rector of Llanddowror. He was a powerful and effective preacher whose zeal and fervour led him at first to ignore parish boundaries and to preach in the open air to great congregations. But though he became a father in God to some of the young men who were pioneers of the Revival, he distrusted their excitement and was outspoken in his comments to them. But certainly at the beginning of the Revival, Llanddowror was a place where wise counsel was given and to which the young men resorted. Of a hypochondriac disposition, he was often at Bath, where both John Wesley and George Whitefield sought him out. Even more remarkable than his career as an evangelist and a preacher was his work for religious education. He saw that no kind of renewal of Christianity could take place amid an ignorant and untutored population. He found that 'where 60 or 80 came into his schools, not above 3 or 4 could say the Lord's Prayer.' The SPCK had founded some ninety-six schools in Wales between 1699 and 1727 and had distributed Welsh Bibles and other books, continuing the work of Thomas Gouge's Welsh Trust (1674–81). Griffith Jones was helped to extend this work by Sir John Phillips, that great encourager, and Madam Bridget Bevan, who has been described as a 'poor man's Countess of Huntingdon'. Beginning with his own school at Llanddowror he began a system of ambulatory religious education, in which the teachers taught reading and instructed in the Catechism, and then moved on to another place. The whole operation was run 'on a shoestring'[3] and much of the teaching was done in barns or in churches (there was a great deal of co-operation, as well as some fierce opposition, from the local clergy). The teachers were poorly paid, between £3 and £4 a year, but they were given some sort of training at Llanddowror and there was no lack of applicants for the demanding work. Jones claimed that within six or seven weeks the brighter children could learn to read Welsh, and there were English schools in Pembrokeshire. Between 1737 and 1761 there were 3,325 schools held in just under 1,600 places, with 153,835 scholars.[4] A conservative estimate is that within twenty-five years some 200,000 had been taught to read, at a time when the population of Wales may have been between 4–500,000. Jones was not only a planner, but a visionary, who looked beyond his own work to the renewal of the whole Church and the 'utter reformation of a degenerate age'.

But it was Howell Harris (1714–73) who was the linchpin of the Revival in Wales, not only as one of the Welsh leaders, but as the one who maintained its connection with the Wesleys and even more with

---

[3] G. Williams, *Religion, Language and Nationality in Wales* (Cardiff 1979) p. 205.

[4] Ibid., p. 207.

Whitefield. He was born in the village where he also died, at Trevecka, near Talgarth in Breconshire in 1714. He came of poor parents, but his brothers were affluent, and the worst sin of his unregenerate youth was a cruel snobbishness towards his home. His conversion came after a period of intense spiritual struggle between Easter and Whitsun 1735. A sense of divine forgiveness came upon him at the Lord's Table and soon afterwards.

I felt suddenly my heart melting within me, like wax before fire, with love to God my Saviour: and also felt not only love and peace but a longing to be dissolved and be with Christ. There was a cry in my soul, which I was totally unacquainted with before — 'Abba, Father!' I could not help calling God my father. I knew that I was his child and that he loved and heard me.[5]

He began to visit friends and neighbours, reading, praying, and exhorting. He took counsel with Griffith Jones who warned him that if he wanted to be ordained he had better walk delicately and give no offence to those in authority. He got across the local vicar, and went ahead with characteristic impetuosity and when he presented himself to the Bishop, despite good testimonials, he was abruptly dismissed. But he pressed on to become the first lay preacher and field preacher of the Revival. The evangelistic demands on his time led him to abandon his teaching work in one of Griffith Jones's schools and henceforth he gave all his time and energy to his itinerancy.

Meanwhile, elsewhere in Wales, other leaders were emerging. The most notable, rivalling Harris in gifts and in prestige, was Daniel Rowlands (1713–91). Unlike Harris, who had sprung Melchizidek-like out of the blue, Rowlands was of clerical family and, when ordained deacon, assisted his brother who was Rector of Llangeitho as their father had been. Though he did not go to a university, he studied hard, and was widely read in theology of an orthodox kind. If the Bible was paramount for his thought, he also revered the Thirty-nine Articles and the Westminster Catechism, while the Athanasian, Nicene, and Apostles' creeds were the framework of his doctrine. He was a powerful preacher, in his youth preaching between two and four-hour sermons which shortened mercifully during his ministry. He was a man of explosive energy, and no enemies denied his utter integrity. He was a much more

    [5] G. T. Roberts, *Howell Harris*, Wesley Historical Society Lectures No. 17 (1951), p. 18; H. R. Harris, *Howell Harris*, n.d.; B. Knox, 'The Wesleys and Howell Harris', *Studies in Church History*, ed. D. Baker 1966; G. Nuttall, *Howell Harris the Last Enthusiast*, University of Wales 1965; D. L. Morgan, *Y Diwygiad Mawr*; R. W. Evans, 'The relations of George Whitefield and Howell Harris, Fathers of Calvinistic Methodism', *Church History*, June 1961.

human person than Harris, and while Harris could rebuke his house-keeper at Trevecka for her 'levity' in drinking tea, Rowlands did not banish good cheer or laughter from his table. Under Rowlands Llangeitho became a centre of counsel, and indeed of pilgrimage, for the converts. He and Harris did not meet until some years after the Revival had begun, when they rubbed one another the wrong way, and there were elements of jealousy and rivalry between them. But in the time of crisis and separation which was to come in the late 1740s, it was Rowlands who held the movement together and who made possible the harvesting of the new revival which began in 1762. Another important convert of Harris was Howell Davis (1716–70) and the even more remarkable William Williams of Pantecelyn (1717–91). Notable leaders of second rank were John Thomas and John Evans.

What strikes one about these pioneers is their youth — 'A Heap of Boys', said Harris. For they were born within a few years of one another and were in their middle and late twenties in the opening years of the Revival. Derec Llwyd Morgan, in his remarkable study, speaks of their ministry, their evangelism, and the Revival itself as a 'great Adventure' and points to a very important element of the Evangelical Revival, its virile appeal to youth. As in the earlier Religious Societies, it was young men and women who were attracted in large numbers, bringing with them the splendid energies and the awkward truculencies of the young, as well as the inevitable problems of young people seeking to live together in a new kind of community experience.

William Williams is known in England only by his fine hymn 'Guide me, O thou great Jehovah', but he was the greatest hymn writer of a revival which, as in England, was inspired and moved on its way by its song. The son of a Nonconformist father and an Anglican mother, he was given a Dissenting-academy education which included the sacred languages, and it has been said that he was the most theological of all the Welsh revivalists. After his conversion he was slow to mature and it was not until after a period of much thought and meditation that he began to exercise leadership, which was most marked in the second phase of the Welsh Revival. He did not think in individualist terms, for the thought of the Church as the Body of Christ was of great importance to him and he found the image of this in the Methodist society, stressing the importance of mutual counselling among those pressing on to Christian maturity. His epic poem, one among a great number of poetical writings, *The Prospect of the Kingdom of Christ,* is a very remarkable piece of spiritual writing, more profound and perceptive than anything written in English, say by Watts or Wesley. It has been called his *summa theologica,* for its theme embraces the whole sweep of divine redemption, and against the background of a Newtonian universe he stresses the unity of creation and redemption in Christ. He seems to blend the Pauline gospel of Romans and Galatians with the themes of Colossians, Ephesians, and the prologue to the Fourth Gospel in an inspiring panorama of the divine economy which began with Covenant and Creation, and found its centre in the redemption of the world by Christ, in the life of the Church as Christ's body and in the consummation of all things in the Kingdom of Christ.

As far as a non-Welsh reader can gather from the commentaries of his compatriots, one wonders if in English theology there would be anything quite like this until Frederick Denison Maurice.

Like the other evangelists, Harris soon had to face the problem of building his converts together, and he may have been put on the track by the brother-in-law of Griffith Jones, Sir John Phillips, the great patron of the Religious Societies. By the beginning of March 1739 Harris had about thirty societies in South Wales (increased to sixty-four by the end of 1740): '10 and above in Glamorganshire, about so many in Monmouthshire, about 15 in Brecknockshire about 10 in Carmarthenshire, and so many in Cardiganshire; 5 in Pembrokeshire: 4 in Radnorshire and Herefordshire'.

Meanwhile Harris had met Whitefield at Cardiff. Harris reported 'The first thing he said to me was "Do you know your sins are forgiven?"' Harris was to become Whitefield's chief helper in a close alliance which was not broken until 1749. Whitefield and Seward made a short trip to Wales in March 1739 and took Harris back to Bristol with him. Harris and he found they were agreed about the Calvinist doctrines and opposed to the 'notions' of John Wesley.

People seem to have mattered more to Harris than ideas, and sharp differences melted away when he met Charles Wesley face to face or sat under a sermon by John. Zinzendorf's eirenicism was a thought-out matter, but Harris simply had a reconciling heart, which was to prompt him to any initiatives towards the Wesleys and the Moravians in coming years. His language was often flowery and emotional, as may be seen in an ungrudging testimony to the powerful preaching of Daniel Rowlands:

Such crying out and heartbreaking groans, silent weeping and holy joy and shouts of rejoicing I never saw. Their Amens and crying Glory in the Highest etc. would enflame your soul . . . 'tis very common . . . for scores to fall down by the power of the word, pierced and wounded or overcome by the love of God and sights of the beauty and excellency of Jesus . . . some lie there for hours, some praising and admiring Jesus, free Grace, Distinguishing Grace . . . you might read the language of a heart running over with love in their heavenly looks . . . others lie wounded under a sense of their piercing Jesus, so that they can hardly bear it.[6]

Soon Harris added to existing commitments the responsibility of spending some weeks each year in London, at first with the Wesleys at the Foundery, and then with the disciples of Whitefield at the Tabernacle. Here he became one of the leaders and took charge after the defection of Cennick to the Moravians in 1746. None the less, Wales was his vocation. 'I believe I am not called to labour among the rich and the great, I am sent among the Hills of Wales, to my poor ignorant, despised Countrymen', he wrote in November 1742. He and his fellow preachers suffered many attacks from many mobs. One of the worst was during his first visit to Caernarvonshire, a traumatic experience which would bring him nightmares to the end of his days. Later at Bala he received an enormous blow on the head which may have left permanent mark on his nerves and mind. But never for one moment would he spare himself. "Tis now about 9 weeks since I began to go round South and North Wales', he wrote in 1748.[7]

I have now visited in that time 13 counties, and travelled mostly 150 miles every week, and discoursed twice every day and sometimes three or four times a day: and this last journey I have not taken off my clothes for 7 nights, and travelled from one morning to the next evening without rest, above 100 miles.

Harris and Rowlands welded the converts and the societies into the Calvinistic Methodist body which in the years 1742–3 developed its own polity, its own technical vocabulary, for a movement now distinct from that of other Methodists. It seems that in Wales there was a higher proportion among the Methodists of ordained clergymen than in England, though some of them were deacons, and they were combined in one association with the lay exhorters. The societies were divided into groups according to their districts which held their own regular meetings where all the smaller societies were represented. Monthly and two-monthly meetings were held and finally an overall Association met at Carmarthenshire in January 1742. Decisions were taken on a more democratic basis than among the Wesleyan societies, but there was still the need for an overall leadership. Harris could not work under Rowlands, and the attempted solution was the invitation to George Whitefield to become their Moderator. He presided at important meetings in 1742 and at the even more fateful gatherings at Watford in the following year when the first United Association of both English and Welsh Calvinistic Methodists met.

---

[6] Harris to G. Whitefield, *Trevecka Letters* i. 81.   [7] *Trevecka Letters*, ii. 21.

Towards the end of the decade trouble arose, at the centre of which
was Howell Harris, and a result was a withdrawal of allegiance from
Harris towards Rowlands. Harris became infected with Moravian
notions, which chimed with his own florid emotionalism, and he began
to preach a rather muddled kind of Patripassianism. Very Celt of very
Celt he was, in the warmth of his emotion. But his affection and his
ebullience carried with them their own defects. There was an instability
about him which the incessant pressures of his energetic labours did not
ease. A series of crises occurred in the late 1740s. He began to
perambulate with a formidable twenty-nine-year-old prophetess, Madam
Sidney Griffith, who had left her drunken husband for a career as a
public soothsayer, and who completely mesmerized Harris. The
relationship was not beyond propriety, though it roused the jealousy of
Mrs Harris (egged on by Mrs Whitefield who had married Whitefield,
as they say, on the rebound from Harris). It caused endless gossip and
led to a breach with Whitefield who denied him the Tabernacle. Matters
eased with the death of Mrs Griffith, but Harris himself suffered an
almost complete breakdown and did not recover until 1752, by which
time his leading supporters had almost all moved over to Daniel
Rowlands as the leader of the movement.

He now retired for a time to Trevecka which he rebuilt as a 'Family'.
It was a community like that of the Moravians, and scores of craftsmen,
skilled artisans, and labourers worked together in an impressive society.
It prospered, and from it he sent five members to the wars, to fight for
Quebec in Canada. He himself, in time of war and threatened invasion,
became an ensign in the Brecknockshire militia and travelled across
England, where his adventures included a preachment in Yarmouth in
full regimentals. Like that other militiaman, Edward Gibbon, he liked
wearing his uniform, and the spell in a military role seems to have done
both men good. Gradually he began to resume old ties and his preaching
tours. It is interesting that through all this time John Wesley did not
waver in his friendship. In these later years he was much in alliance with
the Countess of Huntingdon, who founded her seminary at Trevecka,
close to Harris and his 'Family'.

The continual absences of Whitefield in America and Britain stunted
the growth of his societies in London. There were times when the
Tabernacle seemed a rather disgruntled shadow of the Foundery. And in
their bands and societies, their discipline and in their philanthropy, they
were very alike. The Tabernacle Minutes,[8] some of which have
survived, show a strict discipline to which the leaders were also subject

---

[8] E. Welch, *Two Calvinistic Methodist Chapels 1743–1811*, London Record Society, 1975.

and they kept a watchful eye on marriages. As at the Foundery, there were some trouble makers, sometimes moving from one body to the other. Geographically Whitefield's English societies supplemented the mission of the Wesleys, for they were strong in Wiltshire (where Cennick was the great evangelist), and in the west, especially between Bristol, Gloucester, and Wales.

It is possible to exaggerate the separation between the two kinds of Methodists, and even between them and the Moravians, and to read back into them a hardening of attitudes such as a later century of denominational division would petrify. For the leaders soon resumed friendly relations: Wesley could come to a business meeting at the Tabernacle; Whitefield, Harris, and Ingham were invited to attend Wesley's Conferences. But the different bodies soon developed their own technical terms and jargon and James Erskine wrote pertinently to Harris in 1744. 'If there were not different phrases and ways of speaking between these two Setts, the variety of their sentiments would appear to be much less than they are said to be.'[9]

On 20 August 1766, at John Wesley's Conference in London, there was a great sight: Howell Harris, George Whitefield, and John Wesley sitting side by side. John Wesley, the oldest, must have looked much younger than the other two, the marks of exhaustion plain to see on their countenances and bearing. Whatever other comparisons may be made between these three men, they had this in common, that each one of them had poured out his energy unstintingly and utterly in the service of their common Master. Harris had never let up from those early days when he might be found, half frozen to the ground, asleep by the stile he had been too weary to climb the night before: Whitefield journeying from continent to continent, never refusing a call to preach until that poignant last address on a stairway by a flickering candle. John Wesley, who at eighty-eight set out on an itinerary which would have daunted most men half his age.

The Welsh Revival was largely the achievement of the Calvinistic Methodists, with the Arminians generally confined to the English-speaking parts of South Wales and the Isle of Anglesey. It is a story of depth and richness, and a fine diversity of leadership as well as the fascinating and often heroic story of the rank and file. It is a signal example of how swiftly and deeply a religious movement can permeate and colour a whole culture, and as far as revival is concerned there would be nothing to equal this until, in another century, the Methodists evangelized the islands of Tonga and Fiji.

---

[9] *Trevecka Letters*, i. 141.

ii. *The Countess of Huntingdon*

Selina, Countess of Huntingdon (1717–91),[10] was a great and good woman, and her participation in the work of the Revival was to open its way into new levels of the national life, as well as to forward the growth of the Evangelical Movement within the Church of England. Yet she herself was driven to separate her 'Connexion' from the Established Church and one result of her leadership was to accentuate the divergence between the two wings: Wesley's Methodists and the Calvinist evangelicals.

The conversion of the wife and daughter of an earl could not go unremarked in fashionable society. At its head there was a group of noble ladies, most of them related to one another, and we have seen how they combined to secure a charter for the London Foundling Hospital. Many of them were formidable, like the militant group led by the Duchess of Queensberry, which staged a successful 'sit-in' in Parliament. The Lady Selina was drawn towards the Methodists by her sisters-in-law, the Ladies Elizabeth and Margaret Hastings, who had been much affected by the preaching of Benjamin Ingham whom the Lady Margaret married.

Left a widow at the age of thirty-nine, Selina devoted the rest of her life and all her wealth to the service of God. She began by holding services in her house, to which she invited her aristocratic friends. Once again, George Whitefield was the key. The greater number came to see and hear him, because it was the fashion to hear him preach. The list of those who attended reads like a handful of pages torn from Debrett and Burke. They included raddled old sinners like the Duchess of Marlborough ('God knows we all need mending, and none more than myself'), disdainful beauties like the Duchess of Suffolk, and the earnest young like the Lady Fanny Shirley. And their men came too, statesmen, courtiers, ambassadors, wits, gallants. Only a few were converted, but they included Lord Dartmouth, who with the Countess was able to plead for the Methodists in high places. The conversions of gentry, of affluent merchants, and above all, of William Wilberforce took evangelical influence into levels of national life where the Wesleys did not enter.

Many might mock at George Whitefield, but Chesterfield, Garrick, and Hume were impressed, and however far Lord Bolingbroke might

[10] A. C. H. Seymour, *The Life and Times of Selina, Countess of Huntingdon*, 2 vols, 1839; S. Tytler, *The Countess of Huntingdon and her Circle*, 1907; F. F. Bretherton, *The Countess of Huntingdon*, Wesley Historical Society Lecture, 1940; G. W. Kirby, *The Elect Lady*, 1972.

be from the Kingdom, he recognized integrity when he saw it, and would not, like Warburton, write the evangelist off as a mountebank. The general attitude of high society became an amused, if cynical, tolerance, and they touched the springs of public opinion at least as nearly as did the Bishops. If the leaders of the Church of England really did contemplate at one point getting Parliament to act against the Methodists, they would not have found it easy to move against an opinion which, from the King and Prince of Wales downward, tolerated, and even admired, the Lady Selina and her friends.

John Wesley was on the margin of this. He would preach for her when Whitefield was away, but though he prized the Lady Maxwell among his female correspondents and allowed the Countess of Buchan to name him one of her chaplains, he was not drawn to what he called 'the genteel', and drew his more influential supporters from the middle class, and much preferred his poor. Nor could his lay preachers have followed up such an infiltration. The Countess is said to have dressed Howell Harris in a new suit and powdered wig to meet her drawing-room congregation, and the run of Wesley's preachers were not cut out for that kind of ministry. Not that her Ladyship neglected the poor, ever at her table. Despite often failing health she was always forward to do herself the hard chores of charity. When Charles Wesley's wife was seriously ill with smallpox she dashed to her bedside and helped to nurse her back to health. The congregations in her chapels were drawn from the same rather wide cross-section of English society as were the Methodists generally.

But her really significant achievement was to draw upon the assistance of a remarkable group of young ordained clergymen, fine preachers and good pastors, who were to become the core of the new Evangelical Movement, Calvinist in theology, but determined to be loyal to the discipline of the Church of England. Romaine, Venn, Madan, Haweis, these she made her chaplains and they became regular preachers at her proprietary chapels. Proprietary chapels were to be a useful device for the evangelicals, and the Countess, by buying a house and putting a chapel alongside, seemed to have solved or at least by-passed the problem which faced other Methodists, who could obtain legal protection only by being licensed under the Toleration Act. But by the Conventicle Act a peeress might have her own private chapel, if its doors were not open towards the public, and in it her own chaplains might preach. She sold her jewels to build the first such chapel at Brighton, and followed this with one at Oat Hill, at Tunbridge Wells, and very notably an impressive, but not flamboyant, building in Bath.

Other chapels followed in different parts of the country. The

Countess was greatly attached to Howell Harris and respected his judgement. This led her to a Grand Tour of Wales, and she followed this with a tour of Scotland where she built on the work of Whitefield, who had attracted a number of the Scottish aristocracy. She was conscious of the need for preachers and for the training of a new generation. The result was the college which, in alliance with Howell Harris was erected in close proximity to his 'Family' at Trevecka. Its foundation was intended to be in tune with a Catholic spirit 'for the education of young men of piety, belonging to any denomination: who when prepared were to be at liberty to enter into the ministry: either in the Established Church or amongst other classes of Christians.' Two intimates of John Wesley, Joseph Benson and John Fletcher, were appointed Headmaster and President. The relations between the Wesleys and the Countess had been close and cordial in the beginning when she attended the Fetter Lane Society, and at West Street Chapel a place was always reserved for the Countess 'until the Creed'. But as she became more and more involved with Calvinists like Romaine and Madan, Wesley cooled, and in a peevish note (8 June 1764) Wesley compared her treatment of her Calvinist friends with the disregard of himself and his brother 'as much notice taken of me and my brother as of a couple of postillions'.[11] In a letter to Fletcher (20 May 1768) he criticized Romaine and Madan, and made a reference to 'genteel Methodists' which much annoyed the Countess when it was passed on to her. At this time the strength of Wesley's movement was becoming plain, with over 100 preachers and 30,000 committed members. Public hostility was softening towards Wesley himself, as the references in public periodicals show. A 'Saul hath slain his thousands, and David his ten thousands' atmosphere did not help.

But the great worry of Wesley and of Fletcher at this time was the growth of Antimonianism. Not so much perhaps flagrant breaches of the moral law or self-proclaimed Antinomian groups, which existed, but the Revival was now old enough to produce in some a sort of half-cock evangelical faith, stirring superficial emotion, encrusted in clichés and jargon ('they talk about their inner corruptions as though they were freckles', said Fletcher). The evidence came from all sides and was dismaying.

Deeply convinced that extreme Calvinist doctrine was at the root of much of the trouble, Wesley became more forthcoming about it than he had been for decades. In so doing he fell foul of an ardent young cleric, Augustus Toplady (1740–78), who detested Wesley's Arminianism and

---

[11] Countess of Huntingdon Archives, Westminster–Cheshunt College. E.4.6.

regarded him as a dangerous menace. Toplady had published an edition of the treatise on Predestination by the sixteenth-century Reformer, Jerome Zanchius. Whether he had in mind Jonathan Swift's brilliant 'abridgement' of the tract of the Deist, Collins, or no, Wesley now did something similar to Toplady's 'Zanchius', leaving out enough of it to make the argument sound jejune, and ending with crushing irony: 'The sum of all is this. One in twenty (suppose) of mankind is elected: nineteen in twenty are reprobated. The elect shall be saved do what they will: the reprobate shall be damned. Witness my hand, A--- T---.' But if Wesley had some of Swift's irony, he had little of his humour, and Toplady none at all, and this treatment of his work roused Toplady to an ecstasy of fury. Henceforward it was 'No quarter' on his part, and on the 'old Fox', John Wesley, he turned his not inconsiderable invective.

In 1743 Wesley had made some astonishing concessions to Calvinism for the sake of peace with Whitefield, which led him to ask his preachers at the Conference of 1744 'Have we not leaned too far towards Calvinism?' It was in a fairly militant mood that he now raised the question afresh in the much larger gathering of 1770. And he put before them the following observations, which were intended to cut the ground from under the Antinomians with scriptural evidence.

3. We have received it as a maxim, that 'a man is to do nothing in order to justification'. Nothing can be more false. Whoever desires to find favour with God should 'cease from evil, and learn to do well.' Whoever repents should 'do works meet for repentance' and if this is not in order to find favour, what does he do them for?

Review this whole affair:
1. Who of us is NOW accepted of God? He that now believes in Christ with a loving and obedient heart.
2. But who among those that never heard of Christ? He that feareth God and worketh righteousness according to the light he has.
3. Is this the same with 'he that is sincere'? Nearly, if not quite.
4. Is not this 'salvation by works'? Not by the merit of works, but by works as a condition.
5. What have we been disputing about for these thirty years? I am afraid, about words.
6. As to merit itself, of which we have been so dreadfully afraid: we are rewarded 'according to our works' yes, 'because of our works'. How does this differ from 'for the sake of our works'? And how differs this from *secunda merita operum*? As our works deserve? Can you split this hair? I doubt I cannot.
7. The grand objection to one of the preceding propositions is drawn from matter of fact. God does in fact justify those who by their own confession,

neither feared God nor wrought righteousness. Is this an exception to the general rule? It is a doubt God makes any exception at all.[12]

Even Luke Tyerman, for whom each word of Wesley is as the gentle rain that droppeth down from heaven upon the place beneath, calls it a 'loosely worded statement' and the laconic sentences, intended to stab his preachers' spirits broad awake, were wide open to misunderstanding.

Wesley himself admitted later that the view that good works are a 'condition' of salvation is a doctrine he had himself opposed in controversy with Dr Church, and that he had formerly denounced his view when he found it in the writings of Bishop Bull. He might have added that his brother Charles had vehemently attacked the proposition in a quotation from Tillotson in his university sermon at Oxford in July 1739,[13] and that Whitefield also blamed Tillotson for this belief. Both had said that this was to teach salvation by faith and works, and was a denial of 'sola fide'. In an explanatory gloss which he would circulate among the preachers a year hence and preparatory to the Conference of 1771, he expounds the word 'condition': 'By salvation here I mean final salvation . . . with justification as it means our first acceptance, this proposition has nothing to do'.[14] It would have saved much trouble if he had put this sentence in a year before. Whether his distinction can be theologically sustained is another matter. And if the distinction about merit were 'hair splitting', then was the Conference the place to dispose in a few words of an intricate debate about 'merit' pursued in depth from the fourteenth to the sixteenth century? In a defensive letter to Charles (3 August 1771) he was to return to the subject: 'I do not use the word merit. I never did . . . but I ask you or any other a plain question: and do not cry "Murder": What is the difference between "merere" and "to deserve" or between "deserving" and "meritum". I say still, I cannot tell'.[15]

But if this were so, how did it help his preachers to combat Antinomianism to put before them such a delicate question, when most of them could not even translate 'secunda merita operum'? It is not a carping comment, for we have always to ask what was preached, not by the Wesleys or John Fletcher or by the core of their preachers who were highly intelligent and theologically sensitive, but by the larger number who were not so well equipped. What could they make of it, and how would they 'Get it across' to the Methodist people?

---

[12] *Minutes of Several Conversations* (Leeds 1803), p. 66; Tyerman, *Life of John Wesley,* iii. 72; Coppedge, *Wesley and Predestination,* Pt. III.

[13] T. Albin, 'Charles Wesley's Earliest Evangelical Sermons', (MS 1982), p. 34.

[14] Wesley, *Letters* (ed. Telford), v. 262.   [15] Ibid., v. 269.

The publication of these Doctrinal Minutes (as of some other of the earlier ones (e.g. those of 1745 which contain curious things) was justifiable in view of the 'nothing up my sleeve' frankness of Wesley about all his words and actions, but one asks whether it furthered the good cause when such difficult points were enigmatically and paradoxically stated, and appeared in print 'urbi et orbi'?

At any rate when it reached the Countess, she wept, though whether in anger or pain is not certain. She thought it plain that John Wesley had abandoned 'the grand point of the Methodists, Free Justification' and propounded a heresy 'horrible, worth being publicly opposed, and such as a true believer ought to be ready to burn against'.[16]

Walter Shirley, the kinsman and chaplain of the Countess, was equally outraged, and it may be not uncharitable to suggest that he found in the affair a means to resolve what he must have regarded as the unfortunate situation at Trevecka, where there were already signs of tension between the mainly Calvinist students and the Arminian staff, Benson and Fletcher.

Benson seems to have got across his students about the Baptism of the Spirit, and, because he defended Wesley's 'Minutes', was told he would have to go. The students were asked to write their own opinions about the Wesley 'Minutes' and Fletcher now wrote a long and careful appraisal of them, explaining the most controversial phrases in what he was sure was Wesley's real intention. Thus, speaking of the state of the heathen who had not heard of Christ, he explains that Wesley was not defending natural sincerity, but the light of prevenient grace which even the heathen have through Christ. But he had to admit that at first sight the document 'carries a strong appearance of legality' and that some of the expressions are 'unguarded'. But then, he says, 'Are not some of the "Minutes" of St. Paul "unguarded"? Yet I would not put St. Paul or St. James out of my synagogue.' There must have been an angry interview with the Countess, for Fletcher wrote a sad note to Shirley (7 March 1771) asking if he could have his memorandum back. (She kept it.)

. . . to conclude as Lady Huntingdon declared to me last night with the highest degree of positiveness that whosoever did not fully and absolutely disavow and renounce the doctrine contained in Mr. Wesley's 'Minutes' should not on any terms stay in her college.

To which there could be only one reply: 'I should not act the part of an honest man if I did not absolutely resign my charge and take leave of this seminary.'[17]

---

[16] Simon, *John Wesley, the Master Builder*, p. 288.
[17] Countess of Huntingdon Archives, Westminster–Cheshunt, E.4.7.

Wesley now felt impelled to write a very plain letter indeed to the Countess, telling her things which should have been said long ago, he thought. Perhaps significantly, the letter does not seem to have survived, and one imagines it did not help. On his behalf Shirley felt impelled to write a circular letter to their friends, accusing Wesley of 'dreadful heresy' and teaching 'salvation by works' in a way which struck at the foundations of the Christian religion. He offered to find lodgings for all who would join in a demonstration at the next Methodist Conference in Bristol, when they would demand from Wesley a full and complete recantation.

But they had overreached themselves. Wesley and his preachers were in no sense under the command of the Countess, nor had she any right to gatecrash his Conference without an invitation. The result was a couple of apologetic notes, and the demonstration withered to a deputation of two parsons, two laymen, and two theological students. The Countess was not present. Wesley courteously invited Shirley and his friends to attend his Conference, and after prayer, statements were made on both sides. John Wesley and his preachers agreed to sign a declaration that 'the Minutes are not guarded enough in the way they are expressed', that 'we abhor the doctrine of justification by works as a most perilous and abominable doctrine', and that 'our works have no part in meriting or purchasing our justification, from first to last, either in whole or in part.' Shirley, for his part, a little hesitantly agreed to admit that he had misunderstood Wesley's 1770 'Minutes' statement and sent a letter to this effect in the next days.

Though there were probably warm moments in the debate, both Wesley and Shirley had behaved with courtesy and in an eirenical spirit. It would have been well had matters rested there. But Wesley had already put in hand the printing of a pamphlet by John Fletcher answering the attacking Shirley. The controversy was to linger for another five years, at the end of which serious damage had been done to the good relations between the two parties. The Countess was hardly softened by two further and more amiable letters from John Wesley and continued to believe that he taught salvation by works. But there is a plausible story that after Wesley's death she read the words of his dying declaration, and realizing that she had indeed deeply misunderstood him, wept at the damage that had been needlessly done to evangelical unity.

Only a few weeks after the Conference of 1770 George Whitefield had died in America. This was a great blow. As long as George Whitefield lived he made it plain that the differences between himself and the Wesleys, though real were not fundamental. In his last years he did all that one could do to show his friendship with his partner in the gospel, compassing sea and land to do him service, sitting beside him in Conference, inviting him to preach, preaching for him and celebrating at his side, until as a last gesture he named John Wesley as the one to preach his funeral sermon. And Wesley was eager to respond.

The last years of Whitefield's life were of declining vigour .of body and of mellowness of spirit. When the Tabernacle opened in 1756 he was at the height of his powers, and the great congregations crowded in, including John Byrom, Philip Doddridge, and many other notables. In the next years, when he was not profligately giving his energies to America, he went from one harvest field to another. Nobody could quite keep track of him on his tip-and-run raids to Lancashire or Scotland or Ireland (where he was nearly lynched) and back to the Tabernacle, and the bi-weekly services in her ladyship's house in Cavendish Square. There was in him a deep simplicity and an abiding generosity of spirit. A little naïveté also, for he could never cease to be a little awed at being able to speak with a Countess as a man speaketh with his friend, or, in the case of John Wesley, as an undergraduate speaketh with his tutor. He had neither the leisure nor the learning to be a good pamphleteer, but one or two of his writings, in reply to Bishop Gibson (1744) and about the expulsion of the Oxford Methodists in 1768, are effective and forthright. His young secretary and general dogsbody, Cornelius Winter, left an account of him in his last years which perhaps does not do justice to what he had been in his prime, and one would prefer to believe he was never so grumpily choosy about those who came to seek his help as the young man suggests.

Towards the end Whitefield's preaching suffered from his emotional and nervous exhaustion, became repetitious and garrulous, while the weeping and the gestures with the corners of his gown became merely gimmicky. But there was always fire when he spoke of grace, forgiveness, and the love of Christ. His heart was always moved towards lost sinners. When the comedian, Shuter, then playing the character of Ramble, sat in his congregation, Whitefield (who did not think an attorney could be a Christian, let alone an actor) addressed him, 'And thou, poor Ramble, who hast long rambled from him come thou also. O end thy ramblings by coming to Jesus', a sentence which might have come from Hugh Latimer. Again and again in the work of the Revival in Britain, he had taken the costly initiative, created the daring precedents, those 'irregularities' without which the Evangelical Revival must have been stifled at birth. And wherever he preached, men and women were converted. There are moving testimonies to this effect from some of the greatest of Wesley's preachers, who were among his converts.

But his achievement in America was even more important. It seems clear that America drew him, and touched his heart. In his seven missions in that country he made an unparalleled contribution to the revival of religion. Among the many fruits was the foundation of three centres of higher education. The Orphan House in Georgia became rather an Old Man of the Sea clinging to him, always needing more money, and in its staff and administration failing for lack of the oversight he had not the leisure to provide. His horizons were perhaps limited, and though he rebuked the slave owners of Carolina, he came to accept slaves as a welcome easement of his problems in Georgia. At the end of his life he made it over to the Countess, when it was about to be transformed from an orphanage to a college. When one considered the demands upon a wife, of being married to a Whitefield or a Wesley, of separation and anxiety, and the weariness of travel, one can understand why theoretically the evangelists were in favour of celibacy.

Whitefield really should have married Elizabeth Delamotte, though his letter of proposal and his address to her parents would have put off any sensible woman. His marriage to the widow James seems to have worked as well as could be expected, and one ought not to undervalue either their affection or their happiness.

The 29 September 1770 found him slowly returning to the Deep South. At Newburyport, Massachusetts, he paused. After supper he made for bed, for great weariness was upon him. But he could not resist the crowd round the door, and half-way up the stairs, on the landing, he stopped to speak to them and preached Christ until the candle flickered into the pervading darkness. In the small hours he was taken ill, and died about 6.00 the next morning. The term 'prince of preachers' perhaps pre-existed him, but wherever he had been, there had been the shout of a king.

But if Whitefield's passing left a great gap, the 1770s saw the Countess surrounded by allies, a new generation of preachers, while to the west and south and north a Walker, a Venn, a Grimshaw, a Berridge, a Newton suggested that Whitefield had indeed sown dragon's teeth. Trouble came in an unexpected quarter. In 1774 a large building came on to the market in Clerkenwell, London, and was bought by some evangelical business men who opened it as Northampton Chapel. It was opened in July 1777, but the large congregations aroused the anger of the local curate, the Revd William Sellon, who took action against them in the spiritual court. Fatefully the Countess now intervened, purchased the building, and opened it as the Spa Fields Chapel, a proprietary chapel of her own. But this time she did not get away with it, and lost legal actions which left all her chapels vulnerable. Perhaps if she had cut her losses and backed off the situation might have been saved, but perhaps, too, it was not in her character to do so, and she was forced to seek a licence under the Toleration Act which would turn her chapels into Dissenting Congregations. The effect on the ablest of her evangelical chaplains was devastating. Apart from Thomas Haweis, they were driven to dissociate themselves henceforward from her pulpits and her 'Connexion'. She had now been driven to separate from the Church of England and on 9 March 1783 the first public ordination of ministers in her Connexion was held in Spa Fields, and a Confession of Faith, Fifteen Articles, which in the main abridge the Thirty-nine Articles, was adopted. In 1785 she printed rules for her societies. She prayed, wrote edifying letters, and presided at her household prayers, but she knew that her contribution to the good cause was her unflagging commitment of her time, wealth, and energy. Like that of Count Zinzendorf, her humility did not always break through the aristocratic mould, and there were often traces in her behaviour of the Old Eve. She had her tragedies, in the deaths of her husband and two sons, though it caused her more pain when her sons rejected their mother's religion and her cousin, Lord Ferrers, had been executed for murder. She was always something of an invalid, yet she managed constant and exhausting journeys. She had indeed been a Mother in Israel and had founded a college and a Connexion which were to endure with long and honourable histories. Her last illness came when she was eighty-four, and on her death-bed she was making plans with Thomas Haweis to send missionaires to Otaheite in the southern seas. J. H. Newman was moved

by the sight of a person simply and unconditionally giving up this world for the next . . . she devoted herself, her name, her means, her time, her thoughts to the cause of Christ. She did not spend money on herself: she did not allow the homage due to her rank to remain with herself: she passed these on, and offered them up to Christ. She acted as one ought to act who considered this life a pilgrimage, not a home.[18]

iii. The Evangelicals

It would be easy to exaggerate the extent to which the divisions between the Methodists had hardened in the 1750s and 1760s. Dr Nuttall has wisely said that

[18] J. H. Newman, *Essays Critical and Historical*, vol. i (1910), 'Selina, Countess of Huntingdon'.

with each fresh biography it becomes clearer that, whether Arminian or Calvinist in doctrine, whether Dissenters or clergy of the Establishment, all these men and many others, were working together in no all embracing organizations, but in close bonds of friendship, correspondence and inter-visitation.[19]

None the less, there was a growing difference between the Wesleys and their societies, and those clergy who were determined to avoid all 'irregularities' such as field preaching and an itinerancy, and who thought of their ministry as properly set within the Church of England. That these men were generally Calvinist in their theology added to the divergence. There was a minor crisis for John Wesley in the 1750s, when, following the handing over of Ingham's societies to the Moravians, the question of possible separation was raised by some of his preachers. Had those clerical friends of his who had turned to the Moravians remained with and under his guidance, or had a large number of ordained clergy come into close alliance with him, the history of the eventual separation might have been different. But it is easy to see why this should not be forthcoming. When, in 1764, Wesley wrote to between forty and fifty clergymen suggesting they should all work together, he had only three replies, even though he had suggested 'not a union with regard to outward order. Some may remain quite regular, some quite irregular and some partly regular and partly irregular.'

Those evangelical clergy who did not reply to John Wesley had their own good reasons for not becoming entangled in what they considered dubious devices. We are not to trivialize the importance of 'Regularity' for a Walker of Truro or a John Venn. But more than loyalty to the Church of England came into the picture. These men were first and foremost ordained clergy of the Church of England: their livelihood came to them from within its structure. It would have made immense demands on them to throw themselves into such a wandering existence as that of Whitefield, Harris, or Wesley and to have submitted in some measure to Wesley's direction and control (which he did not suggest) would have put their families under intolerable strains, of which Wesley's own domestic life would be a sad illustration. When, in 1758, Francis Okeley went with Wesley on a sample tour, he hastily withdrew, and Wesley wrote him an astringent note suggesting that 'you have five strong reasons to the contrary. 1. a wife. 2. a mother. 3. children. 4. cowardice. 5. a love of ease'.[20]

---

[19] Nuttall, *Howell Harris,* p. 29.
[20] *Letters* (ed. Telford), iv. 35–6.

The strong case for not itinerating can be best seen in Walker's correspondence with Wesley.

But Wesley, too, must be sympathetically heard. If his great share in the revival was to be sustained and strengthened he simply had to look elsewhere and raise up his order of Methodist Preachers. And if the evangelicals kept clear of overt irregularities, they did take advantage of anomalies, for the hostility of the leaders of the Church, clerical and lay, towards them meant that only very slowly were benefices at their disposal.

There were the perpetual curacies and the proprietary chapels. The Puritans had made strategic use of lectureships which enabled them to have pulpits in key places where they could bypass the incumbents and the liturgy. In fact such lectureships date from the fifteenth century when many European cities, especially in Germany, provided preaching and teaching which offset a too often absentee clergy. In England at the Restoration, they were still of great use, and coming young men, like John Sharp, were thus enabled to make their voices heard.

The senior of the new evangelicals was William Romaine (1714–95). At Oxford he was a noted Hebraist, compiling a massive concordance, one of the group of 'Hutchinsonians' who believed that the original Hebrew text, uncorrupted by the rabbis, was the primary language. He devoted his first university sermon to the demolition of Warburton's *Divine Legation*. His Hutchinsonian views may have led him to oppose the naturalization of the London Jews in an anti-semitic pamphlet on the text: 'These men, being Jews, do exceedingly trouble our city' (Acts 16: 20).

Looking back on these early years, he said of himself:

He was a very, very vain proud man: knew almost everything but himself, and therefore was mighty fond of himself . . . till the Lord was pleased to let him see and feel the plague of his own heart . . . in his despair of all things else, he betook himself to Jesus and was most kindly received.[21]

His conversion came after a period of inner struggle, but after this his preaching was powerful and effective. He became Lecturer at St Dunstan's-in-the-West, a post he held for forty-six years. After a short spell at St George's, Hanover Square, he held no permanent cure, but in 1766 was made Rector of the joint parish of St Andrew-by-the-Wardrobe and St Anne's, Blackfriars, where he laboured for thirty years. Great crowds came to hear him, and at St George's and at St Dunstan's he got into trouble with the affluent godly, annoyed at the intrusion of vulgar squatters in their pews. The result was a nasty little

---

[21] William Romaine, *The Life, Walk and Triumph of Faith*, ed. P. Toon, repr. 1970 p.x.

row at St Dunstan's where the churchwardens (who do not seem to have improved since the days when Izaak Walton was of their number) locked out preacher and congregation, admitting them only on the dot of 7.00, to an unlighted and unwarmed church. Here, so the story goes, he preached to them by the light of a taper, though one feels it must either have been a very long taper or a very short sermon. Though no itinerant, he liked to travel, and became the Countess of Huntingdon's senior chaplain. He went on several other preaching tours, to Cambridge to hear Berridge, to Yorkshire for Grimshaw, and to his native Hartlepool. He was a fairly strict Calvinist and refused to abandon psalms for hymns. But he kept on good terms with John Wesley. His three books on the Life, the Walk, and the Triumph of Faith were much read, and are good evidence of the best kind of the new preaching, on the benefits of Christ, and the new life of the Christian, who battles triumphantly against sin and against temptation.

At the West End of the town, Martin Madan (b. 1726) was the chaplain at the Lock Hospital. After Westminster and Christ Church he was called to the Bar, but going to scoff at, and indeed to mimic, John Wesley he was himself converted. He was not only a fine preacher, but much interested in music, produced in 1760 a lively collection of hymns and introduced an annual oratorio into his chapel. He evidently brooded on the miseries of the unfortunate women admitted to the hospital, but when in 1780 he published his *Thelyphthora, or a Treatise on Female Ruin,* in which he recommended polygamy as a remedy for his social evil, most Christians thought the cure was worse than the disease and he was forced to retire. Among other important chaplains at this hospital were Thomas Haweis and Thomas Scott.

Cornwall, with its miners and its fishers, its smugglers and its wreckers, its isolated communities along bad roads, presented problems for the Methodists, but if some of the fiercest opposition came from here, it was to be the scene of some of their greatest and most enduring triumphs.

Since G. C. B. Davies's study of *The Early Cornish Evangelicals* (1951) nobody can undervalue the contribution to the Revival of a group of clergy of devotion and distinction. George Thompson had taken a law degree from Exeter College, Oxford in 1719, and was presented to the benefice of St Gennys in 1732. He went through a time of spiritual crisis and was converted some time before 1736. He was an attractive personality and was soon on friendly terms with John Wesley and George Whitefield, who visited him in 1743. Associated with him was John Bennet, a hunting and farming parson, who turned to serious religion late in life. Charles Wesley described how at the end of a memorable service in Bennet's church at Laneast in August 1743, when Wesley told the congregation that he had been 'dead to God, asleep in the devil's arms, in a state of damnation for eighteen years: Mr. Meriton added aloud "And I for twenty five": "and I" cried Mr. Thomson "for thirty-five!"; "and I" said Mr. Bennet "for above seventy!"'

Samuel Walker of Truro had been at Exeter College, Oxford, during the time when the Wesleys were there, but made no contact with them. In 1746 he became perpetual curate at Truro, where he was deeply influenced by his friendship with the Presbyterian headmaster, George Conon. He was a preacher of power and directness, and beloved by his large congregation. Like other conscientious preachers of the age, he set store on catechizing and made much use of Religious Societies, which he ran on the strict and disciplined Anglican rules set out by Horneck and Woodward. Although Walker did all he could to keep his flock unspotted from the Methodists, Wesley had great admiration for him, and they had an important and illuminating correspondence in the 1750s, when Wesley was himself much exercised about the relation of his movement to the Church of England. Walker was quite clear in his own mind that the itinerancy was wrong, but for once Wesley was able to talk these things out with a man of judgement and discrimination. Walker was also opposed to Wesley's doctrine of Christian Perfection. His own Calvinist emphasis on the promises of God seemed to him more healthy than the subjective stress on the so-called 'Witness of the Spirit'. But Walker could not but be aware of some of the pressures which the growth of his movement and the opinions of many of his preachers brought on Wesley, and he wrote to his friend, Adam of Wintringham: 'Will he be able to stand his ground? For my part I think not, I fear he hath too high an opinion of Methodism and imagines it will be lost if the preachers leave him which I am fully confirmed they will do, if he will not go with them.'[22]

Walker saw only one corner of England, and did not perhaps begin to understand Wesley's problem which was not so much a theoretical problem as a practical situation. Until 1759 Walker gathered his allies together in a Clerical Club, and it is plain that a small evangelical 'connexion' now existed with contacts over a very wide area. Mention must be made of his friend, Adam of Wintringham, with whom he corresponded for years before the two men met. Adam had gone from Oxford to Wintringham, Lincolnshire, where he remained until he died in 1784. How influential and successful, in a superficial sense, was his ministry may be questioned, but he was a noble and sensitive soul, his

---

[22] Davies, *The Early Cornish Evangelicals*, p. 102.

mind very much in tune with his Cornish friend and the posthumous publication of his *Private Thoughts* had seminal influence.

During the first part of Romaine's London ministry he had two young allies south of the Thames, Thomas Jones of St Saviour's, Southwark, and Henry Venn (1725–97), a former Fellow of Queens' College, Cambridge, who was curate at Clapham and a lecturer within the City. At first he was close to Wesley and the Countess of Huntingdon, but he was always very much his own man and it became of importance for the Evangelical Movement in the north when in 1779 he became Vicar of Huddersfield. The arrival in Huddersfield of an impeccably evangelical incumbent raised a problem for the Methodists, whether they ought not to withdraw their own preachers. But by now there were evident divergences in arrangements for pastoral care, and a compromise was made. Henry Venn went on preaching tours, was glad to be at the disposal of the Countess of Huntingdon as one of her chaplains, and had good relations with the Wesleys. He was an effectual preacher, and perhaps equally skilled as a pastor. Simeon said of him that 'the only end for which he lived was to make all men see the glory of God in the face of Jesus Christ.' Grave weakness of health led him to leave Huddersfield in 1771 for the village of Yelling in Huntingdonshire. Here he was in touch with the Cambridge evangelicals, and the last phase of his ministry was in quality as valuable as any more active phase had been. He and his son were between them to make a splendid contribution to the evangelical cause.

Like the Countess of Huntingdon, the evangelicals were concerned to train a coming generation for the ministry. The Elland, Bristol, and Creaton Societies were formed to provide funds. The immediate problem was to get them trained and ordained in view of the hostility of the university authorities.

In Oxford[23] James Stillingfleet and Thomas Haweis were evangelical dons not easy to put down, and mixed groups of town and gown assembled for devotion at the house of the widow Durbridge, while Haweis as curate of St Mary Magdalen was a focus for vociferous opposition. It was evident to the authorities that an example must be made and the public expulsion of six Methodist students from St Edmund Hall, in 1768, was the result.

The Vice-Principal of the College, Dr John Higson, himself a psychological case, having complained in vain to his Principal about the evangelical vipers in their midst, appealed to the Vice-Chancellor as

---

[23] J. S. Reynolds, *The Evangelicals at Oxford 1735–81*, Oxford 1953; G. R. Balleine, *History of the Evangelical Party* (1951), p. 98; L. E. Elliott-Binns, *The Early Evangelicals* (1953), pp. 353 ff.

Visitor of the College. He and his Assessor, Heads of Houses, Proctor and, Public Orator, descended on the College on 11 March 1768. Amid a jostling, jeering crowd of gownsmen the six students were arraigned.[24]

The charges against Benjamin Kay, Thomas Jones, Thomas Grove, Erasmus Middleton, Joseph Shipman, and James Matthews varied from person to person, but they were charged with the social meanness of their background (a barber, a draper, and — shades of George Whitefield — a tapster) and, in consequence, of illiteracy. They were charged with holding un-Anglican doctrines, with having sat under notorious Methodists like Venn, Newton, and Fletcher and with having taken part in Methodist services in houses and barns and being involved in shocking practices, one of which was listening to extempore prayer 'by a staymaker'.

They were indeed a mixed bag. Of them all only Erasmus Middleton was to become known, as the author of the well-known *Biographia Evangelica*. But he was sinner above all the others in Jerusalem, having, while still a student, officiated in a Chapel of Ease. They were then called on to translate, unseen and on the spot, from the Latin Statutes and the Greek New Testament. Middleton and Kay did well. The examination of the rest was a shambles. Some sort of defence was heard, and testimonials read. But there were hostile depositions, too, and the inevitable result was the solemn expulsion of the offenders in the Chapel.

The sensation was to be prolonged. Sir Richard Hill speedily dashed off a powerful and anonymous pamphlet so damaging that the authorities were urged to answer it. An answer was written by the Public Orator, Dr Nowell, which bore the imprimatur of the Vice-Chancellor. The cause of the six students tended to be smothered by argument whether the Articles of the Church of England taught Predestination. But Hill (who has some claim to be the founder of 'investigative journalism') dug up some curious facts about the mean social background of some contemporary eminences in the Church, overreached himself by charging a Proctor (Westminster and Christ Church) with being a captain in the militia, but scored a bull's eye in his investigation of the murky origins and grisly career of a leading hostile witness. This man was now counter-attacked by the friends of the expelled students as a notorious infidel, and the authorities were forced to haul him in for questioning. He admitted that he had poured scorn on the authenticity of the New Testament miracles, but explained that it

---

[24] *Pietas Oxoniensis, or a full and impartial account of the expulsion of six students from St. Edmund Hall By a Master of Arts of the University of Oxford* [Sir Richard Hill], 1768; *An Answer to a Pamphlet entitled Pietas Oxoniensis*, by Thomas Nowell D.D., Oxford 1768.

was at a college Gaudy and that he was drunk at the time. He was only reprimanded. It was plain that the real offence of the extruded students was that they were Methodists. George Whitefield wrote a lively defence. John Wesley noted it as further proof that Methodists would always be persecuted, but it is noticeable that he did not intervene, because he was pleased that Nowell had cleared Article 17 from teaching Calvinist doctrine. It may be, however, that the authorities had not chosen badly for their public example, for the group, earnest and devoted and of good character as they were, were perhaps of doubtful quality as ordinands; one or two had been about the place a long time, and they were perhaps not quite up to the University. There is some point in Dr Johnson's verdict: 'I believe they might be good beings, but they were not fit to be in the University of Oxford. A cow is a very good animal in the field: but we turn her out of a garden'.

J. S. Reynolds has shown that, despite these things, the evangelicals had not been crushed and that a notable group of future prominent evangelicals were students at Oxford during the next years.

The contrast between the treatment meted out by the university authorities to Methodists in the 1730s and the 1760s is striking. No member of the Holy Club had difficulty in getting ordained, and the provisions of the Conventicle Act were not held over them. Howell Harris is an instance of one whose early irregularities became an insuperable bar to ordination. But now this difficulty was more frequent, the more so as it became known that people like the Countess of Huntingdon and the Elland Society were providing funds for the training of ordinands. In Cambridge there had been a small group nearly contemporary with the Holy Club. William Delamotte of St Catherine's may have been its originator, but the heart of the little company was in St John's College with William Hammond and Francis Okeley.[25] The leaders soon turned towards the Moravians, and it lapsed with the going down of its members. One would suppose that it is accidental that the revival of an evangelical cell came in St John's College, were it not that ideas linger on very unexpectedly in colleges.[26]

Rowland Hill was the sixth son of a baronet, and his elder brother Richard, another notable evangelical, succeeded to the title. Both boys were at Eton, like Charles Simeon, and seem to have been part of an evangelical group at school. Rowland came up to St John's in 1764 and soon began to attract attention, not only by the activities of the group of which he was the leader but by his own preaching activities. The

---

[25] Walsh, 'The Cambridge Methodists', p. 249 ff.

[26] Cf. the persistence in St John's College of the Platonist ideas of Everard Digby, despite the overall Calvinism, in the reign of Elizabeth I.

influence of his affluent family probably shielded him from deprivation of his degree and expulsion from the University. He himself was a brilliant young man, fearless and truculent. He had a portrait of Romaine in his study and turned for help to Whitefield who sent him some splendid letters of encouragement. No doubt for a time the dominant influence on him was his friend and counsellor John Berridge and he may have been led by his example to introduce into the pulpit humour which was not everywhere appreciated.[27] The Countess now took him under her wing, and he became one of her preachers travelling on her 'rounds'. But some witty, if good-humoured, remarks about her got back to the Countess, and she was so offended that she forbade him her pulpits. He had been ordained deacon in 1774, but did not proceed to the priesthood. In 1783 his friends bought for him the Surrey Chapel in Southwark, where he attracted the crowds and fulfilled the remainder of his ministry. He had no bishop's licence, but he refused to be called a Dissenter, and kept to the Anglican liturgy. He kept his friendships, and some of the leading evangelicals made their sole irregularity their practice of preaching for him at Surrey Chapel. With his brother Richard he took an effective share in the Calvinist controversy of the 1770s.

It was important for the evangelical cause in Cambridge when Venn came to Yelling, which was nearer to the University than Berridge's Everton. William Farish of Magdalene persuaded his College to take in the young men sent by the Elland Society. The real breakthrough came when Isaac Milner became President of Queens'. The fine scholar and formidable administrator was able to persuade the College to tolerate an evangelical infiltration which became all important. His influence was only outmatched by the work of Charles Simeon. Simeon must be the name with which an account of the early evangelicals must close, but we may first say something about the three evangelical 'originals', John Berridge, William Grimshaw, and John Newton.

John Berridge (1716–93) was a devoted Christian whose overflowing humour verged on eccentricity and who was, as Bishop Ryle said, 'a comet rather than a planet'.[28] His wit was the trait which endured through the unregenerate and evangelical phases of his life. He began as an able scholar, Senior Fellow of Clare College, reading for fifteen hours

---

[27] There is a letter from Glazebrook complaining about his oddities in the pulpit and of his behaving like a 'buffoon'. But Glazebrook was an ex-collier, the first student at Trevecka, and had himself been severely criticized for feeble humour. Countess of Huntingdon Archives, Westminster–Cheshunt, E.4.6.

[28] J. C. Ryle, *The Christian Leaders of the Last Century*, 1873, ch. VIII.

a day. He said of himself that he 'lived proudly on faith and works' until 1754. He was appointed to the living of Everton, on the borders of Cambridgeshire, Huntingdonshire, and Bedfordshire, in 1755, and underwent a spiritual crisis after which he burned his old sermons and found that 'as soon as I preached Jesus Christ and faith in his blood, then believers were added to the church continually.' He began preaching in the open air and found an ally in Hicks of Wrestlingworth. Between them they began a revival, the fame of which could not be hid, particularly as very soon Berridge's preaching was attended by the kind of emotional scenes which we have seen to be features of the early preaching of the Wesleys and of Howell Harris and others. The Countess of Huntingdon descended on him with her lieutenants and took him off to London, where for a time he preached and travelled. But although he could not be confined to his own parish, he had no liking for the itinerant ministry. He invited John Wesley to preach for and with him, and they were friends, though during the Calvinist controversy of the 1770s Berridge felt constrained to write defending Calvinism. His jokes and his turns of phrase make his letters witty and lively reading. The evangelicals and Methodists, who thought levity a great sin, were restive about his jokes, and there is a long letter of remonstrance from his friend and patron, the merchant John Thornton, upbraiding him on this account and claiming that there was but one joke in the whole Bible (Elijah and the prophets of Baal). In his age, eccentricity mingled with delusion that his arms were made of glass and that he was swelling within his clothes. But he was an endearing friend, and not for nothing, nor out of kindness, did Venn and Simeon make the trip to Everton once a week to dine with John Berridge.

William Grimshaw (1708–63) was educated at Christ's College, Cambridge, but his character and gifts enabled him to become the evangelical apostle of the north, first as a chaplain at Todmorden and then as perpetual curate at Haworth, where his dourness matched the countryside. He was drawn into the Evangelical Revival through the work of Benjamin Ingham and his Yorkshire societies, and the work of the Methodist preacher, John Nelson. He met the Wesleys in 1746 and from then on worked closely with them, sharing their persecutions, writing in their support, and in his preaching and his formation of classes and societies working within the Methodist plan. In his later years he drew back from itinerancy and became critical of tendencies inside the Methodist movement which were drawing away from the Church of England. But Dr Baker claims 'until his death the major portion of his time and energy was thrown into propagating Methodism and he was acknowledged to be, if not second in command after John

Wesley himself, at least third in command.'[29] A man of passionate nature, firmly controlled, he dominated his scene. He was a holy terror to the slothful, and there are splendid stories about him, some of which must be true, of how he dressed as an old woman to get close to those sporting on the village green, of leaving the congregation to sing the 119th Psalm while with his whip he scoured the pubs for absentees, and of scared delinquents cascading out of windows and leaping over walls, in order to flee before him into church.

John Newton (1725–1807) is beyond doubt the most colourful of all these characters. His early career as he described it in detail in his letters and memoirs was a hair-raising saga of disaster. Son of a shipmaster, he went to sea. In the Royal Navy he was a Dick Deadeye, and publicly flogged. In the merchant marine he was so shocking in his profanity that he was near to being thrown overboard as a Jonah. Shipwrecked off the coast of Africa, he became himself a slave to a planter's black mistress and underwent grievous humiliations, crawling to eat roots in the time of great rains, kept in any sort of dignity only by the remembrance of his sweetheart Mary and a copy of the first six books of Euclid which he worked out with a stick on the sand. Then fortune turned and he got home, married Mary, and became master of a ship. He also turned to devotional reading and to prayer and a new way of life. He was now involved in the slave trade, and it must needs be offensive to modern and pious ears to hear him say, 'I never knew sweeter or more frequent hours of divine communion than on my two last voyages to Guinea when I was either almost secluded from society on shipboard or when on shore amongst the natives.'[30]

But it is plain from his frank narrative that slave-trading was widely regarded as a respectable avocation, and he is insistent that he went in his long boat to buy slaves, not to steal them. He afterwards became a firm ally of his friend William Wilberforce, and his testimony against the evil and the cruelty of slavery was much heeded by members of the Government. He had begun to study the Bible and the sacred languages, and after being invalided out of the Navy he sought and obtained orders from the Bishop of London in 1764. He became curate at the village of Olney. There he was joined by that stricken deer, William Cowper. Cowper's mental illness had begun before he met Newton and there is little to be said for the view that Newton's Calvinism was a morbid influence. Newton had now begun to write fine hymns and the two men collaborated in the lovely *Olney Hymn Book* which contains some

---

[29] F. Baker, *William Grimshaw* (1963), p. 144. Ryle, *Christian Leaders of the Last Century*, ch. V.

[30] *The Works of the Rev. John Newton* (1839), i. 26; Bernard Martin, *John Newton* (1950).

treasures. In 1780 he became Rector of St Mary Woolnoth, London, where he remained until his death.

He was not one of the most distinguished preachers of his day, though his bluff manner had its own directness and power. But he knew the human heart, and his own earlier experiences had taught him the strength of divine forgiveness and the hope of newness of life, so that he kept up a flow of spiritual counsel, letters which in themselves were an effective ministry. He continued to write hymns and to preach while he had any strength left, and when he died he had become influential far beyond his parish, in touch with all the evangelical leaders of the day, the friend not only of Charles Simeon, but of William Wilberforce and Hannah More.

Charles Simeon (1759–1836) was not only the most important figure in the consolidation of the Evangelical Movement in Cambridge, but Macaulay could write of him in 1844 as one whose influence was felt in the remote corners of England and whose 'real sway in the Church was far greater than that of any Primate.[31] Although his mature influence was exerted in a ministry extending beyond the scope of this present work, there are important facts to be recorded here. Coming up from Eton to King's College, the arresting moment in his life was when he found himself faced with compulsory attendance at a Sacrament for which he was disastrously unprepared. *The Whole Duty of Man* and Bishop Wilson's *On the Lord's Supper* were decisive for his belated preparation and on Easter Day 1779 he found a lasting peace in his soul. In 1782 he became a Fellow of his College and was ordained on his fellowship, as John Wesley had also been. He sought out those who might guide him, Fletcher of Madeley and Henry Venn. Venn at Yelling became his real spiritual father and together they made a weekly pilgrimage to Berridge at Everton. But Berridge with his bursting energies was too singular and, with his field preaching and his little band of lay helpers, deserved the comment of Charles Smyth that 'it was from his contact with John Berridge that Simeon learned that although the Kingdom of heaven is indeed taken by violence, it is not to be held by indiscipline.' Simeon's part in the Evangelical Revival was, as Smyth clearly demonstrates, that of an evangelist who was an ecclesiastical statesman, much as he would have deprecated the description.[32]

His meetings with John Wesley, though few, show how deeply impressed Wesley was with this young man, and how attractive he found his personality. Simeon showed himself an evangelical leader; he saw

[31] Elliott-Binns, *Early Evangelicals*, p. 365; Charles Smyth, *Simeon and Church Order*, Cambridge 1940.
[32] Smyth, *Simeon and Church Order*, p. 365.

behind and beyond the differences between evangelicals and Methodists about Calvinist points, to a deeper and more compelling unity in Christ, and there is still much to ponder in his comment that Christian truth is not a golden mean, or a half-way between two extremes, but that it lies in both extremes — as we might say, in polarity with one another. In 1783 he was ordained, and began his memorable ministry at Holy Trinity Church. Not since Benjamin Whichcote captured the attention of a whole generation of undergraduates had the incumbent of that parish church been the focus of the University, but Simeon, unlike the smooth Platonist, began with a very rough time. He paid special attention to the young men who might contemplate taking orders, and his famous conversation classes in his rooms each Friday were marvellously influential. His sermon class was a seminal institution, and Simeon in the pulpit, in gown and bands and gloves, became the most striking clerical figure in the University of his day.

The sixteenth-century writer who spoke of 'Anglo-Calvinism' might have presented historical theology with a useful term, for the Calvinist tradition in England from 1560 onward had its own characteristics. And if in the eighteenth century the problems of predestination and reprobation were once again the theme of acrimonious debate, it cannot be too often said that the Calvinists were in the main concerned not about these things, but about the free and sovereign grace of God. There was among the evangelicals a spectrum of opinion, from the moderate Calvinism of the majority, to the stricter doctrines of Romaine and Madan and the more extreme views of Hill and Toplady. But as the movement drew away from the Methodists, Calvinism ceased to be the differential. Rather was it the stress on the depravity of man by sin, and his redemption by the grace of Christ. This was combined with acceptance of the Bible as the Word of God, and, rejecting any Socinian notions, of the inseparable connection between the person and the work of Christ, the sufficiency of his atonement, and the imputation of his merits to believers. And this was not a straitened rationalist scheme, but religion known and experienced in faith, in conversion, and the continuing experience of forgiveness and the sanctifying work of the Holy Spirit.

The historians of the Evangelical Movement all stress that at the heart of it was the Christian home and family devotion. It is perhaps not possible to compare this with what went on in the other fields of the Revival, in Wales, or among the Methodist societies. It may be that the strength of the evangelicals came from clerical families and those of laymen affluent enough to preside over their own households. The Methodists highly valued family prayer, but the Methodist preachers were hardly ever at home, and their elaborate devotions early and late in the day, from 6 o'clock sermons to vigils and watch-nights, catered for humbler people in whose homes was neither quietness nor room for family prayers.[33] But to stress the importance of the home for the evangelicals need not invite invidious comparisons, and there is no doubt that within these Christian families there was an inner strength which passed from one generation to another.

It would be unbelievably complex to compare the similarities and differences between the 'other worldliness' of the high-church tradition of Ken and Law and that of Wesley and his Methodists and of the Evangelicals. But there seems to have been a narrowing of horizons as they moved into the nineteenth century, in a further straitening of Sabbath observance and in the exclusion of poetry and novels. High churchmen, Methodists, and evangelicals alike regarded as a sin of levity what other generations before and since might describe as the saving grace of humour. But we must not underestimate the happiness and joy of evangelical religion at its best, though when, as happens in all religious movements, gospel became law, the result could be grim and boring and indeed disastrously counter-productive on the next generations.

The intellectual battle against scepticism had ended its first phase when the Revival got under way, and the evangelicals made but small contribution to learning.

The works of Venn, Romaine, Wilberforce, and Newton were a contribution to the literature of devotion and one must mention Thomas Scott's commentary on the Bible with its deep influence on the next generation, not least upon John Henry Newman. Joseph Milner's *History of the Church of Christ* (1794) was pietistic in scope and much attacked by other historians, but it, too, was widely read.

In the field of letters James Hervey of Weston Favell made his writings the vehicle of an evangelical fervour which his poor physical frame could not express in action. His *Meditation among the Tombs* (1746) went into twenty editions, while his extraordinary *Theron and Aspasia,* with its florid romanticism, was an immediate success, but proved to have little survival value. More important was the genius of William Cowper whose *The Task* expounds the evangelical world view with beauty, pathos, and — yes, humour.

The Evangelical Revival was nourished in song, and almost every group produced notable hymns. The Moravians had their own historic tradition, to which John Cennick added new glory. The Welsh Revival

---

[33] But see L. F. Church, *The Early Methodist People* (1951), ch. 6.

produced in Williams of Pantecelyn a hymn writer of immense importance for the future of Welsh Nonconformity. The Countess of Huntingdon and Romaine and Madan had their own collections, as did Venn, Berridge, and Toplady. Among scores of similar compilations the *Olney Hymn Book* stands out. Within the narrow compass of its covers are included Christian songs echoing a long tradition — patristic and medieval, as would be made plain later by J. M. Neale. John Newton's 'How sweet the Name of Jesus sounds' is obviously in the 'Jesu, dulcis memoria' succession. Cowper knew all about Luther's *Anfechtung* and some of his best hymns wrestle with the problem of suffering — 'God moves in a mysterious way' and 'Sometimes a light surprises' — but nobody in that age, not even Charles Wesley, excels him in writing of the love of God in hymns like 'Hark my soul, it is the Lord' or 'There is a fountain filled with blood'. It has often been pointed out that the most determined Arminian must be hushed in the presence of Toplady's 'Rock of Ages, cleft for me', with its authentic expression of the 'sola fide, sola gratia, solo Christo' of the Reformation.

23

THE DISSENTERS 1750–1791

THE notion that the older Nonconformist bodies were in decline in the middle of the century, and were rescued by a blood transfusion from the Evangelical Revival, is but half a truth. The Dissenting history would have gone on, with its continuing life rooted in its own tradition, and with its own involutions and developments altogether apart from the Evangelical Revival, just as in the main, the Church of England went its own way. And in fact there were important movements of renewal in areas untouched by the Revival.

Moreover, the exclusion from the Universities of the Nonconformists, the benefits of their own Academies, and their confinement within a narrow section of English culture meant that a great amount of intelligence and character went into the life of their communities, and the second half of the eighteenth century produced, certainly among the Baptists, an impressive number of notable leaders.

In the previous half-century the Baptists had little contact with public life. Now, altogether apart from their infiltration into the Industrial Revolution, already noted, there were more and more ministers and laymen learned enough to be properly honoured with Scottish doctorates, and such distinguished figures as John Ward, a Vice-President of the Royal Society, Andrew Gifford, also famed as an antiquarian and book collector, Thomas Guy, the founder of the famous hospital, Thomas Hollis, who founded two chairs at Harvard among many benefactions, and Joseph Collet, the Governor of Madras. Within the ranks of its ministry Robert Robinson, the two Robert Halls, John Ryland, and William Carey were men of spiritual stature and deep fervour, in whom something of the strength of nineteenth-century Nonconformity is already discernible.

Renewal came in Northamptonshire and Leicestershire, already a great centre of Nonconformity. It was owing to the Countess of Huntingdon that one of her servants, David Taylor, was set free to form a group of societies in Leicestershire and, though he himself became a Moravian, he founded a group of Baptist societies which centred in Barton.

A West Riding Methodist, Dan Taylor, turned away from Methodist doctrine and discipline and worked in Lincolnshire to such effect that he, too, founded societies which when joined with the Barton communities to form a New Connexion of General Baptists, grew and flourished at a time when the General Baptists had largely succumbed to the rising liberal rationalism.

Against the rational background of the age, Deism, the infiltration of Socinian and Arian ideas, which Calvinists of all kinds put down to the sinister influence of Arminian and Baxterian notions, some kind of polarization was inevitable, and it came among the Strict Baptists in the appearance of a vehement hyper-Calvinism. In a hyper-Calvinist succession the Cambridge Independent, John Hussey, begat the Baptists, John Brine and John Skepp, but it was the learned John Gill (1697–1771) whose many volumed theology was the staple of the hyper-Calvinist cause. These men discouraged any evangelical or missionary initiative on the ground that it was a presumption for men to invade the sphere of God's own sovereign grace, and though they did not go unchallenged at any time, their influence was as powerful as it was evangelically enervating.

For a time the moderate Calvinists lacked a coherent counter-movement, but when it came it found an effective weapon in the theology of the American Independent, Jonathan Edwards, about whose evangelical zeal and authentic Calvinism there was no doubt. In England Robert Hall Senior, of Arnesby, took up the challenge in his preaching and his influential printed sermon, *Help to Zion's Travellers* (1781), was perhaps a turning-point. Even more effective was the work of Andrew Fuller (1754–1815), a man of impressive physical frame and no less doughty mind. He had begun his battles as a youth in the little chapel of Soham in the Fens and he became the mainspring of the new evangelical and missionary activity which soon began.

John Sutcliff of Olney in 1784 sent out a call to prayer which resulted in a little movement of renewal. The learned John Ryland and the notable preacher Robert Hall were other leaders of the group which in 1792 founded the Particular Baptist Missionary Society for Propagating the Gospel to the heathen. Of this group William Carey became the central figure and from it the pioneer mission to India originated. It was a missionary enterprise which in zeal and sacrifice is worthy to stand alongside the great missions of the early Christian centuries and those of the monks, the Jesuits, and the Moravians. Sydney Smith might sneer at them as a 'nest of consecrated cobblers', but in vision, integrity, and moral courage the Baptist leaders were hardly equalled among the Anglican bishops. The Methodist missions led by Thomas Coke soon followed, and other societies which were to make the coming age the greatest period of missionary advance in Protestant history.

The Independents had been joined by several Methodist preachers, who had taken Methodists along with them, and John Wesley had learned that it was better to let trouble-makers go in scores rather than upset 'our discipline'. More important were societies which had been formed by Whitefield and above all the chapels, societies, ministers, and students from the Countess of Huntingdon's Connexion, once it had been forced into separation from the Church of England. Almost as important were the numbers of Presbyterian chapels where Calvinism still remained, which either went over as a whole or were composed of faithful remnants who had withstood the infiltration of liberal rationalism.

For among the Presbyterians and Independents unorthodox doctrines had made great headway, following the Salter's Hall debate and as a result of the theological free-for-alls which the Nonconformist academies had encouraged from the best of motives. At least half a dozen Congregational churches were to become Unitarian, when that communion was formally established, and in many other places opinions were bitterly divided.

Moreover, in the last decades of the eighteenth century there were swift, strong currents of thought in which ideas of the seventeenth century began to find new life, ideas which lay deep in Nonconformist history. Their links with the older Puritan colonies were such that they were inevitably in sympathy with the Americans in their struggle for justice and for independence. It brought new vigour into their renewed struggle for the repeal of repressive legislation, the Test Acts of the last century. There was a growing sense of an awakening political life outside Parliament, an appeal to wider public opinion, and a new political radicalism which found a focus in new leaders and in the formation of Constitutional societies. To much of this the Nonconformist leaders gave a sympathetic attention while Anglicans and Methodists were opposed.

It was with the outbreak of the French Revolution and in the furore of its opening stages that the Nonconformists were vociferously involved — to such an extent that Edmund Burke, who had favoured the repeal of the Test Acts, now changed his mind as he became aware of the role played by Nonconformity in the wider political agitation. For this centred in two Nonconformists of stature and influence, both leaders of the new liberal rationalism, Richard Price (1723–91) and Joseph Priestley (1733–1804). Price had been associated with the well-to-do Congregationalism of Stoke Newington and had embraced Arian ideas, though from 1770–1791 he was minister of the Gravel Pit Presbyterian church in Hackney. Price was a mathematician and a pioneer in studies of public finance, of the Public Debt, and of life-assurance schemes. As such he had acted as adviser to the Government and became through these activities, a protégé of Lord Shelburne.

Joseph Priestley was a giant after the manner of Benjamin Franklin, a polymath of a new kind such as the Universities could hardly have bred, nourished in the forward-looking disciplines of the more liberal Nonconformist academies where he had taught, master of many languages, a student of history and a scientist whose studies brought him deserved and lasting fame. He did not, perhaps, shine as a preacher, for a bad stammer interfered with his speaking and he had no cure of souls. He was opinionated and perhaps arrogant, though it might be said he had something to be arrogant about. He and Price, the Yorkshireman and the Welshman, were very different in temperament, and differed entirely in their philosophy: Priestley was a materialist, and a believer in necessity. Price equally vehement in defence of free will. But about the new watchwords 'liberty' and the 'rights of man', both men were belligerently at one. On 4 November 1789, the anniversary of the Glorious Revolution, Richard Price preached in the Old Jewry meeting-house a 'Discourse on the Love of our Country' addressed to the Society for Commemorating the Revolution in Great Britain. But he linked the past with two other contemporary 'Glorious Revolutions', in America and in France. Price, who was in ill health, managed to attend the Society's dinner at the London tavern which sent to the French National Assembly their congratulations. The sermon itself was to have important literary and political consequences, for it drove Edmund Burke to compose his immensely influential *Reflections on the Revolution in France* which in turn provoked the not less seminal *Rights of Man* of Tom Paine.

For a few months the English liberals found it bliss to be alive, but as the Revolution became more chaotic and as the bloodshed and violence grew, as thousands of refugees entered England, and with the outbreak of war with France, there was a national reaction on the side of law and order, and a not unnatural revival of old antagonism against Dissent. Now the mobs took action on another side, and on the night of 14 July 1791 a Birmingham rabble attacked Dissenting meeting-houses, wrecked Priestley's house, burned his papers, and demolished his scientific apparatus. He had to flee to London, whence in 1794 he went to a more congenial America.

The cause of rationalist Dissent received some new accession from the Church of England in the aftermath of the Feathers Tavern Petition, most notable of all Theophilus Lindsey, who opened a Unitarian chapel in Essex Street off the Strand. But with the death of Price in 1791 and the departure of Priestley the movement lacked leaders.

Despite their emphasis on learning, there was a growing lack of candidates for their ministry, and the liberalism of the academies degenerated into a chaotic indiscipline which had grievous repercussions on the Presbyterian churches who ended the century in some disarray.

PART VI

THE ESTABLISHMENT

In a Christian Commonwealth the Church and the State are one of the same thing, being different integral parts of the same whole. For the church has been always divided into two parts, the Clergy and the Laity: of which the Laity is as much an essential integral part and has as much its duties and privileges, as the Clerical member: and in the rule and government of the Church has its share.

EDMUND BURKE *Speech on the Petition of the Unitarians*, 1792

24

THE CLERICS

i. 'Truly Earthed'

MORE influential than the Evangelical Revival was the continuing life of the Church of England. The bitter-sweet music of its jangling bells hovered over the fields and towns as though expressing a sway over the very elements. Within the walls of its parish churches the greater part of the nation was baptized, married, and laid to rest. Through all the changing scenes of life, in trouble and in joy, thither the tribes came up in national crisis or in private need, to reckon with their Maker. Whether the priests were faithful or unfaithful, the liturgy went on, Holy Scripture, prayers, the Word and the Sacraments. And if most of it was as unexciting and unspectacular as daily bread, it was as vital to the continuing life of a Church with roots going back a thousand years. The historian would be foolish indeed who should underestimate its importance.

No room for romanticism here, for the Church of England was as well and truly earthed as any Church in Christendom, and its institutions guarded and guaranteed by law. It was mingled with the life of the nation, less in the Chalcedonian image of Warburton, of an alliance between two entities, each of which kept its properties unconfused and undivided, than the more Eutychian view of Burke of England as one Christian nation.

Norman Sykes suggested that the 'laicization of religion' rather than the secularization of the Church is a fit image for the eighteenth-century Establishment, and we shall consider the laity before we are done. But the clergy themselves were involved at every level of the life of the people. A great part of the income of most incumbents was still connected with tithes. Tithes were an ancient institution, but the untidiness of it as a system was enhanced following the Dissolution of the Monasteries. There was first the widespread impropriation of tithes into lay hands, and the anomalies caused by the commutation of tithes for payment, the *modus,* and still further by the practice of leasing tithes for shorter or longer periods. The great tithes, which came directly from the products of the earth, had often passed into lay hands. The lesser tithes were notoriously difficult to collect and control, as many a parson found when he tried his hand at 'turning a fleece'. But they kept the clergy as sensitive as the farmers to the vicissitudes of harvest, weather, and rising prices. When Samuel Wesley rebuilt his rectory at Epworth, his first care was a long hall in which to store his corn. Yet Parson Woodforde's Diaries show how reasonably well the system could work and he has pleasing pictures of good cheer when payment was accomplished. Too often there were tensions and quarrels, and for centuries there had been intermittent grumbles at the whole system, repudiated altogether by the Quakers in the eighteenth century. When Samuel Wesley caught one of his farmers cropping the ears of his tithe corn, he almost frog-marched him to the market-place to display the perfidy. It did not increase his own popularity. Sometimes quarrels led to the lawcourts, while non-payments could bring a parson to financial straits and even to be 'on the run' or in prison.[1]

Most country parsons had their glebe of several acres. There were many like Henry Fielding's Parson Trulliber who was 'a parson on Sundays but all the other six might properly be called a farmer. He occupied a small piece of land of his own, besides which he rented a considerable deal more. His wife milked the cows, managed his dairy and followed the market with butter and eggs. The hogs fell chiefly to his care, which he carefully waited on at home and attended to fairs'.[2]

On a much more affluent scale was Dr John Taylor of Market Bosworth for whom the chief end of man was 'getting a bull to his cows and a dog to his bitches' and who seems a less clerical figure than his lay friend, Samuel Johnson, who wrote many of his sermons. Bishop Watson of Llandaff worked even more energetically at his estates in the Lake District and sought earnestly the best gifts, the *charismata* of 'Capability Brown'. With this immersion in the bucolic there was a varying political involvement from sharing the work of magistrates and Justices of the Peace, to lively intervention in parliamentary elections, while at the top of the ecclesiastical pyramid were the massive services given to the Crown and Government by the episcopate.

ii. Incumbents and Curates

The clergy were an overcrowded profession, and the stream of ordinands proceeding from the Universities, and sometimes ordained upon spurious titles, swelled the ranks of the unemployed. There was an ugly residue of desperate men who lived on what they could make from clandestine weddings and who would have been no credit to any

---

[1] 'Absconditi', in *Speculum Dioceseos Lincolniensis,* I. ed. R. E. G. Cole (Lincoln Record Society 1913), iv. p. xv.

[2] *Joseph Andrews.*

profession, least of all the cloth. Like other professions, law, medicine, the Army and the Navy, family influence, wealth, and patronage were needful to those who would climb the steep ascent to the higher ranks. From curate to bishop, midshipman to admiral, ensign to general, law student to judge, etc., etc. the ascent was so difficult, and so little dependent on merit as to justify Bentley's famous description of it as a lottery.[3]

Holy orders, however, is not 'just another profession' about which a pragmatic or self-interested behaviour acceptable in secular society may be accepted without question. Ambition, a thrusting disposition, an eye to the main chance, touting and toadying, the use of money and interest for clerical advancement, find little support in the New Testament. Nor could these things be without contaminating effect. Even an earnest young cleric like Richard Kidder could be badgered by his friends into unseemly importunities when an incumbent whom he might succeed was on his death-bed, and there were more shocking examples which were well known.

At the end of the seventeenth century John Eachard had satirically suggested that the ignorance and poverty of the lower clergy had brought the clerical estate into contempt. The modern historian underlines this, more coolly.

A poor clergyman . . . might labour under grievous disadvantages. His poverty could cripple his pastorate in many obvious ways. He would lack books and the society of educated persons; he would have nothing but words to give to the afflicted; he would be driven to supplement his inadequate income by taking on other jobs — one or two additional curacies, perhaps or teaching, hack writing or farming.[4]

Those who criticize the unreadiness of bishops to ordain Methodist preachers and exhorters must not forget the hard, long haul that the leaders of the Church of England had, almost from the beginning of the Reformation, to raise the standards of clerical learning, or minimize the extent to which, in the middle of the eighteenth century, improvement was achieved. But below the ignorance, as has been suggested, was the poverty which the uneven and unequal distribution of the wealth of the Church seemed doomed to perpetuate. Absentee incumbents — the result of pluralism and lay rectors — made the provision of curates a necessity and ensured their depressed economic position.

In vain did the author of *Ichabod* warn: 'What new generation of men

---

[3] G. Holmes, *Augustan England*, 1982; J. Addison, *Spectator*, No. 21 (Everyman edn.), p. 63.

[4] G. Best, *Temporal Pillars* (Cambridge 1964), p. 13.

are these curates? . . . your commission, O my sons, Is "Go ye and teach all nations": not, "Go ye or send your curates to teach all nations."' Curates had no tithes, and were appointed on a fixed stipend and thus at a disadvantage in times of inflation. Some were appointed to do the work of the absentee incumbent: some to assist an infirm cleric, or during a vacancy. Perpetual curates were in a class of their own, and, when licensed by a bishop, had a status which brought them near to that of the beneficed clergy. Most of them were poorly paid despite the Act 12 Anne, c.12, which laid down that curates should be paid sums ranging from £20 to £50; most were nearer the lower figure and many much lower than that.

Nor were the laity without fault, for in many cases licences were deliberately not sought, and there is the disagreeable picture of the neglected Cheddar village described by Hannah More.

I asked the farmers if they had no resident curate: they told me they had a right to insist on one: which right, they told me, they had never ventured to exercise for fear their tithes should be raised. . . Mr. G. the only one of the clergy who came near the place is intoxicated about six times a week and very frequently is prevented from preaching by two black eyes, honestly earned by fighting.[5]

There were a few who successfully laid curacies and lectureships together. The obnoxious William Sellon who had successfully attacked the Countess of Huntingdon's Northampton Street Chapel made his curacy at Clerkenwell the centre of his £1,000 a year empire. But there were others, like Samuel Walker of Truro and Thomas Jones of Craton, whose curacies were models of pastoral and evangelical care.

A little less sanctified and a little less devoted, but attractive too, is the curate of Broxbourne, the Revd. William Jones, whose manifold minor tribulations at the hands of his wife and family never drove from him entirely the joys of his little study where, unbuttoned, he could relax.[6] Fielding has the endearing Parson Adams, who in all his poverty kept his dignity, his humour, and his charity and withal his love of learning, for he was an admirer of Hoadly and doted on his own hand-written copy of Aeschylus. More attractive still is the real-life John Bold, curate of Stoney Stanton in Leicestershire, where he lived faithfully and devotedly for nearly fifty years, living contentedly on one meal a day in one hired room in a farm before whose thronged and open hearth he did his reading. He was also a devoted catechist, from whose parish crime seems to have disappeared. All this on £30 a year, and heaven too.

The impropriation of advowsons, the right to present a candidate for

---

[5] A. M. B. Meakin, *Hannah More* (1911), p. 293.
[6] O. F. Christie, *The Diary of the Rev. William Jones 1771–1821* (1929).

a living to the bishop, added to the complexities of patronage which was exercised by Crown, ministers, bishops, colleges, corporations, and laymen from peers of the realm to simple esquires. Families like the Dixies of Market Bosworth built large rectories and put in incumbents who should keep the place warm for members of the family in what was a rich living. The advowson was a property which could be disposed of, either permanently or for a generation, but the business of marketing, and even auctioning, advowsons was felt to be a scandal, while the practice of taking 'bonds of resignation' brought such practices to the borders of simony, as those earnest evangelicals Thomas Haweis and Martin Madan found when ensnared by the lay patron Kimpton of Aldwinckle, whom financial distress had forced into desperate and disreputable methods.[7]

The beneficed clergy generally did not come from the lower orders of society, though as in every age a bright, exceptional poor man's son might find his way to the top. And indeed a number of eminences, Potter, Warburton, Secker, came from the plebeian class, so that the opprobrium cast by the Oxford authorities on the mechanic background of the expelled Methodist students suggests either humbug or that in the 1770s the social standards of the clerical calling were rising.

As in most lands of the Reformation, there was a noticeable continuity in parsons' families, and sons of the manse continued to play their part in the ministry. There were indeed cases where a ministerial dynasty might fill a living for centuries.

It is impossible to generalize about the characters and competence of the many thousands of the beneficed clergy. The hard-drinking, hunting 'squarson' undoubtedly existed. William Jones acidly deplored the 'keen sportsmen, sharp shooters and mighty hunting Nimrods of the cloth . . . daily advertisements appear for the sale of the next presentations of valuable livings . . . situated in fine sporting countries' — 'plenty of game' — 'A pack of staunch fox hounds kept in the neighbourhood . . .' These men are, of course, rare, charming preachers! But they are rectors, vicars etc. and their poor curates however gifted, zealous and excellent are still 'only the curates'.[8]

Others preferred hunting Methodists and among them were some ugly characters. Among the country parsons the worldly and the devoted might live cheek by jowl. At Loddington in Leicestershire the Revd Nathaniel Heyrich could be ironically described as 'better fitted for this world than the next'. He owed his fame to his profitable skill at whist, and to the fact that he disdained any but the very best society. But

[7] A. S. Wood, *Thomas Haweis* (1957), pp. 126 ff.
[8] *The Diary of the Rev. William Jones*, p. 158.

the devoted Rector of South Croxton rushed about for twenty-seven years in tireless preachments, 'like a flying curate on Newmarket plain'.[9]

Among the richer livings it is obvious that wealth, family influence, and patronage prevailed. Sometimes the iron entered into the soul of the rebuffed and disappointed, like Humphrey Michel, an Oxford graduate, but son of a butcher, who envied his neighbours their wealth, their patrons, and their clerical background, and attacked them as 'velvet cushioned doctors', 'pompous periwigs', and members of a 'foppish fraternity'.[10] Those with poor livings might move in hope of better things, but the most part remained where they were and in Leciestershire 'only one in five resigned to accept a living elsewhere.'[11] There were many with the tenacity of John Bold, already mentioned, and others like Richard Hill who went to the rich living of Thurcaston from Emmanuel College, at the age of forty, to remain there with great devotion for over thirty years, founding a charity school before he died. In fiction Fielding, Sterne, Goldsmith, Smollett, and Jane Austen show a wide range of clerical character, and Parson Adams and the Vicar of Wakefield are offset by the Trullibers and Thwackums. Part of the attraction of Parson Woodforde may be that he comes close to the meridian, the average of pastoral care in his age. We see him as a good, kindly man, always at hand when one of his flock, rich and poor, was in need, playing cards and dining with his social superiors, hating the limelight, not a great preacher, but not a bad one either, without much imagination, perhaps above or below average in his endless descriptions of gargantuan meals, which suggest he derived peculiar pleasure from the prospect of the Messianic Banquet, which shock some readers, but endear him to those who love their Surtees.

iii. Queen Anne's Bounty

The institution of Queen Anne's Bounty was the one signal attempt to deal with clerical poverty.[12] By this relatively simple Act, which was supported by Whigs and Tories, the revenue derived from the payment of first-fruits and tenths to the Crown, was to be given to a corporation which would use the money to raise the value of poor livings. Its value was about £17,000 a year. There were initial problems about collecting

---

[9] VCH Leicestershire, i. 392–3.
[10] J. H. Pruett, The Parish Clergy under the Later Stuarts (Chicago 1978), p. 73.
[11] Ibid., p. 74.
[12] Best, Temporal Pillars; Ian Green, 'The first five years of Queen Anne's Bounty', in Princes and Paupers of the English Church 1500–1800, ed. R. O'Day and F. Heal, Leicester 1981.

the money, and it took many investigations to ascertain the exact financial status and the whereabouts of those livings most in need of assistance. It was decided not to give cash grants, but to make longer-term investments in land. The procedure was to begin with the poorest livings of £10 or less and move upwards until all under £50 had been augmented. The legislation passed with surprising ease.

The Bounty did not remain a royal grant alone, for from the first its Governors encouraged private benefactions. These were forthcoming from humble parishioners to peers of the realm, and in them the clergy played a part. 'In the first century of its existence Queen Anne's Bounty raised over £2,450,000 . . . and made over 6,400 grants to poor livings in England and Wales'.[13]

It is not cynical to add that part of the enthusiasm for the scheme lay in the fact that it was no head-on attack on inequalities, no attempt to assail the rights of property or to remove from the richer preferments to pay the poor. The potent anomalies remained.

It is true that the clergy profited from the growing prosperity, not least in agriculture, and this was accompanied by an enhanced social status, so that the Church once again became a profession into which the aristocracy could profitably put their sons, and the poorer parsons ceased to be treated as inferior servants.

iv. Problems of Reform

The machinery of the Church of England was maladjusted to its pastoral vocation. The famous image springs to mind, of Gulliver stranded on the shores of Lilliput, seeking to lift his head, but unable to do so because he was tied to the ground by thousands of tiny threads, any dozen of which he could have torn out, but which together frustrated all movement. For by reason of many frailties the Church of England was not able to stand upright. Many of these anomalies, abuses, inefficiencies, were the continuation of medieval malpractices, though 'medieval' is a very odd word to apply to the eighteenth century, which despised all things medieval, and one has still to ask why evils which had some colour of defence in the later Middle Ages could still continue to exist in the self-satisfied age of the enlightenment. For the Church in this most rational of centuries was choked by practical irrationalities which had indeed ceased to be merely anomalies, but were so much a part of the life of the Church that neither churchmen nor statesmen dared contemplate attempting their removal. The trafficking in tithes and advowsons could

---

[13] *Green*, p. 231.

and did come near to simony, and many an archdeacon was affronted by practices which in a complicated area touching civil and canon law passed beyond the borders of propriety. About pluralism, non-residence, and nepotism there was no ambiguity. At the lower end of the scale the poorer clergy were driven to pluralism by the need to exist, and this might vary from the simple combination of cures within distance of one another (as when Samuel Wesley added Wroote to Epworth) to places where no spiritual oversight was possible, and where the incumbent had no intention of exercising direct pastoral care, delegating this to his curate. The Visitation returns again and again mention the absence, or decay of parsonages, and the dereliction of churches as side-effects. Alongside the ruinous state of Llandaff Cathedral we may put the sight which met the eyes of Mrs Thrale when she visited for the first time the impropriated living at Bodvil. 'The churches . . . are mean and neglected to a degree scarcely imaginable. They have no pavement and the earth is full of holes, the seats are rude benches. The altars have no rails: one of them has a breach in the roof.'[14] And these things did not only happen in Wales, though undoubtedly Wales was a special case. The poorly paid Welsh bishoprics, remote, difficult of access, were generally regarded as places of transit by aspiring English clergy, and of thirty English bishops in Wales only three had any acquaintance with the Welsh language.

Pluralism was less indefensible when no cure of souls was involved, but the traffic in simple prebends in the cathedrals was at the mercy of interest and family pressures. More difficult to justify was the practice of adding preferments *in commendam* to act as makeweights for the dioceses which were poorly paid, and the attachment of the deaneries of St Paul's and Westminster to Rochester or Oxford or Bristol, or of churches like St James's, Westminster, to the assistant of the Bishop of London was no way to treat such offices.

Family interest, whether exerted by wealthy patrons on behalf of their kin, or by little dynasties of local clergy or simply by bishops attending to the needs of their own relatives and friends and servants, was taken for granted, went almost without comment, and was exercised by good and great bishops like Wake and Sharp. How difficult it was to combat these evils can be seen in the troubles into which Kidder ran when he tried to oppose them at Wells, and became involved in situations which neither Ken before him nor Hooper after him was able to remedy. At Wells, too, there was the dominating influence of Dr Creyghton, son of a former Bishop and Precentor, who secured three or four canonries for

[14] Samuel Johnson, *Diaries, Prayers and Annals,* Yale edn. of the *Works* of Samuel Johnson, ed. McAdam (New Haven 1958), i. 206.

his sons-in-law. An even more difficult situation arose under Bishop Willes (1743–73) and his sons and sons-in-law. His appointments to dignities included the following:

19 Aug. 1749 E. Aubrey (son-in-law): Archdeacon of Wells
 1 Oct. 1753 L. Seaman (son-in-law): Archdeacon of Taunton
31 Oct. 1755 Henry Willes: Chancellor
 6 Aug. 1757 Henry Willes: Precentor
27 April 1758 L. Seaman: Archdeacon of Wells
15 May 1758 William Willes: Chancellor
31 Dec. 1760 William Willes: Archdeacon of Taunton
26 May 1764 Charles Willes: Chancellor
20 Oct. 1764 William Willes: Archdeacon of Wells.

It seems that the chapter had decided to dig its heels in against these genteel mafiosi and kept them away from canonries.[15]

There seems reason to believe that as the century proceeded the difficulty of eradicating the anomalies increased. 'The percentage of episcopal appointments made with long term commendams . . . rose from 46.7% before 1714 to 68.9% afterwards.'[16]

The Church of England had no Council of Trent and its discipline was largely unreformed. We may not string too many 'ifs' of history together, but if the Laudians had triumphed (not in 1660, but in 1640) and the massive theology of the Caroline divines been matched in practice, there might have been a genuine amendment and rooting out of the insidious abuses. We may add another 'if' and suggest that the Restoration was the last time when such an opportunity occurred[17] and that some churchmen seem to have seen this. We may even risk the remark that such a high-church programme might have been preferable to that one day to be achieved by anti-clerical Whigs. This point is supported with some poignancy by a document which appeared in 1663 entitled *Ichabod, or Five Groans of the Church: prudently foreseeing and passionately bewailing her second fall.* The work was ascribed to Thomas Ken after his death, and the attribution tentatively accepted by his biographer, Dean Plumptre.[18]

There are internal traits which support the identification. The author is a high churchman who stresses the importance of episcopacy and the

---

[15] *Life of Richard Kidder,* ed. Robinson, pp. 208–9.
[16] D. R. Hirschberg, 'Episcopal incomes and expenses 1660–1760', in *Princes and Paupers in the English Church 1500–1800,* p. 218.
[17] Best, *Temporal Pillars,* p. 11.
[18] E. H. Plumptre, *Thomas Ken* (2 vols. 1898), i. 55; Benham, *The Prose Works of Thomas Ken,* p. 1.

apostolic succession, and who rejoices in the discomfiture of the Puritans. Like Ken, he is well read in the Fathers and in the councils of the early Church, but is also familiar with the history of the Anglo-Saxon and medieval Church of England. His work closes with a quotation from Gildas. The only difficulty of linking *Ichabod* with Ken is that the first edition was printed 'for J. Greaves' in Cambridge. There, in a marginal reference (p. 30), where the author is attacking 'factious ministers' who face both ways, who 'use the ceremonies and say to . . . confidants — they are a burden to him', there is a marginal reference to

S. H.
H. M.
Dr. JW

which must stand for Samuel Hartlib, Henry More, and Dr John Worthington. This is a bit of Cambridge in-fighting which suggests a closer knowledge of what was going on there than Ken could be supposed to know, though it may have been inserted by the Cambridge printer.

The tract includes a devastating attack on those Puritan clergy who had conformed in 1660 and such bitter antagonism to what he called 'time-serving clergy' as underlines Ken's lifelong antagonism to Latitudinarians. The only other consideration which might tell against Ken's authorship is the attack on the youthfulness of the new generation of ordinands which comes oddly from one who himself was twenty-seven.

The first part of the work is a lament spoken by the Church of England. The second part of the tract attacks abuses

    1. Undue Ordination
    2. An unconscionable simony
    3. Careless non-residence
    4. Loose profaneness
    5. Encroaching pluralities

It begins with an attack on the levity of the new young men accepted in large numbers since 1660.

Where is thy pious spirit, devout Hall? Where is thy gracious temper, excellent Usher? Where is thy even and settled frame, serious Hammond? Where is thy virtuous deportment, famous Morton? Where is thy rational, well weighed and stayed soul, venerable Sanderson?[19]

---

[19] Benham (ed.), *The Prose Works of Ken*, p. 28.

He roots his attack on simony in the pronouncements of church councils and in Acts of Parliament and applies them to the traffic in tithes and advowsons. 'Are tithes of God, or are they not? If they are of God, why do ye buy them of men?'[20] And he quotes the feeble excuses 'Objection. I only laid a wager, bought a horse, married my patron's daughter . . . . I only bought an advowson.'[21] To which he replies:

Is the Church grown so contemptible that it may be bought and sold for the richest rather than a reward for the worthiest?

Will you crouch for the priest's office that you may eat a morsel of bread? Will you all degrade yourselves and buy and sell your sacred persons and employments? Justly would the Catholic Church have degraded you . . .

He ends the section with a devastating quotation from John Jewel against impropriations. The attack on pluralities centres on the neglect of pastoral care.

Do you know that you must watch over the congregations as they that must give an account? so many benefices, so many more hundreds of souls but you must answer for. Do you know what it is to answer to the great God for an immortal soul?. . . you consider not whether some have not accused you whom you never saw. . .

Now, now my people are neglected, my buildings are ruined, my hospitality is lost, my authority is shrunken and fallen and the Church of England is thought to be nothing else but the interest of a few crafty clergymen ordering all things to their best advantage.

This is not mere rhetoric, for he supports his argument about non-residence from councils of the early Church, from the Fathers of East and West, and from Acts of Parliament from Henry VIII to Charles I. He returns to the attack on the abuses of tithing with a formidable array of quotations from Anglo-Saxon and medieval historians. All the time, the neglect of souls is the heart of his indictment.

Fain would they hear that their souls may live, but you are not among them to preach: willing are they to receive the sacrament, but you are not among them to administer it. They are declining in grace but there is none to recover them . . . they miscarry and there is none to oversee them, to watch over them, to look to them.[22]

We may think that a century later such a diatribe would have been dismissed as 'enthusiasm'. In the eleventh century a Hildebrand had led a great counter-attack against simony, and in the thirteenth century St Francis had put the challenge of holy poverty — but these were the very

---

[20] Ibid., p. 34.   [21] Ibid., p. 35.   [22] Ibid., p. 47.

figures picked out for ridicule and contempt by bishops like Stillingfleet and Lavington.

With the suspension of Convocation, the Government was freed from worry about turbulent priests. A Herring and a Secker had no intention of leading a crusade against abuses, nor did they have any consciousness of having made 'the great refusal' by not disturbing the existing disorder. There were, it is true, voices raised from time to time which were more than the grouse of men like William Cole who did not come off well under prevailing conditions. The aged Sherlock disconcerted his London clergy by a vigorous charge against pluralism and non-residence in which he deployed his great knowledge of the law, and he asked with a directness worthy of *Ichabod,* 'Can you deliver the message of Christ as his ambassador to persons to whom you have no access? Can you oversee the flock or feed the church which you have forsaken?'[23] Yet he himself owed much of his ascent to pluralism at every stage, and while he attacked the right of the Archbishop to exercise an option on St George's, Hanover Square, with almost medieval intransigence, he himself handed over St James's, Piccadilly *in commendam* to his assistant Dr Nicholls at the Temple.

Not that Sherlock's admirable sentiments were not preferable to those of the author of the *Apology for the Clergy* written in reply.

'It may be much more for the interest of the church and of religion that men of learning and abilities should officiate in large and respectable congregations and attend the services of cities and cathedrals than that they are obliged to attend personally in their own parishes on the instruction it may be of a few Mechanics or Rustics who may learn as much as they are capable of from the meanest curate.'[24]

Still less convincing must have been the solemn reminders of their pastoral duty to reside, which his clergy received from their pluralist, non-resident bishop, Richard Watson of Llandaff, on his occasional incursions into his diocese. It would be a mistake to accuse either Sherlock or Watson of hypocrisy, for both the high churchman and the Latitudinarian were paragons of that sovereign virtue of the age, 'sincerity'. Rather they witness to the prevalence of ills in a complex situation which no individual example could have changed.

So the old 'medieval' abuses continued, years on, in a Church which had ceased to be deeply shocked by them. For at least the men of the Middle Ages had hung out danger signals. Dante put the nepotist Pope Nicholas III along with the simoniacs in the third *bolgia* of the eighth circle of the *Inferno,* while Bishop Willes of Bath and Wells and his like

---

[23] E. Carpenter, *Thomas Sherlock* (1936), p. 149.   [24] Ibid., pp. 153 ff.

attained their desired haven in the House of Lords. But then, neither the ultimate destination of the one nor the penultimate destination of the other could be mutually exclusive.

Undoubtedly, part of the problem of achieving amendment was the fact that the life of the Church of England was what might be called a 'package deal', in which discipline could not be separated from doctrine and liturgy. The practical anomalies must be seen in relation to other pressures, to the growing demand, as the century proceeded, for some relaxation of subscription to the Thirty-nine Articles, and for a measure of doctrinal and liturgical revision.

More fateful than Bishop Gibson's opposition to the preferment of the Latitudinarian Dr Rundle was his successful blocking of the attempt to elevate Samuel Clarke to the episcopate.

There is no doubt that Samuel Clarke's intellectual gifts were of the highest kind, and though his position about subscription brought down on him the wrath of Whiston, who thought it moral cowardice, he did suffer for his convictions and was cut off from a position of influence which might have been of critical importance. He had devoted a great amount of detailed attention to a revision of the liturgy, down to the smallest details, and it is astonishing how in differing centuries a Hippolytus, a Thomas Müntzer, and a Samuel Clarke could, in the name of orthodoxy, colour their liturgical experiments with their own idiosyncratic theology. In Clarke's revision the Athanasian and Nicene Creeds would have been casualties and the prayers deprived of all Trinitarian associations. The Athanasian Creed had been under fire from the time of Tillotson, and only partly because of the damnatory clauses.

For many, Waterland seemed to have successfully defended the orthodox doctrine of the Trinity, and Gibson, who defended the use of the Athanasian Creed, noted in the fly leaf of his copy of Waterland that he had carefully ascertained that the Swedish Lutherans continued publicly to recite that formulary. The effect of Deist, Arian, and Socinian notions, the growing toleration and rationalism of the age gave impetus to the movement for loosening standards of subscription, since the God of the historic creeds and of the Articles had for many given way to the thought of God as the Supreme Being, the Governor of the Universe.[25]

The pressure for some measure of reform in the matter of subscription came to a head in the Feathers Tavern petition (1772) when some 250 liberals signed, in a tavern in the Strand, a plea that for the Thirty-nine Articles there should be substituted a simple appeal to the Bible as the

---

[25] See Sykes, *Church and State*, pp. 343–5.

source of divine truth. It was a high-powered group, and academically strong, being heavily supported from the University of Cambridge. Among the leaders were Archdeacon Francis Blackburne of Cleveland and Theophilus Lindsey, Vicar of Cleveland. The petition was presented to the House of Commons by Sir William Meredith and was debated on 6 February 1772. The motion was rejected by 217 votes to 72 after a great speech by Edmund Burke, who urged that such a drastic reform should not be enacted at the plea of a minority, but only when it had behind it the support of a majority of lay and clerical churchmen.

After the defeat of the project, Blackburne remained in the Church of England, but Theophilus Lindsey formed the Unitarian Chapel in Essex Street, Strand, *en route* for an impressive memorial in Bunhill Fields. But there were others, like Beilby Porteous and a group of influential friends, opposed to such radical change, who wished a revision of the Articles, at least as regards Article 17, and for some revision of the liturgy.[26] They applied to Archbishop Cornwallis, who replied on behalf of his fellow bishops that 'nothing can in prudence be done'. Others, notably Richard Watson of Llandaff, wished to press for acceptance of Samuel Clarke's revised liturgy, and in contemporary pamphlets there were still more proposals. In the decades of crisis and political change, of American Independence and the French Revolution, it was a plausible argument that drastic change in discipline or doctrine would have roused a tumult and begun a train of events very difficult to control.

In a famous passage, Edmund Burke defended the role of religion in the high places of the nation.

> We will have her to exalt her mitred front in court and parliaments. We will have her mixed throughout the whole mass of life and blended with all the classes of society. The people of England . . . can see without pain or grudging an Archbishop precede a Duke. They can see a Bishop of Durham, or a Bishop of Winchester in possession of ten thousand pounds a year; and cannot conceive why it is in worse hands than estates to the like amount in the hands of this Earl or that Squire.[27]

v. The Bishops

When Sir Adam Fergusson suggested doubt of the propriety of bishops having seats in the House of Lords Johnson replied 'How so, sir? Who is more proper for having the dignity of a peer than a Bishop?'[28]

This was not perhaps the point in time for the Church to remember

---

[26] Ibid., pp. 380 ff.

[27] E. Burke, *Reflections on the Revolution in France* (Harmondsworth 1982), p. 203.

[28] Boswell's *Life of Johnson*, ed. Hill, ii. 171.

the patristic notion that the wealth of the Church is the patrimony of the poor, in an age when there was no talk about the menace of 'triumphalism' and the need for an image of a 'Servant Church'. But none could ignore the disparity and inequality between the richer and the poorer sees, and whether we take the later calculations of the Ecclesiastical Commissioners in 1835 or the earlier figures for 1714 and 1760, the disproportion between Canterbury, York, Durham, and Winchester and Llandaff, St Davids, Rochester, and Bristol shows why the poorer bishops were driven to supplement their incomes by holding deaneries *in commendam*.[29]

But in fact the majority of bishops did not exploit their situation and some of them found it difficult to make ends meet. The charges upon their office were manifold and heavy: aside from their families, the upkeep of their palaces and staff, the expense of living in London during the parliamentary sessions, and the cost of 'journeyings oft'; large benefactions to charity, not grudgingly or of necessity; sizeable bills for food and drink (even the frugal Secker's drink bill was 6.55 per cent of his income: more abstemious commitments might have saved many a bishop from being 'surpriz'd by the gout'). If a bishop loved books, like John Moore of Norwich at the beginning and Richard Hurd of Worcester later in the century, a library could be a costly item. And finally Visitations were cumbered with charges so diverse that the bishop was rarely able to 'break even'.

Granville said that there were 'bishoprics of ease' which were properly reserved for 'men of family and fashion', and the highly connected Cornwallis, North, Barrington, and Manners Sutton attest the return of the privileged classes to the clerical vocation in the latter part of the century. Public hospitality and numerous servants underlined the appearance of affluence, and Burnet himself confessed his failure to bring about the economies he thought desirable. Kept within bounds, it was not perhaps offensive, but Archbishop Potter, sprung from obscurity, with his too many and too ostentatiously paraded servants and liveried postillions, is a contrast with the modest sobriety of Secker, while the flamboyance of Cornwallis (or more particularly of his wife) led to a protest from the Countess of Huntingdon which the monarch seems to have endorsed. William Cole records acid gossip:

The late . . . Bishop of Salisbury is said to have died worth upwards of £150,000 . . . . I can hardly think it probable that he could amass so much wealth. . . . I never heard him accused of avarice: nor did I ever hear that he had any great fortune with any of his four wives.[30]

[29] Sykes, *Church and State*, p. 409; D. R. Hirschberg 'Episcopal incomes and expenses 1660–1760', p. 212.   [30] W. Cole, *The Blecheley Diary*, p. 52.

Of course marriage might always be a side door to clerical affluence. It had been so from the first days of the Reformation when in Germany and England a few such alliances raised eyebrows among clerical colleagues, and there were instances among the Methodist preachers in England and Wales. Cole comments on the fortunes of Thomas Sherlock and Bishop Maddox, 'I hope the laity and the nobility will not envy the clergy their wealth and preferments: especially as the nobility do all they can to heap preferment upon preferment on their own relations.'[31]

A glance at the 'also-rans' who close the chapters of Abbey's delineation of the eighteenth-century episcopate shows that the Bench had its due proportion of amiable nonentities. But there were many who were eminent in learning, wisdom, and pastoral care. We may feel that the bishops in the period between Sancroft and Gibson were more admirable than those a century later, but over the whole period there is a worthy roll of honour. Wesley's comments on bishops are always interesting and he said that Gibson was a great and a good bishop, while he had warm admiration for Horne and Lowth. Even middle-of-the-road archbishops like Herring and Secker had virtues which deserve higher praise than their rather unadventurous administration. In a class of his own, by common consent, was Thomas Wilson, Bishop of Sodor and Man (1663–1755). Appointed bishop in 1698, he faithfully stayed in his diocese and had the good fortune to find in the Isle of Man a people who responded to his vigorous attempts to restore discipline, which he succeeded in doing to a degree unparalleled elsewhere. He built churches, founded libraries, and wrote notable devotional works. His fame spread far beyond these islands, and a Cardinal of France and the Moravian leaders went out of their way to do him honour. He was loved by Roman Catholics and Dissenters as well as by his flock. A number of bishops were scholars, and some were eminent in learning. Lord Hervey's disparaging remarks about 'Greek and Hebrew blockheads' suggest a politician's frustration with the academic mind. But it is true that from the time of Wake and Gibson to that of Warburton learning was grounded in philological and antiquarian precision which had perhaps an Ozymandian quality.

Among the philosopher-bishops George Berkeley and Joseph Butler do not abide question. Others, like Richard Hurd (Lichfield 1774–81, Worcester 1781–1808), had a distinguished place in polite letters.[32] His essays and dialogues display a fluency, percipience, and imagination

[31]. Ibid., p. 53.

[32] J. Butt, *The Mid-Eighteenth Century, Oxford History of English Literature,* xviii. 351–4.

which many found absent from his precise, laconic and, 'off-putting' personal demeanour. But he was much more than a shadow of his bumblingly extroverted friend Warburton, and one must be impressed by the way his monarch leaned upon his counsel. The diaries of Pepys, Evelyn, and Thoresby at the beginning of our period confine our glimpses of the bishops in the main to services and sermons, but the pages of the pale blue-stockings of a century later, of Mrs Thrale, Miss Burney, and Hannah More, show the genial and relaxed side of some who otherwise might have seemed daunting, and show us how congenial a part in a social circle might be played by bishops like Horne and Lowth, and the evangelically minded bishops Shute Barrington and Beilby Porteous. There were always a small number of bishops in the magic circle of Johnson's famous 'Club', of which Bishop Shipley was a notable member.

It has ever been the wisdom of the Church of England to produce in every generation figures who defy all labels and pass through all divisions, inexplicable mutations of the genus 'bishop' who have brought delight and anger to their contemporaries. Such was Richard Watson, Bishop of Llandaff (1737–1816). The uncouth northerner, who made no concessions of outward appearance or manners, whom nerve and ambition had led to 'get up' chemistry and divinity sufficient to enable him to seize the Chairs of Chemistry and Divinity at Cambridge, perhaps underestimated the difficulties of 'getting up' the episcopate. Thinking, like so many others, to pass through his Welsh diocese as a valley of Baca, swiftly and without retrospect, his refusal to toe any party line, and his independence of judgement stopped the way to the further preferment which he was only too conscious that he deserved.

He accordingly spent at least twenty-five years of his thirty-four as Bishop away from his ruined cathedral and non-existent palace, on his estates at Calgarth, Lake Windermere, where he spent his time 'principally in building farmhouses, blasting rocks, enclosing wastes, in making bad lands good, in planting larches'. But he conducted Visitations and Confirmations during his intermittent visits to his diocese and took trouble about his ordinations. Nor may his apologetic services be forgotten, for he wrote doughty defences of the Christian faith against Gibbon and Thomas Paine, and he was to the fore among those who demanded revision of discipline, doctrine, and liturgy. The Bible for him was the religion of Protestants, and there could be no greater contrast between his generation and that of a century before, in his disesteem of the Fathers, whom Gibbon and Middleton had reduced to a babel of discordant bigotries, rather than the revered fountain of wisdom next only to Holy Scripture.

The rehabilitation of the eighteenth-century Church has been most impressive in what concerns the office and work of a bishop. Norman Sykes may have made too much of the appalling difficulties of travel along execrable roads which kept the bishops at home or locked in London, for it was along those very roads that the Methodist preachers made their ceaseless journeyings. But he demonstrated the concern of many bishops about their essential duties, the care of ordinands, the diligence of Visitations, and a new concern for Catechism and Confirmation. Bishops would not again perform the role in politics which they had hitherto exercised, but their services to the State were still very considerable. The involvement in politics, and especially in party politics, inevitably exposed them to pressures and temptations which some found chafing and uncongenial, but Burke had the great point, that the voice of the Church echoed along the corridors of power.

vi. The Practice of Worship

It may be fairly argued that the religion of everyday wayfaring Christians should have occupied far more of these pages than theological controversies, ecclesiastical councils, the doings of the famous, books, in short, Ecclesiastical Man rather than Christian men. But here, alas, is the least ascertainable of all our enquiries — to relate the inner convictions of a silent, and largely inarticulate, majority. We can of course find plenty of human material in diaries and spiritual autobiographies, but the very fact of writing such narratives lifts the author out of the common run. And while statistics of church attendance tell us something, the counting of heads cannot at all distinguish between the formal and the deeply contrite. The figure 'one' for a church attendance may stand for the flighty young women described more than once in the the *Spectator,* who come to church chiefly to stare or to be gazed at, or to show off the latest fashions, or it may stand for the serious devotion of Queen Anne or the solemnity of an 'Amen' from Samuel Johnson.

There were many complaints from the bishops that the Toleration Act had led to members of the Church of England absenting themselves from divine service. It is likely that with ups and downs a slow decline continued, though there were still large congregations. Those absentees for whom evangelical parsons like Grimshaw scoured the pubs and the fields, and the great numbers in the abandoned villages of the Mendips and the industrial areas, came from the poorer classes, while it has often been argued that at the lowest economic levels there were those who had no contact with the Church, which the very poor attended only to get the doles given out at the Communion Services. Calamy's old boatman, who had never even heard of Jesus, points to people completely ignorant of the Christian faith, though there is plenty of evidence of what would now be called 'diffused Christianity'. At the other end of the social scale it is not any easier to judge what was going on in the minds of the prosperous, in many of whom the fashionable rationalism had left a very reduced Christianity and for whom worship was little more than a formal bow to the Supreme Being.

The land was covered with parish churches great and small. Most of them were centuries old, many of them ancient, patched and reshaped many times. From the lank austerity of Sussex Anglo-Saxon, as in Sompting, to the great fabrics of the Fens, of Lavenham, Long Melford, Blythburgh, to the cathedrals and the embellished London boxes of Wren and Gibbs, from tiny village shrines to the splendid dignities of a Beverley Minster, a St Peter Mancroft, a St Mary Redcliffe — there was an immense diversity, linked by common beauty, and the line of the modern poet, 'You are here to kneel where prayer has been valid.'

But eighteenth-century man did not regard his churches with the distant reverence of the modern tourist, guide-book in hand, or of the educated modern custodian alert to every treasure. He who scurries between the gales which seem permanently to blow between the steel and glass temples of Mammon which now occupy the City of London cannot but gasp with wonder and relief when he escapes into another century within the walls of St Lawrence Jewry, St Vedast, Foster Lane, St Andrew-by-the-Wardrobe; or, beyond the liberties, St Giles-in-the-Fields, St Paul's, Covent Garden, and St James's, Piccadilly. Those churches, many of them risen Phoenix-like after the Blitz of 1940, rebuilt, refurnished, glow with light and polished brightness — an immaculateness which perhaps they never had when Benjamin Whichcote, Simon Patrick, John Sharp, or William Wake occupied their pulpits, since in those days great congregations rubbed off some of the bloom.

The Visitation returns dispel romanticism. Many churches were in disrepair and furnishings were often scruffy. Sometimes a member of a vestry might perch upon an unadorned altar, on which others might rest account books, or write school exercises. But there were others concerned to remedy deficiencies which Queen Mary had evidently noted when following her visits to Canterbury she gave fine cloths to the Cathedral. And there were many like Sir Roger de Coverley, who, 'being a good churchman, has beautified the inside of his church with several texts of his own choosing. He has likewise given a handsome pulpit cloth and railed in the Communion table at his own expense.'[33]

[33] *Selections from the Tatler and Spectator*, ed. A. Ross (Harmondsworth 1982), p. 229.

Within the churches medieval brasses, converted chantry chapels, imposing monuments of Tudor and Jacobean worthies, surrounded by effigies of wives and offspring, were reminders of the past, while on the walls a myriad epitaphs commemorated departed clergy and citizens of renown, expressing sentiments which ranged from the pretentious to the poignant. The medieval colours had been overlaid with whitewash, and prominent were the Ten Commandments and the Creed, the Royal Arms, and large notice boards with details of benefactions, an attempt to guard their philanthropies from misappropriation. Something had perhaps been lost with the eclipse of the Laudian tradition, and Bishop Butler's famous charge on the importance of externals suggests a theological defect behind the unconcern. The days when the Herberts and the Ferrars could whip round their wealthy friends and rebuild the church of Leighton Bromswold with a loving attention to detail, which extended even to the drainpipes, seem to have gone. Now wealthy laymen used the skills of an unparalleled wealth of craftsmanship in gold, silver, porcelain, glass and furniture to decorate their own stately homes, and took but little interest in adorning churches, still less in building the new ones which by the last half of the century were badly needed. Secker in 1753 expressed his sorrow that

noblemen and gentlemen will squander vast sums in the gratification of private luxury and vanity . . . and not consider that much smaller sums bestowed upon public works, especially in honour of religion, would gain them the admiration of a whole country.[34]

The church seating reflected the social hierarchy. The Lord of the Manor had the largest pew in the best position, with the highest ramparts, and its amenities ranged from the ability to escape the direct gaze of the preacher, to facilities for comfort, warmth, and refreshment. As the Visitation returns remind us, it was customary to think of Christians in families, and in some parishes the pews corresponded to the numbering of houses. The congregations were often segregated by sex, and though there was always room for the poor, they generally had their place at the back of the church. If we are to judge from handbooks about worship, people were often reluctant to kneel, and there were not often kneeling mats available. In some of the fashionable London churches you had to tip to get a good place, and it was said of St James's, Piccadilly, that 'it costs almost as dear to get a seat as to see a play.'[35] Parson Woodforde's Diary tells us of his troubles with his choir, and of

---

[34] Sykes, *Church and State*, p. 233.
[35] Legg, *English Church Life*, p. 36; W. K. L. Clarke, *Eighteenth Century Piety* (1944), ch. 1.

visits from singers from other churches. But there were few churches with organs, and musical instruments were not generally available.

The caricatures and porcelain figures remind us of eighteenth-century services at their least appealing, with the three-decker pulpit, and the parson bashing his cushioned Bible above the sleepy parish clerk. But there were many services like that at St James, Garlick Hill, of which the *Spectator* wrote 'I heard the service read so distinctly and emphatically and so fervently that it was next to an impossibility to be inattentive. My eyes and my thoughts could not wander.' Samuel Johnson was by no means the only devout Christian who never managed to be in church on time, and there must have been frequent tardy infiltrations at least until the Psalms.

Pluralism had made it impossible for there to be two Sunday services throughout the land – a drastic halving of the ration of worship which seems to have caused no more qualms than has its modern repetition. The service was of Mattins with Ante-Communion and a sermon. There were some afternoon services, at a time once specially earmarked for Catechism, but these were generally without a sermon, and the complaints about parishioners wandering off to other parishes where sermons were available show that most people wanted to hear sermons. In the cities, and not often elsewhere, there were weekday services, but the reiterated appeals from bishops show the neglect of public worship and in the country many a parson was baffled by the non-appearance of a congregation when he tried to put on services for holy days. In London and Westminster in 1714 there were seventy-two churches[36] and chapels with daily services. Churches, then as now, had their ups and downs. It seems that by 1711 the Covent Garden area had lost some of the fervour kindled by the ministries of Patrick and Horneck. Said a letter to the *Spectator:*

I have been for twenty years under-Sexton of this parish of St. Paul's Covent Garden and have not missed tolling in to prayers six times in all these years . . . to my great satisfaction, till this fortnight last past during which time my congregation take the warning of my bell, morning and evening, to go to a puppet show set forth by one Powell under the Piazza . . . there appear among us none but a few ordinary people who come to church only to say their prayers so that I have no work worth speaking of but on Sundays.[37]

The seventeenth century left English Christians a nation of sermon addicts. The London divines, Whichcote, Barrow, South, Tillotson, had appreciative audiences, and set the norm for the next generations. Not only did these outstanding preachers publish their sermons, but so

[36] Legg, *English Church Life*, ch. IV.   [37] *Spectator*, i (Everyman edn.), 45.

did a great number of lesser mortals like the Revd Zachariah Mudge of Plymouth whom Johnson so admired. Sermons became a staple of edifying reading. The example of Parson Woodforde suggests that the rank-and-file preachers throughout the land got their own sermons to a large extent from the sermons of more renowned preachers, though biblical commentaries were also a feature of the age. Samuel Johnson, a discriminating sermon-reader, perhaps underrated Tillotson, but he shrewdly summed up South: 'one of the best, if you except his peculiarities and his violence and sometimes coarseness of language.' The two Latitudinarian preachers Tillotson[38] and Samuel Clarke[39] achieved a lucid, attractive, and unpretentious style which made their sermons easy to read, and easy for others to re-deliver. The range of their themes is much wider than the moralism with which they are associated. But the moralism is certainly there. Tillotson's famous sermon on 'His commandments are not grievous' (1 John 5:3) has had much attention from historians. And it is true that the Latitudinarian emphasis on the need to practise the virtues, on repentance and the abandonment of sin as prerequisites for forgiveness, recalls the semi-Pelagianism of the fourteenth century so that it is no surprise to find Tillotson repeating almost exactly the Nominalist watchword, 'God does not deny grace to the man who does what within him lies, *Facienti quod in se est.*'[40] That Tillotson should stress that the way to heaven is plain and pleasant and not the kind of precipitous ascent pictured by the Calvinists is in itself not alarming or unique. 'Religion never was designed to make our pleasures less' is a startling line from Isaac Watts, and John Wesley began his hymn book with the theme of 'The pleasantness and excellence of religion'. But perhaps a stress on moral achievement had its own points of anguish and uncertainty, especially when its demands were stepped up as by William Law. One would say that nobody would give the Latitudinarian sermons to a man whose sins had found him out, save that this is exactly the place where Samuel Clarke spoke to the condition of an anguished Samuel Johnson.

But many preachers were content to read to their flock the sermons of the famous. Hence the incident in the *Spectator* when Sir Roger de Coverley replied to one who asked 'Who preaches tomorrow?'

The Bishop of St. Asaph in the morning and Dr. South in the afternoon. He then showed us his list of preachers for the whole year where I saw with a great deal of pleasure Archbishop Tillotson, Bishop Saunderson, Doctor Barrow,

---

[38] *The Works of Dr. John Tillotson,* 4th edn., 1704.
[39] *The Works of Samuel Clarke, D.D.,* 4 vols., 1738.
[40] Tillotson, *Works,* p. 77.

Doctor Calamy with several living authors who have published discourses of practical divinity.[41]

Nor should we underestimate what may be called the 'kerugmatic' content of those Latitudinarian sermons. Tillotson and Clarke both have fine passages about the goodness of God, and about the great acts of salvation in Jesus Christ. If Clarke's sermons are arranged in an order which underlines his unorthodox view of the Trinity, he has some quite remarkable passages about the work of Christ, repudiating those who suggest that the Son has averted the wrath of the Father and insisting that our salvation rests in the loving purpose of a God who is all goodness. There is nothing arid or dry about him in the pulpit.

Preaching habits were diverse. The young brothers Wesley preached one another's sermons and anybody else's they found suitable. Samuel Johnson wrote sermons for hire at 2 guineas a time, and he can hardly have been the only one plying this abnegatory trade. Some used notes, others read from manuscripts, though reaction against Puritanism discouraged the extempore and the impromptu. Many of these repeated discourses had been preached at Court, or before the lawyers and notables of the City of London. Some of them must have been well above the heads, if not of the Royal Family, certainly of the Maids of Honour, and even more surely of village congregations, and if many preachers shot their arrows into the air on Sunday mornings, not many landed in the hearts of Tom, Dick and Abigail at the back of the church. Still, it is only too easy and fallacious to underestimate the intelligence of ordinary congregations or the ability of good men and women of simple faith to get to the root of theological matters. Once again Parson Woodforde's sermons may have been somewhere near the average.[42] Woodforde topped and tailed Tillotson's 'His commandments are not grievous' and preached it again and again as a curate and as a parish priest. But the range of his themes is impressive: the relation of reason to revelation, the place of miracles in the Christian dispensation, the meaning of Holy Communion (and a plea for its frequent celebration) were recurring subjects of his edifying discourses. A very different preacher was Laurence Sterne,[43] but he, too, was a great borrower from Tillotson and others. His *Sermons of Yorick* show his mastery of language and his versatility of mind in preachments which he described as a 'theological flap on the heart'. Johnson detested them, and when a friend 'showed him Sterne's sermons "Sir", said he, "do you ever read any

---

[41] *Selections from the Tatler and Spectator*, p. 218.

[42] N. Sykes, 'Sermons of a Country Parson', *Theology*, xxxviii, Feb–May 1939.

[43] *The Sermons of Yorick*, 2 vols., 1760; J. Downey, *The Eighteenth Century Pulpit* (Oxford 1969), ch. 5.

others?" Yes, doctor, I read Sherlock, Tillotson, Beveridge and others". Ay sir, there you drink the cup of salvation to the bottom: here you have merely the froth from the surface.'[44]

There seems some ambivalence about the evidence whether Sterne, in his parish or in York Minster, was an attractive preacher, since he obviously had mannerisms and a curious voice. About the popularity of the preaching of Archbishop Secker there was no doubt, and he had great and appreciative congregations wherever he went. If he does not borrow explicitly from Tillotson, it is because he had so imbibed the Tillotsonian moralism and, though moralism is by no means the whole content of his sermons, they lack any kind of style or sparkle and have a devastating way of expounding the obvious.[45]

Sermon-tasting was among the delights that in that age attracted visitors to the metropolis. Many went the round of the pulpits, from those of the leading Dissenters to the Roman Catholics at the embassy chapels. More exotic fare was provided by the near mountebanks, Orator Henley of the 'gilt tub' and Macaroni Dodd. Henley, like the spiritual chameleon Edward Stanley, offered the heady attraction also of a trendy liturgiosity (to coin a rather needed word).

We have seen how in word and in writing the City preachers at the end of the seventeenth century expounded the Sacrament of Holy Communion, and pleaded for its regular reception. What Patrick, Horneck, Wake, and Tillotson commended was also commended, in lower key, by Hoadly and Samuel Clarke. There does seem to have been a small eucharistic revival, for there are accounts of great sums raised for the poor in the London Communion Services and of large numbers of communicants. They were earnestly supported by the young men of the Religious Societies.

The phrase 'frequent Communion' was in the air, familiar from Roman Catholic writings and the practice and teaching of the Non-Jurors. John Wesley and his friend John Clayton, in the days of the Oxford Holy Club, believed that constant, rather than frequent, Communion was to imitate the Primitive Church. We have already noted the extent to which, where the Wesleys were concerned, the evangelical was also a eucharistic revival.

Visitation returns and other evidence show that in that age Communion was celebrated but seldom, which does not mean that it was in low esteem. Most churches celebrated three or four times a year and at the great feasts, and, as always, Easter drew the largest number of communicants. But the infrequency had much to do with the

---

[44] G. B. Hill, *Johnsonian Miscellanies*, (Oxford 1897, repr. 1966), ii. 429.
[45] Downey, *The Eighteenth Century Pulpit*, ch. 4.

unavailability of clergy and it is notable that in many market towns and cities there was a much higher proportion of monthly celebrations, and in London there were many weekly Communions. It is difficult to assess what proportion of the congregations communicated and the numbers may have been small in proportion to the population: some statistics for thirty Oxford parishes for the period 1738–88 suggest only 5.5 per cent of the population. But the figures are not given for Easter — they are an overall figure for the chief feasts, including Ascension Day. Wickham Legg quotes reliable evidence of a higher percentage than this. Archbishop Herring's Visitation returns show a much higher figure than this in parts of Yorkshire, and Norman Sykes quotes surprisingly high figures for Bangor in Wales.[46]

The frequency of celebration is probably a better guide to the importance of the Sacrament than the number of communicants. Holy Communion is a sacrament from which inhibitions are never absent — people stay away from thoughts of unworthiness, from a sense of guilt, or, like Samuel Johnson, because they took preparation for it very seriously. In remote country areas one would understand that attendance might be minimal and there is evidence of some congregations baulking the expense of wine (with at least one benefaction dealing with this subject).

So, regularly as an incoming and ebbing tide, the worship of the Church drew in its people and discharged them again for the business of daily living. As we said, most of it was unexciting and unspectacular with an enormous range between it at its best and at its worst. With all the defects things worked out much better than the recital of woes would suggest and as in all ages men made the best of what they had no power to mend. It cannot be said that over England as a whole the hungry sheep looked up and were not fed. And then, as always, God had his own ways of circumventing the follies of his people, and never ceased to satisfy the empty soul and fill the hungry soul with goodness.

---

[46] Sykes, *Church and State,* p. 251. R. Currie, A. Gilbert, L. Horsley, *Church and church goers* (Oxford 1977), p. 22. As on the next page it is said that the Catholic population in Britain 'probably fell' about 40 per cent between 1720 and 1780, when in fact it was more probably increasing (see above, p. 190), one may have reservations about this study.

25

THE LAICS

THERE was nothing doctrinaire about the 'laicization' of religion in eighteenth-century England. It had nothing to do with modern notions about the 'wholeness' of the one People of God, the Scriptural *laos*. Nor had it the anti-clerical overtones of the French use of the word 'laïque'. It did not explore the implications of the Priesthood of Believers, as this was acclaimed at the Reformation, still less that apostolate of the laity expounded by the Second Council of the Vatican. It did not probe the mysterious questions 'What is a layman?' 'Who is a priest?' It did not ask (as some have interpreted the Coronation Rite) whether the Supreme Governor of the Church of England was a 'mixed person', a hermaphroditic combination of the two. It had nothing to do with the teachings of Erastus, or what was derided as Erastianism by the high churchmen of the reign of Anne. It was rather the tacit acceptance of a historical situation, which had given the laity power in the Church. And this in a way which blurred earlier distinctions between the spiritual and temporal powers, and led to the lay occupation of a no-man's-land between them.

The patron of a living, the owner of an advowson in a society where patronage and interest prevailed, had an added degree of power. A Sir Wolstan Dixie could treat Market Bosworth as though it were some feudal *Eigenkirche* putting incumbents in and out according to family interest and breaking the rules when he wanted to, as he did in his despotic treatment of his ungainly usher, Samuel Johnson. Dogberry and Mr Bumble, constable or beadle, Vestryman, Justice of the Peace, and up through the civic corporations to the High Court of Parliament itself — each had its own legal standing. At the very top, a godly layman, the Christian monarch, could by proclamation recall the nation to more seemly manners and morals, as well as exercising often decisive influence over the higher clerical appointments. And this latter power was formidably exercised by his ministers, so that it was said that all but three of the Bishops owed their appointment to the Duke of Newcastle. On the other hand the lower clergy had been corporately silenced by the suspension of the Convocations, and the Bishops in the House of Lords were declining in influence. The ability of the Government again and again to block such entirely desirable measures as the provision of bishops for the Plantations show the limits set to clerical initiative. The debate on the Feathers Tavern petition (1772) demonstrated the truth of Lord Hardwicke's famous judgement (1737) that since the Reformation it had been Parliament which enacted or confirmed measures which concerned the laity as well as the clergy.

i. The Good-Doers

The philanthropic movement looked like running out of steam by the middle of the century, but there was a remarkable acceleration before its end. Old ways of doing good persisted, but there were new methods to meet new needs. Trade and industry swelled, and men made fortunes in Russia, the West Indies, the Middle and Far East, and the Americas. Among them there continued to be rich men furnished with ability retiring with time and money on their hands, which they regarded as a solemn responsibility. On the other hand there were new problems, as more and more men and women were pressed into the towns or the new manufactories. The poor were less and less capable of coping with dearth and famine, and high prices and the wars meant the stream of returning cripples and invalids. Those who did good continued to do so from a wide range of motives, and from all strands of belief and unbelief. But one may not leave out of account the impact of the Evangelical Revival. The side-effects of the Methodist movement may have been confined within narrow limits of society, but the Evangelical Movement within the Church of England in the 1780s produced a series of godly men and women of compassion and vision, consciously taking up the challenge to reform the manners and morals of the nation. They were aware that this had been attempted in earlier generations, and they knew about the earlier Society for the Reformation of Manners. They also knew that an attempt to revive something of this kind by the Methodists had not been successful, and they were aware that the head-on attempt at such amendment had been limited by the use of public informers, and vulnerable to the criticism that it only tackled the vices of the poor, while the rich and powerful escaped. When, therefore, in 1787 William Wilberforce and Bishop Porteous agreed to solicit a Royal Proclamation such as earlier sovereigns had used in times of moral crisis, it was with a determination to use it differently. On 1 June 1787 King George III did indeed issue a *Proclamation for the Encouragement of Piety and Virtue*. It was publicized as of yore. Its contents were traditional, save perhaps for a more explicit denunciation of pornographic literature, and few could have denied that in the last decades there had been a slipping of moral standards, from duelling and gambling to the neglect of Sunday observance.

What was new was that Wilberforce and his friends got in touch, one by one, with members of the peerage and aristocracy, asking them to create local associations who would further the reforms adumbrated in the proclamation. The eminent would form the core of his new society and through them Wilberforce hoped to influence and change the attitudes of the ruling class. Not for nothing did Wilberforce write in his diary for Sunday 28 October, 1787; 'God Almighty has set before me two great objects, the suppression of the Slave Trade and the Reformation of Manners.' The measures of practical philanthropy have to be set within this wider context.

Outstanding among the mid–century benefactors was Jonas Hanway, a wealthy merchant who, after making his fortune in an adventurous way in Russia and the Middle East, retired in 1750 and gave his main energies for the remaining thirty–six years of his life to all manner of good works. He was an astringent Governor of the Foundling Hospital in its difficult years, an investigator into conditions in the workhouses (an agitation which led to Acts of Parliament). He found, like other reformers, that each solution opened up new problems; in the case of the Foundling Hospital, that of the employment of the children. He therefore founded, in 1756, the Marine Society to train and supply boys and men for the Navy and the Mercantile Marine, so that during the war years from 1756 onwards more than 10,625 boys and men were kitted out of the cost of £23,500 Hanway was one of the first to show concern about the little chimney sweeps, though it was to take a century to get rid of the use of the 'climbing boys'.

Some of the newer institutions had by now run into difficulties. No new general hospitals were founded in London between 1750 and the end of the century. Apart from the two royal hospitals and Guy's, the running of the rest left much to be desired. Overcrowded and insanitary wards spread, rather than cured, infection, while on the other hand there was widespread closure of wards. The problems of convalescence were hardly tackled, though in 1791 the Samaritan Society was formed for just those needs. On the other hand, there were new specialist institutions of the kind which had been the dream of Nelson and of Bellars: lying–in hospitals, training of midwives, hospitals for smallpox, for cancer, and for lunatics. New institutions were formed in many cities for the care of the blind, the deaf, and the dumb, and the Royal Humane Society was founded in the 1770s.

While the old Charity Briefs fell into disuse, the newer methods of philanthropy by subscription and association proved the most effective way of spreading the burden, and of furthering good causes too complex to be left to individuals.

(a) Penal Reform

The age of projects gave way to the age of reform, to the age of causes which sought to involve public opinion and touch the conscience of the nation. Penal reform was such a cause. The state of the prisons, in the context of the brutal Penal Code, was a notorious evil. Those, like Silas Told or John Wesley, who visited and ministered to the inmates wrote and spoke of the sufferings they found. The 'deserving' poor conferred at least this benefit on the 'undeserving', that more than once those visiting friends who had fallen into misfortune or disgrace were horrified by what they found, and were moved to action.

The debtors' prisons were a concentration of human misery. Gaolers were unpaid and made their living from fees extorted from their prisoners, so that many prisoners remained in prison long after their original debts had been discharged. In this matter General Oglethorpe was a pioneer, and if the experiment of providing refuge for the debtors in the new colony of Georgia was only a very qualified success, he also succeeded in carrying through some remedial legislation. The London jeweller James Nield made the investigation of the debtors' prisons his main objective and in 1773 he founded the Society for the Discharge and Relief of Persons Imprisoned for Small Debts. This, the so-called 'Thatched House Society', had procured the discharge of 16,405 prisoners by the end of the century. In his investigative methods Nield had imitated the great John Howard.

In 1773 John Howard (1726?–90), a Dissenter who had complied with the Test Acts, became High Sheriff for Bedfordshire, and as such responsible for the oversight of the prisons of the county. What he found in them deeply disturbed him and to amend them became the vocation of the rest of his life. His move to get gaolers put on a salaried basis led him to investigate conditions in other counties, and subsequently in other countries. In the end he visited prisons and lazarettos in almost every part of Europe, travelling more than 50,000 miles, investing more than £30,000 of his own money in this work. This was the new methodology of the new age — 'Hearing the cry of the miserable I devoted my time to their relief. In order to procure it, I made it my business to collect materials, the authenticity of which could not be disputed.' In a series of reports which culminated in the famous 'State of the Prisons' (1777) Howard declared the facts, a calm and unemotional recital which made the detailed stories even more moving and horrific, and he well earned the thanks of the House of Commons. Gaolers of the baser sort learned to dread his footsteps, and if his one-man assault on the Bastille failed, he successfully visited hundreds of other prisons. There was nowhere so foul that he was afraid to enter, and again and again he walked where gaol fever raged. There was about him a perpetual stench and his notebooks had to be treated by fire. In the end he died far away in a labour camp in Russia, tending a fevered patient.[1] He had not in fact achieved many reforms, but he had set in train a movement, and other reformers would take up the work — the Quaker Elizabeth Fry with the women prisoners, and Jeremy Bentham and William Wilberforce. Bentham had been impressed by experiments in Russia and produced a project for a 'Panopticon', a penitentiary where prisoners might work and be rehabilitated and given some degree of privacy, albeit being discreetly overseen. Despite the encouragement of Wilberforce and others, neither the First Lord of the Admiralty nor the Dean of Westminster were agreeable to such an institution being erected on their doorstep, and Dean Horsley's refusal to help increased if it did not begin Bentham's disillusion with religion. In the end an attenuated version of his scheme was erected on Millbank.[2]

(b) Slavery

The second public cause was the abolition of the slave trade, the full story of which lies beyond the scope of this volume. But its beginnings, and the development of the movement in the last decades of the eighteenth century has everything to do with the theme of 'Religion in England'.

The leaders were very different in character and outlook, but made a doughty group of champions. In the first half of the century slavery, and the trade in slaves, hardly touched the conscience of the nation. It is true that the thinkers of the Enlightenment deplored slavery, and it was from the writings of Montesquieu that the pioneer Granville Sharp drew his arguments. But it was recognized that there were deep and complex economic issues involved, and stubborn vested interests, and there were those like Edmund Burke who thought abolition a practical impossibility. But the movement for abolition, once launched, spread swiftly. Though it took what seemed to the leaders an eternity of eighteen years to accomplish, it was, in the light of history, an astonishingly short time for such a signal achievement.

As for other great reforms in the coming century, it was necessary to make the facts known, if the governors of the nation were to be moved

---

[1] B. K. Gray, A History of English Philanthropy, 1967 (repr.).
[2] J. Pollock, William Wilberforce (1977), pp. 137–9.

to action. There were three dimensions. There was Africa, still and for some time to come the Dark Continent from whose shadows the bands of slaves unwillingly emerged, brought to the coast along trails of misery and greed. There followed the voyage, the so-called 'Middle Passage' between Africa and the West Indies, in foetid, overcrowded vessels, the stench of which carried for miles at sea. The mortality rate was dreadfully high, but it attracted attention only when a high proportion of the white crews similarly succumbed. And there were the Plantations themselves, the separated families, the grim conditions of men without human rights. But at least here there were witnesses who offset the propaganda of the slave owners and the merchants of cities like Liverpool and Bristol.

Granville Sharp (1735–1813), the grandson of Archbishop John Sharp, made his career the hard way in the City of London and acquired a store of learning in Greek and Hebrew, though *autodidactos*. It was not the French philosopher, Montesquieu, but personal confrontation with the evil of slavery in the person of a London slave, Jonathan Strong, which moved him to action. There were said to be 15,000 such negroes in London, and Sharp battled for years to secure a legal judgement, which was finally given by the judges in the Somersett case in 1772, when it was laid down that 'as soon as any slave sets his foot upon English territory he becomes free.'

Sharp was strongly supported by the Quakers and, when the Abolition Society was formed, they were well represented on the committee. William Warburton, among the churchmen, was an early voice against slavery, which was also denounced by Watson of Llandaff, while Beilby Porteous could rightly claim to have supported the agitation from beginning to end. The ex-slave, ex-slaver, John Newton, made his voice heard and was important for his influence on William Wilberforce and Hannah More. John Wesley, had been deeply stirred by the writings of the American abolitionist Benezet, wrote a useful and vigorous pamphlet and two wise letters of counsel and encouragement to Sharp and to Wilberforce.

At Teston in Kent an important circle centred on the home of Sir Charles Middleton, a former naval person. If a Wolstan Dixie seems to have come straight out of *Ruddigore,* then Middleton reminds us of *H. M. S. Pinafore,* for he married his captain's daughter, ended up as 'Ruler of the King's Navee' (as Lord Barham at the time of Trafalgar) and, of course, as a good evangelical, 'never used a Big Big D—.' His splendid wife was a musician and a painter, a woman of persistent and practical kindness, so that her house was an open refuge for those in distress.

But it was Middleton's former ship's surgeon turned parson, James

Ramsay, who provided the ammunition for the attack. His own first-hand observations of slavery in the island of St Kitts were recorded and defended in two powerful writings in 1784. Two young men visited Teston. The first was a young Cambridge parson, Thomas Clarkson, (1760–1846) a Johnian whose interest began when he penned a Cambridge Prize Essay on the question 'Anne liceat invitos in servitutem dare?'. Though he found it often difficult to get himself out of the picture, he was the first to devote all his time and energy to abolition, was the first historian of the movement, and gave to it all his powers until his health was shattered.

The second was William Wilberforce (1759–1833), the affluent son of a merchant family from Hull, who had been a Commoner at St John's, Cambridge, but done not much more than dabble in learning, though his great gifts were obvious to all who knew him. Small, with a perky nose, he was attractively unhandsome (his enemies said ugly), but he had entered Parliament with all the signs that he was, in the jargon, a 'coming man' who would go right to the top. He lived on the edge of his nerves, and his intermittent and life-long bouts of lethargy may have had a physical cause. His eyesight was weak — he needed a glass and had people to read to him. He was a skilled parliamentarian and could on occasions make superb orations. But if he was loyal to his friends, of whom William Pitt was a chief, he had something of a cross-bench mind and it was not always easy to foretell how he would speak and how he would vote. But there was nobody as fit to lead the campaign in Parliament and it was to be a great thing for him that he had not only the support of Prime Ministers like Pitt and Grenville, but the constant support of Charles James Fox.

The next years were what the hymn calls 'a strait and thorny road where mortal spirits tire and faint'. But there were some wise and wary parliamentary hands among them, like Sir William Dolben and James Stephen, who guided the tactics rather than the strategy. Pitt and Wilberforce knew that high sentiment and moral principles by themselves would not avail without the evidence. So there were the great enquiries, first by the Privy Council and then by Select Committee, examining witnesses and recording evidence which in the end exceeded 10,000 pages. Wilberforce was often ill under the nervous strain, and it was Pitt who, in his place, first moved that abolition be considered. The first great debate was 11 May 1789 when Wilberforce made an impressive speech of three and a half hours. Though his own motives were deeply Christian, he generally spoke of this cause in terms of 'humanity'. But he did on this occasion speak of corporate guilt 'We are all guilty, we ought all to plead guilty'. But the move was side-tracked and the one small victory that year was the Bill of Sir William Dolben limiting the size of slave ships.

Outside Parliament there was the attempt to stir up public opinion on both sides, in the press and in sermons. Petitions were organized, beginning with the radicals in Manchester, but copied by other cities. There were little Wedgwood cameos, a poem by Hannah More, leaflets bearing the detailed picture of the interior of a slave ship. Again and again political events favoured the delaying tactics of their opponents, the French Revolution and the reaction against it, and the fact that so many radical opponents of the slave trade were sympathetic to the Revolution, and the abortive rising of slaves in San Domingo. At last another grand debate took place on 18 April 1791, when, with a speech of four hours' length, Wilberforce moved 'that the Chairman be directed to move for leave to bring in a Bill to prevent the farther importation of African negroes into the British Colonies and Plantations.' There was a fine speech from Fox, but the vote was lost 'Noes 163, Ayes 88'.

Many lost heart altogether after this reverse, and even Wilberforce could not go on raising a matter so sharply defeated. The attempt to found a colony of liberated slaves in Sierra Leone was a disaster, though it brought a new ally in Zachary Macaulay, while at this time when Clarkson's health failed, there was the splendid new accession of the lawyer James Stephen. In April 1792 Wilberforce once again brought the matter to a vote, to be foiled by the amendment of Lord Dundas of the word 'gradual', a positive vote of 230 to 85, but no great victory. By now the abolitionists were becoming wise as serpents: they took advantage of political situations and the war to drive a wedge between the vested interests in the West Indies and in England, by attacking the use of foreign ships and such parts of the slave trade as could be shown to benefit the enemies of England. Meanwhile the trade was carried on, and it has been estimated that 'more slaves had been carried in the seventeen nineties than ever before'.

In 1806 James Stephen, under cover of the struggle against Napoleon, and in the name of economic sanctions, promoted the Foreign Slave Bill which took the opposition by surprise, and divided their ranks. When this Bill was carried, the encouraged abolitionists returned to the main attack in debates in which Fox made one of the finest and last speeches of his career. Now Lord Granville promised to bring in a Bill simply abolishing the trade and he himself made a notable speech at the second reading. The vote in the Lords was 100 to 36 in favour of abolition. The grand finale came 23 February 1807 in an astonishing debate in which many young men spoke supporting the older abolitionists, and it included a cheering, standing ovation for a weeping Wilberforce. The result was indeed overwhelming. 'Ayes 283: Noes 16'. It was a famous victory, but like famous victories generally, not so easy to follow up. The laws had yet to be enforced. None of the abolitionists was willing to stop short of the abolition of slavery itself. So the struggle went on during the remaining years of Wilberforce's life, and final victory came as a last crowning mercy on the eve of his death in 1833.

The attempt which has been made to read the whole story in terms of national self-interest and in reaction to a crisis caused by over-production in the sugar trade has not survived the further examination of the evidence. It may be granted that great nations do not make such gestures entirely disinterestedly, or entirely against the grain of national interest. But this in no way takes away the high motives and purposes of the leaders of the abolitionist movement. William Wilberforce, making due and lawful use of the machinery of politics and law, proved that Christian politics are the art of the impossible.[3]

(c) Sunday Schools

If abolition is an example of philanthropy as a cause, the Sunday Schools show it as a movement. As the charity schools had been at the heart of the increase of charity a century before, so the new Sunday School movement caught the imagination and aroused the energies of men and women deeply concerned for the amendment of the morals and manners of the nation. Though the charity schools continued to exist, the movement had no further momentum, and left untouched great numbers of children who had no effective education at all, and who were being sucked into the accelerating industrial revolution.

From the time of the Reformation, Sunday afternoon had been the usual time for catechetical instruction of the young, so that we need not be surprised to find there had been various attempts to start such Sunday Schools. But now what was in mind was something more than religious instruction; it was to teach the young to read, and, in some cases, to write as well. Robert Raikes (1735–1811), a man already active in penal reform and other philanthropic activities, was able to give the new schools advertisement and publicity through the *Gloucester Journal* which he edited, so that the movement swiftly developed. Raikes and his colleagues hired four women to act as teachers and began with some ninety pupils. In 1794 he described how the children had been divided into classes. 'The children who show any superiority in attainments are placed as leaders of the several classes and are employed in teaching the

---

[3] R. Anstey, *The Atlantic Slave Trade and British Abolition 1760–1800*, 1975; Pollock, *Wilberforce*; E. Royle and J. Walwin, *English Radicals and Reformers 1760–1848*, 1982.

others their letters or in hearing them read.' They met on Sundays from
10.00 until noon, had an afternoon session, and returned after Evensong
for instruction in their Catechism. We have seen how John Fletcher
welcomed the idea at Madeley. In 1788 John Wesley was almost ecstatic
about the Sunday Schools he saw in Bolton le Moor. 'About three I met
between nine hundred and a thousand of the children belonging to our
Sunday schools.'[4] Here there were forty masters who had assistants
whose services were voluntary. The expenses were much less than the
founding of charity schools, but buildings had to be found and there
were some teachers to be paid, even though more and more use was
made of voluntary help. The Sunday School Society was formed, and
Dissenters as well as church men used the new devices. Though
historians are sceptical of some of the claims made — as that by 1785
there were a quarter of a million in the schools — it is just possible that
the claims are justified and that in effect there had been something like a
mass movement. Like the charity schools, the Sunday Schools came
under fire, with charges of indoctrination and brainwashing. Nor could
it be denied that to teach a child to read made it possible for him to read
Tom Paine as easily as the Bible. And as the life of the radical Samuel
Bamford shows, there were soon to be radical and rationalist Sunday
Schools. The old charges made a century before, that it was teaching
children to be dissatisfied with their lowly station in life and that they
became less useful farm hands or manufactory workers, were repeated,
so that one way and another, as Hannah More was to find, an innocent,
laudable, and immensely necessary educational movement ran into all
kinds of trouble. Within the limited means at their disposal and despite
the small learning of many of the teachers, there was much goodness
and much zeal, and probably a good deal and better educational insights
than later sophistication would ever be prepared to admit.[5]

That there had been schools in other parts of the country before
Robert Raikes and that the establishment of Sunday Schools became
such a rapidly growing movement is because it was one of those ideas
whose time had come, an immediate answer, possible in human and
material resources, to an evident social problem: how to deal with
masses of ignorant poor children who, when not labouring the long
hours in the new manufactories, were let loose upon the streets of towns
and villages. The work of the More sisters in the country villages of
Gloucester show that it was not simply an urban or an industrial

---

[4] Wesley, *Journal*, vii. 377.
[5] S. C. Neill in *The Layman in Christian History*, ed. S. Neill and H. Ruedi-Weber
(1963), p. 210; Gray, *History of Philanthropy*, pp. 118 ff; D. Owen, *English Philanthropy*,
pp. 113–15; S. Bamford, *Passages in the Life of a Radical*, 1839.

problem — though even in Cheddar it was to be among the colliers and the workers in the glass-houses that the need was most acute. But in the north and in the textile towns the civic authorities saw the opportunity for the establishment of schools with a zest which in its beginnings crossed the sharp denominational barriers. This was shown by the intricate organization which launched the Sunday Schools in Manchester, Leeds, and Stockport in 1784 with an important undenominational stress.

ii. *Women in Ministry*

The higher education of women had many ups and downs from the days of the Renaissance. Then a Vives and an Ascham had devoted treatises to the theme, and there were a few splendid instances of female learning, the daughters of Conrad Peutinger and the household of Thomas More among them. The Lady Jane Gray, the Princess Elizabeth, and the team who produced the translation of the *Paraphrases of Erasmus* show a combination of religion and learning at Court. During the seventeenth century there were always notable Christian ladies, not forgetting those at Little Gidding and Thomas Ken's friends at Naish, while we have already noted instances of female learning in the courts of William and Mary, and Queen Anne.

Throughout the eighteenth century there was a growth in the attention paid to female education. Despite their economic disadvantages, the Wesley girls were a remarkable bunch. Many of them dabbled in writing and one of them became a member of Samuel Johnson's inner circle. It is obvious that there was much to be done, as Isaac Watts complained, and the ill-written, badly spelled letters of Mrs Doddridge to her husband are perhaps typical of the extent to which the education judged fit for the female sex lagged behind that taken for granted with the males.

The young ladies in the Cotswold villages, many of them daughters of the parsonage whom the young Wesleys cultivated, were a gracious and cultured company, far from unlearned in the literature of spirituality, though the brightest of them all, the lovely Mrs Delany, was perhaps no more than a beautiful and ineffectual angel in the society she graced. But, as the century progressed, more and more ladies were involved in the arts, in painting and music, and in the pursuit of learning. One of the features of the last half of the century was the widening of society by the admission to its ranks of the wives and daughters of the trading and merchant classes. And as this class moved up on the social escalator, there were more and more boarding schools for girls in all parts of the country, like those run by the friends and disciples of John Wesley near Oxford, and, as we shall see, the school of the sisters More. The pages of the *Tatler* and the *Spectator*, the character sketches of Isaac Watts and William Law, the essays in Johnson's *Rambler* show, alas, how many young women were inured to lives of triviality and idleness, a combination of useless vanities which bore sad fruits when, as a way of female existence, it was passed on to the next generation.

But there were also better things at hand, and the age of the blue-stocking was come. If novel-reading became an infectious hobby for women, it was to bear fruit in a remarkable succession of female novelists. Samuel Johnson gained much pleasure from conversation with women who could stand up to him, intellectually, much better than divines or aristocrats. He doted on Elizabeth Carter, the linguist who could translate Epictetus, but also cook a pudding. And this explains his delight and serious respect when one evening a young woman, Sarah Kirby, settled a point in argument by producing *Paradise Lost* from her pocket.

(a) Sarah Trimmer

Sarah Kirby became famous, after her marriage, as Mrs Trimmer (1741–1810). She was the daughter of an Ipswich artist who became instructor to the Prince of Wales, and she became a member of a social group which included the most eminent artists of the day. She married at the age of twenty-one, and had six daughters and six sons, all of whom she educated herself save for the boys' classics, which she had to put out. She got up at 4 a.m. before her marriage, to read poetry, and for the rest of her life rose early to accomplish her vast chores.

Nor was her devotion confined to her home, for from an early age she set aside time for visiting the sick and the poor. There are times when the Church needs, more than almost anything, a sanctified Enid Blyton, somebody who can put clearly and simply in language which normal people (and especially children) can understand, the principles of Christian teaching and behaviour. This she began to do in 1780 in an epitome of the sacred history of the Bible. The work was followed by the *Fabulous Histories* which became famous for its inclusion of an all-time best-seller, the *History of the Robins*. She was delighted when the Sunday Schools appeared for she believed that new methods were needed, which the old charity schools had failed to provide. Her *Oeconomy of Charity* (1786) dealt with some of these problems, attracted great attention, and a large correspondence, and she was called to advise the Queen about starting schools at Windsor.

Like other educational pioneers, she found that other problems were involved, including the need to provide decent clothing for many of the children, and although the utmost use was made of voluntary assistants, teachers had to be paid, so that Mrs Trimmer lost a good deal of money in her ventures. If her moral stories kept well within the structure of an ordered society and inculcated reverence and obedience to authority and contentment with one's lot, there was a wide range of human interest and evidence of a love of nature which may be compared with Hannah More's love of flowers and gardening. She seems to have learned, from French educational works, the use of pictures as a means of teaching the very young. But perhaps most notable of all were her *Charity School Spelling Books — Short Stories of Good and Bad Boys, in Words of One Syllable Only*. So, in one of them, a man says to a poor boy: 'I know of a school where they will not mind your rags, where you may learn to read, and to put heads on pins, and help to make shoes and boots and mend your clothes.' She was a devoted Church of England woman and the Sacrament was of great meaning for her religion, the personal depth of which is evident from the Journal which she carefully kept.

To put the Church of England woman Sarah Trimmer alongside the Evangelical Hannah More need involve no invidious comparisons. Hannah More the spinster, was to display the same massive common sense as the experienced mother of twelve about what the young could understand, and both were to pursue successfully and influentially the two good works of establishing Sunday Schools and of the writing of Christian doctrines and morals in a manner 'understanded of' the children. Both made a great contribution to the amendment of the manners and morals of the nation. It is better not to begin with the simplistic complaints about their 'tunnel vision' or the limitations of minds set in conventional blinkers, but to remember the jargon of the old Jewish tailor, 'Never mind the width, feel the quality!'[6]

She knew people and she knew children, and with kindness, devotion, and great common sense she served her Church and generation better than she knew, far better than those who in a later age thought her somebody to be patronized or dismissed with contempt in favour of the sophisticated rigmarole of much that passes for religious education.

(b) Hannah More

Hannah More (1745–1833) was the fourth of five daughters of Jacob More, a schoolmaster who had come down slightly in the world. The

---

[6] *DNB*, s. v. 'Trimmer' Clarke, *Eighteenth Century Piety*, ch. x.

girls were all lively and intelligent and the eldest, at the age of twenty-one, began a school for girls at Bristol in which all the sisters became involved. With the friendly patronage of Dean Tucker and Dr Stonhouse it prospered and became a celebrated academy to which children came from distant parts and notable families. But Hannah was the prodigy, early taking to all manner of studies — mathematics, Latin, letters in four languages. 'It is not given to every woman to be a hero to her sisters', said Dr M. G. Jones. But this she accomplished, though in fact, they were a loving company. 'What, five women live happily together?' exclaimed Dr Johnson, who turned aside to see that great sight. Of the other sisters we know Martha (Patty), best for her merry wisdom in her *Mendip Annals,* while Sally was the vivacious one, great fun to be with, but rather exhausting. Hannah became well known, for she was a good talker at a time when conversation mattered very much, and she began to write verse and plays which attracted attention. At the age of twenty-three she was betrothed to a middle-aged squire, William Turner, who might have been invented by Jane Austen. After much hesitation, it was broken off, and though she had later offers of marriage, there was no further romance.

They adored Edmund Burke and took an enthusiastic, if not entirely rational, share in his Bristol campaign of 1774, Hannah writing letters and encouraging verses for him. In that year she came to London and was able to enter at once the charmed circle which included Sir Joshua Reynolds and Dr Johnson. But it was David Garrick and his Viennese wife who captured her affection in a life-long friendship. Garrick called her 'nine' because she was a combination of all the Muses, and was responsible for putting on her play *Percy,* which had a good run and was at least more successful than Johnson's *Irene,* though it had no survival value. Memorable was the first encounter with Johnson and their first visit: 'Abyssinia's Johnson! Dictionary Johnson! Rambler's, Idler's and Irene's Johnson! Can you picture to yourselves the palpitation of our hearts?' Hannah had a reputation for flattering, though a good deal of it was a simple capacity to admire (a pretty rare virtue), and if she buttered people up it was always the best butter. And though she once embarrassed Johnson and indeed annoyed him who had moments of intense self-consciousness, he was rather fulsome in his compliments to her, among them the famous affirmation that she 'was the most powerful versifatrix in the English language.'

Whereas the great majority of fashionable women spent their time in tea and sympathy, and in the current social obsession, whist, there was in existence a group of blue-stockings, into which Hannah now entered (Fanny Burney and Mrs Thrale were among her non-admirers). They

included the noble Elizabeth Carter, Mrs Montagu, 'the Maecenas of
Hill St.', and Mrs Boscawen, lettered, but not learned, a hostess who
provided an outer drawing room where cards were played and another
for good conversation. Hannah was quicker, wittier than most of them,
and it began to be the fashion to hush when she held forth. She
developed an enormous range of friendships, many of which she never
relinquished, and which is one of the tributes to her greatness. Long
after her evangelical conversion it was to be shown in the remarkable
fascination which she exercised over Horace Walpole, and the ability to
charm the often savage tongues, not only of Walpole, but of the young
Thomas Babington Macaulay.

It is not easy to trace the stages by which Hannah More tired of this
fashionable world and came to see so much of it as vanity. But there are
those who suspect that, in the end, permissive societies must die of
boredom. And it would be foolish indeed to suppose that she and
another young contemporary, William Wilberforce, in turning to
religion had any thought that they were entering a world with
narrowing, rather than opening horizons, or that they were doing
anything less than surrendering trivial joys for the pearl of great price.
Surely John Newton had something to do with it — a reading of his
Cardiphonia, and then a visit to hear him preach 'and afterwards sat an
hour with him and came home with two pockets full of sermons.' John
Newton was at his best as a counsellor and he turned her towards a
loving God and to the thought that her vocation was to serve him in the
world. David Garrick had humorously excused her from attendance at
Sunday music, and she now began to associate more and more with that
evangelical circle, the Middletons and Wilberforce, which was to be the
core of the later 'Clapham Sect'.

We ought not to think of these men and women as more coherently
organized at this stage than they really were, or that they had some
common platform of rigidly defined beliefs. Hannah, who was perhaps not as gifted a theologian as Mrs Trimmer, did not care to go
into the niceties of Calvinism. She had in any case a wide acquaintance
and friendship with many kinds of churchmen including George Horne,
Horsley, and Beilby Porteous. These were the men who saw how
valuable her gifts might be in their efforts to amend society. In 1788 she
wrote a tract, which was published anonymously, *The Importance of
the Manners of the Great to General Society,* which sold over seven editions
in a few weeks. 'Reform', she said, echoing the programme of
Wilberforce and Porteous, 'must begin with the great or it will never be
effectual.' The booklet appeared everywhere, 'in the houses of all the
Great'. It is not only that by this time she was well known, for the first

impact came when it was anonymous. But it does seem that both as a verse and as a prose-writer she spoke to the literate condition of the age, with a great gift for putting things clearly and without sophistication.

Now it became the 'done thing' for the ladies of the aristocracy to read Hannah More and to cultivate her friendship, from Queen Charlotte through a galaxy of duchesses and ladies. And if it is a period of much name-dropping on Hannah's part, it was mainly among her sisters and in her private journals that she dropped those names and listed her engagements with the Top People. When the *grand peur* of the French Revolution had produced at least a small horror among the ladies of England, she produced *An Estimate of the Religion of the Fashionable World* which was even more popular, not least because it was really hard-hitting and attacked not only the manners of the élite, but their responsibility that bad ways were being transmitted to the young in the shape of the fashionable 'Baby Balls'. One result of the work was a firm friendship with the rather tragic figure of the Duchess of Gloucester. The third work which she placed in the top drawer of society was *Strictures on the modern system of female education with a view to the principles and conduct of women of rank and fortune* (1799). It is long and repetitive, as Hannah invariably was, for, like the Bellman, she had a sound instinct that there were those who had to be informed that 'what I say three times is true!' It had more in common with the writings of the women's liberationist, Mary Wollstonecraft, than she could have known, but it was fundamentally a recall to religion, to praise moral excellence in a disordered and morally confused age. This, too, ran through five editions and was praised by princesses as well as bishops, even if there were some critical theological eyes cast upon some of her statements. Inevitably, and like all the evangelicals, she had begun to attract contemptuous and virulent abuse. The Bishop of London had once jokingly distinguished between Sarah Trimmer and Hannah More by saying that the first had a vocation towards the poor and the second towards the great. But now Hannah More was to find that her effectual calling lay among the under-privileged classes.

In 1784 Hannah More built a cottage at Cowslip Green in Somerset, where she might spend the summer months and devote herself to the gardening in which she and Patty delighted. Five years later, as the latter aptly recorded, 'In the month of August, 1789 Providence directed Mr Wilberforce and his sister to spend a few days at Cowslip Green.'

During the visit, the sisters pressed Wilberforce to make a trip to Cheddar Gorge. (Those who have read his undergraduate journal of his holiday in the Lake District in 1779 will understand why anything like grandeur in scenery appealed to his romantic mind.) They sent him off with a packed lunch. But when he returned he looked serious and shaken, and they noticed that the chicken and the wine were untouched in the carriage. He went straight to his room, but dismissed the reader whom he employed to relieve his weak eyesight. Patty thought he must be ill, but after supper he asked that the servant might be sent out, and then solemnly began: 'Miss Hannah More, something must be done for Cheddar.' Wilberforce had an even sharper eye for people in need than for grand scenery and he had been appalled by what he had seen of poverty and squalor, and had spent most of the day in asking questions. Round the table they talked into the night, and at the end Wilberforce asked the ladies to take on the enterprise while, inevitably in the background, Wilberforce promised that he and his friend Henry Thornton would provide funds, beginning with £40.

At the end of September the two ladies set out. The villages of the Mendip area are set in one of the loveliest and anciently Christian parts of England, the land of stories of Joseph of Arimathea and the Holy Grail, of the death of Arthur, and of the ministry to the poor of the monks of Glastonbury. As today the little bus meanders through the villages amid green pastures and neat cottages, it is hard to realize how much savagery and destitution there was to be found here in the eighteenth century, among the farms, and even more among the mines for coal and calomine and the notorious glass-houses.

The two trim, middle-aged ladies invaded this area, beginning at Cheddar. They could hardly have caused more sensation had they been visitants from another planet, saying 'Take me to your leader!' The leader turned out be a wealthy farmer, himself a coarse product of the environment, who told them that religion was the ruin of agriculture. They made their way from house to house, Patty said, like fortune-tellers, getting the next address at each place where they called. These were more hospitable, and it was as well they did not accept all the universally proffered draughts of whisky and water. There were no resident clergy, but they were able to rent a house at £7 a year. At last, on 25 October 1789, they opened a school for 140 children in a crowded church. The large congregation stared their fill at the legendary two they knew only as 'the ladies'. The parson said prayers and gave a short harangue on the divine right of kings! They were fortunate in securing a splendid teacher, Mrs Baber, who with her daughter ran the school. When she died, the whole village grieved.

Almost the whole parish attended. Her two hundred children followed the corpse . . . every creature had on some little badge of mourning . . . the procession was immensely long, solemn and affecting: no noisy, clamorous grief but a quiet silent sorrow: the footsteps scarcely heard, and the tears running down their poor faces to the ground, their little pocket handkerchiefs not being large enough to contain them.

After the sermon and the interment

the whole concluded with a suitable hymn, sung, or rather sobbed by the children . . . the undertaker, usually callous by profession wept like a child. Thus closed the last scene of a mistress of a charity school who had not a shilling of her own to give.[7]

In the next years the sisters extended the work through the neighbouring villages, bringing in more and more teachers and assistants. Though this lay intrusion into their parishes was startling, and often resented, there were other parsons who greatly helped, and some of them, like the beloved Mr Darrow, of remarkable devotion, while among the lay teachers were several former coal miners, including a crippled pit man who painfully but very effectually mastered his new vocation.

In Cheddar itself the congregation in the parish church grew in a few years from a dozen or so to over 500, sometimes overflowing the church. Notable was the concern of the sisters for the Sacrament. 'Another anxiety we laboured under was, whether our Sunday evening company attended the communion.' They accordingly visited the church on a wet September day, and were glad to find that the number of communicants were 'so many as to prolong the service for nearly two hours'.

The hours of teaching were long and arduous, and progress was inevitably intermittent and slow. But if Patty is anything to go by, the ladies were no dragons, and had a way of coming up with gingerbread and dishes of tea from time to time. The climax of the year was a great feast on the green hillside.[8] 'We left Cowslip Green in the morning with some friends, mounted in a waggon, dressed with greens, flowers, etc. Another followed with the servants, thirteen large pieces of beef, forty-five great plum puddings, six hundred cakes, several loaves, and a great cask of cider.' A grass area had been railed off into which one by one the schools processed while outside some thousands of onlookers stared as well they might. 'Each child had laid at his feet a large slice of beef, another of plum pudding and a cake.' The parson of each parish then said grace and the children 'were permitted to eat as much as their stomachs would hold and talk as fast as their tongues would go.' No doubt to impress the onlookers, there followed a short quiz at which one girl repeated twenty-four verses of the Bible and another

---

[7] M. More, *Mendip Annals*, ed. A. Roberts (1859), pp. 121–2.
[8] *Mendip Annals*, p. 36.

fifteen. 'As the design of the day was to prove to them the possibility of being merry and wise we all joined in singing God save the King!' Thus were 517 children made happy and 'really feasted for the sum of £15'.

Attention had perforce to be given to the problems of clothing the children, and some of the assistant teachers. There were the famous wedding presents, when each girl who had been married during the year ('with a fair character!') was presented with 'five shillings, a Bible and a pair of white worsted stockings'. They also began a benefit society for the older women to which they contributed three-halfpence a week in return for which they got sick benefit and money for lying in (some of them said they would prefer to keep the money for a really good funeral!).

There were difficulties and tensions. Some of the villages held evening meetings for adults at which sermons and Bible were read, and since at this time the schools were concerned not only with Biblical instruction, but with religion, and people were in fact becoming converted, there were the inevitable complaints about enthusiasm and the suspicion of being tainted with Methodism. Hannah More had to use what material was available, and some of the teachers were awkward characters. These tensions and the suspicion and antagonism towards her evangelical self exploded in the nasty Blagdon controversy between the parson and the lay teacher. It swelled into a pamphlet war which won nation-wide publicity. It was a complex business, in which Hannah More was not at her best. Like the athlete in the hymn she

> Bare all she could endure
> And bare not always well

But distressing as it was, and though it led to a serious breakdown in health, she was vindicated by a new bishop, and her esteem in the nation was unharmed as an episcopal chorus assured her. There were day schools and Sunday Schools according to the needs of the villages, and the 'ladies' ventured into the toughest areas, including the apocalyptic setting of the glass-houses, with their roaring furnaces and their well-paid, but riotously profligate, communities. What they had accomplished was an experiment in Christian education, evangelism, and community of signal worth. Wilberforce had admired and studied what the Jesuits had achieved in Paraguay. On its own small scale the achievement of the 'ladies' was also memorable.

Much as the whole enterprise owed to Hannah More and her friends and influence, one suspects that a good deal of the oversight fell on Patty, who was a skilled teacher whose 'pep talk' annual reports on each village are always well worth reading. Moreover the sisters withdrew during the winter months, when snow and floods made such journeyings dangerous to limb and health and when much had to be left to those working on the spot.

Hannah herself was drawn more and more into new and urgent writing activities. There was an obvious ferment of social distress in the land and a growing radical agitation, often anticlerically and certainly anti-ecclesiastically inclined. One consequence of the French Revolution had been the battle between Edmund Burke and Tom Paine, whose *Rights of Man* and *Age of Reason* flooded the land in cheap and popular form and horrified the Christians. 'Our dear Bishop of London', wrote Hannah in January 1793, 'came to me with a dismal countenance and told me I should repent it on my death bed if I who knew so much of the habits and sentiments of the lower orders of people did not write some little thing tending to open their eyes'. The result was her astonishing tract for the time, *Village Politics,* which Dr M. G. Jones aptly called 'Burke for Beginners'. It is a dialogue between Jack Anvil the village blacksmith and Tom Hood the village mason, who has been influenced by the writings of Tom Paine. The chief appeal is to patriotism and the simple argument ends with Jack saying, 'While Old England is safe I'll glory in her and pray for her: and when she is in danger I'll fight for her and die for her.' But she refused the Bishop's invitation to write a direct reply to Paine himself. She had, however, for a long time been exercised by the problem of what to do with her new-made literate communities, and how to counteract the influence of the vast numbers of broadsheets and ballads, the often unsavoury popular literature hawked by the chapmen. She knew about Sarah Trimmer's writings, which were however, relatively expensive. The result was her marvellously success-ful series of cheap *Repository Tracts,* stories, ballads, and Sunday readings of which 114 were published in the years 1795–8. She got her friends to organize them, backed with a subscription list, and some of her eminent evangelical friends, clerical and lay, contributed to them. They were illustrated in the manner of the popular ballads and sold at a halfpenny or a penny a piece. By March 1796 2,000,000 copies had been sold. Not all, or even most, got into the hands of the poor, and some were directly aimed at the middle class. But they deal with a great range of contemporary life, some aspects of which Hannah More described with Breughel-like perception. They are, of course, on the side of the Establishment and there is not a word of criticism of Church and State, though there are stern things said about the responsibilities of the well-to-do. If Hannah More described the dignity of the poor, as in the most famous of all the tracts the *Shepherd of Salisbury Plain,* it was because such devout and godly common men really did admirably exist. She was violently attacked by radicals like William Cobbett who detested this 'Bishop in Petticoats'.

After the Blagdon uproar, things quietened and the schools continued among the Mendip villages. In 1801 the sisters left Bath to join Hannah in a house at Barley Wood and here she spent the last twenty-five years of her life. Here, too, they went about doing good, and brought off yet another evangelical coup. In an appalling winter in 1817 some 300 miners at Shipham were thrown out of work, the brass and calomine unwanted. The ladies organized food and clothing for more than 1,200 men and women, and with other friends bought up the ore and 'stored it until better times'.

She was now an honoured figure in the nation, and a number of the eminent wrote to, or visited, her: bishops and evangelical clergy, the Clapham laymen, the Quaker Elizabeth Fry, Southey, Wordsworth, and Coleridge. In 1809 she felt the need for new adventure and penned a novel, *Coelebs*. It puzzled and dismayed her evangelical friends, whose opinions were hardening against the lawfulness of novel-reading as a Christian diversion. (But then she was really an eighteenth-century person, and never a 'typical' evangelical or indeed a 'typical' anything.) It was slammed by those reviews which were now a sadistic power in the land, and she decided the time had come to break her staff and drown her book. She had to reduce visiting days to two a week and from 1818 to 1825 was generally confined to bed. There followed a bizarre happening worthy of a Gothic novel, for she was imposed upon by 'eight minions' of servants who tyrannized her and stole her goods until at last a posse of stalwart friends rescued her and she moved to Clifton Wood.

As an old lady in her late eighties she lived with memories which were often confused such as with the ancient is often the case, and more remote memories the sharper. But what rich memories they were: her home, her father, and her sisters; Bristol, the school, and Edmund Burke's election, with the letters and the garlands; Sir Joshua and Dr Johnson and the beloved Garricks; the noble ladies, the blue-stockings, and the duchesses, princesses, and the Queen, and visits to a dozen stately homes; Dr Tucker, Dr Stonehouse, and Bishop Porteous. Above all, there were her evangelical friends — John Newton and William Cowper, the Thorntons, the Macaulays, the incomparable 'Wilber', comrade in great battles on behalf of the slaves and the poor, those vile bodies for whom Christ did not disdain to die. But in the background was the great company — thousands and thousands of young faces and figures winding their way in and out of her memory as long ago she watched them make their way around the green hillsides, in companies, on the green grass, sitting at the feet of Jesus.

'A Bishop in Petticoats'? Did she anticipate the future? Rather should we see her as one of a great continuing ministry of women, that goodly fellowship of the prophetesses, which surely joins her with Hildegard of Bingen (versifatrix, teacher, friend of the eminent) and with Monnica and Macrina in the early centuries, for it is uncertain whether she was ever, in the evangelical sense, subject to a conversion experience, but she certainly renounced her culture and her world. Perhaps she had not the spiritual depth of Sarah Trimmer, if their journals are anything to go by. But she was an evangelical genius, her sharp mind always softened by kindness and humour, always ready to shed her introspections for vigorous encounters with the minds of her fellows. If the gesture had its limitations she knew better than anybody else how to break up and distribute the crumbs which fell from the rich man's table.[9]

iii. The Religion of Samuel Johnson

What do they know of Johnson, who only Boswell know? Most of us would answer 'Enough: enough to find endless pleasure in a matchless portrait of one of the greatest of men'. Yet Johnson and Boswell were together only in the last twenty years of Johnson's more than threescore years and ten. 'They spent, as nearly as can be computed, two hundred and seventy days or parts of days in one another's company. Of these a hundred were spent in one continuous stretch when they travelled to Scotland.'[10]

For most of us it is Boswell's Johnson we know; he sets the scenes: the dinners, the journeys, the conversations, the debates, the gossip, the pronouncements, the thronged assemblies, the inns and taverns, above all, the Club. And since this present chapter is about the laity, we may think of that club as a gathering of Christian laymen (give or take a bishop or two), though at differing removes from one another in their devotion.

David Garrick took his religion seriously enough to make nonsense of William Law's (and George Whitefield's) view that no actor could be a Christian. At the request of a pale young curate he wrote notes on how to read the liturgy — a curious document. Garrick might have got away

---

[9] M. G. Jones, *Hannah More*, Cambridge, 1952; A. M. B. Meakin, *Hannah More* 1911; A. Buckland, *Life of Hannah More*, n.d.; A. Roberts (ed.), *Mendip Annals;* F. K. Brown, *The Fathers of the Victorians,* Cambridge 1961.

[10] J. Wain, *Samuel Johnson,* (1980), p. 233.

with his recommended practice of raising the eyes upwards whenever heaven was mentioned, but hardly any imitator. And Garrick, who loved to imitate Johnson's own 'Who's for Poonsh?', was perhaps betrayed by his own Staffordshire accent into misleading the young man into saying 'Dead and Boorried' in the Creed, in perpetuity! Oliver Goldsmith left us classic Christian perceptions in his *Deserted Village* and *Vicar of Wakefield*. Edmund Burke, though sometimes flushed with drink, was one of the profoundest Christian thinkers of his age, however uncongenial to our time may seem his view of a Christian nation as one which has roots and grows like a great tree and is not apt for restructuring by carpentry or engineering. Sir Joshua Reynolds, it seems, kept well clear of public worship, and Johnson's dying bequest was an attempt to jog him into reading his Bible, and to refrain from sketching on Sunday. We see them in Doyle's painting which is a romantic afterthought — laughing, talking, and gesticulating. But are all those faces, we wonder, other than masks in a masquerade? What if one of those masks should slip and we looked through its laughter, to behold a Knight of Sorrowful Countenance?

For in fact, as we now know Johnson through a critical apparatus of scholarly analysis and much new evidence, we are more aware than even his friends could be, that there were precipices, heights, and depths, within his soul, that he knew better than most what in a poignant phrase he called 'the pain of being a man'. No doubt we await a thorough and competent psychological appraisal of Johnson, but up to the present, the witness of different schools of interpretation does not seem to agree. And if here are riddles beyond the capacity of wayfaring men to resolve, there may be comments from the history of the Christian religion which have some relevance.

Indeed a useful starting-point might be the classic study by Archbishop Söderblom, *Humour and Melancholy in Martin Luther*. For in both Johnson and Luther the humour and the melancholy are deep and inseparable. But the humour underlies the whole, and in Johnson it had an immense range from the subtlest of ironies to puns and witticisms and a belly laugh like that of a rhinoceros. But there was also a deep melancholy. And in both men there was something more than *Angst*. Luther coined his own word, *Anfechtung*, with its suggestion of conflict, for in it the fight of faith, the issue of salvation were also involved. It is a conflict which is never done, and may recur at any moment, right up to the last. As Dr Pierce says of Johnson, 'Like the fog that seems to lie offshore, and threatens to return on even the sunniest of days, these dark moods could recur at any time.'[11]

[11] C. E. Pierce, *The Religious Life of Samuel Johnson* (1982), p. 58.

What Boswell said of Johnson was equally true of Luther:

His mind resembled the vast amphitheatre, the Colisaeum at Rome. In the centre stood his judgment, which, like a mighty gladiator, combated those apprehensions that, like wild beasts of the *Arena,* were all around in cells, ready to be let out upon him. After a conflict, he drove them back into their dens: but not killing them, they were still assailing him.[12]

Both men could be physically knocked out by their onset, Luther for hours and days, Johnson for weeks and over long months. Neither Luther's colleagues nor Johnson's friends could ever understand. In the words of Gerard Manley Hopkins,

> O the mind, mind has mountains: cliffs of fall
> Frightful, sheer, no man fathom'd.
> Hold them cheap
> May who ne'er hung there.

Nobody could deny that in all these experiences there was a morbid and pathological element which brought him more than once to the verge of madness. And this dread of insanity was an additional horror, not least because of the vile humiliations to which lunatics were subjected, but because also he prized above all things the gift of reason.

Like Luther, Johnson knew the torment of scruples, the mind overset by trivialities whose disproportion part of the mind could recognize, but which irrationally took control. Yet both men had a great fund of common sense and a hearty disdain of singularities and niggling Puritanism. 'O let us not be found when our Master calls, ripping the lace off our waistcoats, but the spirit of contention from our souls and tongues.'

Doubt is always an element in *Anfechtung,* but for Johnson the sense of guilt was paramount, guilt rooted in almost classically tragic fashion, in his nearest personal relationships. There was guilt about his wife, his 'Tettie' which descended on him as a dark mist when her death caught him off balance, unprepared, emotionally shattered, and which never completely lifted. To the end of his days this was the haunting remorse, for the wasted days and years, the neglect of his long absences, his lack of patience, and for a lost love, and indeed we must believe a happiness the one had given to the other, but which had been somehow choked.

He was guilty about his mother, and found her death a horrific experience: and about his father, in a relationship which had always been going wrong. He was tormented by Michael Johnson's innocent pride in showing off the excellences of his gifted son, and he loathed the

---

[12] *Boswell's Life of Johnson,* ed. G. B. Hill, revd. L. P. Powell (Oxford 1971), II. 106.

drudgery of a small-town bookshop. How deeply he felt was shown when, thirty years on, he went alone to Uttoxeter and stood in the market in the cold rain all one morning because as a youth he had refused his father's command to go there and tend the family bookstall. And he may have felt guiltiest of all about his brother Nathanael, on whose tragedy he was reticent. There were other things too. John Wain in his sensitive study seems to balance them best, but he draws attention to Johnson's sexual frustrations, to the besetting sins of his imagination and fantasies which may have had a masochistic element within them.[13] All this took place within a sombre moralistic creed. When he was two his mother told him of hell, 'a sad place'. Like many others he was bred into the way of duty by *The Whole Duty of Man*. Not that this youth was deeply coloured by religion. He walked in the fields when the church was under repair, and perhaps lost for ever any taste for public worship. At Oxford he was a rather flippant talker against religion, until his devastating encounter with William Law's *Serious Call*. Law's writings certainly influenced him deeply. His own view of the vanity of human wishes — almost turning *Ecclesiastes* into a Christian book — is a reflection of Law's solemn preamble to his *Christian Perfection*. He shared with Law an interest in the shrewd observation of human character and some of his own sketches in the *Rambler* are nearer to those of Law than to those in the *Spectator*! Above all, he took seriously the call to seek perfection, even as living in the world. Like John Byrom, he was to find this not as easy for one who had no King's Cliff to retire to, but lived, in John Wain's apt phrase, a Bohemian existence.

It may be that Law's perfectionism heightened the spiritual tensions which led to a breakdown at the end of his Oxford days. Like the young Luther, he came rather to fear than love God, a just God who took account not only of outward behaviour and demanded integrity in the heart and purity of motive. He may have found some relief in a sermon of Samuel Clarke who would not have men wind themselves too high, yet who accommodated perfection to the spiritually possible. But in his early and middle years Johnson did not take his religion so seriously. The conversation is surely significant which he had with his friend, John Hoole the Indian civil servant, at the very end of his life (20 November 1784). 'He conjured me to read and meditate upon the Bible, and not to throw it aside for a play or a novel. He said he had himself lived in great

---

[13] On the business of the 'Padlock' and the question whether Johnson feared or felt he needed some constraint, and the relation of this to Hester Thrale see Wain, *Samuel Johnson*, ch. 23. 'The Padlock'; K. C. Balderston, 'Johnson's Vile Melancholy', in *The Age of Johnson*, ed. F. W. Hilles, Yale 1964; W. J. Bate, *Samuel Johnson* (1978), pp. 384–5, 387–8, 439–41.

negligence of religion and worship for forty years.'[14] This would seem to suggest a turning-point in his life which may have coincided with the death of his wife. And one wonders if this may not be the meaning of the reference in his last prayer when he asks forgiveness for his 'late conversion'?

Boswell's statement that Johnson was a 'zealous Christian of high Church of England and monarchical principles'[15] perhaps deserves scrutiny. We will not ask what constituted a high-church Anglican to the Laird of Auchinleck! But it is clear that to describe Johnson as a 'high' churchman needs some qualification. He was a stout Church of England man. He believed in episcopacy and in the apostolic succession. He was opposed to the Dissenters and hated historic Puritanism. Though more sympathetic than some, he opposed the Roman Catholic Church. But he did not believe the traditional high-church doctrines about the divine right of kings. His spirituality is different from that of Donne, Herbert, or Andrewes, and anybody who compares his prayers with those of Thomas Ken will be struck by the differences, rather than the resemblances, in Ken's affirmation of joyous love of God: 'Thou, Lord art my hope, my trust, my life, my joy, my glory, my God, my all, my love.'[16]

Despite his wide reading in the great Church of England divines of the seventeenth century, his own theology was much nearer to that of the Latitudinarian age, to its rationalism, to its Newtonian view of God as the self-existent Governor, to its moralism, and a stress on a just God who exactly rewards virtue and punishes vice, and a view of salvation in which the amendment, repentance, and indeed reformation, of the sinner is a requisite of the receipt of grace; and which is underwritten by the sacrifice of Christ, which for some years Johnson thought of (in Augustinian words) rather as *exemplum* than as *sacramentum*.

This affinity with Latitudinarian rather than high-church theology is shown by his indebtedness to the sermons of Samuel Clarke. This is the more remarkable because Johnson had strong views about Trinitarian heresy, believed that Clarke was heretical at this point, and for this reason refused to quote him in his *Dictionary*. From the number of references to Clarke's sermons in his Diaries one must conclude that Johnson set much store by him and recommended his sermons to others.[17] We know that he took careful notes of Clarke's four sermons

[14] Hill, *Johnsonian Miscellanies*, ii. 146.
[15] Boswell's *Life*, ed. Hill, iv. 426–7.
[16] Ken, 'The Practice of Divine Love', *Prose works*, ed. Benham, p. 127.
[17] *Yale Edition of the Works of Samuel Johnson*, vol. 1, *Diaries, Prayers, Annals*, ed. E. L. McAdam Jr. with D. and M. Hyde (Oxford 1958), pp. 105, 122, 129, 132, 155.

on *The Nature, End and Design of the Holy Communion.*[18] It is clear that they are echoed in Johnson's sermons since for him also the Sacrament is primarily a commemoration.

Clarke had asserted that the Sacrament of Baptism is not to be taken as a parallel with Communion, which is not a means of renewing the application of divine forgiveness. But when Johnson asserts that Holy Communion is indeed 'a kind of repetition of baptism'[19] the difference from Clarke is only apparent since for Johnson baptism itself is a covenantal vow and he returns explicitly to the definition (Tertullian? Zwingli?) of *sacramentum* as a soldier's oath. Johnson's expositions of the Eucharist have not the many sidedness of the high-church writers on the Eucharist, Bull, John Johnson, Daniel Brevint, Charles Wesley.

More important for him was the easement of mind which Clarke's doctrine of the sacrifice of Christ brought him, which enabled him to shift the weight from himself and his own endeavours to the mercy of God. In his last illness, Dr Brocklesby tells us,

all his fears were calmed and absorbed by the prevalence of his faith and his trust in the merits and propitiation of Christ.   . . . He pressed me to study Dr. Clarke and to read his sermons. I asked him why he pressed Dr. Clarke, an Arian. 'Because' (said he) 'he is fullest on the propitiatory sacrifice'.[20]

This was not precisely accurate. For Clarke himself sharply attacked the notion of 'propitiation' as it was interpreted in various Protestant orthodoxies, in which at the centre of atonement is the Son of God who by his death assuaged the wrath of God. Clarke himself stressed that it was Almighty God who was in Christ reconciling the world to himself. None the less, Clarke was faithful to the 'theology of the Cross' of Cranmer's liturgy, with its stress on the once-for-all-ness and the sufficiency of the death of Christ. Despite his heterodox view of the divine nature, there is a thoroughly evangelical insistence on what Christ has done for men, in his condescension and in his sufferings.

Johnson's sermons are important material for any appraisal of his theology, but perhaps some of his editors have taken them much more solemnly than Johnson ever did himself. They have spoken of them as though he brooded often and long, playing the sedulous ape to Hooker, Taylor, Baxter, South.

Johnson's Augustan and Restoration economies of thought and expression are part of a far richer pattern, which is also composed of the baroque style of

[18] *The Works of Samuel Clarke D. D.* vol. i, *Sermons* 56–9, pp. 344–69; M. J. Quinlan, *Samuel Johnson: A Layman's Religion* (Madison 1964), ch. 2.

[19] Johnson, *Works* (Yale edn.), vol. xiv, *Sermons*, p. 100.

[20] Boswell's *Life of Johnson*, ed. Hill, iv. 416.

Hooker, the solemn and poetic meditativeness of Jeremy Taylor, and the evangelical urgency of Baxter.[21]

In fact Johnson tossed off those sermons as swiftly as he did his articles for the *Rambler*. 'I myself have composed about forty sermons. I have begun a sermon after dinner and sent it off by post that night'.[22] He sold them (mostly to his friend John Taylor) for 2 guineas a time, and when they were done and he had handed over the copy of his own manuscript which he then tore up, he forgot all about them. The style of Samuel Johnson, whatever we may think of it, is very far from being a mixture in which Hooker, Taylor, and Baxter can be discerned. He has his own solemnities, his own rhythms and cadences.

Not that the sermons are to be despised. Some of them are sonorous analyses of motive, of the springs of human action to which the only parallel can be Joseph Butler's famous sermons in the Rolls Chapel. Now and again there are some astounding aphorisms — like this one, which any young historian might hang in his study: 'We cannot make truth: it is only our business to find it.'

In one sermon (Number 5 on Neh. 33) there is an amazing picture of what human society might be like if men really obeyed the Golden Rule, of what a Christian society really might become. And he firmly rejects the view that this is 'a train of airy phantoms: a visionary scene . . . but which the first survey of the world will shew him to be nothing more than a pleasing delusion.'

The learned commentators on Johnson's sermons do not seem to have sufficiently considered their defectiveness in one important dimension. They are sermons to be read, and read out, but they are not preaching. And though there is a genuine element of Christian instruction, of *didachē*, in preaching, as truly as there is proclamation, *kērugma*, Johnson's sermons are too often moral essays which might have come from the *Rambler*. He preferred reading sermons as he preferred reading plays to seeing them performed. He knew nothing of the art by which a Chrysostom, an Augustine, a Gregory the Great — a Tillotson, Doddridge, or Watts — tailored their words to a living congregation. If he agreed that, as Baxter had said, preachers should sometimes shoot over the heads of their audience, an ordinary Christian listening to Johnson's homilies, would, one feels, be bewildered by the rumble of artillery so far above his head, and if he could follow the compressed argument of the long sentences would be confounded by words like 'succedaneous', 'abruption', 'feculence', words not understood by those unfamiliar with the more exotic corners of Johnson's great *Dictionary*.

[21] Johnson, *Works*, vol. xiv, *Sermons*, p. 11.
[22] Boswell's *Life of Johnson*, ed. Hill, vol. iii, App. F, p. 507.

From his vast reading, his classical learning, his study of the Fathers, of the Anglican divines, and his omnivorous reading of sermons, it is impossible to pick out 'influences'. But at a less pretentious level one may mention his three favourite books, the *Pilgrim's Progress, Robinson Crusoe,* and *Don Quixote.* With *Pilgrim's Progress,* with the thought of life as a long journey, menaced again and again with disaster, with a thousand perceptions about human nature, with the great characters of whom there is a little bit of each in everyman, and with its Christianity, Johnson had obvious affinity. We, who tend to read *Robinson Crusoe* skipping its religion, as Johnson's age did not, may find that Crusoe, not least in his casting accounts before God, on one side the Bad News and on the other the Good, had much to say to Johnson, whose life was always within sound of breakers and the possibility of shipwreck. And in Crusoe he might have found the great anti-Donne principle, that in the end every man is an island entire of itself, every man is cut off from the main. And *Don Quixote,* more than a little daft, whose inner world was his reality — Don Quixote who like himself, though Boswell would have hated the comparison, would live in history inseparable from his Sancho Panza.

With his diaries and prayers we come near to the heart of his religion. There were three or four days which he treated with special solemnity, for which he wrote special prayers and for which he had his own programme. One was his birthday. Another was the anniversary of his wife's death, and since this was near the Easter season, might merge in his greatest commemoration which was Easter Day.

Unless we are to get Johnson's existence out of all proportion, we have to remember that in the Diaries we are overhearing a man in his confessional. The Diaries tell us things about him that perhaps men have no right to know about their fellows, except perhaps a priest. They are a sad, sometimes almost comic, record of successive failure, of broken resolves, of besetting sins at the last almost as potent as at the first. What he confesses is also surprising. There is no mention of sinful deeds. He does not ask to be freed from pride (which he had, though there was little vanity in him), gossip, uncharitable detraction. His chief lament is that he cannot get up in the morning, and has neglected the study of the Bible. Venial enough, but crucial for Johnson, for he knew that it was in the idle hours that the deadliest of his spiritual enemies, the evil imaginations, entered in. Johnson's overall existence is better seen, after all, in Boswell's *Life* than in the diaries.

His private prayers and meditations were dovetailed into his public worship. And here, too, there are unanswered questions. In his deep needs, why did he not make more constant use of the 'means of grace', of opportunities to partake of the Sacrament? Instead of once a year, which was his norm, it would have been possible for him, living in the heart of the City church-land, to have communicated once a month, or even once a week at a time when parish boundaries were flexible. He could, had he wished, have attended daily prayers, twice a day if need be, in the London churches. But he found it easy to stay away. Church attendance in that day was perhaps a less decorous and tidy business than in ours, and he may not have been so unusual in continually turning up late (he had plenty of bad excuses — he hadn't heard the bells, Boswell set him talking), often after the Psalms, the Lessons, even the Creed. This meant that he invariably missed the Confession and the Absolution (is that another un-high-church trait?)

He settled down in the great church of St Clement Danes, and for a time had a pew in the gallery. An examination of his Easter celebrations over a number of years suggests the following pattern. In the early hours of the morning of Easter Day (and probably of Good Friday too) he rose and wrote out a special prayer which he took an hour or so correcting and on which he meditated, and he sometimes added to it a few suitable collects. Then, fasting, or with only a bun and cup of tea (without milk), he took his prayers to church — and Johnson clutching his Prayer Book and his scraps of paper must have been a familiar, and sometimes disconcerting, sight as he moved around and as he wheezed and muttered. In his pew he prayed his prayer and conditionally prayed for his wife and other departed friends who might be upon his mind. Later in the liturgy he left that pew and moved nearer the altar and again prayed and meditated. He then communicated (once he comments he was the last, and on another occasion that the communicants were mostly women) and returned to his pew, where he prayed again. Visitors permitting, he prayed his prayer again on his return home. Though he was a bad attender at church on other Sundays and fitfully made amends by going to prayers during the week, he seems to have devoted Sunday to studying the Bible, in the sacred languages, and to meditation. There was one occasion when he had decided to read Thessalonians in the Greek, but Boswell turned up, and since to meditate with Boswell present was like trying to read in the presence of a bluebottle, an exasperated Johnson stuffed Pascal's *Pensées* into his hand and told him to get on with them.

When we have spoken of Johnson's reading and the effect of it upon him, we should recognize that he got much more from the liturgy than from reading sermons, and it was its mixture of piety and wisdom which sustained him. The preachers whom he often could not, and sometimes would not, hear were a sad anti-climax. We do not know if he

was there when John Wesley preached in 1783 in St Clement's to an
overflowing congregation, or on a much duller occasion when the
preacher droned away, appearing to be reading from a book 'with very
wide margins'. At the day's end he said his prayers and called in his
servant Francis Barber to join in the devotions.

We have yet to mention two great parts of his practice of the Christian
religion, his friendships and his charity. He kept his friendships in repair
and some of them, like John Taylor, went back to his early youth. And
how diverse they were — Taylor, Bennett Langton, Boswell, the
Thrales, Edmund Burke, and Sir Joshua Reynolds — at one moment
surrounded by his companions, at home in polished society, at another
in a setting which would do for *The Beggars' Opera*. And he did not
forget them, but remembered them and mourned them when they
departed. Years after the death of Nugent, who, as a Roman Catholic,
ate an omelette at the club, the sight of an omelette on a table moved
him to a rush of tears. The description of him as a Bohemian is a good
one, but he was a Johnsonian Bohemian, who could plan the great Essex
Street orgy when laughter and conversation went on into the small
hours, with Johnson drinking only lemonade.

But Johnson, the moralist, had no inhibitions for Johnson, the friend.
We may say, in Kierkegaardian phrase, that in his personal relationships there was 'a teleological suspension of ethics'. The man who wrote
the sermons was the one who entirely delighted in the friendships of
Richard Savage and James Boswell. He described Savage in a marvellous
literary portrait of complete candour, but one feels that Savage's vices
and virtues were irrelevant to the reasons why Johnson loved him.
Similarly with James Boswell, whom perhaps no decent father would
have relished as a son's boon companion and from whom he might well
lock away his daughters. But the friendships with this 'young dog',
with all his faults and follies, was indeed Johnson's greatest medicine
and perhaps drew out of the much younger man more goodness than he
knew. That George Psalmanazar had been a cheat and the greatest 'con
man' of all time, whose lying enormities about Formosa sound like a
combination of every university spoof that ever was — mattered not at
all to Johnson who doted on him, and though he took his conversion
seriously and thought him a saint, one feels it would not have made
much difference to Johnson's pleasure in his company had he never
mended his ways. He simply accepted men as human beings, and
perhaps came nearer an attribute of deity not listed by Samuel Clarke
but of which a modern theologian has spoken: God who 'loves this
human life of ours, not only as a moralist approving where it is good or
disapproving where it is bad, but as a poet or an artist loves it, because

he cannot help loving a thing so strange, piteous and enthralling as the story of every human soul must be' (W. R. Maltby). Johnson's Diaries might seem full of his unanswered prayers, but there was one that was abundantly vouchsafed him. He prayed for a compassionate heart. He made a profound and detailed analysis of the rationale of Christian charity, both in his sermons and in his essays, but his compassionate deeds were no fulfilment of a programme, still less were they good works done with the ulterior motive of meriting reward or attaining salvation.

It is commonly saluted as a mark of his genius that Bunyan, at the end of the *Pilgrim's Progress,* puts together, under the guardianship of the great champions, Greatheart, Standfast, Valiant for Truth, a band of old crocks, Mr. Fearing, Mr. Despondency and his daughter Mistress Much-Afraid, Mr. Ready-to-Halt. But in real life Johnson did almost exactly this, in the collection of battered human beings who composed his home and his household. There was blind Ann Williams, a Welsh lady of some culture and a sharp tongue, and Elizabeth Desmoulins, with whom she often quarrelled. There was the misfit Poll, whom Johnson himself described as 'a stupid slut — I could make nothing of her; she was wiggle waggle.' There was his daily breakfast companion Robert Levet, an ex-waiter turned into a quack medico, of some competence, but no affluence. It seems that at the end of his life Johnson thought of adding to the family John Wesley's sister of the 'lean and lanky' Martha Hall, then aged seventy-seven. The members of his household continually scrapped and quarrelled, sometimes egged on by a delighted Johnson 'At her again, Poll! Never flinch, Poll!' And when he returned home it was in the sure knowledge that they would be lined up with their mutual complaints. There would be nothing quite like it until the Mad Hatter's Tea Party. But when he left them for the peace and comfort of his other, equally prized companions, the Thrales in Streatham, he always returned at the weekend to make sure that his ungainly tribe had decent meals. Francis Barber, his negro servant, was a real *Sorgenkind,* to whom in life and death he did abundant good. But when the cat, Hodge, became old and could only eat oysters, or so Johnson thought, it was Johnson who went out to buy them, lest the black man might think such an errand a slight on his dignity.

Unlike Byrom and John Wesley, he did not stand over and against the poor, but identified with them. But it was not poverty, but misery, which most deeply moved him, the human condition, the pain of being a man. For into misery he had been born. And this was no doctrinaire notion about original sin and total depravity, or the 'pessimism of nature' of Hobbes, Swift, or Mandeville. It was being born a sickly infant, only with difficulty saved alive; it was the misery of a doleful countenance and a misshapen body, of a shambling gait and uncontrollable limbs, the misery of poverty and hunger and debt. It bred the grim realism with which he watched his fellow human beings in the streets of London, late at night and in the small hours, hungry and wretched, sleeping on the balks of the shop fronts or huddled together for verminous warmth in the glass-houses, the tottering wrecks of humanity who stumbled past even the poor men's cookshops of 'Porridge Island' off Charing Cross, and the premonitions of the families who would die next winter because of the drought, at which the fine ladies grumbled as the dust spoiled their complexions and ruined their dress.

This took him beyond the charities of a John Byrom or a John Wesley. Johnson it was who loved to leave pennies in the stiff fingers of little sleeping infants, Johnson who, finding a London drab diseased and dying in the Fleet Street gutter, wrapped her in his great coat, put her on his back, carried her home and tended her, and saw that she was nursed back to health. Then, it is said, he put her in charge of a milliner's shop. But there were hundreds of others, most of them rather undeserving than deserving poor, and for some of them he organized whip-rounds and solicited subscriptions from more affluent friends, when he got to the end of his own resources, which he lavishly distributed so that despite his royal pension he generally had but little left. He saw the men and women of the London streets with a Breughel-like perception, and cared for them with a Franciscan heart. He never thought of such deeds as thrown into that heavenly balance, which so affrighted him. He had his own capacity for gratitude and did not mind that those of his own household had little sense of benefits received and grumbled at what they took for granted.

Through his character there ran a deep simplicity which is the hallmark of greatness and indeed of sanctity. His friends did not simply admire him, but were deeply fond of him. Hidden in the hearts of most men, and sometimes the better part of them, is a boy of about twelve, and this was surely true of Johnson with his shouts of laughter, his habit of disconcerting more staid companions by rolling down a grassy hill, climbing a wall or making them run races with him, patting his lamp-posts, treading his paving stones, hoarding his orange peel.

There does not seem to be any convincing evidence that at the end of his life he underwent anything like an evangelical conversion. Hannah More may sound as though she thought he had, but in fact she is describing her friend in her own jargon. Nor should one read much into the fact that he had friendly visits from the Moravian, La Trobe. Still less can one turn his great deliverance from illness in 1783 into a decisive spiritual experience. The critical illness was strikingly similar to that which befell Luther at Schmalkald in 1537. Both men suffered from acute infections, which brought them great pain, and they were so desperately ill that they expected to die. Both found sudden and unlooked for relief in what seemed to each a miraculous deliverance. Both gave solemn and formal thanks to the divine mercy. But, just as in Luther's case this was not regarded as some kind of conversion experience, so there is no reason at all to suppose this in the case of Johnson.

The last weeks of Johnson's life were not free from anguish of mind. There came a moment when Johnson asked Dr Brocklesby:

> Canst thou not minister to a mind diseased?
> Pluck from the memory a rooted sorrow?
> Raze out the written troubles of the brain;
> And, with some sweet oblivious antidote,
> Cleanse the stuff'd bosom of that perilous stuff,
> Which weighs upon the heart?

And he was grimly pleased when his friend continued the quotation

> . . . therein the patient
> Must minister to himself.[23]

No doubt those two laymen, William Shakespeare and Samuel Johnson, knew more about the human condition than the parsons did. But one wonders whether the clergy might not have done more for Johnson? The evidence fails, and it is possible that he privately found consolation and help, though it does not seem likely. The skills of his great friend, the Revd John Taylor, seem chiefly to have concerned what the hymn calls 'the humbler creation'. The Revd George Strahan, Vicar of Islington, looked after him in his last days. His bowdlerizing excisions from Johnson's papers after his death do not suggest a perceptive soul. Had Johnson been a Roman Catholic he would at least have had the recurrent consolations of the Sacrament of Penance, and one feels his name would have been on one of Richard Challoner's slips of paper, to be visited and prayed for, and that he would assuredly have been given some spiritual direction.

An emotional and rational block cut him off from the Evangelicals. He walked past William Romaine's St Dunstan's-in-the-West on his way to St Clement Danes. Had he been able to turn — as at this time Hannah More and Wilberforce turned — to John Newton, he might

---

[23] Boswell's *Life of Johnson*, ed. Hill, iv. 400.

have found one who knew how to turn a man from himself to the one who 'makes the wounded spirit whole'. But those products of the Latitudinarian establishment, the incumbents of the prestigious City churches which clustered round Johnson's dwelling, were not where they were for their skills with sick souls, or for directing the distressed to where lay balm in Gilead. One suspects that John Sharp or Simon Patrick or Anthony Horneck a century before, or the clergy of the Oxford Movement half a century on, knew and cared more about such things. There had perhaps been a high price paid for the 'laicization of society'.

Johnson received his last communion in his house at the hands of the Revd George Strahan on 5 December 1784. Thereafter the horrifying shadows seem to have vanished from his mind. Once again, with great care he had drafted his last communion prayer, simple and moving.

Dec. 5th 1784. Almighty and most merciful Father, I am now as to human eyes it seems, about to commemorate for the last time the death of thy son Jesus Christ Our Saviour and Redeemer. Grant Lord that my whole hope and confidence may be in his merits and in thy mercy: forgive and accept my late conversion, enforce and accept my imperfect repentance: make this commemoration of Him available to the confirmation of my faith, the establishment of my hope, and the enlargement of my charity, and make the death of thy Son Jesus Christ effectual to my redemption. Have mercy upon me and pardon the multitude of my offences. Bless my friends, have mercy upon all men. Support me by the grace of thy holy spirit in the days of weakness and at the hour of death, and receive me at my death to everlasting happiness for the sake of Jesus Christ. Amen.

POSTSCRIPT

THE lines must be drawn somewhere across a roughly chronological study, and it may be admitted that the year 1791 was not, as perhaps the year 1789 was, a grand climacteric. It was a bad year for those fighting to abolish the slave trade, but a good one for the cause of Catholic relief, and a frustrating one for the Nonconformists hoping for the repeal of the Test Acts. It was the year when Europe reeled from the impact of the French Revolution, but if it saw the publication of Thomas Paine's *Rights of Man,* that work lacked as yet its explosive second part and the more scandalous *Age of Reason* lay in the future. It was also the year of the deaths of John Wesley, Richard Price, and William Williams of Pantecylyn.

Every hundred years or so the Christian Church has to evangelize a new humanity and it is worth considering the fact that in 1791 there were hardly any human beings alive who had been on earth in 1688, that within the confines of our study an entire human race had disappeared and been replaced by another.

It is a fundamental rhythm of our existence that

> The busy tribes of flesh and blood
> With all their cares and fears

vanish one by one and that history undergoes a perpetual brain-washing as the memories and experiences of countless individuals are erased. Mortality has therefore relevance to history, altogether apart from the poignant human experiences of dying. We might have begun with the muffled drums of Henry Purcell's music for the funeral of Queen Mary, as near the end of our story we heard the women of Cheddar prepared to forgo their sick benefits for the chance of a better funeral. So that it is change which is constant and stability the illusion, change deep and swift below the surface of things, even amid the famous 'Quieta non movere' of the eighteenth century. Hardly heeded though they were, it was not unseemly for William Law and Samuel Johnson to warn their contemporaries of the transitoriness of earthly hopes and the vanity of human wishes. Not that the course of change is even and uninterrupted. There are decades when a great transformation seems to take place. There are those moments when the board is swept clear of leading figures, as in those years 1710–15 when the bishops Compton, Tenison,

Kidder, Ken and Sharp died. In such times new men take over and this has something to do with unexpected ups and downs, renewals and failures of nerve in history. And of course, as men die, others are born, and we noticed in the story of the Welsh Revival how important it was that its young leaders had been born within a year or so of one another.

We have tried to understand the main preoccupations of men and women of another century. Yet to us, those who plunged so earnestly into the Convocation, Sacheverell, and Bangorian controversies, or into the great argument between the religious and the secular clergy of the English Catholics, or the issues between liberal and orthodox Dissenters, or between the Calvinistic Methodists and the followers of the Wesleys, seem to have got their priorities askew. They seem to belong to that dismal undercurrent of church history in which good men strain at gnats and swallow camels, and tithe mint, anise, and cummin, oblivious of the more serious needs of a world distraught for lack of charity. Sadder still is the prospect of bodies of Christians going their several ways, all claiming that their Master's business was their supreme preoccupation, but in effect excommunicating one another, to their grievous mutual impoverishment, behind invisible curtains of suspicion and hostility, misunderstanding, and ignorance about those whom in that age they did not deign to describe as separated brethren, and fearing, rather than desiring, the consequences of what Dr Sacheverell derided as a 'Mungril-Union'.

The last decades of the century were marked by accelerating change, and its rapid course seems poised over a cataract, at the moment when we abandon the story.

William Sancroft was wont to protest that he was not one of those who 'worshipped the sunrise'. A century later there were very many who rejoiced to do precisely that. Samuel Parr dancing round the Tree of Liberty, Wordsworth and his friends in what seemed a blissful dawn of freedom, and many more excited — and even fevered — by the prospect of great change, urgent for reform in Church and State, and the rough amendment of society. In 1791 two ultimate attitudes to human society were in confrontation between Edmund Burke and Thomas Paine.

But there was continuity as well as change. The Evangelical Revival was far from done. In the next decades the local revivals would splutter and spark and flame like jumping crackers, from village to village, touching miners in their pits and even children in their schools, and becoming more and more involved in the accelerating Industrial Revolution.

The Anglican evangelicals, prominent among them the influential laymen of Clapham, had yet to experience their finest hour. The Sunday School movement began to reveal implications beyond pietism and philanthropy, and foreshadowed far-reaching and national educational change. In Church and State the next half-century was to witness drastic amendment, to sweep away anomalies and abuses in such a way as to make the eighteenth-century fabric hardly recognizable.

But despite all the changes and though their labels altered, ancient tensions remained. There were those who were forward-looking, eager to let a brave new world write the Church's agenda. Others thought that from Old Testament times an identification with the spirit of the age was a hallmark of the false prophet. They would reject the new liberalism in the vigorous affirmation of living tradition in the Oxford Movement. To some, a concentration upon England may seem an unpardonably parochial way of treating the century when, as Chabod has said 'Europe came of age', a continent in which, according to Burke 'no man can be a complete exile'. To others the story of the Church may seem a drab shadow across a glittering culture with its marvellous roll-call of the great, and their creations in music, architecture, letters, science, and philosophy, to say nothing of manifold skills in the fine arts.

But there are those, also, for whom the study of these eighteenth-century Christian men and their doings has been the enthralling occupation of a lifetime of scholarship, and in our century a number of notable historical studies have taken away the reproach of the eighteenth-century Church. We have neither the competence nor the inclination to challenge their judgements. It would not be a historian's, but a theological, comment to suggest that the most devastating criticism of that age would be the marginal gloss, Benjamin Hoadly's controverted text 'my Kingdom is not of this world'. But such a criticism, dire and profound though it might be, would not diminish, but might rather enhance, the true glory of a great company of the good who served their generation according to the will of God, and who, by the quality of their faith and their devotion, made authentic that apocalyptic hope sung and proclaimed in the very middle of that century, in the music of Handel's *Messiah:* 'the Kingdoms of this world are become the Kingdom of our God and of His Christ.'

SELECT BIBLIOGRAPHY

(The place of publication, unless otherwise stated, is London.)

GENERAL STUDIES

ABBEY, C. J. *The English Church and its Bishops 1700–1800*, 2 vols., 1887.
—— and OVERTON, J., *The English Church in the Eighteenth Century*, 1878.
CRAGG, G. R. *Reason and Authority in the Eighteenth Century*, 1964.
CREED, J. M., and BOYS-SMITH, J. S., *Religious Thought in the Eighteenth Century*, Cambridge 1934.
DAVIES, HORTON, *Worship and Theology in England*, 4 vols., Oxford 1961–.
DOBRÉE, B., *English Literature in the Eighteenth Century*, Oxford 1968.
HUTTON, W. H., *A History of the English Church from the Accession of Charles I to the Death of Queen Anne* (Hunt and Stephens, vol. vi).
OGG, D., *England in the Reign of James II and William III*, Oxford 1953.
OVERTON, J., and RELTON, F. *A History of the English Church from the Accession of George I to the end of the Eighteenth Century* (Hunt and Stephens, vol. vii).
SYKES, N., *Church and State in England in the Eighteenth Century*, Cambridge 1934.
WILLIAMS, B., *The Whig Supremacy, 1714–60*, ed. C. H. Stuart, 2nd edn., Oxford 1962.

THE NON-JURORS

GENERAL STUDIES

BROXAP, H., *The Later Non-Jurors*, 1924.
DOUGLAS, D. C., *English Scholars, 1600–1730*, 1951.
GRISBROOKE, W. J., *Anglican Liturgies of the Seventeenth and Eighteenth Centuries* (Alcuin Club, No. 40), 1958.
HAWKINS, L. M., *Allegiance in Church and State*, 1928.
LATHBURY, T., *A History of the Non-Jurors*, 1845.
OVERTON, J. H., *The Non-Jurors: Their Lives, Principles and Writings*, 1902.
WILLIAMS, G., *The Orthodox Church of the East in the Eighteenth Century*, 1868.

BIOGRAPHIES

BROKESBY, F., *The Life of Henry Dodwell*, 1715.
BROXAP, H., *Biography of Thomas Deacon*, Manchester 1911.
D'OYLY, G., *The Life of Archbishop Sancroft*, 2 vols., 1821.
PLUMPTRE, E. H., *Thomas Ken*, 2 vols., 1891.
SECRETAN, C. F., *The Life of Robert Nelson*, 1860.

WALMSLEY, R., 'John Wesley's Parents, quarrel and reconciliation', *PWHS* xxix, Sept. 1953.

WORKS

DEACON, T., *A Compleat Collection of Devotions*, 1734.
HICKES, G., *The Constitution of the Catholic Church, and the nature and consequences of schism set forth in a collection of papers under the late Rt. Revd. G. Hickes, D. D.*, 1716.
—— *Devotions in the Ancient Way of Offices: Reformed by a Person of Quality and published by the Revd. G. Hickes D. D.*, 1701.
KEN, T., *Prose Works*, ed. W. Benham (Ancient and Modern Library) n.d.
KETTLEWELL, T., *Complete Works*, 1719.
LAW, W., See separate Bibliography above, p. 242.
LESLIE, C., *The Theological Works of the Reverend Mr. Charles Leslie*, 2 vols., London 1721.
NELSON, R., *A Companion for the Festivals and Fasts of the Church of England*, 1704.
SPINCKES, N., *The True Church of England Man's Companion to the Closet*, 1721.

LATITUDINARIANS

KIDDER, R., *The Life of Richard Kidder, D. D.*, ed. A. E. Robinson, Somerset Record Society, vol. xxxvii, 1924.
PATRICK, S., *The Hypocritical Nation*, 1657.
—— *A Brief Account of the New Sect of Latitude Men*, 1662, repr. Augustan Society, 100, University of California, ed. A. T. Burrell.
—— *The Parable of the Pilgrim*, 1664.
—— *The Christian Sacrifice*, 1672.
—— *Advice to a Friend*, 1673.
—— *Autobiography*, Oxford 1839.
—— *Works*, ed. A. Taylor, 9 vols., Oxford 1858.
STILLINGFLEET, E., *Irenicum*, 1669.
—— *A Discourse Concerning the Idolatry Practised in the Church of Rome*, 1672.
—— *The Mischief of Separation*, 1680.
—— *Origines Sacrae*, 1680.
—— *Origines Brittannicae*, 1685.
—— *Works*, ed. R. Bentley, 6 vols., 1709–10.
TILLOTSON, J., *Works*, 1704.
—— *Works* (with Life by T. Birch) 3 vols., 1752.

DIVINES OF THE CITY OF LONDON

GENERAL STUDIES

BRETT-JAMES, N. G., *The Growth of Stuart London*, 1935.
CARPENTER, E. F., *A House of Kings: the History of Westminster Abbey*, 1966.

DOBIE, R., *The History of the United Parishes of St. Giles-in-the-Fields and St. George's Bloomsbury*, 1829.
ELLIS, A., *The Penny Universities*, 1956.
ESDAILE, K., *St Martin-in-the-Fields*, 1944.
GEORGE, M. D., *London Life in the Eighteenth Century*, 1976.
LILLYWHITE, B., *London Coffee Houses*, 1963.
MATTHEWS, W. R., and ATKINS, W. M., *A History of St. Paul's Cathedral*, 1957.
MCMASTERS, J., *St. Martin-in-the-Fields*, 1916.
RUDÉ, G., *Hanoverian London*, 1971.

THE HIGH CHURCH PARTY

ATTERBURY, F., *An Answer to Some Considerations on the Spirit of Martin Luther and the Origins of the Reformation*, Oxford 1687.
—— *Memoirs and Correspondence*, ed. F. Williams, 2 vols., 1869.
BENNETT, G. V., *The Tory Crisis in Church and State 1688–1730*, Oxford 1975.
—— 'English Jacobitism, 1710–5', *TRHS* (5th Series) 32, 1982.
CANNON, J. (ed.), *The Whig Ascendancy*, 1981.
EVERY, G., *The High Church Party*, 1956.
GREGG, E., *Queen Anne*, 1980.
HAMILTON, E., *William and Mary*, 1972.
MARSHALL, W. M., *George Hooper*, Sherborne 1976.
PLUMB, J. H., *The Growth of Political Stability in England 1675–1775*, 1967.
SPECK, W. A., *Stability and Strife in England 1714–60*, 1977.
TYERMAN, L., *The Life and Times of Samuel Wesley*, 1866.
WALKER, Obadiah, *Two Discourses concerning the Spirit of Martin Luther*, 1687.
ZEE van der, H. and B., *William and Mary*, 1975.

THE CONVOCATION CONTROVERSY

CONTEMPORARY WRITINGS

ATTERBURY, Francis, *The Rights, Powers and Privileges of an English Convocation Vindicated*, 1700.
—— *The Parliamentary Original and Rights of the Lower House of Convocation cleared*, 1702.
GIBSON, Edmund, *Synodus Anglicana, or the Constitution and Proceedings of an English Convocation*, 1702.
KENNETT, White, *Ecclesiastical Synods and Parliamentary Convocations in the Church of England historically stated*, 1701.
WAKE, William, *The State of the Church and Clergy of England in their Councils, Synods and other public Assemblies*, 1703.

LATER STUDIES

EVERY, G., *The High Church Party*, 1956.
LATHBURY, T., *The History of the Convocation*, 1842.

—— *The Diaries of Bishop Nicolson*, Transactions of the Cumberland and Westmorland Antiquarian and Archaeological Society, NS 1901–6.
Also works of G. V. Bennett and N. Sykes listed above.

THE SACHEVERELL CASE

A Compleat History of the Trial of Dr. Henry Sacheverell (published by Order of the House of Lords), 1710.
Tracts relating to Sacheverell (Cambridge University Library).
The Bishops of Lincoln and Norwich's Speeches in the House of Lords, 1710.
SACHEVERELL, H., *The Character of a Low Churchman*, 1701.
—— *The Communication of Sin*, 1709.
—— *The Perils of False Brethren in Church and State*, 1710, repr. Exeter 1974.
SHARP, John, *A Speech relating to Dr. Sacheverell*, 1710.
HOLMES, G., *The Trial of Dr. Sacheverell*, 1973.

CHURCH OF ENGLAND MEN

BENNETT, G. V., 'King William III and the Episcopate', in *Essays in Modern English Church History in Memory of Norman Sykes*, ed. G. V. Bennett and J. D. Walsh, 1960.
BURNET, Gilbert, *A History of My Own Time*, 4 vols., 1797 (Supplement ed. H. C. Foxcroft, Oxford 1902).
—— *Some Letters containing an account of what seemed more remarkable in Switzerland, Italy, etc.*, Amsterdam, 1686.
DUFFY, E., 'Correspondence Fraternelle: the SPCK, SPG and the churches of Switzerland during the war of the Spanish Succession', in *'Reform and Reformation': Studies in Church History* ed. D. Baker, Oxford, 1979.
EACHARD, J., *The Grounds and Occasion of the Contempt of the Clergy and Religion Enquired Into*, 1698.
FOXCROFT, H. C., *A Life of Gilbert Burnet*, Cambridge 1907.
ROUSE, R. and NEILL, S. C., *A History of the Ecumenical Movement*, 1954.
—— *Mr. Sewell's First Letter to the Bishop of Salisbury*, 1713.
SYKES, N., *Daniel Ernst Jablonski*, 1950.
—— 'The Sermons of Archbishop Tillotson', *Theology*, 1955.

LIVES

BENNETT, G. V., *White Kennett*, 1957.
CARPENTER, E. F., *Thomas Sherlock*, 1936.
—— *Thomas Tenison*, 1948.
—— *The Protestant Bishop*, 1956.
HART, A. Tindal, *The Life and Times of John Sharp, Archbishop of York*, 1949.
—— *William Lloyd*, 1952.
SHARP, T., (ed. T. NEWCOMBE), *The Life of John Sharp, Archbishop of York*, 2 vols., 1825.

SYKES, N., *Edmund Gibson*, Oxford 1926.
—— *William Wake*, 2 vols., Cambridge 1957.
—— 'Queen Anne and the Episcopate', *EHR* 1935.

SERMONS, etc

A *Collection of Cases and Discourses lately written to recover Dissenters to the Communion of the Church of England by some Divines of the City of London,* 1698.
GIBSON, Edmund, *The Bishop of London's Pastoral Letter to the People of his Diocese*, 1728.
—— *The Bishop of London's Second Pastoral Letter. . .* 1730.
—— *The Bishop of London's Third Pastoral Letter. . .* 1731.
—— *A Pastoral letter to the People of his Diocese by way of caution against Lukewarmness on the one hand and Enthusiasm on the other,* 1731.
—— (ed.) *A Preservative Against Popery*, 3 vols., 1738.

THE BANGORIAN CONTROVERSY

BURNET, G. (The Younger), *An Answer to Mr. Law's Letter*, 1717.
DISNEY, J., *Memoirs of the Rev. A. A. Sykes*, 1785.
HOADLY, B., *The Works of Benjamin Hoadly*, ed. J. Hoadly, 3 vols., 1773.
—— *A Defence of the Reasonableness of Conformity*, 1707.
—— *A Preservative against the Principles and Practices of the Non-Jurors both in Church and State*, 1716.
—— *A Sermon on Superstition*, 1717.
—— *The Nature of the Kingdom of Christ*, 1717.
—— *A Plain account of the Nature and End of the Sacrament of the Lord's Supper*, 1735.
LAW, W., *Three Letters to the Bishop of Bangor*, 1762.
RACK, H., 'Christ's Kingdom not of this world': the case of Benjamin Hoadly re-considered, *Studies in Church History*, ed. D. Baker, vol. xii, 1976.
SNAPE, A., *A Letter to the Bishop of Bangor*, 1717.
STEBBING, H., *Remarks upon a position of . . . the Bishop of Bangor concerning sincerity'*, 1718.
SYKES, A. A., *The Innocence of Error asserted*, 1715.
—— *The Difference between the Kingdom of Christ and the Kingdoms of this world. . . Preached in Cambridge, 16 Dec. 1716.*
SYKES, N., 'Benjamin Hoadly' in *'The Social and Political ideas of some English Thinkers of the Augustan Age'*, ed. F. J. C. Hearnshaw, 1928.
TRAPP, J., *The Nature, Folly, Sin and Danger of being Righteous Overmuch*, 1739.

THE DISSIDENTS

BEBB, E. D., *Nonconformity in Social and Economic Life 1600–1800*, 1935.
CALAMY, Edmund, *An Abridgement of Mr. Baxter's History of His life and times*, 2 vols., 1713.

—— *A Continuation of the Account* . . . 2 vols., 1727.

CLARKE, H. W., *History of English Nonconformity*.

COOMER, D., *English Dissent*, 1946.

MANNING, B., *Essays in Orthodox Dissent*, 1939.

PAYNE, E. A., *The Free Church Tradition in the Life of England*, 1944.

SELBIE, W. B., *Nonconformity* (Home University Library), n.d.

WATTS, M. R., *The Dissenters*, vol. 1, Oxford 1978.

PRESBYTERIANS

BOLAM, G., and THOMAS, R., *The English Presbyterians*, 1968.

The Minutes of the Westminster Assembly 1644–9, ed. Mitchell and Struthers, Edinburgh, 1874.

YULE, G., *Puritans and Politics*, 1982.

RICHARD BAXTER

BAXTER, R., *Reliquiae Baxterianae*, ed. Sylvester, 1696.

—— *Autobiography* (Everyman), ed. J. M. Lloyd Thomas, 1925.

—— *A Call to the Unconverted*, 1658.

—— *The Saints Everlasting Rest*, 1659.

—— *Sacrilegious Desertion of the Holy Ministry Rebuked*, 1672.

—— *A Christian Directory*, 1673.

—— *Richard Baxter's answer to Dr Edward Stillingfleet's Charge of Separation*, 1680.

'The Poor Husbandman's Advocate to Rich Racking Landlords', *The Reverend Richard Baxter's Last Treatise*, ed. F. J. Powicke, Manchester 1926.

KEEBLE, N. H., *Richard Baxter*, Oxford 1982.

NUTTALL, G. F., *Richard Baxter*, 1965.

POWICKE, F. J., *The Rev. Richard Baxter under the Cross*, 1927.

CONGREGATIONALISTS

BROWNE, J., *The History of Congregationalism in Norfolk and Suffolk*, 1877.

DALE, R. W., *History of Congregationalism*, 1907.

HILL, C., 'Occasional Conformity', in *Reformation, Conformity, Dissent, Essays Presented in honour of G. Nuttall*, ed. Buick Knox, 1980.

JONES, R. Tudor, *Congregationalism in England*, 1962.

MILLER, Perry, *Orthodoxy in Massachusetts*, 1932.

MORGAN, E. S., *Visible Saints*, Cornell 1963.

NUTTALL, G. F., *Visible Saints*, Oxford 1957.

OWEN J., *Works*, 24 vols., ed. W. H. Goold, repr. 1966.

—— *The Savoy Declaration*, ed. A. G. Matthews, 1959.

TOON, P., *God's Statesman: The Life and Work of John Owen*, Exeter 1971.

—— *Correspondence of John Owen*, 1971.

YULE, G., *The Independents in the Civil War*, Cambridge 1955.

BAPTISTS

BAINES, H. A., 'Signatories to the Orthodox Confession', *BQ* xvii, 1957–8.
DAVIES, Horton, *Worship and Theology in England,* vol. 3, Oxford, 1961.
MONK, T. A., *A Cure for the Cankering Error of the New Eutychians,* 1673.
NUTTALL, G., 'Assembly and Association in Dissent', in *Studies in Church History,* ed. D. Baker, Cambridge 1971.
—— 'Calvinism in Free Church History', *BQ* xxii, 1968.
PAYNE, E. A., 'Who were the Baptists?' *BQ* xvi, 1955–6.
—— *The Fellowship of Believers,* London 1952.
UNDERWOOD, A. C., *A History of the English Baptists,* 1932.
WHITLEY, W. T., *A History of the English Baptists,* 1947.
WINTER, E. P., 'The Lord's Supper, Admission and Exclusion among the Baptists of the seventeenth century', *BQ* xvii, 1957–8.
—— 'The Administration of the Lord's Supper among the Baptists in the seventeenth century', *BQ* xviii, 1960.

QUAKERS

ANDERSON, V., *Friends and Relations,* 1980.
BARCLAY, R., *Apology,* Glasgow 1886.
BRAITHWAITE, W. C., *The Beginnings of Quakerism,* 1912.
—— *The Second Period of Quakerism,* 1919, rev. edn. 1961.
BRAYSHAW, A. N., *The Quakers,* 1953.
FOX, G., *Journal,* Everyman edn.
—— *Journal,* ed. John L. Nickalls, Cambridge 1952.
—— *Journal,* ed. N. Penney. 2 vols., Cambridge 1911.
LESLIE, C., *The Theological Works of the Reverend Mr. Charles Leslie,* vol. ii, 1721.
PENN, W., *Select Works,* 5 vols., 1782.
—— *No Cross, No Crown,* 1699.
PENNINGTON, I., *Works,* 2 vols., 1761.
RAISTRICK A., *Quakers in Science and Industry,* Newton Abbott 1950.
SELBIE, W. B., *Nonconformity* (Home University Library).
VIPONT, Elfrida, *George Fox and the Valiant Sixty,* 1975.

ISAAC WATTS

WATTS, I., *Works,* 5 vols. Leeds, n.d.
—— *Poetical Works,* 7 vols., Edinburgh 1782.
BISHOP, S. L., *Hymns and Spiritual Songs,* 1962.
DAVIS, A. F., *Isaac Watts,* 1943.
GIBBONS, T., *Memoirs of the Rev. I. Watts D. D.,* 1780.
JOHNSON, Samuel, 'Isaac Watts' in *Lives of the Poets,* vol. ii, Oxford 1975.
MANNING, B., *The Hymns of Wesley and of Watts,* 1942.
RUPP, E. G., *Six Makers of English Religion,* 1964.

PHILIP DODDRIDGE

DODDRIDGE, P., *Works*, 10 vols., 1802–5.
DEACON, M., *Philip Doddridge of Northampton*, Northampton 1980.
HUMPHREYS, J. D., *The Correspondence and Diary of Philip Doddridge*, 1829–31.
NUTTALL, G. F., *Calendar of the Correspondence of Philip Doddridge* (Historical MSS Commission 1979).
—— (ed.), *Philip Doddridge*, 1951.
—— *Richard Baxter and Philip Doddridge*, 1951.

THE DISSENTING ACADEMIES

MCLACHLAN, H., *English Education under the Test Acts*, Manchester 1931.
PALMER, S., *Defence of the Dissenters' Education in their Private Academies*, 1703.
—— *A Vindication of the Dissenters in Answer to Mr. Wesley's Defence*, London 1705.
PARKER, I., *The Dissenting Academies in England*, Cambridge 1914.
WESLEY, S., *A Letter from a Country Divine*, 1703.
—— *A Defence of a Letter concerning the Education of Dissenters in their Private Academies*, 1704.

THE ENGLISH CATHOLICS

ANSTRUTHER, G., *The Seminary Priests*, 5 vols., Great Wakering, 1975.
AVELING, H., *Northern Catholics*, 1966.
—— *The Handle and the Axe*, London 1976.
BASSET, B., *The English Jesuits*, 1947.
BOSSY, J., *The English Catholic Community 1570–1850*, 1976.
BURTON, E. H., *The Life and Times of Bishop Challoner*, 2 vols., 1909.
CLANCY, T. H., *English Catholic Books, 1641–1700*, Chicago 1973.
DUFFY, E. (ed.), *Challoner and his Church*, London 1981.
—— 'Richard Challoner and the Salesian Tradition', *Clergy Review*, LXVI, Dec. 1981.
—— 'Poor Protestant Flies: Conversions to Catholicism in Early Eighteenth Century England', in *Studies in Church History*, ed. D. Baker, Vol. 15, Oxford, 1978.
—— 'Ecclesiastical Democracy Detected', I. 1779–87; II. 1787–96, *Recusant History* x, Jan.–Oct. 1970.
—— 'Over the Wall: Converts from Popery in eighteenth century England', *Downside Review* 94, Jan. 1976.
—— 'A rubb-up for Old Soares: Jesuits, Jansenists and the English secular clergy, 1705–15', *JEH* 28, No. 3, 1977.
—— 'Englishmen in Vaine: Roman Catholic allegiance to George I', *Studies in Church History*, ed. S. Mews, vol. xviii, Oxford 1982.

—— 'Peter and Jack: Roman Catholics and Dissenters in eighteenth century England', Friends of Dr. Williams Library Lecture, 1982.

GOTHER, J., *Spiritual Works*, 16 vols., 1718.

—— *Instructions and Devotions for Confession, Communion and Confirmation*, n.d.

LEYS, M. D. R., *Catholics in England 1559–1829*, 1961.

SALES, F. de, *Oeuvres*, Annécy 1893.

THE CISALPINES

CHADWICK, O., *The Popes and European Revolution*, Oxford 1981.

CHINUCCI, J. P., *The English Catholic Enlightenment*, 1980.

THE GORDON RIOTS

HIBBERT, C., *King Mob*, 1958.

RUDÉ, G., 'The Gordon Riots', *TRHS* (5th Series), vi, 1956.

'INWARD RELIGION'

HENDERSON, G. D., *Mystics of the North-East*, Aberdeen 1934.

—— *The Burning Bush*, Edinburgh 1957.

HIRSCH, E., *Geschichte der neueren evangelischen Theologie*, vol. 4, Göttingen, 1975.

KOYRÉ, A., *Mystiques, spiritualistes, alchémistes*, Paris 1955.

KRIEG, G. A., *Der mystische Kreis*, Göttingen 1979.

JOHN BYROM

The Private and Literary Remains of John Byrom, ed. R. Parkinson, Chetham Society, 2 vols., 1854–7.

The Poems of J. Byrom, ed. A. Ward, Chetham Society, 3 vols., 1894, 1895, 1912.

TALON, H., *Selections from the Journals and Papers of John Byrom*, 1950.

THE PHILADELPHIANS

HUTIN, S., *Les Disciples anglais de Jacob Boehme au xvii et xviiime siècles*, Paris 1960.

THUNE, N., *The Behmenists and Philadelphians*, Uppsala 1948.

JACOB BOEHME

BOEHME, J., *Works*, ed. J. Ellistone and J. Sparrow, 3 vols., 1762–84.

—— *Sämtliche Schriften*, ed. Peuckert, 10 vols., Stuttgart, 1955–60.

—— *The Way to Christ*, tr. P. Erb (Classics of Western Spirituality) Toronto, 1978.

BORNKAMM, H., 'Luther and Böhme', *Luther Jahr-Buch* 9, 1927.

—— 'Jakob Böhme' in *Das Jahrhundert der Reformation*, Göttingen 1966.

HANKAMER, P., *Jakob Boehme*, 1924.

HOBHOUSE, S., 'Fides et Ratio', *JTS* xxxvii, 1936.

—— (ed.), *J. Boehme. Studies in his life and theology by H. L. Martensen*, 1949.

KOYRÉ, A., *La philosophie de J. Boehme*, Paris 1929.

MULLER, A. A., 'The Theologies of Luther and Boehme in the light of their Genesis commentaries', *Harvard Theological Review* 63, 1970.

MUSES, C. A., *Illumination on Jacob Boehme, the Work of Dionysius Freher*, New York 1951.

WHYTE, Alexander, *Jacob Behmen*, 1895.

RATIONALISTS AND MORALISTS

GENERAL STUDIES

ALLISON, G. F., *The Rise of Moralism*, 1966.

ATKINSON, G., *The Extraordinary Voyages in French Literature 1700–20*, Paris 1922.

BAHLMANN, D. W., *The Moral Revolution of 1688*, New Haven 1957.

CUNLIFFE-JONES, H., and DREWERY, B., *A History of Christian Doctrine*, Edinburgh 1980.

GAY, Peter, *The Enlightenment*, 2 vols., 1967.

HASARD, P., *The European Mind*, English tr. 1964.

HUNT, J., *Religious Thought in England*, 3 vols., 1871.

PAILIN, D., *Attitudes to Other Religions*, Manchester 1984.

PATTISON, Mark, 'Tendencies of religious thought in England, 1688–1750' in *Essays and Reviews*, 1861.

REDMOND, J., *Reason, Ridicule and Religion*, 1976.

STEPHEN, Leslie, *English Thought in the Eighteenth Century*, 2 vols., 1963.

STROMBERG, R., *Religious Liberalism in 18th Century England*, 1954.

VICKERS, B. (ed.), *The World of Jonathan Swift*, 1968.

YATES, F., *The Rosicrucian Enlightenment*, 1972.

SOCINIANISM

COLLIGAN, J. H., *The Arian Movement in England*, 1936.

MCLACHLAN, H. J. *Socinianism in Seventeenth Century England*, 1951.

NYE, Stephen, *The Explication of the Articles of the Divine Unity, the Trinity and Incarnation*, 1715.

DEISTS

BENTLEY, R., *A Confutation of Atheism*, 1692.

—— *A Discourse upon the Epistles of Phalaris*, 1699.

—— *Remarks upon a Late Discourse of Free Thinking* by Philelevtherus Lipsiensis, 1716.

—— *Eight Sermons,* 1724.

BERKELEY, G., *Works,* ed. A. A. Luce and T. E. Jessop, 1955.

BURCHILL, T. L., *The Sage of Salisbury, Thomas Chubb,* New York 1968.

CLARKE, Samuel, *Works of the Rev. Samuel Clarke D. D.,* ed. B. Hoadly, 4 vols., 1738.

—— *Three Practical Essays,* 1699.

—— *A Discourse concerning the Being and Attributes of God, the Obligations of Natural Religion, and the Truth and Certainty of the Christian Revelation* (Boyle Lectures), 10th edn. 1766.

—— *The Scriptural Doctrine of the Trinity,* 1712.

COLLINS, Anthony, *A Discourse of Free Thinking,* facs. edn. ed. G. Gawlick, Stuttgart 1965.

—— *A Philosophic Inquiry Concerning Human Liberty,* 1717.

CUDWORTH, R., *Sermon Before the House of Commons,* 1647.

—— *The True Intellectual system of the Universe,* 1677.

EDWARDS, J., *Some Animadversions on Dr. Clarke's Scripture Doctrine,* 1712.

—— *Some varied critical remarks on Dr. Clarke,* 1714.

FERGUSON, J. F., *An Eighteenth Century Heretic, Dr. Samuel Clarke,* Kineton 1976.

GASTRELL, F., *The Certainty of the Christian Religion,* 1703.

—— *Remarks upon Dr Samuel Clarke's Scripture Doctrine of the Trinity,* 1714.

HARE, Francis, *The Difficulties and Discouragements Which attend the Study of the Scriptures,* 1714.

JACKSON, John, *Three Letters to Dr Clarke from a Clergyman,* 1714.

—— *A Collection of Queries . . .* 1716.

—— *A Reply to Dr. Waterland's defence of his Queries,* 1722.

LESLIE, Charles, *Tracts against Deism, Works,* vol. 1, 1721.

MANUEL, F. E., *The Religion of Isaac Newton,* 1974.

MIDDLETON, Conyers, *An Enquiry into the Miraculous Powers which are supposed to have subsisted in the Christian Church,* 1747.

O' HIGGINS, J., *Anthony Collins, the Man and His Work,* The Hague 1970.

SHERLOCK, Thomas, *The Tryal of the Witnesses of the Resurrection of Jesus,* 1729.

SULLIVAN, R. E., *John Toland and the Deist Controversy,* Harvard 1982.

SYKES, A. A., *A Modest Plea for the Baptismal and Scripture Notion of the Trinity,* 1719.

—— *The True Foundations of Natural and Revealed Religion,* 1730.

TINDAL, M., *Christianity as Old as the Creation,* Facs. edn., G. Gawlick, Stuttgart 1967.

TOLAND, J., *Christianity not Mysterious,* Facs. edn., G. Gawlick, Stuttgart 1964.

WATERLAND, D., *Works,* 3 vols., Oxford 1823.

—— *A Critical History of the Athanasian Creed* 1728.

—— *Scripture Vindicated,* 1731.

WESTFALL, R. S., *Never at Rest: A Biography of Isaac Newton,* Cambridge 1980.

WHISTON, W., *Primitive Christianity Revived,* 4 vols. 1711.

—— *Memories of the Life and Writings of William Whiston, written by Himself,* 2 vols., 1753.

WHITBY, D., *A Dissuasive from Enquiring into the Doctrine of the Trinity,* 1714.

WOLLASTON, W., *The Religion of Nature,* 1738.

WOOLSTON, T., *Six Tracts of Miracles. The Life of Mr Woolston, with an impartial account of his writings,* 1733.

MORALISTS

BUTLER, J., *The Analogy of Religion* 1906.

—— *Fifteen Sermons,* ed. T. A. Roberts, Oxford 1970.

—— *Works,* ed. J. H. Bernard, 2 vols., 1900.

COOPER, A. A., 3rd Earl of Shaftesbury, *Characteristicks,* 1731.

HUME, D., *Enquiries Concerning Human Understanding,* 1777 edn. rep. L. A. Selby-Biggs; 3rd edn. revd. P. H. Nidditch, Oxford 1922.

—— *The Natural History of Religion,* ed. H. E. Root, 1956.

—— *Dialogues,* (ed.) Kemp-Smith, Oxford 1935.

MOSSNER, E. C., *Bishop Butler and His World,* New York 1936.

WILLEY, B., *The English Moralists,* 1964.

—— *The Eighteenth Century Background,* 1940.

INCREASE OF CHARITY

ALLEN, W. O. B. and MCCLURE, E., *Two Hundred Years: The History of the S.P.C.K.,* 1898.

BARROW, Isaac, *The Duty and Reward of Bounty to the Poor,* 1671.

BASTIAN, F., *Defoe's Early Life,* 1981.

BAXTER, Richard, *Letters to John Eliot,* ed. F. J. Powicke, 1930.

BEECHAM, H. A., 'Samuel Wesley, Senior, New biographical evidence', *Renaissance and Modern Studies,* (University of Nottingham), vii, 1963.

BEEVES, W. A., *Charity Briefs,* 1896.

BELLARS, John, *An Essay towards the Improvement of Physick,* 1714.

COWIE, L., *Henry Newman,* 1956.

DEFOE, Daniel, *The Poor Man's Plea,* 1698.

—— *Giving Alms no Charity,* 1704.

GASTRELL, Francis, *The Religious Education of Poor Children,* 1707.

GRAY, B. K., *A History of English Philanthropy,* repr. 1967.

HORNECK, A., *The Great Law of Consideration,* 3rd edn., 1684.

—— *The Happy Ascetic,* 1693.

—— *The Crucified Jesus,* 1700.

—— *The Glories of the other World,* 1708.

JONES, M. G., *The Charity School Movement,* Cambridge 1964.

KIDDER, R., *The Life of the Rev. Anthony Horneck,* 1698.

MANDEVILLE, Bernard, *The Fable of the Bees,* 1725.

—— *Charity and the Charity Schools,* 1725.

McCLURE, R., *Coram's Children,* Yale, 1981.

NELSON, Robert, *An Address to Persons of Quality and Estate, with an appendix of papers,* 1715 (among the papers is 'a proposal for a charity school for the blackguard boys').

OWEN, D., *English Philanthrophy 1660–1960,* 1964.

PENNINGTON, E. L., *The Rev. Thomas Bray,* Philadelphia 1934.

PULLAN, B., 'Catholics and the Poor in Early Modern Europe'. *TRHS* (5th Series) Vol. 28, 1970.

SWIFT, Jonathan, *Prose Works,* ed. H. Davis, 14 vols., 1939–68.

—— *Of the Poor Man's Contentment.* ed. Davis, Vol. iv.

WOODWARD, J., *An Account of the Rise and Progress of the Religious Societies.* 1701.

EVANGELICAL REVIVAL

GENERAL BACKGROUND

GILLIES, J., *Historical Collections of Accounts of Revival,* repr. Philadelphia. 1981.

TRACY, J., *The Great Awakening,* repr. Edinburgh 1976.

WALSH, J. D., 'The Beginnings of the Evangelical Revival', in *Essays in Modern English Church History in memory of Norman Sykes,* ed. G. V. Bennett and J. D. Walsh, 1960.

WARD, W. R., 'Relations of the Enlightenment and religious Revival in Central Europe and the English speaking world', in *Studies in Church History,* ed. D. Baker, *Reform and Reformation, Subsidia 2,* 1979.

WOOD, A. S., *The Inextinguishable Blaze,* 1960.

—— *The Burning Heart,* 1967.

PIETISM

ALAND, K., *Kirchengeschichtliche Entwürfe,* Gütersloh 1960.

HERMELINK, H., 'Another look at Freylinghausen and his Awakening', *CH* xxxvii, 1968.

NAGLER, A. W., *Pietism and Methodism,* Nashville 1918.

SCHMIDT, M., *Pietismus,* Stuttgart 1972.

—— 'Spener und Luther', *Luther J-B.,* 1957.

—— *Wiedergeburt und neuer Mensch,* Witten 1969.

STOEFFLER, E., *The Rise of Evangelical Pietism,* Witten 1969.

TANIS, J., *Dutch Calvinist Pietism in the Middle Colonies,* The Hague 1967.

WALLMANN, J., 'Pietismus und Orthodoxie', in *Geist und Geschichte der Reformation. Festgabe Hanns Rückert,* Berlin 1966.

THE MORAVIAN BRETHREN

ADDISON, W. G., *The Renewed Church of the United Brethren,* 1932.

BENHAM, D., *Memoirs of James Hutton*, 1856.

Die Guldene Himmelpforte: das ist Bekenntnis des Glaubens der Christlicher Bruder in Behmen und Merhern, Newenstadt 1568.

HAMILTON, J. T., *History of the Moravian Church*, Philadelphia 1967.

HUTTON, J., 'The Moravian Contribution to the Evangelical Revival, 1742–53', in *Historical Essays by Members of Owen's College*, ed. T. F. Tout and J. Tait, Manchester 1902.

PINNINGTON, J., 'Moravian and Anglican', *John Rylands Library Lecture*, Manchester 1969.

TOWLSON, C. W., *Moravian and Methodist*, 1957.

ZEMAN, J. K., *Anabaptists and Czech Brethren*, The Hague 1969.

ZINZENDORF

BEYREUTHER, E., *Studien zur Theologie Zinzendorfs*, Neukirchen 1962.

FORELL, G. W., *Zinzendorf: Nine Lectures*, Iowa 1973.

LEWIS, A. J., *Zinzendorf, the Ecumenical Pioneer*, 1962.

SCHMIDT, M., 'Luther und Zinzendorf', *Luther J-B*, 1951.

GEORGE WHITEFIELD

WHITEFIELD, George, *Works*, 6 vols., 1772.

—— *Letters*, 1771, repr. 1976.

—— *Journals*, repr. 1978.

—— *The Nature and Necessity of Society in General and Religious Societies in particular*, 1737.

DALLIMORE, A. A., *George Whitefield*, 2 vols., Edinburgh 1970–80.

POLLOCK, J., *George Whitefield*, 1972.

TYERMAN, L., *The Life of George Whitefield*, 2 vols., 1877.

WELCH, E., *Two Calvinistic Methodist Chapels 1748–1811*, London Record Soc., 1975.

JOHN WESLEY

The Works of the Rev. John Wesley, M. A., 14 vols., 1856.

The Works of John Wesley (Oxford Edition). This edition is in progress. Volumes so far published are:

Vol. 11 *The Appeals*, ed. G. R. Cragg, 1975.

Vol. 25 *Letters, 1721–39*, ed. F. Baker, 1980.

Vol. 26 *Letters, 1740–55*, ed. F. Baker, 1982.

Vol. 7 *A Collection of Hymns*, ed. F. Hildebrandt, and O. Beckerlegge, 1984.

The Journal of John Wesley, ed. N. Curnock, 8 vols., 1931.

The Letters of John Wesley, ed. J. Telford, 8 vols., 1931.

The Standard Sermons of John Wesley, ed. E. H. Sugden, 2 vols., 1955.

GREEN, R., *The Works of John and Charles Wesley: A Bibliography*, 1895 (an indispensable tool).

—— *Anti-Methodist Publications*.

LIVES OF WESLEY

MOORE, H., *Life of the Revd. John Wesley*, 2 vols., 1824.
SCHMIDT, M., *John Wesley*, 2 vols., Frankfurt, 1953.
—— *John Wesley*, 3 vols., Eng. tr. 1962.
SIMON, J. S., *John Wesley and the Religious Societies*, 1921.
—— *John Wesley and the Methodist Societies*, 1923.
—— *John Wesley and the Advance of Methodism*, 1925.
—— *John Wesley, the Master Builder*, 1927.
—— *John Wesley, the Last Phase*, 1934.
SOUTHEY, R., *The Life of Wesley*, 2 vols., 1824.
TYERMAN, L., *The Life and Times of John Wesley*, 3 vols., 1878.
WHITEHEAD, J., *The Life of the Revd. John Wesley, M.A.* 2 vols., 1796.

SOME WESLEY STUDIES

BORGEN, O. E., *John Wesley on the Sacraments*, Zurich 1972.
COPPEDGE, A., *John Wesley and the Doctrine of Predestination*, Diss. University of Cambridge, 1976.
CROW, E. P., *John Wesley's Conflict with Antinomianism in relation to the Moravians and Calvinists.* Diss. University of Manchester, 1964.
IRESON, R. W., *The Doctrine of Faith in John Wesley and the Protestant Tradition.* Diss. University of Manchester 1973.
KÄLLSTAD, T., *John Wesley and the Bible*, Stockholm 1974.
LINDSTRÖM, H., *Wesley and Sanctification*, Stockholm 1946.
WILLIAMS, C. W., *John Wesley's Theology To-day*, 1966.

THE OXFORD METHODISTS

GREEN, V. H. H., *The Young Mr. Wesley*, 1961.
HEITZENRATER, R. P., *John Wesley and the Oxford Methodists*, Diss. Duke University, N. Carolina 1972.
TYERMAN, L., *The Oxford Methodists*, 1873.

'THE PEOPLE CALLED METHODISTS'

A New History of Methodism, ed. Townsend, Workman, and Eayrs, 2 vols., 1909.
A History of the Methodist Church in Great Britain, ed. R. Davies and G. Rupp, 4 vols., 1965.
CHURCH, L. F., *The Early Methodist People*, 1948.
—— *More about the Early Methodist People*, 1949.
EDWARDS, M., *My Dear Sister*, 1980.
The Journals of Mary Gilbert, 1768.
The Journal of Elizabeth Harper, 1769.
KENT, J., 'Wesleyan Membership in Bristol, 1783', *An Ecclesiastical Miscellany*, Bristol and Gloucester Archaeological Society, vol. xi, 1976.
KIRKHAM, D. H., *Pamphlets Opposing the Methodists*, Diss. Duke University, N. Carolina 1973.

MOORE, H., *The Life of Mrs. Mary Fletcher*, 2 vols., 1818.

STEBBING, H., *A caution against religious delusion. A Sermon occasioned by the . . . Methodists*, 1739.

STEVENSON, C. J., *A History of City Road Chapel*, 1872.

TELFORD, J., *Wesley's Veterans*, 7 vols., 1912.

—— *The Life of Mr Silas Told*, 1786, repr. 1954.

WALSH, J. D., 'Methodism and the Mob in the eighteenth century', in *Studies in Church History*, ed. D. Baker, vol. ii, 1972.

—— 'The Cambridge Methodists', in *Christian Spirituality, Essays in Honour of Gordon Rupp*, ed. P. Brooks, 1973.

There are very many books on John Wesley and on the history of Methodism. Those mentioned here are the ones cited in the present work. Excellent up-to-date bibliographies are regularly published by the Wesley Historical Society in its *Proceedings*.

CHARLES WESLEY

ALBIN, T., 'The Earliest Evangelical Sermons of Charles Wesley' (MS).

BETT, H., *The Hymns of Methodism*, 1913.

BREVINT, D., 'The Christian Sacrament and Sacrifice', in *Hymns on the Lord's Supper*, by John and Charles Wesley, Bristol 1745, repr. 1951.

FLEW, R. N., *Charles Wesley's Hymns*, 1953.

JACKSON, T., *The Life of Charles Wesley*, 2 vols., 1841.

—— *The Journals of Charles Wesley*, 2 vols., n.d.

—— *The Poetical Works of Charles Wesley*, 13 vols., 1872.

RATTENBURY, J., *The Evangelical Doctrines of the Hymns of Charles Wesley*, 1941.

—— *The Eucharistic Hymns of Charles Wesley*, 1948.

WISEMAN, F. L., *Charles Wesley*, New York 1932.

JOHN FLETCHER OF MADELEY

LAWTON, G., *Shropshire Saint*, 1960.

STREIFF, P. P., *John William Fletcher 1729–85*, Frankfurt 1984.

WESLEY, J., *The Life of Fletcher* (*Works*, Vol. xi).

THOMAS COKE

VICKERS, J., *Thomas Coke, Apostle of Methodism*, 1969.

SIDE-EFFECTS OF THE REVIVAL

ASHTON, F. S., *Economic Fluctuations in England 1700–1800*, Oxford 1969.

CHEYNE, G., *The English Malady, or a Treatise of Nervous Diseases*, 1735.

HALÉVY, E., *The Birth of Methodism in England*, Eng. tr., ed. B. Semmell, Chicago 1971.

LEESE, R., *The Impact of Methodism on the Black Country Society. 1743–1860*, Diss. University of Manchester 1972.

SEMMELL, B., *The Methodist Revolution*, 1930.

WALSH, J. D., 'Elie Halévy and the Birth of Methodism', *TRHS* (5th Series), vol, xxv, 1975.

WARNER, W. J., *The Wesleyan Movement in the Industrial Revolution*, 1930.

WEARMOUTH, R. F., *Methodism and the Common People of the Eighteenth Century*, 1945.

SEPARATION FROM THE CHURCH OF ENGLAND

BAKER, F., *John Wesley and the Church of England*, 1970.

GEORGE, A. R., 'Ordination', in *A History of the Methodist Church in Great Britain*, ed. Davies and Rupp, vol. 2, ch. iv.

HARRISON, A. W., *The Separation of Methodism from the Church of England*, 1945.

LAWSON, A. B., *John Wesley and the Christian Ministry*, 1963.

MOEDE, G. F., *The Office of a Bishop in Methodism*, Zurich 1964.

ANGLICAN EVANGELICALS

BAKER, F., *William Grimshaw*, 1963.

BALLEINE, G. R., *A History of the Evangelical Party in the Church of England*, 1908.

BROWN, F. K., *The Fathers of the Victorians*, Cambridge 1961.

DAVIES, G. C. B., *The Early Cornish Evangelicals*, 1953.

ELLIOTT-BINNS, L., *The Early Evangelicals*, 1953.

HILL, Sir Richard, *Pietas Oxoniensis*, 1768.

—— *Logica Wesleiensis*, 1773.

MARTIN, B., *John Newton*, 1950.

—— *The Works of John Newton*, 4 vols., 1839.

NOWELL, T., *An Answer to a Pamphlet Entitled Pietas Oxoniensis*, Oxford 1768.

OLLARD, S. L., *The Six Students of St Edmund Hall expelled from the University of Oxford in 1768*, 1911.

REYNOLDS, J. S., *The Evangelicals at Oxford, 1735–81*, Oxford 1953.

RYLE, J. C., *The Christian Leaders of the Last Century*, 1873.

TOON, P., *The Emergence of Hyper Calvinism in English Nonconformity 1689–1765*, 1967.

THE ESTABLISHMENT

GENERAL WORKS

BURKE, Edmund, *Correspondence*, ed. A. Cobban and R. A. Smith, Cambridge 1967.

—— *Works*, 8 vols. (Bohn Library), 5th edn. 1883–90.

—— *Reflections on the Revolution in France*, ed. O'Brien, Harmondsworth 1982.

BURNEY, Fanny, *Evelina*, Everyman edn.

—— *Diary*, Everyman edn.

BUTT, J., *The Mid-Eighteenth Century*, Oxford History of English Literature, Oxford 1980.

EHRMAN, J., *The Younger Pitt*, 1983.

HOLMES, G., *Augustan England: Professions, State and Society, 1688–1730*, 1982.

JAMES, D. G., *The Romantic Comedy*, Oxford 1963.

LECKY, W. E. H., *The History of England in the Eighteenth Century*, 1887.

MARSHALL, D., *Eighteenth Century England*, 1977.

MCLEOD, H., *Religion and the People of Western Europe 1789–1970*, Oxford 1981.

MCMANNERS, J., *Death and the Enlightenment*, Oxford 1981.

PAINE, Thomas, *The Rights of Man*, ed. H. Collins, Harmondsworth 1982.

PORTER, R., *English Society in the Eighteenth Century*, 1982.

QUINLAN, M. J., *Victorian Prelude*, 1965.

ROYLE, E., and WALWIN, J., *English Radicals and Reformers, 1760–1848*, Brighton 1982.

WATSON, J. S., *The Reign of George III*, Oxford 1960.

WHITE, R. J., *The Age of George III*, 1960.

WILLIAMS, B., *The Whig Supremacy, 1714–60*, 2nd edn., Oxford 1962.

THE CLERICS

BEST, G., *Temporal Pillars*, Cambridge 1964.

COLE, R. E. G. (ed.), *Speculum dioceseos Lincŏlniensis sub. Ep. Guil. Wake et Edm. Gibson*, Part I: *1705–23*, Lincoln Record Soc. 1913.

COLE, W., *The Blecheley Diary*, ed. F. G. Stokes, 1931.

DERRY, W., *Dr. Parr*, Oxford 1966.

HART, A. Tindal, *The Country Priest in English History*, 1959.

—— *Country Counting House*, 1962.

—— *The Curate's Lot*, Newton Abbot 1971.

JONES, W., *The Diary of the Rev. William Jones 1777–1821*, ed. O. F. Clinton, 1929.

LEGG, J. Wickham, *English Church Life from the Restoration to the Tractarian Movement*, 1914.

MIDGLEY, G., 'Orator Henley', the Life of Orator Henley, 1973.

O'DAY, R. O., and HEAL, F., *Princes and Paupers of the English Church*, Leicester 1981.

OLLARD, S. L., *Archbishop Herring's Visitation Returns, 1743*, 5 vols., Yorkshire Archaeological Soc. Vol. LXXIX, 1931.

PRUETT, J. H., *The Parish Clergy under the Later Stuarts*, Oxford 1960.

SMYTH, C., *Simeon and Church Order*, Cambridge 1940.

—— *The Evangelical Movement in Perspective*, CHJ. 1943.

SYKES, N., *Church and State in England in the Eighteenth Century*, Cambridge 1934.

—— *From Seldon to Secker*, Cambridge 1959

—— 'The Sermons of a Country Parson', *Theology* xxxviii, Feb. 1939.

—— 'James Woodforde in his Pulpit', *Theology* xxxviii, May 1939.

The Torrington Diaries, ed. C. B. Andrews, 4 vols., 1934.

TOON, P. (ed.), *W. Romaine. The Life, Walk and Triumph of Faith*, 1970.

TOPLADY, A., *More Work for John Wesley*, 1772.

—— *The Scheme of Christian and Philosophical Necessity Asserted*, 1775.

WARBURTON, W., *The Divine Legation*, 2 vols. 1745.
—— *The Alliance between Church and State*, 2 vols., 1727.
—— *The Doctrine of Grace*, 1762.
WARNE, A., *Church and Society in Eighteenth Century Devon*, Newton Abbot 1969.
WOODFORDE, James, *The Diary of a Country Parson*, ed. J. Beresford, 5 vols., Oxford 1968.
WOODS, A. S., *Thomas Haweis*, 1957.

THE LAICS

ANSTEY, R., *The Atlantic Slave Trade and British Abolition*, 1975.
BUCKLAND, A., *The Life of Hannah More*, n.d.
CLARKE, W. Lowther, *Eighteenth Century Piety*, 1944.
JONES, M. G., *Hannah More*, Cambridge 1952.
MEAKIN, A. M. B., *Hannah More*, 1911.
The Mendip Annals (M. More). ed. Roberts, 1859.

SAMUEL JOHNSON

The two major sources are

The Yale Edition of the works of Samuel Johnson, 10 vols. New Haven 1958.
Boswell's *Life of Johnson*, ed. G. B. Hill, 6 vols. rev. L. F. Powell, Oxford 1971.

Useful sources included in

G. B. Hill, *Johnsonian Miscellanies*, 2 vols., Oxford 1897.

EDITIONS OF JOHNSON'S SINGLE WORKS

The Lives of the Poets, Oxford 1973.
Rasselas (Penguin) 1979.
The Early Biographical works of S. Johnson, ed. Fleeman, 1973.
Johnson's Juvenal, ed. N. Rudd, Bristol 1981.

BIOGRAPHIES AND STUDIES

W. J. Bate, *Samuel Johnson*, 1978.
C. F. Chapin, *The Religious Thought of Samuel Johnson*, 1982.
J. L. Clifford, *The Young Samuel Johnson*, 1958, *Dictionary Johnson*, 1979.
C. E. Pierce, *The Religious Life of Samuel Johnson*, 1982.
M. J. Quinlan, *Samuel Johnson, a Layman's Religion*, Madison, 1964.
S. C. Roberts, *Dr Johnson and Others*, Cambridge 1958.
J. Wain, *Samuel Johnson*, 1980.
T. F. Wharton, *Samuel Johnson and the Theme of Hope*, 1984.

INDEX